Dreamweaver® MX 2004
in 10 Simple Steps or Less

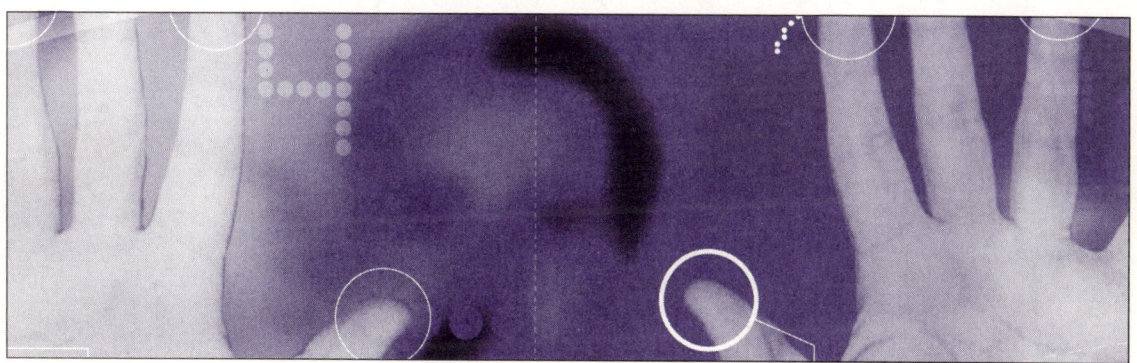

Dreamweaver® MX 2004
in 10 Simple Steps or Less

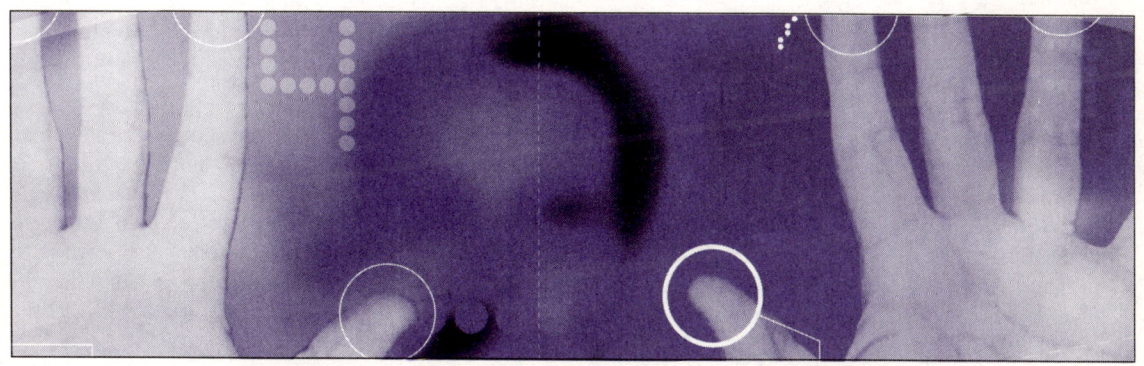

Joyce J. Evans

WILEY
Wiley Publishing, Inc.

Dreamweaver® MX 2004 in 10 Simple Steps or Less

Published by
Wiley Publishing, Inc.
10475 Crosspoint Boulevard
Indianapolis, IN 46256
www.wiley.com

Copyright © 2004 by Wiley Publishing, Inc., Indianapolis, Indiana

Published simultaneously in Canada

ISBN: 0-7645-4348-2

Manufactured in the United States of America

10 9 8 7 6 5 4 3 2 1

1O/QS/QU/QU/IN

For general information on our other products and services or to obtain technical support, please contact our Customer Care Department within the U.S. at (800) 762-2974, outside the U.S. at (317) 572-3993 or fax (317) 572-4002.

Wiley also publishes its books in a variety of electronic formats. Some content that appears in print may not be available in electronic books.

Library of Congress Control Number: 2004101968

To my loving family for all their support and care.

Credits

Acquisitions Editor
Chris Webb

Developmental Editor
Sharon Nash

Production Editor
Felicia Robinson

Copy Editor
Joanne Slike

Editorial Manager
Kathryn Malm

Vice President & Executive Group Publisher
Richard Swadley

Vice President and Executive Publisher
Bob Ipsen

Vice President and Publisher
Joseph B. Wikert

Project Coordinator
Ryan Steffen

Graphics and Production Specialists
Beth Brooks
Carrie Foster
Lauren Goddard
Jennifer Heleine
LeAndra Hosier
Kristin McMullan
Lynsey Osborn

Quality Control Technicians
John Greenough
Brian Walls

Book Designer
Kathie S. Schnorr

Proofreading
Sossity Smith

Indexing
Sherry Massey

About the Author

Joyce J. Evans is a training veteran with over 10 years of experience in educational teaching, tutorial development, and Web design. She has spoken at conferences such as Macromedia MAX 2003 and TODCON. Joyce has received Editor's Choice Awards for her book *Fireworks 4 F/X and Design* and has authored numerous computer books, including *Dreamweaver MX (and MX 2004) Complete Course*, *Web Design Complete Course*, and *Fireworks MX (and MX 2004): Zero to Hero*.

Joyce is a Team Macromedia Volunteer and her work is also be featured in the Macromedia Design/Developer center and the MX Developers Journal magazine. She can be reached at Joyce@JoyceJEvans.com. Her personal Web site is www.JoyceJEvans.com, and her design business, Idea Design (www.je-ideadesign.com), has clients such as a Century 21 and prominent colleges in Florida and is a subcontractor for a local service provider. Joyce also actively teaches new students how to use the Macromedia Studio products.

Joyce lives with her husband, teenage son, dog, and cat in the Tampa Bay area in Florida. When Joyce isn't doing Web design, she can be found at the beach or managing her Real Estate investment company.

About the Contributors

Murray R. Summers wrote Part 10, on templates and Library items.

Paul Vachier wrote Part 9 on using CSS styles and Part 11 on working with code.

Brad Halstead contributed to Parts 1, 3, and 4.

Caleb John Clark contributed to Part 2.

Acknowledgments

The task of writing these long computer books is a daunting one, and it is a process that requires significant contributions from many people who help these projects see their way to completion. For this project, I need to thank the entire team at Wiley, including Sharon Nash and Chris Webb, as well as all the myriad others involved in preparing, designing, and producing the books there.

I also need to thank my family for their patience during the writing of the book. In particular, my husband, Martin, and son, Derek, deserve credit for tolerating the time I had to devote to the preparation of this book. They took up much of the housework and meal preparations.

I'd also like to thank each of the contributors who wrote a portion of the book or contributed to a specific part.

I'd also like to thank the crew at Macromedia who work so diligently to produce such a superb application. Special thanks go to Heather Hollaender, who always made sure I had the resources I needed, and to Scott Unterberg for the privilege of being included in the beta testing.

Contents

Introduction

Dreamweaver is the industry leader as a layout editor. Dreamweaver MX 2004 makes your job of building Web pages even easier. In *Dreamweaver® MX 2004 in 10 Simple Steps or Less* You'll discover how to use the new features, as well as the old ones, to achieve specific tasks.

This book is a recipe book providing you with quick, digestible examples of how to perform specific tasks using Dreamweaver MX 2004. These tasks range from simple tasks such as defining a Dreamweaver site to complex tasks such as creating dynamic content.

This book isn't a tutorial for Dreamweaver MX 2004. It is designed to be a useful reference when you are actively engaged in building your Web applications and need quick answers to the question "How do I do this in Dreamweaver MX 2004?" For most tasks of low and medium complexity, you will likely find an example in this book. Completing complex tasks can often be achieved by combining more than one sample task from the book.

tip

- If you want to build a Web site step-by-step, you might consider *Dreamweaver MX 2004 Complete Course* by Joyce J. Evans (John Wiley & Sons, 0-7645-4304-0), or if you want to use Dreamweaver MX, Fireworks MX, and ColdFusion MX, check out *Web Design* by Joyce J. Evans (John Wiley & Sons, 0-7645-3752-0).

About the Book

This book is divided into 13 sections.

Part 1: Building the Foundation

This section provides tasks that help you use the Dreamweaver MX 2004 interface as well as set up your workspace. You'll find tasks to define a site, set up testing browsers, and much more.

Part 2: Using Text and Images

This section shows you how to add and format text, as well as how to add images. Topics such as adding links and alternative text are also covered here.

Part 3: Working with Tables and Site Management

In this section you'll find tasks that teach you how to use tables to display data but primarily to use as a layout tool. You'll also find tasks for checking links and using other site management tools.

Part 4: Mastering Frames

The tasks in this section teach you how to build and use a framed site. You'll also find a task to help you make the frames–no frames choice.

Part 5: Working with Forms

This section provides tasks that teach you how to add forms to your documents. There is also a task on how to validate your forms

Part 6: Working with Layers

In this section. you'll learn how to use layers to organize your content. Layers are a great substitute for tables and are used for positioning0 in CSS-P (Cascading Style Sheets Positioning) layouts.

Part 7: Making Your Site Interactive Using Behaviors

This section provides tasks to show you how to use behaviors such as rollovers and pop-up menus, how to build a photo album, and much more.

Part 8: Using External Media

This section provides tasks that illustrate how to use external media such as Flash, QuickTime, and others. You'll also get tips on how to view external media in Internet Explorer's new browser.

Part 9: Styling with CSS Styles

CSS Styles is one of the hottest new feature enhancements in Dreamweaver MX 2004. You'll find tasks that show you how to use CSS styles easily to format your text or layout.

Part 10: Automating with Library Items and Templates

Library items and templates both make Web site development much faster. Develop once and apply to every page in your site. In this section, you'll find tasks that show you how make new templates, apply templates, and much more.

Part 11: Working with Code

Working with the actual code can be quite intimidating to new users. The tasks found in this section will help demystify this process for you. There are times when you'll want or need to work directly with code. You may be surprised how easy it can be to work with code in Dreamweaver MX 2004.

Part 12: Setting Up Web Applications

This section provides tutorials on how to prepare to build dynamic sites. You'll learn how to set up (Internet Information Server (IIS), Personal Web Server (PWS), and ColdFusion, as well as how to set up your site to use these technologies.

Part 13: Making Your Site Dynamic

The tasks in this section require that you perform the tasks in Part 12. Here you'll learn how to build dynamic pages and applications. A starter site is provided for your use so you can actually add dynamic content as you do the various tasks.

Finally, the complete source code for each task can be found on the companion Web site at `www.wiley.com/compbooks/10simplestepsorless`. Some of the tasks provide sample files for you to use. With sample files, the tasks take on more of a hands-on approach for concepts that may be more difficult to grasp.

Conventions Used in This Book

As you go through this book, you will find a few unique elements. We'll describe those elements here so that you'll understand them when you see them.

Text You Type and Text on the Screen

Whenever you are asked to type in text, the text you are to type appears in bold, like this:

Type in this address: **111 River Street**.

When we are referring to URLs or other text you'll see on the screen, we'll use a monospace font, like this:

Check out `www.wiley.com`.

Icons

A number of special icons appear in the margins of each task to provide additional information you might find helpful.

note

- The Note icon is used to provide additional information.

tip

- The Tip icon is used to point out an interesting idea or technique that will save you time, effort, money, or all three!

caution

- The Caution icon is used to alert you to potential problems that you might run into.

cross-reference

- Although this book is divided into tasks to make it easy to find exactly what you're looking for, few tasks really stand completely alone. The Cross-Reference icon provides us the opportunity to point out other tasks in the book you might want to look at if you're interested in this task.

Part 1: Building the Foundation

Changing the Workspace

Dreamweaver MX 2004 gives you the option of two different workspaces depending on whether you are a visual designer or prefer to code by hand.

1. Choose Edit ➪ Preferences (Ctrl/Command+U) to open Dreamweaver Preferences.

2. Select General under the Category heading to activate the proper panel to change the workspace.

3. Click the button labeled Change Workspace, as shown in Figure 1-1, to open the Workspace Setup dialog box, shown in Figure 1-2.

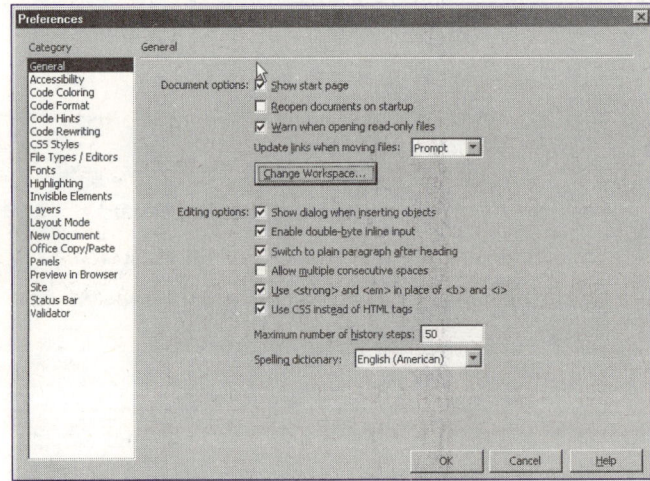

Figure 1-1: Dreamweaver 2004 Preferences dialog box

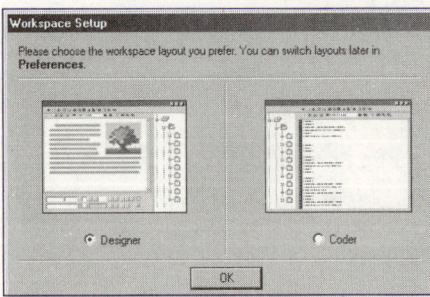

Figure 1-2: Workspace Setup dialog box

4. Make your selection between the two available options:

- *Designer layout.* Multidocument interface with panels on the right-hand edge, as shown in Figure 1-4.

note

- If this is your first time opening the preferences, General is selected. The preferences dialog box remembers where you last were in the categories and highlights that entry when the preferences are opened (Step 2).

cautions

- Once you make a change to the Workspace Setup dialog box and press the OK button, you are committed; there is no way to cancel the change request (Step 5).

- If you change your workspace after customizing it, Dreamweaver does not retain that customization and returns the panels to their factory state when the workspace is changed and the preferences are saved (Step 9).

- *Coder layout*. Multidocument interface with panels on the left-hand side, as shown in Figure 1-4 (right side). You can still work in Design view if you desire.

5. Click the OK button to activate your selection. A warning dialog box appears, as shown in Figure 1-3.

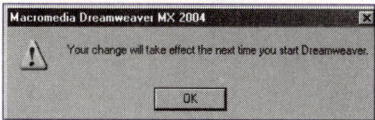

Figure 1-3: Warning dialog box

6. Click the OK button to close the Warning dialog box and return to the Preferences dialog box.

7. Click the OK button on the Preferences dialog box to close it.

8. Select File ⇨ Exit to shut down Dreamweaver MX 2004.

9. Restart Dreamweaver MX 2004 to see and use your new workspace, shown in Figure 1-4.

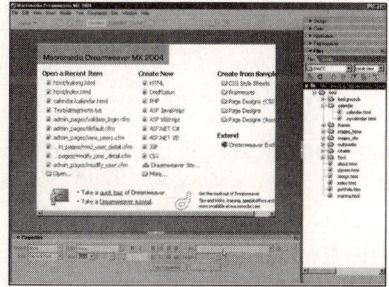
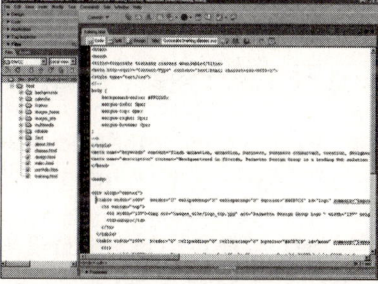

Designer   Coder

Figure 1-4: Dreamweaver MX 2004 workspaces. The image on the left uses Designer layout and image on the right uses Coder layout.

Task **1**

cross-reference

- See Task 3 for information on using the integrated panel sets and customizing the panel groups.

Using the Start Page

The Start Page is a new feature in Dreamweaver MX 2004. It opens by default each time you open Dreamweaver and offers a list of quick links for frequently used items.

1. Open Dreamweaver. The Start Page, shown in Figure 2-1, appears.

notes

- What shows in the Open a Recent Item category depends on what you've opened recently (Step 2).

- The Start Page is only visible when there are no other documents open.

- You need to register with Macromedia before you download any extensions (Step 5).

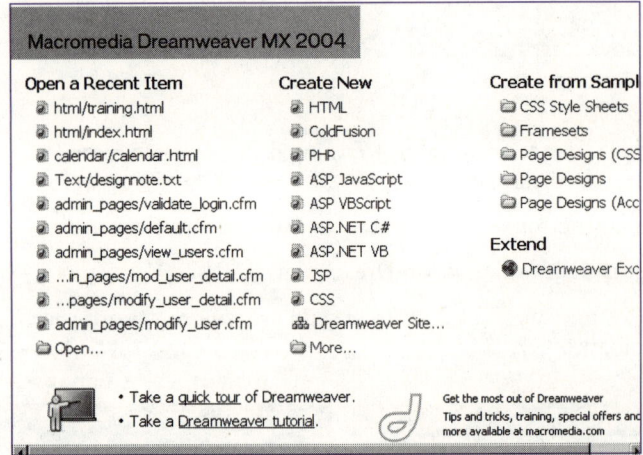

Figure 2-1: The Start Page that appears when you first open Dreamweaver

2. Click any link in the Open a Recent Item category to open it. At the bottom is a link to open the Open dialog box to navigate to files.

3. The Create New column has links to quickly create a new document, such as Hypertext Markup Language (HTML), Cascading Style Sheets (CSS), ColdFusion, and so on. When you click one of these links, the proper code is added for the page. For instance, if it's a CSS page, /* CSS Document */ appears in the document in Code view. If you click the More icon, the New Document dialog box opens, where you can choose from all the available options (see Figure 2-2).

4. In the Create from Sample column, you can choose from CSS Style Sheets, Page Designs, and more. These are the same options you find in the New Document dialog box (File ➪ New).

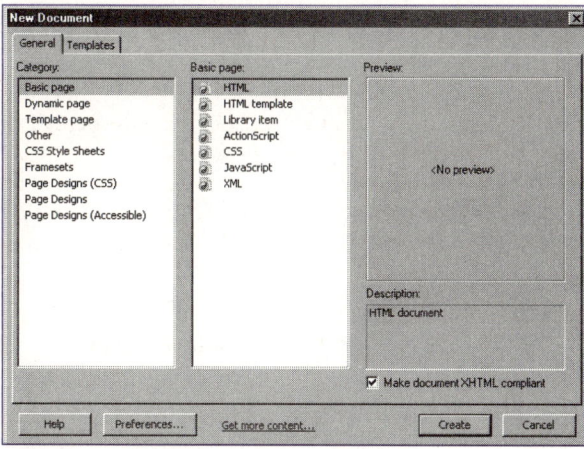

Figure 2-2: The New Document dialog box

5. The Extend area connects directly to the Dreamweaver Exchange if you have an active connection.

6. On the left bottom side of the Start Page, you'll see links to a tour of Dreamweaver and a Dreamweaver tutorial. You need to be online for the tour, but the tutorial is part of the Help system.

7. On the right bottom of the Start Page is a link directly to Macromedia for Dreamweaver for the latest updates, tutorials, and news.

8. You can choose not to show the Start Page on startup by selecting Edit ➪ Preferences, General category (see Figure 2-3). Uncheck the Show Start Page option to turn it off, and click OK to close the Preferences dialog box.

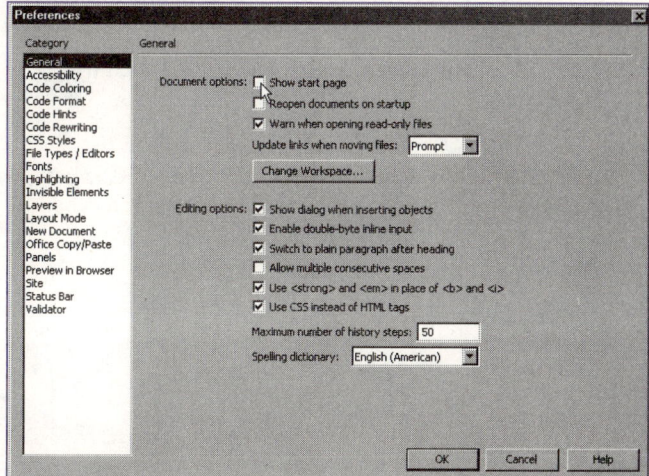

Figure 2-3: The Preferences dialog box showing the Show Start Page option

cross-reference

▪ Refer to Task 4 for more information on opening and saving documents.

Moving Panels into Different Groups

Dreamweaver is all about customization, allowing you to configure your setup in accordance with your taste and workflow. A panel may be opened, closed, grouped with other panels, or made to use its own panel group. Before configuring the panels and groups, you need to know the names of the panel group features, shown in Figure 3-1.

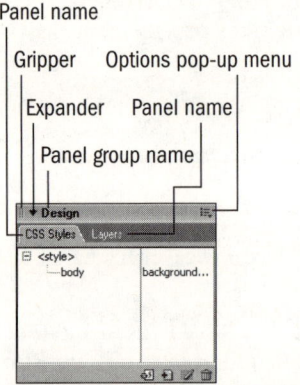

Figure 3-1: The common features of the panel groups

1. To move a panel from one group to another, expand the current group by clicking on the group's expander arrow (or simply click the name). Click the Panel Options pop-up and select Group Panel Name With ➪ Panel Group. The currently active panel is moved to the selected group.

2. To make a panel use its own group, expand the current group by clicking on the group's expander arrow. Click the Panel Options pop-up menu, and select Group Panel Name With ➪ New Panel Group, as shown in Figure 3-2. The currently active panel is moved to a new panel set of its own.

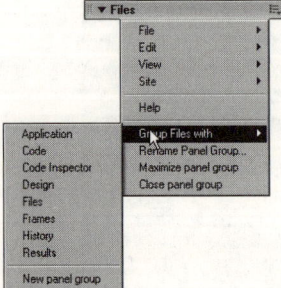

Figure 3-2: The Options pop-up menu showing the panel group options

3. To rearrange panel groups, click the panel heading by the gripper and drag it to the desired new location. When you see the solid blue (or black) line where you want to move the panel, release the mouse button.

4. To rename a panel group, expand the current group by clicking on the group's expander arrow. Click the Panel Options pop-up menu, and select Rename Panel Group. In the Rename Panel Group dialog box that appears, type in the new name, then click the OK button.

5. To close a panel group, expand the current group by clicking on the group's expander arrow. Click the Panel Options pop-up menu, and select Close Panel Group.

6. To adjust the height of a panel group, expand the current group by clicking on the group's expander arrow. Move your cursor down into the below panel group bar, and it changes to a resize cursor. Depress the left button and drag to get the desired height.

7. To undock a panel group, grab its gripper and drag off to the right or left to detach it from the other groups.

8. To redock the panel group, grab its gripper, drag over the other groups, and look for a dark thick line to indicate its current drop position. If the thick line does not appear, you are either not using the gripper to dock the group or you don't have the group in dock-able position. The thick line is shown in Figure 3-3.

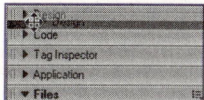

Figure 3-3: Docking position indicator for panel groups

9. To hide all the panels, choose View ⇨ Hide Panels or press F4. You can also simply click the tab attached to the left of the panel sets. Click tab or name to open or close the panel groups.

cross-reference

▪ Refer to Task 16 for customizing the Insert bar.

Opening, Creating, Saving, and Closing a Document

Before you can begin editing a document, you need to know how to create or open one for editing. Once the editing is done, you need to know how to save it so you don't lose your changes to the edited file.

1. To open an existing document, choose File ⇨ Open (Ctrl/Command+O). The Open dialog box appears. Navigate to the folder that contains the file you want to open, select the file, and click the Open button.

2. To create a new document, choose File ⇨ New (Ctrl/Command+N). The New Document dialog box opens, as shown in Figure 4-1.

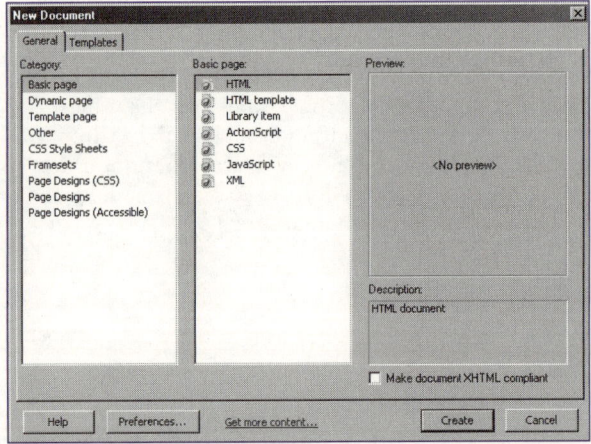

Figure 4-1: New Document dialog box

3. Choose the General tab, and a list of categories is displayed, showing the available pages for each category. These lists are ordered intuitively; if you wish to create a dynamic page, click the Dynamic Page category and select the desired file from the list. You can make the new document XHTML-compliant by placing a check in the Make Document XHTML Compliant check box. Click the Create button on the New File dialog box to create the file and open it for editing.

4. To save an open existing page, select File ⇨ Save (Ctrl/Command+S). The page is saved.

5. To save a newly created file, select File ⇨ Save As (Ctrl/Command+Shift+S). The Save As dialog box opens, as shown in Figure 4-2. Navigate to the desired folder, type in a name for the document, and click the Save button on the Save As dialog box.

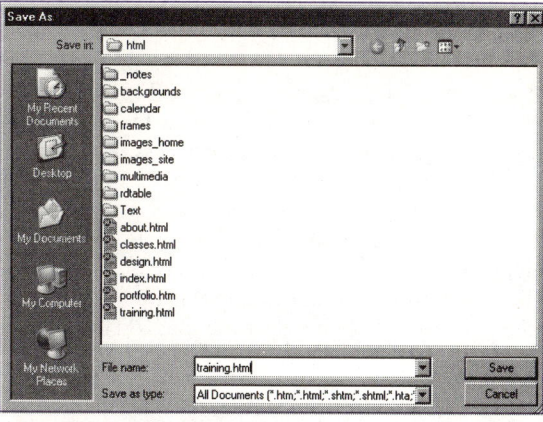

Figure 4-2: Save As dialog box

6. To close the currently active document, choose File ➪ Close (Ctrl/Command+W). If the file has been modified, a Save Changes dialog box opens, prompting you to save the changes prior to closing the document (see Figure 4-3).

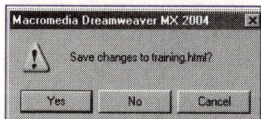

Figure 4-3: Save Changes dialog box

7. If the document is a new document, clicking Yes to the Save Changes dialog box opens the Save As dialog box. If the document is an existing document, clicking the Yes button on the Save Changes dialog box saves and closes the document.

8. Clicking the No button on the Save Changes dialog box closes the document without saving changes.

9. Clicking the Cancel button on the Save Changes dialog box cancels the closing of the document and leaves the document open for further editing.

10. Notice the title bar in Figure 4-4. When changes have been made to an open document since it has last been saved, an asterisk is added to the end of the document's name.

Asterisk added

Macromedia Dreamweaver MX 2004 - [Corporate training classes available (html/training.html*)]
File Edit View Insert Modify Text Commands Site Window Help

Figure 4-4: An asterisk added to the page name to indicate it needs saving

cross-reference

▪ Refer to Tasks 10 and 11 for defining a site.

Setting Accessibility Preferences

With the growing importance of the U.S. government's Section 508 compliance guidelines, which deal with Web site accessibility for the disabled, Dreamweaver MX 2004 has implemented several useful accessibility dialog boxes that you can use.

notes

▪ Macromedia DevNet has a great 508 section at www.macromedia. com/macromedia/ accessibility.

▪ Checked is enabled and Unchecked is disabled (Step 3).

▪ Dreamweaver MX 2004 doesn't need to be restarted to effect the changes to the selections that you made (Step 5).

▪ If you are using tables for layout, simply type **Layout Table** in the Summary box (Step 7).

1. Choose Edit ➪ Preferences (Ctrl/Command+U) to open Dreamweaver Preferences.

2. Choose Accessibility under the Category heading. This activates the proper panel for accessibility preferences (see Figure 5-1).

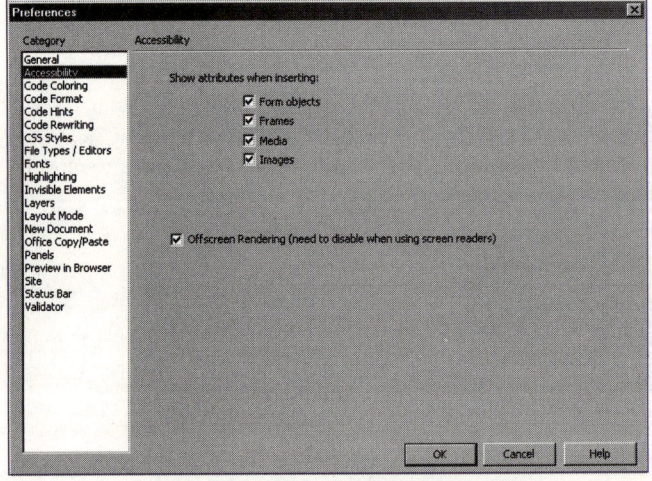

Figure 5-1: Dreamweaver MX 2004 Accessibility Preferences

3. The top four elements of this dialog box control accessibility features for the elements specified: Form Objects, Frames, Media, and Images. These controls affect the content of your Web pages at time of insertion by you. In most instances, enabling the accessibility feature tells the parent dialog box to display a new dialog box, where you can enter the required information. For this task, select Images.

4. The last item, Offscreen Rendering, is for controlling Dreamweaver MX 2004's accessibility so that persons using a screen reader can use them. If using a screen reader, the Offscreen Rendering option needs to be disabled.

5. When you've configured the preferences to your liking, click the OK button to activate your selections.

6. Open a new page, choose Insert ⇨ Image, and navigate to any image on your computer. Select and open it to insert into the document. As soon as you insert the image, the Image Tag Accessibility Attributes dialog box opens, as shown in Figure 5-2. Fill in the alternative text and click OK.

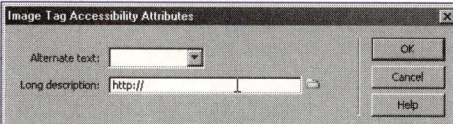

Figure 5-2: The Image Tag Accessibility Attributes dialog box opens automatically every time you insert an image.

7. Now choose Insert ⇨ Table. Note that the table accessibility options are displayed at the bottom of the dialog box, as shown in Figure 5-3.

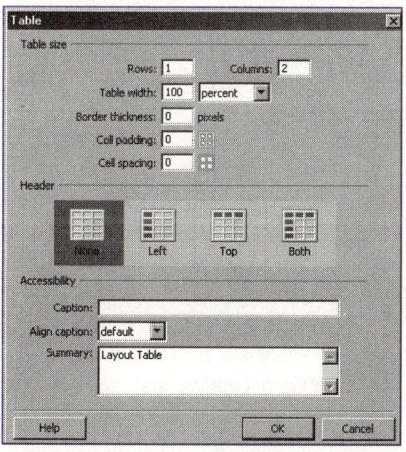

Figure 5-3: The Insert Table dialog box showing the Accessibility area

cross-references

- Refer to Task 47 for adding alternative text.

- Refer to Task 46 for inserting images (Step 6).

Setting Up External Editors

Dreamweaver MX 2004 can be configured to open many different file types, but it also allows you to configure other installed applications as the default editor for any file type you define.

1. Choose Edit ➪ Preferences (Ctrl/Command+U) to open Dreamweaver Preferences.

2. Choose File Types/Editors under the Category heading to activate the proper panel to configure the external editors, as shown in Figure 6-1.

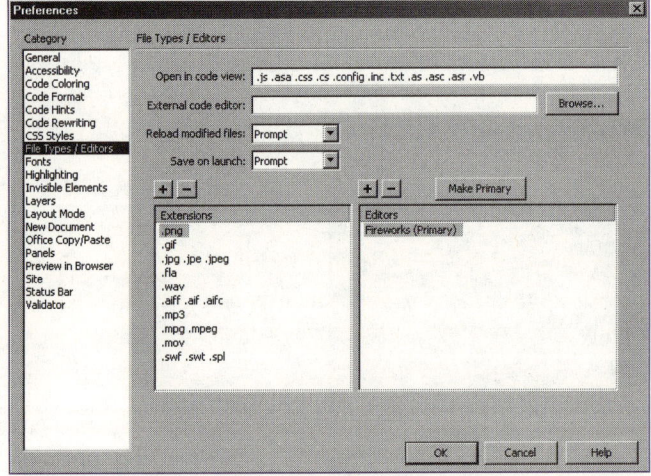

Figure 6-1: Dreamweaver MX 2004 File Types/Editors Preferences

3. Configure or change the default external editor by clicking the Browse button beside the field entitled External Code Editor. Then use the Select External Editor dialog box to locate and select the desired application. Click the Open button to assign it, as shown in Figure 6-2.

4. At the bottom of the dialog box are two list boxes that can be used to add or remove file extensions (in the left box) and add or remove default and alternate editors (in the right box) for each file type in the left pane.

5. Add a new file type by clicking the Add (+) button and typing the desired extension, including the period. Then press Enter. Or you can select a file type already in the list.

---

note

- If this is your first time opening the preferences, General is selected. The preferences dialog box remembers where you last were in the categories and highlights that entry when the preferences are opened (Step 2).

- Once the External Code Editor has been defined, the Edit ➪ Edit with External Editor menu entry changes to Edit ➪ Edit with {*Application*} (Step 3).

- Although Dreamweaver has greatly improved its CSS capabilities, TopStyle is the premier CSS editor (www.topstyle.com) (Step 7).

- Removing a file type also removes the associated editors for that file type (Step 10).

- Defining a primary editor for file types such as FLA or PNG populates the associated Property inspector with an Edit button. This button allows you to edit the desired asset from within Dreamweaver by launching the external editor.

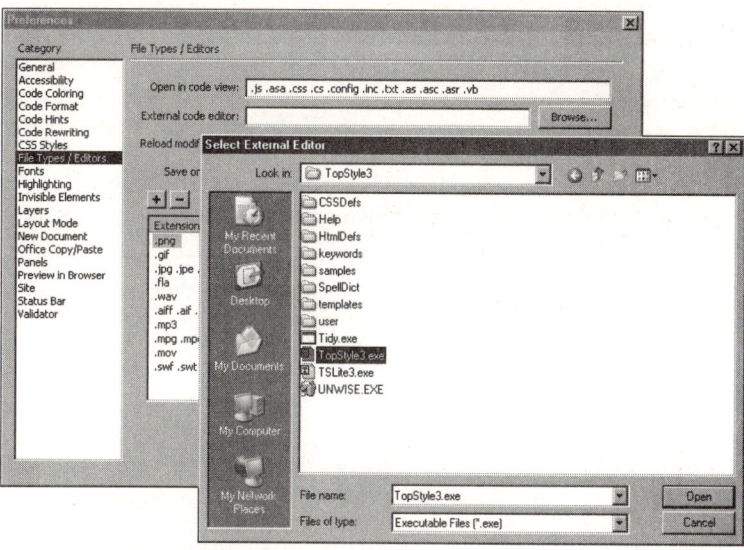

Figure 6-2: Select External Editor dialog box

6. Add an editor for this file type by clicking the Plus (+) button above the right box to open the Select External Editor dialog box.

7. Navigate to the desired editor (locate the EXE file), and select the Open button to assign that editor to that file type.

8. You can define more than one editor for a file type; repeat Step 7 for each editor for that file type.

9. To make one editor the primary editor for a file type, select the file type in the left-hand list box, then select the desired default editor in the right-hand list and click the Make Primary button.

10. To remove an editor for a file type, select the file type, then select the editor that is to be removed and click the Minus (–) button. To remove a file type, select the file type and click the Minus (–) button.

cross-reference

▪ Refer to Task 56 for editing with Fireworks (or preferred editor).

Setting Up Testing Browsers

As Web developer, one of your many jobs is to test your project in as many browsers as possible that are used by your target market. Dreamweaver allows you to define a primary and secondary editor, but you can configure and use many other browsers as well, right from within the Dreamweaver environment. However, unless you have multiple operating systems, you can only install one version of Internet Explorer on your machine.

To set up testing browsers, follow these steps:

1. Choose Edit ➪ Preferences (Ctrl/Command+U) to open Dreamweaver Preferences.

2. Under the Category heading, choose Preview in Browser to activate the proper panel to modify the Preview in Browser list (see Figure 7-1).

notes

- During installation of Dreamweaver, some installed browsers are detected automatically (Step 2).

- On Windows machines, Internet Explorer is configured to be the primary browser and you activate it by pressing F12.

- Leaving the Primary and Secondary Browser check boxes blank still allows you to preview your documents using that browser, just not by using a shortcut key (Step 6).

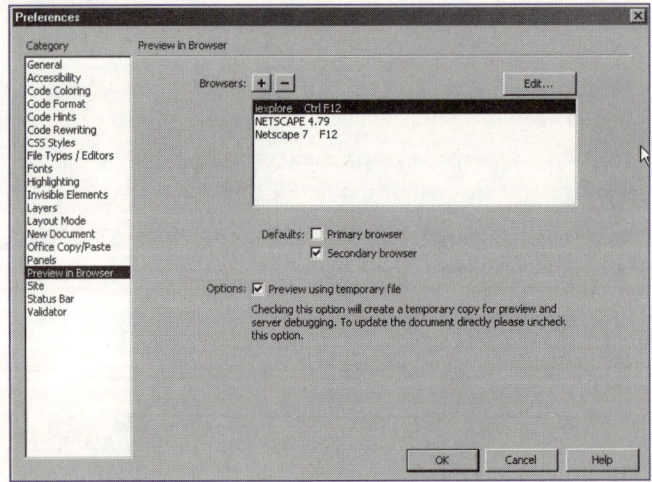

Figure 7-1: Preview in Browser preferences

3. Click the Plus (+) button beside Browsers to open the Add Browser dialog box, shown in Figure 7-2.

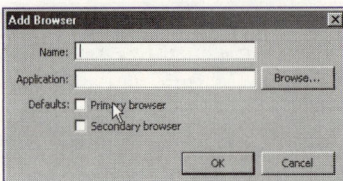

Figure 7-2: Add Browser dialog box

caution

- If you remove the primary browser, none will replace it until you tell Dreamweaver to use another one. This could prevent the F12 shortcut key from functioning in Dreamweaver (Step 7).

4. Use the Browse button to open the Select Browser dialog box. Navigate to the folder the browser was installed in and select its application (an EXE file normally). Click the dialog box's Open button to select the application and close the Select Browser dialog box.

5. Name the browser by typing the desired name in the Name field. Use something meaningful to you.

6. If you wish to define this newly configured browser as the primary or secondary browser, check the primary or secondary fields.

7. To remove a listed browser, select the browser and click the Minus (–) button.

8. Select a browser from the list and click the Edit button. The Edit Browser dialog box opens, allowing you to configure the displayed name of the browser, change the path to its executable, or define this browser as the primary or secondary browser. Click the dialog box's OK button to effect changes made, as shown in Figure 7-3.

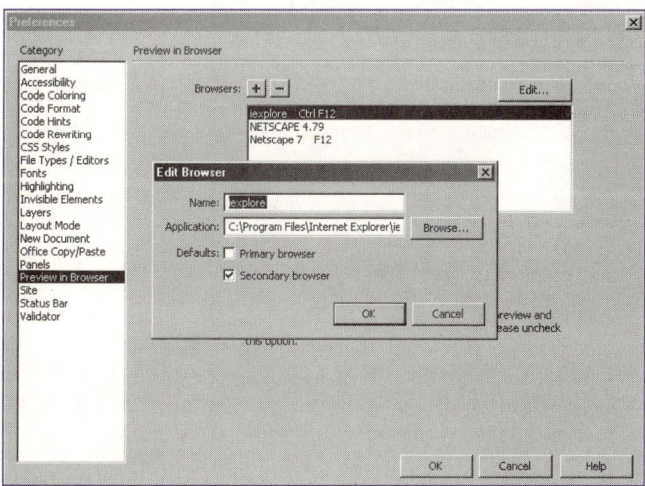

Figure 7-3: Edit Browser dialog box

9. To set the primary preview browser, select it from the list and select the Defaults: Primary Browser check box. To set the secondary preview browser, select it from the list and select the Defaults: Secondary Browser check box.

10. To tell Dreamweaver to preview the current document in the browser using a temporary file, check the Options: Preview Temporary File check box. If you leave it unchecked, the document will be previewed in the actual file. Click OK.

cross-reference

▪ Refer to Task 80 to learn how to check browser compatibility.

Adding or Removing Keyboard Shortcuts

Because it provides a defined set of keyboard shortcuts for many of the commonly accessed menus and functions, Dreamweaver is very accessible. However, although the shortcuts are fairly comprehensive, they may not suit your needs. Therefore, customization is allowed and even encouraged to suit your workflow.

1. Choose Edit ⇨ Keyboard Shortcuts to open the Keyboard Shortcuts dialog box, as shown in Figure 8-1.

Rename Set — Export Set as HTML
Duplicate Set — Delete Set

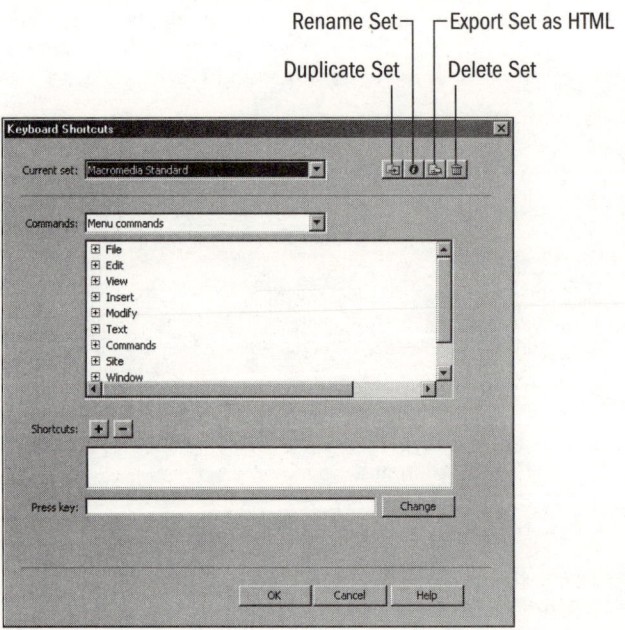

Figure 8-1: Keyboard Shortcuts dialog box

2. Choose a set from the Current Set drop-down menu that you wish to duplicate and customize. Select the Duplicate Set button and provide the duplicated set with a new name in the Duplicate Set dialog box. Click OK.

3. Choose the appropriate Commands group for the item for which you are changing or adding the shortcut key. Expand the item container by clicking the Plus (+) button beside it, and locate the desired item. Some have shortcuts assigned and some don't.

4. Add or remove shortcuts by clicking the Shortcut, then the Plus (+) or Minus (–) button, respectively.

5. To add a keyboard shortcut to an entry with none already defined, position your cursor in the Press Key field and depress your desired shortcut. Letter or number shortcuts must include the Ctrl/Command key and can contain Shift or Alt/Option keys.

6. Click the Change button.

7. Once all desired changes have been completed, click OK.

8. Save a copy of your customized keyboard shortcuts by clicking the Export Set as HTML button. Provide a filename and click the Save button in the Save as HTML File dialog box, as shown in Figure 8-2.

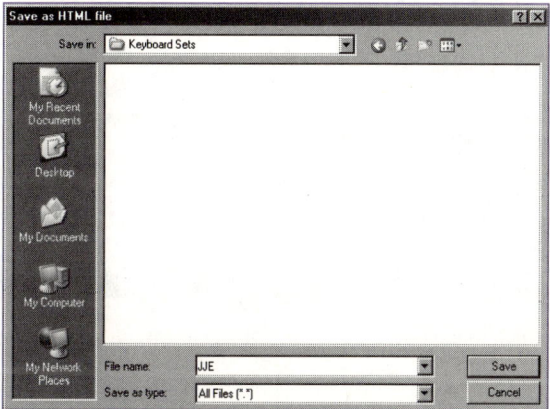

Figure 8-2: Save as HTML File dialog box

9. Delete a customized set of keyboard shortcuts by depressing the Delete Set button and completing the Delete Set dialog box, as shown in Figure 8-3.

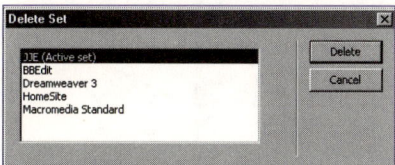

Figure 8-3: Delete Set dialog box

10. Click the OK button of the Keyboard Shortcuts dialog box to effect the changes and close the dialog box.

Task **8**

Dreamweaver's Various Workspace Views

Dreamweaver MX 2004 is built with flexibility in mind. It is designed for both the visual designer and the coder, or a combination of both. In this task you'll see what the working views are and how to access each.

1. Open any file in Dreamweaver.

2. Locate the Document toolbar, which is on top of the document window by default (see Figure 9-1).

notes

- If you select something in Design view and switch to Code or Split view, it is highlighted for you (Step 3).

- You can click and drag the divider bar to give more or less space to the code (Step 4).

Document toolbar

Figure 9-1: The document window with the Document toolbar on top

3. Click the Code button. Figure 9-2 shows all the code in the current page.

4. Select the Split View icon. You'll now see code and your design visually, as shown in Figure 9-3.

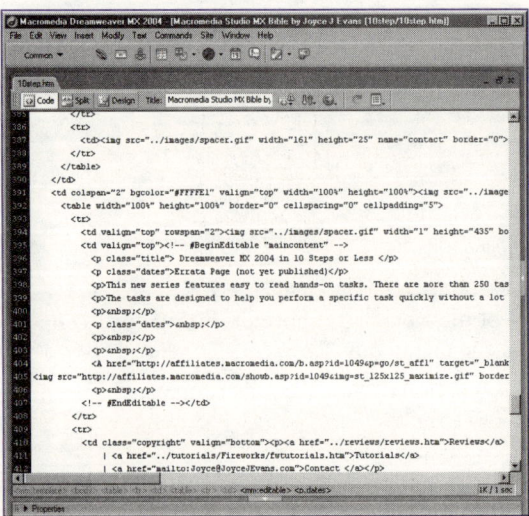

Figure 9-2: The Code view of the open document

Task **9**

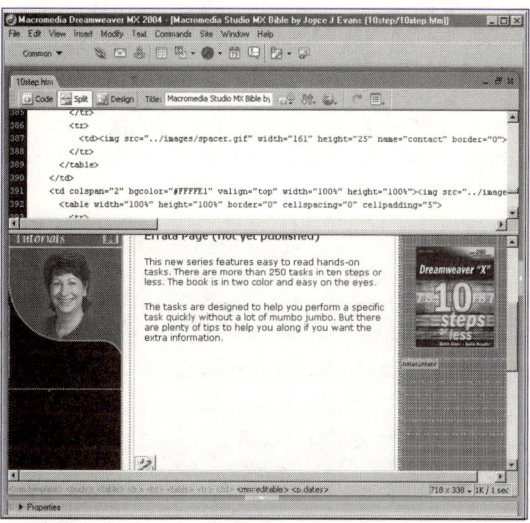

Figure 9-3: The Split view showing code and design elements

5. Click the Design View icon, and as in Figure 9-4, only your layout is displayed.

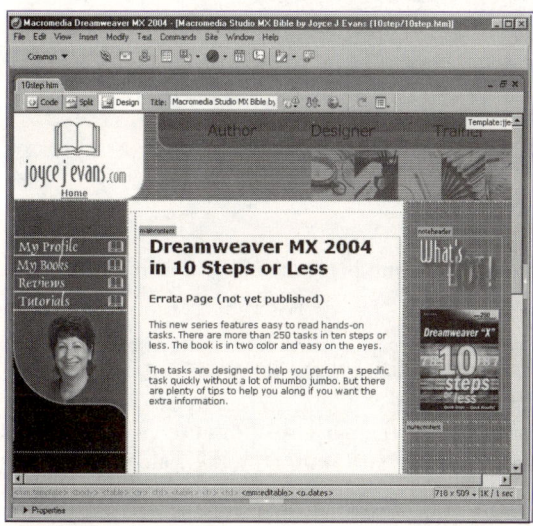

Figure 9-4: The Design view

6. You can also move the position of the Document toolbar. Click and drag its gripper, and move the toolbar to a new location, such as next to the main menu or above or below the Insert bar. There is one problem, however. When you close Dreamweaver and open it again, it doesn't remember the change (as of the initial release of Dreamweaver MX 2004).

cross-reference

▪ Refer to Task 71 to see how to access and use the different layout modes.

Defining a Site Using the Site Wizard

Dreamweaver offers two modes of creating a site definition: Basic and Advanced. Basic mode is great for people new to defining sites, whereas Advanced mode is for people generally a little more familiar with File Transfer Protocol (FTP) configuration.

1. Choose Site ⇨ Manage Sites, and click New ⇨ Site to open the New Site dialog box. Be sure to select the Basic tab to bring the wizard to the foreground, as shown in Figure 10-1.

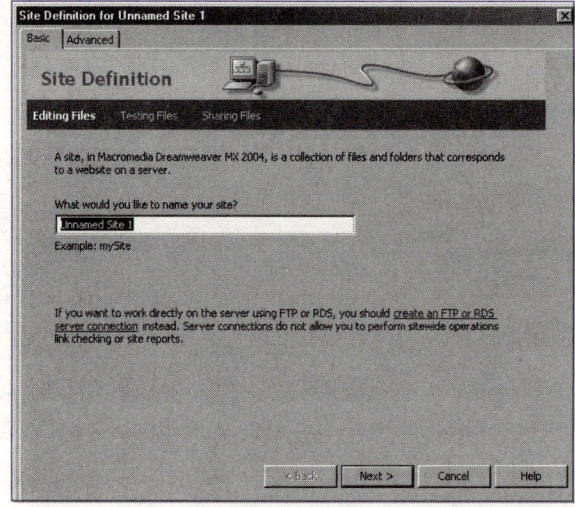

Figure 10-1: New Site Wizard dialog box

2. Type a name for your new site and press the Next button on the dialog box.

3. Choose No, I Don't Want to Use a Server Technology or Yes, I Want to Use a Server Technology. If you choose the latter, a drop-down menu appears, asking you what technology to use. Make your selection from the drop-down menu. For the purpose of this exercise, choose no server technology and click the Next button on the dialog box.

4. Decide how you wish to work with your files. For the purpose of this task, select Edit Local Copies on My Machine, Then Upload to Server When Ready (Recommended). Click the Browse button and navigate to the folder where your files are located (see Figure 10-2). Click Next.

cautions

- Anything goes here, but give your site a name that makes sense to you (Step 2).

- Choosing any method other than the top one may lead to frustration. Because their individual configurations are so broad across networks, the final two methods lack support (Step 4).

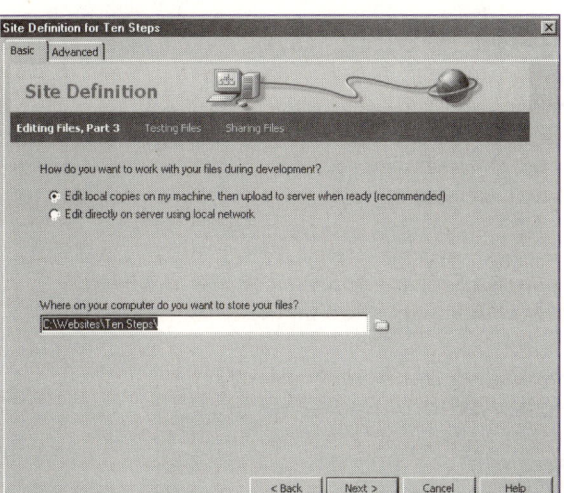

Figure 10-2: The Editing Files, Part 3 dialog box

5. The Sharing Files dialog box appears, with a message that reads, How Do You Connect to Your Remote Server? The options are as follows:

   • None

   • Local/Network

   • FTP

   • RDS

   • SourceSafe Database

   • WebDAV

   For the purpose of this exercise, choose None. You'll add remote server information in another task. Click Next.

6. A summary is displayed showing most of your configuration information for this site. Click the Done button on the dialog box to close the wizard and make the new site the active site.

cross-references

▪ Advanced site creation is discussed in Task 11.

▪ See Task 218 for defining a remote and testing server (Step 5).

Defining a Site Using the Advanced Tab

After creating a few Web sites, you may find the Wizard mode of Web site creation doesn't give you quite the control of the configuration that you desire or the setup speed. Dreamweaver provides an Advanced tab with all the pertinent fields grouped in categories, so that you can more quickly or accurately define a site.

1. Choose Site ⇨ Manage Site, and click New ⇨ Site to open the New Site dialog box. Be sure to select the Advanced tab, as shown in Figure 11-1.

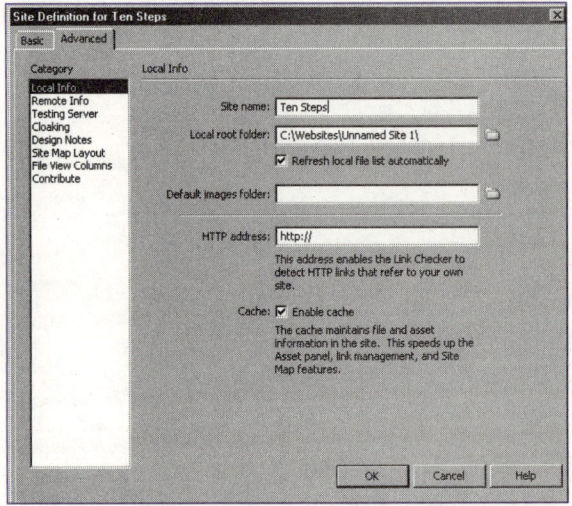

Figure 11-1: New Site dialog box, with Advanced tab showing

2. Select the Local Info category, and complete the details of this category.

3. Type a descriptive name for your site.

4. Use the Browse button beside the Local Root Folder field to browse to your desired new site location on your hard drive. Enable or disable the Refresh Local File List Automatically check box. If enabled, the Files panel file list automatically refreshes periodically.

5. Browse to a default images folder for your site if you want images not in the currently defined site to be copied to the defined site folder.

6. Specify an HTTP address. Then, when you are using absolute links on your page, Dreamweaver will know to validate these HTTP-referenced assets as local files.

notes

- Enabling Refresh Local File List Automatically is a performance hit for Dreamweaver, so disable it unless you have a pretty fast computer with lots of memory (Step 4).

- If you do not define the Default Images folder, Dreamweaver will prompt you each time you try to use an image outside of the local defined folder (Step 5).

- If you do not define the HTTP address, Dreamweaver will not be able to verify local links that are referenced by absolute URLs and will report unknown or broken links (Step 6).

- Enabling the site cache is a performance hit to Dreamweaver because the cache is rebuilt quite often (Step 7).

7. Enable the cache by selecting the Cache: Enable Cache check box. This tells Dreamweaver to build and use a site cache for this site, which allows you to use the Assets panel. It also allows Dreamweaver to more efficiently manage the links in the local site. Figure 11-2 shows the completed Local category.

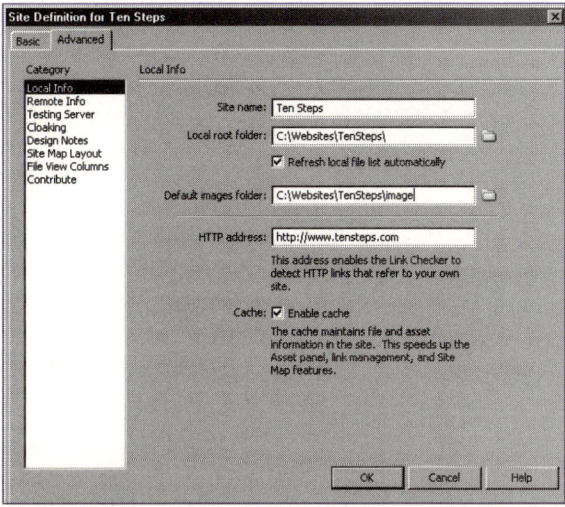

Figure 11-2: The Advanced dialog box with fields filled in

8. Select the Testing Server category and choose None from the Server Model drop-down menu if you are creating an HTML-based Web site. Make the appropriate selection in this category to match your chosen language.

9. Click the OK button on the Site Definition dialog box to create the basic HTML site and close the Site Definition dialog box.

10. Open the Files panel. Your new site is added to the Site list and it will be the active site.

cross-reference

▪ See Task 218 for defining a remote and testing server (Step 8).

Task

Adding Files and Folders in the Files Panel

When you open a new file from the main menu or the Start window, the files are not saved. When you create them via the Files panel, they are saved automatically.

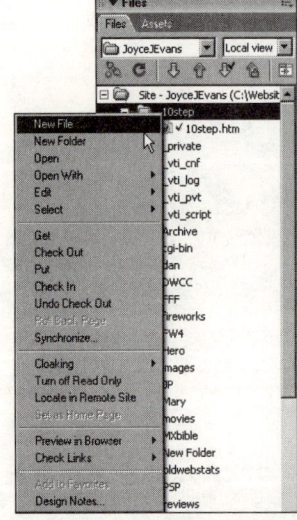

Figure 12-1: The Files panel with a selection made

1. Activate the Files panel (F8) or select its name in the docked panel area.

2. Right-/Control+click a folder to which you want to add a file or folder, as shown in Figure 12-1.

3. Select New File (or New Folder), as shown in Figure 12-1.

4. An untitled document name appears and is highlighted. Type in a file or folder name. (See Figure 12-2.)

5. Press Enter/Return or click anywhere in the document to accept the change.

6. If you want to rename the file/folder, right-/Control+click the name, select Edit ⇨ Rename, and type in a new name (see Figure 12-3).

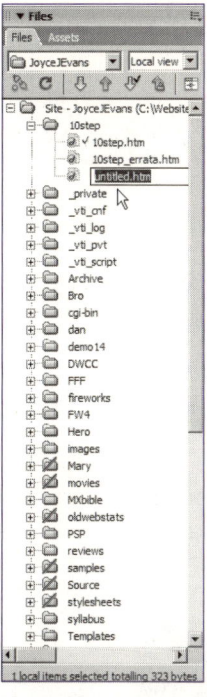

Figure 12-2: The new folder added

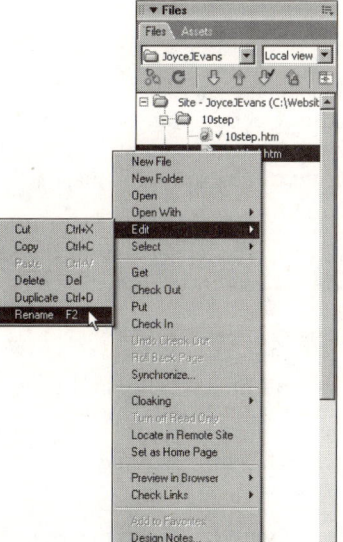

Figure 12-3: Editing the filename

cross-reference

- Refer to Task 4 for other ways of adding files.

Setting the Page Properties

If you are creating a very small site or just a page or two, you may find it easier to set your page properties using the Page Properties dialog box. The preferred method is using external style sheets. Page Properties adds embedded styles and affects the current page only.

1. Open a document.

2. Click the Page Properties button in the Property inspector or choose Modify ⇨ Page Properties (Ctrl/Command+J) to open the Page Properties dialog box, shown in Figure 13-1.

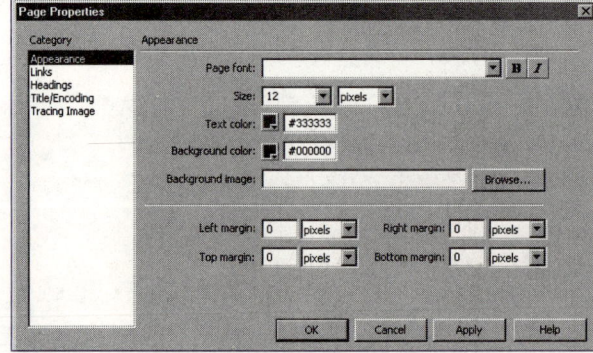

Figure 13-1: Page Properties dialog box

3. The Appearance category is selected by default unless you've previously selected another category. You can select the font family, size, and color you'd like for the page. This category also allows you to select the background color and navigate to a background image if you are using one.

4. If you want the page to abut against the top and left sides, type o into each of the Margin fields. A blank field does not mean zero. Each browser has a default margin.

5. Select the Links category. Here you can set the link colors by using the Color Picker or by typing in the hexadecimal number in the applicable field.

6. Select the Headings category. Here you can set the size and color of each heading.

7. Select the Title/Encoding category (see Figure 13-2). Fill in a title for your site and select an encoding method if appropriate. Encoding is grayed out if you don't have other character sets for other languages.

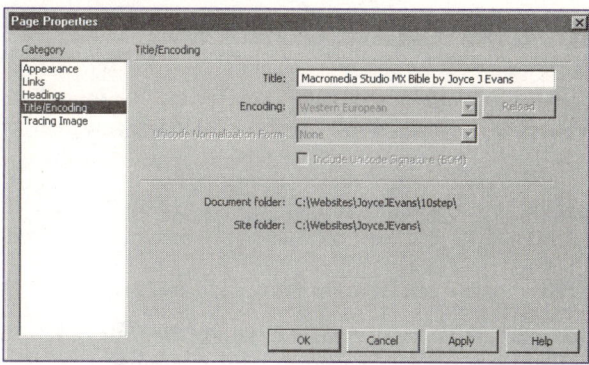

Figure 13-2: The Title/Encoding category

8. Select the Tracing Image category, and use the Tracing Image Browse button to locate and choose a tracing image for the page. Set its transparency using the Image Transparency slider. Figure 13-3 shows a tracing image set at 40% opacity.

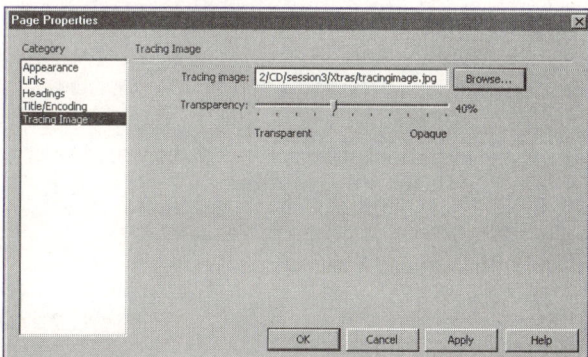

Figure 13-3: The Tracing Image category selected and filled in

9. Click the OK button on the Page Properties dialog box to effect the changes and close the dialog box. Clicking Cancel only cancels changes made since the dialog box's Apply button was last pressed or reverts to the state the fields were in prior to the dialog box being opened.

10. Choose File ➪ Save (Ctrl/Command+S) to save the changes to the page.

cross-references

- Refer to Part IX for using CSS styles to define your Page Properties.

- Refer to Task 31 to learn how Dreamweaver adds styles using the Property inspector and Page Properties.

- Refer to Task 165 for converting the embedded styles into an external style sheet.

Adding and Changing Colors

Adding and changing colors in Dreamweaver is quite easy. The simplest way to know when you have a color option is by the small color box that appears next to certain options.

1. Open a new document by clicking HTML in the Start Page, from the Create New Column.

2. In the Property inspector, click Page Properties.

3. With the Appearance category selected, click inside the little box next to Text Color. The Color Picker opens and your cursor changes into a dropper. Pass the cursor over a color and notice the hexadecimal number changes, as shown in Figure 14-1.

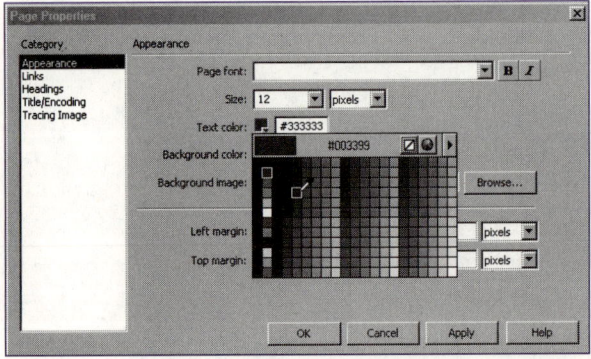

Figure 14-1: The Color Picker open and a color being selected

4. Cancel the Page Properties and look in the Property inspector. Notice a Text Color field is available. It doesn't matter if the field is grayed out. You can click in the box and select a color from the Color Picker, as shown in Figure 14-2.

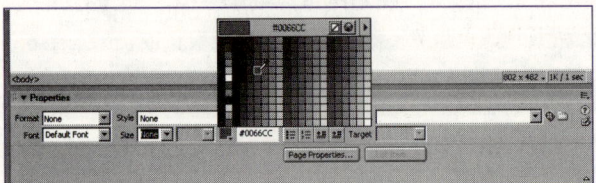

Figure 14-2: Selecting a color from the Property inspector

5. Figure 14-3 shows the relevant styles for a style sheet. You can click the color boxes here as well, including those that only have an outline because they currently have no color set.

Task 14

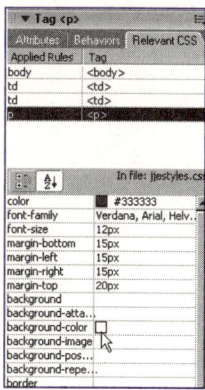

Figure 14-3: The Tag inspector showing the relevant CSS for a style sheet

6. Click any color box, and then click the Options pop-up menu in the top right corner. You can select other color options here, as well as select Web Safe, as shown in Figure 14-4. Keep in mind, however, that the Web Safe option shifts any color selection you make to the nearest Web-safe color.

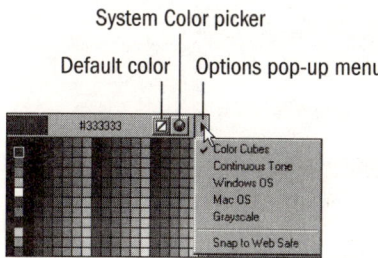

Figure 14-4: The Color Picker's Options pop-up menu

7. You can also click the box with the red slash for the default color or click the System Color Picker icon. In the System Color dialog box, you can enter specific RGB (Red, Green, Blue) colors and add custom colors to your palette.

cross-reference

• Refer to Task 173 for changing link colors using CSS styles.

Using the Insert Bar to Add Common Objects

Dreamweaver offers many different methods of performing the same function. With this in mind, you can use either the Insert menu item or the Insert bar to enter just about anything on the page.

1. First, you must create a new document or open an existing document (choose an HTML document for this task).

2. The Common category is selected by default, as shown in Figure 15-1.

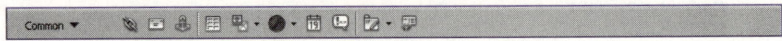

Figure 15-1: Insert bar showing the Common category

3. Select the Date object, as shown in Figure 15-2.

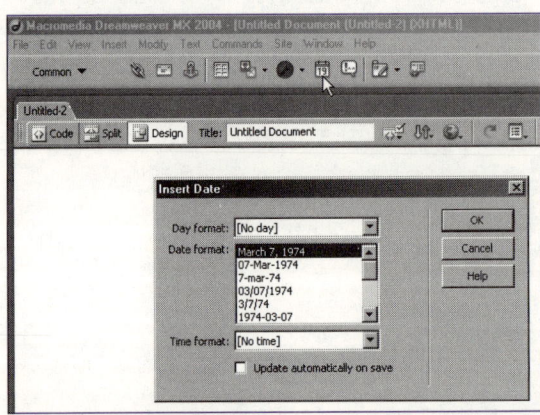

Figure 15-2: Selecting the Date object in the Common category of the Insert bar and the Date dialog box

4. The Insert Date dialog box opens, as shown in Figure 15-2.

5. Change the date formats to whatever format you want, and click OK to close the dialog box. The date is inserted at the current cursor position, as shown in Figure 15-3.

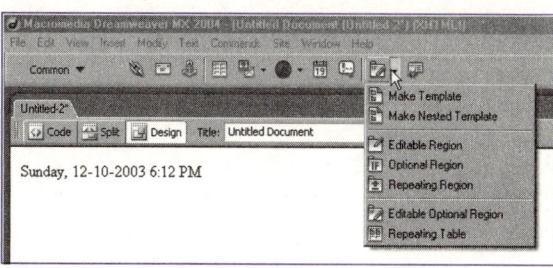

Figure 15-3: Date inserted

6. Notice that some of the objects have little arrows next to them. These objects have menus with additional objects available. When you select an object from a menu, the icon changes to the last object used. Figure 15-3 shows the Template menu opened.

7. To change categories, click the down arrow next to the Common category name, as shown in Figure 15-4.

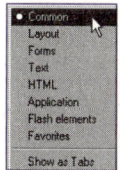

Figure 15-4: The various categories of the Insert bar

8. Experiment with the different items in the various Insert bar categories to get familiar with what types of objects are available from each.

9. Click the Show as Tabs option at the bottom of the Category menu. All the categories now display as tabs. To return back to the menu, right-/Control+click the Insert name and select Show as Menu.

cross-references

- Refer to Tasks 10 and 11 for defining a new site.

- To open an existing file, review Task 4 (Step 1).

Adding Favorites to the Insert Bar

One of the new features of Dreamweaver MX 2004 is a Favorites category in the Insert bar. You can now customize this category for the way you work.

1. Open a new document. The Insert bar isn't activated unless a document is open.

2. Right-/Control+click the Table icon, as shown in Figure 16-1. You can actually right-/Control+click any icon.

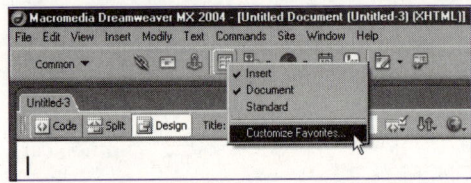

Figure 16-1: Right-/Control+click the Table icon in the Common category of the Insert bar

3. Select Customize Favorites. The Customize Favorite Objects dialog box opens, as shown in Figure 16-2.

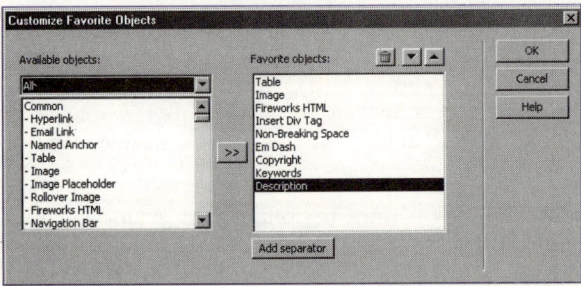

Figure 16-2: The Customize Favorites dialog box

4. You can choose to see all the objects in a list or select individual categories. For now leave All selected.

5. Select an object. I selected Table, since I use it frequently.

6. Click the >> button between the Available Objects and Favorite Object boxes to add the object.

7. Repeat for all the objects you frequently use. I didn't add things like form elements because it's easier to simply open the Forms category. You'll need to decide which objects you'd like quick access to.

notes

- If you frequently use one of the Server technologies, you can select it from the Available Object menu and add it to your Favorites category for quick access (Step 4).

- You can only add single objects to the Favorites category (not menu lists).

8. Select an object and use the up or down arrow to rearrange the order or press the trash can to delete an object. If you want to place a separator between objects, select the object that will be in front of the separator, then click the Add Separator button, as shown in Figure 16-3.

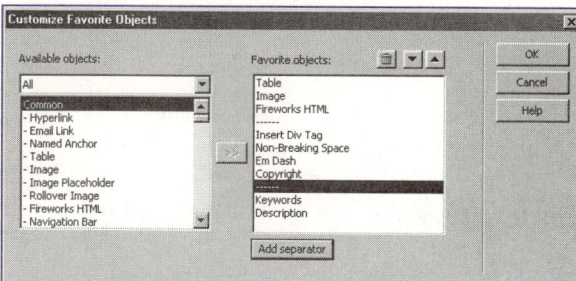

Figure 16-3: Separators added

9. Click OK when you are done.

10. View your new Favorites category (see Figure 16-4).

Figure 16-4: Favorite objects added to the Favorites category of the Insert bar

cross-reference

▪ Refer to Task 15 for using the Insert bar.

Task 16

Selecting Invisible Elements

There are a lot of elements, such as anchors, scripts, comments, and so on, that you can't visually see in your document. But there is a way to be able to easily select these elements.

1. Open a new page or one with invisible elements in it.

2. Choose Edit ⇨ Preferences.

3. Select the Invisible Elements category, as shown in Figure 17-1.

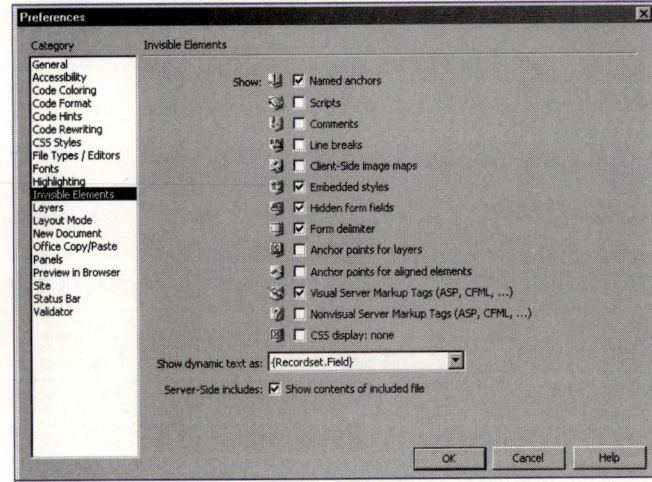

Figure 17-1: The Invisible Elements category of Preferences

4. Select any additional elements for which you'd like the gold anchors to show, or deselect any you don't care about.

5. At the bottom you'll see an option to show the contents of an include file. An *include file* is an image, page, and so on that is linked to from the document. If you want to see this file visually in your document, keep it selected.

6. Click OK to close the dialog box when you are done.

7. To view, click the Anchor icon in the Common category of the Insert bar. Type a name into the Anchor dialog box, as shown in Figure 17-2. You aren't really linking an anchor tag; it's just a quick invisible element you can add.

notes

- You may want to select Scripts if you use them frequently so you can easily select and edit them (Step 4).

- An anchor tag provides a link from text to another location in the same page (Step 7).

- If you see a check by Invisible Elements and you select it, you will actually be deselecting it (Step 8).

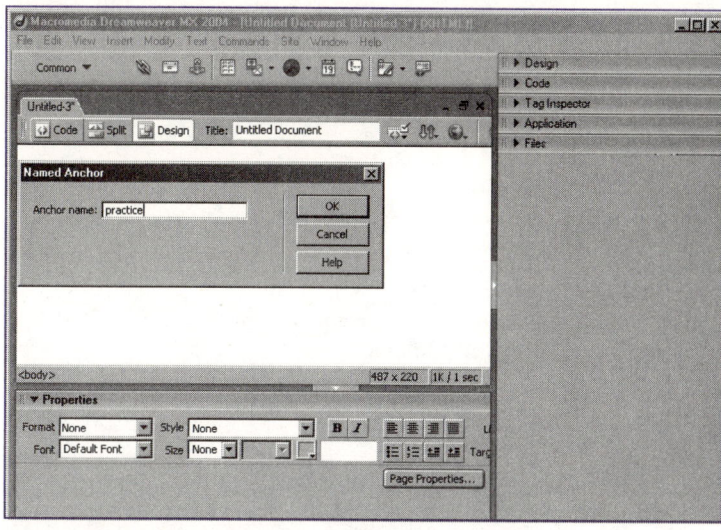

Figure 17-2: An anchor tag being added

8. If you can't see the gold anchor symbol, choose View ➪ Visual Aids
    and select Invisible Elements. It's selected if there is a check mark
    by it.

9. A page with just the anchor tag added is shown in Figure 17-3. You
    can select these gold symbols and edit the element they represent.
    The properties appear in the Property inspector when the gold
    symbols are selected.

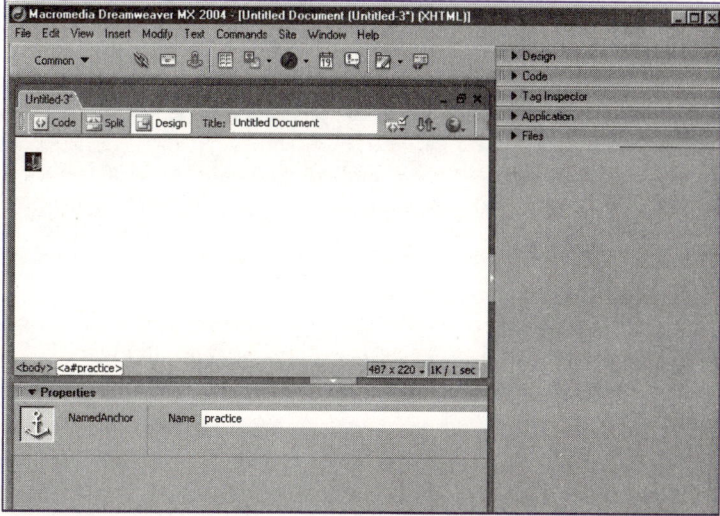

Figure 17-3: The invisible element of an anchor tag is represented by the gold symbol
in the document

10. Close this practice page.

cross-reference

▪ You'll use a lot more invisible elements in Part XI, on
coding.

Modifying Meta Data Content

Meta data tags are used in the head of the document for several reasons—for instance, to help search engines prioritize your page and to help the visitor's browser determine how to display your page.

1. Open the Files panel (F8) and open an existing file or create a new file.

2. To open the Head Content Display area, choose View ⇨ Head Content (Ctrl/Command+Shift+W). Each head block element is visually represented by a selectable icon, as shown in Figure 18-1. They are added just below the Document toolbar.

Figure 18-1: Head content—displayed

3. Position your cursor in this new pane, and its background color changes from gray to white. This means the text is editable (see Figure 18-2).

4. Select the Meta icon (second from left) and switch to Code view. You'll see that there are no keywords or descriptions yet. But if you opened a page with keywords and description added, that portion of the code would be highlighted and you could edit it directly in Code view.

Task **18**

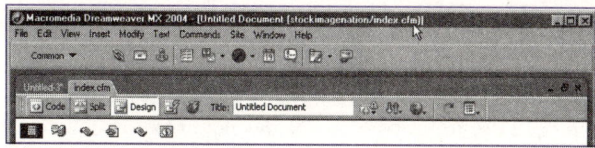

Figure 18-2: Head content—editable

5. Select Insert ➪ HTML ➪ Head Tags, and a pop-up menu appears with head block tag choices: Meta, Keywords, Description, Refresh, Base, and Link. Each of these items inserts different content in the head block of the document.

6. For the purpose of this task, choose Insert ➪ HTML ➪ Head Tags ➪ Description. A dialog box opens, as shown in Figure 18-3.

Figure 18-3: Description dialog box

7. Type in the desired description for the page and click the OK button.

8. After you click OK, the inserted meta data tag for Description is inserted in the proper place and it is highlighted in both Code view and Head Content view. If the Property inspector is open, you will notice that it displays the Description properties, as shown in Figure 18-4.

9. You can open Split view (which shows a split screen with Design view) and Code view to see the meta data tag currently highlighted and properly positioned.

cross-reference

▪ Opening an existing file is discussed in Task 4 (Step 1).

Configuring Design Notes

Design Notes are a useful productivity tool individually assigned to each Web page that you can use to let your fellow developers know information about the file, to remind yourself about important information regarding the file. There are also automatic Design Notes made by Dreamweaver that stores special information maintained by Dreamweaver and other Macromedia products. This task deals with how to make your own Design Notes.

notes

- Enabling Design Notes for sharing is important when developers are working in a group so that they can know at a glance what the status of the file is or read important information from a codeveloper regarding the file (Step 4).

- Design Notes are not exclusive to Dreamweaver. Flash and Fireworks use them as well; so if your site has a note associated, chances are that either of those programs wrote the Design Note. This occurs because either program records specific information that is used for round-tripping the data from the page (Step 5).

1. Choose Sites ➪ Manage Site to open the Edit Sites dialog box, as shown in Figure 19-1.

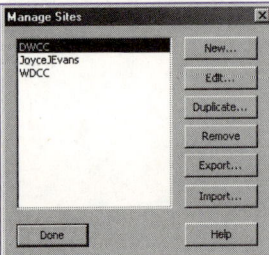

Figure 19-1: The Manage Sites dialog box

2. Select the site for which you want to configure Design Notes, and click the Edit button.

3. Click the Advanced tab of the Site Definition dialog box and select the Design Notes category, as shown in Figure 19-2.

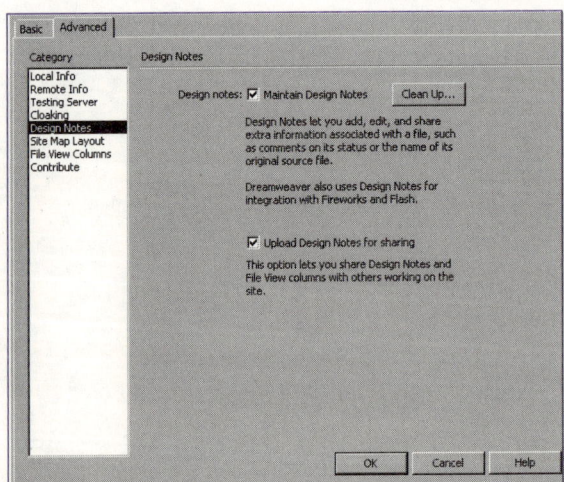

Figure 19-2: Design Notes category of Site Definition dialog box

4. By default, Design Notes are enabled and uploaded to the server for sharing. If you do not desire the sharing of your Design Notes because you are the only one editing the site, remove the check from the Upload Design Notes for Sharing check box.

5. Uncheck Maintain Design Notes to disable Dreamweaver from using Design Notes.

6. Click the Clean Up button. As shown in Figure 19-3, once this option is clicked, a dialog box warns you that existing Design Notes will be deleted. Click the dialog box's Yes button to delete the notes; click the No button to leave them intact.

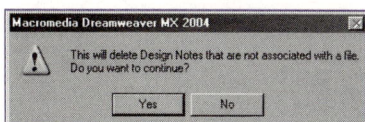

Figure 19-3: The warning that appears when you click the Clean Up button

7. Save the settings by clicking the OK button of the dialog box. This saves the changes and closes the Site Definition dialog box. Clicking the Cancel button does not save the setting changes made.

8. Click the Done button on the Manage Sites dialog box to close it.

cross-reference

▪ See Task 20 for more information on using Design Notes.

Task **20**

Assigning Design Notes

Design Notes allow you to save file-specific information for future use or for the use of a team member. Once you get into the routine of using them for your files, you will find that you can return to the site a year later and still know all about each page to which you have assigned a Design Note.

1. Open the Files Panel (press F8, or select it in the panel group area).

2. Select the file to which you want to assign a Design Note and double-click to open it. From the Options pop-up menu, select File ⇨ Design Notes to open the Design Notes dialog box, as shown in Figures 20-1 and 20-2.

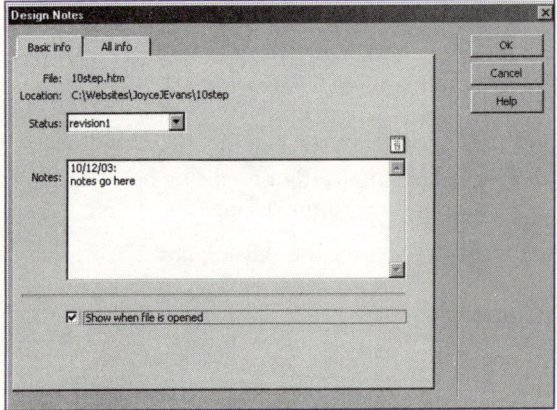

Figure 20-1: Design Notes dialog box—Basic Info tab

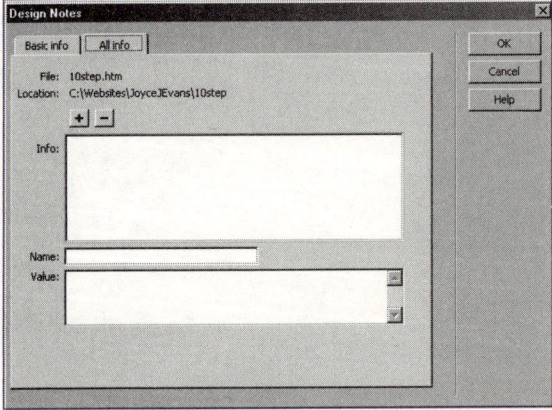

Figure 20-2: Design Notes dialog box—All Info tab

3. To declare the document's current status, use the Basic Info tab. Here you can select a predetermined state in the Status drop-down menu, such as revision 1 and so forth.

4. Click the Date icon to assign a date. Type in your notes in the Notes field. Set the Design Note to always open when the related file is opened by selecting the Show When File Is Opened check box. Click OK to close the dialog box.

5. Click the All Info tab to insert customized Design Note categories.

6. To add a Design Note key, type the name in the Name field. To assign a value to the named key, select the name in the Info field and type the value in the Value field. The Info field populates with `Key name=value`.

7. To add additional key name/value pairs, select the name/value pair in the Info field and click the Plus (+) button above the Info field.

8. To remove a key name/value pair, select the name/value pair in the Info field and click the minus sign (–) button above the Info field.

9. Click the OK button of the Design Notes dialog box to save changes and close the dialog box.

10. To view the Design Note that doesn't open when the document opens, choose File ➪ Design Notes.

cross-reference

- Refer to Task 82 for uploading your files to a server.

Configuring File Check In and Check Out

When you are working in a group environment and multiple people are accessing files on the site, it soon becomes apparent that you could end up with data loss because of users overwriting each other's files. Luckily, Dreamweaver has a feature that prevents the inadvertent editing of a file by more than one person at a time.

note

- Leaving Check Out Files When Opening disabled causes a dialog box to appear that asks you to View, Check Out, or Cancel. Selecting View opens a read-only copy of the file. Selecting Check Out checks the file out if it is currently checked in. Cancel closes the dialog box (Step 5).

1. Choose Sites ⇨ Manage Sites, and click New ⇨ Site to open the Manage Sites dialog box.

2. Select the site you want to configure Check In and Out for and click the Edit button.

3. Click the Advanced tab of the Site Definition dialog box, and select the Remote Info category, as shown in Figure 21-1. If you don't see anything except one field, you'll need to select FTP from the drop-down list.

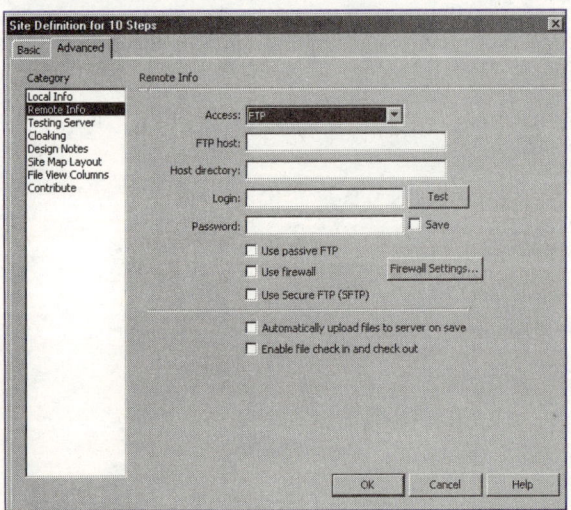

Figure 21-1: Remote Info category of the Site Definition dialog box

4. Select the Check In/Out check box to enable the Check In and Out feature. When this option is checked, three other fields appear that require completion.

5. Select the Check Out Files When Opening check box. If this is left unchecked, you will be prompted each time to check the file out or simply view it each time you attempt to open a file (see Figure 21-2).

6. Type a unique name for yourself in the Check Out Name field. This field is used to show who currently has the file checked out in the Files panel.

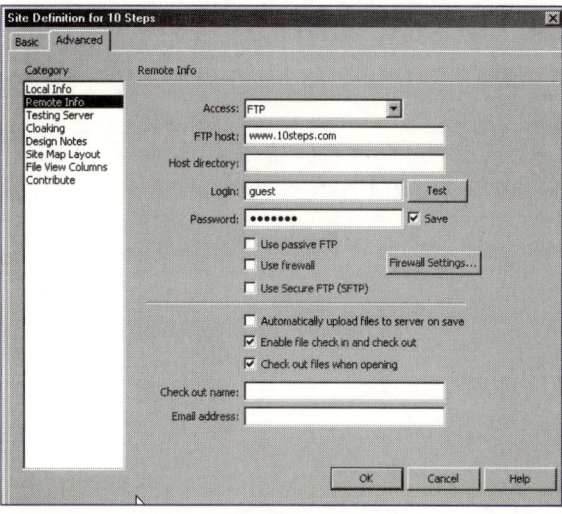

Figure 21-2: Checked-in file dialog box

7. Type your valid e-mail address in the Email Address field. This field is used by Dreamweaver so that another user can contact you if he or she needs access to a file that you have checked out. Once completed, the Site Definition dialog box should look something like Figure 21-3.

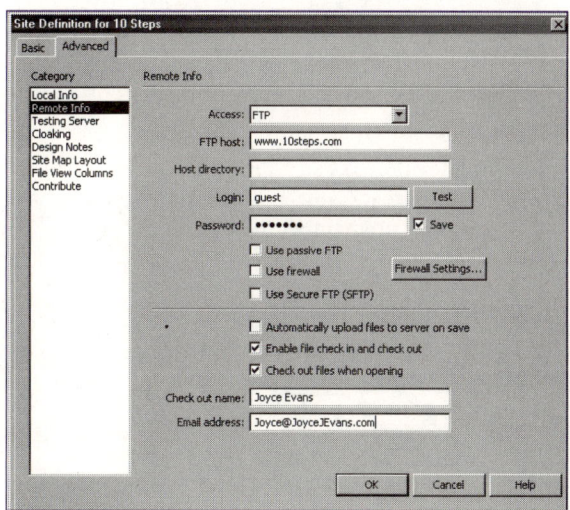

Figure 21-3: Check In and Out properly configured

8. Click OK to close the Site Definition dialog box. Clicking Cancel cancels all changes made to this section of data entered.

9. Click the Manage Sites dialog box's Done button to close the Manage Sites dialog box.

cross-references

- Refer to Task 22 for information on using File Check In and Check Out.

- Refer to Task 218 for setting up a remote server (Step 3).

Using Check In and Check Out

When multiple developers are editing the same site, overwriting one another's work becomes a troublesome issue, and data loss may occur if the team is not very careful. Dreamweaver provides Check In and Check Out capabilities to reduce this possibility to almost zero.

note

▪ If the file is checked out by another team member, you are prompted to contact the other author. Overwrite his or her checkout or to open a read-only copy of the file (Step 4).

1. Open the Files panel using Window ➪ Site (F8). See Figure 22-1 for a reference of the Files panel buttons.

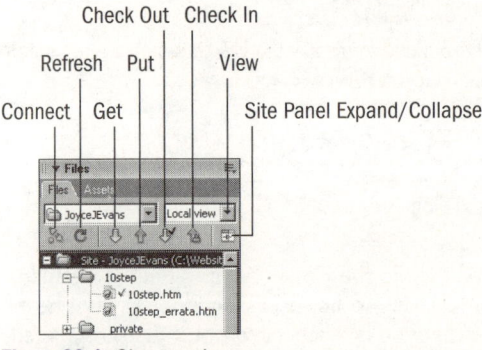

Figure 22-1: Site panel

2. To connect to the remote server, click the Connect button in the Files panel.

3. To check out a file, select the file and click the Check Out button in the Files panel.

4. If a file is checked out by a team member, a dialog box opens, asking you if you would like to open a read-only copy (View), check the file out yourself (overriding your team member's checkout), or cancel the operation (see Figure 22-2).

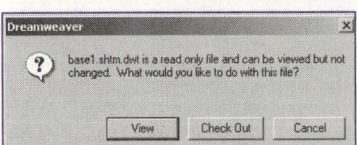

Figure 22-2: Check Out prompt

cautions

▪ A remote server must be defined in the Site Definition for Check In and Check Out to be enabled and to function (Step 2).

▪ Check In and Check Out must be configured in the Site Definition for the Check In/Out capabilities to be enabled and to function (Step 3).

▪ You must have a default e-mail client configured that can talk to the operating system. Otherwise, clicking the e-mail link will not function as desired (Step 5).

5. If the file is checked out by another team member, expand the Files panel and click the team member's e-mail link to send an e-mail asking the current status of the file and to check it back in if the team member is done with it. The e-mail link is shown in Figure 22-3.

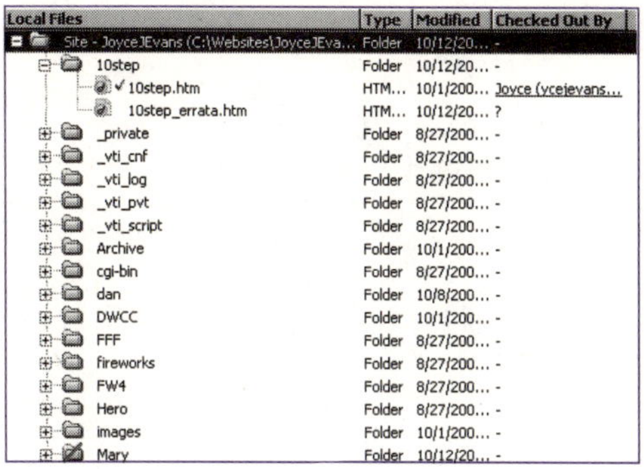

Figure 22-3: The Files panel expanded to display the link to e-mail a team member regarding a file that has been checked out

6. To check in a file, select the file and click the Check In button on the Files panel.

Task 22

cross-reference

- Refer to Task 21 for information on configuring Check In/Out.

Task **23**

Setting the Home Page

The home page of your site needs to be set for Dreamweaver to generate a site map. In this task you'll tell Dreamweaver what the home page of your site is.

1. Open the Files panel.

2. From the Site menu, select the site you want to work on, as shown in Figure 23-1.

note

▪ The home page in this instance isn't the default of the entire site. The default.cfm page for this site redirects to the index.cfm page inside the stockimagenation folder (Step 3).

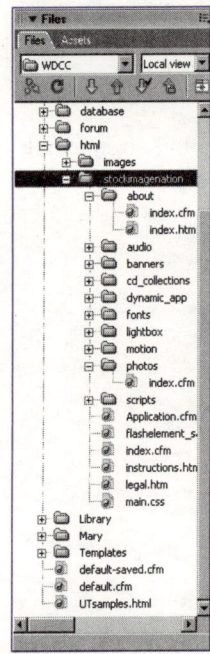

Figure 23-1: The site is selected and open in the Site panel

3. Select the file that will be the home page of your site (see Figure 23-2). Each server has a document name that it is configured to use as the default page for folders and domains that it hosts. This could be, for example, home.asp, default.htm, or index.htm.

4. Select the Files Options pop-up menu arrow to open it.

5. Select Site ⇨ Set as Home Page, as shown in Figure 23-3.

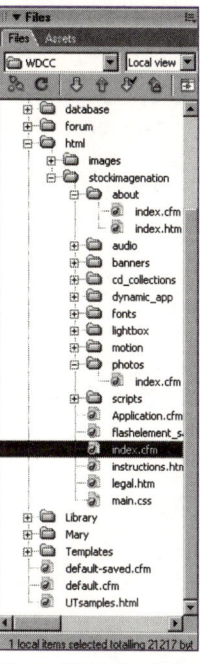

Figure 23-2: The index.cfm file of the main site folder is selected

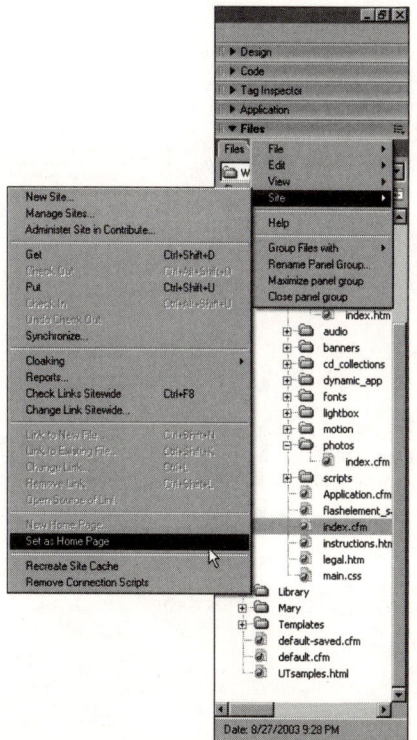

Figure 23-3: Setting the index.cfm file as the site's home page

cross-references

- Refer to Task 10 or 11 for defining a site (Step 2).

- Refer to Task 24 for configuring the site's site map.

24

Configuring the Site Map Layout

Each server has a document name that it is configured to use as the default page for folders and domains that it hosts. Examples include home.asp, default.htm, or index.htm. With that in mind, you need to tell Dreamweaver what the default home page is for your site so that the site map can be maintained based on the root file.

1. Choose Sites ⇨ Manage Sites to open the Manage Sites dialog box.

2. Select the site to configure the Home Page for and click the Edit button.

3. Click the Advanced tab of the Site Definition dialog box, and select the Site Map Layout category, as shown in Figure 24-1.

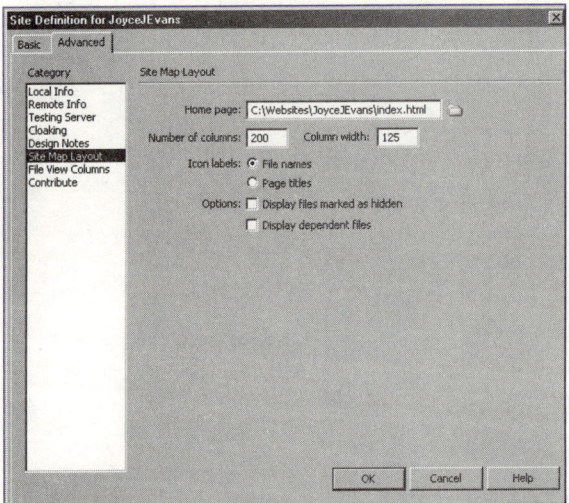

Figure 24-1: Site Map category of Site Definition dialog box

4. In the Home Page field, type the name of the root default document that your host advised you to use for your domain. If the file already exists, you can use the Browse button to locate the file.

5. Change the Number of Columns field to reflect the number of columns that you wish displayed per row of the site map.

6. Change the Column Width field to reflect the amount of space in between each object on a row.

7. Choose between File Names or Page Titles for the Icon Labels.

notes

▪ Be sure to contact your host to find out what default names they have configured for their server that your domain is hosted on.

▪ You may want to adjust this depending on whether you use filenames or page titles for the Icon Labels field (Step 6).

▪ Icon labels are the labels for the file icons in the Site Map view. Some people work better with filenames, others with page titles. Try both to develop your own preferences (Step 7).

▪ Again, develop your own style for the site map. Hidden files work well for some and not others. The same goes for dependant files. Hidden files set to display are shown in italics in the site map (Step 8).

▪ If the specified home page does not exist in the current site definition, you will be prompted to allow Dreamweaver to create the file for you. Choose Yes to do so (Step 9).

8. Two options are available for the site map: Display Files Marked as Hidden and Display Dependant Files. Display Files Marked as Hidden displays hidden files in the site map that may throw the view off. Display Dependant Files displays the filename of each asset, including links, associated to each page, so the site map may become complex in a hurry. The completed Site Definition category is shown in Figure 24-2.

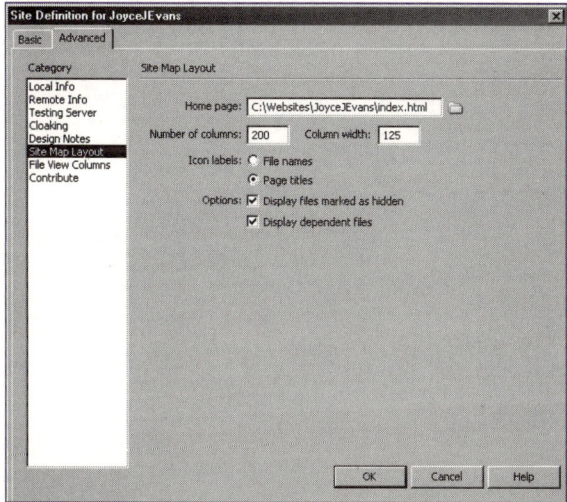

Figure 24-2: Completed Site Map Layout category

9. Click the OK button of the Site Definition dialog box to save the settings and close the dialog box. Click OK to close the Site Definition dialog box; then click Done.

10. To view the site map, click the Expander icon in the Site panel. Click the Site Map icon's arrow and select Map Only. You'll see the map of your site if the links are set up. Figure 24-3 shows a site that has index files inside of multiple folders—that's why there are so many index.cfm (ColdFusion) files.

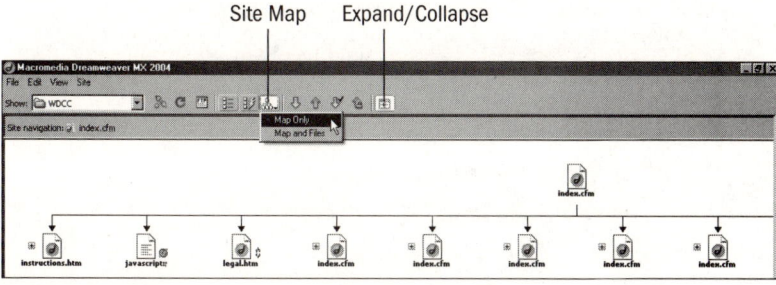

Figure 24-3: A site map of a site with multiple folders containing index pages

Sharing and Retrieving Site Definitions

Dreamweaver allows you to export and import site definitions. This allows you to perform your own backup, as well as to share site definitions with fellow developers.

note

- Exporting your site definitions is part of your daily backup chores to avert disaster should anything bad happen to your Dreamweaver installation or your hardware.

- If the site definition exists, the newly imported site definition is renamed with a trailing digit after it, starting at 0 (Step 6).

1. Choose Sites ⇨ Manage Sites to open the Manage Sites dialog box.

2. Select the site that you wish to export, and click the Export button, as shown in Figure 25-1.

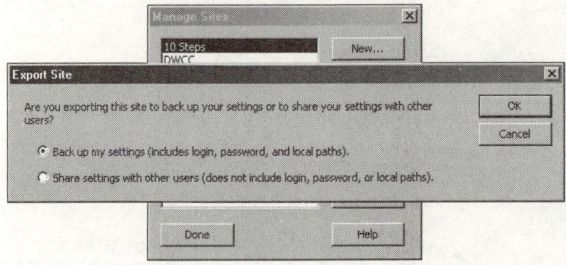

Figure 25-1: Export Site dialog box

Two options are available:

- *Back Up My Settings (Includes Login, Password, and Local Paths).* This is for backup purposes and for sharing with other users of the site.

- *Share Settings with Other Users (Does Not Include Login, Password, or Local Paths).* This is used for sharing the site definition with other developers that require their own login accounts.

3. Select either radio button and click the OK button. The Export Site dialog box appears, where you can save the file (.ste) to a location of your choosing (see Figure 25-2).

4. Click the Done button on the Edit Sites dialog box, and you are done with exporting the current site definition.

5. To import a previously exported site definition, choose Sites ⇨ Manage Sites to open the Manage Sites dialog box.

caution

- Be sure to save the file in a location outside of Dreamweaver's folders and outside the site folders so that you can locate it easily to back it up to floppy or to import it again in case of lost site definitions or if reinstallation is required (Step 3).

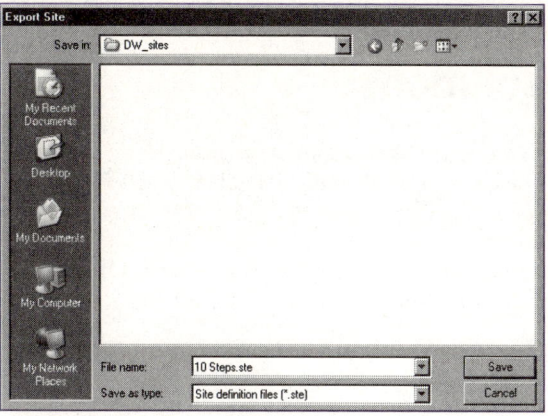

Figure 25-2: Save the exported STE file

6. Select the Import button in the Manage Sites dialog box. Using the Import Site dialog box, navigate and locate the desired STE file to import. Once selected, click the Open button. If the exported definition has the login, password, and local paths saved and the path exists, the import is finished. Click the Done button to close the Edit Sites dialog box.

7. If the imported site definition does not contain login, password, or local paths, when it is imported, the Choose Local Root Folder dialog box opens for you to choose the desired path to set the site definition to as its root, as shown in Figure 25-3.

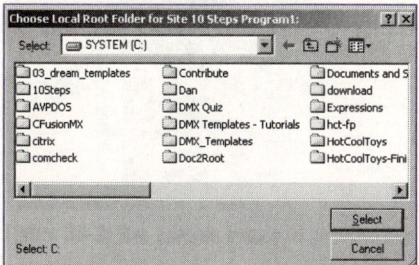

Figure 25-3: Choose Local Root Folder dialog box

cross-reference

- Refer to Task 218 to configure the Remote Server category of the Site Definition dialog box to insert your FTP connection information (Step 7).

Testing the Page Using Different Monitor Resolutions

Before you go live, an important test to conduct is to check the page on different monitor resolutions, such as 640 x 480, 800 x 600, and 1,024 x 768. With the following method, you can perform this test from within Dreamweaver:

1. Open a document from the Files panel (Ctrl/Command+O) and note the Window Size Selector on the document's status bar.

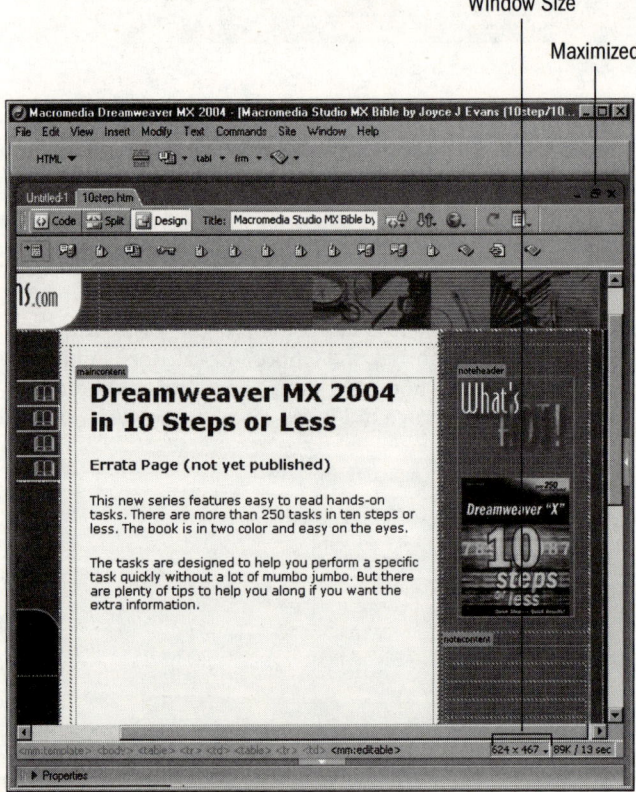

Figure 26-1: Window Size Selector

2. Undock the document window (click the Minimize/Maximize icon) and click the Window Size Chooser to open the menu. The menu displays the predefined settings and an Edit Sizes entry, as shown in Figure 26-2.

3. Select the desired window size from the list, and the document window resizes to the chosen setting. If the screen is incapable of displaying the selected size, a pop-up menu appears, advising you of the problem (see Figure 26-3).

note

- This method applies to all workspaces. This method cannot be used when the document window is maximized in the Dreamweaver MX 2004 or HomeSite workspaces or when the document is using Code view or Split view.

- When you are using Code view, the Window Size Chooser is removed from the status bar.

- When you are using Split view (Code/Design), the Window Size Chooser is visible, but all resolutions are disabled except for the Edit Sizes selection.

caution

- You cannot preview a resolution that your current desktop resolution cannot display.

Window Size

Minimized

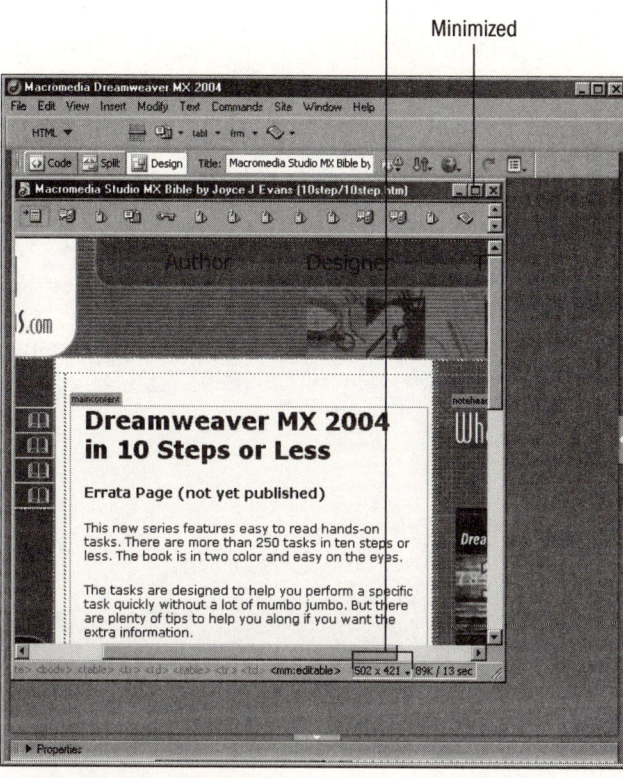

Figure 26-2: Window Size menu

Figure 26-3: Dreamweaver Warning dialog box

4. To add window sizes to the list, click the Window Size Chooser, and select Edit Sizes from the menu. The Preferences panel opens to the Status Bar category.

5. Scroll to the bottom of the list. To add a new size, click below the last item and you'll see a rectangle outline. Type the width, press Tab, type the height, press Tab, and type the description (this is used by the Window Size Chooser).

6. Click the OK button to effect the changes and close the Preferences panel.

7. The Window Size Chooser is populated with the newly added window size, and it is available immediately for use.

cross-reference

▪ Refer to Task 7 for setting up testing browsers.

Task 27

Using the Reference Panel

You can look up a lot of different information in the Reference panel. If you have a tag selected, the appropriate reference will open when you open the Reference panel.

1. Open Code view of a document and select the `<meta>` tag, as shown in Figure 27-1. You can simply click to place your cursor inside the tag or select the entire tag.

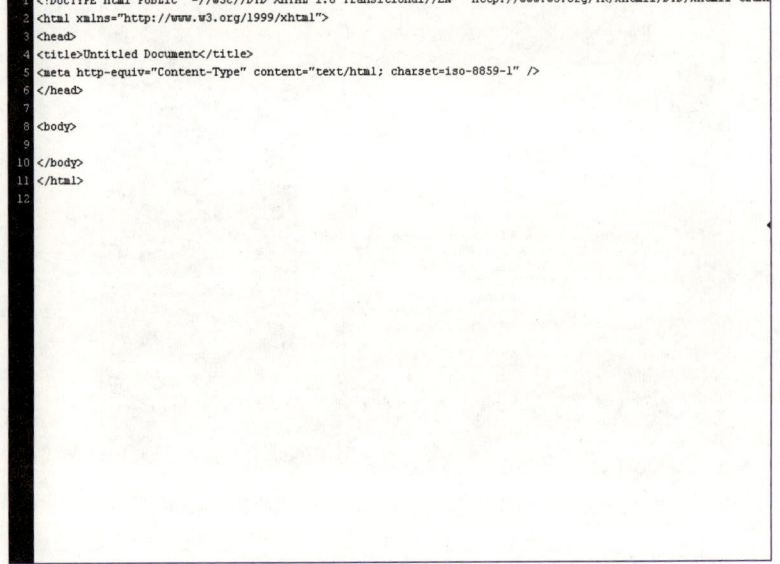

```
1  <!DOCTYPE html PUBLIC "-//W3C//DTD XHTML 1.0 Transitional//EN" "http://www.w3.org/TR/xhtml1/DTD/xhtml1-trans
2  <html xmlns="http://www.w3.org/1999/xhtml">
3  <head>
4  <title>Untitled Document</title>
5  <meta http-equiv="Content-Type" content="text/html; charset=iso-8859-1" />
6  </head>
7
8  <body>
9
10 </body>
11 </html>
12
```

Figure 27-1: The `<meta>` tag selected

2. Press F1 to activate the Reference panel. The O'Reilly HTML Reference opens with the META page activated, as shown in Figure 27-2.

3. You can select another tag (such as `<body>`) and press F1 to automatically bring up the associated information in the Reference panel (see Figure 27-3).

Task **27**

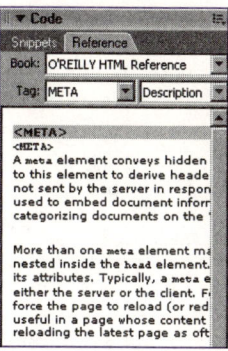

Figure 27-2: The Reference panel open

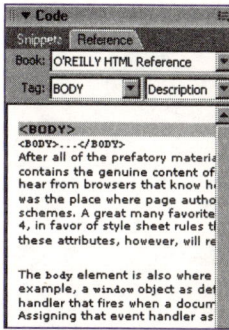

Figure 27-3: The changed panel

4. You can access a number of different types of references by selecting a book from the Book drop-down menu, as shown in Figure 27-4.

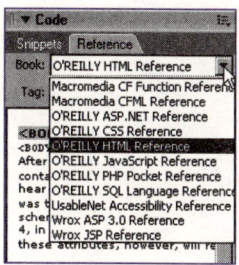

Figure 27-4: The Book drop-down menu

5. You can also select specific tags from the Tag drop-down menu.

cross-reference

• Refer to Task 2 for using the Start Page to access online help.

Part 2: Using Text and Images

Adding Text

Text is the most basic type of content to add to a document. Working with text in Dreamweaver MX 2004 is a lot like working with a word processing application like Microsoft Word, so if you've ever typed on a computer before, you shouldn't find this too hard. Once you can add text, I'll show you how to modify it in the tasks that follow in this part.

1. Open a new HTML document. To do so, in the Start Page, under Create New, select HTML, as shown in Figure 28-1.

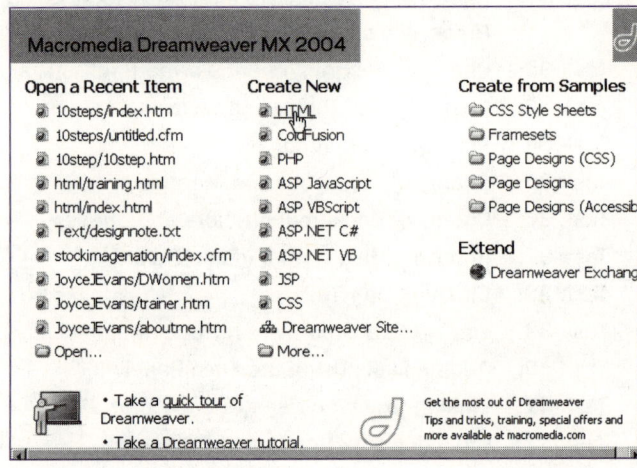

Figure 28-1: The Start Page

2. Or, if you have other documents open (or changed your preferences not to show the Start Page), select File ➪ New. A new document dialog box appears.

3. Select the Basic page category and HTML for the Basic page, and click Create (see Figure 28-2).

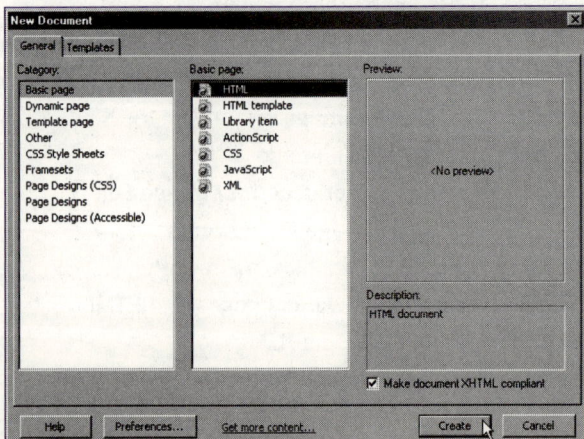

Figure 28-2: New Document dialog box

4. Make sure your new document is being viewed in Design view. If it isn't, click the Design view icon above the Document window, as shown in Figure 28-3.

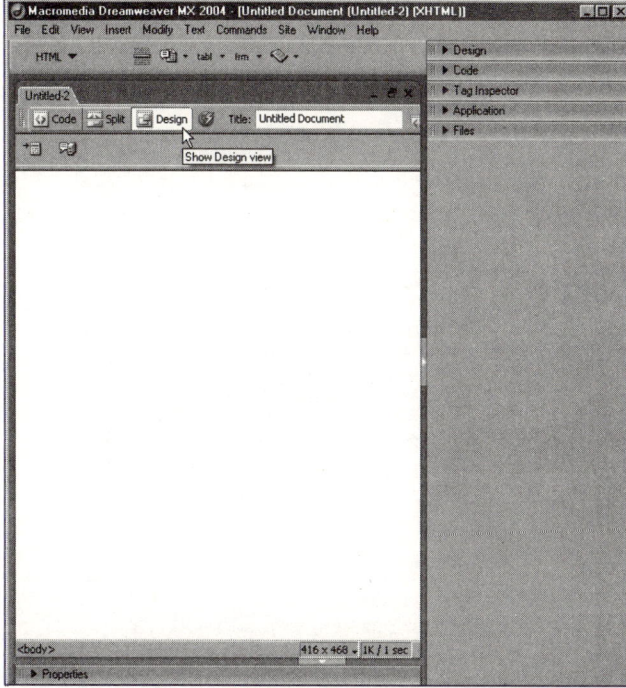

Figure 28-3: Blank document in Design view

5. Click once in the document to place your cursor, and make sure the cursor is blinking in the upper left corner of the document, as shown in Figure 28-3.

6. Notice the Property inspector, labeled Properties, at the bottom of the page. This is where you can control text in the tasks that follow. For now, everything is set at default settings. If you don't see the Property inspector, choose Window ➪ Properties.

7. Start typing. You should see text appear.

8. In the Title field above the middle of your document, replace "Untitled Document" with a name of your choosing. Use **Adding Text Page** if you don't know what to type. It's good to get in the habit of titling every page you work on. Titles are displayed in the top center of most browsers and "untitled" in the title bar looks unprofessional.

9. Select File ➪ Save to save your document.

tip

- You can often save yourself a lot of typing time by copying and pasting text from other applications, such as e-mail, Web pages, or Word documents, directly into your Dreamweaver documents. Line breaks should be maintained, but not the formatting (Step 4).

cross-reference

- See Task 37 for more information on importing text from Microsoft Word.

Formatting a Paragraph

The Formatting Paragraphs feature is used primarily for creating consistent headers for text documents. Most text you're going to work with will be in the default paragraph setting called None, and you will change font, color, size, placement, and so on using the other settings in the Property inspector or by using the preferred method of CSS styles (see Part 9).

1. Type a title, and then type a few words of text under it.

2. Select the title by clicking and dragging the mouse over it, as shown in Figure 29-1.

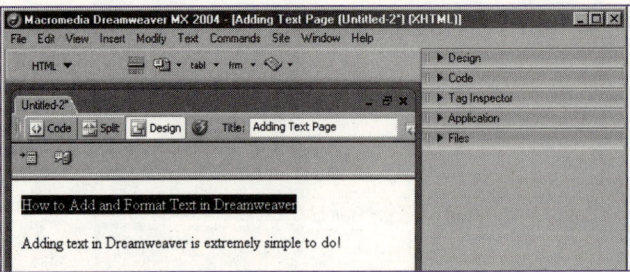

Figure 29-1: Selected title text

3. Click the arrow next to the Format field in the Property inspector and select Heading 1. Your title should get bigger and bolder. (The Format choice None is a default setting, and the Paragraph setting does not format selected text.)

4. Experiment with the other header sizes.

5. An unusual paragraph format is called Preformatted. To apply it, select the text under your title. Then in the Format menu in the Property inspector, select Preformatted. This makes your text mono-spaced and allows you to type more than one space or line break and have the spaces display. In normal text only one space or line return will display in a Web browser.

6. Try typing several spaces and line returns.

7. Select File ➪ Preview in Browser (F12) to see how it looks. If Dreamweaver does not have a Web browser listed, select Edit Browser List and use the Plus (+) button to add a browser. Figure 29-2 shows how the preformatted text appears in a browser.

caution

▪ Don't be alarmed if your text doesn't always appear in Web browsers exactly like you see it in Dreamweaver. This has to do with the way different Web browsers and computers interpret Web pages. You must do what the pros do and test your pages on different computers to make sure your layouts are acceptable.

Figure 29-2: Preformatted text with spaces and breaks in a browser

8. Select the preformatted text and switch it back to None in the Format bar.

9. Preview it in a browser to see the effect of preformatting text (see Figure 29-3).

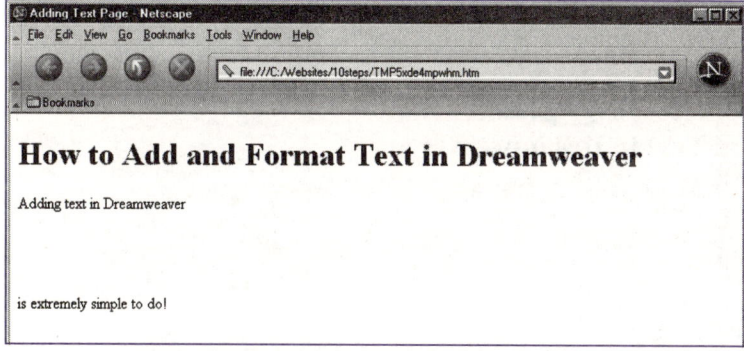

Figure 29-3: Preformatting removed from the sentence

tips

- Double-click text to select the entire row. To select blocks of text, place the cursor at the beginning of your desired text, and then hold the Shift key down and click the cursor at the end of the desired text (Step 1).

- You can get multiple spaces to show up in regular text by adding nonbreaking spaces. Choose Insert ➪ HTML ➪ Special Characters ➪ Non-Breaking Space (Step 4).

cross-references

- See Task 30 for changing the font, size, and color of text.

- See Task 160 for formatting the paragraph tag using CSS styles.

Changing the Font, Size, and Color of Text

In this task, you explore the basic modification of text in the Property inspector. Dreamweaver MX 2004 now uses styles to modify text, which is a new standard for HTML on the Web. But don't worry about it if you're a beginner or used older versions of Dreamweaver, because you won't notice much of a difference when modifying text in Design view. (On the other hand, if you look at the code, you will notice a big difference.)

1. Type some text to modify.

2. Select part of the text to modify and leave some unselected so you can see changes in context to default text (see Figure 30-1).

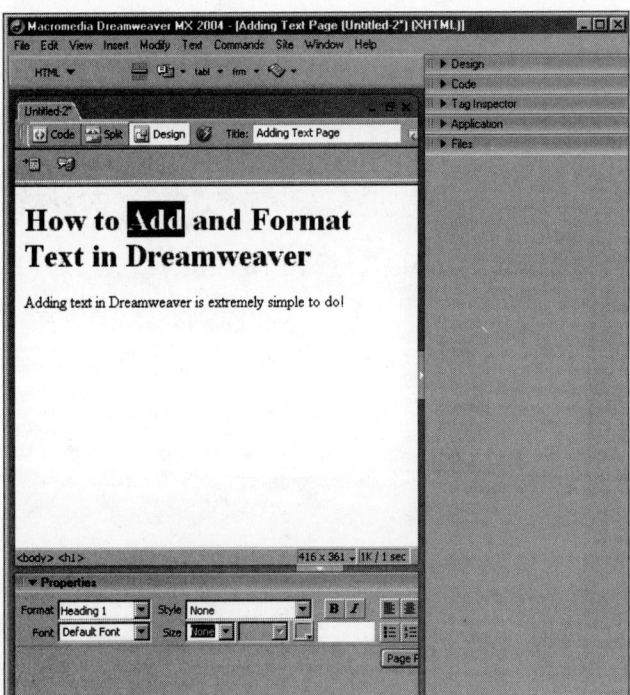

Figure 30-1: Selected text

3. Make sure you can see the Property inspector (Window ⇨ Properties), as shown in Figure 30-2.

Figure 30-2: Property inspector

4. Click the arrow for the Font field and select Arial, Helvetica, Sans Serif. Notice that the text changed from serif (curly-ended text) to sans serif (straight-ended text).

5. In the Size field, click the arrow, and from the menu, select 36. Your text should enlarge to 36-pixel font. You can also type a font size number directly into the Size field. The size choices of medium, xx-large applies sizes that are relative to the default font size of the user's browser, which is usually three (three is about 12 pixels). Figure 30-3 shows a page with the selected text set to a large size.

tip

· Keeping text 10 to 12 points provides good read-ability and is the size users are accustomed to for long blocks of text (Step 5). You can change the settings from Pixels to Points in the Property inspector.

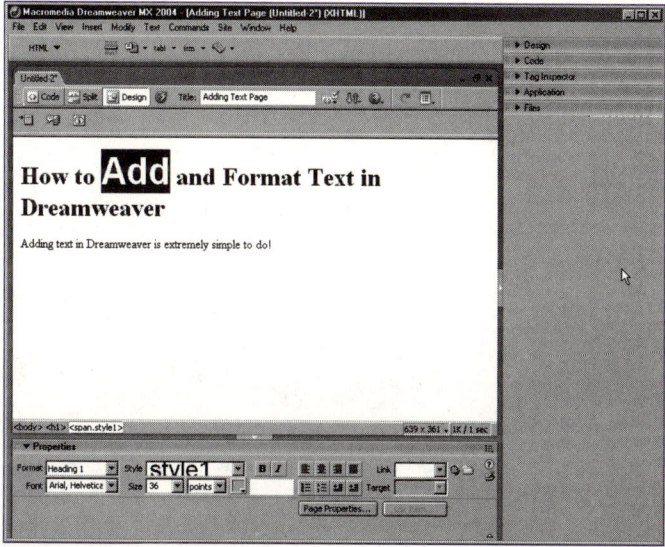

Figure 30-3: Page with large text

6. With your text selected and your size at 36, click the Pixels menu to the right of the Size field and select the percent symbol (%). Your text should get much smaller, because you've set it for 36 percent. Percents and the other choices in this menu let you size your text whatever way you feel most comfortable.

7. With text selected, click the Text Color box and choose a blue color swatch (see Figure 30-4).

cross-reference

· Refer to Task 32 for chang-ing text alignment, format-ting lists, and indenting.

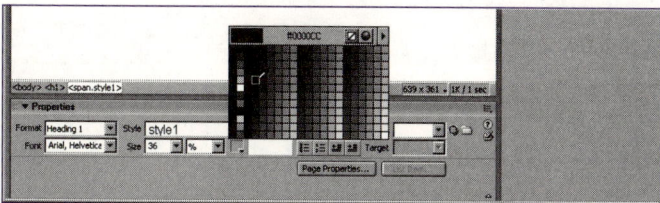

Figure 30-4: Page with altered text and settings in Property inspector

Understanding How Dreamweaver Adds Styles Using the Property Inspector and Page Properties

Dreamweaver MX 2004 performs text formatting differently than in earlier versions. Previously, HTML styles were added, as well as font tags. These tags are now deprecated (that is, they are being phased out). To keep in line with current standards, Dreamweaver uses styles, applied via the Property inspector or the Properties dialog box. The caveat here is that when you use the Property inspector or Page Properties, the styles are embedded in your document. This is just fine for one page but not the best way to go for an entire site.

1. Type a few lines of text.

2. Select half of the text.

3. Using the Property inspector, change the font, size, and color as shown in Figure 31-1.

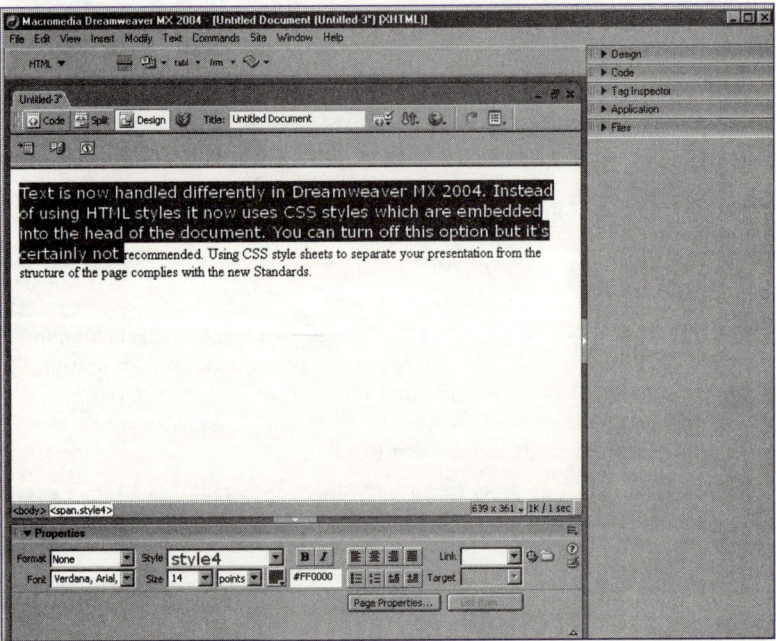

Figure 31-1: The Property inspector showing a font, size, and color change

4. Click Split view, and scroll to the top of your document. Look just below the <meta> tags and you'll see the style embedded in the page, as shown in Figure 31-2.

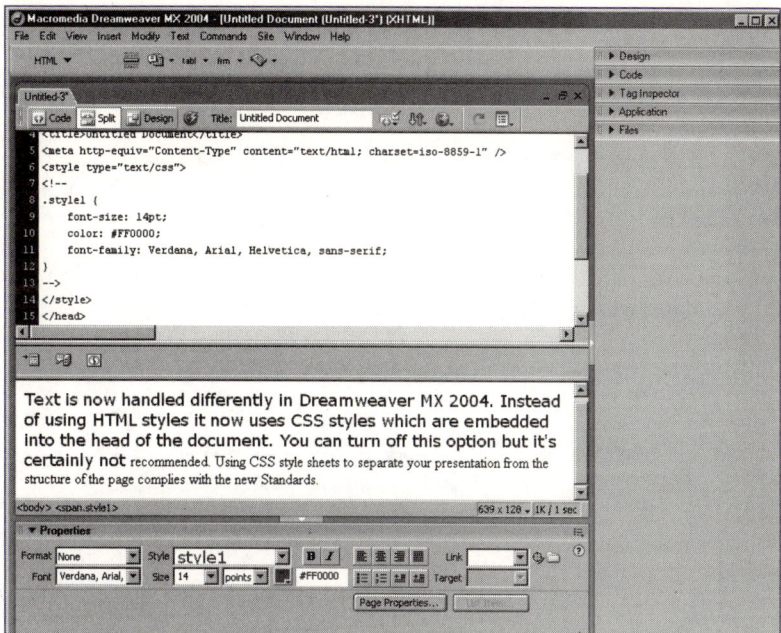

Figure 31-2: A new style named style1 is added to the head of the document

notes

- Style1, Style2, and so on aren't very descriptive. While in Code view, you can change the name. But remember to also change the span class tag that precedes the text.

- Be careful using unnecessary <span> tags; they add to your code unnecessarily. When you add an inline style, however, it can't be avoided (Step 5).

5. Scroll down to the body code and look in front of the text. The style1 is applied to the text using a <span> tag, as shown in Figure 31-3.

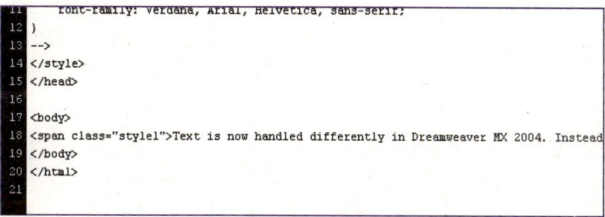

Figure 31-3: A <span> tag is added to the reformatted text

cross-references

- Refer to Tasks 28 to 30 for formatting the text (Steps 1-3).

- Refer to Task 165 for converting an internal (embedded) style into an external Style Sheet (Step 4).

Task 32

Changing Text Alignment, Formatting Lists, and Indenting

Changing alignment, formatting lists, and indenting are some other basic text modification options in the Property inspector. These tools are often used to format bulleted and numbered lists, frequently asked questions, and quotes.

1. Type or copy and paste several lines of text to experiment with, adding paragraph returns between lines, as shown in Figure 32-1.

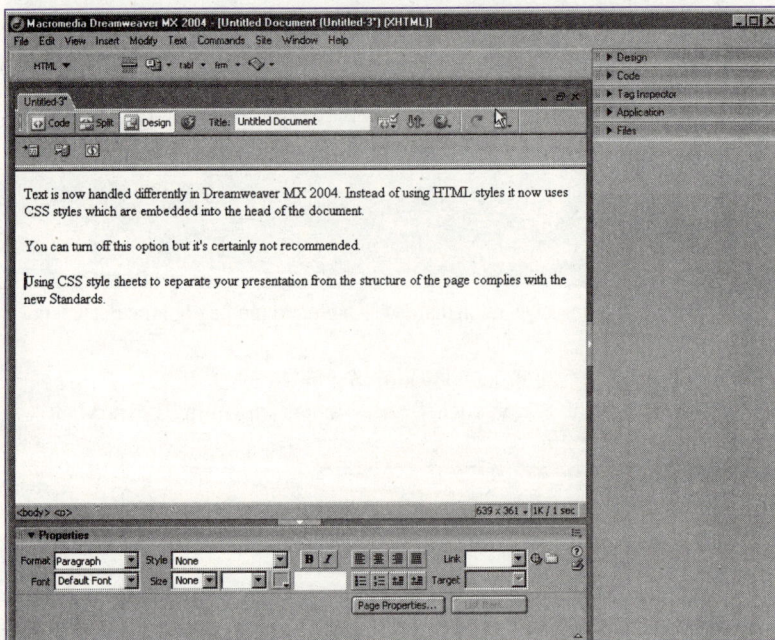

Figure 32-1: Several lines of text with paragraph spaces between them

caution
- Be consistent when you use bullets, numbered lists, or standard left-justified text (Step 6).

2. Click the Align Right button to the right of the Link field in the Property inspector to align everything to the right. This gives the left edge a "ragged" look, as shown in Figure 32-2.

3. Click the Align Right button to get the text back to normal.

4. With text selected, click the Unordered List button below the Left Align button to make a bullet list (see Figure 32-3).

5. Select your bullet list and click the Unordered List button to toggle off the list.

6. With the text selected again, click the Text Indent button to the left of the Target field in the Property inspector. This indents the selected text.

7. Now click the Justify button above the Text Indent button to align the end of the lines of text. This is good for displaying long quotes.

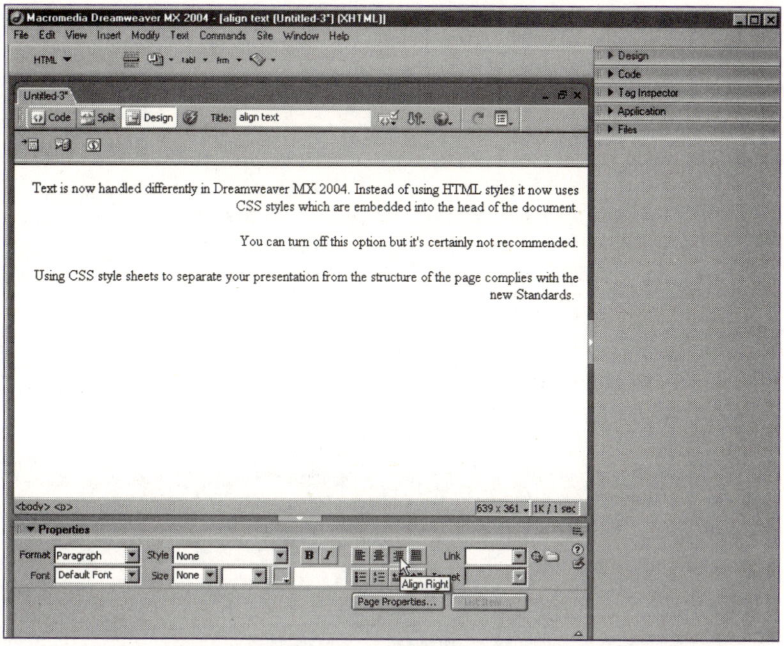

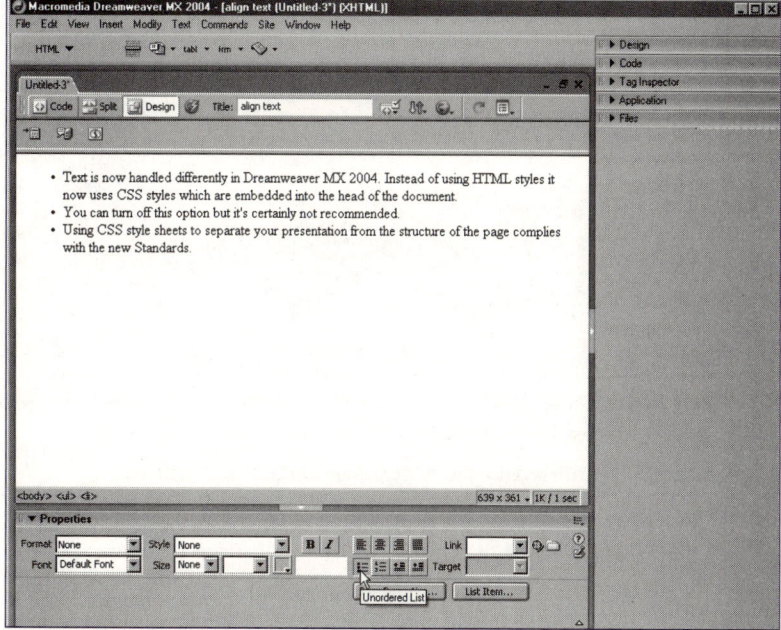

Figure 32-2: Text aligned right with the Property inspector

Figure 32-3: Bullet list and the Property inspector

tips

- If you need text to play with and you don't want to type, go on the Web and search for "Lorem ipsum dolor" to find "Greek" text (Step 1).

- Bulleted lists facilitate users scanning short blocks of text (Step 5).

cross-references

- See Task 30 for changing the font, size, and color of text (Step 8).

- Refer to Task 169 for formatting lists using CSS.

Changing and Renaming Styles

You can change styles, or rename them, in the Property inspector. Changing styles is a time-saver with large blocks of text, and renaming them becomes important when you start to get a lot of different styles in a document.

1. Type or cut and paste several lines of text to experiment with. Don't use the Enter/Return key between lines of text just yet.

2. Select the top half of your text.

3. Change the Font Size to 18 pixels.

4. Choose a good blue using the Text Color button. Figure 33-1 shows the text changed in the Property inspector.

notes

- Adding formatting using the Property inspector automatically creates a CSS style that is embedded in the document. Check your code in the head and you'll see the style.

- Styles are automatically made when you change the properties of text, such as font or size (Step 2).

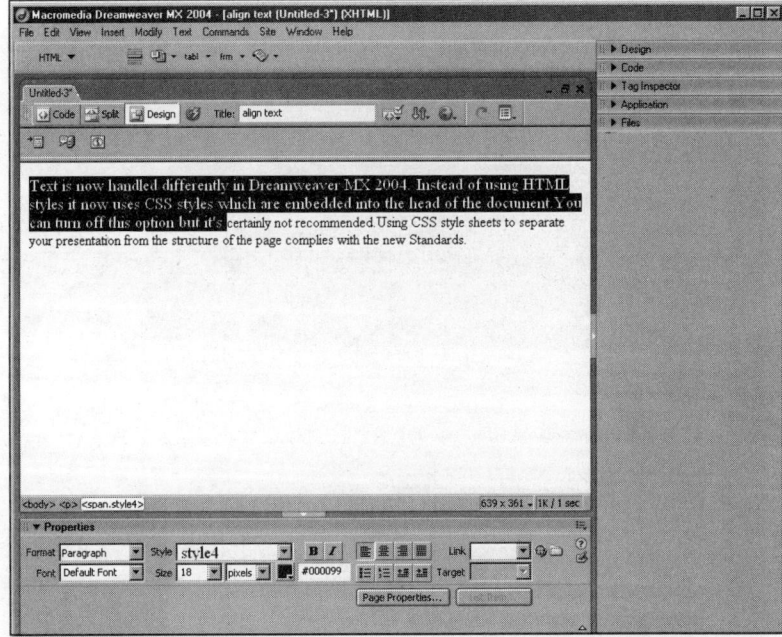

Figure 33-1: 18-pixel blue text selected and changed using the Property inspector

5. Select the bottom half of your text and make it 10 pixels.

6. Click your cursor in the top text, which is 18 pixels. Notice the Property inspector shows the style name. For my document, it says "style4."

7. Click the Style menu drop-down list in the Property inspector and select Rename, as shown in Figure 33-2.

8. In the Rename Style dialog box, type the name of the color of the style you are renaming in the New Name field—for example, **Blue** (see Figure 33-3). Don't use spaces in style names. A good alternative is to use a capital letter between words.

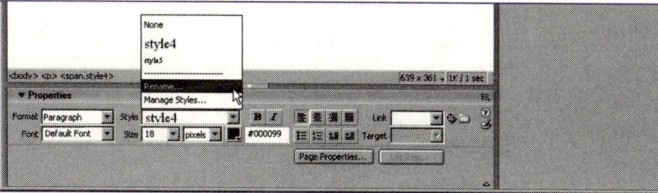

Figure 33-2: Renaming the style and entering a new name

9. A results window may appear under the Properties window letting you know what has happened. You can close it by opening the Options pop-up menu and selecting Close This Panel. Figure 33-3 shows the Results panel open.

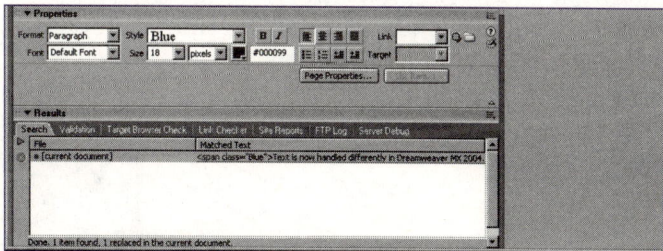

Figure 33-3: Properties and Results inspectors

10. Select your small text and select the new style from the Style menu.

tip

▪ Keep your styles well managed, as they are a very important part of page layout.

cross-reference

▪ See Task 166 for editing CSS Styles using the CSS panel.

Making a Definition List

Definition lists are a little-known text format that is not in Dreamweaver's Property inspector. Definition lists are set up glossary-style, with terms flush left and indented definitions under them (called a "hanging indent"), and you set them up without using tables or styles. This format is also good for bibliographies, where the author's name is flush left and the subsequent lines of text are indented.

1. If you already have text typed you want to use for a definition term, position your cursor where you want the beginning of your list to be. Otherwise, type the term now.

2. Choose Text ⇨ List ⇨ Definition List. You may not notice any change, or a slight shifting of the text. Don't worry; this is normal.

3. Click at the end of your term to position the cursor. Press Enter/ Return. Type your definition. Notice that it is automatically indented, as shown in Figure 34-1.

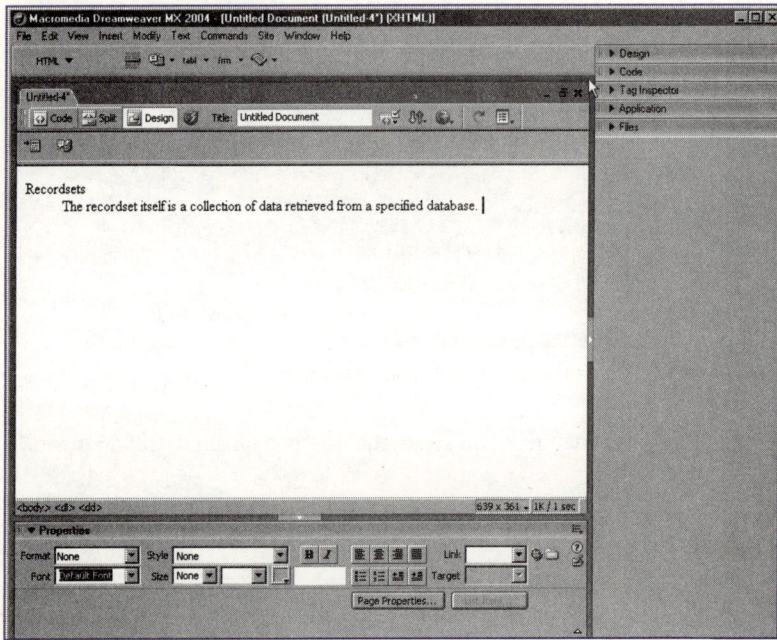

Figure 34-1: A term and its definition

4. Position your cursor at the end of your definition, press Enter/ Return, and type the next term.

5. Press Enter/Return and type the definition of the term, as shown in Figure 34-2.

6. To make your list more attractive, select each term and bold it, as shown in Figure 34-3.

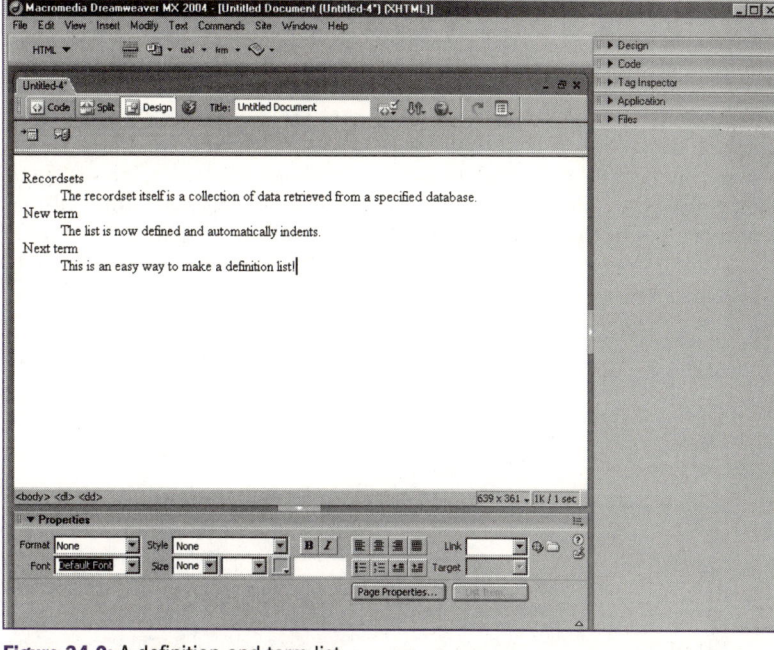

Figure 34-2: A definition and term list

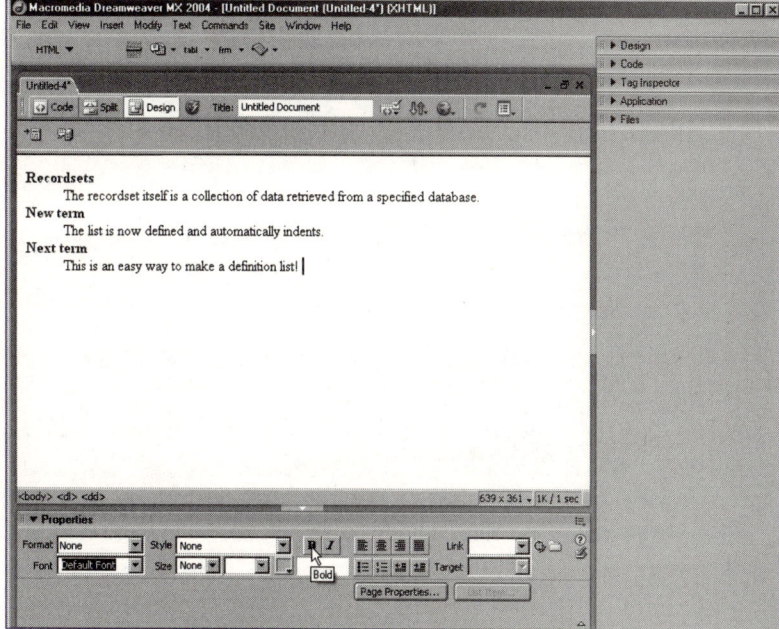

Figure 34-3: The terms bolded

cross-references

- Refer to Task 32 for changing alignment, formatting lists, and indenting text.

- Refer to Task 160 for formatting specific tags using CSS (Step 7).

7. You could also change the font. But keep in mind that formatting the list this way is not considered the best practice. You can and should format using external CSS style sheets.

Task **35**

Changing Page Font and Margins

If you often use the same font and size on a page and don't want to have to keep changing it from the default, you can change the default text for the entire page. And, yes, Web pages have margins! Well, sort of. You can control how far all content on your pages is from the outside edges of a user's browser. This is handy when you need to either get content right up close to edges, as with a full-screen animation, or when you want margins on every page, as with a long text document.

note

- The Left Margin and Top Margin settings are for Internet Explorer. Right and Bottom Margin settings are for Netscape (Step 8).

1. Open a blank HTML page.

2. Select Modify ➪ Page Properties. Or click the Page Properties button in the Property inspector.

3. Click the Appearance Category in the Page Properties dialog box, as shown in Figure 35-1.

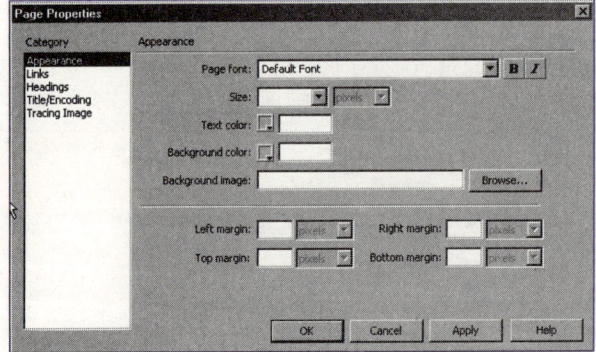

Figure 35-1: Appearance selected in Page Properties

4. Click the Page Font drop-down menu and select Arial, Helvetica, Sans Serif.

5. Click the Size menu drop-down list and select 18.

6. Click the Text Color box, pick a suitable blue, and leave the background fields at their defaults.

7. Click once in the Left Margin field and enter **72**. Pixels should automatically appear to the right.

8. Repeat this for the Top, Right, and Bottom Margin fields. Your Page Properties dialog box should look like Figure 35-2.

9. Click OK.

cautions

- Wild text colors can make a Web page hard to use (Step 3).

- Small margins make large blocks of text hard to read (Step 5).

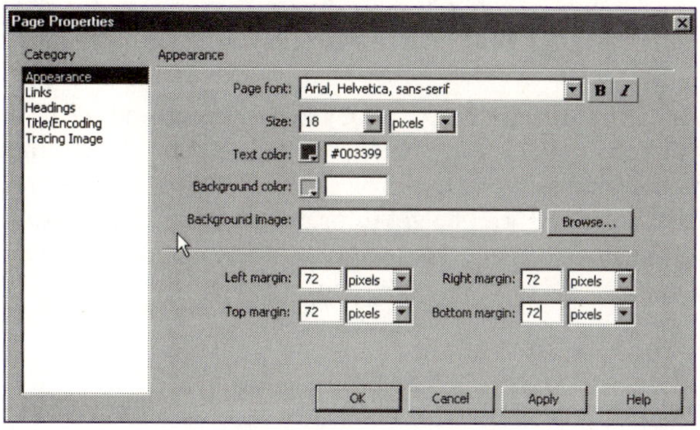

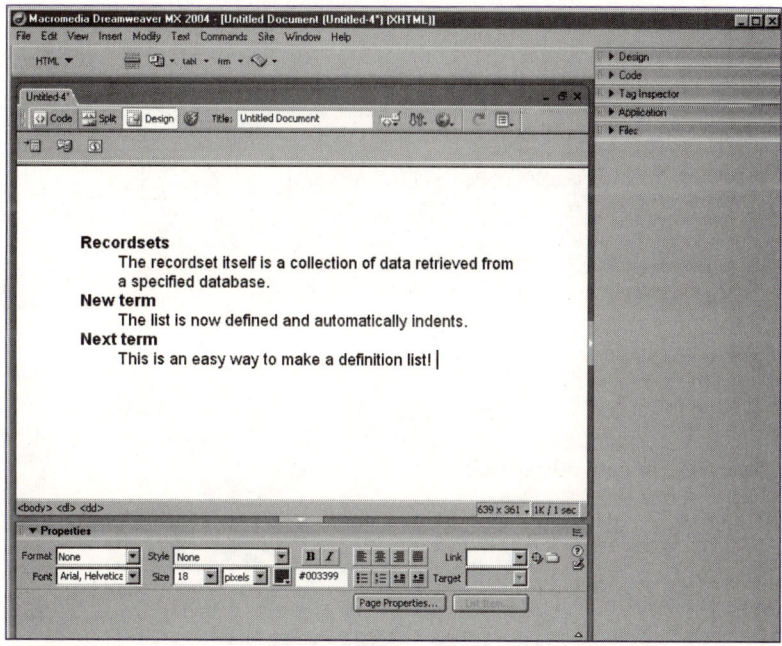

Figure 35-2: Page Properties dialog box with values

10. Start typing, and you should see some big differences. Your text is big and blue and about an inch from all the sides of a browser, as shown in Figure 35-3.

Figure 35-3: New font and margin defaults

tip

- Set margins to 0 on all sides to remove all browser default margins (Step 7).

cross-reference

- See Task 179 for setting margins using CSS.

Task 36

Changing Background Colors and Images

If you want to change the entire background of a page, you can either change the solid color or add an image. Images can be "tiled," meaning they repeat to fill whatever size the user makes his or her browser, or they can be one large image. Gray or dark backgrounds can be good for use with lots of photos, and washed-out tiled backgrounds can provide texture to a site.

1. Type or paste a few lines of text on a blank page.

2. Select Modify ➪ Page Properties. Or click the Page Properties button in the Property inspector.

3. Click the Appearance category in the Page Properties dialog box, as shown in Figure 36-1.

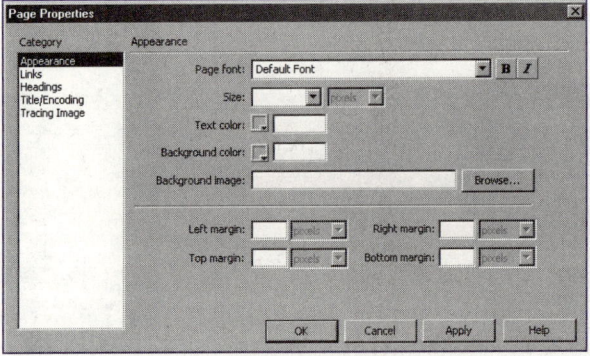

Figure 36-1: Appearance selected in Page Properties

4. Click the Background Color box and pick a suitable blue.

5. Click OK and look at your page. You should see a solid blue background, as shown in Figure 36-2. Note the effect a background can have on readability.

caution

- Big background images can sap a Web browser's memory (Step 10).

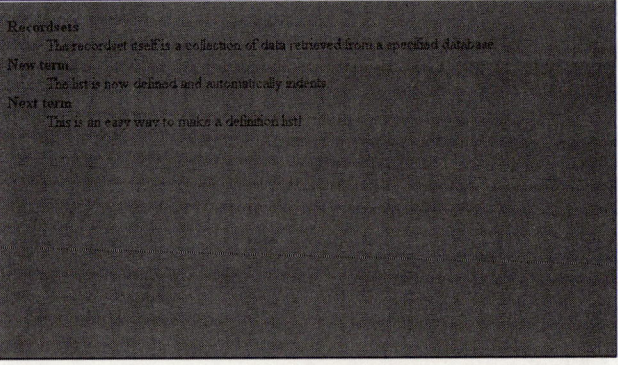

Figure 36-2: Page with blue background and text

6. Select Modify ➪ Page Properties. Or click the Page Properties button in the Property inspector.

7. Click the Background Image Browse button.

8. Navigate to any GIF or JPEG file on your computer, select it, and click OK. If you need an image, navigate to your Dreamweaver application directory, and then select Samples ➪ GettingStarted ➪ 1-Design ➪ Assets ➪ Images ➪ preview.jpg.

9. Click OK to close Page Properties. Figure 36-3 shows the image (preview.jpg) tiled over the text. Your blue background is still there, but the image overrides it. Of course, it overrides the text as well. This is an example of what *not* to use.

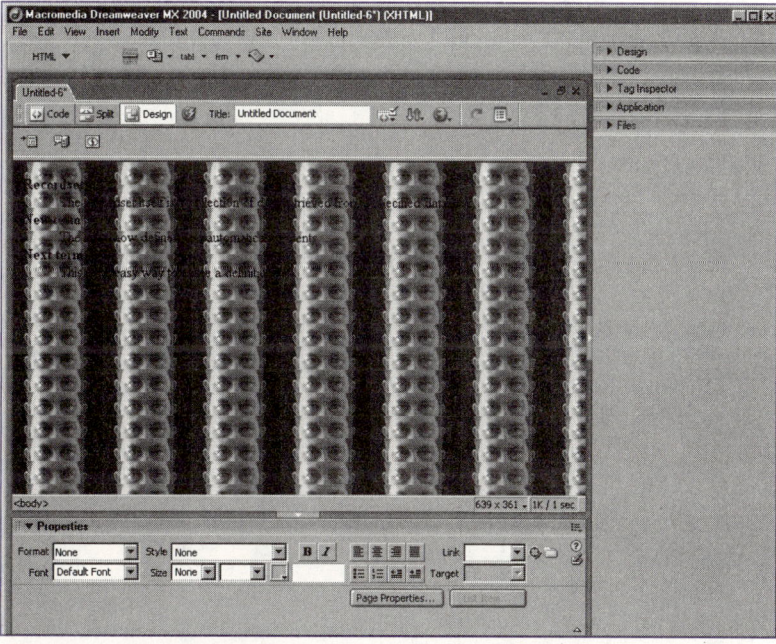

Figure 36-3: The sample image of preview.jpg tiled behind the text

10. Experiment with other images. Keep in mind that textures usually fight less with the text.

tip

- Background colors drastically affect the readability of text. Try to maintain contrast with the content of your page (Step 5).

cross-reference

- Refer to Task 170 for using CSS for background images. Using CSS, you can make an image tile or not tile.

Importing Text from Microsoft Word

Why retype something that's already been typed in Microsoft Word? Just import it and let Dreamweaver do a little housecleaning of the converted HTML. This tool is a real time-saver if you have a lot of text in Word that needs to be converted to HTML.

If you're on a PC, just use Steps 5 to 7 to import any DOC file you want to use. On a Mac, you've got to save your file as an HTM file in Microsoft Word first.

1. In Word select File ⇨ Save As in the document you want to import.

2. Choose Web Page from the File Type (PC) or File Format (Mac) Menu.

3. Type a new filename with something like "import" in the name so you can find it if you forget where you saved it.

4. Save the file.

5. In Dreamweaver on Mac or PC, select File ⇨ Import Word Document.

6. On a PC, navigate to any Word file and open it. The Open dialog box is shown in Figure 37-1.

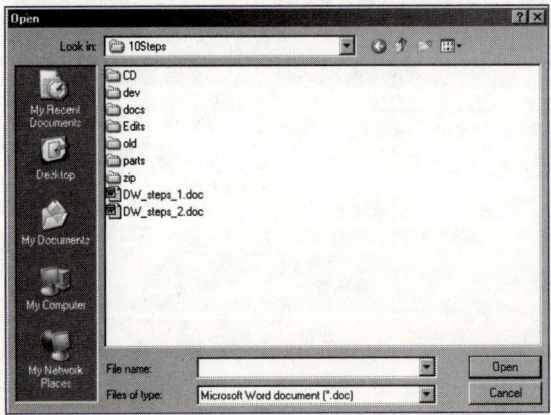

Figure 37-1: Open dialog box with a Word file selected

7. The file is automatically added to your Dreamweaver document. Figure 37-2 shows an imported Word file that has images in it. Notice it maintained its formatting.

8. Select Commands ⇨ Clean Up Word HTML. A Clean Up Word HTML dialog box appears, as shown in Figure 37-3. Select and deselect from the list which options you'd like to clean up. This example selected everything.

notes

-   Because the sample Word document had images, an additional dialog box opens, asking for a description for the images (Step 7).

-   Microsoft Word 2000/ 2002 have much cleaner HTML code than previous versions (Step 10).

caution

-   Not all formatting will survive the trip into Dreamweaver (Step 3).

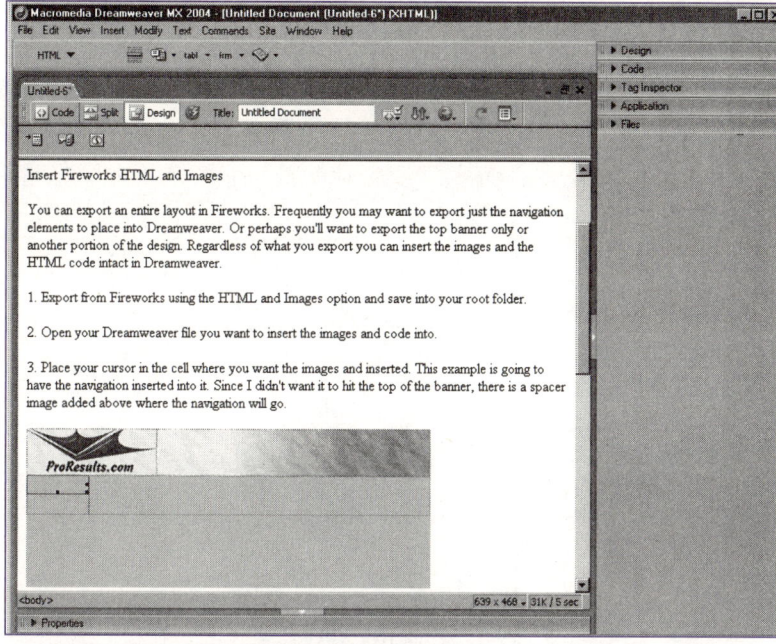

Figure 37-2: A formatted Word document with images imported into Dreamweaver

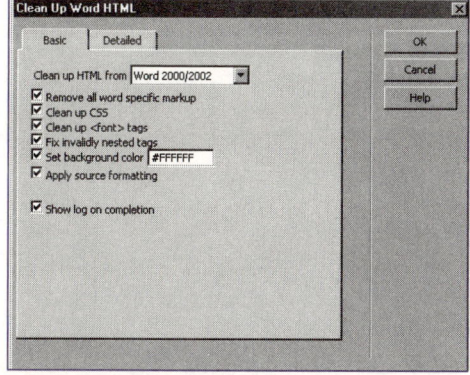

Figure 37-3: Clean Up Word HTML dialog box

9. Click OK. A warning appears, as shown in Figure 37-4. Click OK, and you're done.

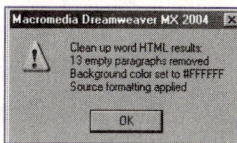

Figure 37-4: Warning dialog

cross-reference

■ Refer to Task 28 for adding text (Step 4).

Cleaning Up HTML

Believe it or not, HTML and XHTML can get dirty, particularly as a result of lots of editing in a document or the use of nonstandard code by some other program or programmer. "Dirt," in this case, can be redundant font tags or empty tags. But not to fear: Dreamweaver will automatically clean house for you.

1. Open a document you've done a lot of editing on.

2. Depending on your document, select Commands ⇨ Clean Up HTML or select Commands ⇨ Clean Up XHTML.

3. Check to make sure the default settings shown in Figure 38-1 are checked.

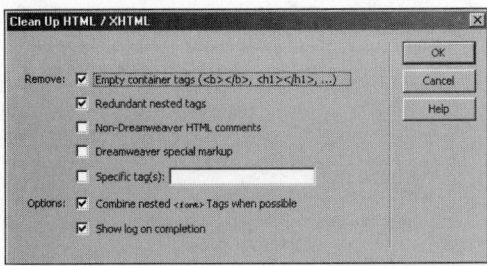

Figure 38-1: Clean Up HTML/XHTML dialog box

4. Selecting Non-Dreamweaver HTML removes any custom comments you've made or code not generated by Dreamweaver. Selecting Dreamweaver Special Markup removes Dreamweaver template code, which will detach any template page from its template. Use these features with care. For this task, leave the default settings the way they are and click OK.

5. A Clean Up Summary box appears, telling you what Dreamweaver cleaned up (see Figure 38-2). Or, if the code is not that dirty, it may tell you that there is nothing to clean, which is also good.

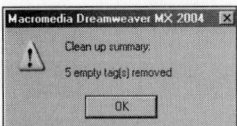

Figure 38-2: Clean Up Summary

6. If the page is based on a template, a warning appears, saying that the change can't be performed (see Figure 38-3).

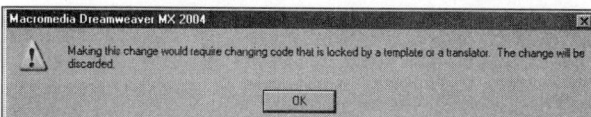

Figure 38-3: A warning opens if a file based on a template is being cleaned

7. If it's a template, open your template and run the Clean Up HTML command. Save the template. Click Update, as shown in Figure 38-4. Click Close when the procedure completes.

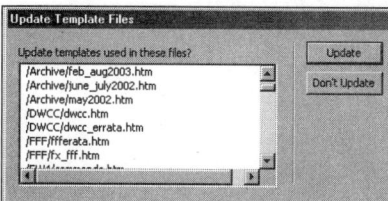

Figure 38-4: The Update dialog box for the changed and cleaned template file

8. Select File ⇨ Preview in Browser to make sure your document still displays the way you want to.

9. Select Edit ⇨ Undo Clean Up HTML if something displays incorrectly.

tip

- It's a good idea to clean up all pages when you are finished editing them (Step 1).

cross-references

- Refer to Task 7 for setting up your testing browsers.

- Refer to Part 10 for working with templates.

Linking to a Dreamweaver Document

This task covers how to link a text or graphic to another Dreamweaver document that is on your computer. You use this method to link Web sites to pages within the same site, usually via a menu. To ensure that your links work properly when you upload the site to a server, be sure to have all your site files in a root folder and define the site in Dreamweaver. Use the same file structure in your root folder that you will use on the Internet.

1. You'll need at least two pages so you can link them from each other. Download the task39 folder from `www.wiley.com/compbooks/ 10simplestepsorless`.

2. Open the Product Info Page.

3. Open the Home_Page.htm file.

4. Figure 39-1 shows both the product and the home page open in Dreamweaver. Notice the tab and name. To make the home page the active one, select its name (if it isn't already). Click in the document and type **Home Page**.

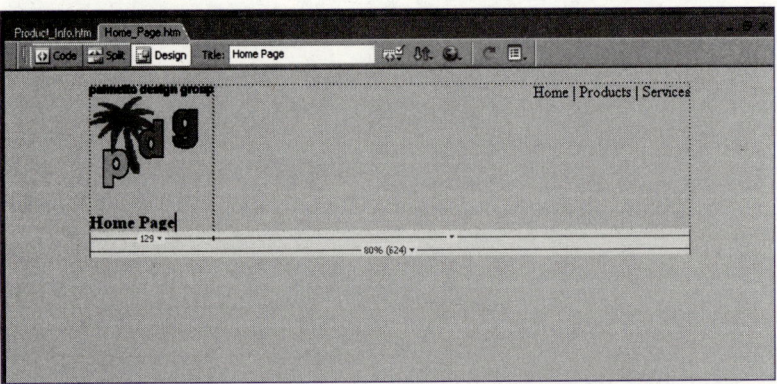

Figure 39-1: The home page selected and text typed into the document

5. Select the Products name in the link area. In the Property inspector, click the Browse folder button to the right of the Link field to find the file you're going to link to (in this example, navigate to task39\ Product_Info.htm) and click OK. Figure 39-2 shows the Products link selected, as well as the Browse for File and Point to File icons.

Browse for file

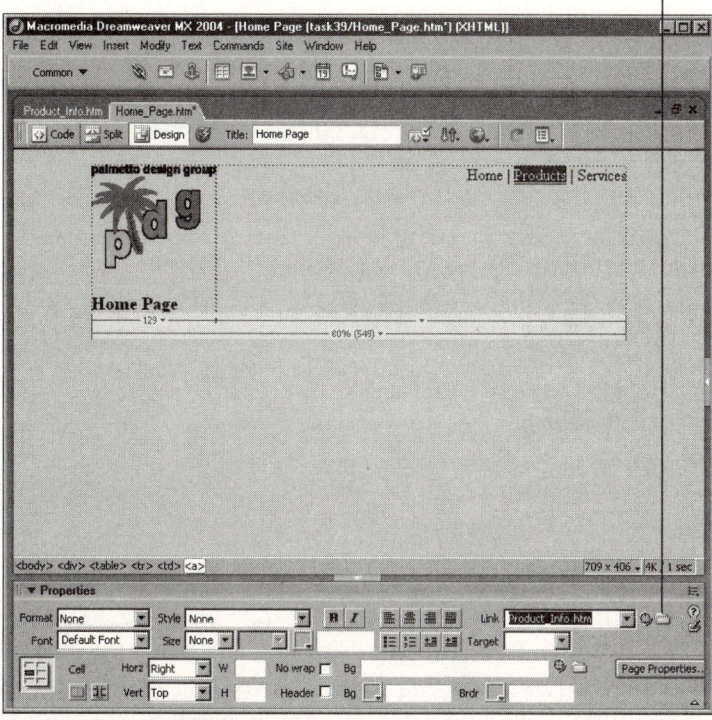

Figure 39-2: Browse for File and Point to File icons in the Property inspector

6. Check the link field of the Property inspector, and you'll see the link added, as shown in Figure 39-3.

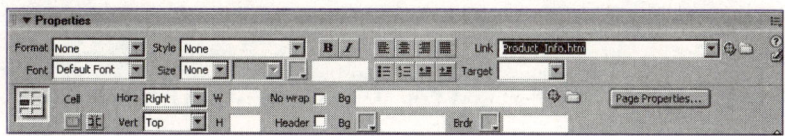

Figure 39-3: Property inspector with a completed link

7. Leave the Target pop-up menu blank for a simple link.

8. Select File ➪ Preview in Browser to try your new link. When you click Products, you should be taken to the Products page.

cross-references

- Refer to Tasks 10 and 11 for defining a site.

- Refer to Task 40 for linking using the Files panel (Step 6).

40 Adding Links Using the Files Panel

The easiest way to add links is to use the Files panel.

note

- If you've used links before, they will appear in the Link drop-down list and you can select them (Step 6).

1. Select the site you want to work on in the Site panel drop-down menu. You can use the sample in the task39 folder at www. wiley.com/compbooks/10simplestepsorless.

2. Click the Plus (+) button next to folders that may contain the pages you want to link to, as shown in Figure 40-1.

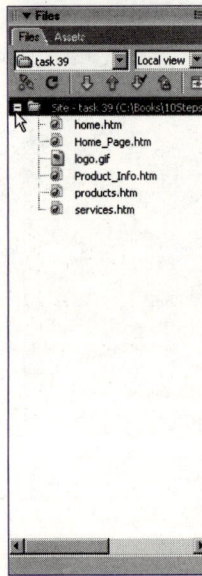

Figure 40-1: The folders are expanded, showing the HTM files to link to

3. Double-click the filename of the document you need to add links to (Home_Page.htm). It opens.

4. Select the text or image you want to add a link to. If you are using the task39 sample pages, select the word Products, as shown in Figure 40-2.

5. In the Property inspector, to the right of the Link field, you'll see a circle icon with something like a crosshair in it named Point to File. Click and drag this icon to the filename in the Files panel you want to link to, as shown in Figure 40-3.

6. Notice in the Property inspector that the link is added for you automatically (see Figure 40-4).

Figure 40-2: *Products* is selected and ready to get a link added to it

tips

- Dreamweaver's site management tools automatically update local links if you move files or rename them.

- Links you've used previously in a site can also be accessed in the Assets panel. With text or an image selected, select the Link category, select the desired link, and click the Insert button.

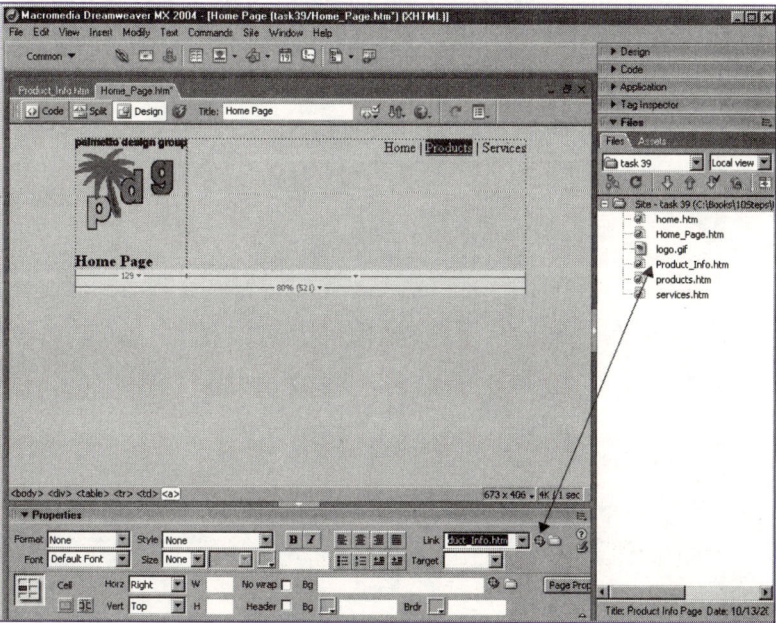

Figure 40-3: Using the Point to File icon to select an HTM page in the Files panel

cross-reference

- Refer to Task 45 for using the Assets panel.

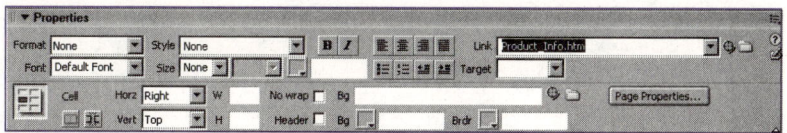

Figure 40-4: The link is added to the link field

Linking to a Web Page Outside Your Site

The Web is all about links. Here's how to link a text or a graphic to a Web page that is not yours.

1. Surf to a Web page you'd like to link to.

2. Copy the entire address (URL) of the page in the browser's address bar.

3. Open a Dreamweaver document from your defined site (you can use sample in the task39 folder at `www.wiley.com/compbooks/10simplestepsorless`).

4. Make sure you can see the Property inspector, as shown in Figure 41-1.

note

- When linking to a page outside of your site, you need the full URL, including the `http://` part (Step 8).

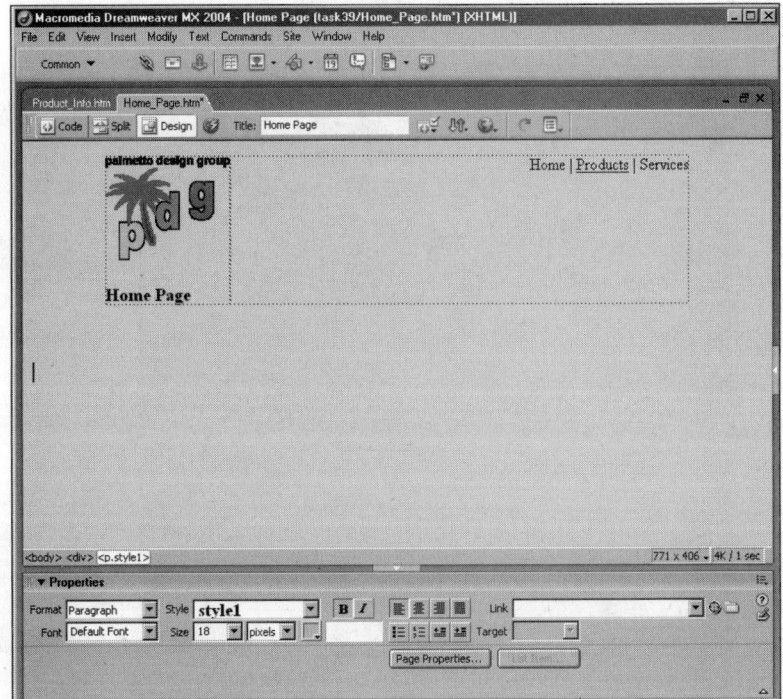

Figure 41-1: Property inspector

caution

- A link will break if the address of the Web page you linked to is changed or taken down (Step 1).

5. Select the text you want to use as the link, as shown in Figure 41-2.

6. Or, select a picture by clicking it once, as shown in Figure 41-3.

7. Place your cursor in the Link field in the Property inspector.

8. Select Edit ⇨ Paste (Ctrl/Command+V) to place the address in the white Link box or field. You should see the URL you copied from the Web page you want to link to in the box, as shown in Figure 41-4.

9. Leave your target blank if you want the link to appear in the same browser page that your page was in. You may also want to change the target to _blank so your page stays up and the link opens in a new browser window.

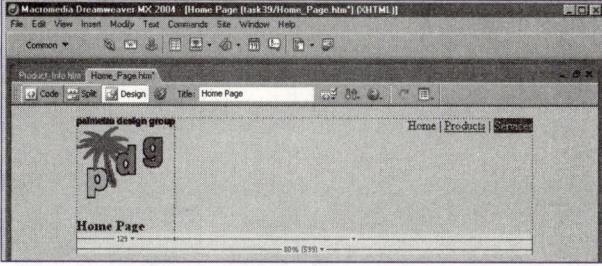

Figure 41-2: Selected text

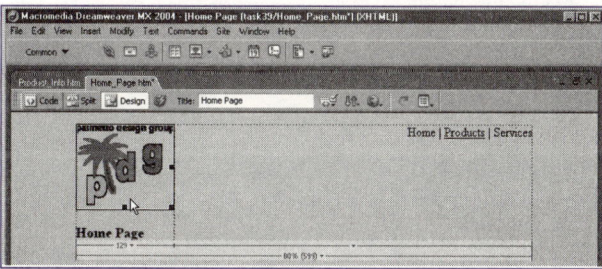

Figure 41-3: Selected graphic

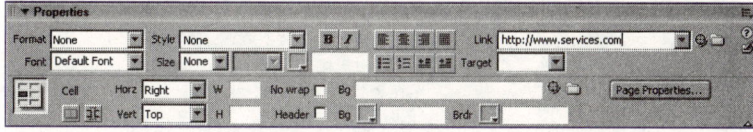

Figure 41-4: Document and Property inspector with a completed link

tips

- Don't use the word "here" as a link. Use text that will describe what the link leads to (Step 3).

- Linking to other Web pages, and hopefully getting them to link to you, is a good way to get more traffic and an increase in some search engine results (Step 5).

cross-references

- Refer to Task 42 for changing link colors and properties (Step 5).

- Refer to Task 47 for adding alternative text to images (Step 4).

42

Changing Link Colors and Properties

Ever wonder why so many links on the Web are blue? It's because the default setting for Web pages and browsers is blue. But you can change the colors of the *Up state* (what you see when the page loads), as well as the colors when you click a link, have visited a link, or roll over a link. You can also change the font and size of links. Changing link properties is desirable when your design clashes with the standard blue link color or when you want larger links in a menu, for example.

1. Open a page with a text link in it, and select a link to modify.

2. Select Modify ⇨ Page Properties. Or click the Page Properties button in the Property inspector (see Figure 42-1).

Figure 42-1: Page Properties button

3. Click the Links category in the Page Properties dialog box, as shown in Figure 42-2.

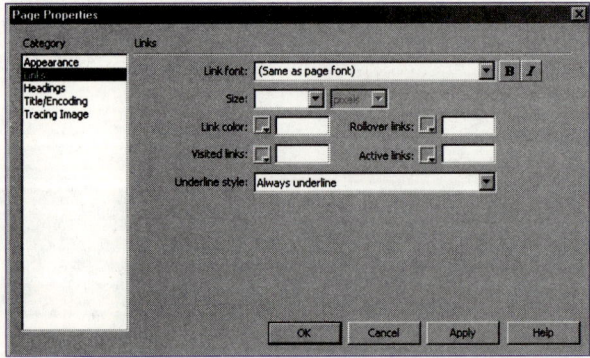

Figure 42-2: Links selected in Page Properties

4. Click the Link Font menu triangle and select Arial, Helvetica, Sans Serif.

5. Click the Size menu triangle and select 24.

6. Click the Color buttons to the following colors:

Link Color	Blue	This is the color of a link when the page first opens.
Visited Links	Red	This controls the colors of links you've been to.
Rollover Links	Yellow	This controls the color when the mouse is over the link.
Active Links	White	This controls the color when you click a link.

7. Leave the Underline Style set at Always Underline. The changed settings are shown in Figure 42-3.

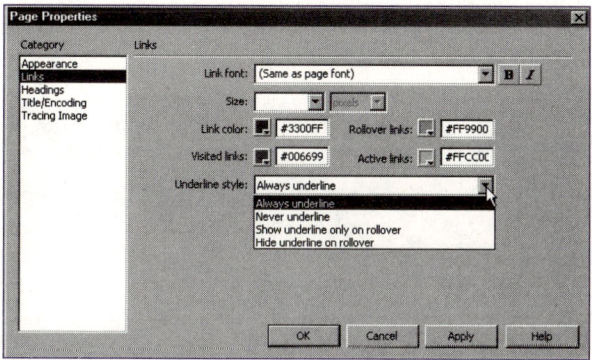

Figure 42-3: Page Properties with link settings

8. Click OK.

9. Select File ⇨ Preview in Browser (F12) to see your page in a Web browser.

10. Now roll over the link, click and hold the mouse down, click and let go, and so on to experiment with your new link.

tip

- Because blue links are so common, they have become a standard that users recognize the quickest.

cross-references

- Refer to Task 30 for changing the font, size, and color of text (Step 10).

- Refer to Task 173 for changing link colors using CSS.

Adding an E-mail Link

An e-mail link allows you to create a link on text or on a picture that causes a user's e-mail software to start up and display a new message with your address in it. E-mail links are used to facilitate your users communicating with you. They are often listed prominently on the first page and on all pages of your site near the bottom of a page. However, they do not work with all users' computers, so it is customary to also add a text link with the actual e-mail address so users can still see your address even if their computers will not work with your link.

1. Open a document.

2. Select an image you want to use as your e-mail link (see Figure 43-1).

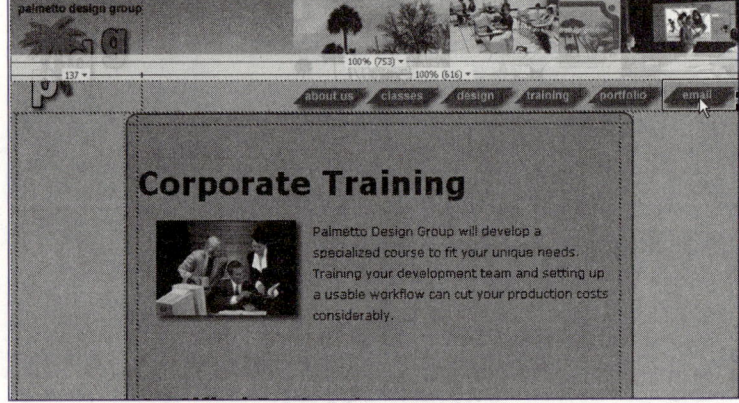

Figure 43-1: Selected e-mail image link

3. In the Link field, type **mailto:yourname@domain.com**, as shown in Figure 43-2.

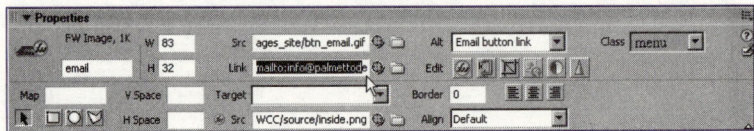

Figure 43-2: The e-mail link added to the Link field of the image

4. Click to insert your cursor at the bottom of your page or wherever you'd like to place a text link.

notes

• When linking an image, be sure you also have your alternative text added in the Property inspector (Step 2).

• You can type the address into the page, then use the Insert ⇨ Email Link option. Your e-mail in the first field will be filled in automatically (Step 5).

• Some sites don't provide an e-mail link. This is a practice that baffles me. If you don't want consumer contact, then why do you have a Web site?

• You can use descriptive text for the link, such as Contact Us, instead of the e-mail address. But some users don't have their browsers setup to use an e-mail link, so the e-mail text is a good idea (Step 6).

5. Choose Insert ➪ Email Link. Or select the Email Link button in the Insert bar's Common category. An Email Link dialog box appears, as shown in Figure 43-3.

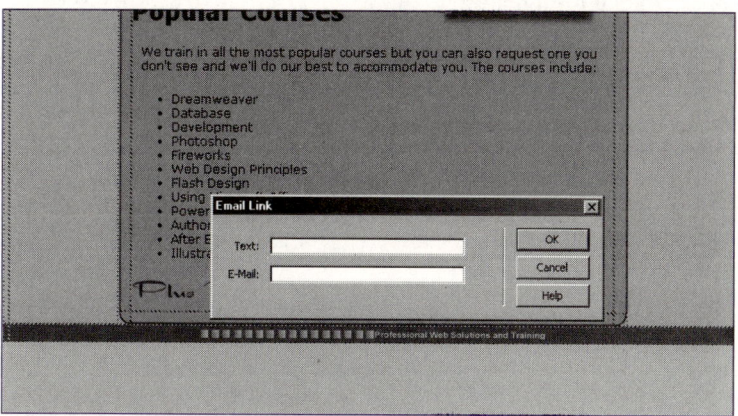

Figure 43-3: Email Link dialog box

6. Make sure the e-mail address is in both the Text and Email fields if you want the linking text to be the e-mail address, and click OK. For this method of adding an e-mail link, you don't use the mailto: in front of the address; just type in the e-mail address, as shown in Figure 43-4.

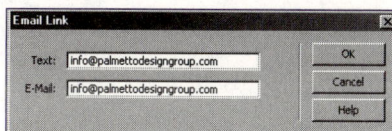

Figure 43-4: E-mail link

7. Select File ➪ Preview in Browser (F12), and click the link. If your browser is hooked up to your e-mail, it should boot up and display a new e-mail addressed to the address you entered.

cross-reference

▪ Refer to Task 45 for using the Assets panel, where you can access e-mail links previously used in the site.

Task **44**

Adding Anchor Links

A nchors are a special kind of link that links to content within a document. They are good for linking a list at the top of a page to expanded content below, so you can see all the list items before you click. Common uses of anchors are to link a glossary of terms and their definitions, or to link a list of frequently asked questions (FAQs) to their answers. You can also link text in one part of the document to another part. Making anchor links is a two-step process. First you name the anchor; then you link it.

note

• You aren't adding the link but naming the area before the link. This will make more sense as you complete this task (Step 2).

1. Open a document you want to link one part of with another section in the same document.

2. Place your cursor at the beginning of the text that you want to use as the anchor link to take the user to the desired location in the page (see Figure 44-1). This is the destination—where you want users to end up when they click a link in another part of the page.

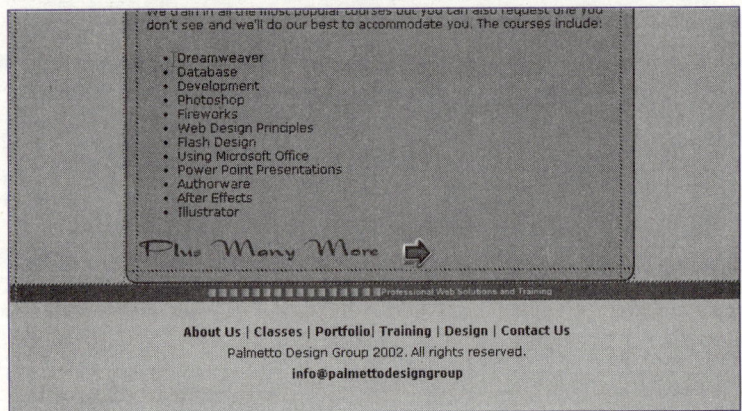

Figure 44-1: The course list users will be taken to when they click a link at the top of the page

3. Click the Named Anchor button in the Common category of the Insert bar, or select Insert ➪ Named Anchor.

4. Type a short name, with no spaces, in the Named Anchor dialog box, shown in Figure 44-2, and click OK. You should see an anchor symbol appear where your cursor was.

5. You may need to change your preferences if you want to see the anchor tag in the document. Choose Edit ➪ Preferences and select the anchor tag option, as shown in Figure 44-3.

6. Select the text you want the user to click.

7. In the Property inspector's Link text area, type a **#** sign and the name of the anchor, with no spaces, exactly like you typed in the Named Anchor dialog box (see Figure 44-4).

8. Select File ⇨ Preview in Browser and try your link.

Task **44**

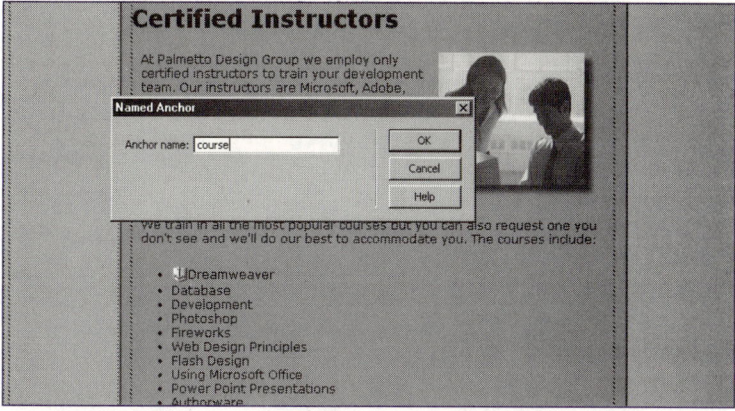

Figure 44-2: Named Anchor dialog box with short name and the resulting yellow anchor tag

tip

■ If you don't see the gold anchor tag, choose View ⇨ Visual Aids ⇨ Invisible Elements (Step 4).

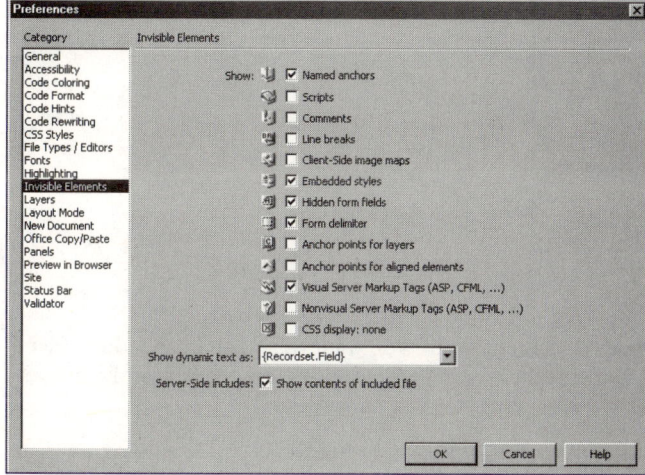

Figure 44-3: Setting the preferences to show the anchor tags

Figure 44-4: List link and Property inspector with anchor link

cross-reference

■ Refer to Task 15 for using the Insert bar (Step 3).

Using the Assets Panel to Manage Assets

When you define a site, all the images and assets in that site will be available in the Assets panel. You can also add your most used elements to a Favorites category.

1. Open the Files panel and click Assets to make it the active panel. If you don't see a list of images, click the first icon, which is the Images icon. The image list is displayed, as shown in Figure 45-1.

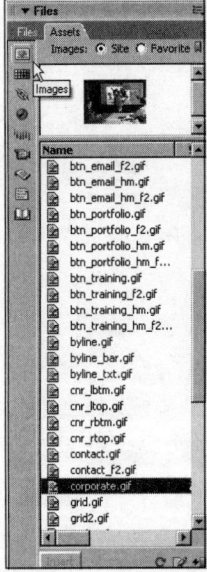

Figure 45-1: The Assets panel showing the image assets

2. Click in your document where you want to add an image; then select an image name in the Assets panel. You'll see a preview of the image in the top window.

3. Click the Insert button, as shown in Figure 45-2. Depending on your preferences, you may see a dialog box to add alternative text. If not, be sure to add the alternative text in the Property inspector.

4. Notice the other categories. Click the Links icon and you'll see any links currently used in the site. You can insert a link using the same method you used for the image. There are also categories for Colors, Flash, Movies, Libraries, and Templates.

5. If you add assets to your site, you may need to click the Refresh icon in the bottom of the Assets panel.

6. To make a custom Favorites list, select an asset you want to make a favorite.

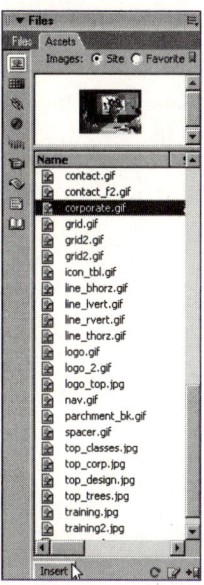

Figure 45-2: The Assets panel showing the image selected and the Insert button

7. Click the Add to Favorites icon at the bottom of the Assets panel, as shown in Figure 45-3. Click OK on the warning that comes up confirming your addition.

Add to favorites

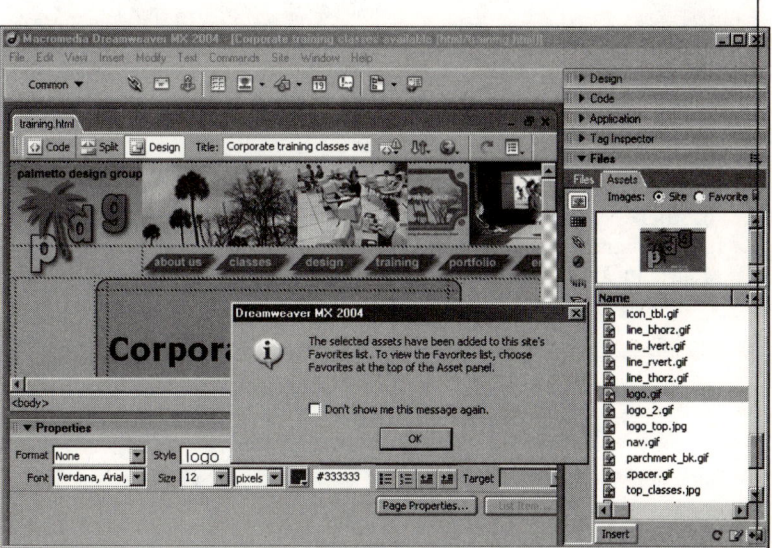

Figure 45-3: Favorites button highlighted, as well as warning

8. Click the Favorites radio button at the top of the Assets panel to view your favorites.

tip

• When you gather more then a few favorites, use the New Favorites Folder button, three buttons to the left of the Add Favorites button (Step 7).

cross-reference

• Refer to Task 47 for adding alternative text (Step 3).

Task 46

Inserting Images

Inserting graphics like photos and buttons into documents is one of the basic skills needed for controlling a page's layout.

note

- If you navigate to an image outside the site you are using, a dialog box appears, asking if you want to save it to your current site. Normally you'll click Yes and navigate to the appropriate site folder to save it there (Step 3).

1. Place your cursor where you want the graphic to be.

2. Click the Images icon, shown in Figure 46-1, in the Common category of the Insert bar, or select Insert ⇨ Image.

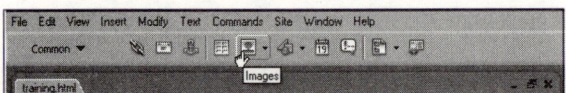

Figure 46-1: Images icon in the Common category of the Insert bar

3. Navigate to a GIF or JPEG image on your computer in the dialog box that appears. If you don't have any graphics, navigate to the directory where your Dreamweaver application is, then select Samples ⇨ GettingStarted ⇨ 1-Design ⇨ Assets ⇨ Images ⇨ homeMain.jpg, and click OK.

4. The image you selected appears in your document where you cursor was. Notice that the Property inspector changes to properties of the image, as shown in Figure 46-2.

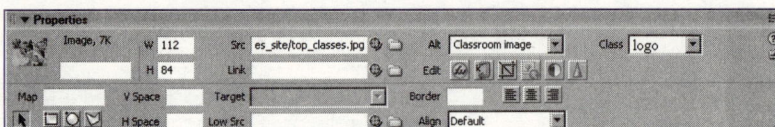

Figure 46-2: Linked picture and Property inspector dialog box

5. Select File ⇨ Preview in Browser and see how your image looks.

6. Another way to insert images is to use the Assets panel. Click the Images icon to view the images in your defined site, as shown in Figure 46-3.

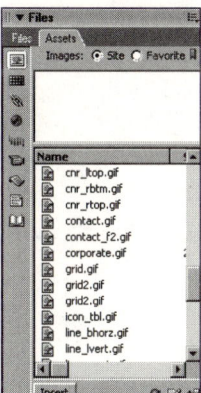

Figure 46-3: The Assets panel with the Images category selected

7. Scroll through the list to select the image you want to insert. You can see a preview to be sure it's the correct image, as shown in Figure 46-4.

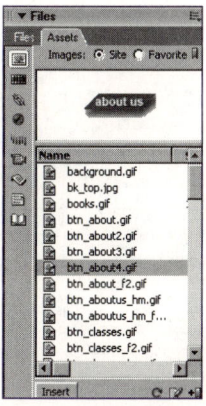

Figure 46-4: The preview seen when an image name is selected

8. Select the image name and click the Insert button.

9. The image is added to your page. In the Property inspector, type in alternative text in the Alt field.

tips

- Change the alignment of a picture to get text to flow around it (Step 5).

- You can use a photo management application to automatically make small thumbnails and large pictures and then bring them into Dreamweaver (Step 3).

cross-reference

- Refer to Task 47 for adding alternative text to images (Step 9).

Task 47

Adding Alternative Text to Images

Whenever you add any kind of image to your page, you should add alternative text. This is so screen readers can read it for the visually impaired. In addition, alternative text may be displayed while a picture loads or if the user has images turned off.

1. Select an image (if you've just inserted an image, it is already selected).

2. Look in the Property inspector. You'll see an Alt field, as shown in Figure 47-1.

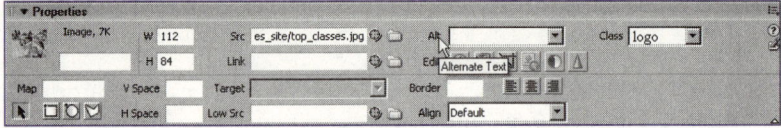

Figure 47-1: The Alt field is present when an image is selected

3. Type in some descriptive text.

4. Click the drop-down menu and notice that there is an `<empty>` selection available, as shown in Figure 47-2. Click this whenever you insert a spacer image or a layout graphic, such as a corner image of a table.

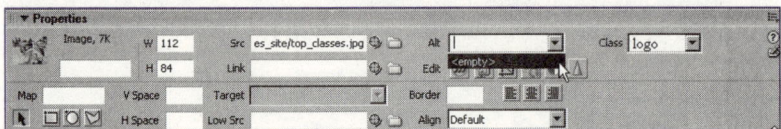

Figure 47-2: The `<empty>` option, as shown in the Property inspector

5. To be reminded automatically to enter alternative text, you can change a Preferences setting. Choose Edit ➪ Preferences and select the Accessibility category.

6. Select the Images option, as shown in Figure 47-3, and click OK.

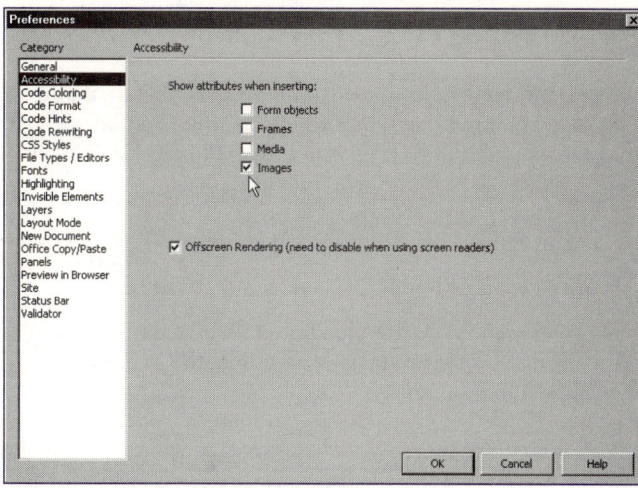

Figure 47-3: The Preferences dialog box showing the images option selected in the Accessibility category

7. Insert an image, and the dialog box shown in Figure 47-4 opens. Add your alternative text and click OK.

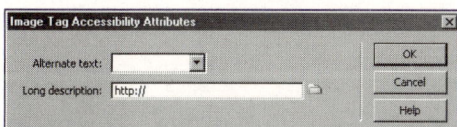

Figure 47-4: The Image Tag Accessibility Attributes dialog box

8. You will also notice a field for descriptive text. Click the yellow folder and navigate to a text file containing a larger description of an image.

cross-reference

- Refer to Task 46 for inserting images (Step 1).

Adding or Removing Image Borders

At times you may want to add a border to an image. You can do that in Dreamweaver. Keep in mind that when you add a link to an image, you may see a dark blue border around it indicating it is a link. This border, however, is removable.

1. Insert an image, or select a previously inserted image.

2. Use your favorite means of linking and add a link to the image.

3. Preview in a browser and note the blue border. Links are normally underlined, so when you use an image with a link, the line surrounds the image, as shown in Figure 48-1.

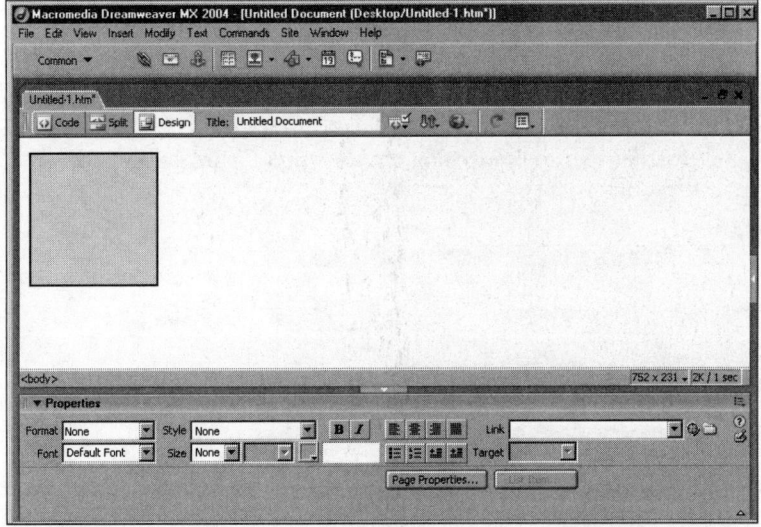

Figure 48-1: An image with a link added, as shown in Dreamweaver

4. In the Property inspector, type **0** for the border, as shown in Figure 48-2.

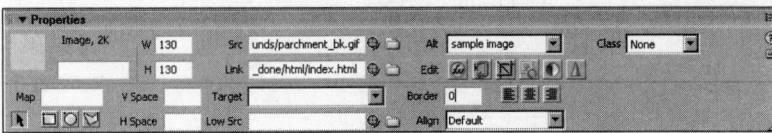

Figure 48-2: The Property inspector with a border of 0.

5. To add a border, type in a number such as **3** in the Border field (see Figure 48-3). The numbers represent the thickness in pixels, so 3 is 3 pixels.

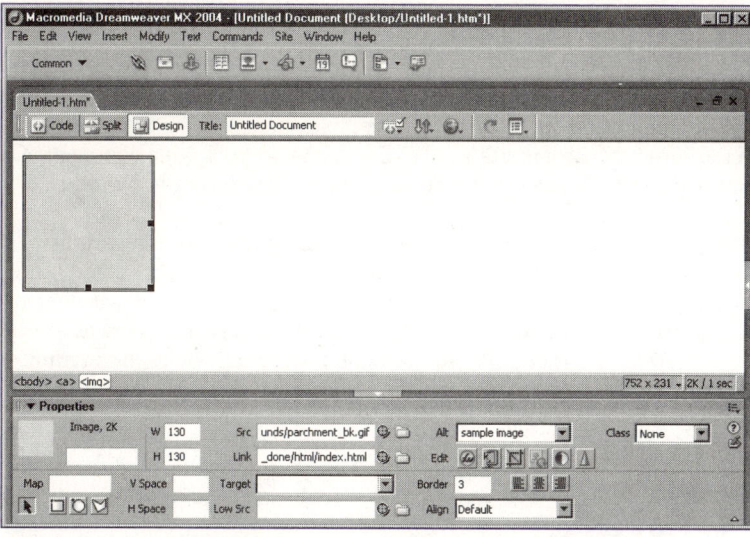

Figure 48-3: A 3-pixel border added in the Property inspector

6. Deselect the image. You should see a thick black border around an unlinked image, as shown in Figure 48-4.

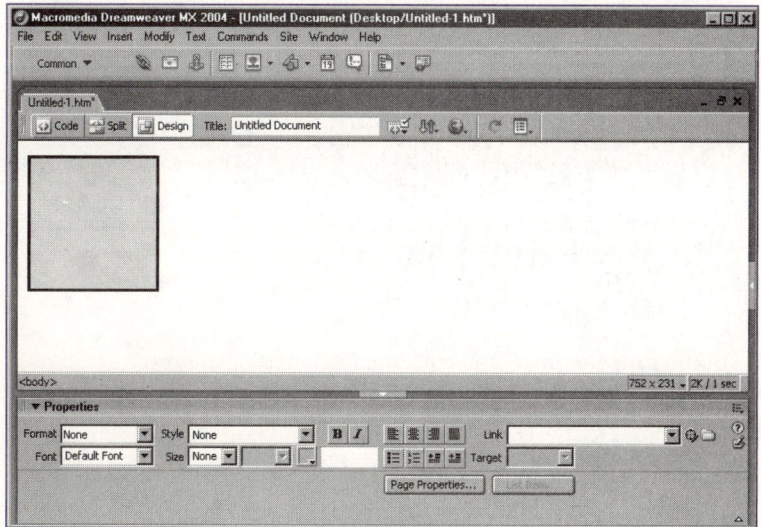

Figure 48-4: Bordered image

7. Select File ⇨ Preview in Browser and try the link. The border might appear a slightly different color and size. This is normal.

cross-references

▪ Refer to Task 46 for inserting images and Task 40 for adding links (Step 1).

▪ Refer to Task 171 for controlling borders styles and border colors using CSS (Step 7).

Aligning Images

Alignment of images is a bit tricky because there are so many options. Although most graphics can be controlled using tables and their alignment left untouched from the automatic default, it's good to know how to work with alignment. This is especially true with images that have other text or images bordering them.

1. Open a document that has at least one image and some text right next to it. The first alignment you'll learn is the most basic and is one you'll use frequently. Notice that text does not always flow around a picture like you'd like it to, as in Figure 49-1. There's a very easy way to fix this, and it doesn't require table formatting, styles, or anything fancy.

Lorem ipsum dolor sit amet, consectetuer adipiscing elit. Mauris nonummy elit a turpis pretium vestibulum. Donec laoreet, massa sed imperdiet nonummy, mi nisl luctus leo, luctus tincidunt nibh augue vel sapien. Donec ac augue a ligula bibendum hendrerit. Class aptent taciti sociosqu ad litora torquent per conubia nostra, per inceptos hymenaeos. Donec mollis ligula a nibh. Donec ipsum neque, dignissim ut, luctus quis, pellentesque eget, dolor. Praesent pharetra. Vestibulum ante ipsum primis in faucibus orci luctus et ultrices posuere cubilia Curae; Phasellus cursus, eros in accumsan tincidunt, tortor urna scelerisque mi, quis condimentum libero orci vel mauris. Fusce feugiat elementum mi. Mauris ornare. Suspendisse potenti. Donec et lorem non ligula tempus consequat. Vestibulum ante ipsum primis in faucibus orci luctus et ultrices posuere cubilia Curae; Donec vel massa nec ipsum pretium porta.

Duis nibh mi, dapibus eget, rhoncus id, lobortis eget, diam. Quisque aliquam. Sed tristique quam ut ligula. Integer neque diam, malesuada id, molestie quis, porttitor sit amet, pede. Nullam consectetuer volutpat pede. Phasellus at sem. Donec quis velit. Morbi mollis nonummy pede. Nullam posuere, felis non tempor luctus, neque massa aliquet purus, ut sollicitudin velit sapien ut massa. Proin ante sapien, luctus eu, lacinia nec, consequat tincidunt, pede. Quisque elementum, nunc ultricies ullamcorper mollis, ante ligula accumsan erat, sed porta lorem odio vel velit. Sed mollis, lectus a vehicula congue, nibh arcu aliquet mi, eget imperdiet nisl ipsum sed augue. In ut justo. Vestibulum viverra interdum nisl. Maecenas bibendum mi non ligula. Proin vulputate nunc eu ante.

Figure 49-1: Image and text at default

2. Select the picture.

3. In the Property inspector, click the menu triangle next to the Align field, and from the menu, select Left (see Figure 49-2).

4. Now select Right from the Align menu, and note the difference.

5. Table 49-1 shows all the different alignments and what they do. Experiment with them to get the effect you are after.

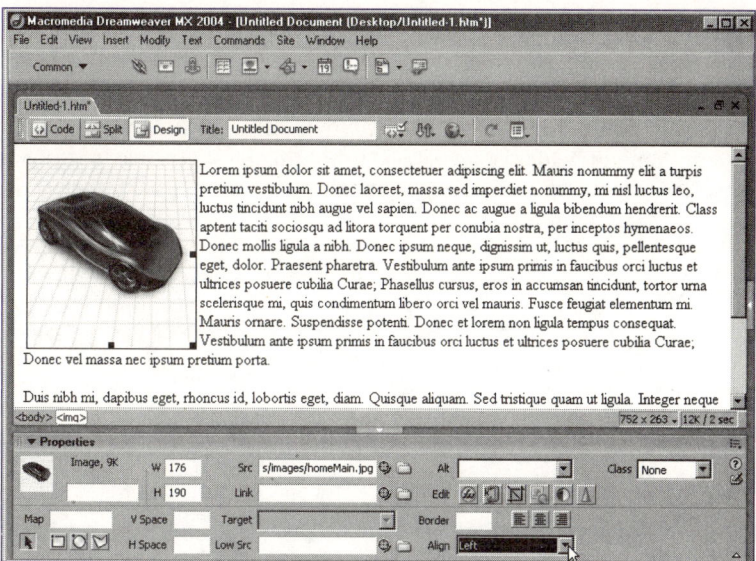

Figure 49-2: An image with Left alignment applied

Table 49-1: Alignment Attributes

Property	Function
Default Alignment	The browser default; usually denotes bottom.
Baseline	Bottom-aligns the images with the baseline of the first line of text.
Top	Top-aligns the top of the image with the first line of text.
Middle	Middle-aligns the middle of the image with the baseline of the first line of text.
Bottom	Bottom-aligns the bottom of the image with the baseline of the first line of text.
TextTop	Top-aligns the top of the image with the top of the first line of text.
Absolute Middle	Middle-aligns the middle of the image with the middle of the first line of text.
Absolute Bottom	Bottom-aligns the bottom of the image with the bottom of the first line of text.
Left	Aligns the image flush left on the page or cell; text is on the right.
Right	Aligns the image flush right on the page or cell; text is on the left.

Task 49

tips

- Left- or right-align graphics to have text flow around them (Step 1).

- If you are aligning just images in a table, set the alignment to the cell, not to the images (Step 4).

cross-reference

- Refer to Task 70 for aligning table cells.

Task 50

Using Image Placeholders

Placeholders are areas that act like graphics where you don't yet need an actual image. They are useful when you want to lay a page out and get an idea of the size of graphics before you create or insert them. Or you may need a placeholder that someone else on your design team can use as a guide when creating the real image content.

notes

- The default image icon will change to the Placeholder icon in the Insert bar. The icon that appears is the last one you've used (Step 2).
- Click in the color box to change the color (Step 5).

1. Position your cursor where you want the placeholder to be.
2. In the Common category of the Insert bar, click the arrow of the Images icon and select Image Placeholder (see Figure 50-1). Or choose Insert ➪ Image Object ➪ Image Placeholder.

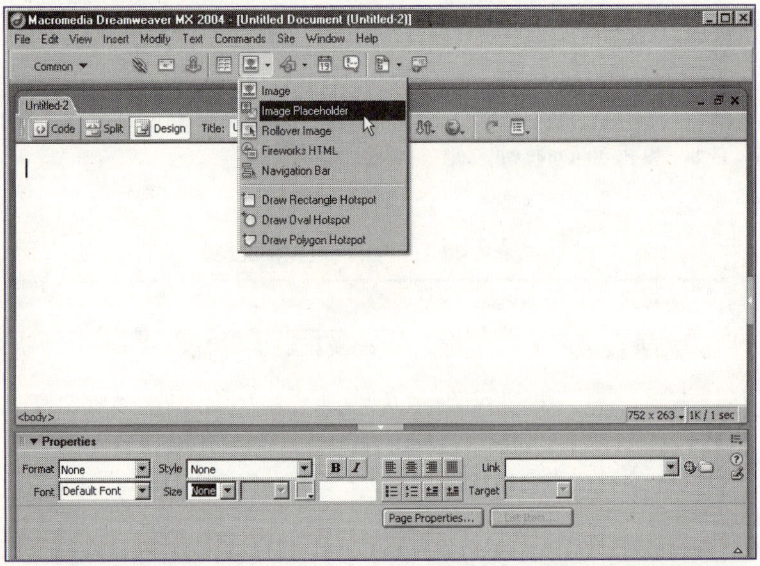

Figure 50-1: Common Insert bar with the Image button triangle highlighted

3. In the Image Placeholder dialog box, type **TestPlaceholder** in the Name field (or whatever you want to name it).
4. Type **300** in both the Width and Height fields.
5. Change the color if you'd like from the default gray.
6. Click OK. The completed dialog box is shown in Figure 50-2.
7. A gray placeholder is inserted into your document, as shown in Figure 50-3.
8. Click the placeholder once to select it.
9. Change the size of it by clicking and grabbing an edge, or the black square on an edge, and moving the mouse.
10. Double-click the placeholder to replace it with an image that is completed and ready to replace the placeholder.

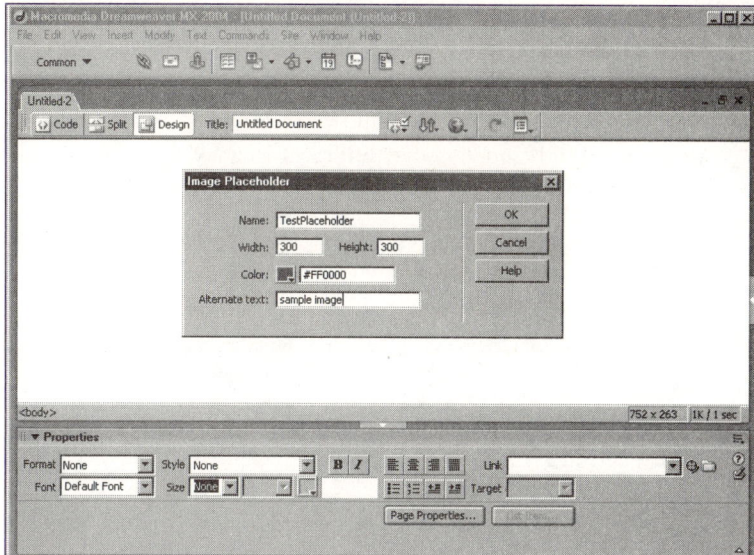

Figure 50-2: Image Placeholder dialog box filled out

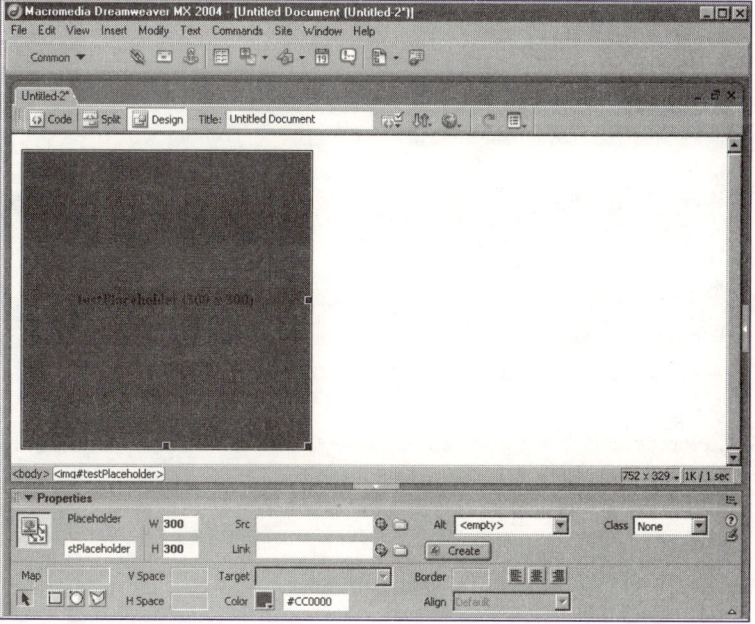

Figure 50-3: Placeholder in document

tip

- Use the exact pixel dimensions of your placeholder images in your real graphics, and your layout will stay the way you made it (Step 8).

cross-reference

- Refer to Task 51 for replacing the placeholder using Fireworks (Step 9).

Replacing a Placeholder Image Using Fireworks

Dreamweaver is tightly integrated with Fireworks, making it easy to add or edit images directly from Dreamweaver.

1. Open a Dreamweaver document that has the placeholder you want to replace, as shown in Figure 51-1.

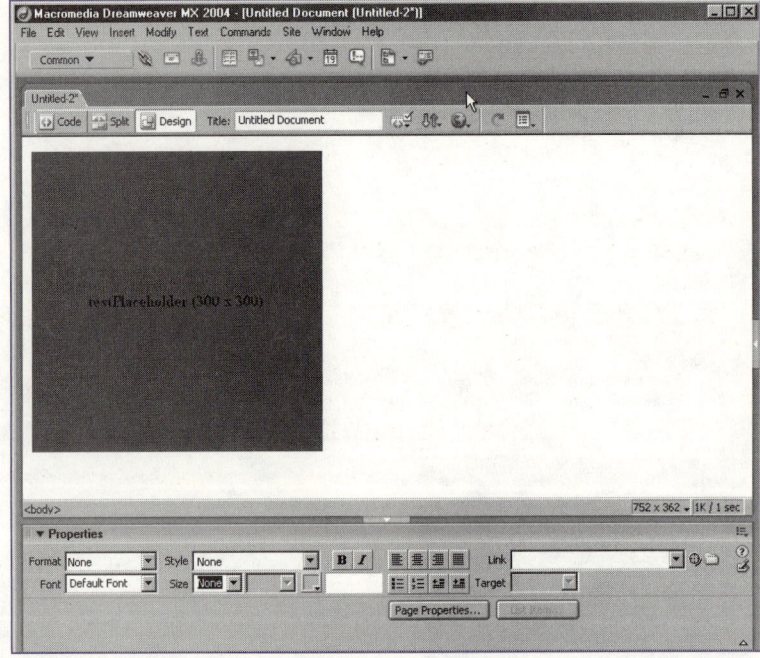

Figure 51-1: Placeholder image added to a document

2. Select the placeholder image.

3. Click the Create button in the Property inspector, as shown in Figure 51-2. This opens Fireworks.

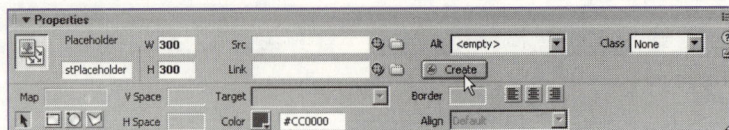

Figure 51-2: Create button in the Property inspector

4. Design your image. In the Optimize panel, be sure to set your optimization settings. When you are finished, click Done, as shown in Figure 51-3.

Figure 51-3: The Done button, as shown in Fireworks

5. The Save dialog box opens. Navigate to where you keep your site's source files and save this PNG.

6. The Export dialog box appears. Using the settings you made in the Optimize panel, the image is exported in the appropriate GIF or JPEG format. Navigate to the folder in your root site where you want to save the image.

7. Click Save. You are returned to Dreamweaver, and your new GIF or JPEG image is inserted into the document in place of the placeholder.

8. If you have an image ready to replace the placeholder with (and don't need to create one), double-click the placeholder in the Dreamweaver document.

9. Navigate to your replacement graphic in the Select Image Source dialog box and click OK.

cross-reference

▪ A free tutorial on optimizing images in Fireworks can be found at www. JoyceJEvans.com in the Tutorials ➪ Fireworks section.

Task **52**

Changing the Brightness and Contrast of an Image

You can change the brightness and contrast of an image directly in Dreamweaver. Use this tool instead of using a graphic application when you need to make slight changes to an image. Keep in mind these changes will be permanent, so you'll need to make a backup of your image first.

1. Before you edit an image in Dreamweaver using the Brightness/ Contrast feature, make a copy of the image first and save it in a separate folder.

2. Open a Dreamweaver document with the image you want to edit.

3. Click once on the image so it is selected, as shown in Figure 52-1.

Figure 52-1: Image selected on a page

4. Click the Brightness/Contrast button in the Property inspector, shown in Figure 52-2, or select Modify ⇨ Image ⇨ Brightness/ Contrast.

5. A warning appears, notifying you that the change will be permanent (see Figure 52-2). Because you made a backup copy, click OK.

6. Click and drag the Brightness slider bar to the right for more brightness or to the left for less.

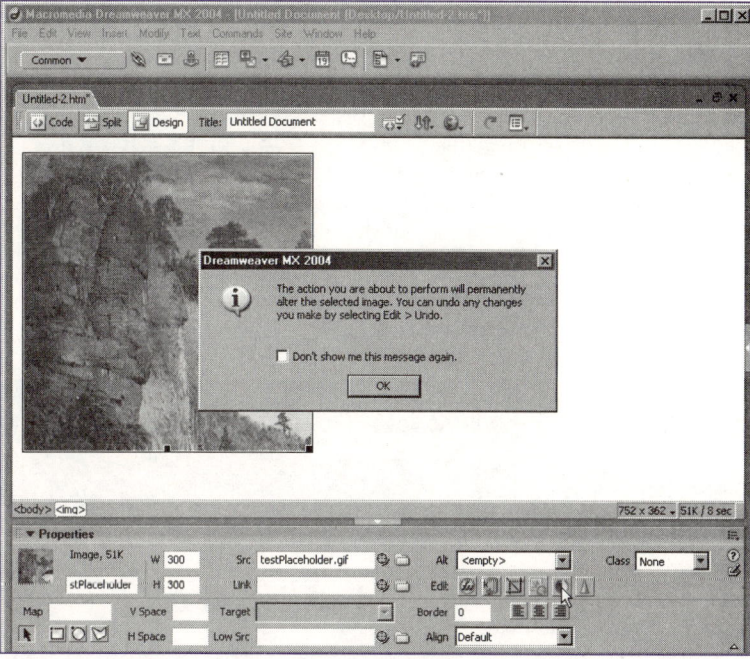

Figure 52-2: Brightness/Contrast button and warning dialog box

tip

- When you are managing a lot of images, it's best to use an image editing program and establish a consistent brightness and contrast for all the images of similar types on a page (Step 2).

7. Click and drag the Contrast bar to the right for more brightness or to the left for less, as shown in Figure 52-3. You can also type values directly in the Brightness or Contrast fields.

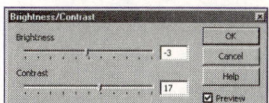

Figure 52-3: Brightness/Contrast box with -3 and 17

8. Watch the changes to your image take place. The settings I used made the picture a bit darker but with more contrast.

9. If you like what you see, hit OK. If not, alter the settings.

10. Select Edit ⇨ Undo Brightness and Contrast to see the difference.

cross-reference

- Refer to Task 56 for editing images in Fireworks, where you have much more control.

Cropping an Image

Y ou can crop an image directly in Dreamweaver. This is helpful when you are dealing with images you did not make in Fireworks, or graphics you need to make small changes to. But like brightness and contrast changes, these changes are permanent. So you'll make a backup of your image first.

1. Before you edit an image in Dreamweaver using the Crop feature, make a copy of the image first and save it in a separate folder.

2. Open a Dreamweaver document with the image you want to edit.

3. Click once on the image so it is selected.

4. Click the Crop button in the Property inspector, shown in Figure 53-1, or select Modify ➪ Image ➪ Crop.

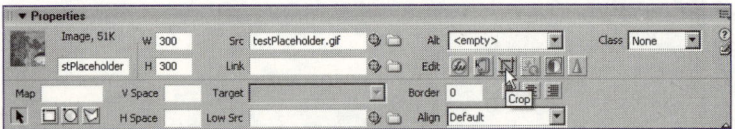

Figure 53-1: Crop button in Property inspector

5. A warning appears, notifying you that these changes will be permanent. Because you made a backup, click OK.

6. Your graphic is now surrounded by a new kind of frame, or marquee, with square black handles, as shown in Figure 53-2.

Figure 53-2: Crop marquee around graphic

---

note

- You don't need to have any image editor at all to use this feature.

caution

- Cropping images can change the layout of your page. Make sure to check your work in a browser (Step 1).

Task 53

7. Click and drag the edges of the marquee. To constrain the resize, drag in from one of the corners. A marquee making an image smaller is shown in Figure 53-3.

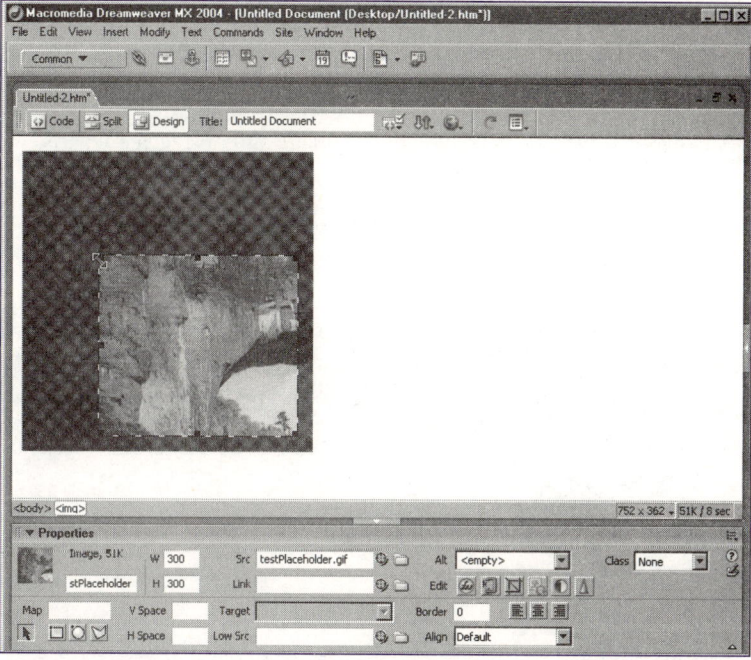

Figure 53-3: Crop marquee tighter on the graphic

8. When you have the crop you like, double-click in the middle of the graphic. The result is shown in Figure 53-4.

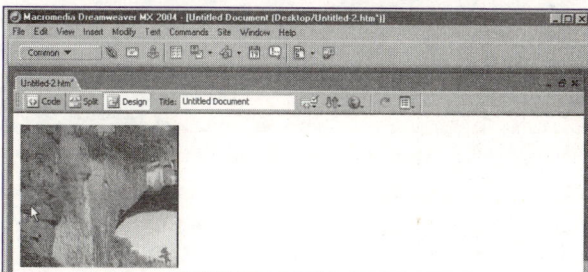

Figure 53-4: Cropped graphic

cross-reference

• Refer to Task 56 for editing images in Fireworks, where you can crop down or up (Step 9).

Task **54**

Sharpening an Image

Y ou can sharpen blurry images directly in Dreamweaver. Sharpening images works well when you have just a slightly blurry photo or graphic. This tool can only do so much good, so don't get your hopes up too high. You'll make a backup file first, because these changes are permanent to the image file.

note
- You don't need to have any image editor at all to use this feature (Intro).

1. Before you edit an image in Dreamweaver using the Brightness/ Contrast feature, make a copy of the image and save it in a separate folder.

2. Open a Dreamweaver document with the image you want to edit.

3. Click once on the image so it is selected, as shown in Figure 54-1.

Figure 54-1: An image needing sharpening has been selected

caution
- Sharpness sometimes makes things worse. When in doubt, do very slight sharpness, or none at all. If the edges start to turn white, you've probably gone too far (Step 6).

4. Click the Sharpen button in the Property inspector, shown in Figure 54-2, or select Modify ⇨ Image ⇨ Sharpen.

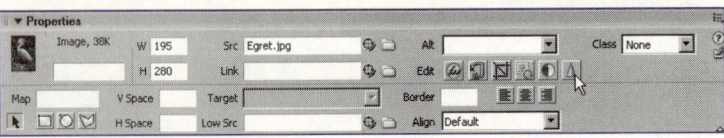

Figure 54-2: Sharpen button in Property inspector

5. A warning appears, notifying you that these changes will be permanent. Because you made a backup, click OK.

6. In the Sharpen dialog box, drag the slider to the right until it reads 4 in the field (see Figure 54-3). The scale is 1 to 10. A high setting above 5 usually makes the quality worse.

Figure 54-3: Sharpen dialog box set to 4

7. The edges are a good place to see the effects of sharpening. Experiment with the settings. Figure 54-4 shows the setting at 10. As you can see, it's far too much.

8. Redo the setting to whatever looks good, and click OK.

9. Select Edit ⇨ Undo Sharpen to see the effect.

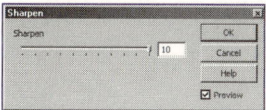

Figure 54-4: Sharpening set at 10 to demonstrate oversharpening an image

cross-reference

▪ Refer to Task 59 for editing images in Fireworks. Sometimes you want to apply more sharpening, then add a tiny bit of blur. You can do this in Fireworks (Steps 8 and 9).

Setting Fireworks as Your Image Editor

Fireworks can be used to edit all your graphics. This is recommended because of the great integration between Dreamweaver and Fireworks. If you created your images in Fireworks, you probably saved the native file. This is a Fireworks PNG format and remains totally editable.

1. In Windows, select Edit ➪ Preferences. On a Mac, select Dreamweaver ➪ Preferences.

2. Select File Types/Editors from the Category area on the left, as shown in Figure 55-1.

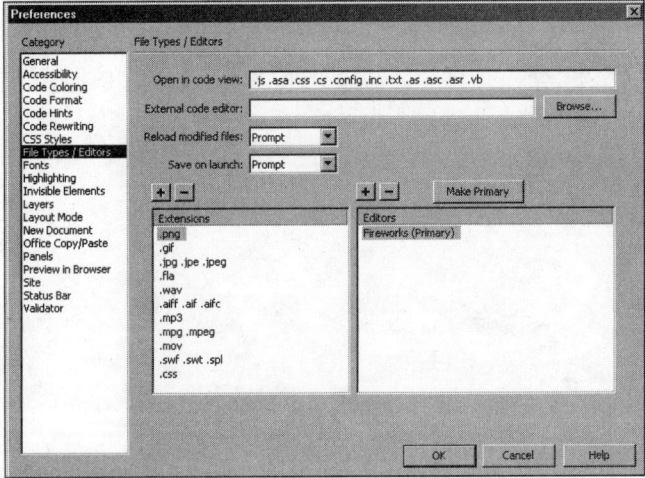

Figure 55-1: Preferences with File Types/Editors selected

3. In the Preferences dialog box, click .png in the Extensions window.

4. Look in the Editor window and check whether you see Fireworks (Primary). If so, you're all set.

5. If not, select anything that is there that you don't want, and click the Minus (–) button. Now click the Add (+) button above the Editors window. Navigate to your Fireworks application EXE file, select it, as shown in Figure 55-2, and click Open.

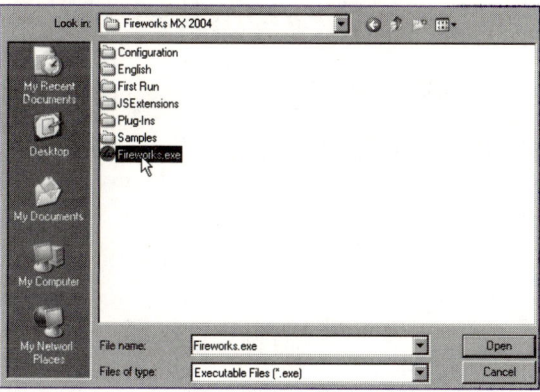

Figure 55-2: Selecting fireworks.exe on a PC

6. If it doesn't say Primary automatically, click the Make Primary button in the File Types/Editors window so you see Fireworks (Primary) in the Preferences dialog box.

7. Repeat Steps 5 and 6 for the extensions .gif, .jpg, .png, and .jpeg. This sets Fireworks to be your primary editor for all graphics used on the Web.

8. Click OK

9. In your document, click an image once to select it, then click the Fireworks button, shown in Figure 55-3, in the Property inspector to edit that image in Fireworks.

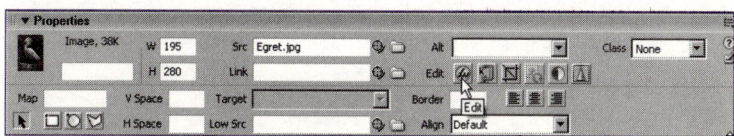

Figure 55-3: Fireworks button in Property inspector

cross-reference

- Refer to Task 56 for editing images using Fireworks.

Editing an Image in Fireworks

It is always better to use a tool made specifically for the job than one made for many jobs, or primarily for another job. Dreamweaver can edit images, but it was not made specifically to perform this task. Fireworks, on the other hand, is made specifically for editing images for the Web, and it works great in conjunction with Dreamweaver.

note

- You can also edit tables that were exported from Fireworks and inserted into Dreamweaver.

1. Make sure Fireworks is set as your primary image editor for .png, .gif, and .jpg. (Refer to Task 55.)

2. In your Dreamweaver document, click the image you want to edit once to select it, as shown in Figure 56-1.

Figure 56-1: Selected image

3. Click the Fireworks button in the Property inspector, as shown in Figure 56-2.

4. If the image was not created in Fireworks or you've moved the source file since exporting, a Find Source warning appears, as shown in Figure 56-3.

5. If you have a source image, navigate to it. Otherwise, click Use This File.

6. Edit your document in Fireworks. For editing such as brightness/contrast, color adjustments, and so on, use the Effects list in the Property inspector (see Figure 56-4). Effects are undoable in Fireworks.

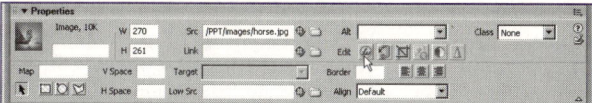

Figure 56-2: Fireworks button in the Property inspector

7. Click Done and you are returned to Dreamweaver. If you used a source PNG file, it is updated along with the exported file.

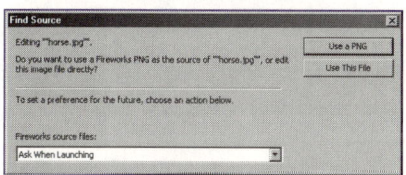

Figure 56-3: Find Source warning

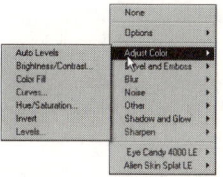

Figure 56-4: The Effects list in Fireworks

tip

▪ Create a directory outside your Web page directory for original graphics, and always keep the source files for your site there (Step 4).

cross-reference

▪ Refer to Task 58 for inserting Fireworks HTML.

Optimizing Graphics in Fireworks

Fireworks has a useful tool for optimizing graphics for which you do not have the source files. Optimizing images makes them download quicker by reducing their file size. Graphics optimization is a permanent change, so you need to make a backup of your file first.

1. Make a copy of the actual image file on your computer. Using your computer's operating system (Windows on a PC or OSX on a Mac), select the image you want to edit once. Then select Duplicate (or, on a PC, Edit ➪ Copy, then Paste; and on a Mac, File ➪ Duplicate).

2. In Dreamweaver, click the image you want to optimize once to select it, as shown in Figure 57-1. The sample image is actually a PNG file, but it'll be optimized now in Fireworks.

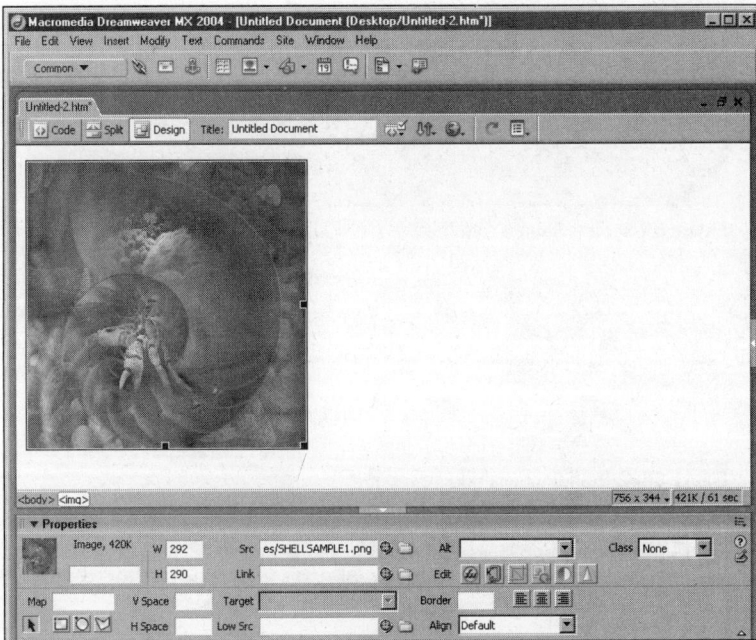

Figure 57-1: Selected image

3. Click the Optimize in Fireworks button in the Property inspector, as shown in Figure 57-2, or select Commands ➪ Optimize Image in Fireworks.

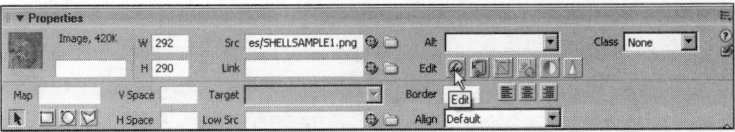

Figure 57-2: Optimize button in Property inspector

4. In the Find Source dialog box that appears, click Use This File. But if you happen to have the source file, be it a PNG or PSD or whatever, by all means select it.

5. In the Optimize Fireworks dialog box's Format menu, select JPEG for photographs and images with many colors, or GIF for buttons and other graphics with limited colors. Select a quality setting for JPEGs and the number of colors to be used for GIFs.

6. Click the Preview tab, shown in Figure 57-3, to see the results of your settings in the Optimize panel.

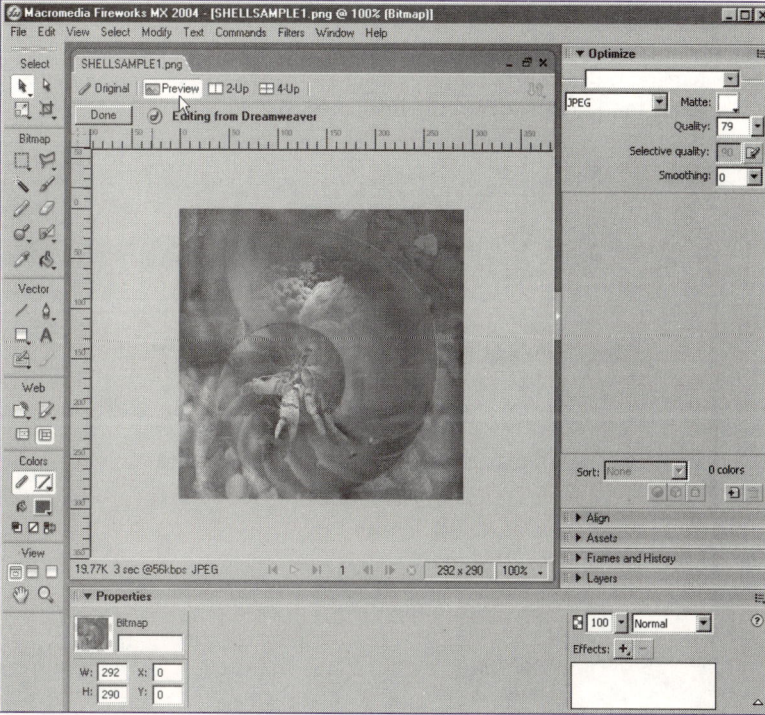

Figure 57-3: Optimize dialog box

7. When you are satisfied, click the Done button. If you used an original file, it is saved and the exported file is saved and appears in Dreamweaver.

tips

- Optimize thumbnail photographs to around 40 to save download time. Then optimize a larger image using 60 if you click the thumbnail (Step 2).

- If you have a lot of images to optimize, use Fireworks' batch process to quickly do them all at once and export to a folder for use in Dreamweaver (Step 3).

cross-reference

- Refer to Task 56 for editing images with Fireworks.

Inserting Fireworks Images and HTML

In Fireworks you can export just images. But there are times when you make buttons or other objects that have behaviors attached to them. For instance, a button may have a rollover or a swap image behavior attached. You can even add the links in Fireworks. If you want to maintain the JavaScript (which is what is used for the behaviors), you'll need to export as HTML and Images. Once you've exported a file with HTML and Images, you can insert it all into a Dreamweaver layout.

note

- Slicing does not reduce the image's size; it just breaks it up and facilitates layout (Step 3).

1. Position your cursor where you want to insert the Fireworks HTML.

2. Select Insert ⇨ Image Objects ⇨ Insert Fireworks HTML.

3. In the Insert Fireworks HTML dialog box, shown in Figure 58-1, navigate to where you exported your Fireworks HTML and Images, choose the HTM file (not the images files), and click OK.

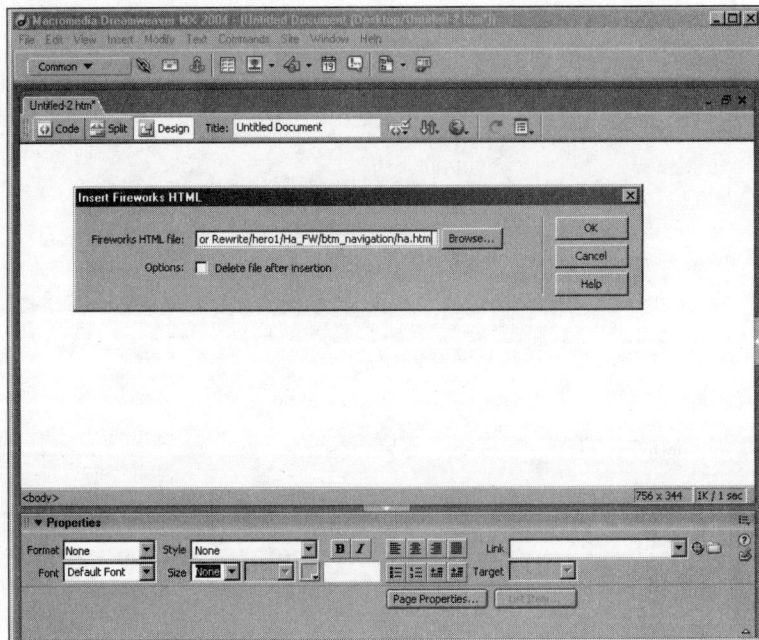

Figure 58-1: Insert Fireworks HTML dialog box

caution

- Keep complex sliced Fireworks exports in separate directories, because they can create a lot of images that will clutter directories with other images in them (Step 4).

4. If your Images and HTML are located outside the directories where your Web site is, a warning appears, shown in Figure 58-2, that asks you if you want to copy the HTML files into your site folder. If so, click Yes.

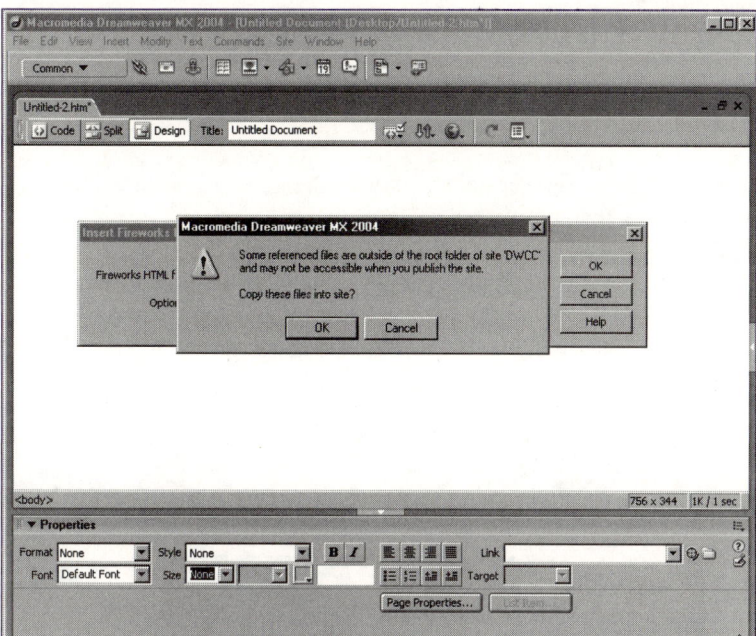

Figure 58-2: Warning about copying HTML

tip

- Fireworks is great at making sliced graphics. Slicing is useful when you have a large graphic or want to slice up a circle into parts for easier page loading (Step 1).

5. In the Copy Image Files To dialog box, shown in Figure 58-3, navigate to the directory in your Web site where you want to store your Fireworks HTML and Images, and click OK.

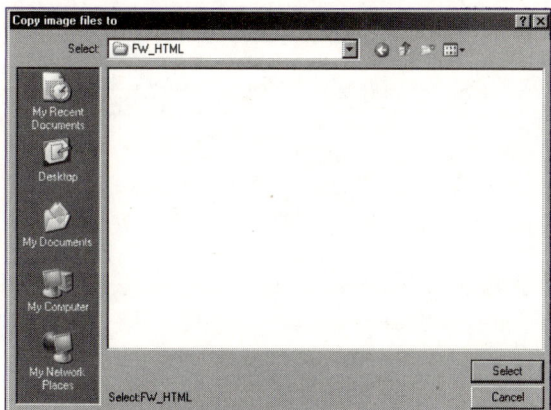

Figure 58-3: Copy Image Files To dialog box

cross-reference

- Refer to Task 59 for editing Fireworks HTML.

6. Your Fireworks HTML and Images appear in the Dreamweaver document.

Editing Fireworks HTML

Once you learn how to import Fireworks HTML into your Dreamweaver documents, you may need to edit the HTML.

1. Open a Dreamweaver document with the Fireworks images and HTML that you want to edit.

2. Select the entire image in Dreamweaver by placing the cursor to the right of the table containing the images and then dragging left. Be sure to select the entire table. You'll know you did it right if you can see the Edit button in the Property inspector, as shown in Figure 59-1.

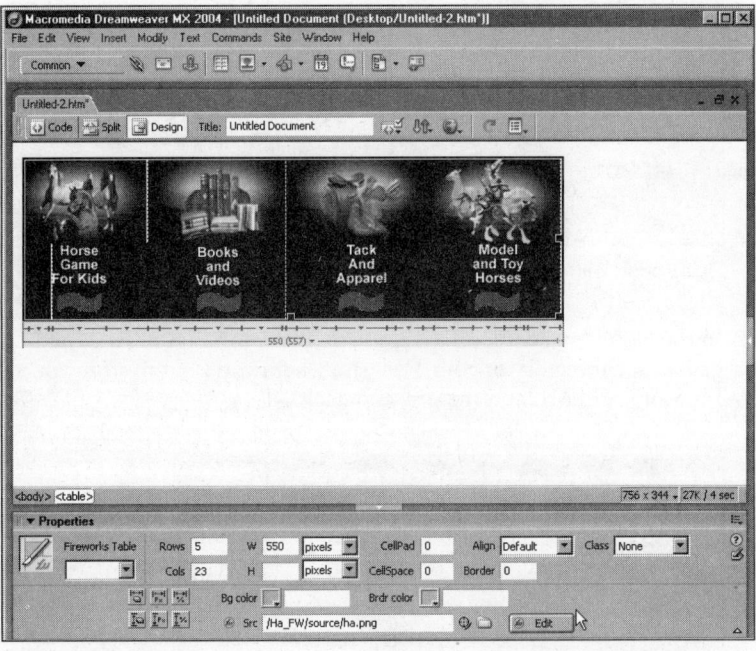

Figure 59-1: Entire image selected with Edit button in Property inspector

caution
- If you have troubles or get warning boxes, make sure the Src field in the Property inspector is referencing the right PNG file. Or try starting an export from the beginning in Fireworks (Step 3).

3. Click the Edit button in the Property inspector. You may get a dialog box asking you to locate the source PNG file. You'll need to know where it is to use this technique.

4. In Fireworks edit your graphic (see Figure 59-2). To see the changes without committing yet, select File ➪ Update HTML if you want to see the changes in Dreamweaver. You can keep editing in Fireworks or click Done. This brings you back to Dreamweaver, where your images and HTML have been updated.

Figure 59-2: Fireworks with image to edit

5. The edited file appears back in Dreamweaver, as shown in Figure 59-3.

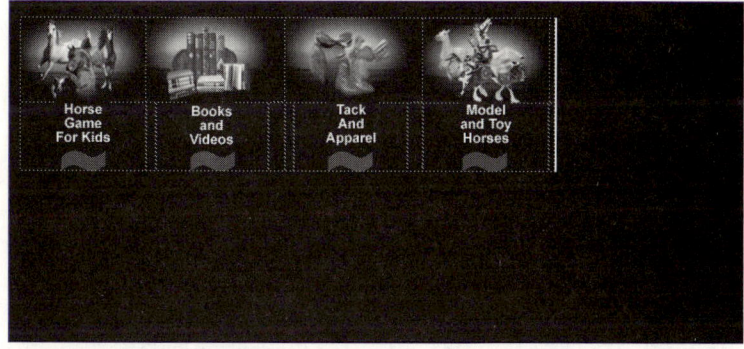

Figure 59-3: Edited image in document

tip

- To save time, do as much work in Fireworks as you can, including previewing your work in a browser. Then when you have what you want, update the Dreamweaver HTML (Step 1).

cross-reference

- Refer to Task 58 for inserting Fireworks HTML.

Making an Image Map

Image maps are graphics with areas you define that link to other pages. Image maps are very useful when you want to display an actual map of something that has several spots you want users to be able to click, such as a map of neighborhoods in a city with pages of real estate listings linked to each area.

1. Open a Dreamweaver document with the image for which you want to make an image map.

2. Select the image, as shown in Figure 60-1.

note

- The image map name goes in the Map field just above the hot spot icons in the Property inspector (Step 4).

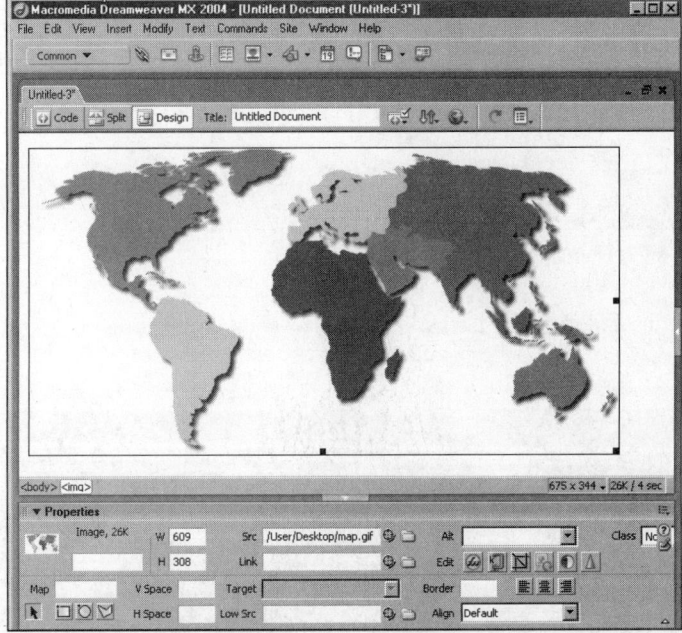

Figure 60-1: Image selected

3. Click the Oval Hot Spot tool in the Property inspector, and draw a medium-sized circle or rectangle on your graphic—whatever you need.

4. Click the hot spot (indicated by blue) once to select it (see Figure 60-2). A reminder opens telling you to name your hot spot for better accessibility. Enter a link in the Link Field in the Property inspector, or use the Browse to File button to navigate to a file. Be sure to add the alternative text and name the image map.

5. Repeat Steps 3 and 4 to draw and link with the Rectangle and Polygon tool on either side of the Oval Hot Spot tool. To use the Polygon tool, you click in several places to make a shape until the shape is closed on all sides. Figure 60-3 shows three hot spot shapes added.

6. Select File ➪ Preview in your browser to try your links. The shapes you drew will be invisible, but your mouse will change to a hand, indicating a link, if you pass over them.

cautions

- Image maps add a lot of weight to your page if they are large. Use them only if it's the only way.

- Image maps are not obvious to users, so you have to explicitly instruct them to click different parts of the image (Step 1).

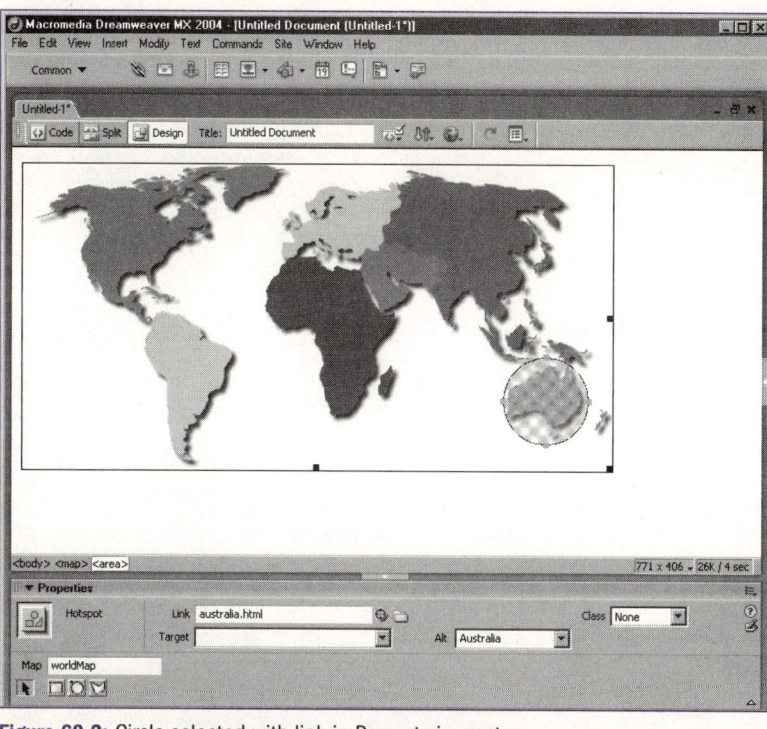

Figure 60-2: Circle selected with link in Property inspector

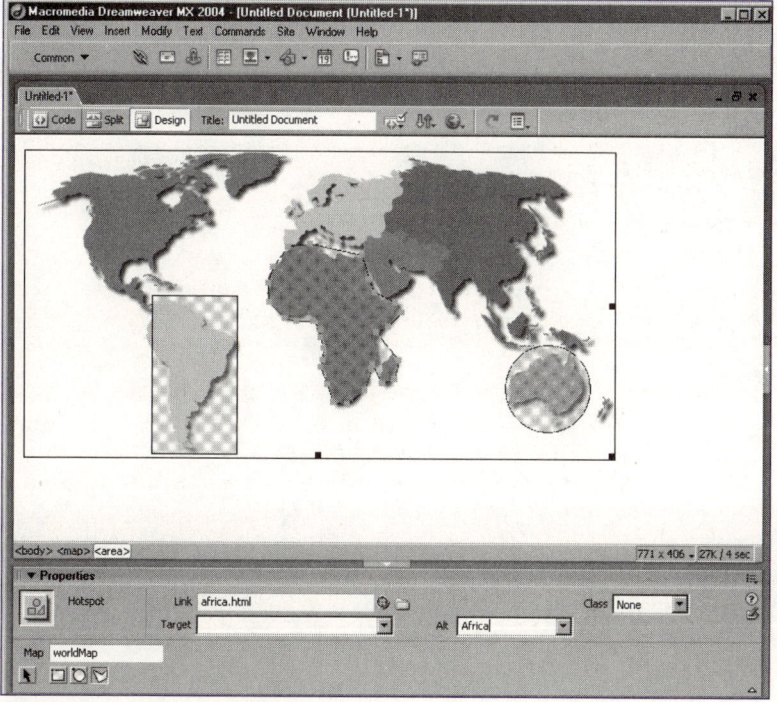

Figure 60-3: Image with three hot spot shapes

cross-reference

- Refer to Task 47 for adding alternative text.

Part 3: Working with Tables and Site Management

Inserting a Table

Originally, tables were designed for tabular data (text and numbers represented in a format much like a spreadsheet). Along the way, designers figured out that tables were an excellent way to format page content on the Web page. Basically, a table is a series of rows and columns that make up an area of the page.

1. Open a document from the Files panel or create a new document and save it.

2. Click the Table icon in the Common category of the Insert bar to open the Insert Table dialog box.

3. Rows tells the interface how many rows you want the table to contain; Columns tells the interface how many columns you want for each row. Cell Padding is the padding inside the cell between the cell walls and the content and affects above, below, left, and right of the cell content. Cell Spacing is the spacing between each cell's adjoining wall, not inside the cell, and similarly affects all sides of the cell. Width is specified in a value and units. Available units are pixels or percent. Border is the size of the border separating the cells and surrounding the table as a whole.

   For the purpose of this task, populate the Insert Table dialog box with the following values (also see Figure 61-1):

   Rows: 3

   Columns: 4

   Width: 600 Pixels

   Border: 1

   Cell Padding: 5

   Cell Spacing: 5

4. Click the OK button to insert the table into the open document at the current cursor position.

5. Select Code view to see what Dreamweaver MX 2004 inserted into your document, as shown in Figure 61-2.

6. Adjustments can be made using Code view (if you are careful), or you can select the `<table>` tag in the Tag Selector to open the Table Property inspector.

notes

- Alternatively, you can use File ➪ Insert to open the Insert Table dialog box (Step 2).

- The Insert Table dialog box is sticky; it automatically populates with the last data used in the creation of a table (Step 3).

- If using CSS, you should specify the cell padding, cell spacing, width, and border using CSS for finer control of the table and its cells (Step 3).

- If you have set Accessibility Preferences for Tables to On, another dialog box opens, prompting you for Caption, Caption Alignment, Summary, and Table Headers (Step 4).

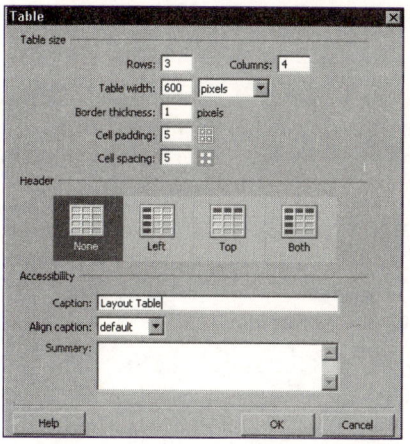

Figure 61-1: Completed Insert Table dialog box

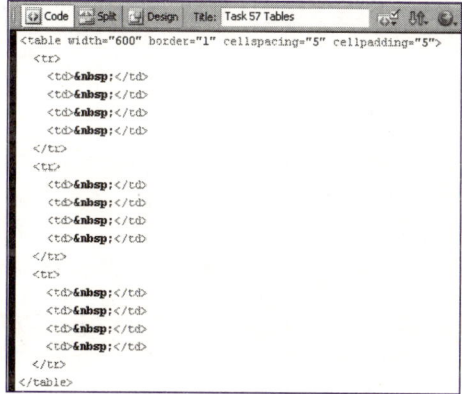

Figure 61-2: Code view of inserted table

7. Depending on where you have your cursor in the table or what you have selected in the Tag Selector, different Property inspectors will open, allowing you to edit content related to the selected item.

8. Once the table is inserted in the document, adding content to the cells is simply a matter of positioning your cursor in the desired cell and typing away or adding an image.

9. This page is used in the next few tasks, so name it **task61.htm**.

cross-reference

- See Task 4 for instructions on opening or creating a document.

Task **62**

Selecting Table Elements

Once the table is defined, you need to be able to select the various elements, such as the table itself, one or more rows or columns, or a single cell to set the properties. Dreamweaver MX 2004 gives you a number of methods. Choose which one is easiest for you.

1. To select a table:

   - Click the Table Width (View ➪ Visual Aids ➪ Table Widths) bottom arrow (see Figure 62-1).

   - Click anywhere inside the table, and then select the `<table>` tag from the status bar.

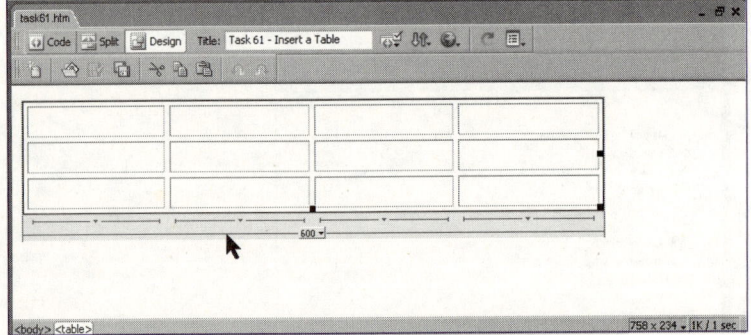

Figure 62-1: A table with the Table Widths Visual Aids showing and the `<table>` tag highlighted

   - Click outside of the table and drag the cursor over the edge of the table.

   - Choose Modify ➪ Table ➪ Select Table.

   - Right-/Control+click the table, and from the contextual menu, hover over Table and click Select Table.

2. To select a row:

   - Click in any cell within the row you want to select. In the Tag inspector, click the `<tr>` (table row) tag.

   - Roll the cursor over the edge of the row until the small arrow appears, then click. Hold down the Ctrl/Option key, and repeat to select multiple rows, even noncontinuous rows.

   - Click inside the first cell of a row and drag across to select the entire row. Continue dragging down to select multiple rows.

notes

- Click and drag means to hold the left button down while doing the drag (Step 2).

- If you have an image that fills a cell, it may be difficult to select the cell itself. Use the Tag inspector when this happens (Step 4).

3. To select a column:

   • Use the Table Width column arrow to open the Column Header menu, and choose Select Column (see Figure 62-2).

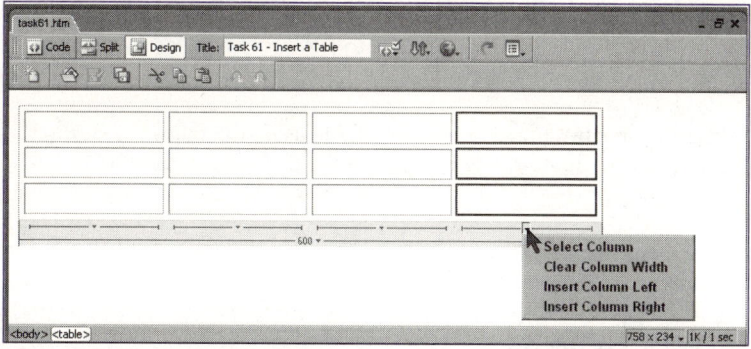

Figure 62-2: The Column Header menu

   • Hover the cursor over the top of the column you want to select. Once you see the vertical arrow, click. Hold down the Ctrl/Option key, and repeat to select multiple columns, even discontinuous columns.

   • Click inside the first cell of a column and drag down to select the entire column.

4. To select a cell:

   • Click in any cell to select it.

   • Ctrl/Option+click each cell you want to select, even discontinuous cells.

   • Click inside the cell and drag across and/or down to select multiple continuous cells.

   • Click in a cell and select the `<td>` tag in the Tag inspector.

5. To move from cell to cell, use the Tab key. This is especially useful when a cell is collapsed because of lack of content.

cross-references

• See Task 71 for instructions on using the Extended mode in making selections.

• See Tasks 61 and 63 for inserting a table and modifying the number of rows and columns.

Task 63

Adding and Removing Table Rows or Columns

It never fails. Just when you think you have defined the table structure completely, you find out that you need to add more rows or columns to accommodate the desired content.

note

- The same menu options are selectable from the context menu in Design view by right-/Command+ clicking in the cell (Steps 3 through 6).

1. Insert a table by choosing Insert ⇨ Table using the following settings for the Insert Table dialog box, or use the table you created in Task 61.

   Rows: 3

   Columns: 4

   Cell Padding: 5

   Cell Spacing: 5

   Width: 600 Pixels

   Border: 1

   Click the OK button on the Insert Table dialog box and save the page using File ⇨ Save As.

2. Using Design view, position your cursor in the cell on row 2, column 2.

3. To insert an additional row, select Modify ⇨ Table ⇨ Insert Row (Ctrl/Command+M), and a new row is inserted above the current cursor position. (See Figure 63-1.)

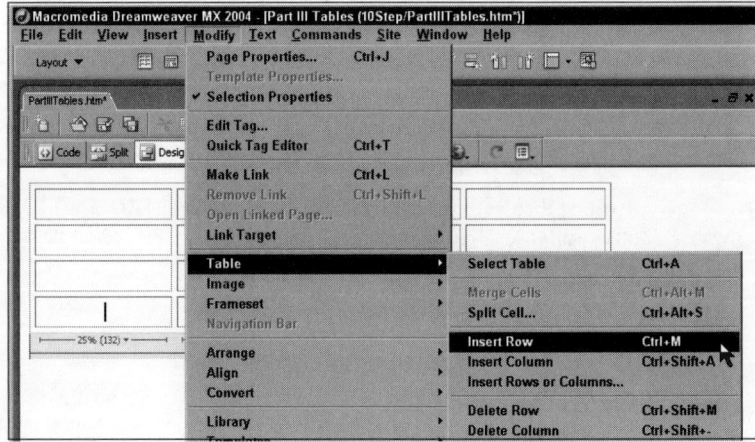

Figure 63-1: The Modify Table menu with Insert Row selected

caution

- The inserted column or row takes the same format as the current one (the column or row that the cursor is in). If you have merged or split a cell in the column or row (see Task 64), the inserted element includes a merged or split cell.

4. To delete the currently selected row, select Modify ⇨ Table ⇨ Delete Row (Ctrl/Command+Shift+M).

5. To insert an additional column, select Modify ⇨ Table ⇨ Insert Column (Ctrl/Command+Shift+A), and a new column is inserted before the current cursor position. To delete the currently selected column, select Modify ⇨ Table ⇨ Delete Column (Ctrl/CommandShift+-) and the column is removed.

6. Sometimes you may not want the row or column inserted before the currently selected cell, or you may want to add more than one row/column at a time. To open the Insert Rows or Columns dialog box, select Modify ⇨ Table ⇨ Insert Rows or Columns. The Insert Rows or Columns dialog box appears, as shown in Figure 63-2.

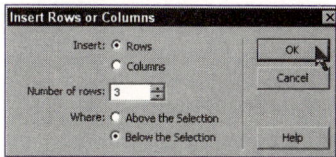

Figure 63-2: Insert Rows or Columns dialog box (rows)

7. This dialog box allows you to set the number of rows or columns to insert, as well as specify their position, relative to the current cursor position. The dialog box changes depending on your selection of what to insert. Figure 63-3 shows the columns version.

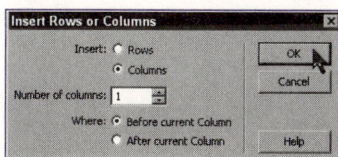

Figure 63-3: Insert Rows or Columns dialog box (columns)

8. Select Rows, 3, and Below the Selection, as shown in Figure 63-2. Once you have made your desired selections, click the OK button to effect the desired change and close the dialog box.

9. The table on the page should consist of six rows and four columns (see Figure 63-4). Once this is accomplished, save the page.

Row 1, Col 1	Col 2	Col 3	Col 4
Row 2			
Row 3			
Row 4			
Row 5			
Row 6			

Figure 63-4: The table with the rows inserted

cross-references

- See Task 4 for instructions on opening or creating a document.

- Refer to Task 61 for inserting tables (Step 1).

Task **64**

Merging and Splitting Table Elements

Formatting tables sometimes involves combining columns and/or rows to make a combined cell that can be used for a special image slice or another kind of content for the page.

1. Insert a table using Insert ⇨ Table using the following settings for the Insert Table dialog box, or use the table you created in Task 61.

    Rows: 6

    Columns: 4

    Cell Padding: 5

    Cell Spacing: 5

    Width: 600 Pixels

    Border: 1

    Click the OK button on the Insert Table dialog box and save the page using File ⇨ Save As.

2. To select a group of cells to merge, use Design view and position your cursor in the cell on row 2, column 2. Click the left button and drag over to column 3, row 5; then release the mouse button to select the cells, as shown in Figure 64-1.

Row 1, Col 1	Col 2	Col 3	Col 4
Row 2			
Row 3			
Row 4			
Row 5			
Row 6			

Figure 64-1: Selected cells

3. To merge the selected cells, click the Merges Cells icon, shown in Figure 64-2, in the Property inspector or use the shortcut keys (Ctrl/Command+Alt +M).

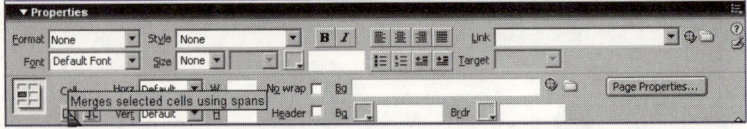

Figure 64-2: The Merge icon in the Cell area of the Property inspector

4. The merge is performed, leaving the merged block highlighted, as shown in Figure 64-3. Save your work here.

Row 1, Col 1	Col 2	Col 3	Col 4
Row 2			
Row 3			
Row 4			
Row 5			
Row 6			

Figure 64-3: Merge completed

5. Splitting previously merged cells is a little more complex because Dreamweaver doesn't recognize that a merged cell can consist of both rows and columns. Each operation must be performed independently. Position your cursor in the previously merged cell.

6. To split the rows out, select Modify ➪ Table ➪ Split Cells or click the Split Cell icon in the Property inspector. The Split Cell dialog box opens, as shown in Figure 64-4. Dreamweaver automatically populates the quantity field if it can determine the value. Click the OK button to split the rows.

7. To split the columns, select the four newly split rows (rows 2 through 5, column 2) individually (Dreamweaver cannot perform this function on a combination of rows). Then select Modify ➪ Table ➪ Split Cells. The Split Cell dialog box opens. Click the OK button and repeat for each row that is still split.

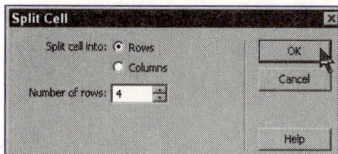

Figure 64-4: Split cells dialog box (rows and columns versions)

8. Save the page once it looks like the original again.

cross-references

-   See Task 4 for instructions on opening or creating a document (Step 1).

-   See Tasks 61 and 63 for inserting a table and modifying the number of rows and columns (Step 1).

Importing Tabular Data

One of the frustrating items in static Web page development is inserting the client's spreadsheet data into a page. The old method was to print the spreadsheet, create a table in Dreamweaver, and type all the data into each cell by hand. Dreamweaver offers you an easier method of getting that data onto your page using Import Tabular Data. Dreamweaver can import tabular data that uses just about any character to separate the values. Internally, it directly supports Tab, Comma, Semicolon, and Color, while providing an Other type that you can specify in the dialog box.

1. Create a new document and save it using the filename **Task65.htm**.

2. Create a spreadsheet in your favorite spreadsheet application, fill in about three or four columns in ten rows, and save the file as comma-separated values (.csv). Alternatively, if you use Outlook or Outlook Express, to export the Address Book in CSV format, you open the Address Book, select File ➪ Export ➪ Other Address Book, choose Text File (Comma Separated Values), select the Export button, and then follow the prompts.

3. You can use the following sample data instead of building a spread-sheet. Type the lines as shown into a text document. Be careful to insert the commas after each entry. (Or you can use the file task65data.txt.)

```
Sample data that you can use:
Datum,First Name, Last Name
1,Brad,Halstead
2,Joyce,Evans
3,Brenda,Gillis
4,Megan,Gillis
5,Hugh,Gillis
6,Denise,Gillis
7,Linda,Martell
8,Paul,Martell
9,Teddy,Bear
```

4. To import the data into the page, select File ➪ Import ➪ Tabular Data. This opens the Import Tabular Data dialog box, shown in Figure 65-1.

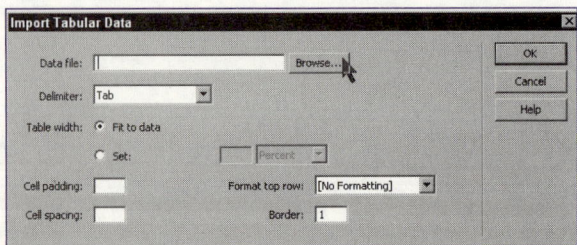

Figure 65-1: Import Tabular Data dialog box

5. Use the Browse button to locate the file you wish to import. Note that the delimiter may change to the desired value. If it does not, select the delimiter from the Delimiter pop-up list. You can use a custom delimiter by selecting Other from the pop-up list and then specifying the value in the field that appears. For this task, select comma as the delimiter if using the previous sample data.

6. Set the table width options by selecting Fit to Data or Set. If using Set, you can specify the width of the table in a percentage or pixel value. For this task, select Fit to Data.

7. Set the desired Cell Spacing, Cell Padding, and Border values as desired. For this task, set the values to 5, 5, and 1, respectively.

8. The interface gives you the opportunity to format the top row. The choices are [No Formatting], Bold, Italic, and Bold Italic. You would only use this if the data set has a header row already defined (as in the sample data set). For this task, choose Bold from the pop-up menu. The dialog box should look similar to Figure 65-2.

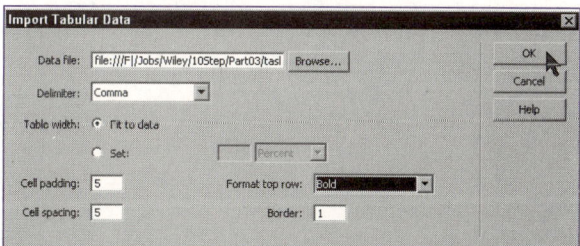

Figure 65-2: Import Tabular Data dialog box—completed

9. Click the OK button on the dialog box to import the data and close the dialog box. The resulting page should look like Figure 65-3.

Datum	First Name	Last Name
1	Brad	Halstead
2	Joyce	Evans
3	Brenda	Gillis
4	Megan	Gillis
5	Hugh	Gillis
6	Denise	Gillis
7	Linda	Martell
8	Paul	Martell
9	Teddy	Bear

Figure 65-3: Imported Data Set page

10. Save the page for future use by pressing Ctrl/Command+S.

cross-reference

• See Task 4 for methods of creating a new file (Step 1).

Sorting Table Data

With the ability to add rows and columns or to import tabular data comes the responsibility of sorting the data on the page. If the table is small, then cutting and pasting by row may be the easiest method for you. However, once the data set gets larger, you will want an automated method of performing this function. Use the file you created in Task 65 for this task.

1. Insert a new row at the bottom of the table by positioning your cursor in the bottom right cell and pressing the Tab key. In this new row, type the following data into the columns (see Figure 66-1):

```
10
Brad
Gillis
```

notes

- If you have applied background colors to the rows to make alternating colors, having the Keep All Row Colors the Same after the Sort Has Been Completed check box selected may cause an alternating color scheme to go awry (Step 6).

- The dialog box has a Help button that you can press to get further information on what each field of the dialog box does.

Datum	First Name	Last Name
1	Brad	Halstead
2	Joyce	Evans
3	Brenda	Gillis
4	Megan	Gillis
5	Hugh	Gillis
6	Denise	Gillis
7	Linda	Martell
8	Paul	Martell
9	Teddy	Bear
10	Brad	Gillis

Figure 66-1: The table with the additional row added

2. To sort the data, position your cursor in the table (if it isn't there already) and select Commands ⇨ Sort Table to open the Sort Table dialog box, as shown in Figure 66-2.

caution

- You must position your cursor in the table or the menu selection will be disabled (grayed out) [Step 2].

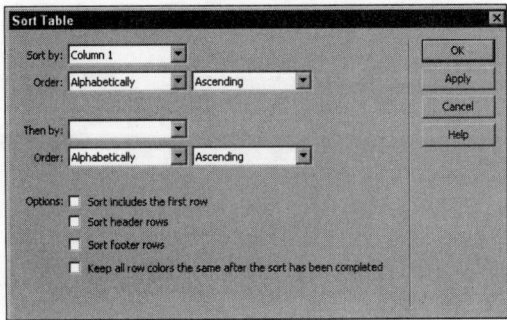

Figure 66-2: Sort Table dialog box

3. From the pop-up list, select the column you wish to be the primary sort column. Select the order method (numerically or alphabetically) and direction (ascending or descending) from their pop-up lists. For this task, sort by Column 2, Alphabetically, and Ascending, respectively.

4. Secondary column sorting is performed by selecting the desired column number in the Then By field, and choosing the sort method and order. For this task, select Column 3, Alphabetically, and Ascending, respectively.

5. If your data has no header row for the columns, place a check in the Sort Includes First Row check box. If your data table contains THEAD or TFOOT attributes, you can enable these in the same dialog box to have them affected by the sort. If you wish to keep the currently defined row colors with the row as it moves, check the Keep All Row Colors the Same after the Sort Has Been Completed check box. For this task, leave all four options disabled (unchecked).

6. Click the Apply button on the dialog box to effect the changes and leave the dialog box open for further modifications. You can use this button to see what the results will be before committing and using the OK button.

7. Change the Sort By field to Column 1 and the Then By field to Column 3, and click the Apply button. Look at the table. Notice that the row order is 1, then 10, then 2, and so on; this is because 1 and 10 both start with a 1 and the Sort Order is specified as Alphabetically.

8. Change the first Order field to Numerically, and click the Apply button on the Sort Table dialog box. Look at the table. The data is sorted in order now by number 1 through 10 in the Datum column.

9. Change Sort By to Column 3 and the Order to Alphabetically. Change the Then By to Column 2. Leave the rest the same and click Apply. (See Figure 66-3.) Now the data is sorted by Last Name and then First Name.

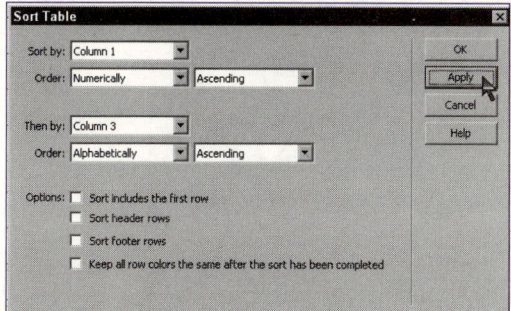

Figure 66-3: The dialog box filled in

cross-references

- Refer to Task 65 for inserting tabular data.

- See Tasks 61 and 63 for inserting a table and modifying the number of rows and columns (Step 1).

10. Click the OK button on the Sort Table dialog box to effect the changes and close the dialog box. Save the page.

Formatting a Table

Dreamweaver MX 2004 has a number of predefined table designs that you can apply to your existing tables. Of course, they are schemes thought up by Macromedia folks, but you can customize them. The advantage of using a scheme is to provide an easier method of grouping data.

1. Use the table you sorted in Task 66 or, alternatively, insert a 3-column, 11-row table into a document so that it looks like Figure 67-1.

Datum	First Name	Last Name
9	Teddy	Bear
2	Joyce	Evans
10	Brad	Gillis
3	Brenda	Gillis
6	Denise	Gillis
5	Hugh	Gillis
4	Megan	Gillis
1	Brad	Halstead
7	Linda	Martell
8	Paul	Martell

Figure 67-1: Data Set table

2. Position your cursor in any of the table cells and select Commands ⇨ Format Table open the Format Table dialog box, as shown in Figure 67-2.

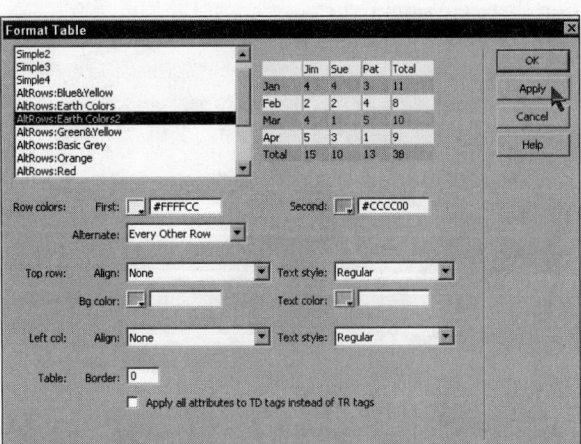

Figure 67-2: Format Table dialog box

3. Play with the various settings in the Format Table dialog box, and use the Apply button to see the changes but leave the dialog box open for further editing. Done playing? Then let's continue.

4. Choose Simple 3 from the Table Format selection list. For Row Colors, change Alternate: from <do not alternate> to Every Other Row. Notice in Figure 67-3 that the preview changes to reflect your selection (this occurs for most of the settings that you have control over). In the Second Color field for Row Colors, type the value **#DFDFFF** and press the Tab key to effect the change.

	Jim	Sue	Pat	Total
Jan	4	4	3	11
Feb	2	2	4	8
Mar	4	1	5	10
Apr	5	3	1	9
Total	15	10	13	38

Figure 67-3: The preview

5. For the Top Row group, change Align to Center, Text Style to Bold, BG Color to **#3399CC**, and Text Color to **#FFFFCA**.

6. For the Left Col group, change Align to Left, and change Text Style to Italic.

7. For the Table group, change Border to 0 and leave Apply All Attributes to TD Tags Instead of TR Tags unchecked. The completed dialog box should look like Figure 67-4. Once your settings match those of the figure, click the OK button to apply the changes and close the dialog box.

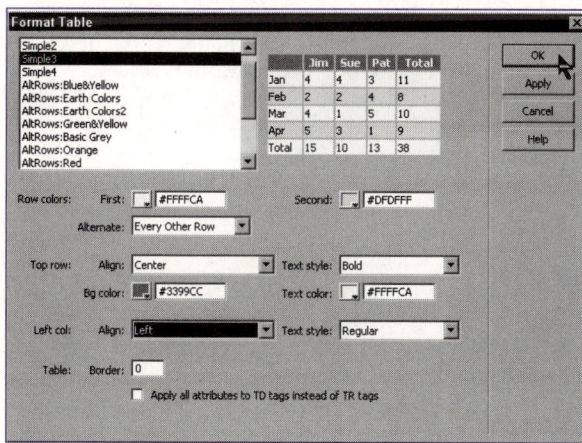

Figure 67-4: Table Format dialog box—Completed

8. Open the Property inspector (if it isn't already) to make changes to the table cell padding or cell spacing to get the look you want. (To select the table, use the Tag Selector to select the `<table>` tag, and the Table Property inspector opens.)

9. Save the document as **Task67.htm** using File ⇨ Save As.

tip

- Using a stronger color (either darker or brighter than the colors of the rows) for the heading row will make the headings obvious to the reader (Step 5).

cross-references

- Refer to Task 65 for inserting tabular data.

- Refer to Task 66 for sorting data.

- See Tasks 61 and 63 for inserting a table and modifying the number of rows and columns (Step 1).

Nesting Tables

When using tables to design a Web page layout, you sometimes need to insert another table in one of the parent table's cells. This is called *nesting* tables. A nested table may not align properly because it "floats" in the containing cell according to that cell's parameters. This task teaches you how to insert a nested table into an existing table cell and maintain alignment to the top of the containing cell.

note

▪ Aligning a nested table at the top of the containing cell is the most common layout. However, you may choose any other alignment (middle, bottom, or baseline) to create specific layout effects.

1. Create a new document (Ctrl/Command+N) and save it as **Task68.htm** (Ctrl/Command+S).

2. Insert a table on the page, using the following specifications: Rows: 2, Columns: 3, Cell Padding: 5, Cell Spacing: 0, Width: 600 pixels, and Border: 1.

3. Select the top row and merge the cells for the header of the document. Your document should look like Figure 68-1.

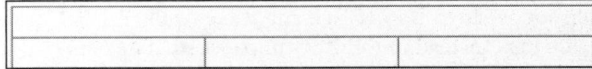

Figure 68-1: Inserted and merged table

4. Position your cursor in row 2, column 1 (bottom leftmost cell), and insert another table using the following specifications: Rows: 4, Columns: 1, Width: 150 pixels, Border: 0, Cell Padding: 0, and Cell Spacing: 0. Your document should look like Figure 68-2.

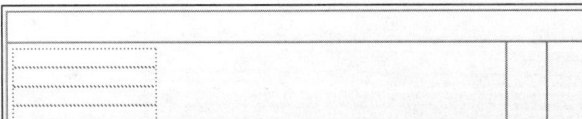

Figure 68-2: Nested table

5. Add some text to the bottom center cell (enough to make the cell larger than the nested table), and add a couple of sentences to the bottom right cell. Notice that the bottom left and bottom right cell contents float with the expansion of the bottom center cell, as shown in Figure 68-3. Preview the document in your browser using F12 (primary browser) or Ctrl/Command+F12 (secondary browser). Close the browser when you are finished looking at the page.

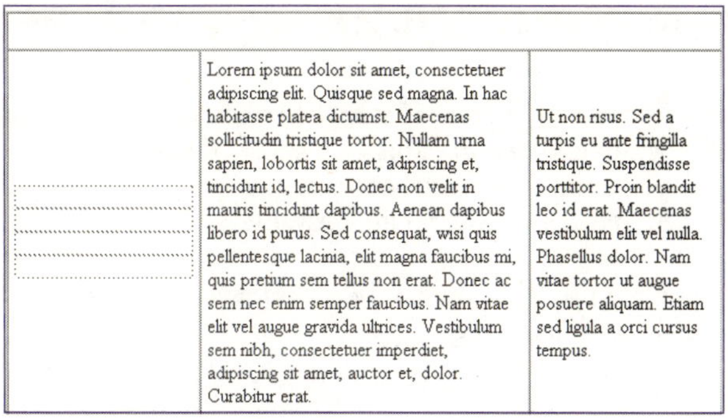

Figure 68-3: Nested table issue

tip

- Generate dummy text at www.lipsum.com (Step 5).

6. Position your cursor in the bottom left cell—the one that contains the nested table. You may need to expand the Property inspector to see all the elements. If so, click the expand/collapse arrow in the lower right of the Property inspector.

7. Change the Vert selection from Default to Top, change the Width (W) from blank to 150, and press the Tab key to effect the changes. Notice that the inner table goes to the top of the cell and the outer table cell shrinks to the size specified.

8. Repeat steps 6 and 7 for the bottom right outer table cell. The content in the right cell repositions to the top of the containing cell, and the bottom middle cell expands to take up the remainder of the allotted space, as shown in Figure 68-4.

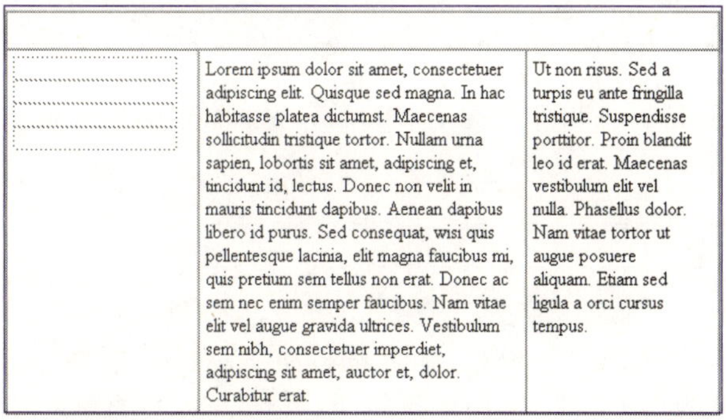

Figure 68-4: Completed task

cross-references

- See Task 70 for more on aligning cells (Step 7).

- See Tasks 61 and 64 for table insertion and merging tasks (Step 1).

9. Save the page and preview it in your browser using F12 or Ctrl/Command+F12. Close the browser and the Dreamweaver document when you are finished.

Manipulating Table Width and Height

P art of developing good table structure is knowing when and how to adjust the table or a cell's width and height. This task details the methods of setting, clearing, converting to percentage, and converting to pixel measurements. It shows how to adjust the table cell width and height values.

1. Create a new document (Ctrl/Command+N) and save it as **Task69.htm** (Ctrl/Command+S).

2. Click the Table icon in the Common category of the Insert bar to insert a table on the page. Use the following specifications: Rows: 2, Columns: 3, Width: 600 Pixels, Border: 1, Cell Padding: 5, and Cell Spacing: 0.

3. You can use your cursor to click and drag the borders of both the table and its cells to change the size. To change the overall size of the table, select it by clicking on a border or on the <table> tag in the Tag inspector. When the table is selected, it has a dark border with small squares, as shown in Figure 69-1. Click and drag on a square to change the width or height of the table.

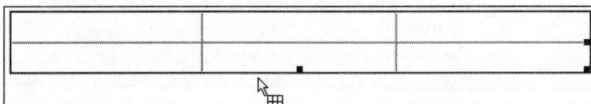

Figure 69-1: A selected table

4. Click inside a cell and then hover the cursor over a cell border. The cursor changes to two parallel lines, as shown in Figure 69-2. When the lines appear, you can click and drag the cell border to another location. If you hover a little longer, a ToolTip pops up, giving you more options.

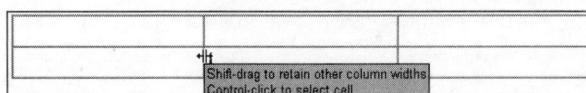

Figure 69-2: The cursor ready to move a cell border and showing the ToolTip

5. Click and drag the table and cell borders until the table looks close to Figure 69-3. Notice that the heights and width of the table and individual cells are added and changed as you drag the border.

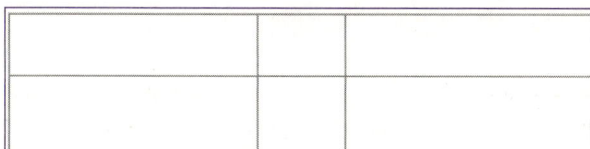

Figure 69-3: Modified table

6. Using the Tag Selector, choose the <TABLE> tag to select the entire table. Open the Property inspector and note that the W and H fields now contain a value, with the unit of measurement specified as Pixels, as shown in Figure 69-4. Similarly, if you position your cursor inside a cell of the table, you can select the <TD> tag from the Tag Selector and view the cell's dimensions in the Property inspector. You can fine-tune these values using manual entries in the Property inspector.

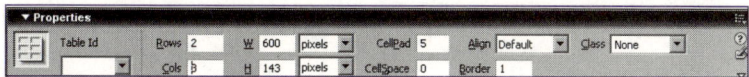

Figure 69-4: Table Property inspector

7. With the <TABLE> tag still selected, use Modify ➪ Table ➪ Convert Widths to Percents. This converts all widths (table and individual cell) from pixel-based to percentage-based. The same holds true for the menu items Convert Widths to Pixels, Convert Height to Pixels, and Convert Height to Percent. Choose Convert Widths to Pixels to convert all widths in the table (table and cells) to fixed pixel dimensions.

8. To clear the cell widths, select the <TABLE> tag using the Tag Selector and then select Modify ➪ Table ➪ Clear Cell Widths. This clears all widths set in the table or cells of the table.

9. To clear the cell heights, select the <TABLE> tag using the Tag Selector and then select Modify ➪ Table ➪ Clear Cell Heights. This clears all heights set in the table or cells of the table.

Steps 8 and 9 are excellent methods for tearing down the table to its basic form to figure out where something is astray in the table markup.

cross-reference

▪ See Tasks 61 and 64 for table insertion and merging tasks (Step 1).

Aligning Tables and Cells

An entire table can be aligned to the left, right, or center of the Web page. The contents of individual table cells are aligned in relation to the table itself.

notes

- Aligning a table means that the table will float according to that alignment in the browser. Preview the right-aligned table in your browser and notice that it stays on the right side of the browser window, regardless of the width of the browser (Step 3).

- Alternatively, you can use the Text ⇨ Align menu items to set the cell alignment using a `<div>` tag (Step 5).

1. Create a new document and save it as **Task70.htm**.

2. Insert a table using the following specifications: Rows: 2, Columns: 3, Cell Padding: 5, Cell Spacing: 0, Width: 600 pixels, and Border: 1. Using the Tag Selector, select the `<TABLE>` tag and open the Property inspector if it's not already open (Ctrl/Command+F3). Figure 70-1 shows the Property inspector and the table attributes.

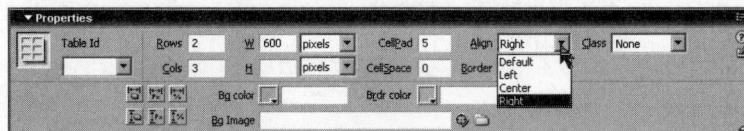

Figure 70-1: The Property inspector when a table is selected

3. Click the drop-down arrow for Align to see the available choices for aligning the table on the page. The choices are Default, Left, Center, and Right. Choose Right, and the table shifts to the right of the page, as shown in Figure 70-2.

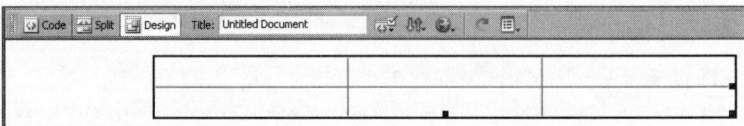

Figure 70-2: Table—Right-aligned

4. Position your cursor in a cell (row 1, column 2), and the Property inspector should populate with the cell properties as seen in the Property inspector shown in Figure 70-3.

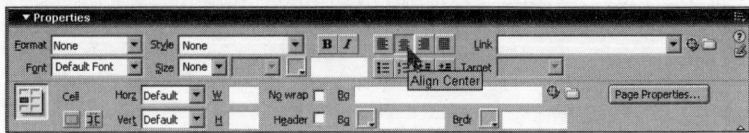

Figure 70-3: Property inspector when a cell is selected

5. There are two ways to select the horizontal alignment for the cell or cells:

- Select one of the Align icons in the Property inspector to change the cell's alignment using a `<div>` tag.

- Select the Horz pop-up menu to set the cell's horizontal alignment as applied to the `<TD>` tag itself or the `<TR>` tag (the `<TR>` tag only if you currently have a whole row selected). The choices are Default, Left, Center, and Right.

6. Type some text into the first cell in row 1 and click the Center icon. Then type some more text into the third cell in row 2 and choose Left using the Horz pop-up menu. Figure 70-4 shows aligned text in the right-aligned table.

| Lorem ipsum dolor sit amet, consectetuer adipiscing. | |
| | Ut non risus. Sed a turpis eu ante fringilla tristique. Suspendisse porttitor. Proin blandit leo id erat. Maecenas vestibulum elit vel nulla. |

Figure 70-4: Right-aligned table with a center-aligned and left-aligned cell

7. Using the icon generates a `<div>` tab in the HTML code, whereas using the pop-up menu generated an `align` attribute. Figure 70-5 shows the code for the cells.

```
<tr>
  <td><div align="center">Lorem ipsum dolor sit amet, consectetuer adipiscing.</div></td>
  <td> </td>
  <td> </td>
</tr>
<tr>
  <td> </td>
  <td> </td>
  <td align="left">Ut non risus. Sed a turpis eu ante fringilla tristique. Suspendisse porttitor.
  Proin blandit leo id erat. Maecenas vestibulum elit vel nulla. </td>
</tr>
```

Figure 70-5: HTML code for the cell alignment

8. Select the Vert pop-up menu to set the cell's vertical alignment as applied to the `<TD>` tag itself or the `<TR>` tag (the `<TR>` tag only if you currently have a whole row selected). The choices are Default, Top, Middle, Bottom, and Baseline.

cross-references

- See Tasks 61 and 64 for table insertion and merging tasks (Step 2).

- You can also use CSS to assign attributes to both tables and cells. See Part 9 for the many options available with CSS (Step 6).

Switching Table Modes

Developing a table and moving around in the cells of a table is often easier when you switch to the Layout or the Expanded table mode. In this task, you use a tracing image to see how these modes work.

1. From the Start Page, in the Create New column, click HTML. Title your document **Horse Adventures**.

2. Click the Page Properties button in the Property inspector to open the Page Properties dialog box. In the Appearance category, set all of the margins to 0 (zero). Select the Tracing Image category, then click the Browse button next to the Tracing Image field and navigate to the Task 71 folder. Choose the task71image.jpg file and click OK. Move the Transparency slider to about 40 percent and click OK. The image is now in your document.

3. Choose the Layout category of the Insert toolbar and click the Layout button. The dialog box shown in Figure 71-1 opens, giving you tips on the two drawing tools available. You can check the Don't Show This Window Again option if you don't want the box to open every time you choose Layout. Click OK to close it.

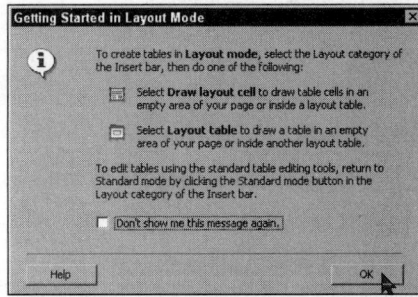

Figure 71-1: Getting Started in Layout Mode opening message

4. Click the Draw Layout Table icon and place your cursor (now a crosshair) in the upper left corner. Drag to cover the entire document.

5. Check the Property inspector to see the available options, shown in Figure 71-2. The properties are different in Layout view. You have the option of typing in a value for a fixed width or selecting Autostretch, which automatically makes your table stretchy. (Stretchy tables are discussed in the next task.)

Figure 71-2: The Property inspector for a Layout Table

6. Click the Draw Layout Cell icon in the Insert toolbar and drag around the horse banner in the tracing image. Notice that after you draw a cell, there are lines marking where other cells would be generated automatically. They are white lines and may be difficult to see.

7. Click the Draw Layout Cell icon again, and drag a cell around the puzzle's picture. Notice that the white lines have automatically moved to generate new cell areas. (See Figure 71-3.)

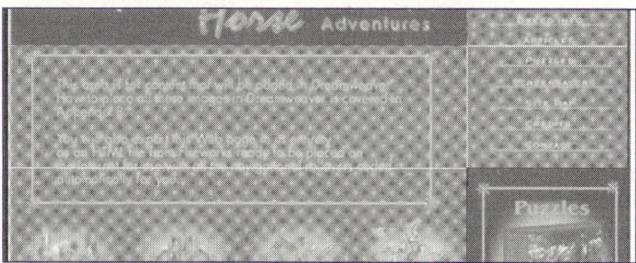

Figure 71-3: A portion of the document showing the generated cells

8. The generated cells aren't placed in the best place. Click the Standard button. Select the two cells on the right that contain the navigation lines. Merge these cells by clicking the Merge Cells icon in the Property inspector.

9. Click the Expanded button and notice that the boundaries between the cells are more distinct. This is especially helpful when one of the cells has collapsed and you want to insert content into it.

cross-references

▪ See Task 4 for instructions on opening or creating a document.

▪ See Tasks 61 and 64 for table insertion and merging tasks.

Making a Stretchy Table

The Autostretch table (also called fluid or stretchy table) expands or contracts to fit the size of the browser window. An advantage is that the table always reflects the size of the browser window—there are no blank areas unless you want them. A disadvantage is that as the cells expand, the cell content can shift. So Autostretch tables aren't useful when you need to keep cell contents in the same place.

1. Open a new document and title it **Task 72 Stretchy Table**. Open the Page Properties dialog box, and set the background color to a color of your choice.

2. Create a table with three rows and four columns. Make the table width 100 percent. Set the border thickness to 2 pixels so that you can see the cells. Set the cell padding and spacing to 0. The Insert Table dialog box is shown in Figure 72-1. Click OK to insert the table.

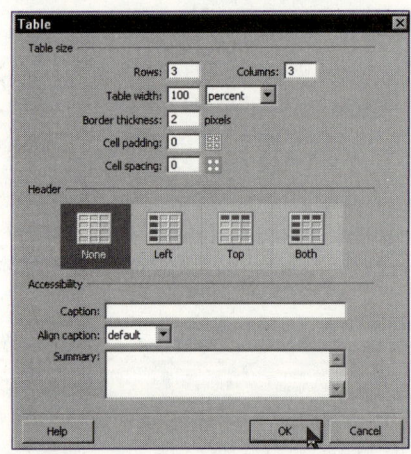

Figure 72-1: The Insert Table dialog box with the values filled in

3. Select the table. In the Property inspector, change the Align value to Center. This allows the table to float in the center of the page. Change the Brdr color to a color that contrasts with the table background, as shown in Figure 72-2.

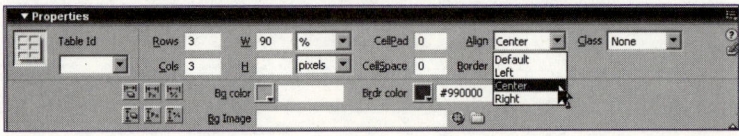

Figure 72-2: The Property inspector for the table; the Align pop-up menu is showing

note

- The default column widths are proportional to the table—that is, if you have four columns, each one will default to 25 percent unless the content forces a different column size. You can specify the column sizes to be different percents of the table. For example, this table could have columns of 20 percent, 50 percent, and 30 percent.

caution

- When you are using default column widths, content always overrides. So if you insert an image that is 50 percent of the page into a cell, that cell's column width will increase at the expense of the other column widths.

4. Preview the page in your browser. Change the width of the browser and note how the cells expand and contract. Figure 72-3 shows an example.

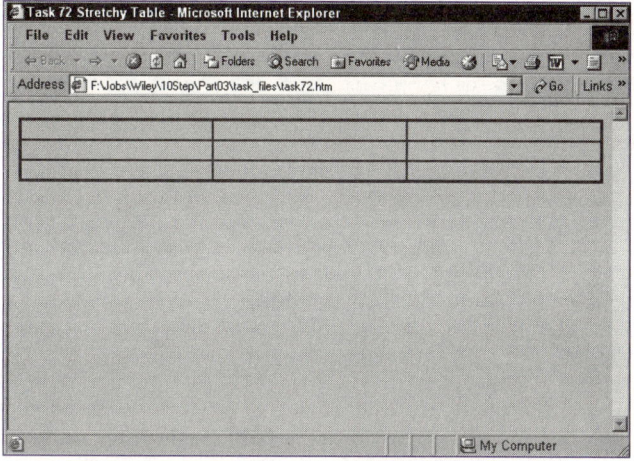

Figure 72-3: The Autostretch table in Internet Explorer

5. Select the table again, and in the Property inspector, change the width to 80 percent. Preview in your browser and note that the table now floats in the middle of the browser window. It is indented on each side by 10 percent of the browser window.

6. Reset the table width to 100 percent. Click in the center of the document to deselect the table. Then open Page Properties (click the button in the Property inspector) and set all of the margins to 0, as shown in Figure 72-4.

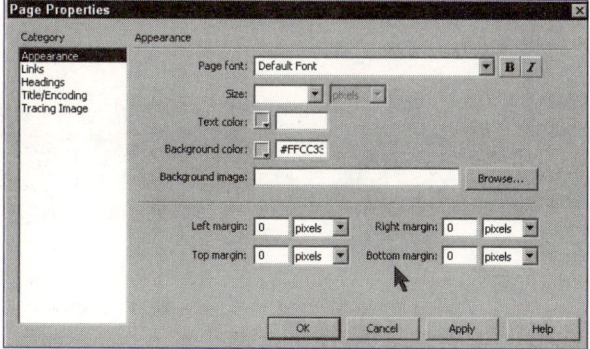

Figure 72-4: Setting the page margins in the Page Properties dialog box

7. Preview in your browser again and note that the table now fills the entire browser window with no space on the sides or top.

8. Save your document as **task72.htm** if you want.

cross-references

- See Task 61 for inserting a table and Task 70 for more on table alignment.

- Tasks 73-75 show how to make other kinds of tables.

Task 73

Making a Fixed-Width Table

A fixed-width table is a specific size no matter what size the browser window is. It is usually employed to organize graphic content—content that has to maintain a specific size and relationship of the elements. For example, a large image should be split up into segments to decrease the perceived downloading time. Then a table is used to realign the image, as you will do in this task.

1. Open a document and insert a table with three rows and three columns. Set the cell spacing, cell padding, and border to 0. The table width should be 640 pixels.

2. The image you will reassemble is in the Task 73 folder. There are nine slices to the ChessShadow image. Position your cursor in the first cell in row 1. Click the Image icon in the Common category of the Insert toolbar. Browse to the topRowCol1.jpg image, select it, and click OK.

3. You can see in the Property inspector that this image is 210 pixels wide and 161 pixels high. Set the border to 0. Since the table should reflect the exact size of the image, select the cell that the image is in by clicking on the `<td>` in the Tag inspector. Make the following changes to the cell properties: Horz = Left, Vert = Top, W = 210, H = 161. The table should look like Figure 73-1.

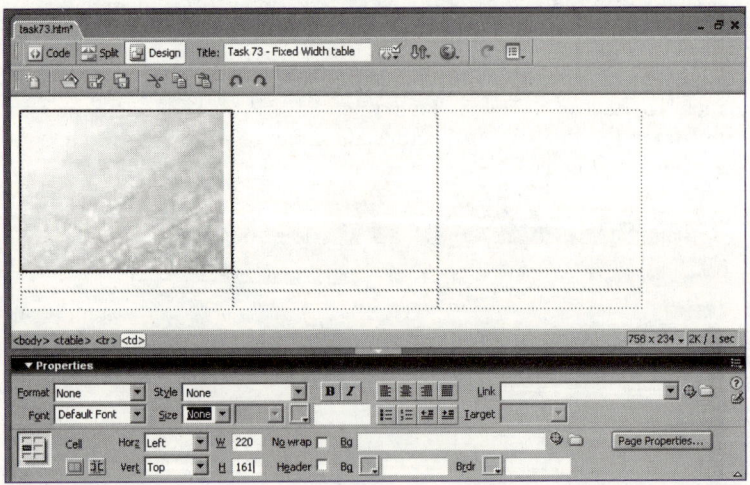

Figure 73-1: The first image is inserted into the top left cell and the cell properties set

4. Tab to the next cell and insert the topRowCol2.jpg image. Select the cell by tapping the right arrow, and set the cell properties as you did in Step 3.

5. Tab to the next cell (top right) and insert the topRowCol3.jpg image. Note that it is a little wider—220 pixels. Set the cell properties accordingly.

6. Insert the rest of the cells in the table. The images are midRowCol1.jpg, midRowCol2.jpg, midRowCol3.jpg, botRowCol1.jpg, botRowCol2.jpg, and botRowCol3.jpg.

7. Set the cell properties to reflect the image sizes.

8. When you are finished, select the entire table and align it to the right. Preview in your browser. The table should look like Figure 73-2. All of the images are back together into one smooth picture.

Figure 73-2: The completed image with all of its slices looks like one image

9. Save your table as **task73.htm** if you want.

cross-references

- See Task 61 for inserting a table and Task 70 for more on table and cell alignment.

- Tasks 72, 74, and 75 show how to make other kinds of tables.

Making a Hybrid Table

The best table of all is a hybrid; it uses both fixed-width and Autostretch attributes. By designating certain columns to be a fixed width and one column to be Autostretch, you can control how the fixed areas appear in all browsers. The column that is set to Autostretch fills whatever space is left in a browser window after the fixed columns are in place.

note

- It's a good idea to use spacer gifs to force column widths to stay at the desired width.

1. Open a new Document and title it Task 74–Hybrid Table. Use the Page Properties to set the margins to 0.

2. Insert a five-row by three-column table. Set the table width to 100 percent, the border to 2, the cell spacing to 0, and the cell padding to 5. Choose a background color for the table and a contrasting color for the border. The example uses #FF9933 for the background and #336600 for the border.

3. Select the first column and set the width to 150 pixels. Then merge the first two columns in the top row into one column and merge the bottom four rows in the first column. The table should look like Figure 74-1.

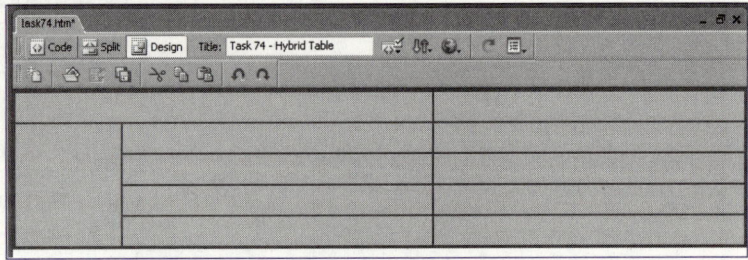

Figure 74-1: The table with columns and rows merged

4. In the top left cell, insert the image logo.gif. Select the cell, and using the Property inspector, set the cell Horz alignment to Left and the Vert alignment to Top. Next to the logo image, insert the company.gif image.

5. In the remaining cell in the first column, insert the image navbar.gif. Preview the document in a browser. The right column has no content yet, so it has collapsed, as shown in Figure 74-2.

caution

- If you specify a column width that is smaller than the image it holds, the image will simply be truncated. All browsers adhere to the column width specification.

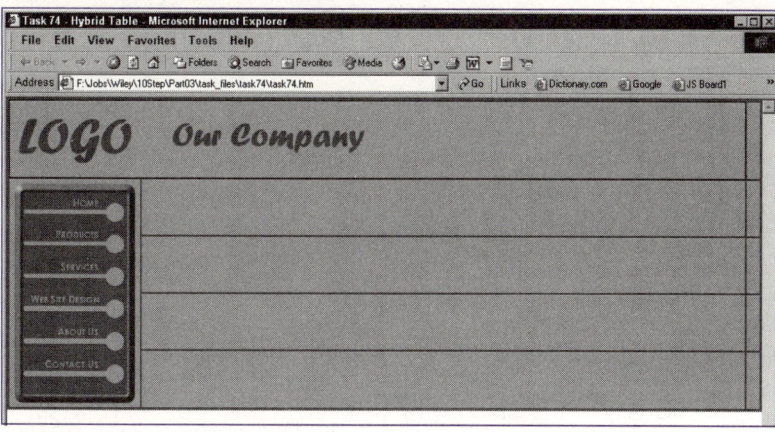

Figure 74-2: The left column contains the navigation bar, but the right column has collapsed

6. In real life, images or text would be inserted in the right column to maintain its size. For now, you'll use a spacer.gif to keep it open to 100 pixels. Click in the top right column. Then click the Insert Image icon. Browse to your task74 folder and select spacer.gif. Click OK.

7. Use the Property inspector to set the width of the spacer.gif image to 100 pixels. You could also set the background of the column to #336633 to make the column more obvious.

8. Preview again in a browser. Change the width of the browser window and notice how the first and third columns maintain their widths while the middle column changes size in response to the changes in the browser window.

9. Save your page as **task74.htm** if you wish.

cross-references

- See Task 4 for instructions on opening or creating a document.

- See Task 61 for inserting a table and Task 70 for more on table and cell alignment.

- Tasks 72, 73, and 75 show how to make other kinds of tables.

Making a Table with Rounded Corners

Tables with rounded corners are a popular table design. The rounded corners are achieved by using four corner images, and then background images for the outline. In this task you make a fluid rounded table.

notes

- This is actually a very small image; it's 2 pixels wide by 26 pixels high. By placing it in the background of the cell, it tiles to fill up the available space. The height was determined by the top corner images, which are 26 pixels high.

- If you have cells with no background color, you missed a spacer image. Add it and the cells show the background color.

1. Open a new document. Click the Insert Table icon and use these values: Rows = 3, Columns = 3, Width = 70 Percent, Border = 0, Cell padding = 0, and Cell Spacing = 0.

2. Click in the top left cell and insert the image cnr_ltop.gif from the task75 folder. Note its width—14 pixels. Select the cell by pressing the right arrow key. In the Property inspector, add these values: Horz = Left, Vert = Top, and W = 14. Press Enter/Return. This collapses the entire column so you don't have to add the width value to the bottom left corner.

3. Click in the top right cell and insert the image cnr_rtop.gif from the task75 folder. Note its width—14 pixels also. Select the cell, and in the Property inspector, add these values: Horz = Right, Vert = Top, and W = 14. Press Enter/Return.

4. Click in the bottom left corner cell and insert the image cnr_lbtm.gif. Select the cell and set the Property inspector as you did in Step 3 except make the Vert alignment Bottom. In the bottom right corner, insert the image cnr-rbtn.gif and set the cell properties. The table should look like Figure 75-1.

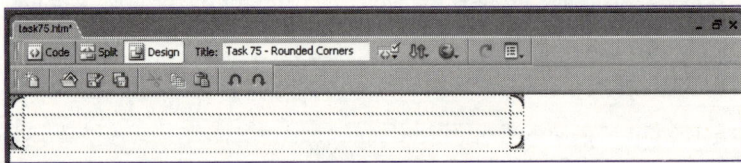

Figure 75-1: The round corners inserted into the table

5. Select the center cell of the top row. Set the W to 100%—be sure to manually type in the percent sign. The center column now fills up 100 percent of the available space. The table itself uses 70 percent of the available space of the browser window, and this cell uses 100 percent of the available space of this table.

6. Set the Bg of the cell to the line_thorz.gif image and set the Vert alignment to Top. To prevent the cell from collapsing, insert a spacer image and size it to 20 pixels wide (W) and 13 pixels high (H). Repeat for the bottom center cell, except use the image line_bhorz.gif and set the Vert alignment to Bottom.

7. Click in the left cell of the middle row. Set the Bg to the line_lvert.gif image and set the Horz alignment to Left. Insert a spacer that is 14 pixels wide and 20 pixels high. Repeat for the right cell of the middle row, using the line_rvert.gif image and setting the Horz alignment to Right.

8. Click anywhere in the rounded-corner table, and click the `<table>` selector tag. In the Property inspector, set the Bg color to #8C9DB1.

9. Preview your table in a browser. It should look like Figure 75-2.

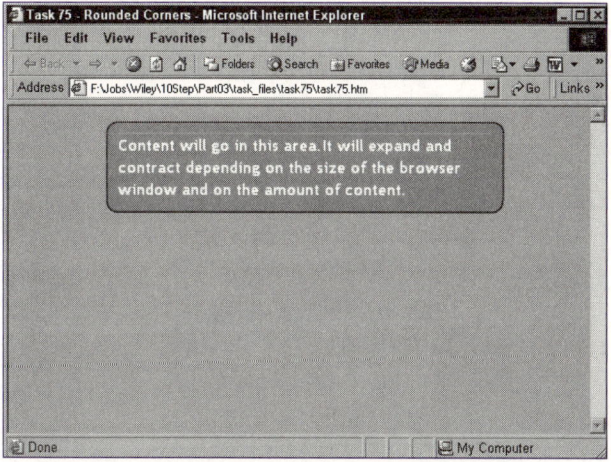

Figure 75-2: A table with round corners

cross-references

▪ See Task 4 for instructions on opening or creating a document.

▪ See Task 61 for inserting a table and Task 70 for more on table and cell alignment.

Task **76**

Cloaking

note

• Folders on the remote site can also be cloaked. This eliminates the remote cloaked folders and files from all operations just like local cloaking does.

For your site to be seen by others on the Internet, it has to be uploaded to an Internet server. Dreamweaver does this very nicely. There will be, however, parts of your site that you don't want available on the Internet—for example, your templates folder or your original images. To avoid having these uploaded, you can specify *cloaking*. Cloaking not only excludes cloaked folders and files from Get and Put operations, but also from Check In and Check Out, synchronizing, and performing sitewide operations such as checking links.

1. Select the Files panel in the Files panel group and open the site you want to upload. Cloaking is one of the categories in the Advanced Site Definition process, so you may already have enabled it. To check, click the Files Options pop-up menu and select Site ⇨ Cloaking. If Enable Cloaking is checked, as shown in Figure 76-1, you're set.

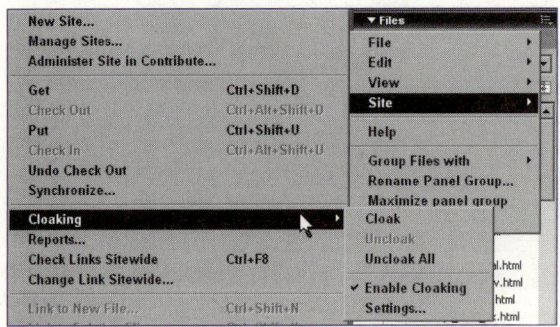

Figure 76-1: The Files Options pop-up menu showing that cloaking is enabled

2. If cloaking is not enabled, select Cloaking ⇨ Settings to open the Settings dialog box, as shown in Figure 76-2. Check the Enable Cloaking option. Click OK.

caution

• You cannot cloak individual files of a type other than what you have specified in the Preferences. You also cannot cloak all of the folders in a site, nor an entire site.

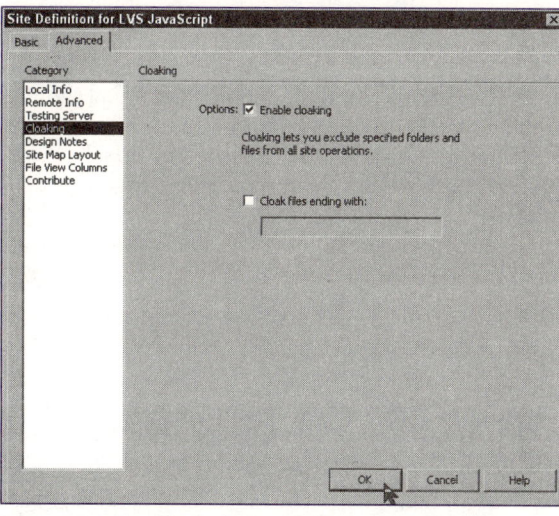

Figure 76-2: The Site Definition dialog box for cloaking

3. To cloak all of the files in a folder, select the folder in the Files panel. Open the Files Options pop-up menu (or right-click for the context-sensitive menu in Windows) and select Cloaking ⇨ Cloak. The cloaked folder now has a red slash through its folder icon, as shown in Figure 76-3.

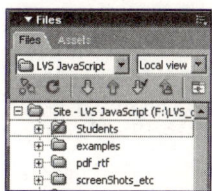

Figure 76-3: The Cloaked Folder icon

4. If you cloak the Templates folder or Library items, you'll get a warning message telling you that cloaking doesn't affect your local use (see Figure 76-4). These items are only excluded from Get and Put operations. That is how it should be.

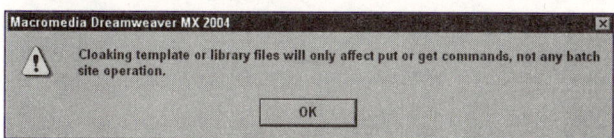

Figure 76-4: The warning message when you cloak the site's Templates folder

5. You can also check the Cloak Files Ending With: box to have all file types ending in your specification automatically cloaked. For example, you can cloak all of your original graphics files. To specify this, check the box and type **png** in the text area.

cross-references

- See Task 11 for setting up a site using the Advanced method.

- Task 82 describes the process of uploading your site to your server.

Testing Links

Prior to putting your site live on the Internet, one thing that you should do is a link check. A link check verifies that the links to images and files in your Web site are functional so that your visitors don't get the proverbial "404 Page Not Found" error or broken image symbol from one of your page's links.

1. Open an existing site and open a document from the Files panel to enable all features of the link check system.

2. Select Window ⇨ Results to open the Results panel. Click the Link Checker tab. The Link Checker Results panel is shown in Figure 77-1.

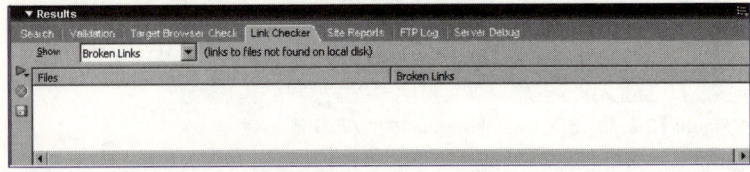

Figure 77-1: Results panel—Link Check tab

3. Select the green arrow on the left side of the panel, and three options are presented to you: Check Links in Current Document (disabled if no document is open in Dreamweaver), Check Links for Entire Site, and Check Links for Selected Files/Folders in Site (this one requires that you have files/folders highlighted in the Files panel to check links on a group of files). For the purpose of this exercise, choose Check Links for Entire Site. The check links routine is run and a report is generated in the Results window. Checking an entire site can take a while. If you need to stop the check, click the Stop icon (red circle with an X in the center under the green arrow).

4. Use the Show pop-up menu to select which link report to display. Available options are Broken Links, External Links, and Orphaned Files (only available if you do a link check on the entire site). For the purpose of this task, select the Orphaned Files report, as shown in Figure 77-2.

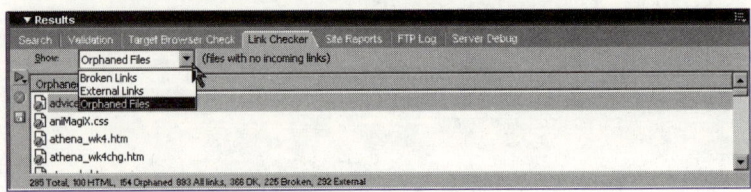

Figure 77-2: Orphaned Files report

notes

- No pages need to be opened for the link check to function sitewide or on selected files (Step 1).

- An alternative method is to choose Site ⇨ Check Links Sitewide (Ctrl/Command+ F8) from the Files panel or File ⇨ Check Page ⇨ Check Links; the latter method needs a page open for the menu item to be enabled and active. If you use one of these methods to check your links, the Results panel is opened for you to the proper tab to display the report (Step 2).

- The Link Checker checks three link conditions. Broken Links (links to files that don't exist locally on your hard drive for the site), External Links (links that reference external HTTP links on the Internet), and Orphaned Files (files in your site that Dreamweaver cannot find any reference to from your pages of the site) (Step 4).

caution

- When you are deleting orphaned files, Dreamweaver doesn't check JavaScript refer- enced links, so make sure you have a backup prior to deleting orphaned files (Step 5).

5. Double-click any of the files listed to open the file for editing. Right-/Control+click the Results display area to open the context menu, shown in Figure 77-3, which allows for more options to be performed. For the purpose of this task, right-click and choose Save Results from the context menu.

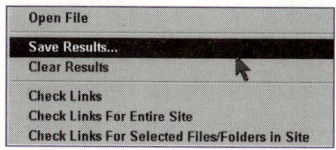

Figure 77-3: Results panel context menu

6. The Save As dialog box opens to allow you to name the file that you wish to save the report to. Alternatively, you can use the Disk icon on the right-hand side of the Results panel to save the report to disk.

7. Name the file **LinkReport.txt** and click the Save button on the Save As dialog box, which saves the file to the specified location. If you saved the file to the site, the Files panel is updated to show the file. All results are sent to this file, Broken Images, External Links, and Orphaned Files, so the task of saving the report need only occur once.

8. Right-click the results pane again and choose Clear Results to clear the report from the Results panel. Doing this allows the report to run fresh each time and to provide you with the most accurate results possible.

9. Open the LinkReport.txt file from the Files panel. You can print the file, pass it to others by uploading it to the server, or review it yourself. The file will look similar to Figure 77-4.

```
LinkReport.txt - Notepad
File  Edit  Format  Help
Broken Links:

aniMagiX.js        ' + img + '
aniMagiX.js        ' + img + '
athena_wk4.htm     /adm/redirect/www
athena_wk4.htm     /adm/img/popup/tripodsm.gif
athena_wk4.htm     /bin/email_when_updated/display_form
athena_wk4.htm     images/dynamic.gif
athena_wk4.htm     java-week4.html
athena_wk4.htm     java-index.html
becky-menu.js      "+location+"
becky-menu.js      "+location+"
btry_cls.htm       #FFFFFF
cubes.htm          C:\Dokumente und Einstellungen\Evelyn\Desktop\cubesend.jpg
cubes.htm          C:\Dokumente und Einstellungen\Evelyn\Desktop\cubeback.jpg
doris_posit.htm    greyreliefb.gif
doris_posit2.htm       greyreliefb.gif
doris_posit2.htm       temptation1.jpg>
</span>
```

Figure 77-4: LinkResults.txt sample

cross-reference

▪ See Task 42 for information on editing links.

Validating the Site

For the Web pages to display properly in browsers, the HTML code needs to contain valid syntax. Keep in mind that it is better to err on the side of being overly strict than to err on the side of allowing bad markup. Many different tag-based languages are supported, such as several versions of HTML, XHTML, CFML, JSP, WML, and XML.

1. Open an existing site and open a document from the Files panel to enable all features of the validation system.

2. Select Window ⇨ Results (F7) to open the Results panel. Click the Validation tab, as shown in Figure 78-1.

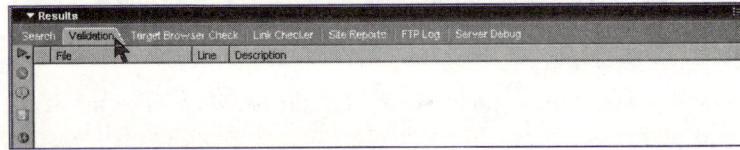

Figure 78-1: Results panel—Validation tab

3. Click the green arrow on the left side of the panel. Four options are presented to you: Validate Current Document, Validate Entire Site, Validate Selected Files in Site, and Settings. The panel also contains five icons on the left side. From top to bottom they are as follows: the selection arrow (green); the Stop button to cease the operation once started; the Info button to provide more information on an error message in the results pane; the Save to Disk icon, which allows you to save the report to disk; and the Browse Report button, which opens the report in HTML format in the default browser. For the purpose of this task, select Settings to open the Preferences dialog box to the Validation tab, as shown in Figure 78-2.

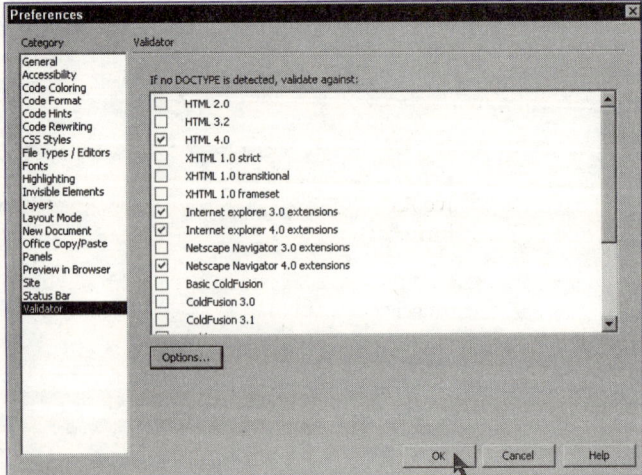

Figure 78-2: Preferences panel—Validation category

notes

- Validation settings are configurable in the Properties using Edit ⇨ Properties (Ctrl/Command+U) or from the Validation tab in the Results panel (Step 5).

- WML stands for Wireless Markup Language, JSP for Java Server Pages, and CFML for ColdFusion Markup Language (Near intro).

- These are systemwide settings. If you change the document type from HTML to CFML, you need to change the "validate against" settings to validate the new document types (Step 6).

4. Select the desired specifications from the list in the Validate Against area. A check means the option is enabled; no check means it is disabled. Once you are satisfied with your selections, click the Options button to open the Validator Options dialog box, as shown in Figure 78-3.

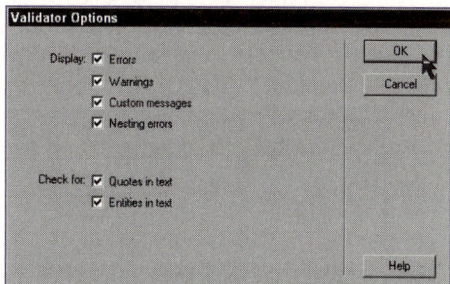

Figure 78-3: Validator Options dialog box

5. Typically I leave the settings here as default. You can enable or disable settings as desired, since you may not care about warnings or custom messages but do care about errors and nesting errors. Click the OK button on the Validator Options dialog box to effect any changes you made and close the dialog box. Click the OK button on the Preference dialog box to effect the changes made and close the dialog box.

6. Select the Results Panel—Validation dialog box selection button (green arrow) and select Validate Entire Site from the available items. The validation routine runs and a report is generated and displayed in the Results panel.

7. Select an error message, and select the More Info button on the Validation Tab sidebar to open the error message in full. Click the OK button on the Description dialog box.

8. Select the Save Report button to open the Save As dialog box. The file is in XML format, so you can save it with the default filename or you can specify another. Be aware that changing the file type will not change the XML contents.

9. To preview the results in a browser session, select the Browse Report button, and the results are displayed in a new browser session. From here, you can use File ⇨ Save As to save the Web page to your local site so that it is in HTML format.

10. The contextual menu is very similar to that covered in Task 77. Most menu options are available here, as well as the Clear Report selection from the Results Options menu.

cross-reference

▪ See Task 38 for help in cleaning up the HTML.

Checking Accessibility

Making your site accessible to as many people as possible is not only the right thing to do but is also the law for many types of organizations. Dreamweaver MX 2004 has a built-in system that helps you add the appropriate tags and labels to various elements. The accessibility standards are set by the World Wide Consortium (W3C). For an extensive study of the standards, go to their Web site at www.w3c.org. It's pretty heavy reading but very informative.

notes

- These are systemwide settings. If you change them for a one-time occurrence, don't use the Save button (Step 6).

- There is no way to preview this page in the browser other than by selecting the saved report and pressing F12 from the Files panel (Step 7).

- More and more accessibility is becoming the standard. Familiarizing yourself with the terminology and using the required items today will make you an asset to your clients. Also, for more information on accessibility issues, refer to the chapter on accessibility in *Using Dreamweaver MX 2004* and the Dreamweaver MX 2004 help files.

1. Open an existing site and open a document from the Files panel to enable all features of the Accessibility system.

2. Select Window ⇨ Results to open the Results panel, and click the Site Reports tab, as shown in Figure 79-1.

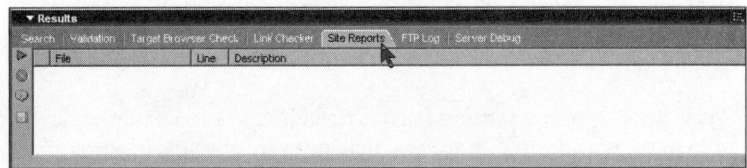

Figure 79-1: Results panel—Site Reports tab

3. Click the Reports icon (the green arrow) to open the Reports dialog box, as shown in Figure 79-2.

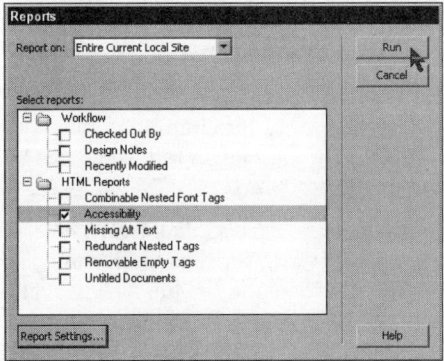

Figure 79-2: Reports dialog box

4. Select the Report On: value from the pop-up menu. Choices are as follows: Current Document, Entire Current Local Site, Selected Files in Site, and Folder (Folder opens a new segment of the dialog box, allowing you to browse to the desired folder to run the report on). For the purpose of this task, select Entire Current Local Site.

5. Expand HTML Reports by clicking the Plus (+) symbol beside it if it isn't expanded already. Place a check in Accessibility. Note that the Report Settings button becomes enabled. Click the Report Settings button to open the Accessibility dialog box, as shown in Figure 79-3.

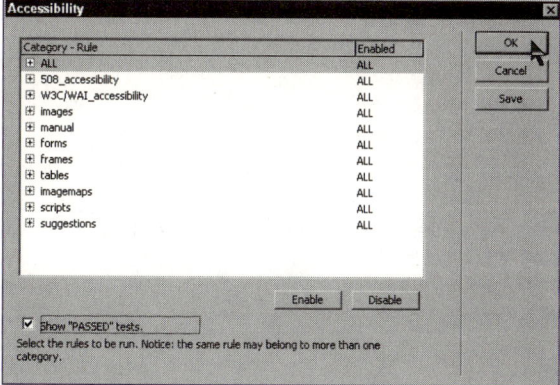

Figure 79-3: Accessibility dialog box

6. You can enable/disable the tests that interest you or your client through this interface. Placing a check in the Show "Passed" tests check box will add the passed items to the report as well as the failed items. Click the interface's Save button to save your settings if you want to use these settings globally. Click the OK button on the dialog box to effect the changes and close the Accessibility dialog box. Click the Run button on the Reports dialog box to run the reporting routine against your settings and close the Reports dialog box. The Reports panel opens (if it's closed) at the Site Reports tab with the results of the test.

7. As before in Tasks 77 and 78, the Stop button (the red button with a white X) stops the processing of the report, and the More Info button opens the Reference panel to the referenced item for further description. With the Save Report button, you can save the data from the report as an XML file by using the Save As dialog box.

8. The contextual menu is very similar to that covered in Tasks 77 and 78. Most menu options are available here, as well as Clear Report (right-/Control+click the Results panel). Use Clear Report after you've made changes and followed the report's guidance.

cross-reference

▪ See Task 5 for setting accessibility preferences.

Checking for Browser Compatibility

Once you decide which browsers your audience is most likely to use, you have the ability in Dreamweaver to test for those specific browsers. A new feature in Dreamweaver MX 2004 is the Check Target Browsers feature. Check Target Browser tests the code in your document to see if your tags, attributes, and CSS properties are supported by your target browsers.

notes

- Target browser checks are not updated constantly. After changes are made to the code, you may want to run the check manually.

- Scripts are not checked.

1. To select your target browsers, select the Target Browser Check menu in the Document toolbar and select Settings, as shown in Figure 80-1.

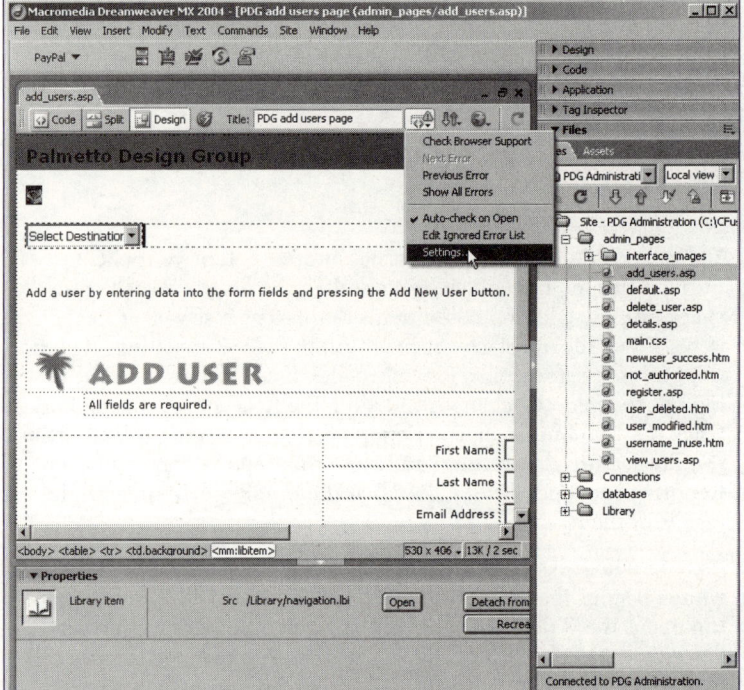

Figure 80-1: The Target Browser Check menu in the Document toolbar

2. Select the check box for each browser you want to support. Set the minimum version for each browser, as shown in Figure 80-2.

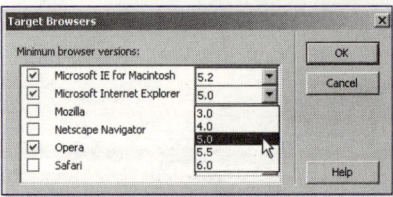

Figure 80-2: The browsers list

3. Switch to Code view or to Split view. If you see any red wavy lines, they indicate an error. Pass your cursor over the underlined word and you'll see a ToolTip specifying the problem and the associated browser, as shown in Figure 80-3. Warnings are not marked in Code view.

```
47  <style type="text/css">
48  <!--
49  body,td,th {
50      color: #006699;
51  }
52  -->
53  </style></head>
54
55  <body leftmargin="0" topmargin="0" marginwidth="0" marginheight="0">
56
57  <table width="100%" height="700" border="0" cellpadding="0" cellspaci
58    <tr valign="top">
59      <td width="635" height="350" class="background"><h4>        Palmett
60        <!-- #BeginLibraryItem "/Library/navigation.lbi" -->
61        <script language="JavaScript" type="text/JavaScript">
62  <!--  The Script tag is not supported. [Opera 2.1]
63  function MM_jumpMenu(targ,selObj,restore){ //v3.0
64    eval(targ+".location.'"+selObj.options[selObj.selectedIndex].value+
65    if (restore) selObj.selectedIndex=0;
66  }
67  //-->
```

Figure 80-3: Code view showing a browser error

4. If you want to see the error report for the entire document, select the Check Target Browser icon and select Show All Errors. The Results panel opens, as shown in Figure 80-4. Errors have red exclamation marks, warnings have a yellow exclamation mark, and messages have word-balloon icons.

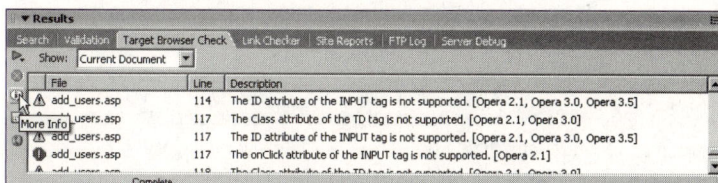

Figure 80-4: The Results panel showing all the errors in the open document

5. Click the More Info icon to the right of the Target Browser Check panel (in the Results panel) to see messages that are too long to read in the panel.

6. Double-click an error message to jump to that specific error; the code will be selected in Code view.

7. To run the browser check on the entire site, select the site folder in the Files panel, then choose File ⇨ Check Page ⇨ Check Target Browsers. The Results panel displays the results.

8. If you want Dreamweaver to ignore a specific error, right-/Control+click the red-underlined code and select Ignore Error. That specific error will then show up as a warning instead.

tip

• An error indicates code that may cause serious problems in your target browsers. A warning indicates code that won't display properly. A message indicates code that isn't supported but won't have a visible effect in the browser.

cross-reference

• Refer to Task 7 for setting up your testing browsers.

Testing Your Site Locally

After creating all the pages, adding your content, validating the markup, and checking your links and accessibility, it's time for some testing before you go live with it. What testing do you need to do locally before publishing the site? You need to test it using various browsers from your computer and preferably different operating systems and platforms, such as Windows and Mac. This requirement depends on what you have coded your pages for, what technologies you have used to build the site, and who your targeted visitors are.

notes

- Using a temporary file bypasses requirements of includes and other file types *only* on this one file. If you click a link on the page to another page of your site, the requirements come into play again, and you could end up with broken images or other errors on the page (Step 3).

- For the PC, browsers that I test are Internet Explorer, Netscape 6.21, Netscape 7, Opera 7.02 and Mozilla. For the Mac, you should check in Internet Explorer, Netscape 6.x, Opera, and Safari (Step 10).

1. Open an existing site and open a document from the Files panel.

2. Select Edit ➪ Preferences (Ctrl/Command+U) to open the Preferences dialog box. Select the Preview in Browser category, as shown in Figure 81-1.

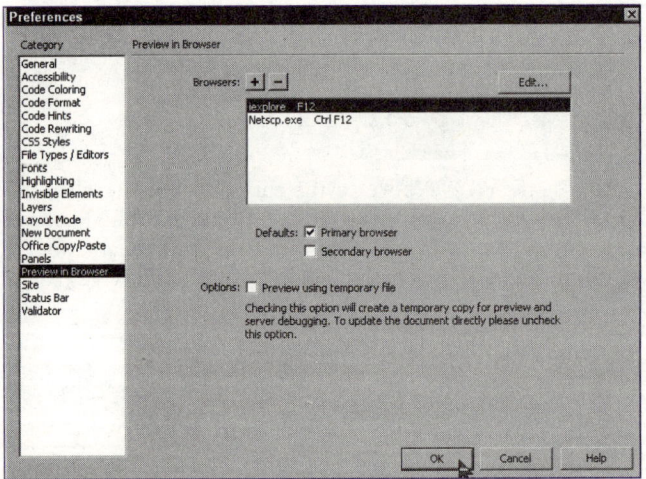

Figure 81-1: Preferences dialog box—Preview in Browser category

3. If you have a local server such as Apache or IIS installed, uncheck the Preview Using Temporary File option and click the OK button on the dialog box to effect the change and close the dialog box.

4. Using the Files panel, select a file from the list and then select File ➪ Preview in Browser and select the desired preview browser from the list.

5. Alternatively, select a file in the Files panel, right-/Control+click to open the context menu, select Preview in Browser, and select the target browser from the list.

6. Another method is to open the file for editing. Select View ⇨ Toolbars ⇨ Document and make sure there is a check beside it. If there is no check, then the Document toolbar has been disabled, so make the selection again to display the Document toolbar, as shown in Figure 81-2.

Figure 81-2: Document toolbar

7. Select the Preview/Debug in Browser button (Globe), and choose the browser of choice from the selection list, as shown in Figure 81-3.

Figure 81-3: Preview/Debug in browser selection list

8. All the methods mentioned in Steps 4 through 7 will open the page selected in Open in the chosen browser.

9. With the page open in the browser, give your entire site the once-over and note anything odd so that you can investigate and repair it after your preview session.

10. Repeat this process for each browser that you have installed.

cross-reference

• See Task 7 for information on adding additional browsers to the browser list and configuring the primary and secondary browsers (Step 2).

Task 82

Uploading Files to the Server

After creating your site and performing all the tests you need done locally, it's time to upload the files to your hosting server for everyone to view. This will give you a broader spectrum of issues that may be encountered by the site visitors. Uploading files from your local site to the server is accomplished using Dreamweaver MX 2004 FTP, which offers different methods of file transfer depending on the site configuration.

note

▪ To see both the remote and local files at the same time, click the Expand/Collapse icon (Step 7).

1. Select an existing site using the Site panel. For an overview of the Site panel, see Figure 82-1.

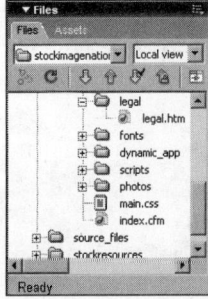

Figure 82-1: Site panel

2. Select the Connects to Remote Hosts button.

3. Select the root folder at the top of the file list in the Files panel.

4. Select the Put File(s) button. All the site files are uploaded to the remote server.

5. If you delete your local files or want to download the files from the server for any reason, switch to Remote View, select the topmost folder, and select the Get File(s) button. All the server files are downloaded to the folder specified by the local site configuration.

6. If you're using the Check In/Out feature for codeveloping the site or for contributing users, select the root folder and use the Check Out File(s) option to check out all files on the server. This renders the site uneditable by your coworkers until you check the files back in. To check the files back in, select the root folder and use the Check in File(s) button (see Figure 82-2).

caution

▪ Whenever you make mass changes to the files on your remote server, make sure that you have local backups of the old version in case errors occur.

7. Using either method, you can transfer one file at a time, a group of files, or the whole site. To select a single file, click it once in the Files panel's Local view and use the appropriate button to transfer the file. To transfer a group of files/folders, hold down the Alt/Option key, click each file/folder that you wish to transfer, and press the appropriate transfer method button.

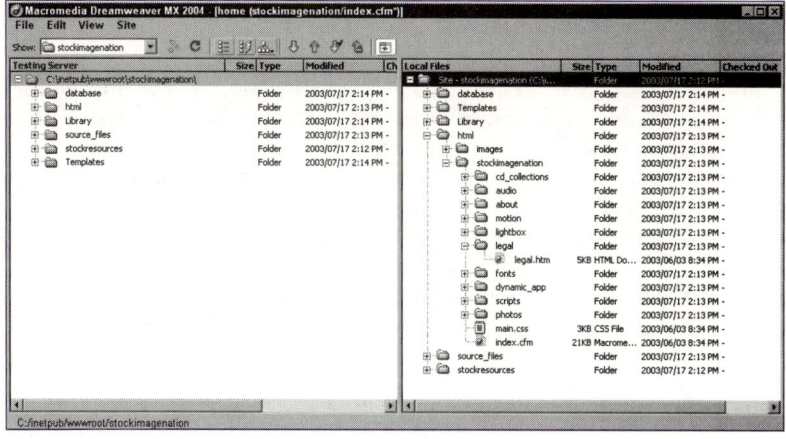

Figure 82-2: Files panel expanded

8. At times you won't want to transfer all files but just the changed files. To perform this function, select Edit from the Files Options menu.

9. The menu selections here allow you to perform the following file selections: Select All (selects all files in the site for transfer), Select Checked Out Files (selects all files that are currently checked out on your system), Select Newer Local (requires an Internet connection, as it compares the local file date/time stamp against the host file date/time stamps and selects the newer one on the local machine), Select Newer Remote (requires an Internet connection, as it compares the local file date/time stamp against the host file date/time stamps and selects the newer one on the host machine), and Select Recently Modified (brings up the Select Recently Modified dialog box, shown in Figure 82-3).

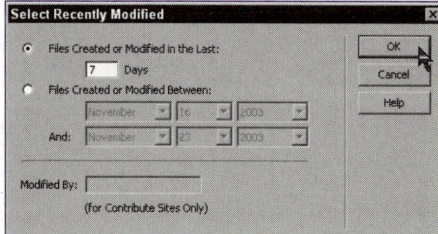

Figure 82-3: Select Recently Modified dialog box

10. The Recently Modified dialog box is pretty self-explanatory. You can choose between Files Created or Modified in the Last XX Days or Files Created or Modified between MM–DD–YY and MM–DD–YY in conjunction with the optional field Modified By, which is grabbed from the File Design Notes (if they are turned on in the site configuration).

cross-references

▪ If no files or folders exist, see Task 21 and 22: (Step 6).

▪ See Task 218 for remote server configuration details (Step 7).

Testing Your Site Online

O ne of the last tests you need to perform with your newly created and uploaded site is to do an online performance test, have it checked by the Dreamweaver newsgroup users, and run it through a couple of online validation engines to make sure everything is working prior to announcing the site is live.

notes

- You should validate against the same doctype as stated in the DOCTYPE line in your page. Not all online validators are equal in their doctype detection routines (Step 4).

- You only need to do a Bobby test if you are worried about accessibility (Step 5).

- Using the guidelines outlined at www.dwfaq. com/Tutorials/Misce llaneous/site_ check_please.asp, post a message to the Dreamweaver support forum at news:// forums.macromedia. com/macromedia. dreamweaver requesting a site check. Be specific about what you are looking for, such as functionality on PC and Mac browsers V4+.

1. Open your browser and clear its history and cache (both memory and hard drive). The menu items for these functions differ from browser to browser, so read your browser's F1 help files if you don't know how to perform these functions.

2. Point to the URL of your Web site and run through the site with the installed browsers on your machine. Make notes of any issues that you notice, and correct them after your preview of the site or as you go—the choice is yours.

3. The next step is to validate each page against the W3C HTML/ XHTML Validator located at http://validator.w3.org/. If you use the Address field, you must either type the HTTP address or copy it from your browser address bar and paste it in the Address field at that page. Alternatively, you can use the Browse button for the local file field and point to the file on your local hard drive to validate. Click the Validate button to validate the page, and the validator engine displays a report of its findings, as shown in Figure 83-1. Print this out and make any necessary repairs. If you've done your job right, the report will display and give you link information so you can post a validation image on your Web site. Only do this if the entire site validates! Repeat this process for each Web page on your site.

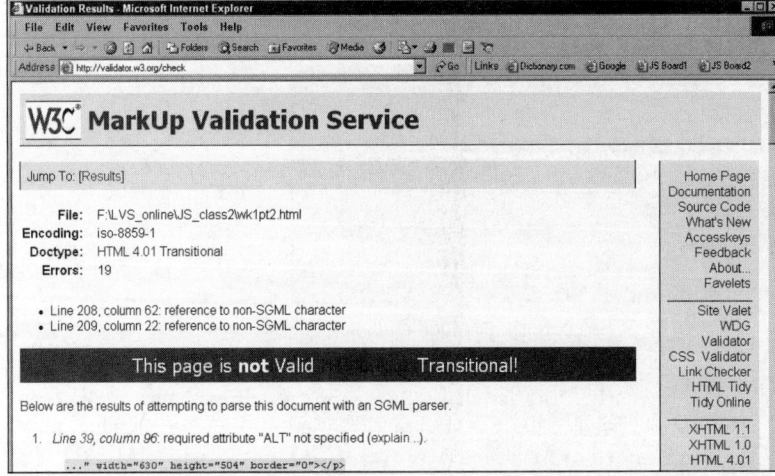

Figure 83-1: W3C HTML/XHTML Validator report

4. The next step is to validate each page against the W3C CSS Validator located at http://jigsaw.w3.org/css-validator/. You can download the validator to do local tests, which would be faster, or

you can validate using the URI, Text Area, or Upload File options on this page. This validator checks CSS files, so make sure that you upload the external CSS file to validate it. The report will be similar to the one in Figure 83-2.

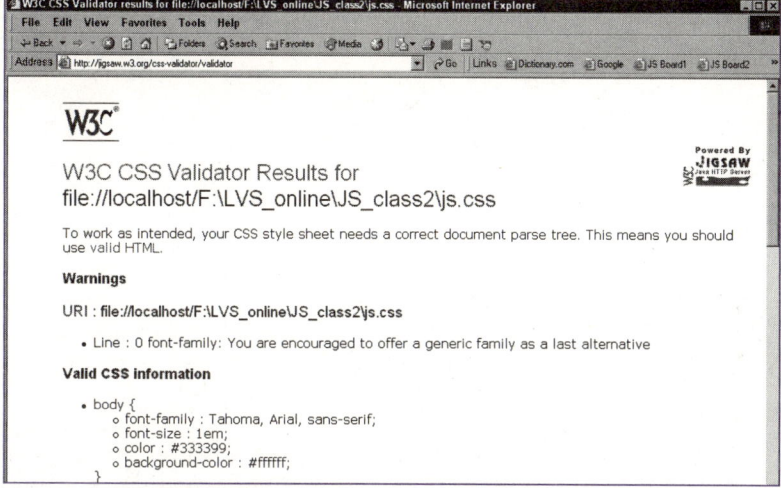

Figure 83-2: W3C CSS Validator report

5. The next step is to validate each page against the Bobby Validator, located at `http://bobby.watchfire.com/bobby/html/en/index.jsp`. You have the choice of validating for Section 508 guidelines or Web Content Accessibility Guidelines (WCAG). (Section 508 refers to the Rehabilitation Act Amendments of 1998; WCAG is from the W3C.) Choose 508 and enter the URL of a page of your site, and press the Submit button to generate the report, as shown in Figure 83-3.

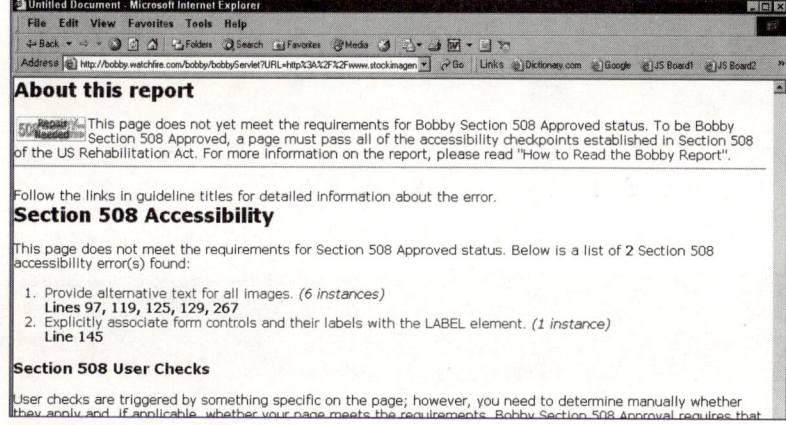

Figure 83-3: Bobby Accessibility report—508

cross-reference

- See Tasks 81 to 83 for local testing routines and getting the files to the server (Step 2).

Part 4: Mastering Frames

Task **84**

Making the Frame–No Frame Choice

U sing frames for a site's design is extremely controversial. People either hate them or love them. You'll see some facts—both pro and con—here so you can make an informed decision. The negative reactions are often remnants of the early days of frames, when abuses such as too many frames on a page were common. Many of the drawbacks and what were once valid reasons not to use frames have been reversed with techniques that overcome or solve the problem.

notes

• Some consider not seeing
   the URL a disadvantage,
   and it does make the page
   hard to bookmark (Figure
   84-1).

• This is a pretty moot
   point, since browsers after
   Netscape 2 and Internet
   Explorer 3 support frames
   (Step 2).

1. Consider the pros of using frames:

    • Unchanging content: Frames have the ability to keep certain
       areas of the screen unchanged instead of the entire page changing
       for each content change.

    • Certain areas of the page can scroll while other areas don't.

    • An unchanging bottom element: Frames can be used to "float"
       unchanging content at the top and left edges of a browser, as well
       as at the bottom.

    • Complex nested frame layouts allow for very complex layouts. If a
       site is properly designed, you can't even tell it is using frames.

    • Portions of a frameset can be printed and/or saved separately by
       right-/Control+clicking in the desired area and selecting from the
       contextual menu, shown in Figure 84-1.

Figure 84-1: The contextual menu of a frame

    • Hidden page references: Only the frameset URL is seen in the
       browser's title bar.

2. Now consider the drawbacks of using frames:

    • Authoring of pages is more complex because of multiple HTML
       pages in a frameset.

    • Search engines issues: Some spiders have a problem indexing a
       framed site.

- Older browsers don't support frames.

- A framed page can be difficult to bookmark.

3. Evaluate your site's needs. Would it benefit from frames? If so, you'll need to decide if you can live with the drawbacks.

4. Avoid using an excessive number of frames, especially ones with scroll bars. Too many scroll bars is not only distracting but very unprofessional looking, as shown in Figure 84-2. Don't laugh; I bet you've seen sites like this—I have. In this section of the book you'll learn how *not* to do this.

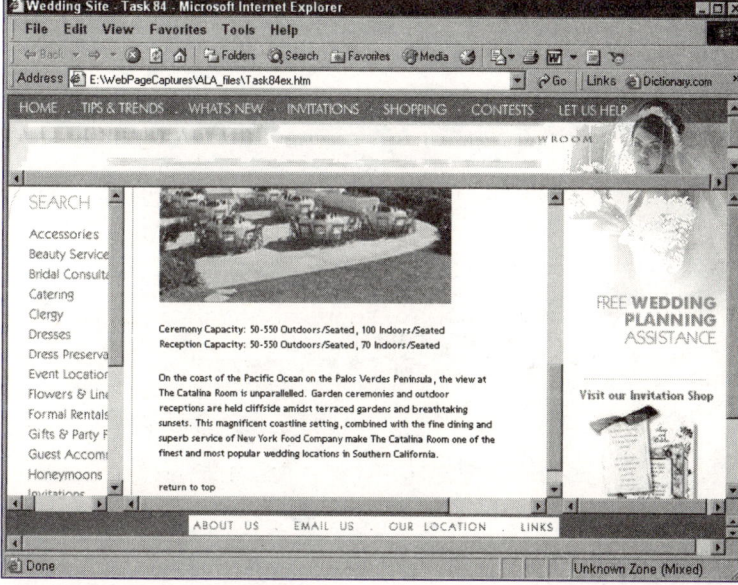

Figure 84-2: A poor use of frames

cross-reference

- Refer to Task 95 to learn how to overcome the indexing problem (Step 2).

Using a Predefined Frameset

The use of frames can lead to nothing but problems and confusion for some developers. Reading this section alone will make the book a worthwhile purchase if you have need to use frames with your Web site. Macromedia has included 15 different preconfigured framesets for your use or modification. Like many items in Dreamweaver MX 2004, these predefined framesets are available in a couple of different locations.

notes

- If you have accessibility enabled for framesets, an accessibility dialog box opens (Step 1).

- Adding a title to individual pages of the frameset has no effect on the browser unless the page is accessed directly outside of the frameset (Step 2).

- Meta data should be added to the frameset defi- nition page as well as to each unique page of the frameset (Step 3).

1. To use a predefined frameset, choose File ➪ New, General tab, Framesets category, and select the desired frameset from the Framesets list, as shown in Figure 85-1. For the purpose of this exercise, choose Fixed Top and click the Create button on the New Document dialog box to create the frameset and close the dialog box.

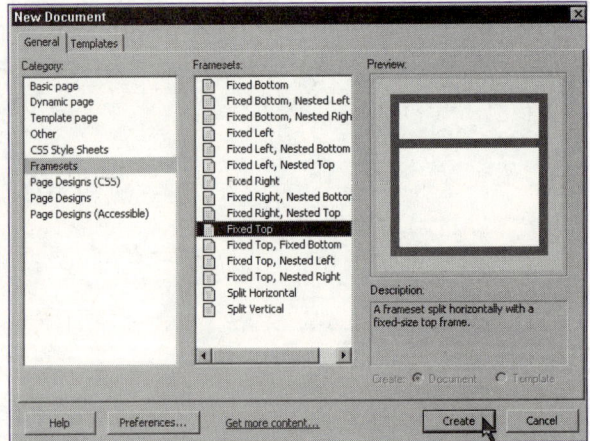

Figure 85-1: New Document dialog box—Framesets

2. In the Title field of the Document toolbar, immediately enter the title of the document. This title will be displayed for all the pages in your entire site that use this frameset. For this task, enter a title of **Frameset-10 Steps** and press the Enter/Return key.

3. Close the frameset without saving any changes. We'll now move on to the second method of using Frameset Stationary.

4. Create a new HTML document using the Welcome screen, Create New HTML. Immediately save the page using CTRL+S [Command_S] and use a filename of **Task85Fset2.htm**. These are just practice files so save them somewhere you can find them and delete them later.

5. To create the Frameset, use Insert ➪ HTML ➪ Frames ➪ Top. Notice that the Frameset is exactly the same as the first method, except this method requires an open document to work. You created one of the pages in the frameset.

6. Close the frameset without saving any changes. We'll now move on to the third method of using Frameset Stationary.

7. Create a new HTML document using the File ⇨ New menu item (select the General tab, Basic Page category, HTML from the Basic Page column, and then click the Create button). Immediately save the page using Ctrl/Command+S, and use a filename of **Task85Fset3.htm**.

8. The third method of creating a frameset uses the Insert toolbar. In the Layout category, the second to the last icon is for frames. Click the down arrow to access the Frames pop-up menu (see Figure 85-2) and select Top Frame. Notice that the frameset is exactly the same as the first two methods, except this method also requires an open document to work.

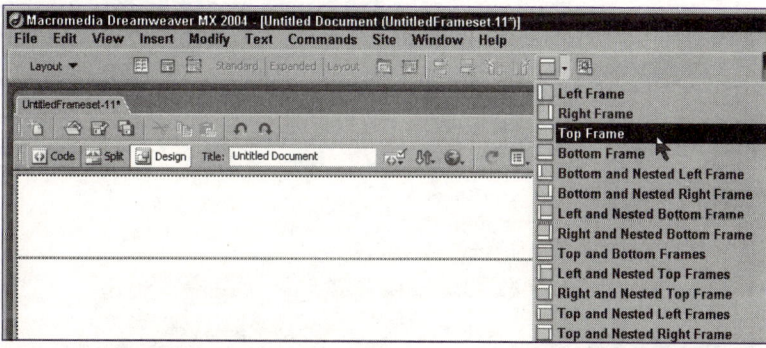

Figure 85-2: The Frames pop-up menu in the Insert toolbar, Layout category

9. In all cases, when the main frameset page is open and no frames are selected, the Property inspector shows the Frameset attributes (see Figure 85-3). You can also open the Frames panel to view the frameset for manipulation by choosing Window ⇨ Frames (Shift+F2).

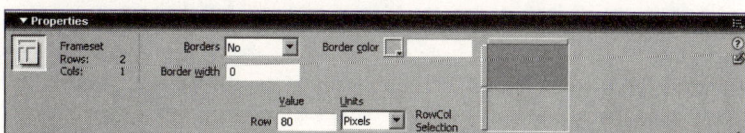

Figure 85-3: The Property inspector with the frameset attributes displayed

10. Another tip for working with frames: It is always a good idea to set Dreamweaver to display frame borders whether or not you have them defined, since it will make selecting content to edit much easier. To do this, choose View ⇨ Visual Aids ⇨ Frame Borders.

cross-reference

• See Task 87 for instructions on saving the frameset and its pages (Step 8).

Making a Custom Frameset

Sometimes you want to make a custom frameset that the predefined sets just don't cover to your satisfaction. You could start with a predefined frameset and customize it, or you can build the frameset from scratch, which you will do with this task.

1. Create a new HTML document using the Welcome screen or the shortcut Ctrl/Command+N.

2. Position your cursor anywhere in the document, and select Modify ⇨ Frameset ⇨ Split Frame Up to split the page on the horizontal axis to generate a top and bottom frameset split equally (see Figure 86-1).

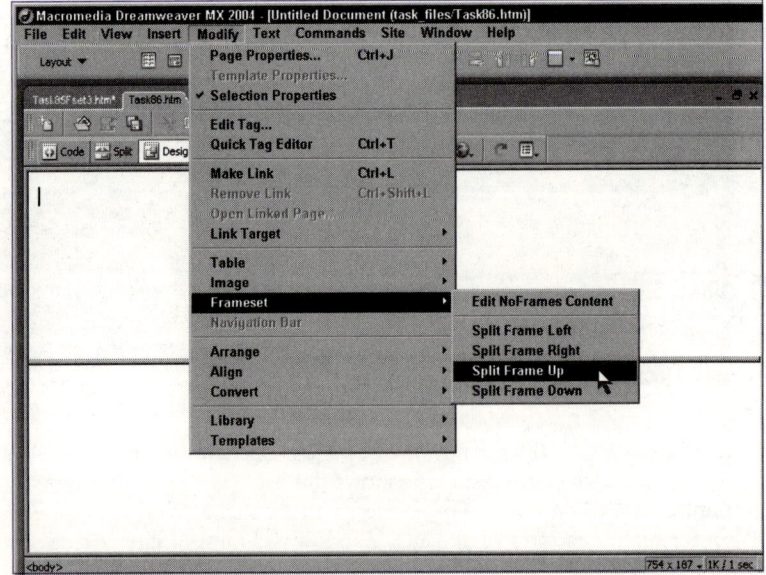

Figure 86-1: Split the new document horizontally

3. Now grab the left-hand edge of the frame and drag it out (press and hold the left mouse button to drag) to roughly the center of the document to make a four-panel frameset, as shown in Figure 86-2. Release the button to release the frame border.

4. Grab the border you just created, slide it all the way to the left or right edge of the document, and release it. The border leaves the frameset.

5. Position your cursor in the top frame and select Modify ⇨ Frameset ⇨ Split Frame Left. This splits only the top frame into two side-by-side frames while leaving the bottom frame alone. Repeat with the bottom frame, but make sure the vertical border is not aligned with each other, as shown in Figure 86-3. Alternatively, you can use the frameset toolset in the Layout toolbar to add a new frame.

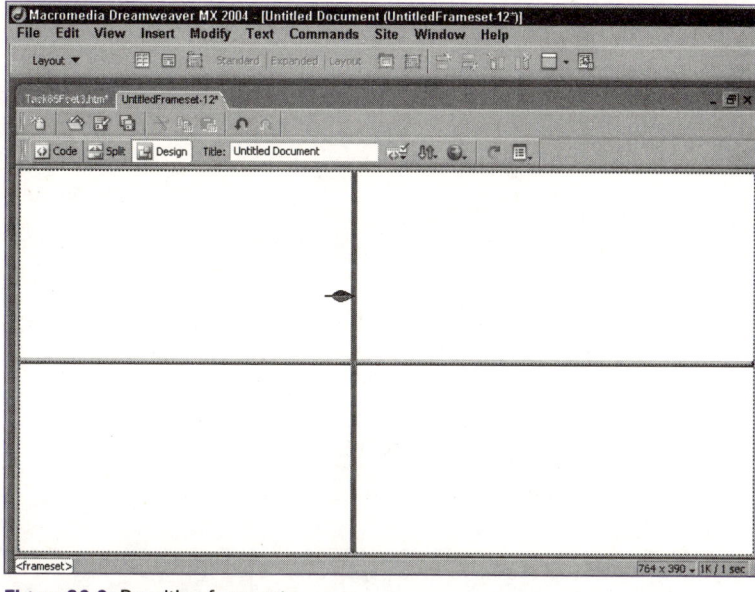

Figure 86-2: Resulting frameset

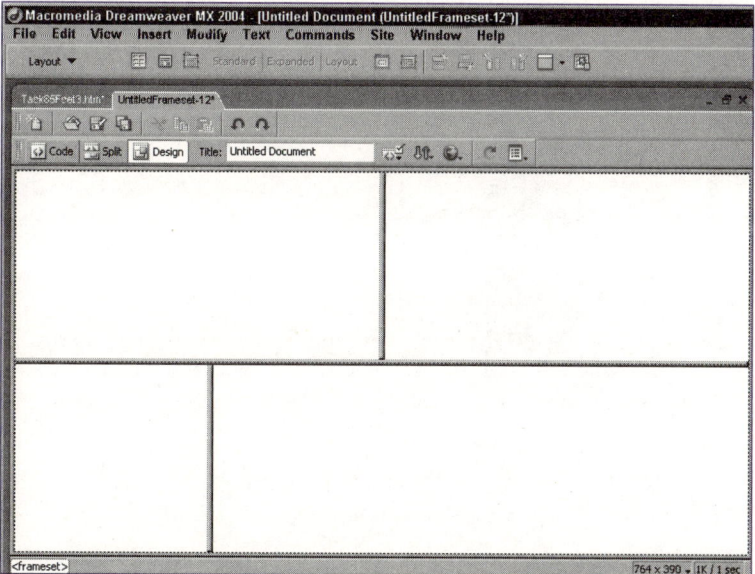

Figure 86-3: Split frames example

6. You can repeat this process as often as you like, keeping in mind that each frame requires a unique page reference.

7. Experiment using the three methods to split a frame. While you have the Frames panel open, click on the various areas of it to see which frame is selected and how it is highlighted.

8. Close this document when you are finished exploring the Frames panel and the methods of splitting frames.

cross-reference

▪ See Task 4 for instructions on opening or creating a document.

Saving a Frameset

Now that you have the creation of a frameset and frames mastered, it's time to start learning how to save these frames. This is the biggest problem area for people using Dreamweaver when they first start to work with frames.

1. Choose File ➪ New ➪ Framesets, select Fixed Top, and click the Create button. You can also use the Welcome screen. For framesets, click Framesets in the Create from Samples area, choose Fixed Top, and click the Create button.

2. Save the frameset using File ➪ Save All. Because this frameset consists of three pages (the main frameset page, the bottom page, and the top page), the Save dialog box will open three times. Dreamweaver shows which page is the active page with a special hashed border, as shown in Figure 87-1. The first save is for the frameset. Name this page **task87set.htm**.

notes

- Name your frames with meaningful names (Step 4).

- Notice that you only need to save the frameset page (task87set.htm) once. The frame pages change, but usually the frameset doesn't (Step 3).

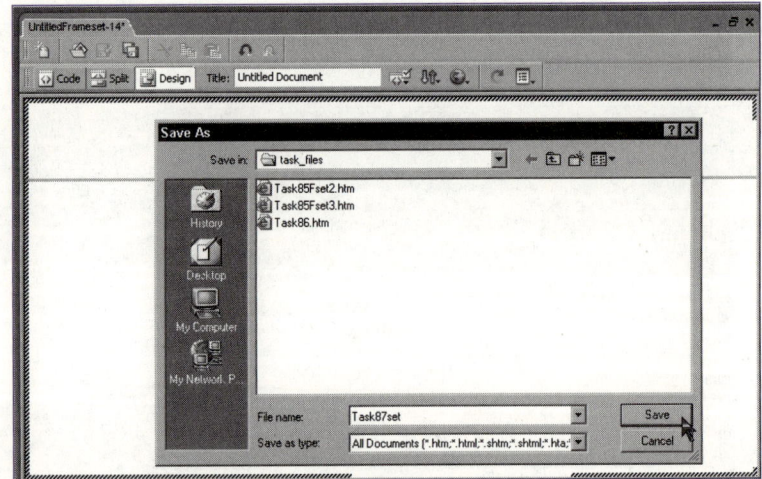

Figure 87-1: The border is surrounding the entire frameset

3. The second dialog box opens, and the appropriate frame is high-lighted with the special indicator border, as shown in Figure 87-2. Name this page **Task87bottom.htm**.

caution

- You cannot make a template of the frameset page (the base page that defines the frameset). Although it is possible with some fiddling, there is absolutely no point in making the frameset a template, since it is referenced only once.

Task 87

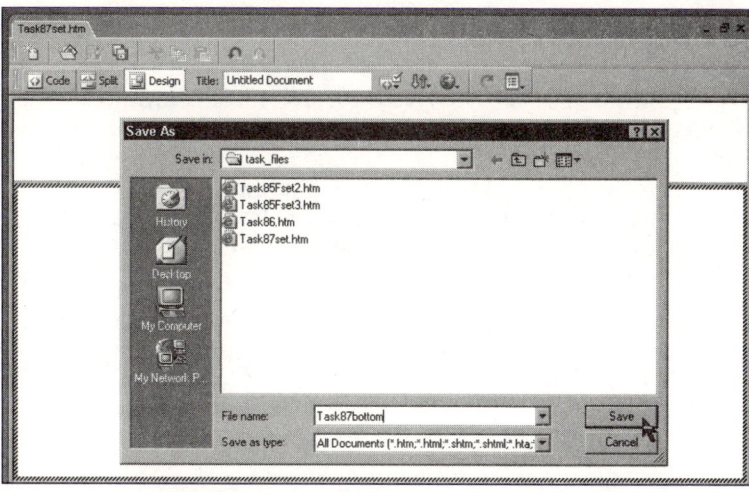

Figure 87-2: Active frame (bottom) highlighted

4. The third dialog box opens and the appropriate frame is highlighted with the special indicator border. Name this page **Task87top.htm**.

5. The frameset code is complete. Highlight the frameset and switch to Split or Code view to see the HTML code, as shown in Figure 87-3.

```
<frameset rows="87,*" cols="*" framespacing="0" frameborder="NO" border="0">
  <frame src="Task87top.htm" name="topFrame" scrolling="NO" noresize >
  <frame src="Task87bottom.htm" name="mainFrame">
</frameset>
<noframes><body>
</body></noframes>
```

Figure 87-3: The HTML code for the frameset you've just saved

6. Now it is safe to edit the content of each of the frames. Position your cursor in the top frame, and type **Top Frame Content**. Press Ctrl/Command+S to save the changes to the page. Position your cursor in the bottom frame, and type **Bottom Frame Content**. Press Ctrl/Command+S to save the changes to the page.

7. You might ask how to force a save of the frameset if it changes. Simply select File ⇨ Save All again, or click the Save All icon in the Standard toolbar.

8. Close all open documents. If you are prompted to save any, select No.

cross-reference

▪ See Tasks 85 and 86 for more instructions on creating a frameset (Step 1).

Editing Frames

Once you create your initial frameset, you can still alter it. You can drag the borders to resize, add or change borders, and modify scrolling options and margins.

1. Open the frameset you created in Task 87 (Task87set.htm), or create a new frameset using the Create from Samples: Framesets in the Welcome page.

2. To access the properties for the entire frameset, you need to select it. In Design view you can place your cursor over the outer border; when you see a double arrow (the drag cursor), click. You can tell the entire frameset is selected when you see the dotted line around the edges, as shown in Figure 88-1.

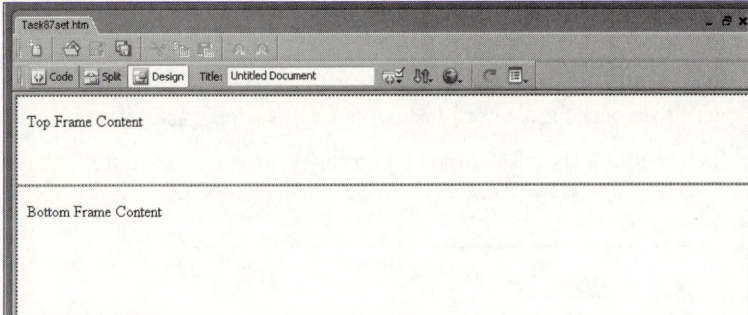

Figure 88-1: The frameset is selected

3. You may find it easier to select the frameset in the Frames panel (Shift+F2). Click the outer border in the Frames panel. Again, when the entire frameset is selected, you'll see the dotted lines in the main Document window and a bold black outline in the Frames panel.

4. Once the frameset is selected, you'll see the various options in the Property inspector (see Figure 88-2). Here you can change the Border properties as well as the row values. There is also a visual row/column selector.

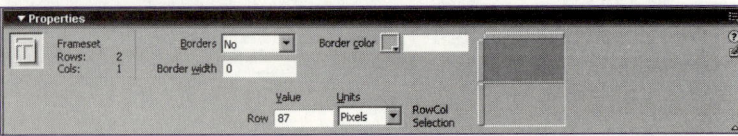

Figure 88-2: The Property inspector showing the properties of the frameset

5. Select one of the frames in the Frames panel.

6. You can edit the scroll, margins, and border properties, as well as add a CSS style sheet or add and edit styles, using the frame attributes in the Property inspector (see Figure 88-3).

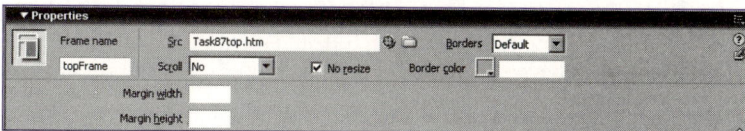

Figure 88-3: The Property inspector showing the properties of the top frame

7. If you simply click inside a frame, the Text Property inspector is activated.

8. You can close your file without saving.

cross-references

- Refer to Task 89 for the specifics of the frameset properties (Step 4).

- Refer to Task 90 for the specifics of the frame properties (Step 6).

- Refer to Part 9 for using CSS styles (Step 6).

- Refer to Part 2 for using the Text Property inspector (Step 7).

Setting the Frameset Properties

You can use the Property inspector to precisely size rows and columns, as well as to control the border for all the frames.

1. Open the file you created in Task 87 (Task87set.htm), or choose File ➪ New ➪ Framesets, select Fixed Top, and click the Create button. Make sure you have the frame borders visible.

2. You'll most likely always have the Property inspector open, but if not, choose Window ➪ Properties. Or if you've simply collapsed it, click on its name to open it again. There is a tiny arrow in the bottom right corner; be sure it is pointing down so you can see everything in the Property inspector.

3. While in Design view, select the frameset border in the Frames panel (Shift+F2). The Property inspector with the frameset properties is shown in Figure 89-1.

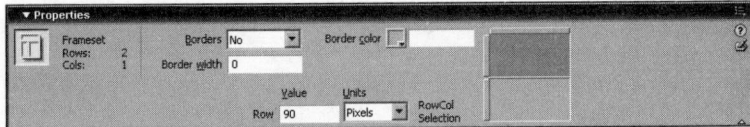

Figure 89-1: The Property inspector open and expanded

4. Look in the Property inspector. On the right, you'll see RowCol Selection for the frameset. Click the Row tab (side) or the Column tab (top) of the row or column you want to modify. This task has two rows and no columns, so only the Row selection is available.

5. To specify a specific pixel size of a row or column, enter a number into the Value text box and select Pixels from the Units drop-down menu. Figure 89-1 shows the top frame set at 90 pixels.

6. To specify as a percentage, enter a number from 1 to 100 and select Percent from the Units drop-down menu (see Figure 89-2). Choosing Percent keeps the top frame at that percent of the browser window's size.

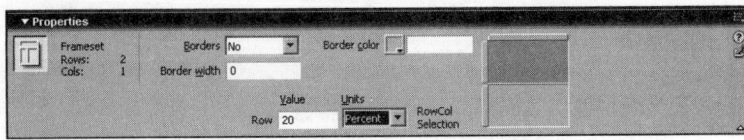

Figure 89-2: A value of 20 percent entered for the top frame

7. To specify the size of a frame relative to the other columns or rows, select Relative from the Units drop-down menu. To set the size to be the remainder of the space available, type **1** into the Value field, as shown in Figure 89-3. To scale the frame relative to the other rows or columns, type the scale factor in the Value text box.

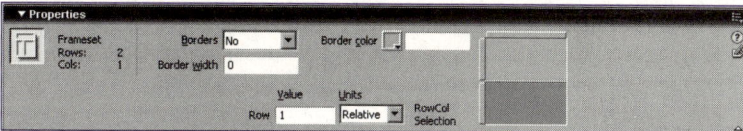

Figure 89-3: The bottom frame is relative; it will fill the remaining space in the browser window

8. Frame borders are set as invisible by default, and this is what you'll use most of the time. But if you require a border for your frameset, select Yes from the Borders pop-up menu and then enter the border amount in pixels in the Border Width field. To set the border color, click on the Border color box and select a color.

cross-reference

- See Tasks 85 and 86 for more instructions on creating a frameset (Step 1).

Setting Frame Properties

In Task 89 you learned how to set the properties for a frameset. Now you'll learn how to set properties for the individual frames. You can have fixed or flexible frames. Some can have scroll bars while others don't—it's up to you.

1. If you have no document open, the Welcome screen is visible with some great shortcut links. In the Create from Samples section, click Framesets. Select any frameset and click the Create button.

2. Change the title in the Document toolbar from Untitled to a descriptive name for your page.

3. Since each frame has its own HTML file, each one also has its own page properties. Click inside one of the frames in Design view and choose Modify ⇨ Page Properties.

4. The Appearance category opens by default (see Figure 90-1). You can set your page font, size, and text color here. You can also use a background image and background color. Left and Top Margins are for Internet Explorer, and Top and Bottom Margins are for Netscape. If you want no margin at all (not even the browser default), type in **o** for all four fields (if you are supporting both browsers). Click the Links and Headings categories if you want to set their styles.

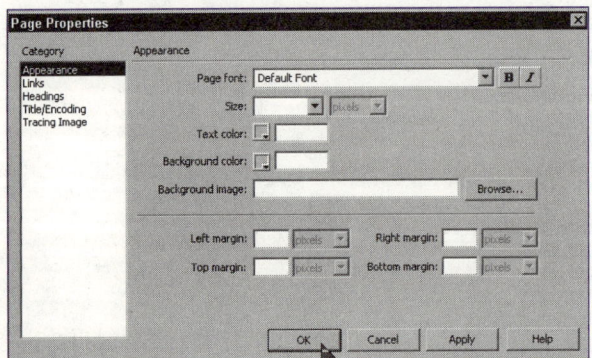

Figure 90-1: The Appearance panel

5. In the Property inspector you can also set the frame name in the Frame Name field. But you have to select the frame, not just click inside it. You can press the Alt/Option and then click inside the frame to select it, or click in the frame in the Frames panel. In Figure 90-2, notice the dotted lines in the document, the frame name in the Property inspector, the bolded outline in the Frames panel, and the highlighted `<frame>` tag in the Tag Selector. There are many ways to determine if the frame is actually selected.

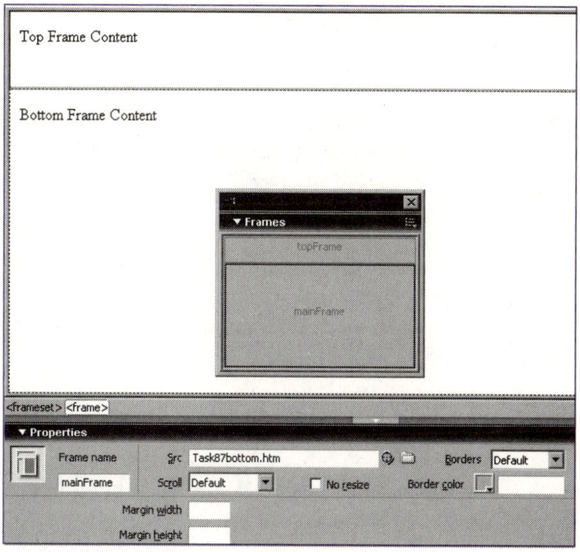

Figure 90-2: The mainFrame selected

6. You can load any page into the frame. In the Property inspector, the Src field is where you can type the path to any page. Or use the Browse icon to navigate to the file and select it. You can also use the Point to File icon (Tasks 39 and 40) and drag it to the desired file in the Files panel.

7. While the frame is selected, you can add a border. If you've made border settings for the frameset, anything you do to the frame's border will override the settings you made for the frameset.

8. Set your desired scroll settings. The options are as follows:

   - *Default.* The choice is up to the browser (not a reliable option).

   - *Yes.* Scroll bars are present regardless of content amount.

   - *No.* No scroll bars even if the content exceeds the frame's limit. This option makes your page look seamless but can mean that some of your page isn't visible.

   - *Auto.* Scroll bars only appear if the content exceeds the frame area.

9. A frame can be resized by the user by default in a browser. If you want to disallow this, check the Resize option in the Property inspector. It's a good idea to use this option in a frame that contains your navigation.

10. You can control the margins of a frame by entering the pixel amounts in the Margin Width and Margin Height fields. If you leave these fields blank, the default is about 6 pixels for height and width and 15 pixels for top and bottom.

cross-reference

- Refer to Task 94 to learn how to have search engines index your frames site properly (Step 3).

Adding Content to Frames

You can get content into your frames a couple of different ways. You can either design the page you want to load into the frame separately or build it directly into the frame. A sample frameset, task91set.htm, and the associated files are available in the Task91 folder on the Wiley Web site (www.wiley.com/compbooks/10simplestepsorless).

notes

- A dotted line around the inside of the frame indicates it is selected. You'll also see the `<frame>` tag bolded in the Tag Selector (Step 4).

- For additional pages you want to load in these frames, refer to Tasks 92 and 93 (Step 7).

1. Open a new document and create the content you'd like in your first frame. If it's your navigation area, for example, then make a page with just the navigation. It's OK to use tables or whatever you'd like. It's just a normal HTML page. Save the page.

2. Create a new page for each frame of your site. It's pretty typical to have an HTML page for a banner, one for navigation, and one for content. The content frame is the one that you will load your site's HTML pages into. Create all necessary pages and save. The sample navigation page, task91nav.htm, is shown in Figure 91-1.

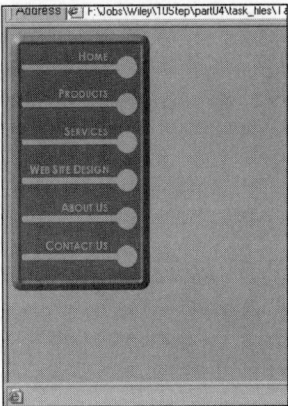

Figure 91-1: An HTML page containing navigation

3. Create a frameset that suits your needs (the predefined frameset Fixed Top Nested Left works well), and save it into your root folder of the site you are building.

4. Press the Alt/Option key and click inside the first frame to select it.

5. Open the Files panel and select your root folder from the defined sites list. Expand the menu so you can see the HTM/HTML files you want to link to. See Figure 91-2.

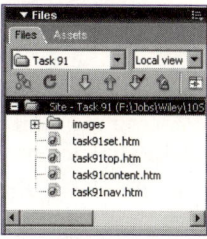

Figure 91-2: The Files panel with the root folder expanded

6. In the Property inspector, click on the Point to File icon, drag it to the filename (task91nav.htm in the sample file), and release the mouse button. Check the Link field in the Property inspector (see Figure 91-3); the path name is added automatically.

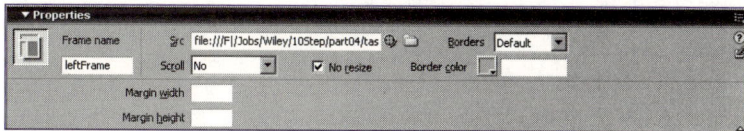

Figure 91-3: The Property inspector with the link added

7. You can use this method for each frame.

8. Optionally, you can build your initial pages for each frame directly in the frame. Click inside a frame and add your images, text, and tables like you would any HTML document.

9. Choose File ⇨ Save All to save each of your pages.

cross-reference

- Refer to Tasks 85 and 86 for creating framesets (Step 3).

Linking in Frames

Linking between the frames is what gives many new designers (or designers new to frames) a lot of grief. It isn't so bad once you understand how it all works and what the target names refer to. When a user clicks a link in one frame (your navigation frame, for example), a page opens into the specified frame.

1. Open a frameset with content for this exercise. If you'd like, you can copy the task92 folder from the partIVfolder (www.wiley.com/compbooks/10simplestepsorless) to your hard drive. Define this folder as a site in Dreamweaver and open task92set.htm.

2. Select the icon (or any image or text you want to act as a link). For this example, select the Home image, as shown in Figure 92-1.

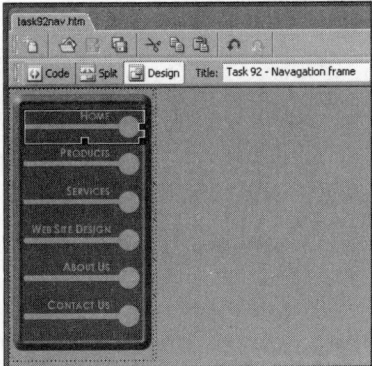

Figure 92-1: The Home image selected in the sidebar

3. In the Property inspector, next to the Link field, drag the Point to File icon on the index.htm file and release the mouse, as shown in Figure 92-2

caution

- Make sure that you specify a target whenever you are using frames. The default is that the new page loads into the current frame. If you forget to state your target, you may have your home page loading into your navigation frame (Step 6).

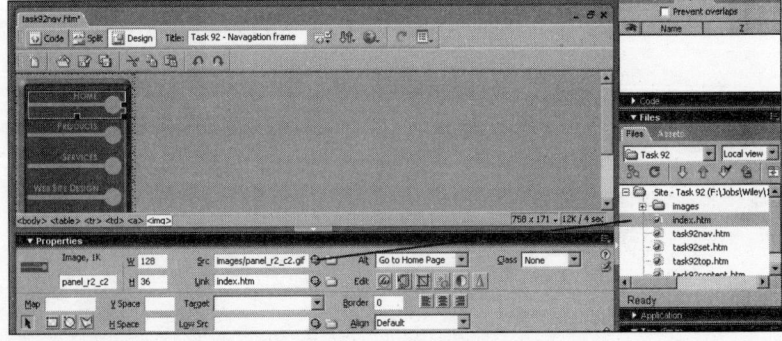

Figure 92-2: The Point to File icon used to select the illustration.htm file in the Files panel

4. Click the down arrow next to the Target field to access the menu.

5. Select contentFrame, since the content frame is where you want the index.htm file to appear when the user clicks the Home link.

6. Save and test the page in a browser. Click the Home link and note that index.htm page is loaded into the content frame, as shown in Figure 92-3. It's as easy as that.

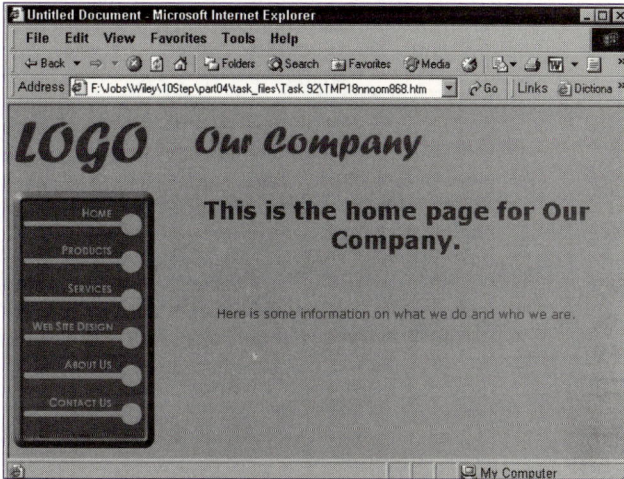

Figure 92-3: The link clicked as seen in a browser

7. Following are other options for the target option other then your site's frames. You should know these in case you ever want to use them.

   • *_blank*. Opens the linked file into a new browser window

   • *_parent*. Opens the file into the parent frameset of the current frame

   • *_self*. Opens the file into the same frame you are linking from, replacing its content

   • *_top*. Opens the linked file into the outermost frameset of the current Web page

8. Open index.htm by double-clicking its name in the Files panel. Highlight the word NEXT.

9. Use the Point to File icon, link to the index2.htm file, and release the mouse.

10. From the Target drop-down menu, select _self. This opens the linked file into the same frame and replaces the original index file. Choose File ➪ Save All and test in your target browsers.

cross-references

▪ Refer to Tasks 10 and 11 for defining a site (Step 1).

▪ Refer to Task 93 for linking to more than one frame with the same link image/text (Step 7).

Linking to Two Frames with One Link

You can use one link to change the contents of more than one frame at a time. In this task you see how to use a top navigation link to change the content in the sidebar and the content area at the same time.

1. Open a frameset with content for this exercise. If you'd like, you can copy the task93 folder from the Part 4 folder (`www.wiley.com/compbooks/10simplestepsorless`) to your hard drive. Define this folder as a site in Dreamweaver, and open index.htm.

2. Click the Design icon in the top navigation area to select it (see Figure 93-1).

notes

- `<shameless plug>`
  This is a file used in my
  Dreamweaver MX Complete Course book, where you can learn step-by-step how to build an entire site.
  `</shameless plug>`
  (Step 1).

- Double-click a filename in the Files panel to open it (Step 1).

- An image is used for this example, but a text link works just as well (Step 2).

- The Behaviors panel is in the Design panel; select its name to activate it. Or you can use the keyboard shortcut key of Shift+F3 (Step 1).

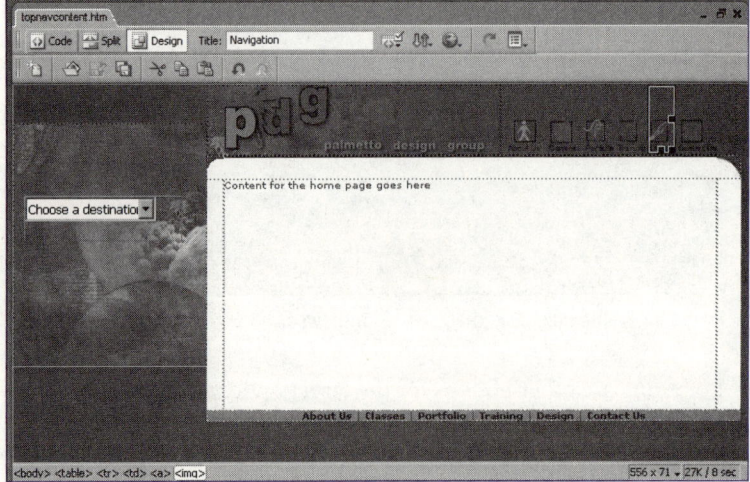

Figure 93-1: The frameset with the design icon selected

3. Open the Behaviors panel (Window ⇨ Behaviors) and click the plus sign (+) for Add Behavior. From the menu select Go to URL.

4. Select the frame "sidebar" and click the Browse button to navigate to the sidebarcontent.htm page, as shown in Figure 93-2. Select it and click OK.

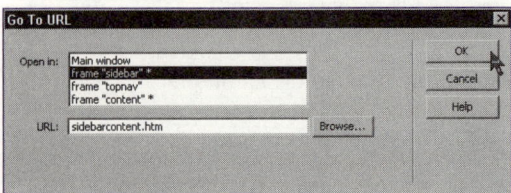

Figure 93-2: The Go to URL dialog box

5. Next, select the frame "content," click the Browse button, and navigate to illustration.htm; select it and click OK.

6. You can see the behavior added in the Behaviors panel, as shown in Figure 93-3. Click the down arrow and select onClick (or whatever event you want to use).

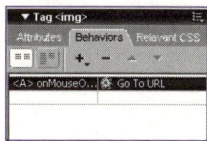

Figure 93-3: The Behaviors panel with the Go to URL behavior added

7. Choose File ⇨ Save All and preview in a browser.

8. Click on the Design icon to see the sidebar and the content frames change, as in Figure 93-4.

Figure 93-4: The changed frames, as shown in a browser

cross-reference

▪ Task 92 shows you how to change to just one frame.

Coding a Frameset to Be Found by Search Engines

One of the biggest arguments against using frames is that the search engine spiders don't index your site properly. With a little care and preplanning, you can eliminate this factor.

notes

- This is the page that users without frames will use. But there are very few browsers that don't support frames, so this technique is more useful for getting indexed by search engines (Step 3).

- Go to www. searchenginewatch. com to learn more about getting your site indexed to your advantage (Step 3).

- The page title is also displayed—don't forget to add a page title to every single one of your site's pages or the user will simply see "untitled.htm". Another reason to title your pages is that the title frequently helps in the search engine placement. So use your best keywords in the title (Step 3).

1. Open a frameset page, or use the one completed in Task 93.

2. Choose Modify ⇨ Frameset ⇨ Edit NoFrames Content.

3. In the document that opens, shown in Figure 94-1, type a description of your site. You can add images or whatever you'd like.

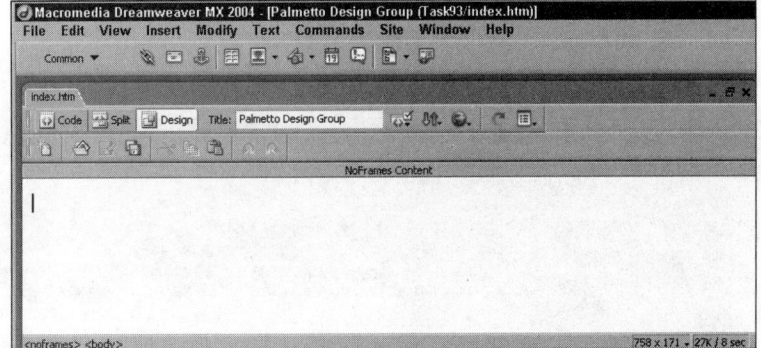

Figure 94-1: The page that opens when you edit NoFrames Content

4. Add a list of links to every page in your site that you want the search engine to index (see Figure 94-2). Use an absolute URL (www.mysite. com/myfile.htm) in the Link field in the Property inspector.

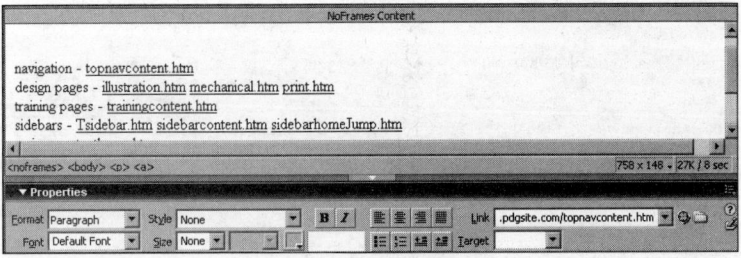

Figure 94-2: The NoFrame page with the links added

5. In the Insert bar, select the HTML category from the drop-down menu (Common is the default). Click on the Meta toolset (second to the right), and select Keywords. The Keywords dialog box opens.

6. Type in the keywords you think someone would enter into a search engine to find your site. Put the most important first and separate by commas, as in Figure 94-3. This is an extremely important part of getting a good index placement. Click OK when you are done.

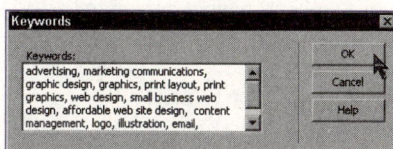

Figure 94-3: The Keywords dialog box filled in

7. In the Insert bar, HTML category, click the Meta Toolset icon again and select Descriptions.

8. In the Descriptions dialog box, shown in Figure 94-4, type in a description of your site. This is what is frequently displayed in the search engine listing. Click OK when done.

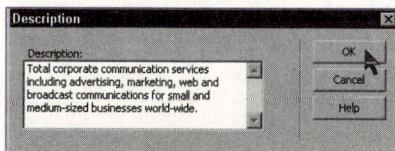

Figure 94-4: The Description dialog box

9. Save and close the page.

cross-reference

▪ See Task 18 in Part 1 for more information on meta content.

Preventing Your Site from Being Framed

note

- When a page that contains this JavaScript is linked from within a frame, it will automatically direct the browser to load it in the parent window (Step 4).

Users with a framed site can link to your site and have your site load into their frame. This often confuses people because they can't tell that an outside site page has loaded, since they are still in the same framed site. It is especially confusing if one of your interior pages loads without your frameset. You can prevent this from happening by writing a bit of JavaScript into the head of your document. This JavaScript is designed to break out of someone else's frames.

1. Open your frameset and click on Code view.

2. Near the top locate the `<head>` tag. Figure 95-1 shows the `<head>` section of the illustration.htm page from Task 93.

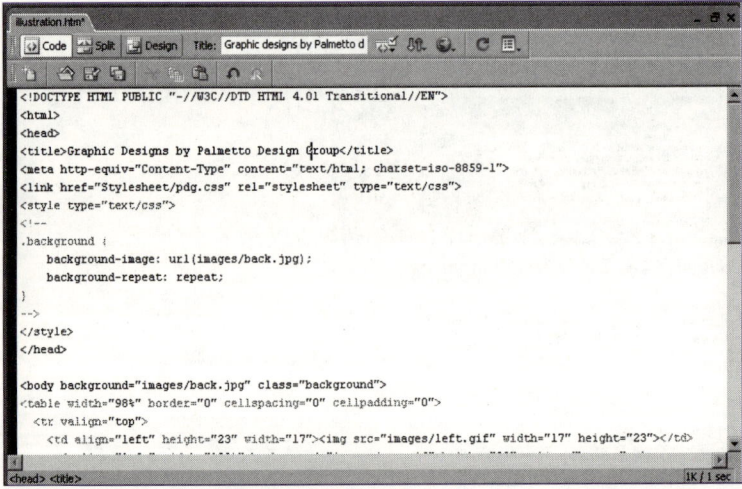

Figure 95-1: The `<head>` tag in code view

3. Place your cursor in front of the `</head>` tag (the closing head tag), press Enter/Return, and add the following code. For your convenience, a code.txt file is provided for you at www.wiley.com/ compbooks/10simplestepsorless in the task95 folder.

caution

- Copy the JavaScript code very carefully. A mistake can prevent your page from loading.

```
<script language='JavaScript' type='text/JavaScript'>
 if (top.location != self.location) {top.location =
self.location};
</script>
```

This code checks the `location` value (the URL) of the document in the browser window. If the `location` value of the `top` document in the browser doesn't match the `location` value of `self`, it means the page is framed and the script will do its magic and bust you out. Figure 95-2 shows how the added code should look.

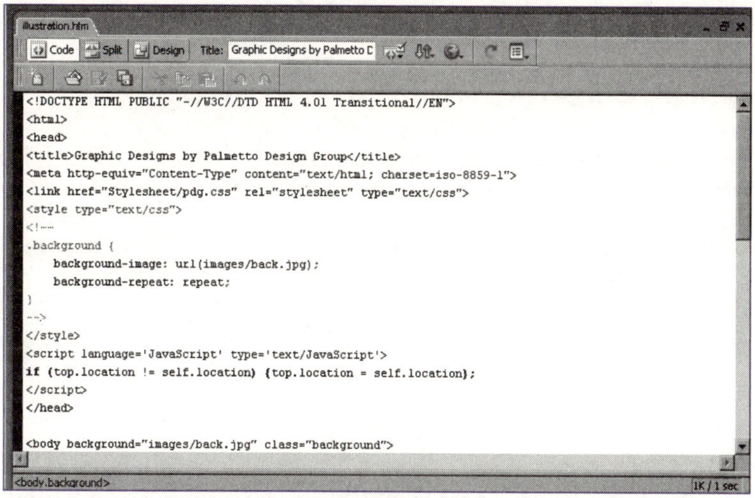

Figure 95-2: The code added to the head of the document

4. Add this code to every page in your site that you don't want to be framed. If you use a template for content pages, you'll only have to enter it once.

5. To do a quick test, you should upload a sample framed page to your site and link to a page that has this bit of JavaScript. Then click on the link and see if your page gets framed.

cross-references

- Refer to Task 96 to learn how to prevent your pages from loading without the frameset.

- Refer to Part 10 for working with templates (Step 4).

Preventing an Interior Page from Being Accessed without the Frameset

In Task 95 you learned how to prevent your site (framed or not) from being inserted into someone else's frames. But what happens if someone finds one of your interior page links? For example, let's say the search engine listed one of your content pages and someone clicked on it. The user would get the correct page, but most likely with no navigation or identifying information. Once you get a visitor to your site, you certainly don't want to lose the visitor for lack of navigation. You can prevent this by using a bit more JavaScript.

1. Open a page that goes into your frameset. The example is the contenthome.htm page from Task 93.

2. Open Code view and find the `<head>` tag near the top. This page already has a `<script>` tag that was added by Dreamweaver when setting a behavior. You can either type in another set of script tags or just insert the JavaScript into the section that is already there. Since it saves some typing, you'll no doubt do the latter.

3. Place your cursor in from of the word `function` and press the Enter/Return key. This is where you'll type in the line of JavaScript (see Figure 96-1).

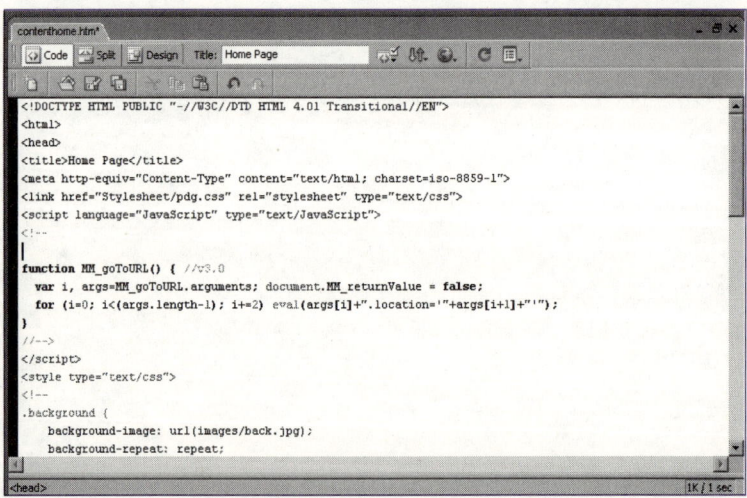

Figure 96-1: Ready to type JavaScript code into the document

4. Type this code, replacing "index.htm" with the name of your frameset—for example, task92set.htm—so it looks like the code in Figure 96-2.

```
if (top.location == self.location) {top.location =
'index.htm'};
```

Task **96**

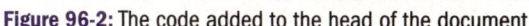

```
Illustration.htm*                                                    _ ∂ x
 Code   Split   Design   Title: Graphic Designs by Palmetto C   ⟳ M. ⊕.  C ▣.

<!DOCTYPE HTML PUBLIC "-//W3C//DTD HTML 4.01 Transitional//EN">
<html>
<head>
<title>Graphic Designs by Palmetto Design Group</title>
<meta http-equiv="Content-Type" content="text/html; charset=iso-8859-1">
<link href="Stylesheet/pdg.css" rel="stylesheet" type="text/css">
<style type="text/css">
<!--
.background {
    background-image: url(images/back.jpg);
    background-repeat: repeat;
}
-->
</style>
<script language='JavaScript' type='text/JavaScript'>
if (top.location != self.location) {top.location = self.location};
</script>
</head>

<body background="images/back.jpg" class="background">
<head>                                                          1K / 1 sec
```

Figure 96-2: The code added to the head of the document

5. This code checks to see if the location value (URL) of the topmost document in the browser window matches the location value of the document (self). If so, it is not framed and the entire frameset page is loaded into the browser window.

6. Test on your server. Type in the URL to a page within your frameset that you added this code to, and watch it load your frameset.

cross-references

▪ See Part 10 for using templates (Step 1).

▪ Task 95 shows how to add JavaScript code using the `<script></script>` tags (Step 2).

Part 5: Working with Forms

Adding a Form

Forms are useful when you want to interact with or collect information from a user. To use a form in Dreamweaver, you'll need a set of `<form>` tags, which you'll learn about in this task.

notes

- Forms require a script to process the form. Frequently, a CGI script is used and provided by your server. But you can also use server-side technologies such as ASP, ASP.NET, ColdFusion, PHP (PHP: Hypertext Preprocessor), or JSP (Step 1).

- The default method for the form is POST, which is most often used. Leave it selected in the Property inspector (Step 3).

- Form names should not contain any spaces. Use an underscore to separate words, and don't use any special characters (Step 5).

1. To prepare your workspace to add your first form, open a new, basic document by selecting HTML from the Create New column of the Start Page (File ⇨ New ⇨ Basic Page ⇨ HTML, and click Create). Then switch to Split view, as shown in Figure 97-1, so you can see the code as you enter your `<form>` tags.

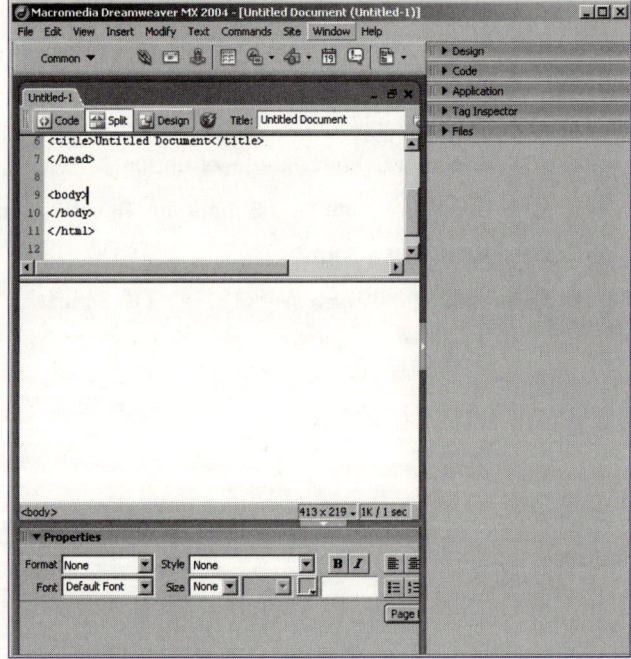

Figure 97-1: Split view

2. In the Insert bar, click the Forms category to access the Forms panel.

3. Click the Form icon and check the code. Notice the following code (also see Figure 97-2):

```
<form name="form1" method="post" action="">
</form>
```

4. You see a red dotted line in the document area. If you don't, choose View ⇨ Visual Aids ⇨ Invisible Elements. The red dots represent the form block that will contain your form elements, such as a text field.

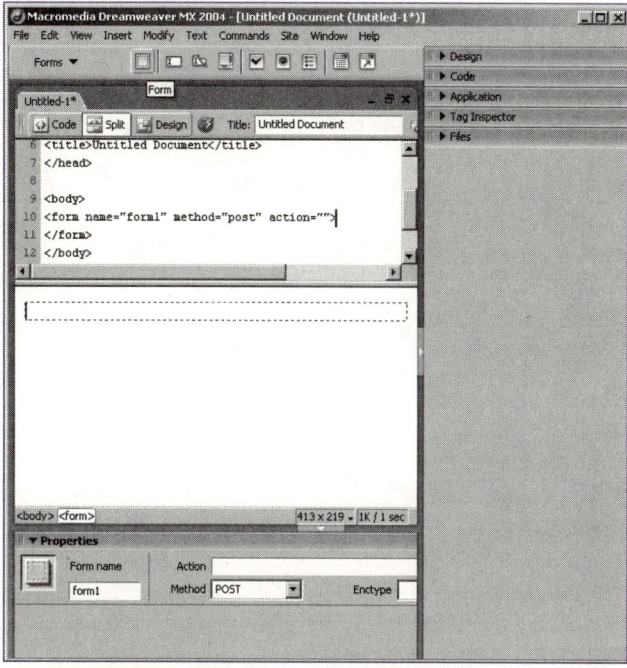

Figure 97-2: The Forms panel and the code in Split view

5. In the Property inspector on the left, you'll see a Form Name field, shown in Figure 97-3. Enter a name for the form. For this exercise, type **example_form**.

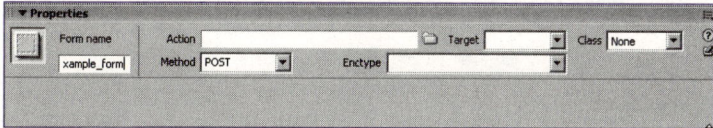

Figure 97-3: The Property inspector showing the Form Name field filled in

6. Check the code. You'll see that name and ID are added. Each contains the name example_form (or whatever name you enter in the Property inspector).

7. Save the file as **task97.htm**, or leave it open for the next task.

cross-references

• Form elements are added in Tasks 98 to 106 (Step 4).

• task97.htm is saved in the task97 folder on the Web site (Step 7).

Inserting Form Elements

In this task you use a table within the form block to line up the form elements neatly. A table isn't necessary, but it does make your form neater and easier to read.

1. Open the page that you created in Task 97, or open the task97.htm file from the partV task97 folder at www.wiley.com/compbooks/ 10simplestepsorless. Click inside the red dotted lines to place your cursor into the form block.

2. Choose Insert ➪ Table and use the following settings for the Insert Table dialog box (also see Figure 98-1):

   Rows: 8

   Columns: 2

   Cell Padding: 0

   Cell Spacing: 10

   Width: 500 Pixels

   Border: 1

   Click the OK button on the Insert Table dialog box.

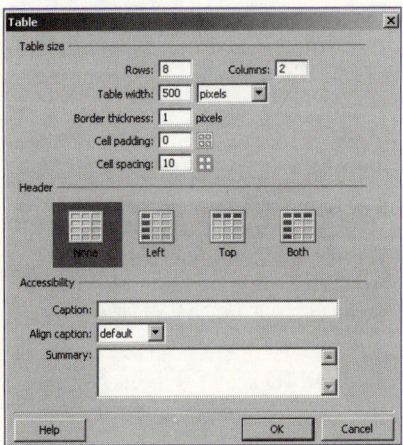

Figure 98-1: The Insert Table dialog box filled in

3. Click in the upper left cell of the first row to place your cursor. Type a label for a form element here. Type **Name** for this exercise.

4. Click in the right column of the first row. In the Forms panel (click the Forms category—or tab—in the Insert bar), click the Text Field icon.

5. While the text field is still active, look at the Property inspector. You'll see the available attributes for this element. In the TextField box, highlight the name and type **visitor_name** (or an appropriate name for your element), as shown in Figure 98-2.

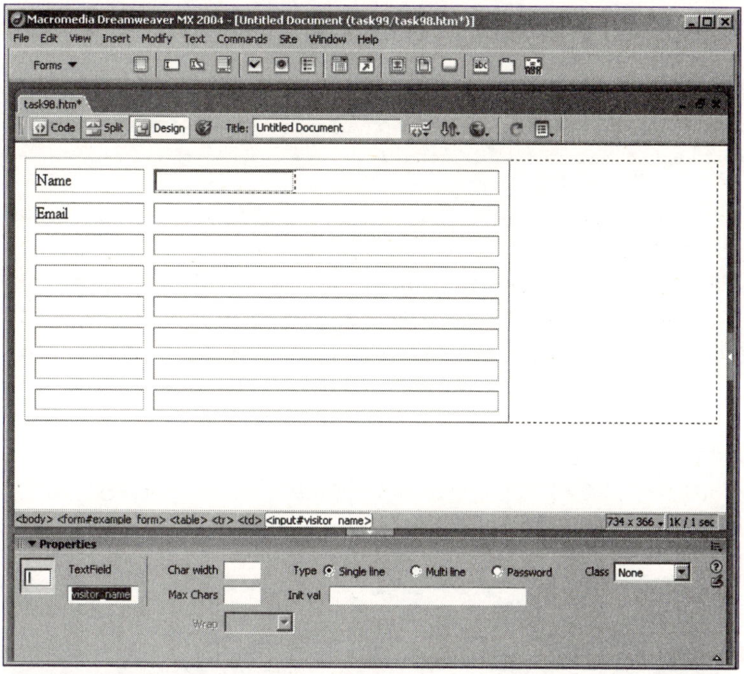

Figure 98-2: The TextField element added to the form and named in the Property inspector

6. To customize how wide the text field will be, type a number in the Char Width field in the Property inspector. For this exercise, type **30**. If you want to limit the amount of characters a user can type in, enter that amount into the Max Chars field.

7. Check the code. You see `size=30` has been added to the `<input>` tag.

8. Insert your cursor in the left cell of the second row and type **Email**. In the right column of the second row, insert another text field (Steps 3 to 6), changing the field name to **email**. Save as **task98.htm**.

cross-reference

▪ See the tasks in Part 3 for specific information on using tables (Step 1).

Adding a Form with Check Boxes

Check boxes are used in a form when you want a user to select one or more options. The exercise in this example uses the task98.htm file in the Part 5 task99 folder at www.wiley.com/compbooks/10simplestepsorless.

1. With the task98.htm file open, place your cursor in the left cell of the third row.

2. Type **Please send information on these services:** (or an appropriate label).

3. Place your cursor in the right cell of the third row, and click the Checkbox button in the Forms panel (Forms tab or category of the Insert bar).

4. While the check box is still selected, go to the Property inspector and type **web_design_services** in the CheckBox Name field, as shown in Figure 99-1.

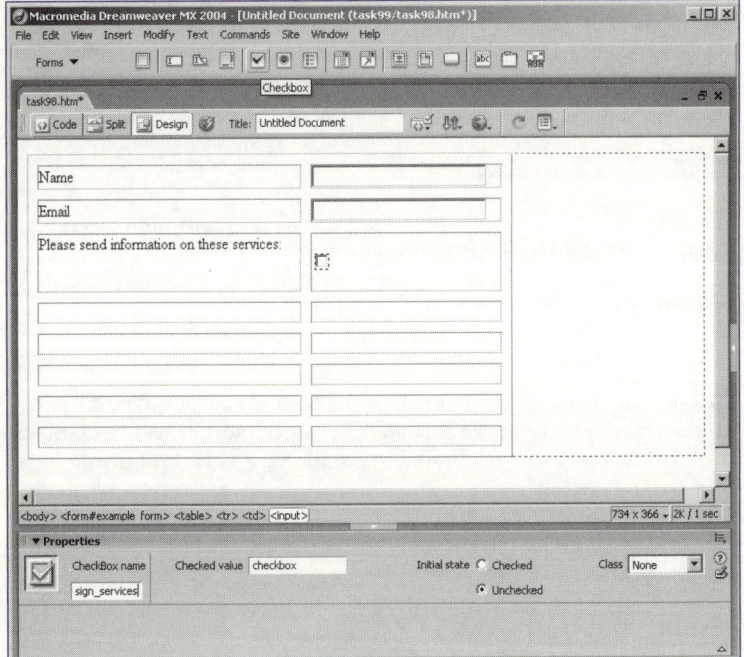

Figure 99-1: The label for the check box and the first check box added

5. In the CheckedValue field, type **web_design_services**.

6. Be sure the Initial State field has Unchecked selected, as shown in Figure 99-2.

7. In the document, to the right of the check box, type **Web Design Services**, as shown in Figure 99-3.

8. Press Shift+Enter/Return and add another check box. Repeat Steps 4 to 7, using the name **web_design_training**.

notes

- Whatever you type in the Checked Value field will be sent with the user's form data when this check box is selected (Step 6).

- Shift+Enter/Return adds a space (not a paragraph) between the check boxes. Enter/Return adds a paragraph space (Step 8).

- You can add as many check boxes as you desire. Users can then select as many as they want (Step 9).

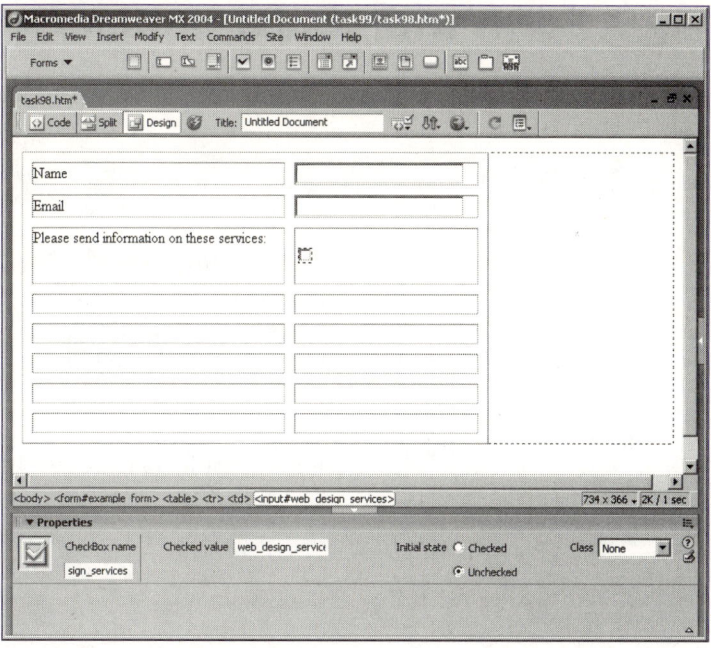

Figure 99-2: The Property inspector showing the attributes added for the first check box

9. Repeat Step 8 and substitute **Web Hosting**.

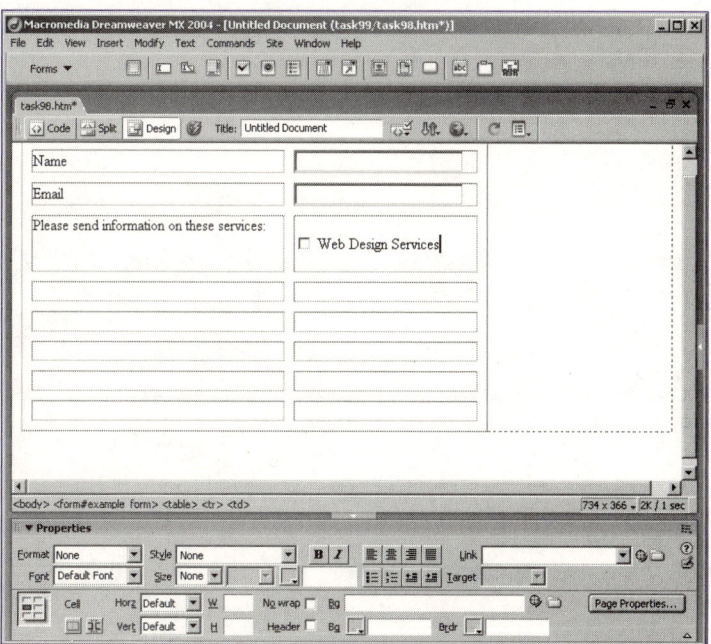

Figure 99-3: The first check box label and name are added

cross-reference

- Refer to Tasks 100 and 101 for adding radio buttons.

10. Save the file as **task99.htm**.

Adding a Form with Radio Buttons

Radio buttons are used when you want to limit the user to just one choice from a list of options.

1. Open the task99.htm file from the Part 5 task100 folder at www. wiley.com/compbooks/10simplestepsorless.

2. Place your cursor in the left cell of the fourth row and type **My organization is:**.

3. Place the cursor in the right side of the fourth row. From the Forms panel (Insert bar, Forms category or tab), click the Radio Button icon.

4. While the radio button is selected, go to the Property inspector. In the Radio Button field, type **organization**, as shown in Figure 100-1.

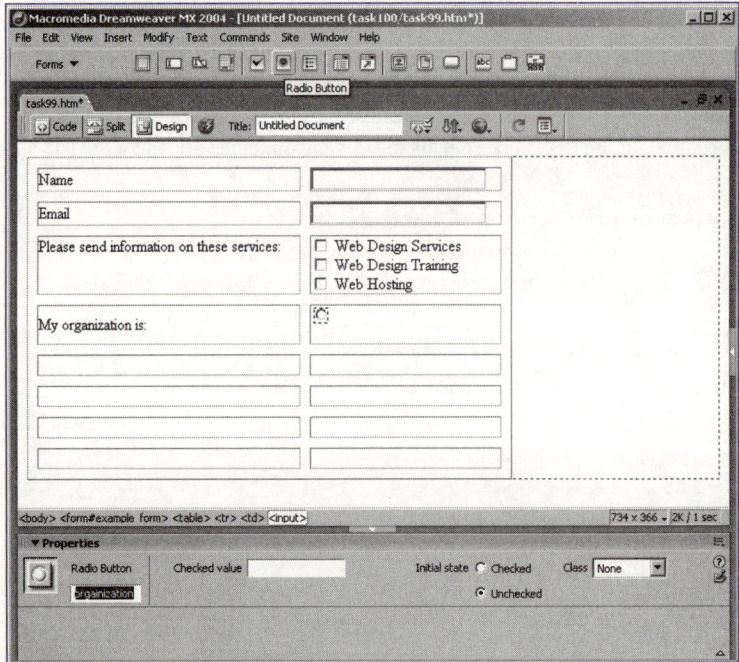

Figure 100-1: The label and first radio button added

5. In the Checked Value field, type **small_business** and leave Unchecked selected (see Figure 100-2).

6. In the document, type **Small Business** to the right of the radio button.

7. Press Shift+Enter/Return and repeat Step 4, then Step 5, except change the Checked Value to **corporation**. Repeat Step 6 and change to **Corporation**.

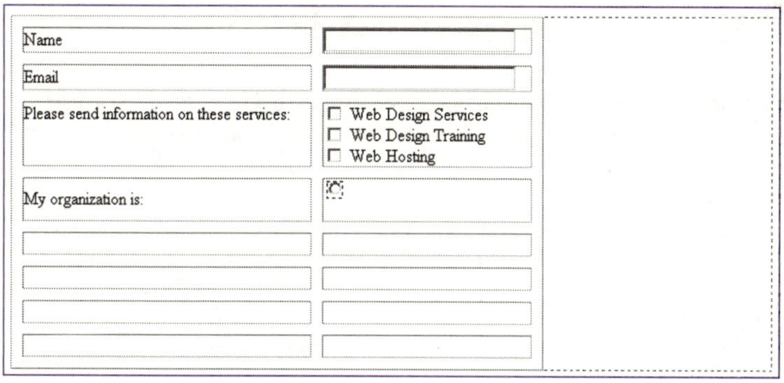

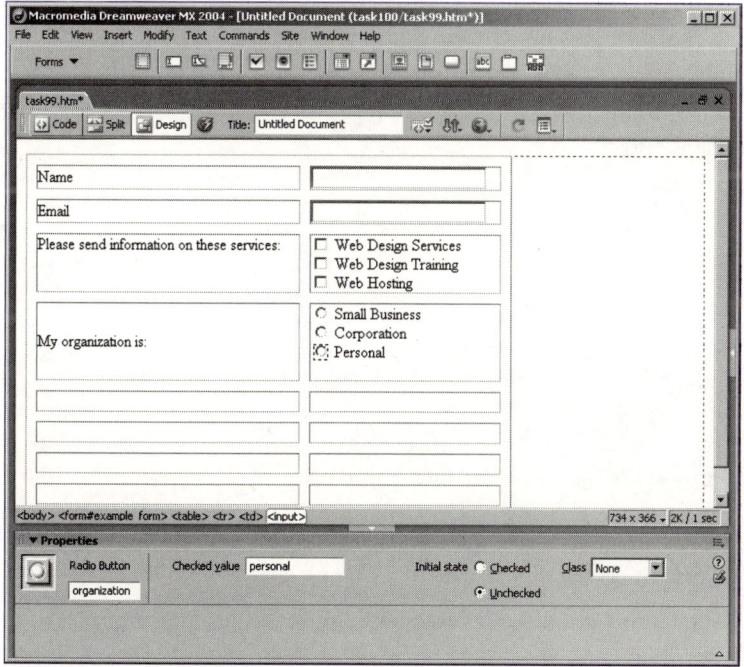

Figure 100-2: The Property inspector showing the Radio Button and the Checked Value fields filled in

8. Press Shift+Enter/Return and repeat Step 4, then Step 5, and change the Checked Value to **personal**. Repeat Step 6 and change to **Personal** (see Figure 100-3).

Figure 100-3: All three radio buttons completed

cross-references

- You can also use the Radio Button Group icon to add multiple options, as shown in Task 101 (Step 6).

- This form won't work as is. You'll need to add an action and method, as shown in Task 107 (Step 8).

Adding a Radio Button Group

There are two different methods for inserting radio buttons into a form. You can either use the single Radio Button or use the Radio Group option. You decide which is easier for you or suits your needs better.

1. Open task101.htm from the Part 5 task101 folder at `www.wiley. com/compbooks/10simplestepsorless`.

2. Place your cursor in the left cell of the fourth row and type **My organization is:**, as shown in Figure 101-1.

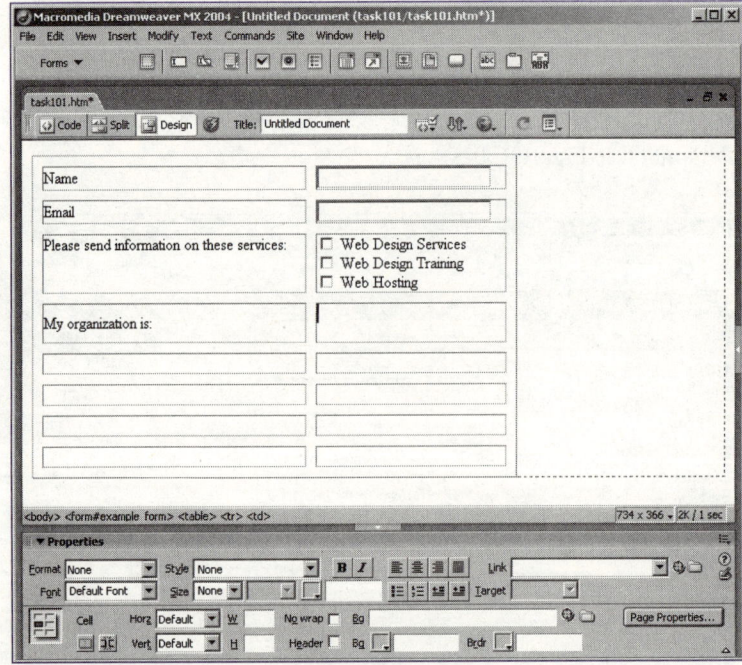

Figure 101-1: The label added for the radio buttons

3. Place the cursor in the right side of the fourth row. From the Forms panel (Insert bar, Forms category or tab), click the Radio Group icon.

4. The Radio Group dialog box opens. For the name, type **organization** (see Figure 101-2).

5. In the Label column, select the first word *radio*. Change the name to **Small Business**, as shown in Figure 101-3.

6. Press the Tab key to get to the value column, and type **small_business**.

7. Repeat Steps 5 and 6 for the next row, except change the label to **Corporation** and the value to **corporation**.

8. To add a third radio button (or more), click the plus sign (+) and type **Personal** for the label and **personal** for the value, as shown in Figure 101-4.

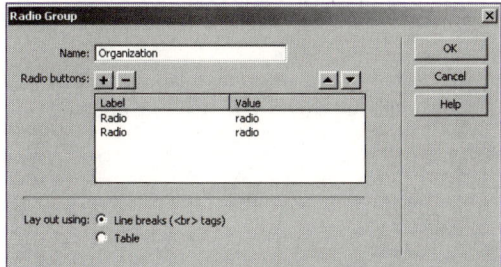

Figure 101-2: The Radio Group dialog box with all the buttons filled in

9. At the bottom of the dialog box, select Layout Using Line Breaks (`<br>` tags).

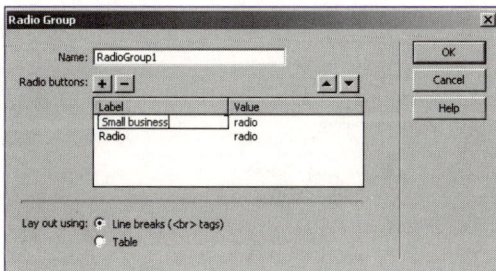

Figure 101-3: The label named for the first radio button in the group

10. Click OK to close the Radio Group dialog box.

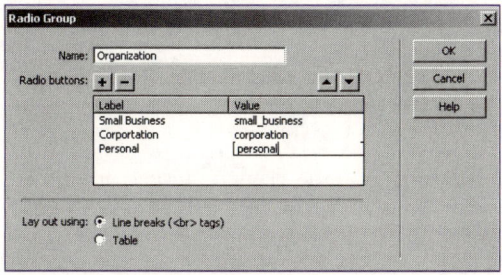

Figure 101-4: All three radio button labels and values set

cross-reference

▪ Refer to Task 100 for inserting individual radio buttons.

Task **102**

Adding a Drop-Down Form List

A drop-down form list shows one line of text—usually a description of the menu. When users click on the menus down arrow, they are presented with a list from which they can select one or multiple options.

notes

- Notice in the Property inspector that the height is 1. This means one line of text will show. Also note that you can choose to select an option that allows the users to select multiple options (Step 5).

- The value is typically the same as the item label, but it doesn't have to be (Step 7).

- You can rearrange any item by selecting it and pressing the up or down arrow in the List Values dialog box (Step 8).

- You can always edit the list values by clicking the List Values button in the Property inspector (Step 9).

1. Open task101.htm from the Part 5 task102: folder at www.wiley. com/compbooks/10simplestepsorless.

2. Place your cursor in the left cell of row 5 and type a label name of **Select the option that best describes who you are** into the cell.

3. Place your cursor in the right cell of row 5.

4. From the Insert bar, Forms category or tab, click the List/Menu icon (see Figure 102-1).

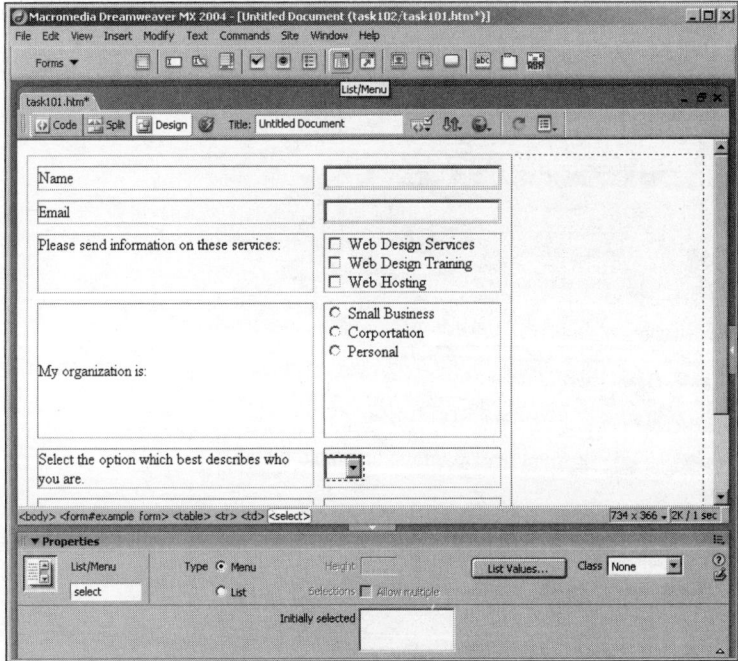

Figure 102-1: The drop-down form list added to a form

5. While the menu is still selected, go to the Property inspector. In the List/Menu field, name your list **who_I_am**. In the Type area, select List, as shown in Figure 102-2.

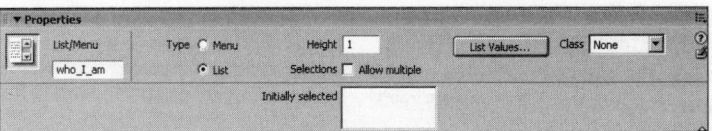

Figure 102-2: The Property inspector showing the options for the drop-down list/menu

Task **102**

6. To add the list items, click the List Values button in the Property inspector. The List Values dialog box opens.

7. Click under the Item Label text and type a name for your list. For this exercise, type **Who I am**. Click under the value and type **who I am** (see Figure 102-3).

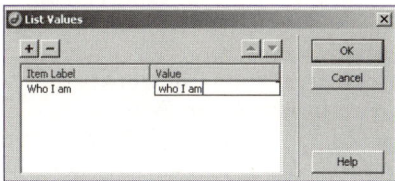

Figure 102-3: The List Values dialog box showing the name of the list

8. Click the plus sign (+) to add more item labels and values. You can use these if you'd like:

> **Individual** (value: who_individual)
>
> **Corporation** (value: who_corporation)
>
> **Student** (value: who_student)

9. When you are finished adding items, click OK to close the List Values dialog box. Figure 102-4 shows the filled in List Values; you can also see the menu in the form.

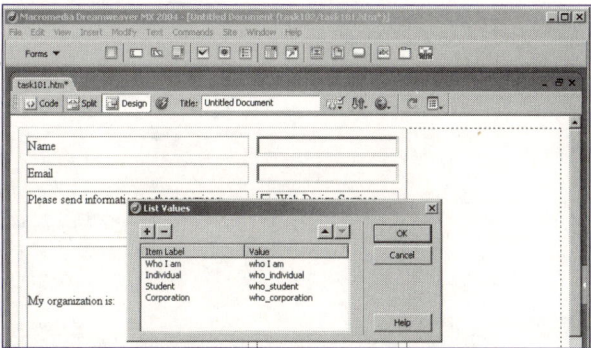

Figure 102-4: The List Values dialog box filled in for this exercise

10. In the Property inspector, select the menu description (Who I am) for the Initially Selected field. Save the file as **task102.htm**.

cross-reference

- See Task 103 for a scrolling list that allows multiple selections and shows more than one line of text.

Task 103

Adding a Scrolling List

A scrolling list is useful because it can display one or more options, and then offer users even more options if they scroll through a list.

1. Open task102.htm from the Part 5 task103 folder at `www.wiley.com/compbooks/10simplestepsorless`.

2. Place your cursor in the left cell of row 6, and type a label name and the following instructions: **PC users, press your Control key and select all options you'd like more information on. Mac users, press the Command key and click.**

3. Place your cursor in the right cell of row 6.

4. From the Insert bar, Forms category or tab, click the List/Menu icon.

5. While the menu is still selected, go to the Property inspector. In the List/Menu field, name it **information**. For the Type, select List; for the Height, type in **4**; then select Allow Multiple for the Selections option, as shown in Figure 103-1.

notes

- In the Label area, you can move from field to field by pressing the Tab key. To add or delete a field, press the plus or minus signs (Step 6).

- The value is typically the same as the item label, but it doesn't have to be. I add a prefix to indicate what the form information is so it can be identified when received (Step 7).

- You can rearrange any item by selecting it and pressing the up or down arrow in the List Values dialog box (Step 8).

- You can always edit the list values by clicking the List Values button in the Property inspector (Step 9).

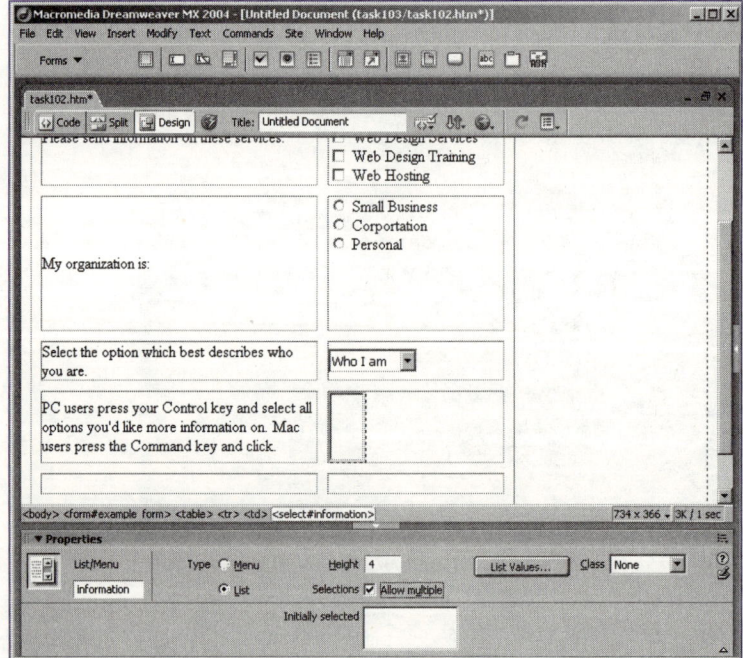

Figure 103-1: The Property inspector showing the options for the drop-down list/menu

6. To add the list items, click the List Values button in the Property inspector. The List Values dialog box opens.

7. Click under the Item Label text and type your first item. For this exercise, type **Web Design Services**. This is the name that will be visible in the browser. Click under the value and type **web design services** (see Figure 103-2). This is what you'll see when the form is received.

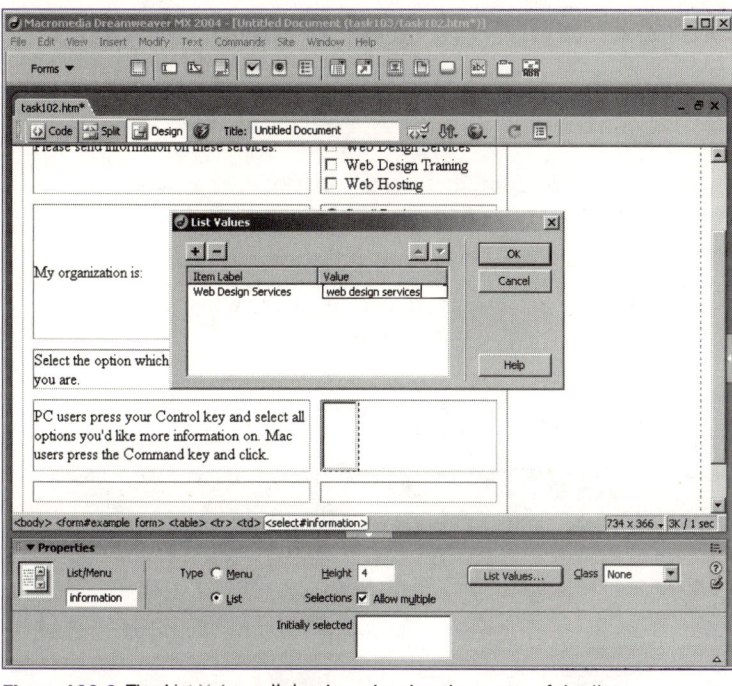

Figure 103-2: The List Values dialog box showing the name of the list

8. Click the plus sign (+) to add more item labels and values (use the Tab key). If you'd like, you can use the following, using the same name for both the item label and the value (except add **info** in front of the label name for the value):

> Dynamic Web sites
>
> Static Web sites
>
> Hosting
>
> Web design training
>
> Flash training
>
> Dreamweaver training
>
> Server technologies

9. When you are finished adding items, click OK to close the List Values dialog box.

10. In the Property inspector, in the Initially Selected field, Shift+select the first four items you want to be seen initially. Or Ctrl/Command+click any four items you want to be visible initially. Also be sure that Allow Multiple is selected. Save the file as **task103.htm**.

cross-reference

- See Task 102 for a drop-down list.

Adding a Submit and Reset Button

The Submit button is used to actually send your form.

1. Open task103.htm from the Part 5 task104 folder at `www.wiley.com/compbooks/10simplestepsorless`.

2. Place your cursor in the right cell of the row 8.

3. From the Insert bar, Forms tab click the Button button. Figure 104-1 shows the button added to the form.

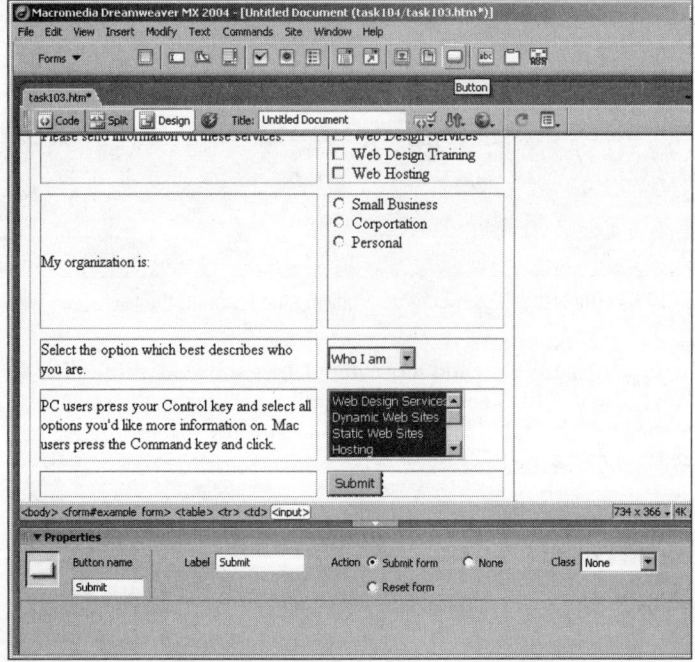

Figure 104-1: The button added to the form

4. Select the button in the document.

5. In the Property inspector, leave the button name Submit. In the Label field, change it to **Send Now**, as shown in Figure 104-2.

6. In the Property inspector, for the Action option, select Submit Form (see Figure 104-3).

7. Place your cursor to the right of the Send Now button; press the spacebar to add a space.

8. In the Forms category, select the Button button.

9. In the Property inspector, change the button name to **Reset**. In the Label field, change it to **Reset Form**.

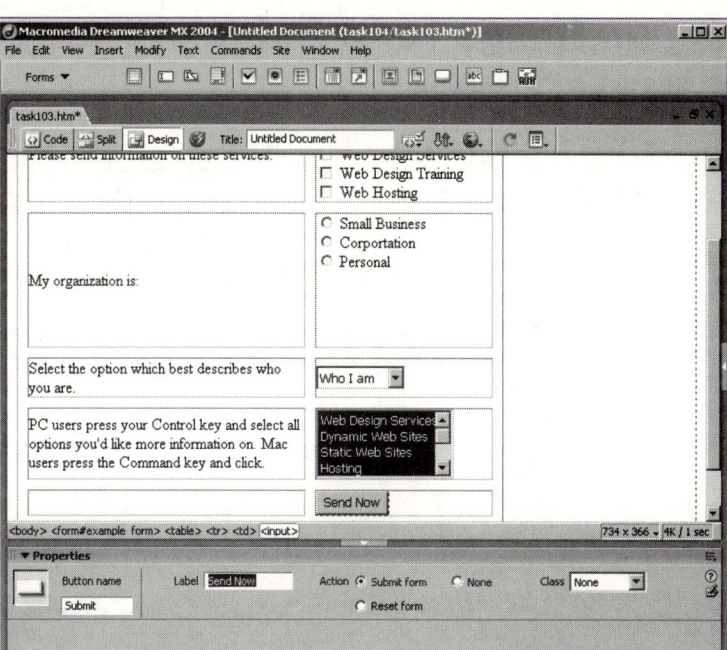

Figure 104-2: The Property inspector showing the button attributes

10. For the Action option, select Reset Form (button is shown in Figure 104-3), and save the file as **task104.htm**.

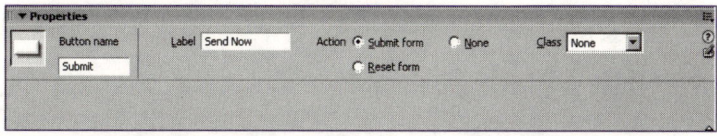

Figure 104-3: The Submit Form action selected in the Property inspector

cross-reference

- Refer to Task 105 for using an image instead of the default button (Step 2).

Using an Image for a Submit and Reset Button

You can use your own custom images for Submit and Reset buttons. Two are provided for you in the folder in the Part 5 task105 folder at www.wiley.com/compbooks/10simplestepsorless.

1. Copy the task105 folder to your hard drive. Open the task105.htm file from this folder.

2. Place your cursor in the right cell of row 8.

3. In the Insert bar, Forms tab, click the Image Field icon.

4. Navigate to the task105 folder and select btn_submit.gif, as shown in Figure 105-1. Click OK.

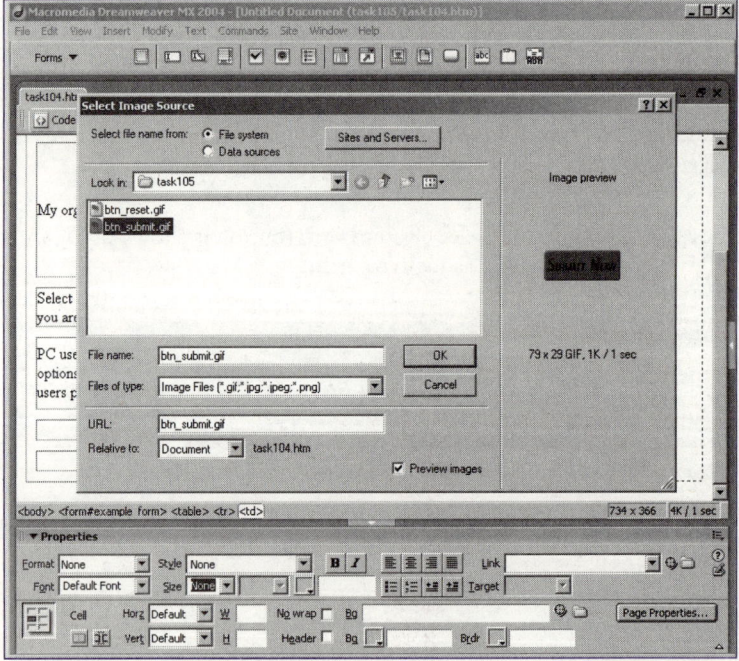

Figure 105-1: The button image being selected

5. With the button selected, go to the Property inspector. Change the ImageField name to **Submit**.

6. Add alt text of **Submit the form now**, as shown in Figure 105-2.

7. Place your cursor to the right of the Submit button and add a space.

8. Repeat Steps 3 to 6, using the btn_reset.gif, ImageField name of **Reset** and alt text of **Reset the form**.

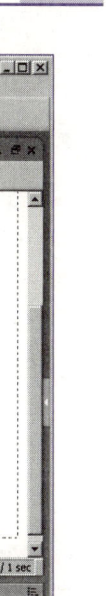

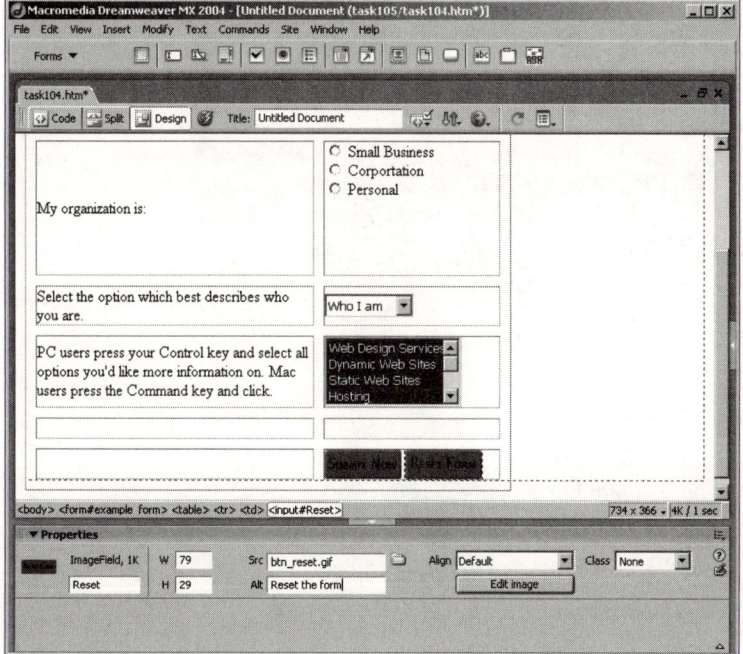

Figure 105-2: The Property inspector showing the attributes of the image

9. Save the file as **task105.htm**.

cross-reference

- Refer to Task 104 for using standard Submit and Reset buttons with no images.

Figure 105-3: The Reset and Submit graphic buttons added to the form

Task **106**

Validating a Form

Validating a form is done using a Dreamweaver behavior. The validation is performed client-side, which means that the form entries are checked prior to the form actually being sent. The Validate Form behavior checks specified text fields to be sure the user filled in certain fields or provided a specific type of data.

notes

- The Validate Form behavior does not need to be attached just to a button but can be attached to any text field or the entire form. To attach to the form, select the <form> tag using the Tag Selector (Step 2).

- Since the behavior will only work on text fields, any text fields you have in the document will be listed in the Named Fields area (Step 5).

- When you select Email Address, the validation will check for the proper formatting, including an @ symbol (Step 9).

- To test the validation, open the saved file in a browser and skip the name. Then press Submit (Step 5).

1. Open task106.htm from the Part 5 task106 folder, which is located at `www.wiley.com/compbooks/10simplestepsorless`.

2. Select the Send Now button.

3. Open the Behaviors panel. It's grouped in the Tag Inspector panel group. If you don't see it, choose Window ➪ Behaviors or Shift+F3 to open the Behaviors panel (see Figure 106-1).

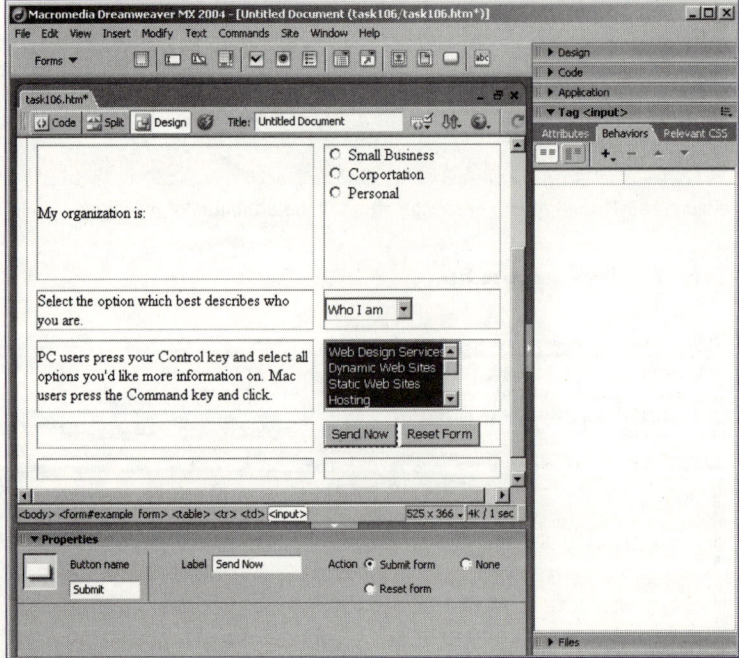

Figure 106-1: The Behaviors panel

4. Click the plus sign (+) and select Validate Form, as shown in Figure 106-2.

5. The Validate Form dialog box opens. Select the "text 'visitor_name' in form 'example_form'" line in the Named Fields area.

6. Select Value: Required to require a name.

7. Select Accept: Anything (see Figure 106-3).

8. Select "the text 'email' in form 'example_form'" line.

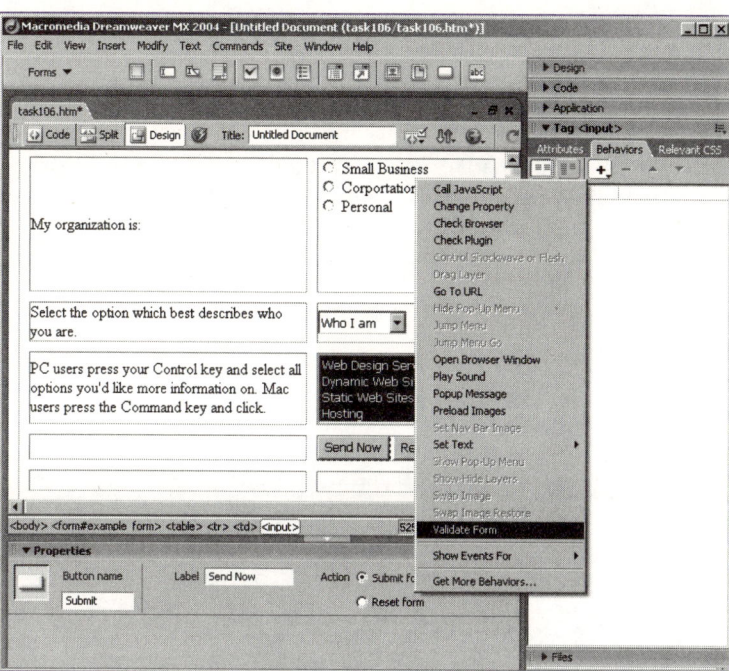

Figure 106-2: The Behaviors menu

9. Select Value: Required and Accept: Email Address.

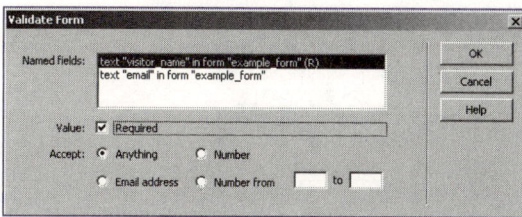

Figure 106-3: The Validate Form dialog box with the values filled in for the name field

10. Click OK and save as **task107.htm**. Figure 106-4 shows the Validate Form dialog box filled in for the Email Address field.

cross-reference

• Refer to Task 98 for adding text fields.

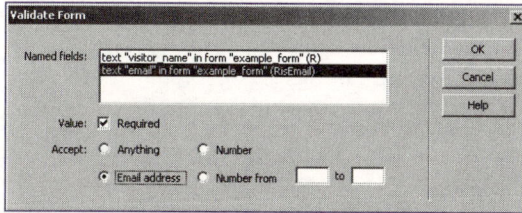

Figure 106-4: The Validate Form dialog box with the values filled in for the Email Address field

Making the Form Work Using a CGI Script

notes

• Data is collected from input fields or menus, lists, radio buttons, or check boxes.

• The standards are determined by the W3C (World Wide Web Consortium). You can find them at www.w3.org.

• The form methods are as follows:

POST. Embeds the form data in the HTTP request and is the most secure option.

GET. Limited to a total of 8,192 characters. If the amount of characters exceeds this number, it will result in errors. Because values are readily visible in URLs, it isn't a very secure method of sending.

DEFAULT. Uses the browser's preferred or default method, which is usually the GET method.

In this section you've learned how to make a form. You'll need to add a method and an action to the `<form>` tag to make it work—or to get the form to submit the entered information to you.

1. Open task106.htm from the Part 5 task106 folder, which is located at www.wiley.com/compbooks/10simplestepsorless.

2. Click anywhere in the form and select the `<form>` tag from the Tag Selector, as shown in Figure 107-1. Notice also that the Property inspector has changed to reflect the form properties.

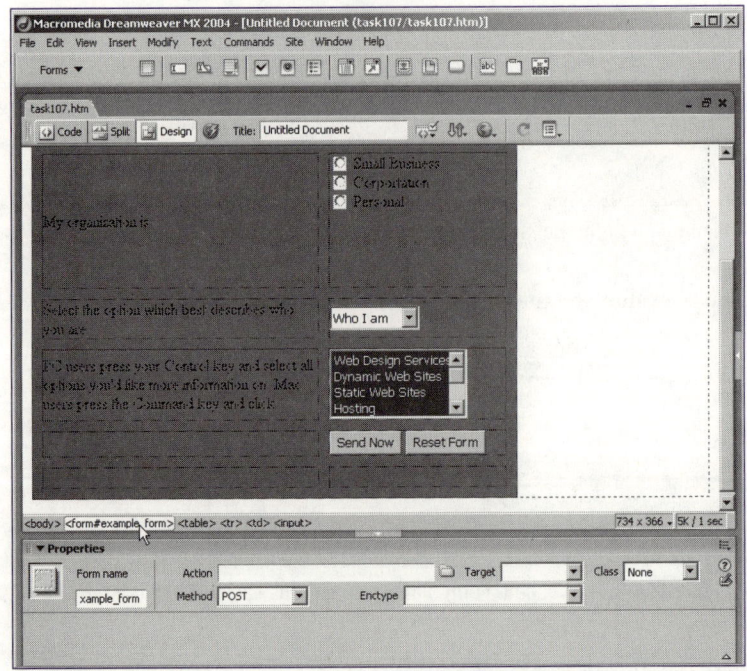

Figure 107-1: The `<form>` tag selected and the Property inspector showing the form properties

3. In the Action field, you can simply add an e-mail address using mailto:, as shown in Figure 107-2, but this is not recommended. It's not a secure method of transferring data.

4. The preferred action is to link to a CGI FormMail script. Most hosting companies have a standard CGI FormMail script, so you'll need to get the URL from your hosting server. These scripts can send the form's data to multiple recipients and even link to a thank-you page after they submit.

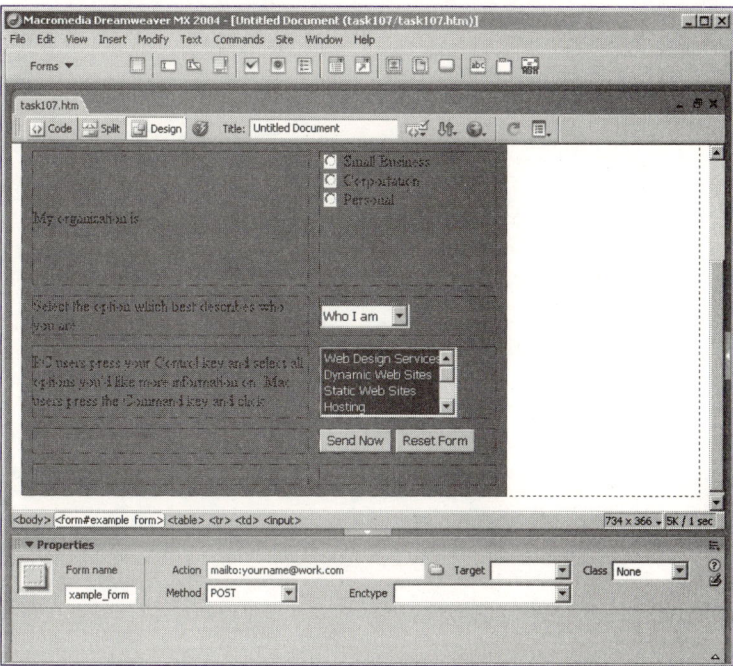

Figure 107-2: The mailto: method of submitting the form

Task 107

tip
- Dreamweaver also has a target option to specify the destination browser location (blank window, parent window, etc.) to be used.

5. The next bit of information you need is the method you want to use to transmit the data to the server. There are several, as shown in Figure 107-3. For this example, select POST.

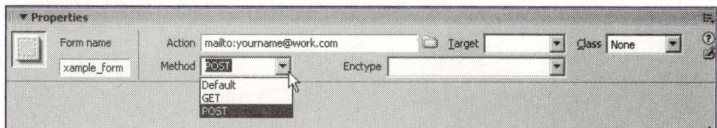

Figure 107-3: The list of available form methods, as shown in the Property inspector

6. In the Property inspector, select a MIME type for the data that is submitted. The standard option is application/x-www-form-urlen-code and is used with the POST method, so select it, as shown in Figure 107-4.

cross-reference
- In Part 13 you'll see how to use forms to add information to a database or retrieve information from a database.

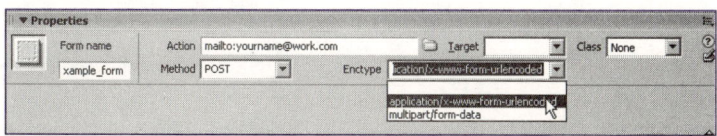

Figure 107-4: The standard MIME option set

Part 6: Working with Layers

Drawing or Inserting a Layer

Adding a layer to your document is pretty simple using Dreamweaver. You can do it visually or by the numbers.

1. Open a new document or one you'd like to add a layer to.

2. To draw a layer, use the Insert bar and select the Layout category from the menu. Select the Draw Layer icon, as shown in Figure 108-1.

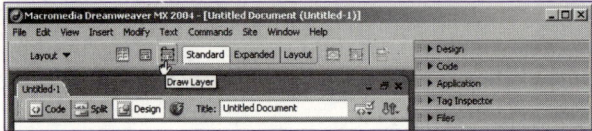

Figure 108-1: The Insert bar showing the Layout category and its objects

3. The cursor has changed to a crosshair. Drag to draw a layer any size, and release the mouse when done.

4. The small box on the outside (top left corner) is the selection handle (see Figure 108-2). You can click and drag to move the entire layer.

5. A yellow anchor is added for each layer. If you don't see it, choose View ⇨ Visual Aids ⇨ Invisible Elements. The anchors show you the position of the code. If the anchors are at the top of the page, the `<div ID>` tags will be below the `<body>` tag.

6. Click the selection handle to select the layer.

Handle

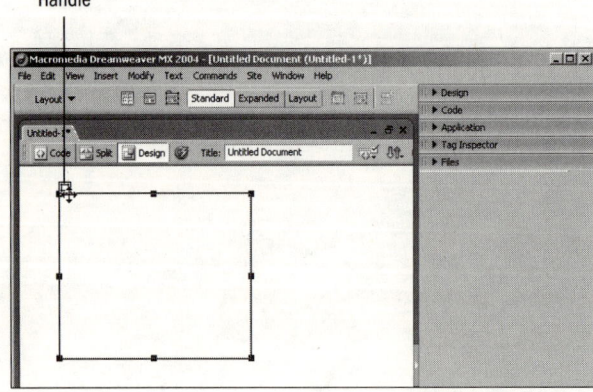

Figure 108-2: The selection handle used to move the layer

7. Check the code. You see that name and ID are added. Each contains the name of example_form (or whatever name you enter in the Property inspector).

8. When the layer is selected, you'll see eight black resize handles. You can click and drag to alter the layer's size.

9. To insert a layer, click to place your cursor where you want the layer, then choose Insert ⇨ Layout Object ⇨ Layer. The default layer size (Edit ⇨ Preferences) is added to the document.

10. Click inside a layer, choose Insert ⇨ Image, and navigate to the image you want to insert. Or you can simply type inside the layer to add text, as shown in Figure 108-3. You can do anything in a layer that you can do in any HTML page.

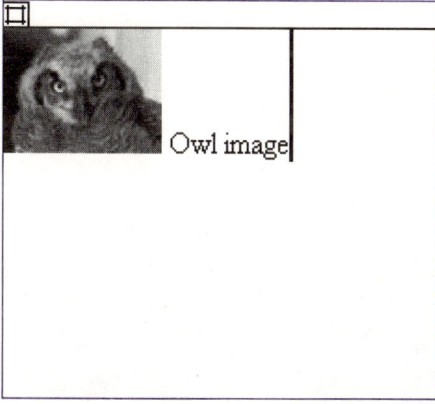

Figure 108-3: An image and text added to a layer

cross-reference

▪ Refer to Task 110 for setting a layer's default properties (Step 9).

Using CSS Layers from Fireworks

A real time-saving function in Fireworks is the ability to export images from Fireworks as CSS layers. Once exported, they can then be imported into Dreamweaver as layers with the content already in the layers.

1. In Fireworks put your content either into separate layers or frames. If all your objects are in one layer, you can select what you want to move to layers, and then select Commands ⇨ Document ⇨ Distribute to Layers.

2. Or if you want each object in a separate frame, select all objects, and then from the Frames Options pop-up menu, select Distribute to Frames, as shown in Figure 109-1.

Figure 109-1: Distributing objects into separate frames via the Frames Options pop-up menu

3. Once the images are in separate layers or frames, choose File ⇨ Export, and from the Save as Type menu, select CSS Layers. From the Source menu, select Layers or Frames. Click Save when you've finished with all the options (see Figure 109-2).

4. In Dreamweaver, open the document you want to import the CSS layers to. In the Common category of the Insert bar, from the Image menu, select Fireworks HTML (see Figure 109-3). Or choose Insert ⇨ Image Objects ⇨ Fireworks HTML.

5. Navigate to the folder you exported the CSS layers to, and select the HTM file. You can delete the original file after insertion if you want. When you are done, click OK.

6. Open the Layers panel with F2, or open it from the Design panel group. Notice that all the layers you exported are now layers in this document.

7. Select one of the layers and notice in your document that the layer is selected and the layer handle is visible, as shown in Figure 109-4. This is a quick and easy way to get images already in layers into Dreamweaver.

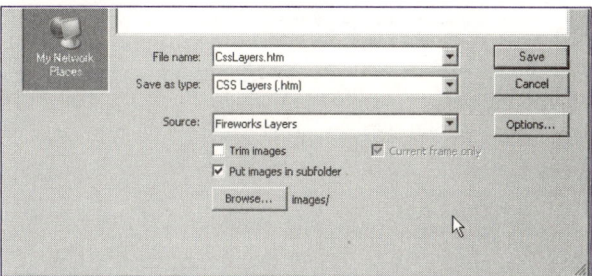

Figure 109-2: Exporting as CSS Layers from Fireworks

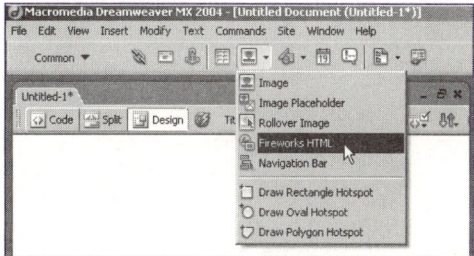

Figure 109-3: The Insert Fireworks HTML option in the Insert bar

8. Change the ID name in the Property inspector for each layer. By default, the Fireworks name is given to the layer and the ID is the same. Each ID has to be unique, so you'll need to change it.

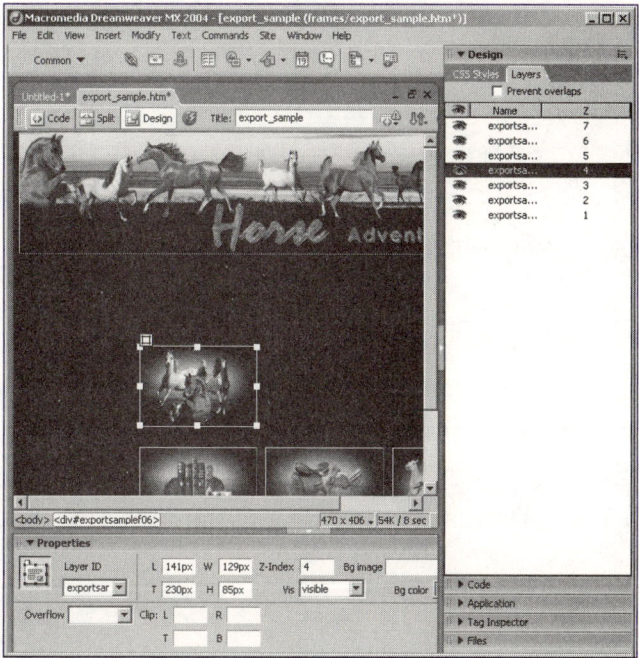

Figure 109-4: The layers imported into Dreamweaver and ready for positioning and for styles to be added

tip

▪ ID names can't be the same as layer names.

cross-reference

▪ Refer to Tasks 179 to 181 for positioning layers using CSS styles.

Setting Layer Properties

Y ou can control quite a few properties for a layer. For instance, you can set a layer's position, its visibility, and its size.

1. Draw or insert a layer.

2. In the Property inspector, locate the Layer ID field. Type in a one-word name, with no spaces or special characters, as shown in Figure 110-1.

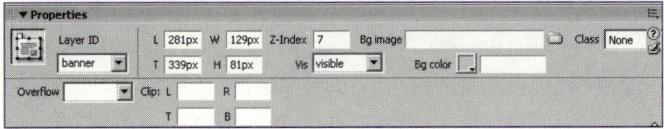

Figure 110-1: The Layers Property inspector showing the layer named

3. The default tag for a layer is `<div>`. The other option is `<span>`. These two tags make the layer work in both Netscape 4.x and Internet Explorer 4 and up browsers.

4. Now set the position of the layer. To specify how far from the left edge you want the layer to be, enter a value in pixels in the L field in the Layers Property inspector. Then set the position for the top of the layer in the T field, as shown in Figure 110-2.

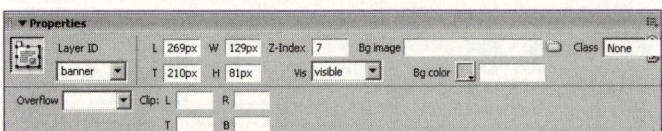

Figure 110-2: The layer's position, as shown in a Dreamweaver document and the Property inspector

5. If you want to specify a specific width and height, enter it into the W and H fields in the Layers Property inspector.

6. The Z-Index field determines the stacking order of the layers. The highest number is on top. Change the number to the order you'd like.

7. You can add background images to layers. With the layer selected, go to the Layers Property inspector and click the Browse button to navigate to the image you want to use for the background. Figure 110-3 shows a background image path in the Property inspector.

notes

- You don't have to change the default layer name of a layer (layer1, etc.), but giving them meaningful names makes locating a specific layer easier (Step 2).

- The name is coded as ID. ID is a CSS selector and can be used for any script that references this layer (Step 2).

- The `<span>` tag is an inline wrapper for a small amount of content (Step 3).

- You can visually set the position by dragging a layer where you want it. The L and T coordinates are added automatically (Step 4).

- Instead of an image background, you can add a color background by clicking the Bg color box and selecting a color (Step 7).

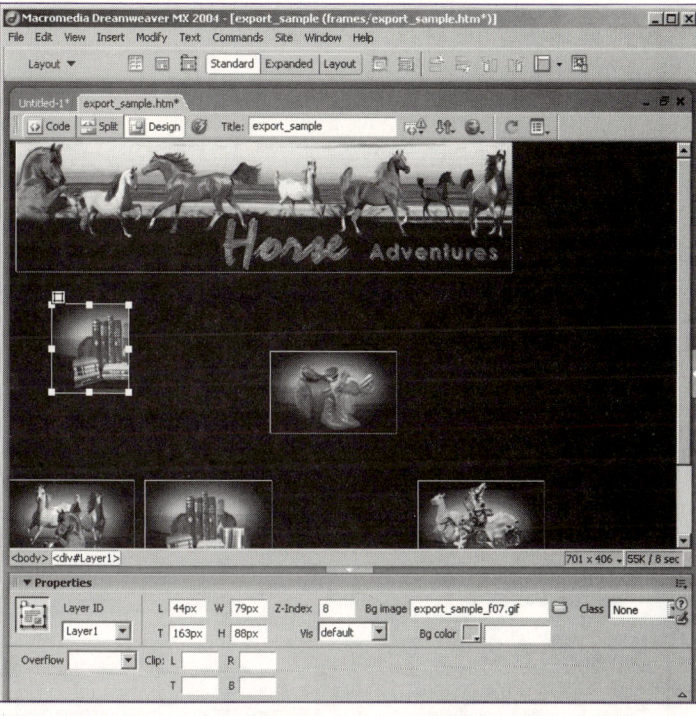

Figure 110-3: The Property inspector showing a background image added

8. In most browsers, the default visibility of a layer (Default) is that it is visible. To be sure every browser interprets this setting correctly, select Visible from the Vis field. To hide the layer, select Hidden.

9. Select one of the overflow options. These options control what happens to content if it doesn't all fit in a layer. Some browsers render the content differently, especially when the overflow is text. The options are as follows:

> *Visible.* The layer's size increases if needed to show all the content even if it covers another layer.

> *Hidden.* The content that doesn't fit won't be seen.

> *Scroll.* Browsers that support layer scroll bars will have a scroll bar to access overflow content.

> *Auto.* The scroll bar will appear if needed by browsers that support layer scroll bars.

10. In the Clip fields, enter the left (L) and top (T) and right (R) and bottom (B) coordinates of the area of the layer you want to be visible. Remember that these coordinates are relative to the layer, not to the document.

cross-references

- See Task 108 for drawing and inserting layers (Step 1).

- See Task 111 for using the Layers panel to rearrange layers (Step 6).

Managing Layers

When you have a lot of layers or if layers are on top of each or invisible, it gets quite difficult to select or move them. The easiest way to access a specific layer is by using the Layers panel.

notes

- When the layer is invisible and you select it in the Layers panel, it becomes visible. But the code isn't changed. As soon as you select another layer (or deselect the current layer), it returns to invisible (Step 3).

- You can visually set the position by dragging a layer where you want it. The L and T coordinates are added automatically.

1. Open any document with multiple layers. If you need a file to practice on, download the task111 folder from the Part 6 folder at www.wiley.com/compbooks/10simplesteps.

2. To access the Layers panel, choose Window ➾ Layers or press F2. The Advanced panel group opens, and the Layers panel is active. You'll see all layers in the document listed, as shown in Figure 111-1.

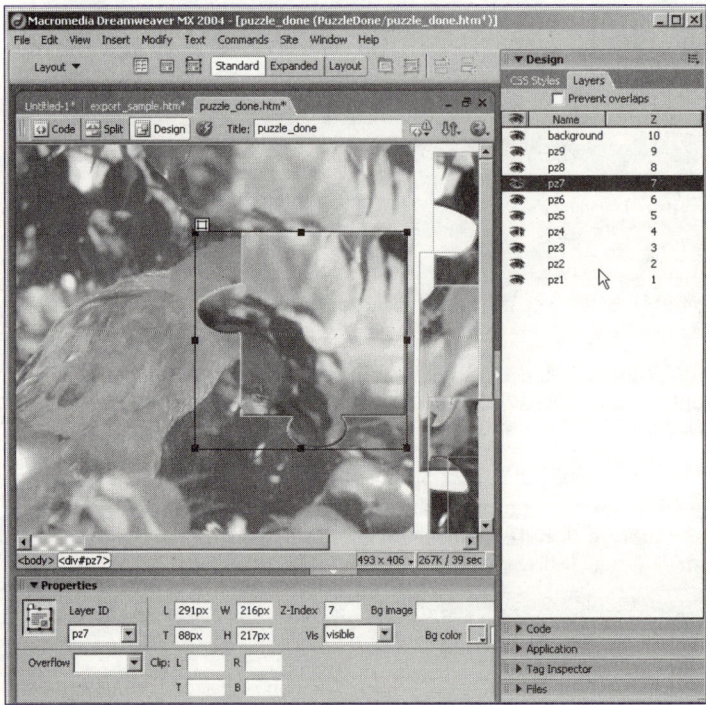

Figure 111-1: The Layers panel

3. Click any layer to select it. You'll see the selected layer in the document even if it's invisible.

4. If you want to change the visibility code, you can click the eye icon to toggle between visible and invisible, as shown in Figure 111-2.

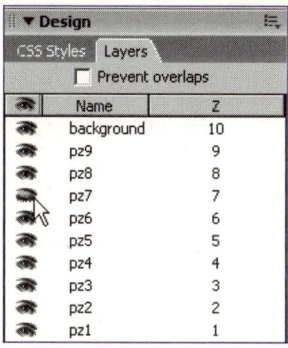

Figure 111-2: The visibility of a layer toggled off in the Layers panel

5. It's a good idea to give each layer a unique name other than layer 1, layer 2, and so forth. To name a layer, you can enter it in the Layer ID field when you create the layer (or select it) or you can double-click its name in the Layers panel and type in a new name, as shown in Figure 111-3.

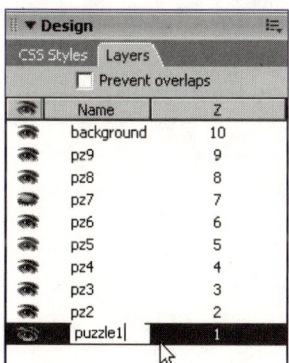

Figure 111-3: The layer name double-clicked and a new name entered

6. To change the stacking order (which layer is on top and in front), you can click and drag it to a new position in the Layers panel. The Z column lists the z-index position of each layer. The higher the number, the closer to the top. Or the Z layer can be changed in the Property inspector, as shown in Figure 111-4.

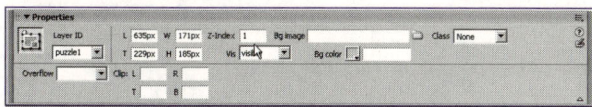

Figure 111-4: The z-index in the Property inspector

cross-reference

▪ Refer to Task 116 for hiding and showing layers.

Aligning Layers Using Rulers and Grids

Dreamweaver provides rulers and grids to help you align your layers with precision. Any layer nested inside another will move with the parent layer.

1. To turn on rulers, choose View ➪ Show. The rulers are visible in the document, as shown in Figure 112-1.

Figure 112-1: Rulers visible in the document

2. To select the unit desired, choose View ➪ Show and select either Pixels or Inches.

3. For a grid, choose View ➪ Grid ➪ Show Grid (see Figure 112-2).

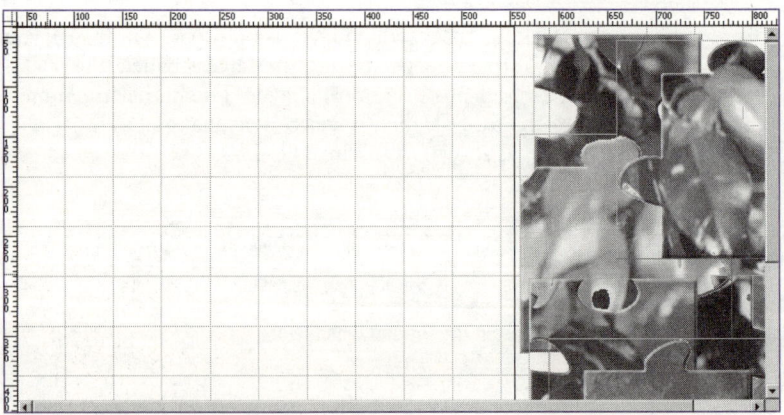

Figure 112-2: The rulers and the grid are visible

4. To change the default settings of the grid, choose View ➪ Grid ➪ Grid Settings (see Figure 112-3).

5. To change the grid color, click in the color box and select a color.

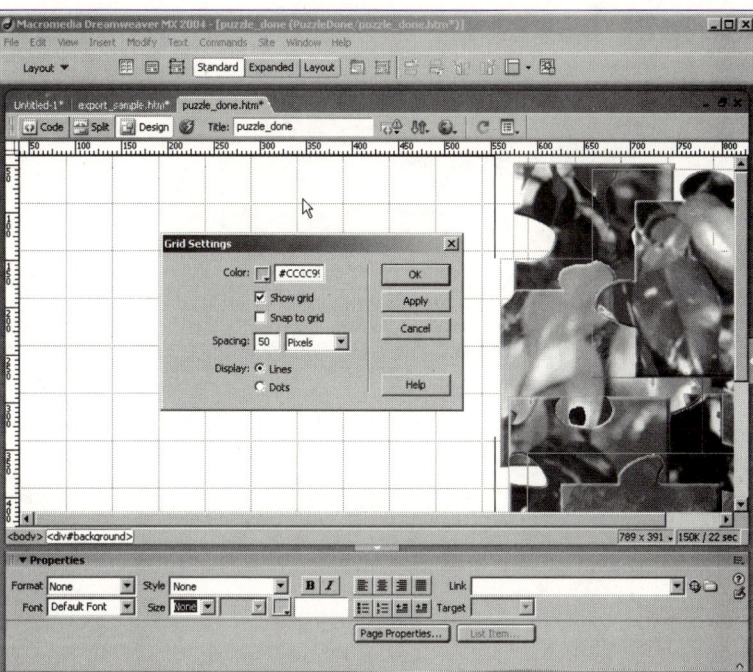

Figure 112-3: The Grid Settings dialog box

6. You can choose to show the grid or make objects snap to a grid inter-section by selecting the corresponding option.

7. Enter an amount of spacing in the Spacing field. To change the unit of measurement, click the arrow for the drop-down menu and choose Pixels, Inches, or Centimeters.

8. Specify whether you would like the grid to display as lines or dots.

9. Click OK when you are done. Figure 112-4 shows the grid with some of the settings changed.

10. You can now drag your layers and objects into position.

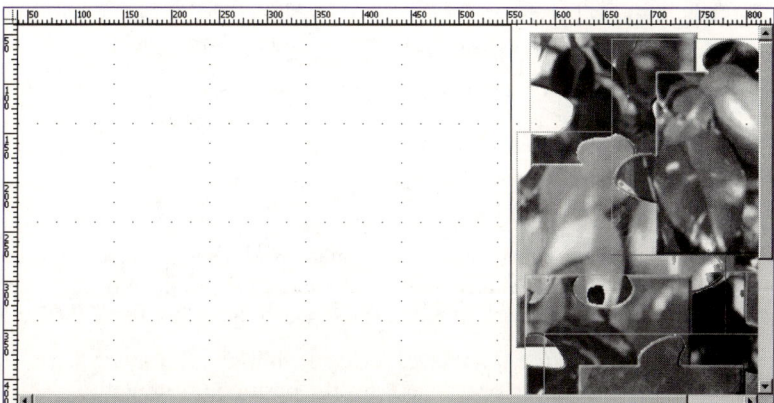

Figure 112-4: The document window with the grid settings changed

cross-reference

▪ See Task 14 for selecting colors (Step 8).

Nesting Layers

Nesting a layer is when you put one layer inside of another. You can nest as many layers as you'd like, but be aware that the more complex you make the layering, the longer the page will take to render.

1. Draw or insert a layer, as shown in Figure 113-1.

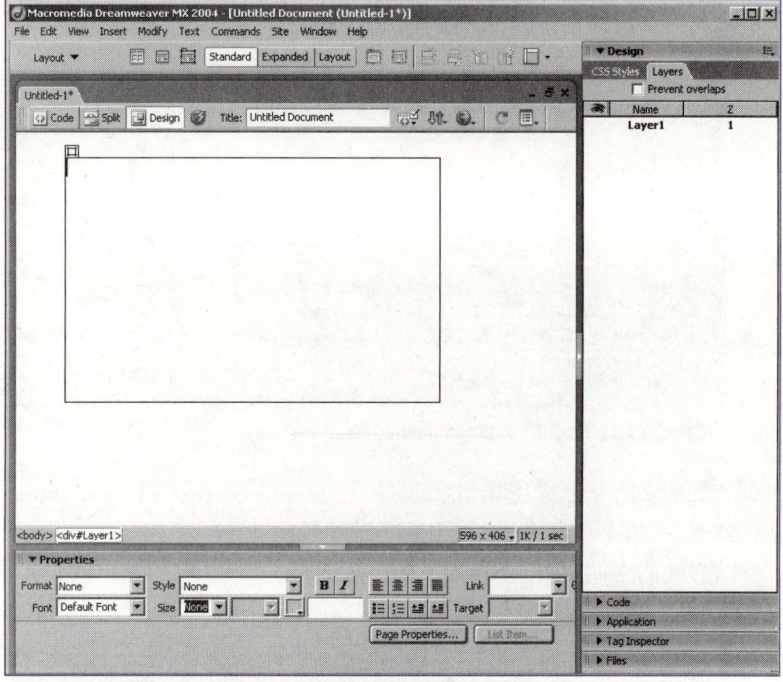

Figure 113-1: A layer drawn in a new document

2. Click inside the layer and draw or insert another layer, as shown in Figure 113-2.

3. Switch to Code view and note the code. Notice that both layers drawn or inserted in Dreamweaver have an absolute position, as shown here:

```
<div id="Layer1" style="position:absolute; left:54px;
top:27px; width:397px; height:251px; z-index:1">
  <div id="Layer2" style="position:absolute; width:200px;
height:115px; z-index:1"></div>
</div>
```

4. Open the Layers panel. Notice the child layer, which is indented below the parent layer to indicate it is nested (see Figure 113-3). The main container or layer is considered the parent, and the one inside is considered the child.

5. With the nested (or child) layer selected, go to the Layers Property inspector and set the coordinates for the position (or drag into place). Remember, the position is relative to the layer, not to the document.

notes

- Nested layers are used to group layers. A nested layer moves with its parent. It also inherits the parent's visibility (Step 2).

- If you don't see the layer's anchors, choose View ➡ Visual Aids ➡ Invisible Elements. You also need to set the invisible element preference to see layer anchors (Step 5).

- When you add a layer using the Insert ➡ Layout Object DIV tag, it is not absolutely positioned. Although it is a DIV tag like Dreamweaver layers, it is a block or content element.

caution

- Not all browsers render the relative position of parent and child layers, so test thoroughly in the browsers you need to support (Step 4).

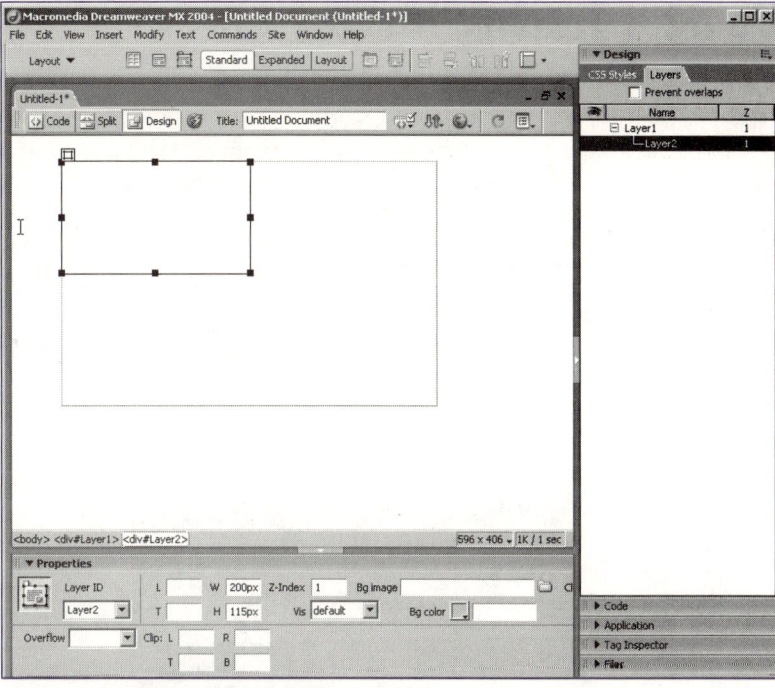

Figure 113-2: A layer drawn inside another layer

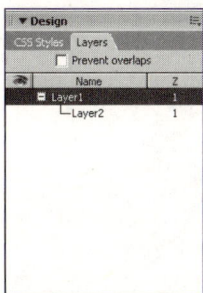

Figure 113-3: The Layers panel showing the parent and the child layers

6. Notice the gold anchor inside the parent layer (see Figure 113-4). This indicates the layer is nested.

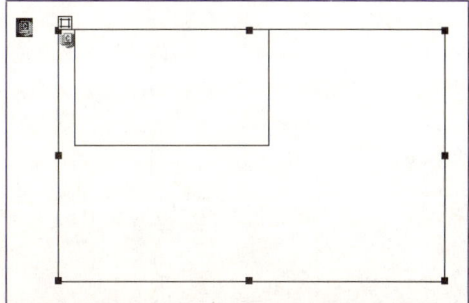

Figure 113-4: The anchor inside the parent layer

cross-references

▪ Refer to Task 108 for drawing and inserting layers (Step 1).

▪ Refer to Task 178 for inserting DIV tags.

Using a Tracing Image

Web designs are frequently mocked up in a graphics program such as Fireworks. These mock-ups can be exported as a GIF, JPEG, or PNG and used in Dreamweaver as a placement guide (tracing image) to place the graphics, text, and tables.

1. If your mockup, comp, or sample design image isn't a GIF, JPEG, or PNG, export it in Fireworks or save as one of the file formats in the graphics editor of your choice.

2. To add the tracing image to your document in Dreamweaver, choose View ⇨ Tracing Image ⇨ Load (see Figure 114-1).

3. In the Select Image Source dialog box, navigate to the tracing image you want to insert, select it, and click OK.

notes

▪ Instead of using the Insert menu to insert the tracing image, you could insert it using the Page Properties dialog box (Step 5).

▪ Totally transparent is 0 percent and opaque is 100 percent (Step 6).

▪ The tracing image cannot be seen by the browser (Step 8).

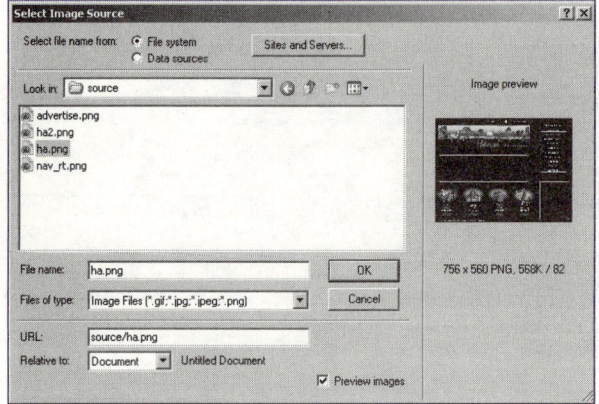

Figure 114-1: The Select Image Source dialog box

4. The Page Properties dialog box opens, as shown in Figure 114-2.

5. Select the Tracing Image category. This is the same Page Properties dialog box that you access by choosing Modify ⇨ Page Properties or by clicking the Page Properties button in the Property inspector.

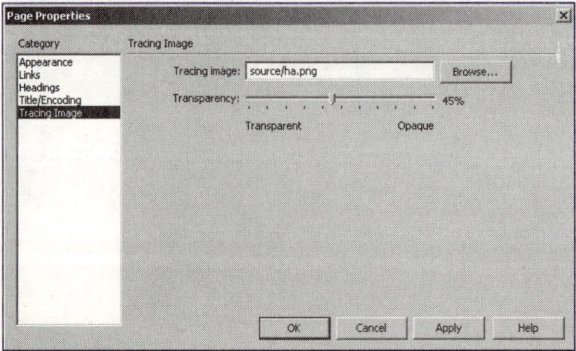

Figure 114-2: The Page Properties dialog box

6. Move the Transparency slider until you achieve the desired effect.

7. Click OK to close the Page Properties dialog box. Figure 114-3 shows the tracing image at 45 percent in the document.

8. If you ever want to hide the tracing image, choose View ⇨ Tracing Image and select Show to deselect (uncheck) it, as shown in Figure 114-4.

Figure 114-3: The Tracing Image category

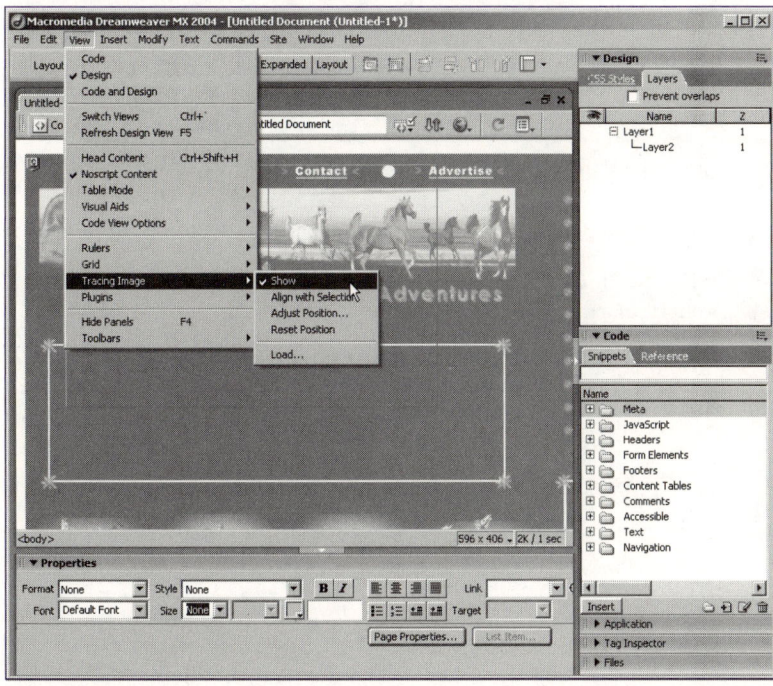

Figure 114-4: The View menu

cross-reference

▪ Refer to Task 13 for using the Page Properties dialog box.

9. If you need to edit the transparency or replace the tracing image, choose Modify ⇨ Page Properties ⇨ Tracing Image category and edit as desired.

10. Click OK.

Task

Layers and Netscape 4.x

When a user resizes his or her browser, all layers lose their positioning in Netscape 4.x and will align to the left of the browser. The solution is to force Netscape to reload the page if the browser is resized.

1. With your document containing layers open, choose Edit ⇨ Preferences.

2. Select the Layers category, as shown in Figure 115-1

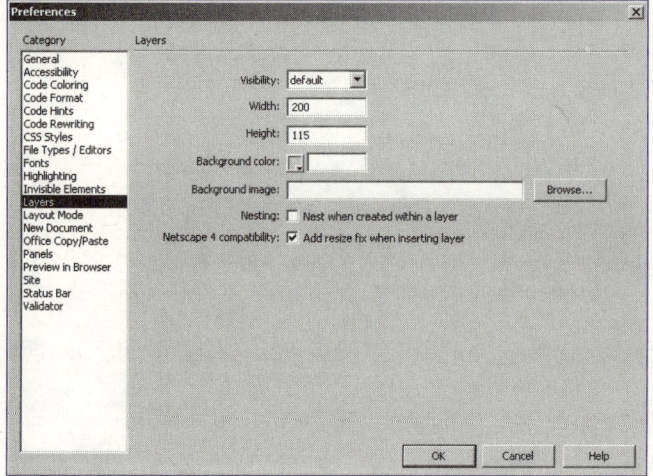

Figure 115-1: The Edit Preferences dialog box showing the default settings

3. For now, don't worry about the default settings.

4. In the Nesting field (Nest When Created in a Layer), select the field. A check mark appears, as shown in Figure 115-2.

5. Check the Netscape 4 Compatibility option (Add Resize Fix When Inserting Image) and be sure it is selected. If it isn't, do so (see Figure 115-3).

---

notes

- The Tab preference default is the `<div>` tag. It is the most compatible (Step 3).

- The resize fix is added to the `<head>` code where the first layer appears (Step 5).

- The outside layer is the parent; the nested layer is the child. The child layer inherits its parent visibility (Step 5).

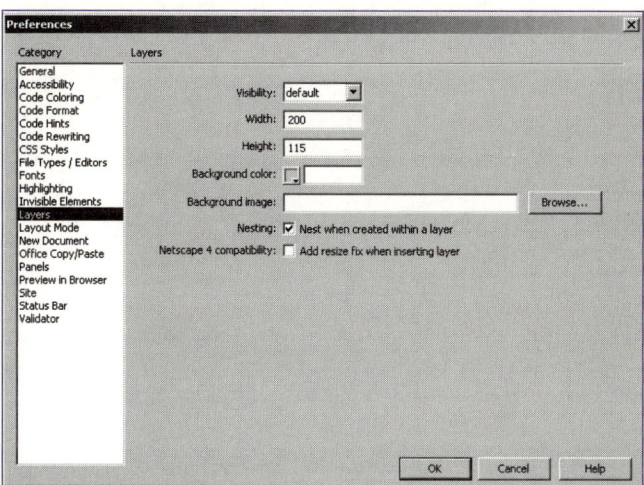

Figure 115-2: Nest When Created in a Layer option is selected

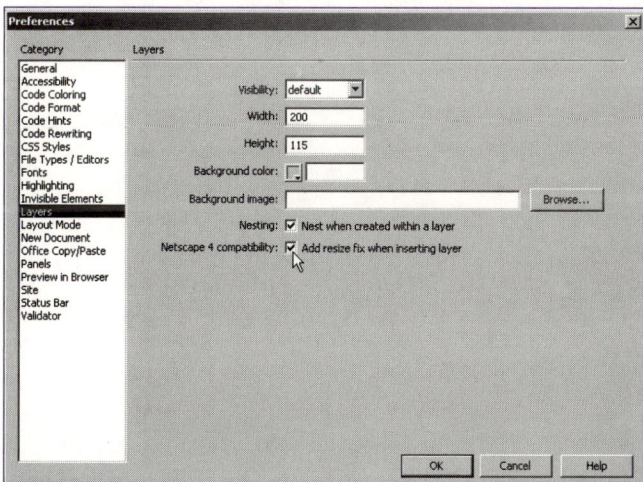

Figure 115-3: The Edit Preferences dialog box with changes made to the Layers preferences

6. Click OK to close the Edit Preferences dialog box.

cross-reference

- Refer to Task 114 for adding a tracing image to the layer.

Using the Show or Hide Layers Behavior

You can choose to show or hide a layer by triggering an event (such as clicking a button). An example of showing a hidden layer is a menu using buttons. You can click or mouse over the button and magically see a submenu. This is done by using an invisible layer that becomes visible when the user performs the specified event.

notes

- The Show-Hide Layers dialog box shows a list of all layers in your document (Step 4).

- The onClick event is the default. Since you don't want the user to have to click to see the menu, you changed the event to onMouseOver (Step 8).

1. Copy the task116 folder in the Part 6 folder on the companion Web site (www.wiley.com/compbooks/10simplesteps) to your hard drive. Open task116.htm. The starting file is shown in Figure 116-1.

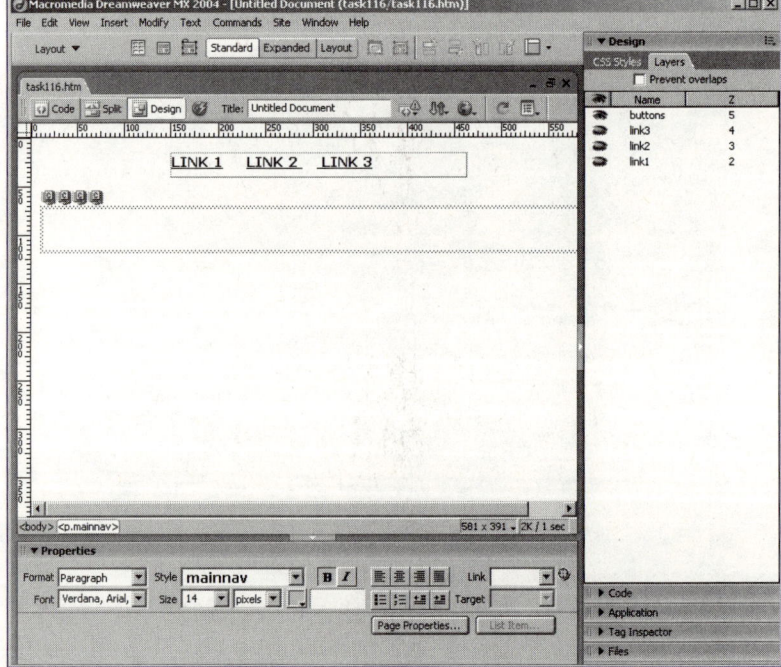

Figure 116-1: The sample file with three buttons and three layers added

2. Select the Link 1 text in the navigation area. You could select any image, button, or text.

3. In the panel group area, click the Tag Inspector panel to expand it. Then click Behaviors. You can also activate the Behaviors panel by pressing Shift+F3.

4. Click the arrow next to the plus (+) sign, and select Show-Hide Layers, as shown in Figure 116-2.

5. When users passed their mouse over the link text, you want them to see the submenu that corresponds to the link. In the Show-Hide dialog box, select link1 and press the Show button.

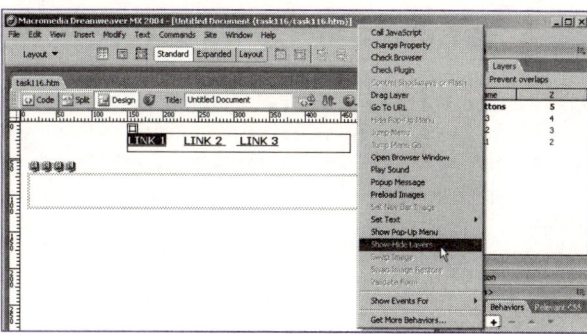

Figure 116-2: Selecting Show-Hide Layers

6. When users mouse over the link, you want the link1 layer to be visible but not the link2 layer and link3 layer.

7. Click the link2 layer and the Hide button; then select the link3 layer and click the Hide button. Click OK to close the dialog box. Figure 116-3 shows the layers with the show and hide settings applied.

8. Look in the Behaviors panel; you'll see the behavior added to the Client Side list. Click the onClick text, and a down arrow appears. Click it and select onMouseOver.

9. Repeat for the remaining links, except make the corresponding layer of each visible. Save the file and test in a browser.

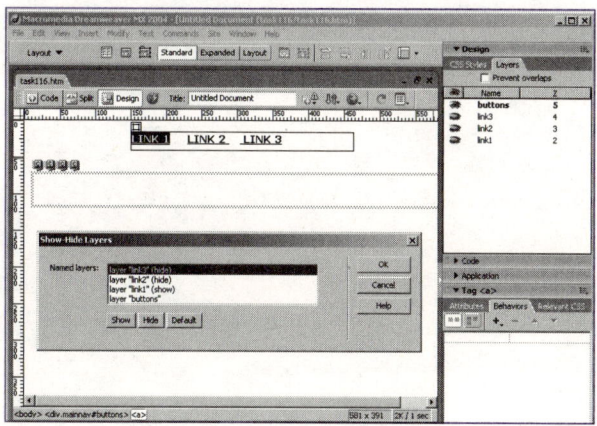

Figure 116-3: The layers with the visibility selected

cross-reference

▪ Refer to Task 110 for setting layer visibility (Step 2).

Task **117**

Changing a Layer's Content Dynamically

You can replace the content in a layer with new content dynamically. Anything you can code in HTML—such as images, text, scripts, and so on—can be used in the layer. The sample file for this task contains three links and one layer that displays different content for each link. This comes in handy when you have a disjoint (remote) rollover that is different sizes. Since rollovers use images only and they have to be the same size, this technique solves the problem. Not only do you not have to use an image for text, but you can use any size you desire for each link.

1. Insert and name your layers, or copy the task117 folder from the Part 6 folder to your hard drive from the companion Web site (www.wiley.com/compbooks/10simplesteps) and open task117.htm.

2. Insert text, image, or buttons to trigger the dynamic content. Skip this step if you are using the sample files.

3. Choose Window ➪ Behavior to activate the Behaviors panel, or select it from the Selections panel group.

4. Select your trigger image or text (Link 1) and click the plus sign (+). From the list, select Set Text ➪ Set Text of Layer, as shown in Figure 117-1.

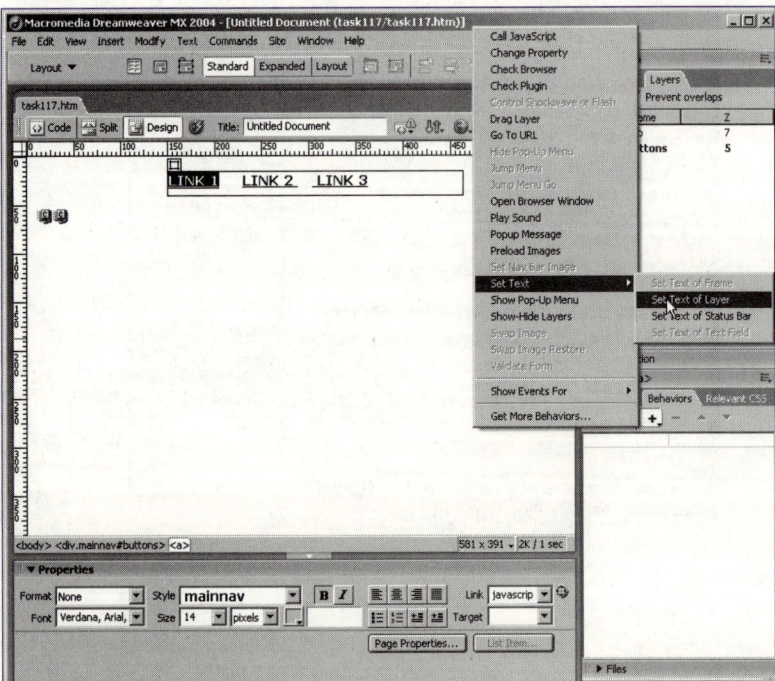

Figure 117-1: The Add Behaviors list of options

5. The Set Text of Layer dialog box opens.

6. Click the Layer drop-down menu and select the target layer (info for the sample, as shown in Figure 117-2).

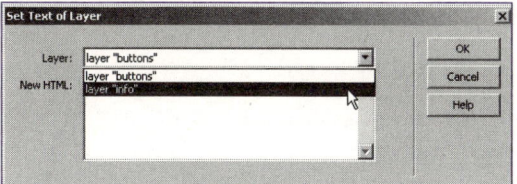

Figure 117-2: The Layer field drop-down list

7. Enter the text you want to appear or the HTML code of the layer's content. For the sample document, open the *code to paste.txt* file in the task117 folder and copy the top section of code. Paste into the New HTML section of the Set Text of Layer dialog box, as shown in Figure 117-3.

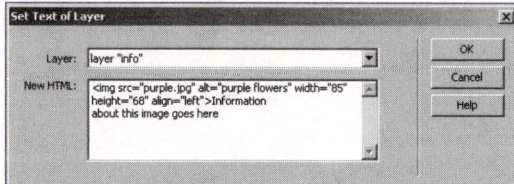

Figure 117-3: The code pasted into the New HTML field

8. Select the next link (Link 2 for the sample) and repeat, except enter different content into the New HTML field. For the sample, copy and paste the second section of code from the *code to paste.txt* file.

9. Repeat for all links or triggers.

10. You can attach multiple behaviors to the same trigger. Since the info layer is hidden, you need to add a Show-Hide Layer behavior to each link (trigger). Select the info layer and click Show, then OK for each link for the example file. Save and test in your test browsers. The finished file is shown in Figure 117-4.

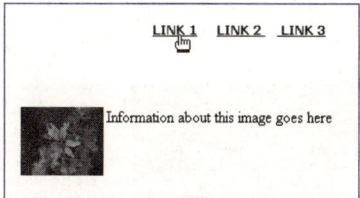

Figure 117-4: The finished file, as shown in Netscape 7

Task 117

cross-references

- See Task 121 for creating remote rollovers.

- See Task 116 for adding a Show-Hide Layer behavior (Step 10).

- A finished file can be found in the task117 folder named task106_done.htm (Step 10).

Making a Layer Draggable

You can code your layers so that users can actually move your layers in their browsers. This is commonly used for puzzles and for shopping carts, where someone can drag the selected item into a cart.

1. Create all your layers and insert the images.

2. Select the `<body>` tag from the Tag Selector (in the status bar).

3. Press Shift+F3 to activate the Behaviors panel (in the Selections panel group).

4. Click the plus (+) sign for Add Behavior. From the menu, select Show Events For ⇨ 4.0 and Later Browsers (see Figure 118-1). Select it if it isn't already.

notes

- When making puzzles, leave the movement unconstrained (Step 6).

- The default is Entire Layer, which is probably what you'll most often use (Step 7).

- You'll need to know how to write JavaScript to take full advantage of the Advanced portion of the Drag Layer dialog box (Step 8).

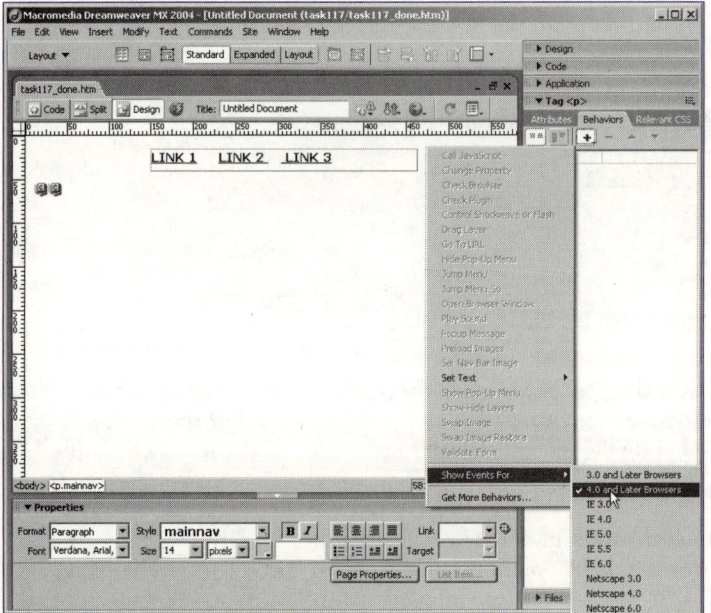

Figure 118-1: The Show Events For menu option

5. Click the Add Behavior button again (+) and select Drag Layer. The Drag Layer dialog box appears, as shown in Figure 118-2.

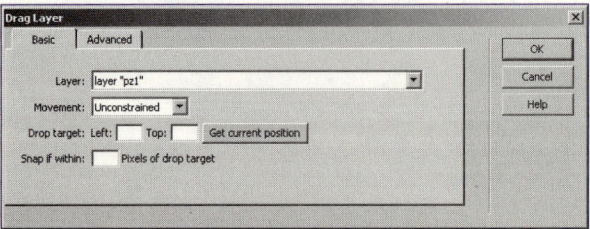

Figure 118-2: The Drag Layer dialog box

6. In the Layer drop-down menu, select the layer you want to be draggable. There are several options for dragging the layer:

- *Movement*. Unconstrained doesn't limit the layer's movement; Constrained does. If you select Constrained, you can add the specific coordinates for the allowed movement.

- *Drop Target*. If the layer is supposed to be moved to a specific point, enter its coordinates in this field. To get the exact coordinates, you can click the Get Current Position button. This assumes the layer is currently in the correct position already.

- *Snap If Within*. If you want the layer to snap into position when it gets close to its destination, enter a pixel amount in this field. For instance, if the user drags a layer and it's within 10 pixels of the target, it will snap into place.

7. Click the Advanced tab and designate what you are making draggable (the entire selected layer or an area within the layer). If you select Area within Layer, you'll be able to enter the specific coordinates of the area you want to be draggable (see Figure 118-3).

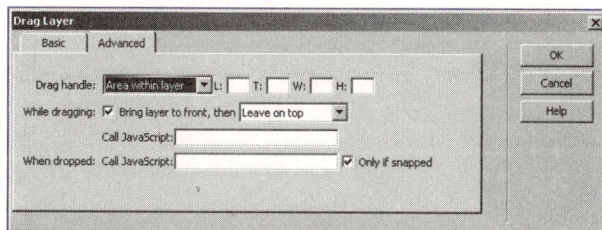

Figure 118-3: The Advanced tab of the Drag Layer dialog box showing the Area within Layer option selected

8. The other options available in the Advanced portion of the Drag Layer dialog box are as follows:

- *While Dragging*. Select to either bring the layer to the top after dragging or to return it to its original z-index, which you select from the drop-down menu. You can also type in or paste JavaScript code that will activate while the layer is being dragged. For instance, the JavaScript could track the movement and suggest hints such as "you're getting closer."

- *When Dropped*. Allows you to enter JavaScript code that activates when the layer is dropped. For instance, when the layer is moved, JavaScript can produce a window that says "Good Job" or "Try Again" or whatever. If you select the Only If Snapped option, the JavaScript won't activate unless the layer is snapped into position.

9. Click OK when you are finished.

cross-reference
- See Task 108 for creating layers and inserting images (Step 1).

Part 7: Making Your Site Interactive Using Behaviors

Adding Behaviors

Behaviors in Dreamweaver are powered by JavaScript code, which runs in a browser without the need of a plug-in. The JavaScript is triggered by an event such as onClick or onMouseOver (and plenty more). When the event occurs, it triggers an action (a predefined function) to occur. Dreamweaver calls this event and action a *behavior*.

1. Open the Behaviors panel, shown in Figure 119-1, using one of the following methods:

   - Use keyboard shortcut of Shift+F3.

   - Choose Window Behaviors.

   - Open the Tag Inspector (F9) in the docked panel group area and select Behaviors to make it active.

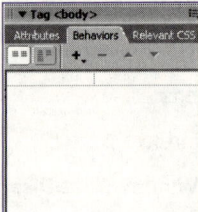

Figure 119-1: The Behaviors panel

2. Click the Add Behaviors button (+), as shown in Figure 119-2.

3. Move your mouse down to the bottom of the Behaviors list over Set Events. Then select Show Events For and select the browser or browser group you are designing for (see Figure 119-3).

4. Select the Add Behaviors button again, and select the behavior you want to add.

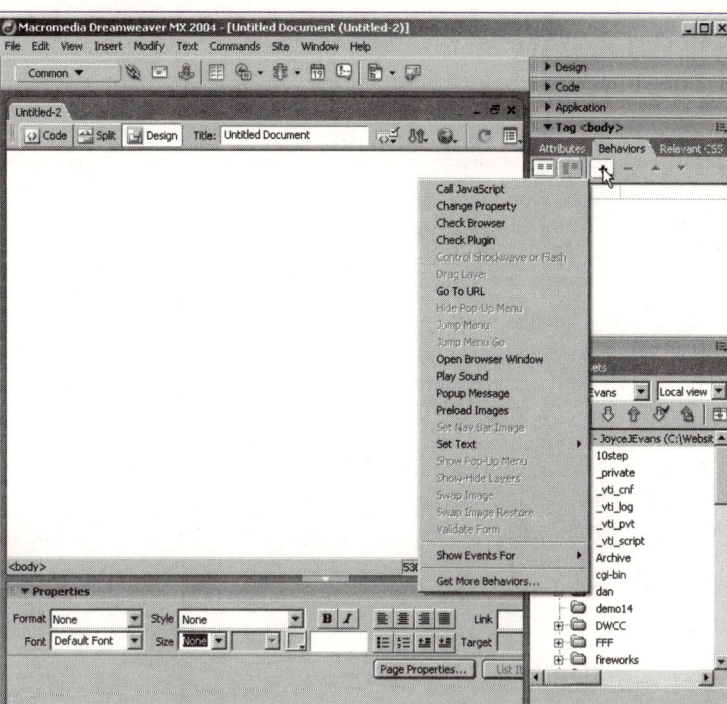

Figure 119-2: The Behaviors list

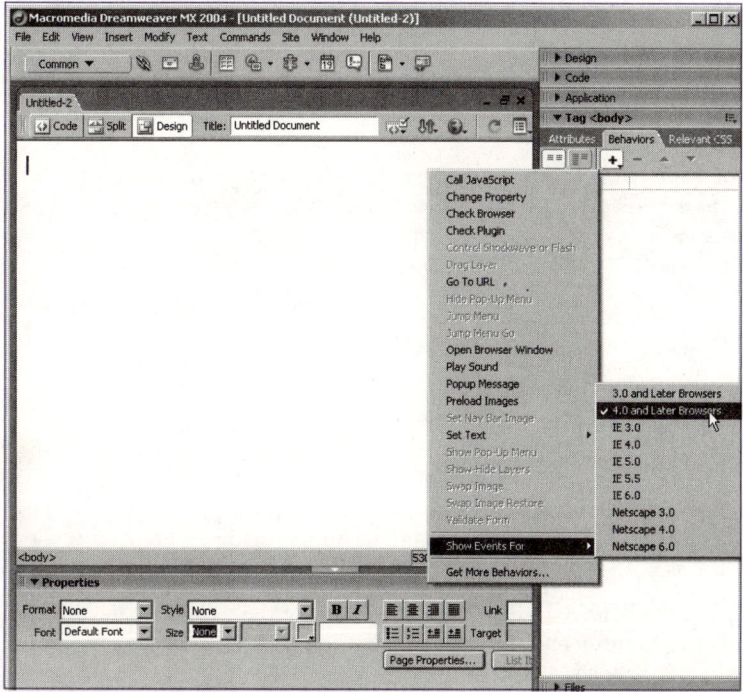

Figure 119-3: Changing the browser to get the specific behaviors needed

cross-references

- Refer to Tasks 120 to 129 for adding specific behaviors (Step 4).

- Refer to Tasks 136 and 137 for downloading and installing extensions (Step 4).

Making a Rollover Button

Rollovers are extremely popular and are a great visual clue to a link. Users are well aware that when the button or text changes color or form, it's a link. The use of Dreamweaver behaviors makes creating rollovers a pretty simple task.

1. In Fireworks or your image editor of choice, create a button for the Up state (what users see when they first arrive at a site) and a second button the same size for the Over state.

2. Insert the image into your document in Dreamweaver and select it, as shown in Figure 120-1. In the Property inspector, name the button.

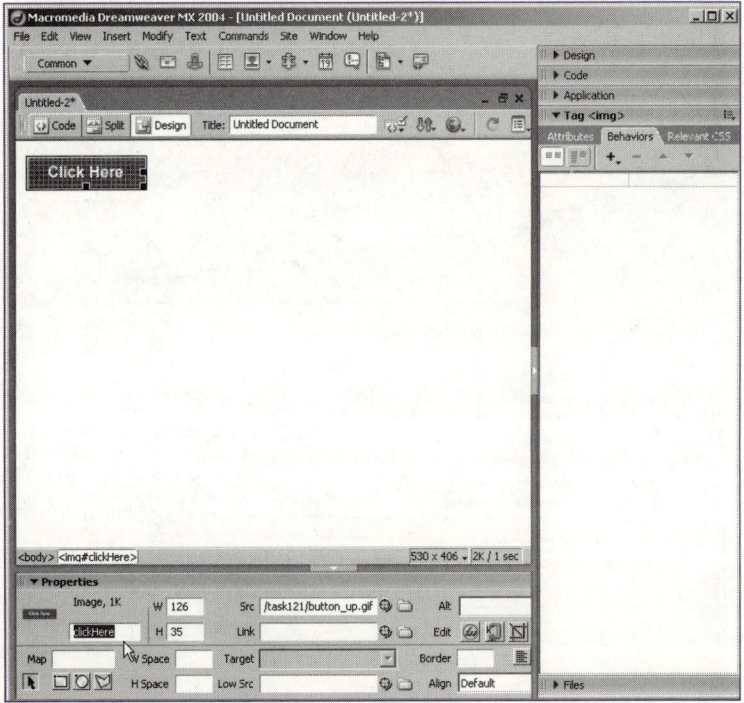

Figure 120-1: A button is added to the Dreamweaver document

3. Open the Behaviors panel (Shift+F3).

4. Click the Add button (+).

5. From the list, select Swap Image. The Swap Image dialog box opens. The selected image name should be highlighted (see Figure 120-2). If it is not, select the image name you want.

6. The Set Source To field is for the image of the rollover. Click the Browse button and navigate to the image you want to swap for the rollover; then select it and click OK.

notes

- I make all the images for my Web sites using Macromedia Fireworks MX 2004 (Step 1).

- Rollovers typically have a change of button and/or text color (Step 1).

- If your image doesn't have a name, select it and add a name in the Image field in the Property inspector (Step 5).

- The behavior is being attached to the button/ image that will trigger the Swap Image (rollover) action (Step 5).

- An instance where you might not want the Preload Images option selected would be if you were using an animated rollover (Step 7).

- If you can't see the arrow, just select the event name and it will appear (Step 9).

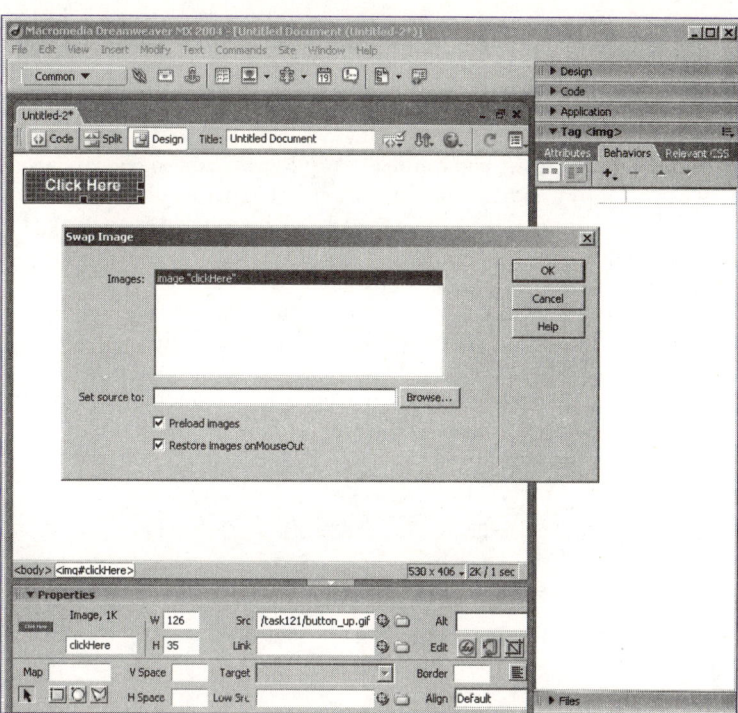

Figure 120-2: The Swap Image dialog box with the image name selected

7. At the bottom of the Swap Image dialog box, you'll notice two options selected by default: Preload Images and Restore Images onMouseOut. Leave them selected for most cases (see Figure 120-3).

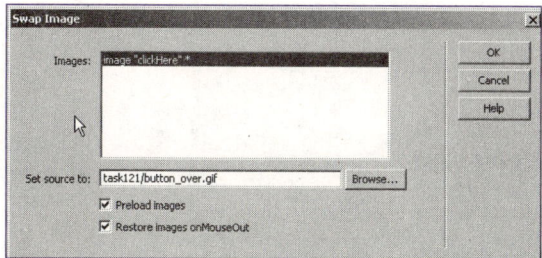

Figure 120-3: The Swap Image dialog box

cross-reference

- Refer to Task 119 for accessing the Behaviors panel (Step 3).

8. Click OK to close the Swap Image dialog box.

9. In the Behaviors panel, click the plus (+) sign next to Client Side to expand it. You see two behaviors added. The event on the left side should be onMouseOver. If you want to change the event, click the arrow in the center and select the event you want from the list.

Making Remote Rollovers or Swapping Multiple Images

By combining behaviors, you can make a rollover that also displays another image in a location other than the button or trigger image. If you want to display text using this method, the text needs to be exported as an image to use in Dreamweaver.

notes

- The images need to be named so you can identify them for adding behaviors (Step 3).

- Leave the two boxes at the bottom checked (Preload and Restore options) for both images (Step 8).

- If you roll over the remote image, nothing happens because the behavior is attached to the button only (Step 9).

1. Insert the two images you want to use—the trigger image and the target (remote) image. If you'd like, you can download the task121 folder in the partVII folder, from www.wiley.com/compbooks/ 10simplesteps. Sample images (button_up.gif and remote.gif) are provided for you to practice on, as well as the completed task. Figure 121-1 shows the button and the target image in the document.

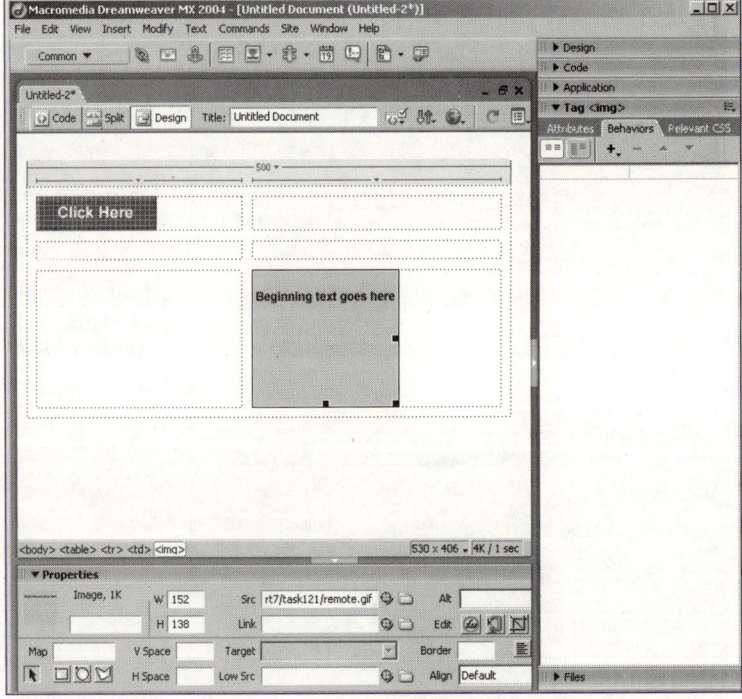

Figure 121-1: The practice file with both images inserted

2. Select the button image, and in the Name field in the Property inspector, name it **button_up**. Select the remote image and name it **remote_up**.

3. Select the trigger image (button for this sample), open the Behaviors panel (Shift+F3), and click the Add button.

4. Select Swap Image from the list. In the Swap Image dialog box, you see both of your inserted images listed.

5. In the Set Source To field, click the Browse button and navigate to the rollover image. For this example, select button_over.gif (see Figure 121-2). Click OK.

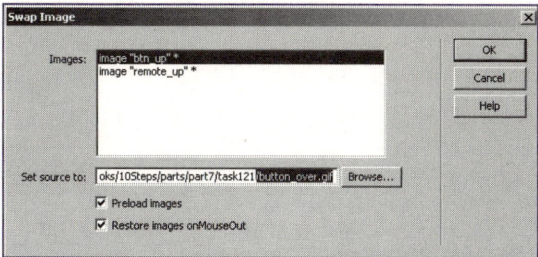

Figure 121-2: Setting the source in the Swap Image dialog box

6. While still in the Swap Image dialog box, select the remote image from the Images list.

7. Click the Browse button for the Set Source To field, and navigate to the rollover you want to appear in the remote area. For this example, select remote_ovcr.gif and click OK.

8. Click OK to close the Swap Image dialog box.

9. Save and preview. If you'd like you can preview task121.htm by rolling your mouse over the button. Notice the text changes to gold and the remote image's text changes to the text that applies to the button—both at the same time, as shown in Figure 121-3.

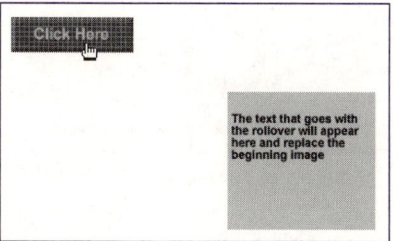

Figure 121-3: The multiple rollovers, as shown in a browser

cross-reference
- Refer to Task 120 for making a rollover button.

Editing a Behavior

Once you've applied a behavior, the event is added to the Behaviors panel and can be edited. The behaviors you add in this part of the book are client-side behaviors, and you add the scripts to your document's code. Of course, you don't have to physically type the code. Dreamweaver does that part behind the scenes for you.

1. Attach a behavior to an image or a button.

2. Open the Behaviors panel (Shift+F3), as shown in Figure 122-1.

Figure 122-1: An image selected and the Behaviors panel open

3. Click the down arrow between the event and the action. If you can't see the arrow, click in the left side (the event name) and it will appear (see Figure 122-2).

4. Select the event you'd like to trigger your action.

5. Double-click the action name to reopen the specific dialog box for that action. Figure 122-3 shows the dialog box for the Swap Image behavior.

notes

- If it isn't an image that has a link, add a null link (**javascript:;**) into the Link field in the Property inspector (Step 1).

- If your screen is smaller, such as on a laptop, the arrow may not be visible automatically (Step 3).

Task **122**

Figure 122-2: The available events for the specific behavior and browser you've chosen

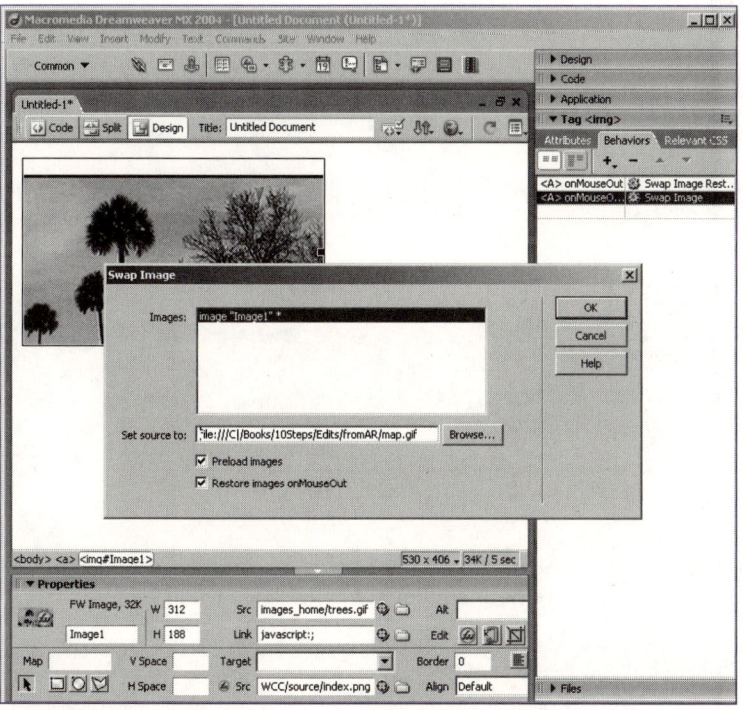

Figure 122-3: The event double-clicked and the appropriate dialog box open

6. Make any changes you'd like and close the dialog box.

7. If you'd like to delete a behavior, select it and then click the Remove Event button (–).

cross-references

- Refer to Task 119 for attaching behaviors (Step 1).

- Refer to Task 123 to choose the browsers you are supporting (Step 3).

Task **123** **Choosing a Browser Model**

An event is added to the Behaviors panel each time you add a behavior. There is a default event for each behavior, which is based on the browser type you've selected.

1. Open the Behaviors panel (Shift+F3).

2. Click the Add Behaviors button (+).

3. Pass your mouse over the Show Events option and then click the browser you are supporting. For this exercise, select 3.0 and Later Browsers, as shown in Figure 123-1.

notes

* The browser model you select determines which events and actions will be available. For example, Internet Explorer 3 has only 13 different tags that can receive an event handler, whereas Internet Explorer 6 has 94 (Step 3)!

* You can go to the Macromedia Exchange to get more behaviors.

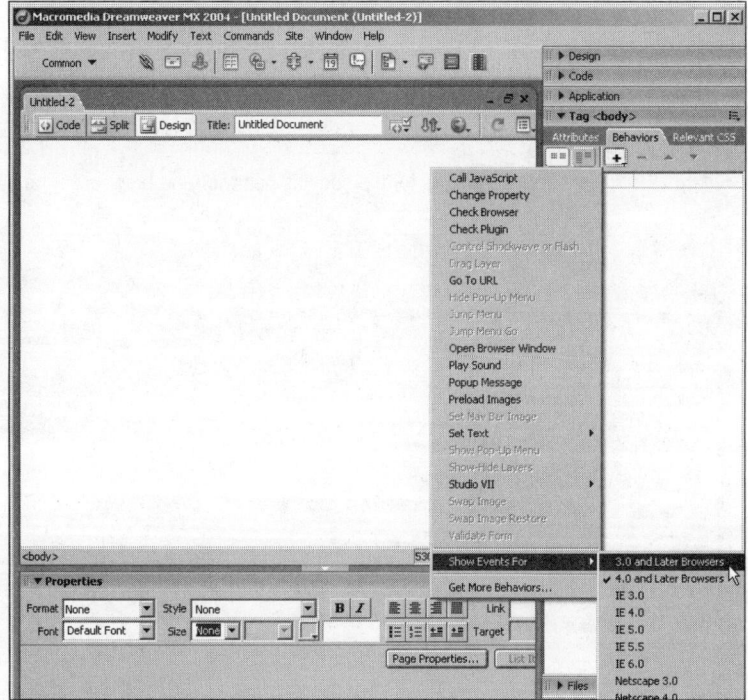

Figure 123-1: The Show Events For menu

4. Click the Add Behavior button (+) and note the available behaviors. The grayed-out options are not available, as shown in Figure 123-2.

5. Click the Add Behavior again, move over Show Events For, and select 4.0 and Later Browsers.

6. Click the Add Behavior button (+) again and notice the additional behaviors available.

7. Once you add a behavior and click the drop-down menu for events (see Figure 123-3), you'll see the largest differences among browsers.

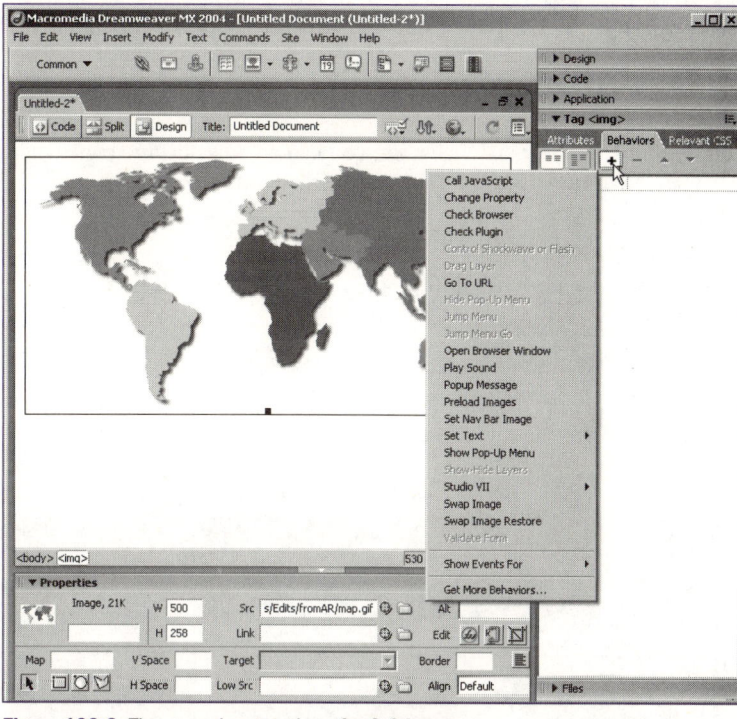

Figure 123-2: The grayed-out options for 3.0 browsers

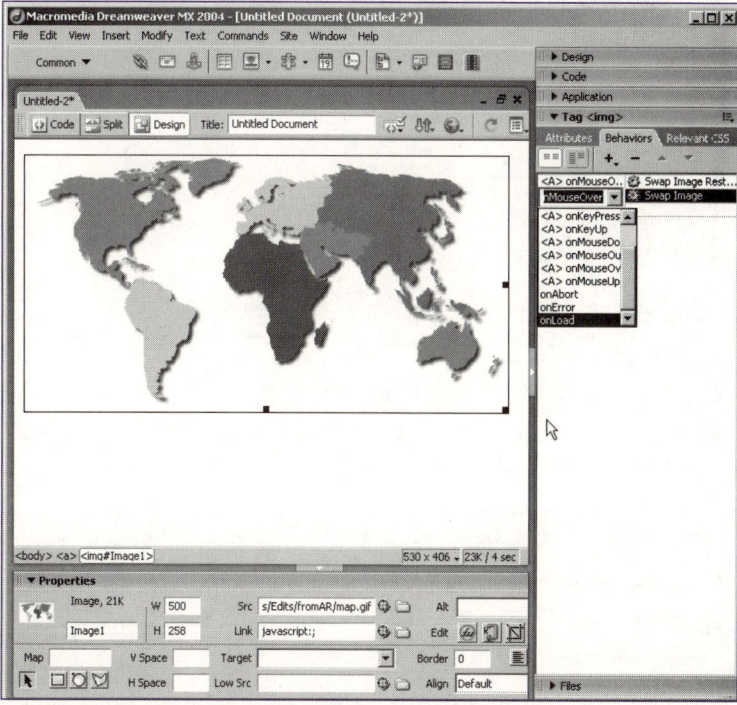

Figure 123-3: The Events drop-down list

cross-references

- Refer to Task 119 for multiple ways of accessing the Behaviors panel (Step 1).

- Refer to Task 122 on editing behaviors to learn about the Events drop-down menu (Step 7).

Changing Properties of a Specific Tag Dynamically

U sing the Change Property behavior, you can change specific tags dynamically when an event occurs.

1. Select the object, which will trigger the action.

2. Open the Behaviors panel (Shift+F3) and click the Add Behavior button (+).

3. Select Change Property.

4. In the Change Property dialog box, select the type of object. Click the drop-down menu to see the list of available objects (see Figure 124-1).

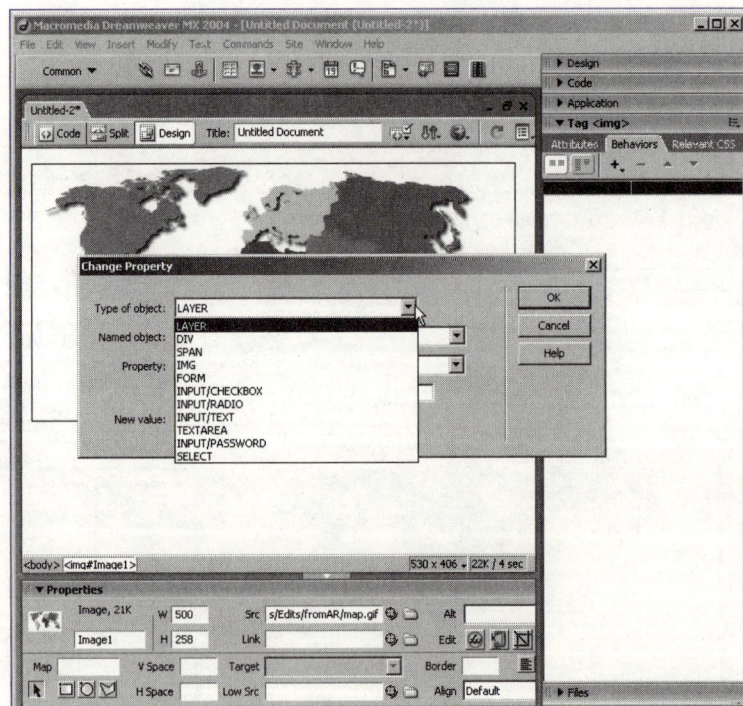

Figure 124-1: The Type of Object list

5. Choose the name of the object from the Named Object field.

6. Click the Select radio button to select it, as shown in Figure 124-2.

7. Click the down arrow for the browser version and select the one you want, as shown in Figure 124-3.

8. From the Select menu, select the property you want to change (see Figure 124-4).

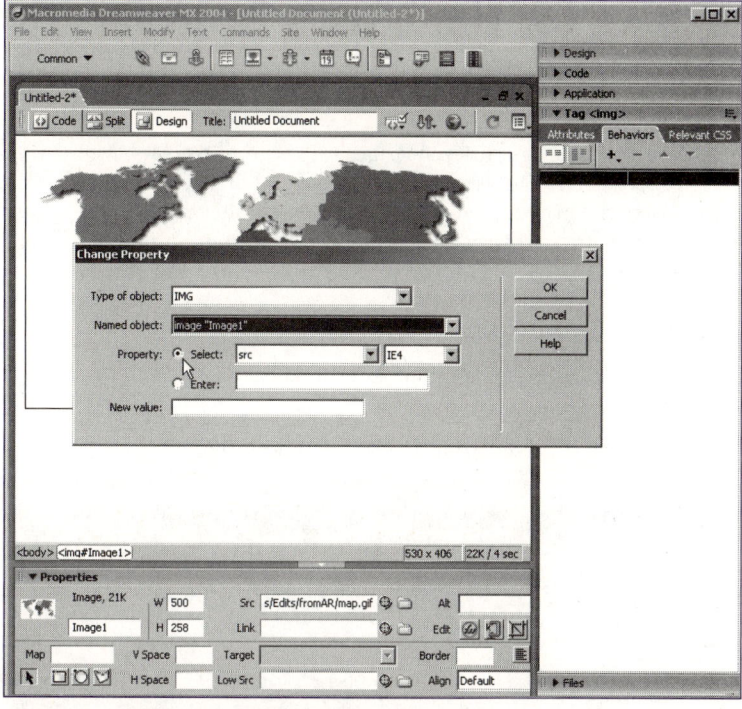

Figure 124-2: The Select option selected

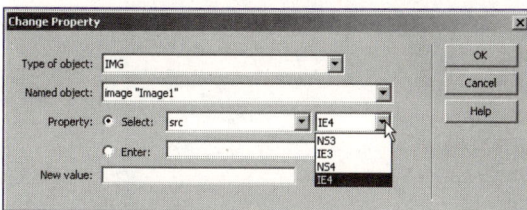

Figure 124-3: The browser list

9. If the property you want to change isn't in the list and it's one that you can change for the browsers you support, select the Enter option and type in the property.

10. In the New Value field, type in the new property value. Click OK to close the dialog box.

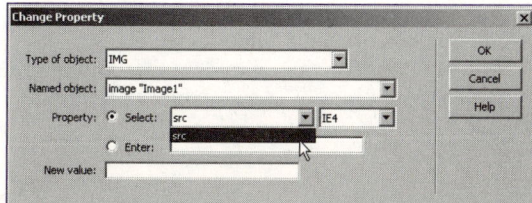

Figure 124-4: The Select list for Internet Explorer 4

cross-reference

▪ Refer to Task 146 for getting more extensions and behaviors.

Checking for the User's Browser Version and Type

S ome developers design different pages for certain browsers. Many developers design special styles and style sheets for several different browsers. But in order to display the proper page or the proper style sheets, your site needs the ability to detect which browser the user is using. Although this can be tricky and not without its problems, Dreamweaver helps streamline the process.

1. Select the object to trigger the action.

2. Open the Behaviors panel (Shift+F3) and click the Add Behavior button (+).

3. Select Check Browser from the list (see Figure 125-1).

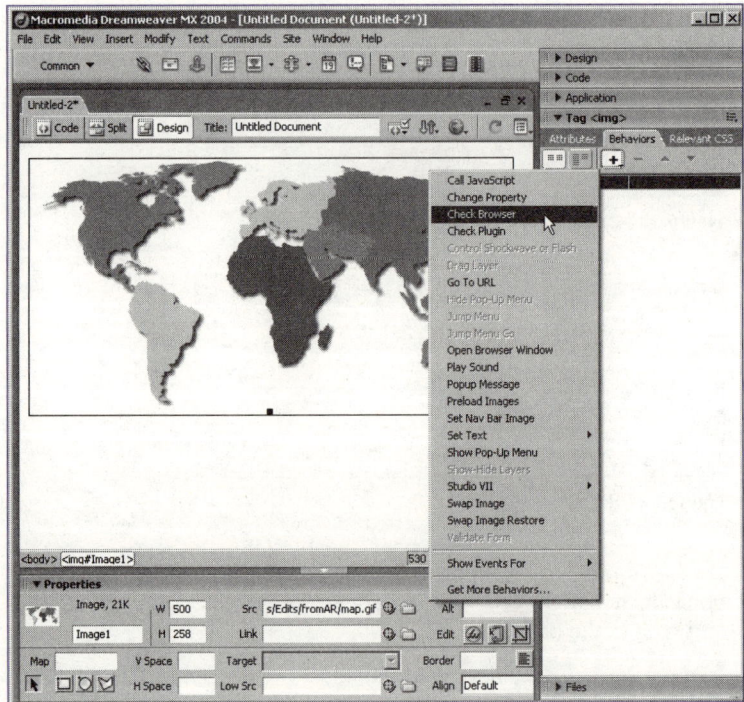

Figure 125-1: The Check Browser behavior being selected

4. In the Check Browser dialog box, the first field you see is for Netscape Navigator. Enter the version number you'd like, and in the next field, select which page you want the user to be sent to. The options, shown in Figure 125-2, are as follows:

   • Stay on This Page

   • Go to URL

   • Go to Alt URL

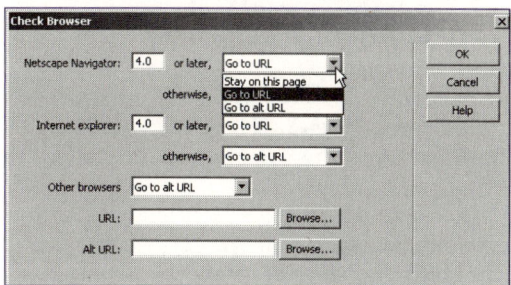

Figure 125-2: The options for Netscape Navigator

5. The Otherwise field is where you select the redirection (see Figure 125-3).

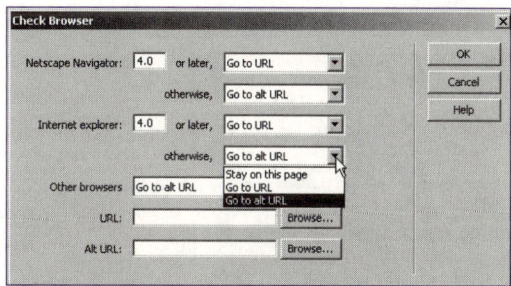

Figure 125-3: The Otherwise option for redirecting the browser

6. Repeat Steps 4 and 5 for Internet Explorer.

7. For other browsers, select the page you want them to view, as shown in Figure 125-4.

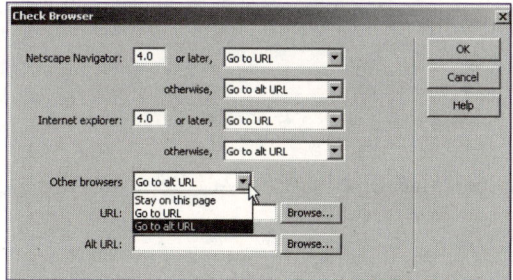

Figure 125-4: Selecting where you want other browsers to be directed

8. Enter the URL into the URL field that you specified in the browser fields, or click the Browse button and select the file.

9. Enter the alt URL in the Alt URL field, or click the Browse button and select the file.

10. Click OK to close, save, and test.

cross-reference

• Refer to Task 136 for getting more extensions and behaviors.

Checking for Installed Plug-ins

When you use media that requires a plug-in to display it, you'll want to check and see if the user has the required plug-in available. You can then send the user to a URL to get the plug-in or to another URL to view the media if the user has it installed already.

1. Select the `<body>` tag of your document from the Tag Selector (see Figure 126-1). Then click into an empty part of the document, making sure you don't select any objects.

notes

- Five of the most commonly used plug-ins are offered by default: Flash, Shockwave, LiveAudio, QuickTime, and Windows Media Player (Step 3).

- You can also click the Browse button to navigate to the file you want to use for the URL field (Step 5).

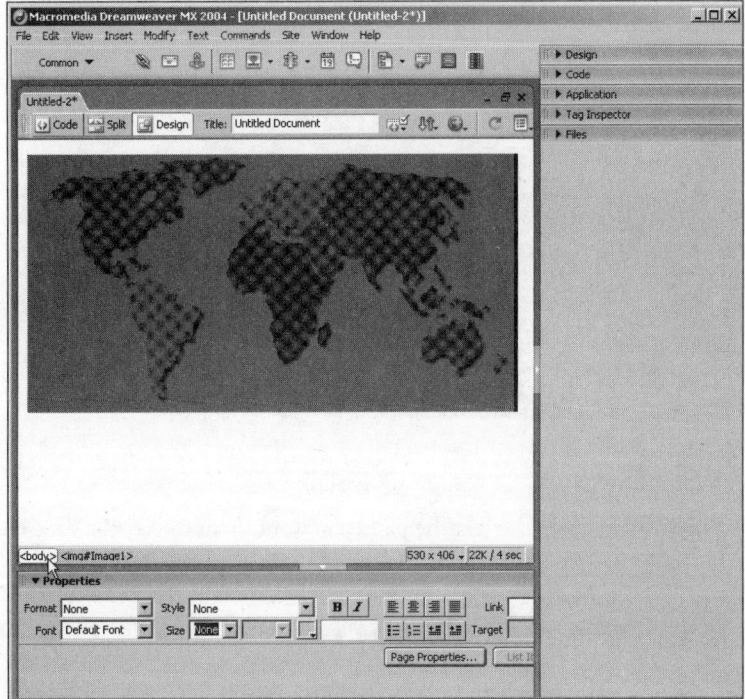

Figure 126-1: The `<body>` tag selected in the Tag Selector

2. Open the Behaviors panel (Shift+F3), click the Add Behavior button, and select Check Browser from the list.

3. In the Check Plugin dialog box, click Select and select the plug-in from the drop-down menu, as shown in Figure 126-2.

4. If the plug-in you want to check for isn't in the list, select Enter and type in the plug-in name.

5. In the If Found, Go to URL field, enter the URL to which users with the required plug-in will be directed.

cautions

- Installing plug-ins can turn users away from your site. Be careful of which ones you use.

- Internet Explorer doesn't do cross-browser detection very well. For Windows users it can detect Flash and Shockwave only, and on a Mac it can't detect any at all!

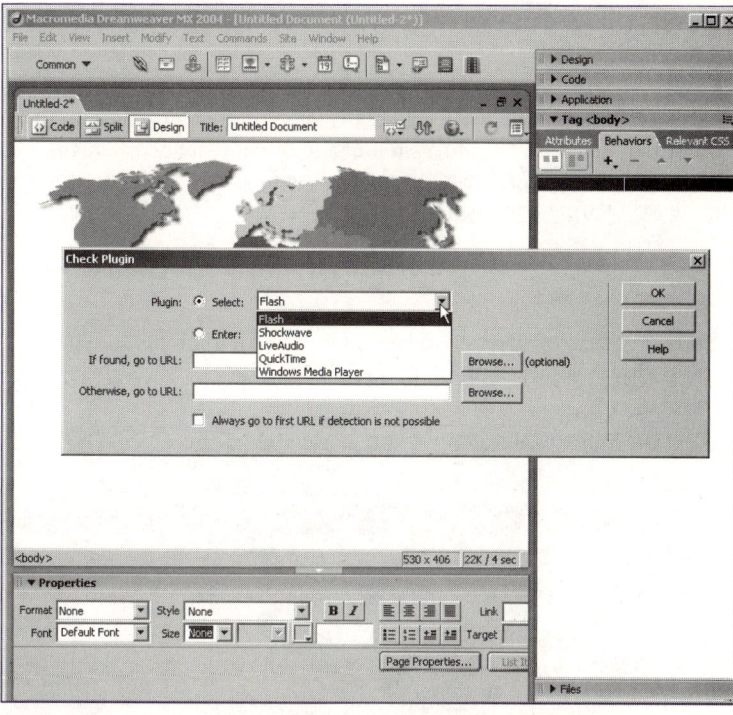

Figure 126-2: The Check Plugin dialog box showing the plug-in options

6. Leave the If Found, Go to URL field empty if you want users to remain on the current page.

7. For users without the plug-in, enter the URL of the plug-in download into the Otherwise, Go to URL field.

8. Enable the Always Go to First URL If Detection Is Not Possible option if you'd like (see Figure 126-3). If left unselected, users will be directed to the "Otherwise" URL, mentioned in the previous step.

9. Click OK to close the Check Plugin dialog box.

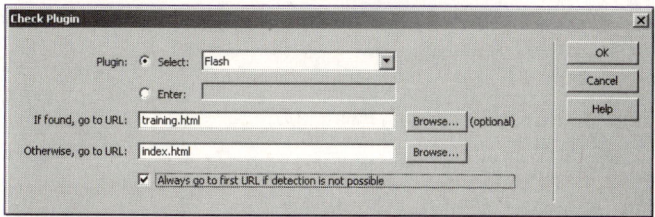

Figure 126-3: The Check Plugin dialog box filled in

cross-reference

▪ Refer to Task 145 for adding a Flash movie to your document.

Task 127

Opening a New Browser Window

This task uses a Dreamweaver behavior that opens a new browser window. You can control the size and the features available in the new window. This task is handy when you are linking to a site outside of your site or when you have a notice or something you'd like to display in a separate browser window, while leaving the originating page still open.

1. Select the text or image you want to use as the trigger to open a new browser window.

2. In the Property inspector, add a null link in the Link field. Type **javascript:;**, as shown in Figure 127-1.

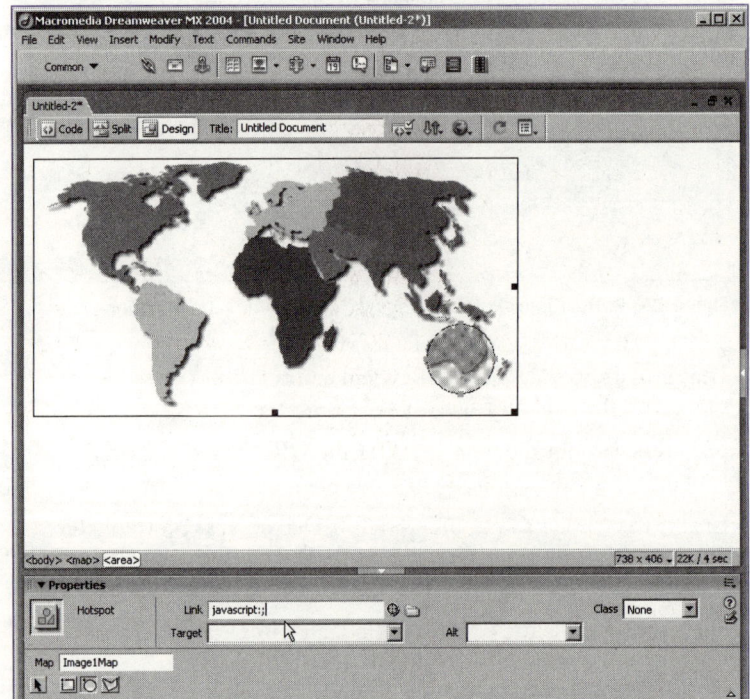

Figure 127-1: The null link added

3. Open the Behaviors panel (Shift+F3).

4. Click the Add Behavior button (+).

5. Select Open Browser Window from the list.

6. In the Open Browser Window dialog box, click the Browse button for the URL to Display field. Navigate to the document you want to load in the new window, select it, and click OK.

7. Type in the height and width you'd like the window to be.

8. Select any available options you'd like to be included in your new browser window from the Attributes list, as shown in Figure 127-2.

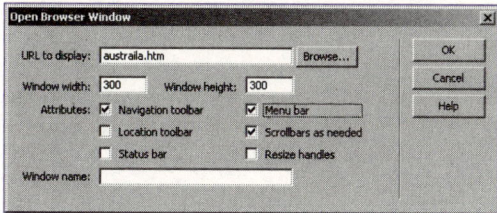

Figure 127-2: The Open Browser Window dialog box

9. In the Window Name field, type in a name. Click OK to close the Open Browser Window dialog box.

10. Check the Behaviors panel and be sure the event is set to onClick.

cross-reference

▪ Refer to Task 122 to change events (Step 10).

Adding a Pop-Up Message Window That Displays a JavaScript Alert

This behavior is used to display a JavaScript alert. They are simple text messages to provide information. You can use any valid JavaScript function call, property, or global variable.

notes

- This behavior requires a knowledge of JavaScript.

- You can't control how the JavaScript alert looks; that's determined by the visitor's browser.

- If you want to embed a JavaScript expression, place it inside braces ({ }). To display a brace, precede it with a backslash (\ {) [Step 5].

1. Select the `<body>` tag, as shown in Figure 128-1, and click into the document, being careful not to select any objects.

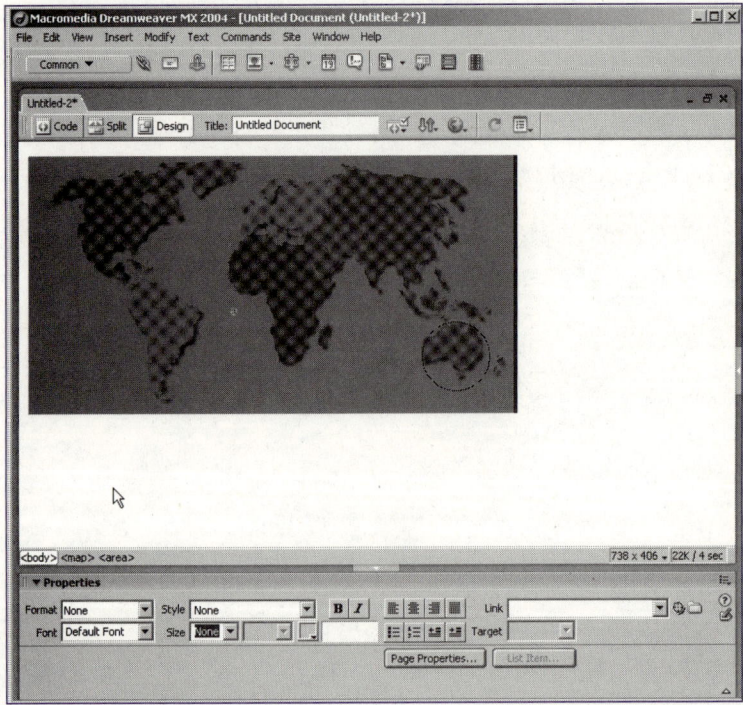

Figure 128-1: Select the `<body>` tag first

2. Open the Behaviors panel (Shift+F3) and click the Add Behavior button.

3. Select Popup Message from the Behavior list, as shown in Figure 128-2.

4. Type your message in the Message box, as shown in Figure 128-3.

5. Click OK to close the Popup Message dialog box.

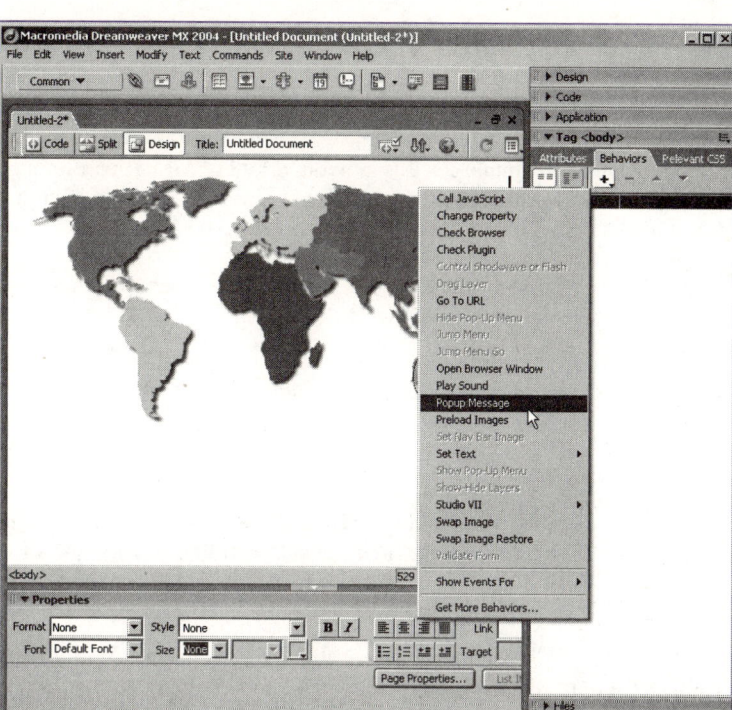

Figure 128-2: The Behavior list with Popup Message selected

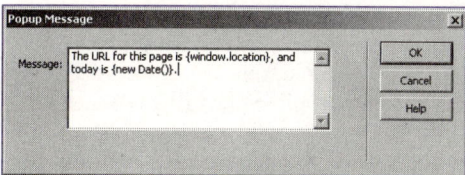

Figure 128-3: The Popup Message dialog box

6. In the Behaviors panel, note that the event is onLoad. You can change this if you want.

cross-reference

• Refer to Task 127 for opening a new browser window.

Making a Simple Pop-Up Menu

Pop-up menus are simple to create in Dreamweaver. You can attach the menus to any image or to text. The Pop-Up Menu behavior allows you to add menu and submenu items. The menu itself is generated by HTML. If you want to use an image for the menu, you can do so using the Fireworks Pop-Up Menu; however, it isn't available with the Dreamweaver Pop-Up Menu behavior.

notes

- For our example, the text "Large Appliances" wouldn't have a link because it's just a category name, which will have submenus.

- If you add menu items after an indented one, it will be indented as well. To make a list name outdented, click the Outdented Item button (Step 6).

- You can see a preview of the text color and the cell color as you make changes (Step 7).

- After you add the menu look, you can reedit as many times as necessary (Step 10).

1. Select the text, button, or image you want to add a menu to; then open the Behaviors panel (Shift+F3).

2. Click the Add Behaviors button (+) and select Show Pop-Up Menu. If you haven't yet saved your document, you are prompted to do so now. When the Show Pop-Up Menu dialog box opens, the Content tab is active.

3. In the Text field, type the menu name you'd like to appear in the menu. For example, you could type **Large Appliances**. If it's a menu item you want to use as a link, click the yellow folder to the right of the Link field and navigate to the file you want the link to open. Select a target from the Target field if you are using frames.

4. Click the Add Item Menu button (+) above the Text field. You notice your menu item name and link are added to the large white box area.

5. To add an additional menu items, repeat Steps 3 and 4. For example, you could add **Refrigerators**, **Stoves**, and **Small Appliances**.

6. Select the word Refrigerators (or any item you'd like to be in a submenu). Click the Indent Item button. Notice that it is now visually indented in the menu list. For this example, repeat for the word Stoves. Figure 129-1 shows the Content dialog box filled in.

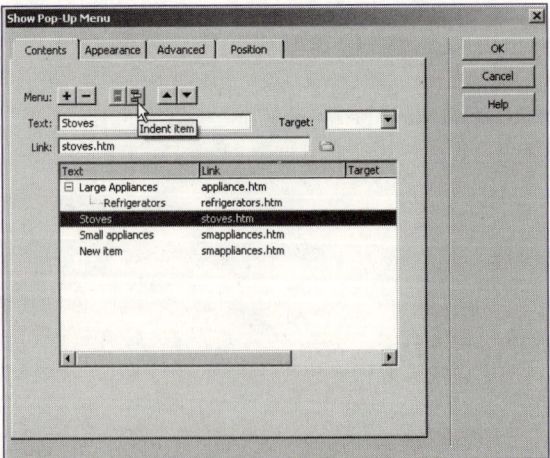

Figure 129-1: The Content for the menu is filled in and Refrigerator indented to be a submenu item

7. Click the Appearance tab. Select if you want the menu to be vertical or horizontal; then select your font style. Select the colors you want for the Up and Over states of the links. The cell color is the color you see behind the text.

8. Click the Advanced tab (see Figure 129-2). If you use the default settings of Cell Width and Height, the menu is sized according to the size of the text you entered. Access the drop-down list and select pixels if you want to enter a specific size for the menu. The next three fields allow you to adjust how the menu looks by entering how many pixels you want for Cell Padding and Spacing and if you want the text indented. The Menu Delay is how long it takes the menu to close when the user mousses off. The remainder of this window is where you set how your borders will appear (or if they will).

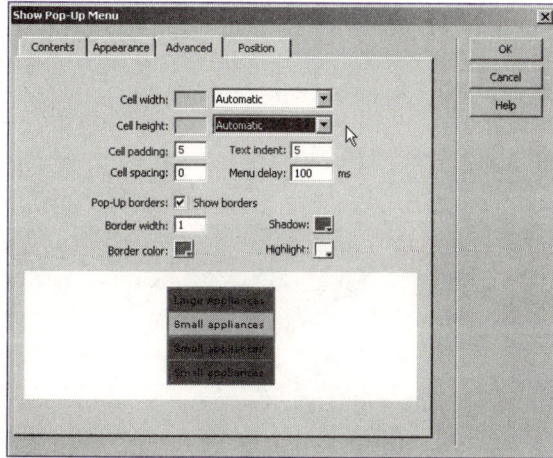

Figure 129-2: The Advanced tab of the Show Pop-UpMenu dialog box

9. Click the Position tab. In this window you set the position of the menu relative to the image it is attached to. Select how you want your menus to appear from the visual icons. The coordinates are set automatically, but you can alter them by entering them yourself. You normally will leave the Hide Menu onMouseOut event checked. Click OK to close the Show Pop Up Menu dialog box.

10. Save and test in a browser. Pass your mouse over the image and you see your menu.

cross-reference

• You may need to edit the position by double-clicking on the event in the Behaviors panel. Refer to Task 122 for editing behaviors (Step 3).

Inserting and Editing a Fireworks HTML Navigation File

I n Fireworks you can easily add swap image behaviors to your buttons, add links, and add alt text. If you want to make large navigation systems, it may be faster to do so in Fireworks and then insert them into Dreamweaver. The Fireworks behaviors are compatible with Dreamweaver and can be edited.

1. Design your navigation in Fireworks.

2. Optimize your navigation and export HTML and Images.

3. In Dreamweaver, insert your cursor where you'd like the navigation inserted.

4. In the Insert bar, Common category, select the Image icon, and from the menu, select Fireworks HTML (or choose Insert ⇨ Image Objects ⇨ Fireworks HTML), as shown in Figure 130-1.

notes

- You can add your links in Fireworks if you'd like. For the example files, the links are the null link of `javascript:;`.

- If you have Fireworks and want to export the navigation yourself, the source file of nav.png is included in the task130 folder.

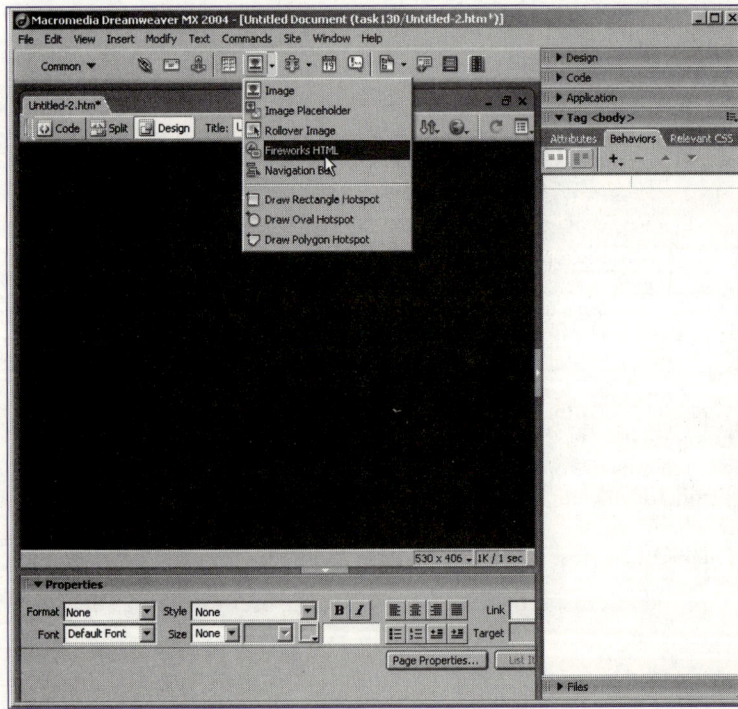

Figure 130-1: The Insert Fireworks HTML menu option

5. Browse to the file you exported. If using the sample files, select ha.htm. You can choose to delete the original HTM file if you want to. Click OK to close the dialog box and insert the navigation.

6. Select one of the buttons. Open the Behaviors panel (Shift+F3) and notice the behaviors show up. You can change the events or edit the behaviors if you'd like to right here in Dreamweaver (see Figure 130-2).

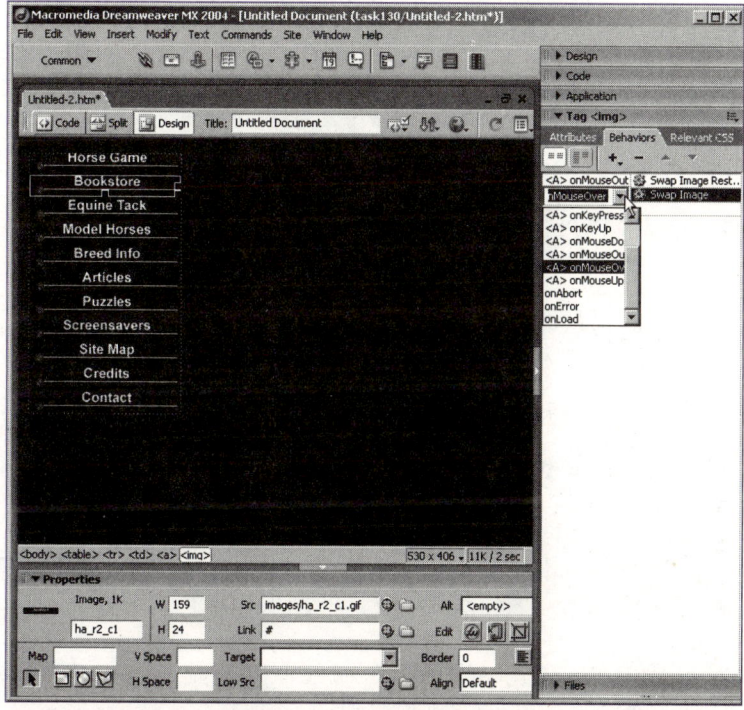

Figure 130-2: The navigation inserted and the behaviors shown in the Behaviors panel

7. With a button selected, look at the Property inspector. You can add your link here, add alt text, and so on, as shown in Figure 130-3.

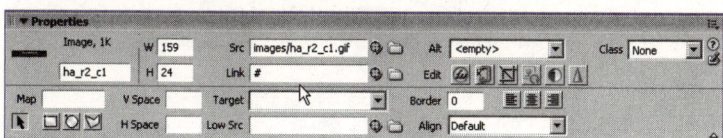

Figure 130-3: The Property inspector showing the link area where you can edit your links

cross-reference
- Refer to Task 122 for editing behaviors.

Making a Drag-and-Drop Object

You can allow users to move elements on your page by dragging them. It's very useful and interactive for tasks such as trying clothes on a model or placing items into a shopping cart and is frequently used for moving puzzle pieces. I've also seen this behavior used for decorating a Christmas tree, and I've used it for a children's site where they could drag tack (saddles, etc.) onto a horse to see how it looked. For this exercise you can download a sample puzzle file (task131 folder) with no behavior added from www.wiley.com/compbooks/10simplesteps.

notes

- The Drag Layer function has to be called before a layer can be dragged; therefore, it is attached to the body so that it is called when the page loads (Step 3).

- You should use the Constrained movement option for interface elements such as sliders (Step 7).

- The Advanced tab of the Drag Layer dialog box is where you can select a specific drag handle, as well as the position where you want the layer to be. You can even attach a JavaScript to the action (Step 9).

1. Add layers and their contents that you want to make moveable into your document. Or you can get a starter file from the task131 folder at www.wiley.com/compbooks/10simplesteps. Open the task131.htm page from the sample folder.

2. Open the Layers panel (F2) and notice all the layer names. You can change the names if you'd like. Figure 131-1 shows the layers in the sample file.

Figure 131-1: Sample puzzle file being used for this example

3. Select the <body> tag from the Tag Selector.

4. In the Behaviors panel (Shift+F3), select the Add Behavior button.

5. From the Behavior list, select Drag Layer.

6. In the Drag Layer dialog box (Basic tab), the Layer field shows all layers in your document (see Figure 131-2). Select one.

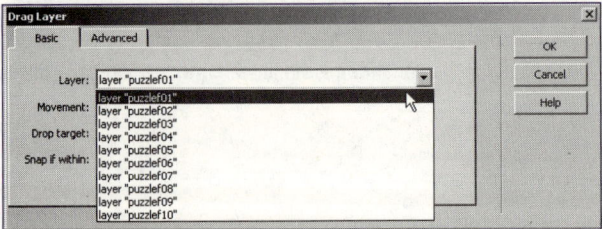

Figure 131-2: The Drag Layer dialog box showing all the layers in the document

7. Click the large Get Current Position button. This gets the coordinates of the puzzle piece (or any other object) while it is in its proper position (or in its current position in the document).

8. Repeat Steps 6 and 7 for all the layers except the large image of the puzzle. In the sample file, the large puzzle image is puzzlef10; don't apply the behavior to it.

9. In the Snap If Within field, enter a pixel amount. This allows the piece to snap in place when it gets close. Click OK to close the Drag Layer dialog box.

10. Save and test the puzzle. Be sure each piece is moveable; it's very easy to miss one. Back in Dreamweaver, select one layer at a time and move all the pieces to the right of the puzzle base, as shown in Figure 131-3.

Figure 131-3: The puzzle with all the pieces moved to the right side

Task **131**

tip

- When moving layers, you may not be able to see or select the handle. When this happens, use your keyboard arrow keys to get the layer in a position where you can drag the handle.

cross-reference

- Refer to Task 108 for adding layers (Step 1).

Adding Text That Is Seen in the Status Bar

The Set Text ⇨ Set Text of Status Bar behavior is used to display a message in the Status bar of the browser.

1. Don't select anything for this behavior if you want the message in the Sstatus bar to be the same at all times.

2. In the Behaviors panel (Shift+F3), click the Add Behavior button (+) and select Set Text ⇨ Set Text of Status Bar, as shown in Figure 132-1.

notes

- Frequently this is used to display company information or name in the status bar (Step 1).

- If you want the text in the Status bar to disappear when the user moves off the image or text, add another behavior of Set Text ⇨ Set Text of Status Bar and leave the Text field blank. In the Behaviors panel, change the event to onMouseOut (Step 10).

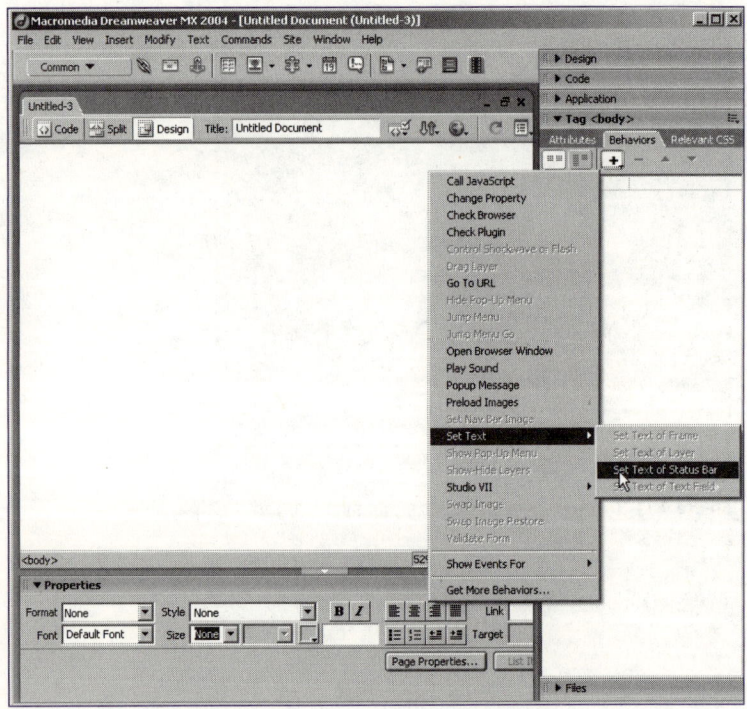

Figure 132-1: The Behavior list showing the Set Text behaviors

caution

- Most browsers have the Status bar as an option, so don't put critical content here—they may not see it (Step 6).

3. In the Set Text of Status Bar dialog box, type the text you want to appear in the Status bar of the browser, as shown in Figure 132-2.

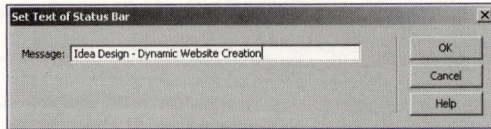

Figure 132-2: The Set Text of Status Bar dialog box

4. Click OK.

5. Notice in the Behaviors panel that the event is onLoad (see Figure 132-3). The text will show as soon as the page loads.

Figure 132-3: The Behaviors panel with the Set Text of Status Bar behavior added

6. Save and preview.

7. Alternatively, you can select an image or text to trigger the behavior.

8. If you use this option, you'll need to add a null link (**javascript:;**) in the Link field in the Property inspector.

9. Repeat Steps 2 to 4.

10. In the Behaviors list, click the arrow in the middle and change the event to onMouseOver. Save and test.

cross-reference

▪ Refer to Task 122 for editing a behavior (Step 10).

Task 133

Making a Navigation Bar

Navigation, or nav, bars are a series of images (usually some sort of button or tab) used as links to navigate your site.

1. Insert your graphics for your navigation bar into your layout. Select your first image. Or you can download the task133 folder from www.wiley.com/compbooks/10simplesteps, open the index.html page, and select the Home button.

2. In the Behaviors panel (Shift+F3), click the Add Behavior button (+) and select Set Nav Bar Image. The Set Nav Bar Image dialog box opens with the Basic tab active, as shown in Figure 133-1.

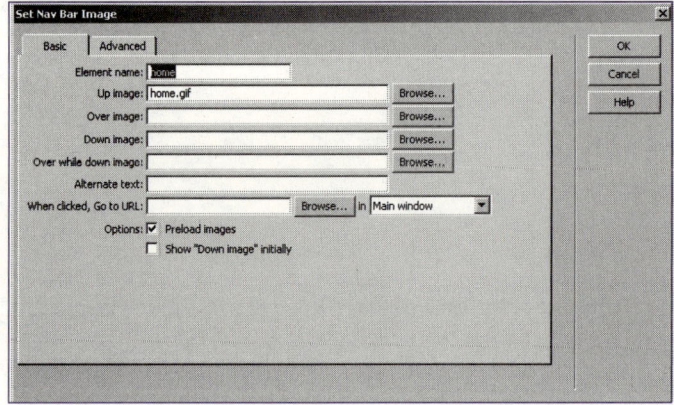

Figure 133-1: The Set Nav Bar Image dialog box with the Basic tab active

3. Enter a name for the button, such as **Home**. Click the Browse button to select the Over image (the image that appears as a mouse passes over). The sample filename is home_f2. Also select the Down image (the image that appears after an image is clicked), which is home_f3 for the sample, and/or the Over while Down image (the image that appears when a mouse passes over an image that has already been selected). Enter the URL that will be displayed when the button is clicked in the When Clicked, Go to URL field, or click the Browse button to navigate to and select the file.

4. It's a good idea to leave the Preload Images option checked. If you don't, the rollover images will not load until the user mouses over, which may cause a delay.

5. Select the Show Down Image Initially option. When the home page is selected, the Down state will show. The default behavior is that when the page is selected, all the other links will return to their Up state. Figure 133-2 shows the Set Nav Bar dialog box filled in.

6. Click OK when you are done with the Home button. In the sample files, the services.html and the products.html pages are already created for you. In your site you'll need to have your files ready so you can link as well as add the Set Nav Bar behavior to each page. If you

are using a template to add the navigation, be sure to make the navigation area editable so you can add the behavior to each page.

7. Repeat Steps 3, 4, and 6 for each of the buttons. Notice you skip Step 5 because you don't want all the images to appear down, just the home page for now. Figure 133-3 shows the dialog box for the Products button of the sample page.

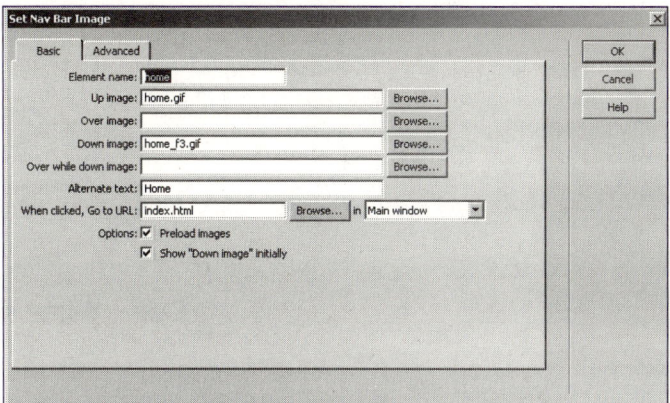

Figure 133-2: The Set Nav Bar dialog box filled in

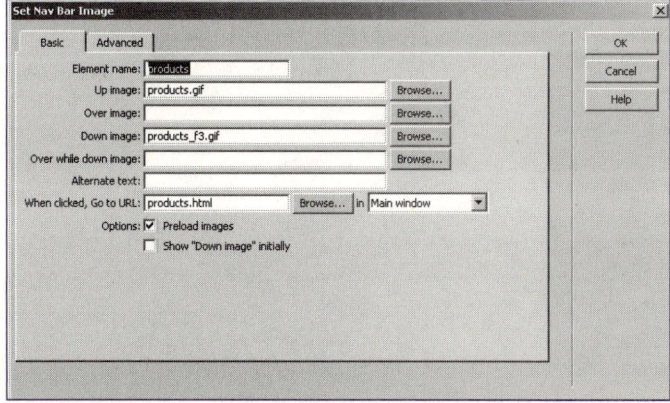

Figure 133-3: The Set Nav Bar dialog box for other buttons

8. Open the file for each button (such as products.html), select the appropriate button (Products), and in the Behaviors panel, double-click the Set Nav Bar Image behavior to edit it. Select the Show Down Image Initially option.

9. Save all your pages and test in a browser (see Figure 133-4). When you click a button, the page loads. The button clicked will be in the Down state, indicating the page is active, and all the other buttons will return to their Up state.

Figure 133-4: The nav bar in a browser

cross-reference
- Refer to the task133_done folder inside the task133 folder for the completed files.

Task **134**

Changing Text in a Layer Dynamically or Adding Submenus Dynamically

You can change text in a layer by clicking on a trigger. A file is provided for your practice (task134.htm) in the task134 folder at www.wiley.com/ compbooks/10simplesteps. The sample demonstrates the popular effect of using a layer to display a submenu under a button.

note

- For the sample file, copy the code from the task127.html page and paste into the New HTML field (Step 6).

1. Before you add the Set Text of Layer behavior, add your layer or layers to your document. If you use the provided sample file, open the Layers panel (F2) and select layer 1 to see it, as shown in Figure 134-1.

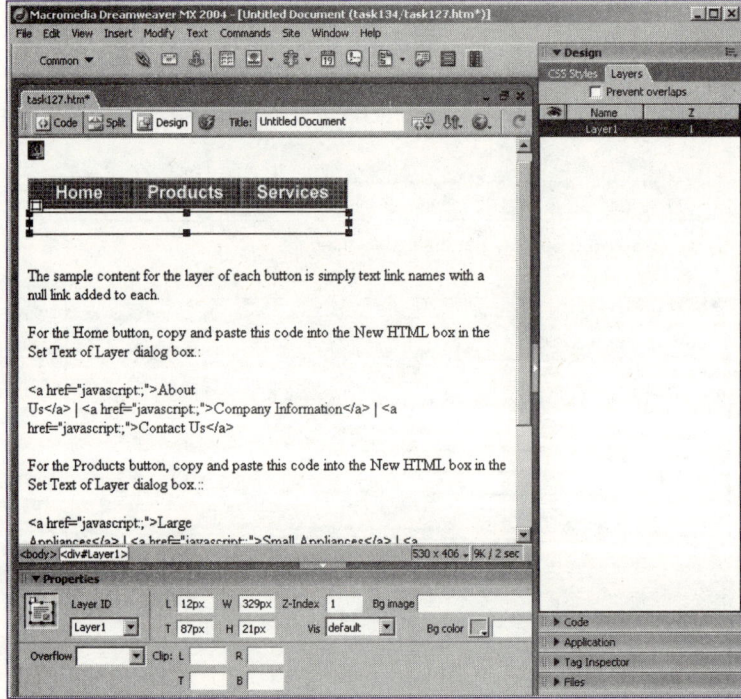

Figure 134-1: The sample file with a layer added

2. Type what you want to go into the layer, and then select it and cut it. For the sample file I put the code you need for the layer on the sample page, so you can simply copy the text for the Home button for this task.

3. Select the trigger image. In the sample file, select the Home button.

4. Open the Behaviors panel (Shift+F3), click the Add Behaviors button (+), and select Set Text ⇨ Set Text of Layer option. There are other behaviors already present in the sample file.

5. In the Set Text of Layer dialog box, check that the correct layer is displayed in the Layer field. Click the down arrow to select a different one. Since there is only one layer in this file, it is selected by default.

caution

- If you are copying from Design view, be sure to check the Code view to get all the code for the layer. For instance, the beginning and ending href code for my links was not selected in Design view (Step 2).

6. Paste (Ctrl/Command+V) the HTML code you cut or copied into the New HTML box, as shown in Figure 134-2.

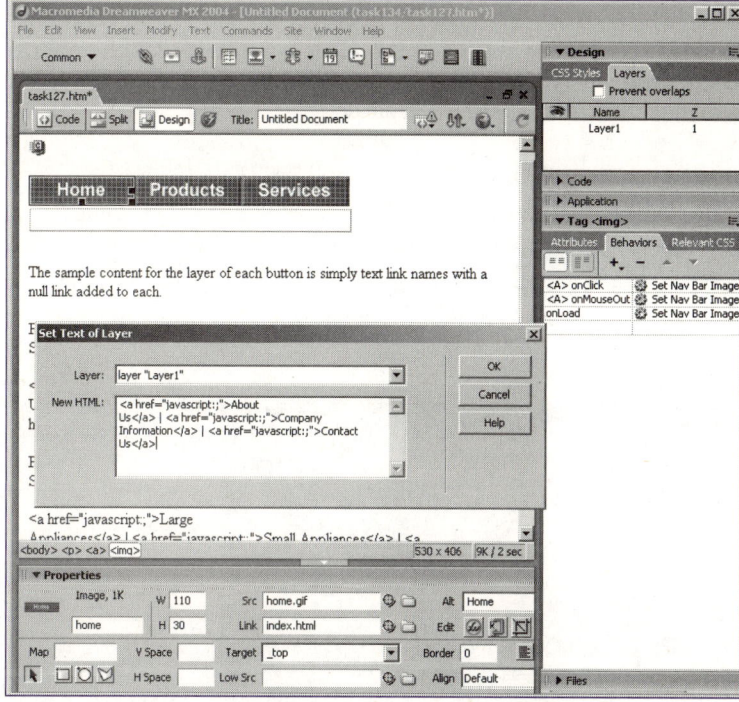

Figure 134-2: The Set Text of Layer dialog box filled in

7. Click OK when you are done.

8. Repeat for the other two buttons in the sample file.

9. Save and preview in a browser. Figure 134-3 shows how the menu looks in a browser.

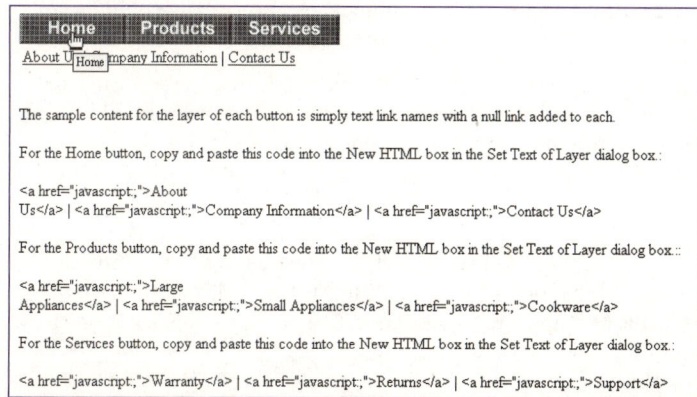

Figure 134-3: Menu as seen in a browser

cross-reference

▪ Refer to Tasks 108 and 110 for inserting layers and editing their properties (Step 1).

Task 135

Making a Photo Album

Since so many people now own digital cameras, there are more and more people who have images they want to display online. The Web Photo Album extension is a fast and easy way to do this. This extension makes thumbnails of all your images and even generates a separate page for each one, as well as the navigation to move among the pages of images.

1. Place all the images you want to use into a separate folder.

2. Give each image a meaningful name if you'd like to place names below each image. Otherwise, it doesn't matter.

3. Open a new document and choose Commands ⇨ Create Web Photo Album. The Create Web Photo Album dialog box opens, as shown in Figure 135-1.

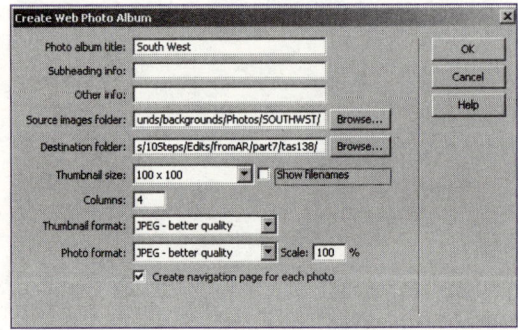

Figure 135-1: The Create Web Photo Album dialog box

4. Give your album a title and subtitle if desired.

5. Browse to select your source folder containing your images and then your destination folder where the processed thumbnails and HTM pages will be saved.

6. Then decide on and enter a thumbnail size, how many columns you want to appear in the layout, and the optimization quality you need.

7. Select Create Navigation page for each photo, if you want the navigation to be included. Click OK when the dialog box is filled in. The image used in Figure 135-1 is a filled-in dialog box.

8. In Dreamweaver, click OK on the message of the photo album being created. Figure 135-2 shows the message telling you it is done.

9. Your document in Dreamweaver now shows a table containing the thumbnails. Preview in a browser. Figure 135-3 shows the page of thumbnails as it appears in Netscape 7.

Figure 135-2: The Album Created message box

Figure 135-3: The automatically generated page of thumbnails previewed in a browser

10. Click any thumbnail and a new page opens with navigation included, as shown in Figure 135-4.

Figure 135-4: The larger view of the image with navigation

cross-reference

▪ Refer to Task 136 for finding more extensions.

Task 136 Getting More Extensions

You can add a ton of functionality to Dreamweaver by using extensions. *Extensions* are scripts that add additional tools to Dreamweaver. There are lots of sites that offer both free and commercial extensions. The first place to start looking is the Macromedia Exchange (www.macromedia.com/cfusion/exchange). You need to register before you download any extensions, but it's easy and pretty fast.

notes

- When you arrive at the Exchange, take a look at the information available. You see the category of the extension, which can help in your search for other similar extensions. You also see the name of the extension, along with the author, date, and version. The rating is pretty important; it is determined by previous users of the extension (Step 4).

- The developer's URL is very important. You want to check the specific developer's site to be sure you are getting the latest and greatest extension. For example, there is a new version to the extension you are downloading now (although this one works fine). You can continue to see how getting extensions is done, but you want to get the latest version later (Step 4).

- You don't have to download to the Downloaded Extensions folder; you can save them anywhere you'd like (Step 7).

- In the right column of the Exchange are options for your favorites, alerts, and uploads in the Your Exchange area.

1. Access the Dreamweaver Exchange using one of these methods:

   - From the Start page, select Dreamweaver Exchange from the Extend category of the page.

   - Choose Commands ➪ Get More Commands.

   - In the Behaviors panel (F2), click the Add Behaviors button (+) and select Get More Behaviors.

   - Choose Commands ➪ Manage Extensions to open the Extension Manager. Click File ➪ Go to Macromedia Exchange.

   - Go directly to www.macromedia.com/cfusion/exchange.

2. If you've never registered at Macromedia, do so now. The registration page is shown in Figure 136-1.

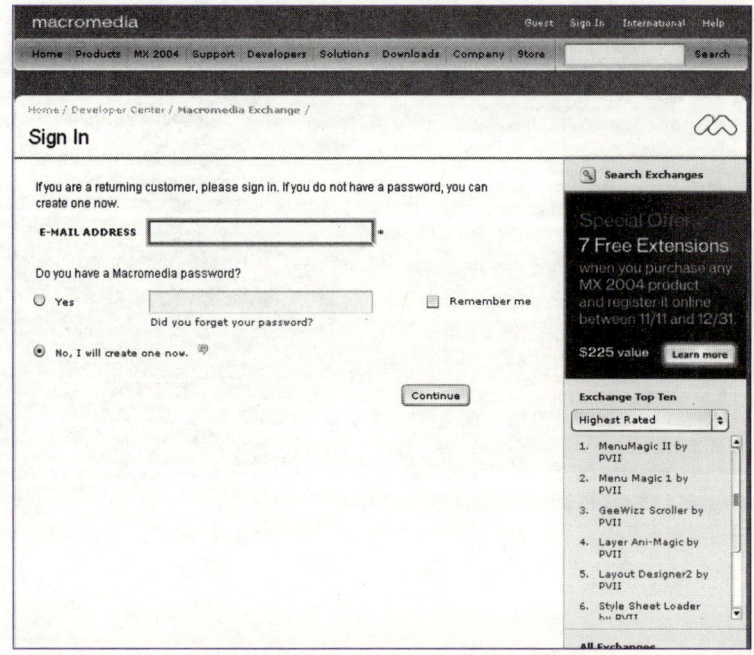

Figure 136-1: The registration page for the Macromedia Exchange

3. After you are registered and logged in, you'll be at the Exchange page. Click the down arrow for Browse Extensions. Select any category, as shown in Figure 136-2.

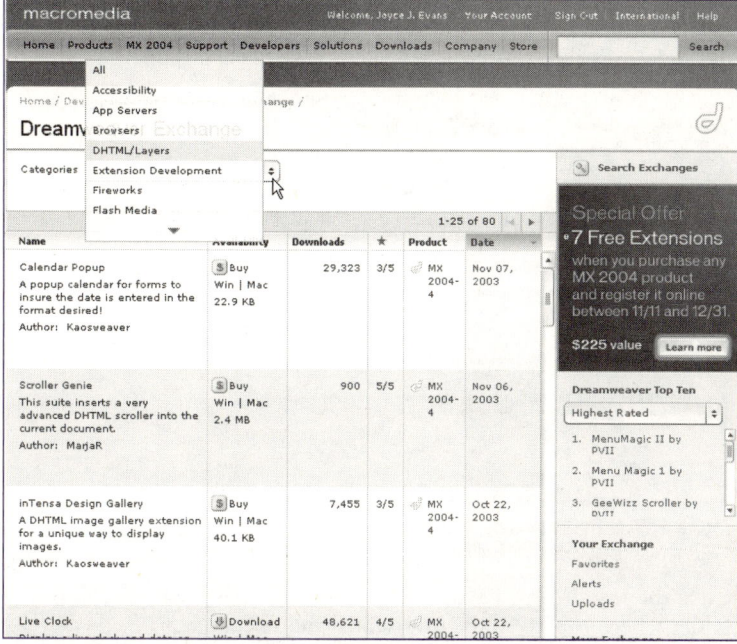

Figure 136-2: The Dreamweaver Exhange

4. If you know the name of the extension you want, click the Search Exchange link at the top of the right column (see Figure 136-2). Type the name of the extension into the Search field and select the Exchange you want to search. Click the Search button.

5. If the search returns more than one entry, find the one you are looking for and click the Buy or Download button. You can click an extension name to get more detailed information.

6. For the free downloads, click OK for the Save This File to Disk option.

7. Navigate to the Dreamweaver MX 2004 program folder and open the Downloaded Extensions folder. Click OK.

cross-reference

• Refer to Task 137 for installing your downloaded extensions (Step 7).

Task **137**

Installing Extensions

1. In Dreamweaver, save and close any open documents.

2. Choose Commands ⇨ Manage Extensions. The Extension Manager opens, as shown in Figure 137-1. Of course, how yours looks depends on the extensions you have or don't have installed.

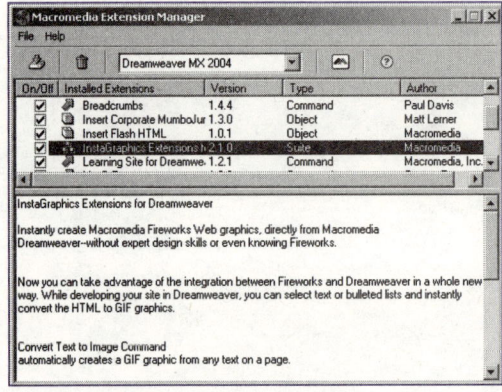

Figure 137-1: The Extension Manager

3. Click the Install New Extension icon (green arrow), navigate to the folder where you saved the extensions, and select one.

4. Agree to any disclaimers or license agreements.

5. Alternatively, you can use Windows Explorer and double-click the extension's filename, as shown in Figure 137-2. Accept the license agreement. The Extension Manager opens automatically, and the extension is installed.

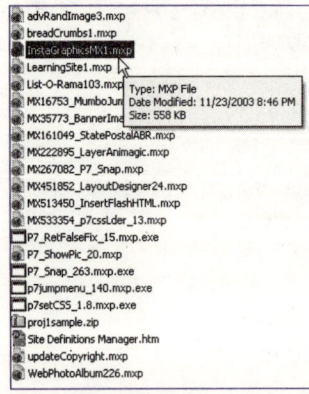

Figure 137-2: Installing extensions from Windows Explorer

6. In the On/Off column of the Extensions Manager, you can temporarily inactivate some of your extensions by clicking to deselect them. A dialog box opens, saying that it has been disabled, as shown in Figure 137-3.

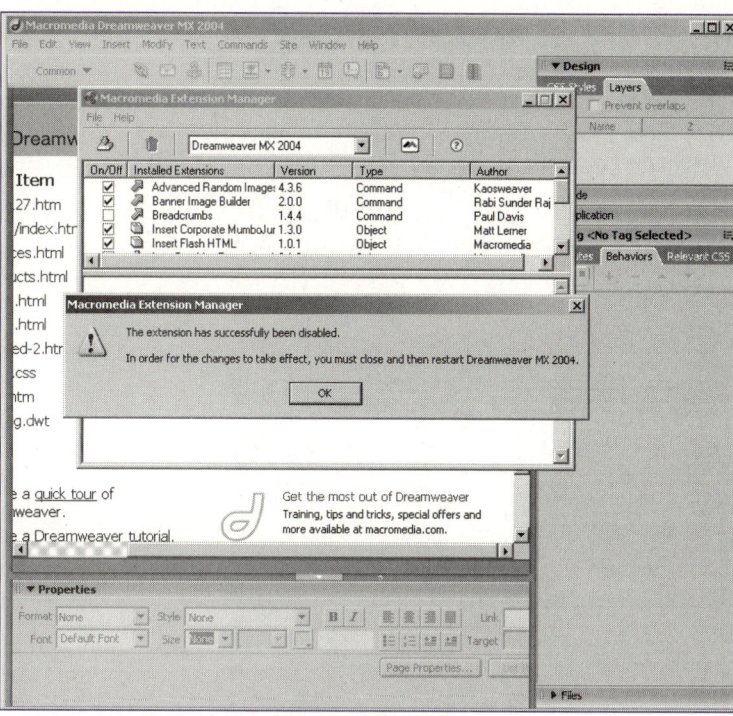

Figure 137-3: Turning off an extension

7. To actually delete an extension, select it and click the trash can icon to uninstall it.

8. Select an extension; in the area below the extension list, you see some details and/or instructions for using the extension, as shown in Figure 137-4.

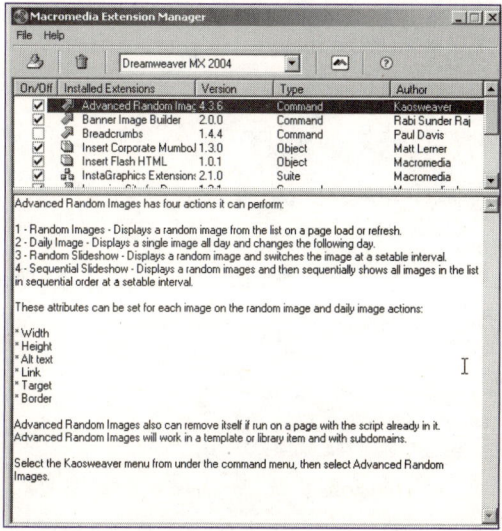

Figure 137-4: Extension detail

cross-reference

- Refer to Task 136 for how to acquire extensions (Step 1).

138

Displaying Random Images

The Banner Image Builder extension is used to display images randomly. You can set the interval between the images changing, plus each image can have a link attached to it. You can also use this extension to make JPEG animations.

notes

- Put all your images in the same folder, and then optimize and size in Fireworks prior to running this command.

- To make JPEG animations, you need to set the rotation to a much faster speed. You can use 0.1, 0.001, and so on.

1. Go to the Dreamweaver Exchange and get the Banner Image Builder 2.0.0 extension. It's made by Rabi Sunder Raj.

2. In Dreamweaver, choose Commands ⇨ Manage Extensions (see Figure 138-1).

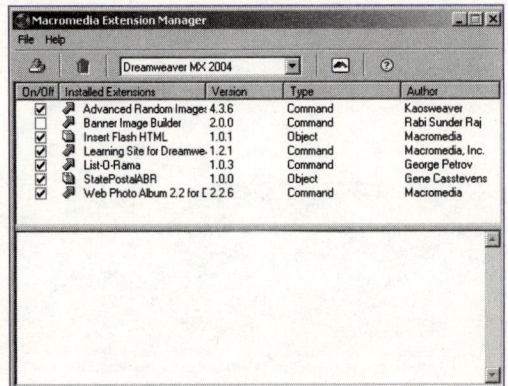

Figure 138-1: The Extension Manager open

3. Click the Install button and navigate to the folder you saved your extension into. Select the Banner Image Builder extension. Click Install, as shown in Figure 138-2.

4. Choose Commands ⇨ Banner Image Builder. The Banner Image Builder 2.0.0 dialog box opens.

5. Navigate to each image you want to be included in your rotating image display.

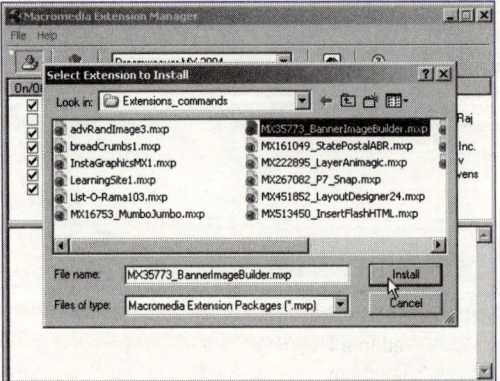

Figure 138-2: Installing the Banner Image Builder extension

Task **138**

6. Add a URL to each image if you want to link the various images to a separate page.

7. Set the target and the rotation speed. A filled-in dialog box is shown in Figure 138-3.

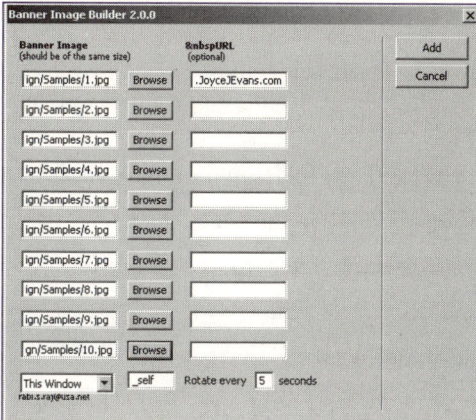

Figure 138-3: The Banner Image Builder 2.0.0 dialog box filled in

8. Click Add to build the image banner.

9. The first image is now visible in your document. Preview in a browser. Although I can't show you the rotation in a screenshot, you can see the image as viewed in a browser in Figure 138-4. This image rotates with a new one every 5 seconds.

Figure 138-4: The first image as viewed in a browser; it rotates every 5 seconds, which was set in the Build Banner Image dialog box

cross-reference

- Refer to Task 136 for down-loading extensions from Macromedia Exchange.

Building an Image Gallery

Download and install the Show Pic Layer extension by PVII. If there is an .exe at the end of the extension name, delete it and then install as normal. Download the starter files from the Part 7 task139 folder at www.wiley.com/compbooks/10simplesteps. These files include the thumbnails for the gallery.

notes

- I've used placeholder captions and descriptive text. Be sure you change this for your gallery images.

- In the Insert Show Pic dialog box, there is an option for Park Avenue. This is a for sale design package from Project Seven (www.projectseven.com).

1. In the Common category of the Insert bar, you see an icon on the end of the row (looks like a filmstrip). Click it, and then perform the following steps (see Figure 139-1):

   - Browse to the full-size image (large folder in the sample files).

   - Browse to select the shim.gif image in the same folder.

   - Enter the position (Top 109 and Left 150 for the sample files).

   - Enter a text caption and descriptive text.

   - Click OK to create the Show Pic layer.

   There is a transparent image in the layer right now. If you click anywhere else, the layer disappears. That's OK. Later you see how the Show Pic extension replaces the shim with a larger image of the thumbnail.

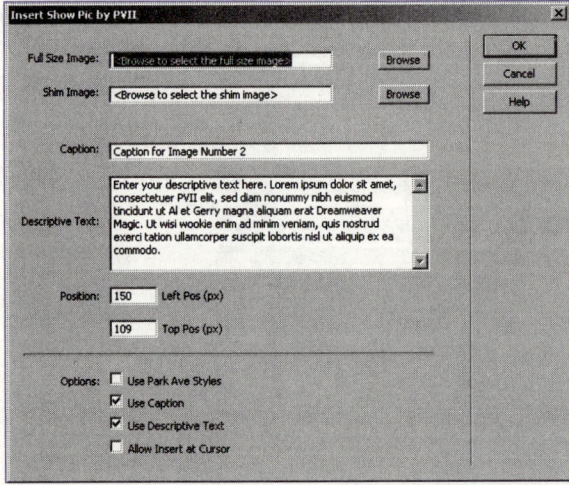

Figure 139-1: The Insert Show Pic dialog box filled in

2. Repeat Step 1 for all the layers you need.

3. To have the first image show when the page loads, select the <body> tag from the Tag Selector.

4. Open the Behaviors panel (Shift+F3) and click the Add button. Select Studio VII ⇨ Show Pic by PVII.

5. In the dialog box, browse to your first image and select it. The layer name should be P7ShowPL1, but check it to be sure. The dialog box should look like Figure 139-2 for the sample file.

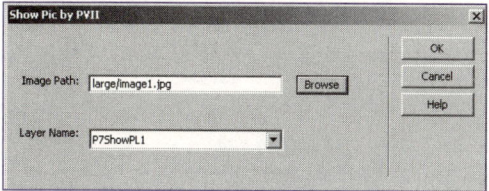

Figure 139-2: The Show Pic behavior dialog box filled in

6. Check the behavior in the Behaviors panel and be sure the event is set to onLoad. Now you can preview in a browser, and it should look like Figure 139-3.

Figure 139-3: As seen previewed in a browser

7. To apply the Show Pic behavior to each thumbnail, select the first one, and in the Behaviors panel, click the Add button, and then select Studio VII ⇨ Show Pic by PVII.

8. In the dialog box, navigate to the first image and select the first layer. Repeat for the second image, only navigate to the second image in the large folder and select the second layer. Repeat for each layer.

9. Be sure the event for the behavior added to the thumbnails is onClick, as shown in Figure 139-4.

10. Preview in a browser. Select each thumbnail, and the larger image replaces the placeholder.

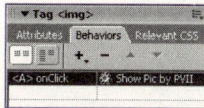

Figure 139-4: The onClick event

cross-references

- Refer to Tasks 136 and 137 for downloading and installing extensions.

- Refer to Task 122 for editing behaviors.

Building a Photo Album Using Design Templates

A newer version of the Photo Album extension is available at the Dreamweaver Exchange. This version is much nicer than the one that ships with Dreamweaver, and it has a lot more control.

notes

- After you add the folder of images, you can select the image and see a preview. If you don't want it, add it to the Exclude side.

- It's quick and easy to convert a folder of large photos into thumbnails using the Fireworks batch command. You can size and optimize the images all in one batch.

1. Go to the Dreamweaver Exchange and locate the WebPhotoAlbum226 extension. You can type the name into the search engine. Download it and save it into your extension folder.

2. Choose Commands ➪ Manage Extensions and install the WebPhotoAlbum226 extension. Accept the licensing agreement.

3. Open a new page and choose Commands ➪ Create Web Photo Album 2.2.

4. Choose the type of album you'd like. The first option requires you to have Fireworks installed, but it's also the option with the best features. The options are shown in Figure 140-1. Click Next.

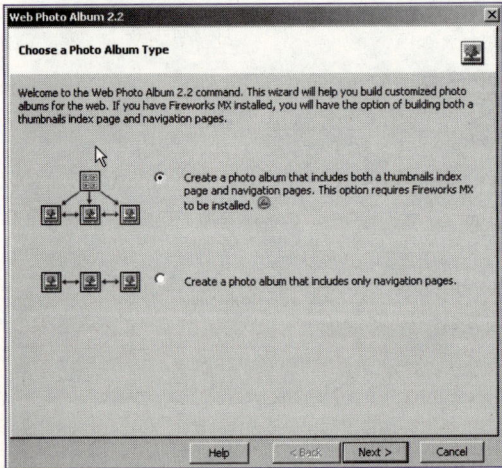

Figure 140-1: The first step is to choose the type of album you'd like to build

5. The next dialog box allows you to use a custom template page or to choose from one of the many that ship with Dreamweaver. You can also go to the Exchange to get more. The theme selection dialog box is shown in Figure 140-2.

6. Select the folder of images you'd like to add, or select individual images. You can also change the rotation of the images if you need to. Once you've selected your images, click Next.

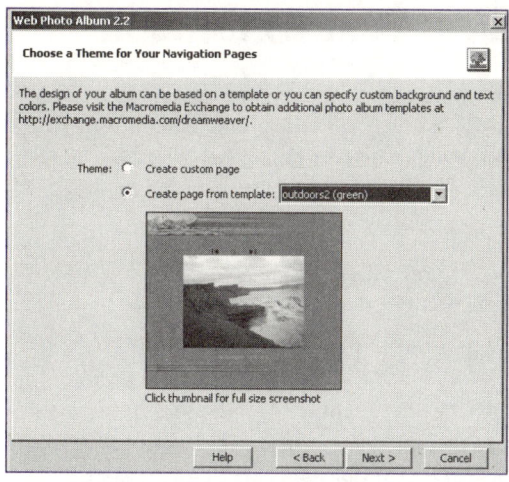

Figure 140-2: Select a theme for the look of your photo album

7. Select the destination folder, and add a title to the photo album. Select the optimization for your images. Select the navigation style you like. You can even be prompted to add a caption to each image. You can also have the file size listed with the image. When you are done making all your selections, click Next.

8. Set the size for your thumbnails and their optimization settings, along with the number of columns you want displayed on the page. Click Next. Look over the Summary and click Finish. The images process in Fireworks, and you'll get a message that the album created successfully. Your browser then opens, as shown in Figure 140-3.

Figure 140-3: The album thumbnail page opens in a browser

cross-reference

■ Refer to Tasks 136 and 137 for getting and installing extensions.

Using a Shopping Cart Extension

With a free extension you can easily add a shopping cart to your Web site. It's an easy, fast, and inexpensive way to add the ability to sell from your site. Before you begin this task, you need to go to www.PayPal.com and register to get a free account.

note

• A paid shopping cart is available from WebAssist, which gives you many more features and is not just for PayPal (Step 1).

1. Go to www.webassist.com/Products/products.asp. Click the WA PayPal eCommerce toolkit link. Click the Get Now icon and follow the instructions to download the extension.

2. Install the PayPal303.mxp extension and close the Extension Manager.

3. Place your cursor where you want to add an Add to Cart button. In the Category drop-down list in the Insert bar, select PayPal (its own category is added when you install the extension), and then click the Add to Cart button. In the Insert PayPal Add to Cart Button dialog box, type in your PayPal account e-mail address into the PayPal Account field. Click Next.

4. Either select one of the button options or click the Yes, I Would Like to Create My Own Custom Button option (see Figure 141-1). If you want to use your own custom button, type in the URL of the image and click Next.

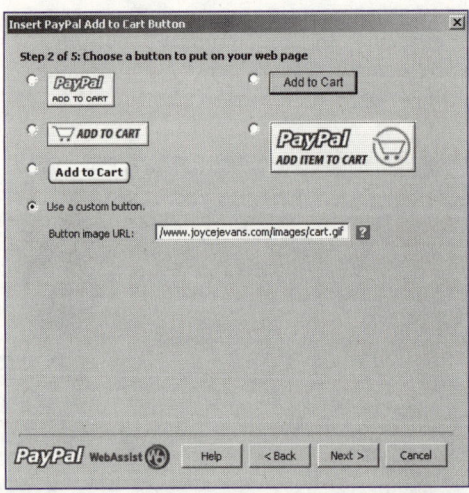

Figure 141-1: The Insert PayPal Add to Cart Button dialog box

caution

• If you do not have a secure server for your logo and you use one, users will see a warning when they enter PayPal about secure and unsecure items. It in no way makes the site unsecure, but it could scare your buyer away. Do not use a logo unless you can put it on a secure server somewhere (Step 6).

5. In the Item Name/Service field, type your item's name. In the Item ID field, you can enter an ID name/number if you'd like. Type in the price of the item, and select the currency type. Select any of the remaining options you'd like to include, and click Next.

6. If you want to use a custom logo on the PayPal page, enter the URL into the URL field and click Next.

7. If you want the user to be sent to a success or an error page, create them, add their links into the appropriate fields, and click Next.

8. Click the Finish button.

9. If you want to add a View Cart button, place it in a different cell or outside of the first form you added the Add button to. Click the View icon in the Insert bar, as shown in Figure 141-2.

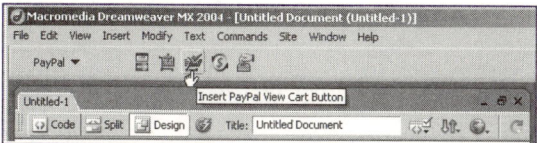

Figure 141-2: View button in the Insert bar

10. Add your PayPal e-mail, click Next, and select the button you want to use, or enter the URL of a custom button and click Next. Click Finish. Figure 141-3 shows custom shopping cart icons added to a page.

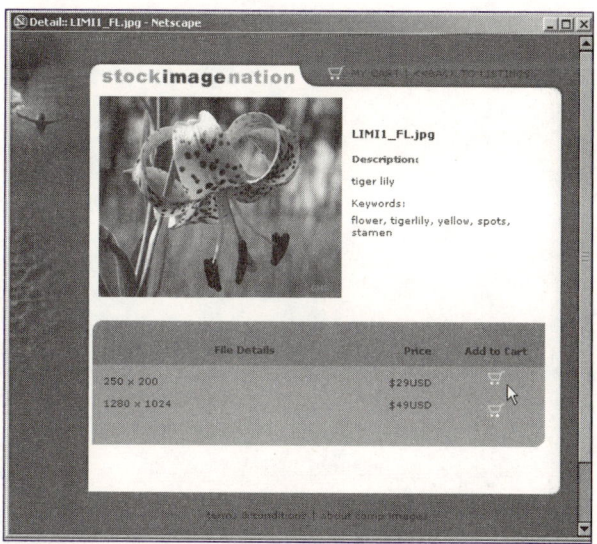

Figure 141-3: The Add to Cart and View Cart buttons added to a Web page

cross-reference

- Item IDs are frequently used if you are pulling your images from a database. Refer to Part 12 for using ColdFusion to access a database (Step 5).

Part 8: Using External Media

Task 142

Inserting a Flash Element (Image Viewer)

Important NOTE:

At the time of the writing of this book the new Internet Explorer browser was not released yet. The tasks in this part of the book will be affected by the new browser. The new browser will display a pop-up message that the user will need to click to confirm that they want to execute the media item on your page. Macromedia should have a utility released to solve this problem by the time you get this book so be sure to go to http://www.macromedia.com/devnet/activecontent/ *for the utility and more information.*

Dreamweaver MX 2004 shipped with one Flash element called the Image Viewer. Flash Elements are prebuilt elements to aid you in quickly developing Rich Internet Applications. I expect that more will be available by the time this book is released. Go to www.macromedia.com/cfusion/exchange to find more. If you've never used the Exchange, you need to register first.

1. You don't need to do anything to use the Image Viewer that shipped with Dreamweaver MX 2004. But if you've downloaded new Flash Elements, you'll need to install them first using the Extension Manager (Commands ⇨ Manage Extensions). The Extension Manager is shown in Figure 142-1.

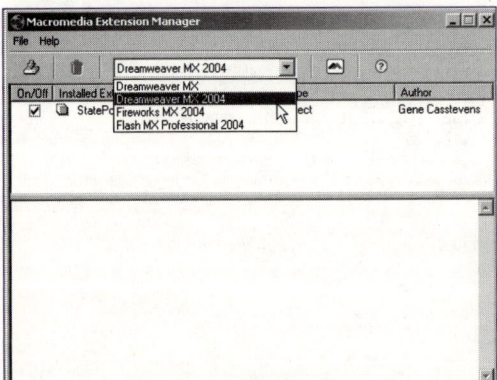

Figure 142-1: The Extension Manager

2. Open a new HTML page or any other page that you'd like to add the Image Viewer or other Flash Element to.

3. Insert your cursor where you'd like the Flash Element to be placed.

4. In the Insert bar, from the category list, select Flash Elements, as shown in Figure 142-2. You can also choose Insert ⇨ Media ⇨ Image Viewer if you prefer that method.

5. From the Flash Element category, select the Image Viewer icon (see Figure 142-3).

---

notes

- Go to www.macromedia.com/devnet/activecontent for the Macromedia utility for media objects to work properly in the new Internet Explorer browser

- It's easier to organize if you have the images you want to use in the Image Viewer in a separate folder.

- You'll be able to edit the Image Viewer using both the Property inspector and the Tag inspector without even owning Flash.

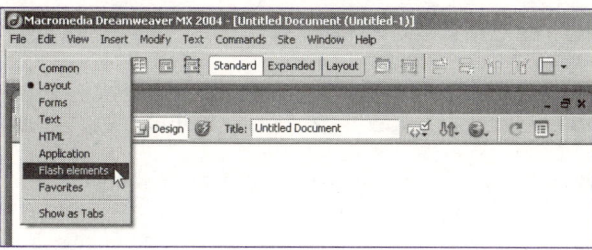

Figure 142-2: The Flash Element category of the Insert bar

6. The Save Flash Element dialog box opens. Select or create a folder and name your new movie.

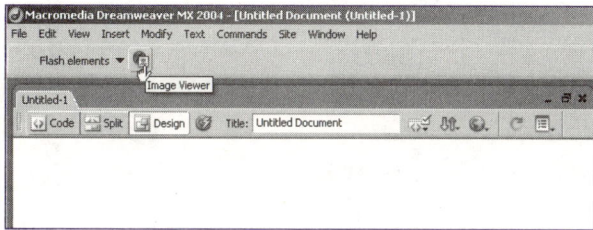

Figure 142-3: Selecting the Image Viewer icon

7. Click OK.

8. A large gray box appears in your document, as shown in Figure 142-4. Also note that the Tag inspector changes to Tag <object> and a new panel labeled Flash Element is present. The Property inspector has also changed.

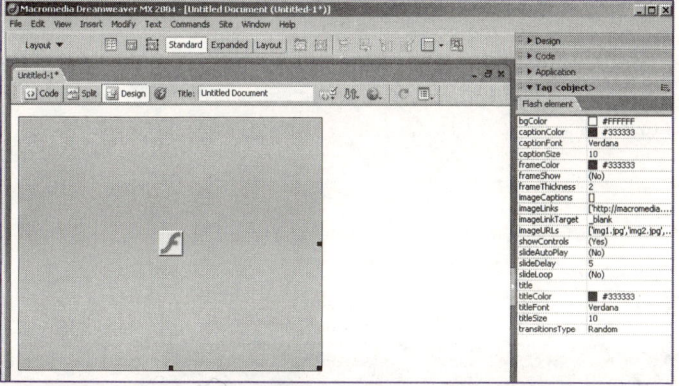

Figure 142-4: The Flash Element is inserted and the Flash Element panel appears

9. Preview in a browser. All you see so far are the controls to move through slides. You'll now need to configure the Image Viewer.

cross-references

- Refer to Task 143 to edit the Image Viewer and to link to the slides you want to appear.

- Refer to Tasks 136 and 137 for downloading and installing extensions.

Editing the Image Viewer

Once you have inserted the Flash Element, chances are you'll need to edit the properties. At this writing, only the Image Viewer is available.

1. In Design view, select the Flash Element (gray box), as shown in Figure 143-1.

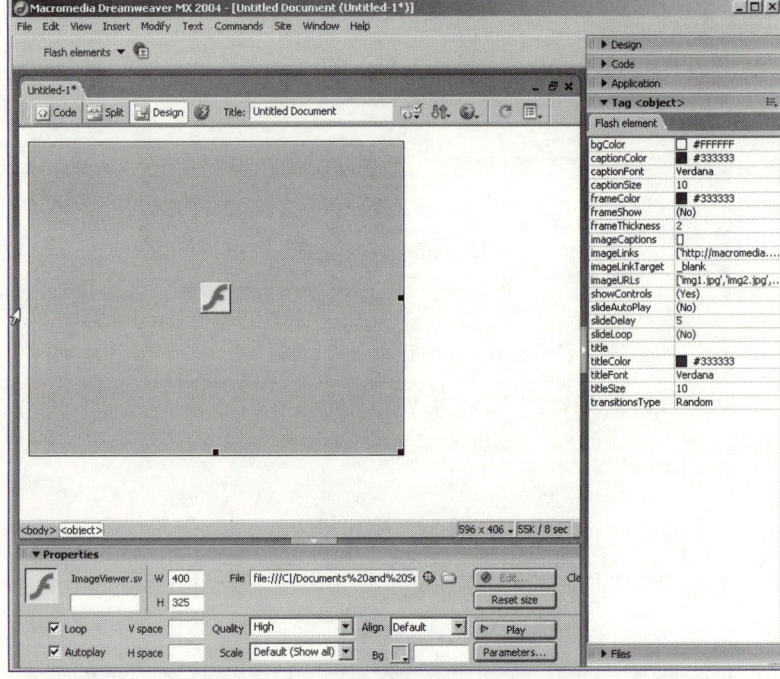

Figure 143-1: The Image Viewer selected in the document

2. If you'd prefer to edit in Code view, click within the Flash component's name (see Figure 143-2).

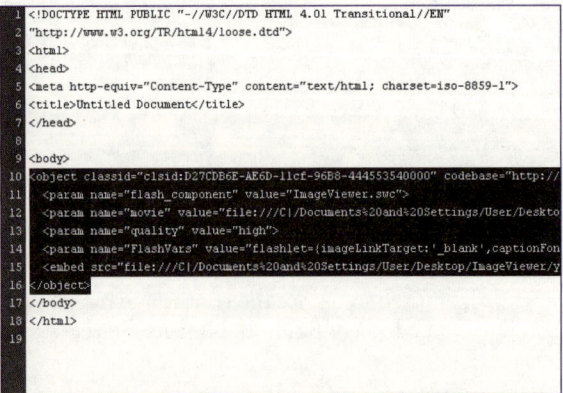

Figure 143-2: The Flash Element selected in Code view

3. Open the Tag Inspector (Windows ➪ Tag inspector). You can view and modify the attributes of the Flash Element in the Tag inspector. Figure 143-3 shows the Title attribute selected and modified.

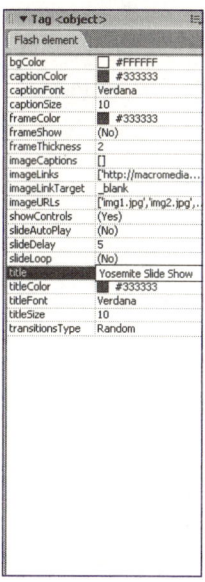

Figure 143-3: The Title attribute being modified

4. To edit an attribute value, select it and type a new value. If the value is predefined, select it from the menu to the right of the attribute-value column.

5. For the Image Viewer, enter the URL for each image. Figure 143-4 shows the URL for each image being added. Click inside the right area and you'll see the little Edit icon. Click it and you can access the Edit 'imageURLs' Arrary dialog box.

6. If you are drawing data from a database, click the Dynamic Data button to the right of the attribute and select a source.

7. Modify any other attribute you'd like to change.

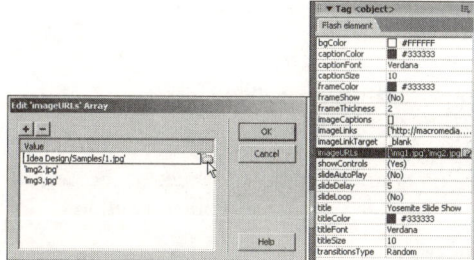

Figure 143-4: Modify the URL in the Tag inspector and/or the Edit 'imageURLs' Array dialog box

tips

- In the Edit 'imageURLs' Array dialog box, if you click the first URL, you see the yellow folder on the right appear and you can navigate to the image file and select it.

- The Property inspector has limited attribute editability, but it does have a Preview button, so you can preview the Flash Element in Design view.

cross-reference

- Refer to Task 142 for inserting the Image Viewer or any other Flash Element.

Making Media Objects Accessible

Many designers now need to make all the elements of their Web pages accessible. You can configure Dreamweaver to prompt you to fill in accessibility information every time you insert a media object.

1. To make your media object accessible, choose Edit ➪ Preferences ➪ Accessibility category and select Media (see Figure 144-1).

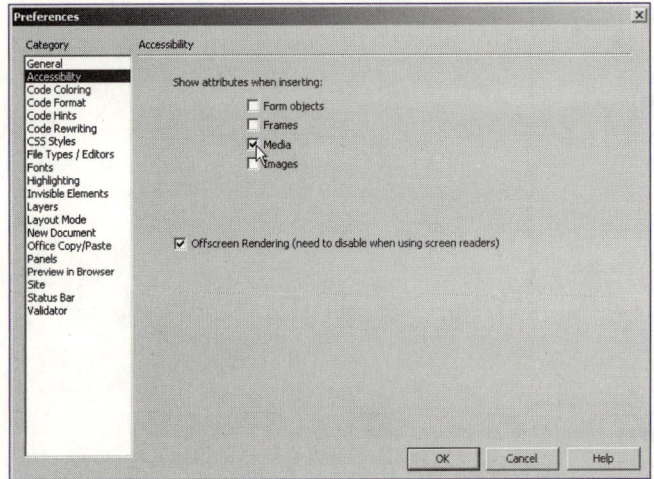

Figure 144-1: The Preferences dialog box showing the accessibility options

2. Click OK to close the Preferences dialog box.

3. In the Common category of the Insert bar is a Media icon. When you click on any of the Media options to insert it into your document the Object Tag Accessibility Attributes dialog box appears, as shown in Figure 144-2.

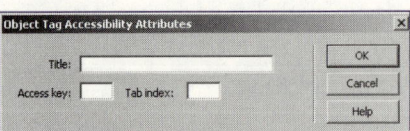

Figure 144-2: The accessibility options

4. In the Title field, enter a name for the media object.

5. In the Access Key field, enter a one-letter access key.

6. In the Tab Index field, enter a number for the tab index of the object. This specifies the order the user can tab through objects and links.

7. You don't have to be automatically prompted to add accessibility parameters; you can do so from the Tag inspector panel. Select the List view in the Attributes panel, and then select the CSS/

Accessibility option You can enter your parameters here, as shown in Figure 144-3.

Figure 144-3: The Attributes panel showing the CSS/Accessibility Category view of the properties

8. You'll see any parameters you've already entered. To add additional parameter values, click in the right column and enter the value.

9. Click the List View icon to display all the parameters from all the categories. You can enter additional parameter values here as well.

cross-reference

- Refer to Task 5 for setting other accessibility preferences.

Adding a Flash Movie to an HTML Page

Using Dreamweaver to add a Flash Movie (SWF) file to an HTML page is as easy as clicking a button.

1. Prepare or obtain a Flash movie you'd like to use in your HTML page.

2. Click in your document to place the cursor in the position where you want to insert the Flash movie.

3. Choose Insert ➪ Media ➪ Flash, or from the Insert bar, Common category, click the arrow on the Media icon and select the Flash icon (see Figure 145-1).

notes

- Go to www.macromedia.
  com/devnet/
  activecontent for
  the Macromedia utility
  for media objects to work
  properly in the new Internet
  Explorer browser.

- Save or put the SWF file
  into your root folder—
  perhaps in a media folder.

- You can change attributes
  and edit some of the Flash
  properties in the Attributes
  panel.

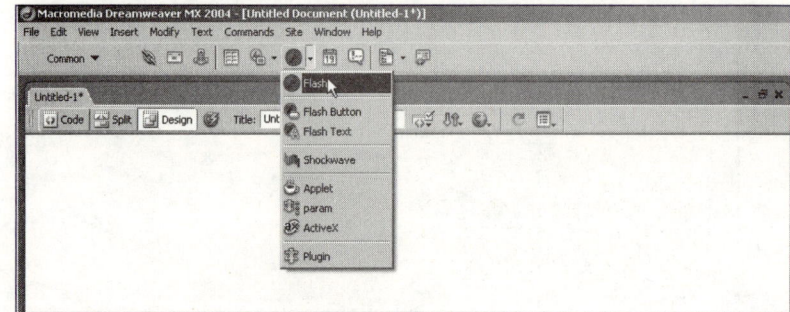

Figure 145-1: The Insert bar and the Media icon

4. Navigate to the SWF file, select it, and click OK.

5. If you've set accessibility features, enter a title, access key, and tab index in the Object Tag Accessibility Attributes dialog box (see Figure 145-2).

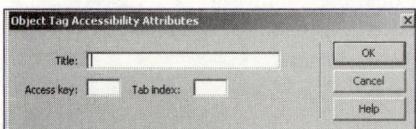

Figure 145-2: The Object Tag Accessibility Attributes dialog box

6. You'll notice a placeholder image has been added to your document. With the image selected, go to the Property inspector and note that the width (W) and height (H) are filled in automatically (see Figure 145-3). Take the time to familiarize yourself with the other properties you can set right from the Property inspector—such as the quality of the movie and whether or not you want it to loop.

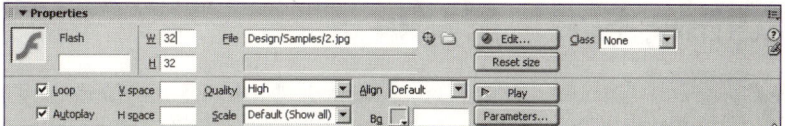

Figure 145-3: The Property inspector showing the Flash media object's parameters

7. You can play the movie right in your document by clicking on the Play button (see Figure 145-4).

Figure 145-4: The Flash movie in Dreamweaver when the Play button was clicked

8. Stop the movie by clicking the Stop button.

cross-reference

- See Task 146 for editing the Flash movie (Step 5).

Editing Flash Media

You saw in Task 144 that you can preview the Flash movie right in Dreamweaver. Now you'll see that you can access Flash from within Dreamweaver as well.

1. To edit Flash media from within Dreamweaver, select the object.

2. In the Property inspector, click the Edit button (see Figure 146-1). Or you can select the placeholder image, press Ctrl/Command, double-click, and select Edit with Flash.

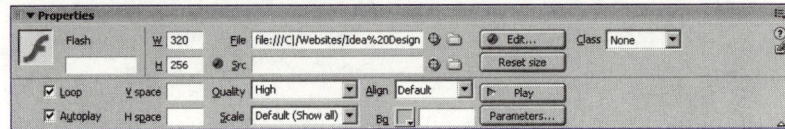

Figure 146-1: The Edit button in Dreamweaver

3. If Flash can't find your source file, you are presented with the Open dialog box. Navigate to your FLA file, select it, and click OK.

4. Optionally, you can tell Dreamweaver before you edit where to find the FLA file. In the Property inspector, click the Browse folder to the right of the SRC field, navigate to the FLA file, and select it (see Figure 146-2).

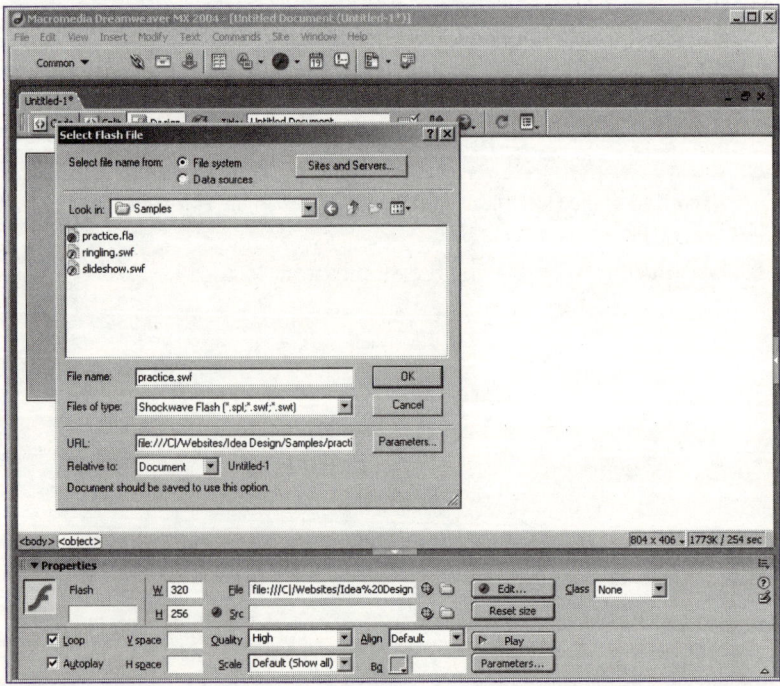

Figure 146-2: Browse to find the source file

5. Once the FLA is located, Flash will open. Make any changes you desire.

6. When you are finished, click the Done button (see Figure 146-3). Once you click Done, any changes made will be saved to the source FLA file.

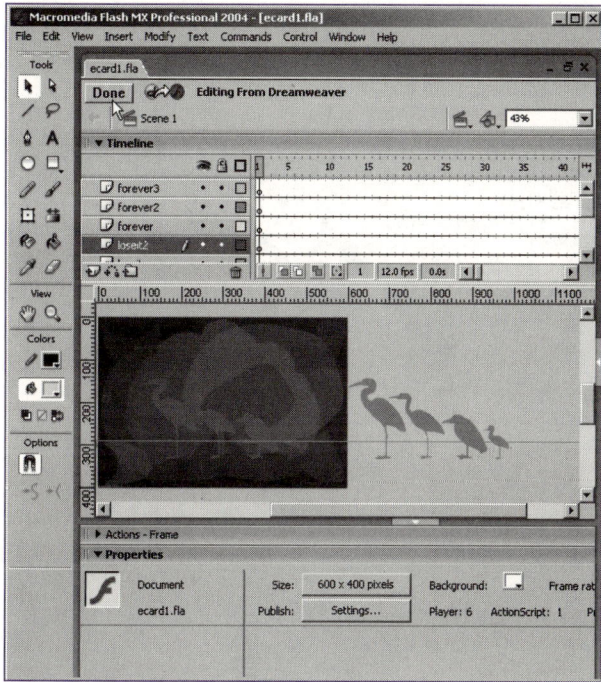

Figure 146-3: The Done button in Flash

7. You are returned to Dreamweaver with the changed image.

cross-reference

- Refer to Task 145 for inserting Flash media.

Adding a Flash Button

You don't even need to own Flash to be able to include Flash buttons in your designs. Dreamweaver ships with 44 buttons to choose from. Flash buttons can animate and even include sound and still keep the file sizes quite small.

1. Save the document you are going to use Flash buttons in.

2. In the Insert bar, Common category, Media menu, select the Flash Button icon (second from the top, as shown in Figure 147-1).

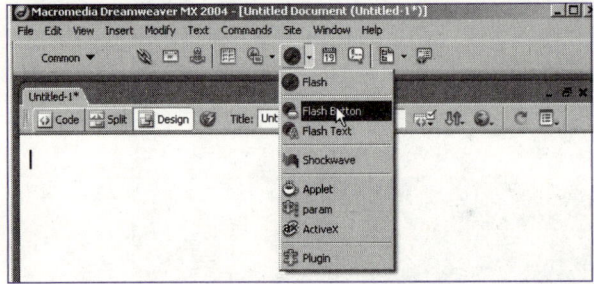

Figure 147-1: The Media list

3. The Insert Flash Button dialog box opens (see Figure 147-2). Select a style from the Style window.

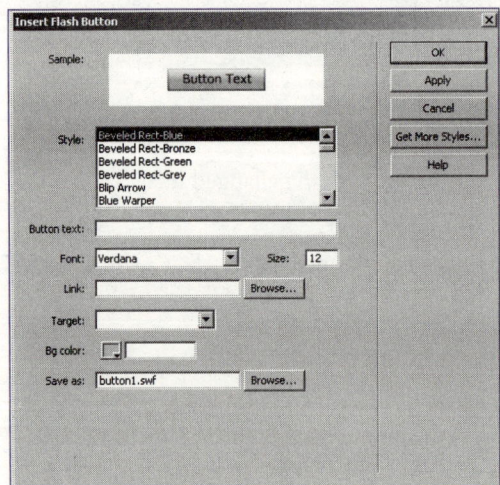

Figure 147-2: The Insert Flash Button dialog box

4. In the Preview pane, you see a sample of the selected style. Run your cursor over the button to see the effect. You can also click to see the Down state.

5. Enter the text you want on the button in the Button Text field. Dreamweaver will ignore any text that doesn't fit on the button.

notes

- Go to www.macromedia.com/devnet/activecontent for the Macromedia utility for media objects to work properly in the new Internet Explorer browser.

- The Done button is only present when you are editing from Dreamweaver (Step 4).

- To preview sound, you have to preview in a browser (Step 4).

- The Get More Styles button takes you to the Dreamweaver Exchange, where you can download additional Flash buttons and a lot of other behaviors made by third parties (Step 10).

caution

- Flash objects don't handle site relative links correctly unless the Flash button is stored in the same folder as the page it is being linked to (Step 8).

6. Select the Font Type from the drop-down list. In the Size field, type the size in points of your desired text.

7. Click the Apply button to see the button and text sample in your document without closing the dialog box. If the text doesn't fit, change the font and/or size.

8. If the button is linking to a URL, type it into the Link field or click the Browse button to select the file. If it is linking to a frame within a framed site, type in a target in the Target field.

9. Click in the Background color box, and select the color of the page the button is being inserted into if it's something other than white.

10. In the Save As field, name the button; then click the Browse button and navigate to the folder where you want the button saved (see Figure 147-3). When you are finished, click OK.

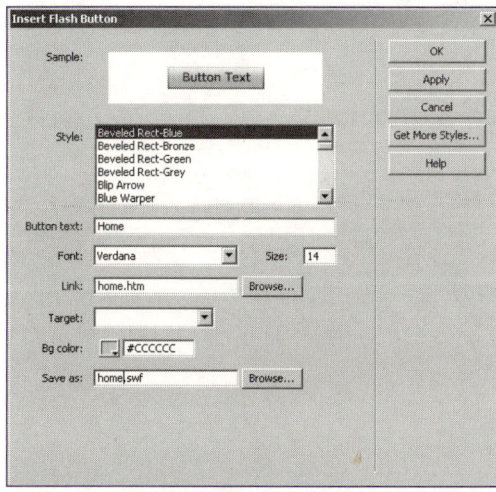

Figure 147-3: The Flash Button dialog box fully filled in

cross-reference

- Refer to Task 148 for editing a Flash button.

Task 148 Editing a Flash Button

You can control a lot of properties in a Flash button. You can use several methods to open the Flash Button dialog box in order to make changes to buttons.

1. After you've inserted a Flash button into your document, you can still make changes to it if you change your mind about any of the properties you've set.

2. Select the button and click the Edit button in the Property inspector, as shown in Figure 148-1, or double-click the button to open the Flash button to open the Insert Flash Button dialog box.

notes

- The text you type on a Flash button is embedded with the movie, so users don't have to have the font installed on their machine (Step 3).

- If you edit a button that you get from the Macromedia Exchange, you'll need the font installed in order to change its size (Step 3).

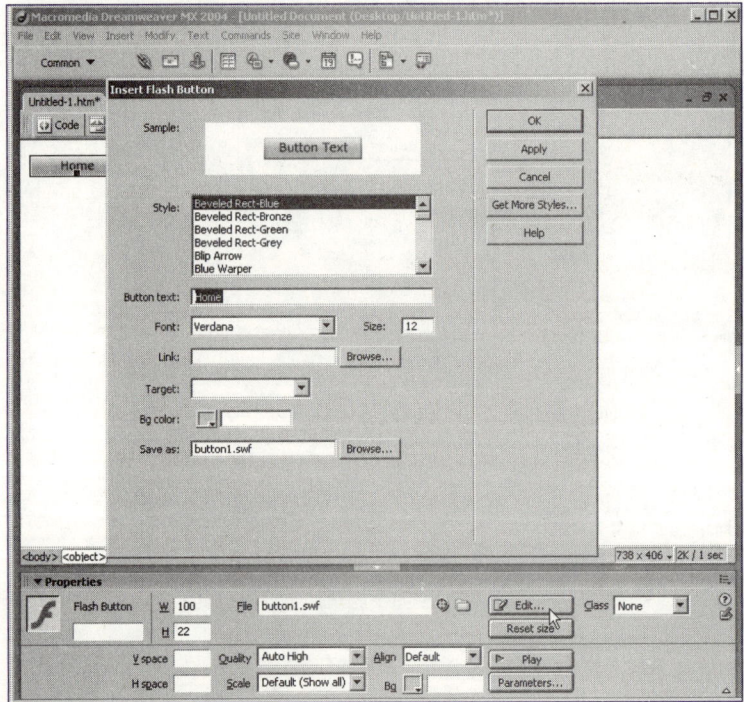

Figure 148-1: The Insert Flash Button dialog box

3. Make any changes you'd like, such as changing the font, the size, or the URL.

4. When you are finished, click OK.

5. In the Property inspector, you can resize the button by entering new numbers in the width (W) and height (H) fields (see Figure 148-2). Or you can drag the handles on the button to resize it visually.

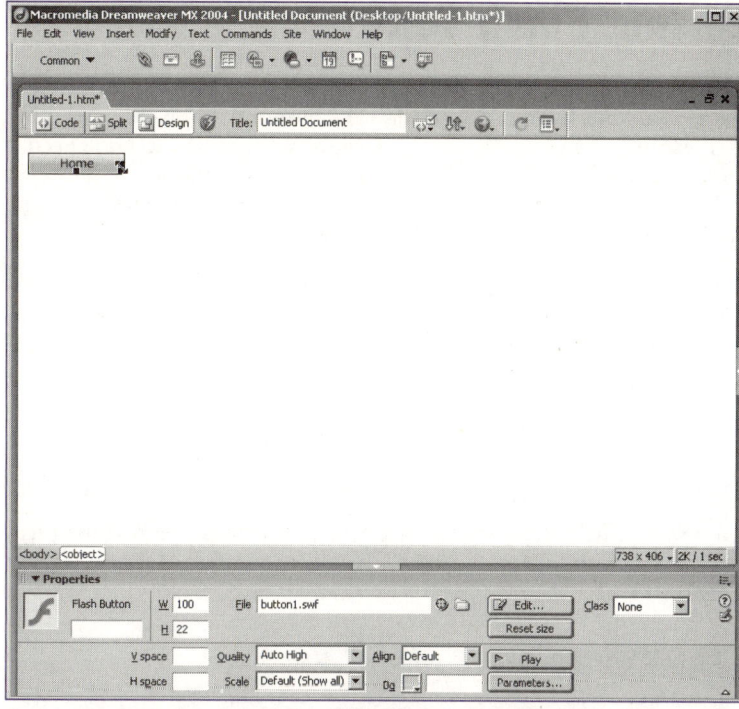

Figure 148-2: The Property inspector showing the Flash Button properties

6. You can also select the quality setting of the Flash button by selecting the drop-down menu in the Quality field (see Figure 148-3).

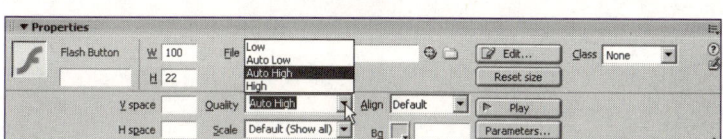

Figure 148-3: The Quality drop-down list

7. Click the Play button to test your Flash button, and click the Stop button when you are finished (see Figure 148-4).

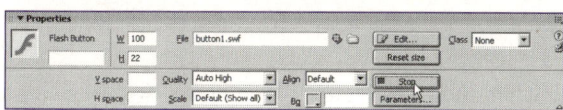

Figure 148-4: The Stop button being selected

cross-reference

- Refer to Task 147 for inserting a Flash button.

Inserting Flash Text

Agood way to achieve great-looking titles is to use Flash text. The best way to use special fonts in your page design and ensure that the user sees the proper font is to use an image (usually a GIF). Using Flash text can result in even smaller file sizes. The drawback is the possibility that someone may not have the Flash Player installed; but with about 98 percent market penetration for the Flash Player, the possibility these days is rather slim.

notes

- Go to www.macromedia. com/devnet/ activecontent for the Macromedia utility for media objects to work properly in the new Internet Explorer browser.

- Though I prefer my text in small doses, there is really no limit to the amount of text that is allowed (Step 4).

- Below the Text field, Show Font is selected by default. This shows your font. If you want the text to use the user's default font. uncheck this option (Step 7).

- You can type in the hexa-decimal number if you have a specific one you want to use. Or you can move your cursor to your document and click a color in it to select it (Step 7).

- Flash text is like a Flash button as far as needing to be saved in the same folder as a file it is linking to (Step 7).

1. Save the page you want to insert Flash text into. Choose Insert ⇨ Media ⇨ Flash Text. Or use the Insert bar, Common category, Media icon, and click the arrow to access the menu and select the Flash text icon.

2. A list of your system's installed TrueType fonts are available in the Font menu. Select the one you want to use.

3. In the Size field, type the size, in points, that you want the text to be.

4. In the Text field, type your text. You see a very small representation of the text with no regard to the size you've entered, as shown in Figure 149-1.

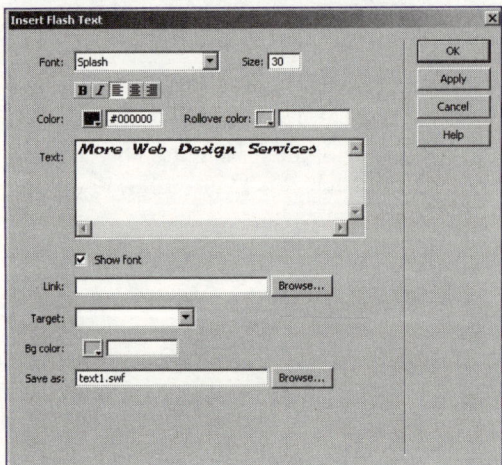

Figure 149-1: The Text field with text typed in

5. Select the B button if you want the text bold, or select I for italic. Select one of the positioning icons.

6. Click the Apply button, shown in Figure 149-2, at any time to view the results in the document. You can then make adjustments to the size, and so on.

7. Click the color box and select a text color. If you want the text to have a rollover effect, click in the Rollover Color color box and select another color.

8. If the text is linking to a URL, type it into the Link field or click the Browse button to select the file. If it is linking to a frame within a framed site, type in a target in the Target field.

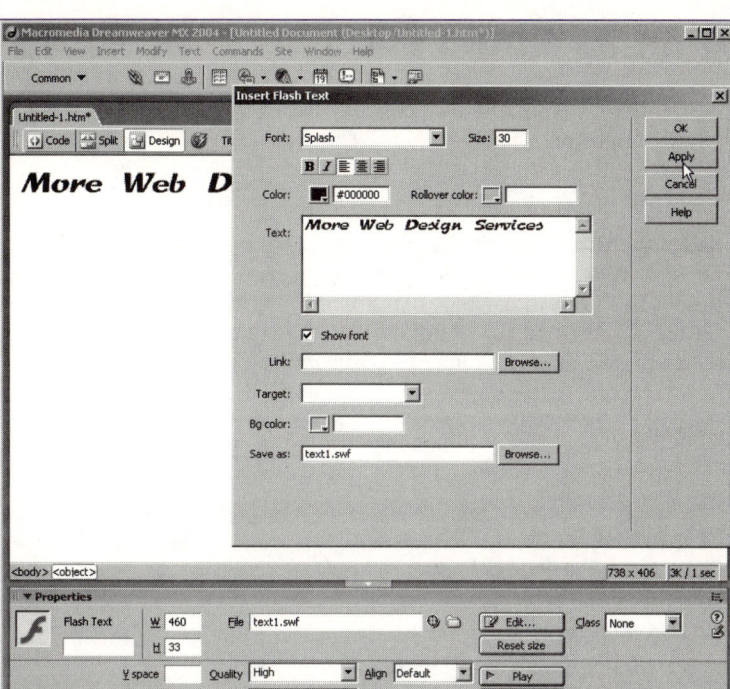

Figure 149-2: The Apply button was clicked and the result is seen in the document while the Insert Flash Text dialog box is still open

9. In the Save As field, name the text. Then click the Browse button and navigate to the folder where you want the button saved.

10. When you are finished, click OK. The text is added to the document, as shown in Figure 149-3.

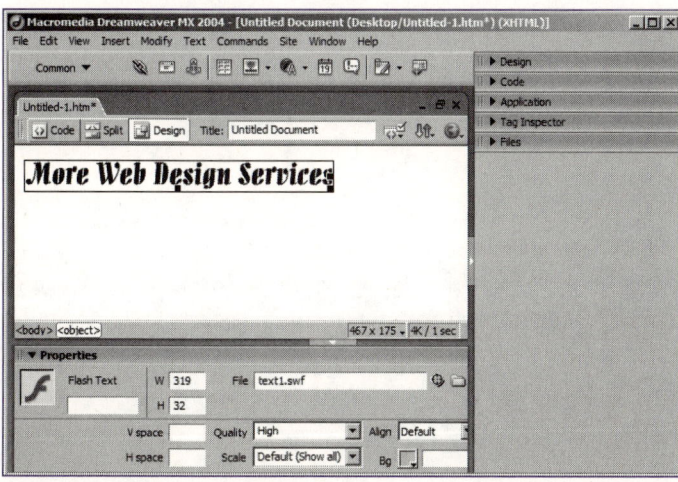

Figure 149-3: The finished Flash text

cross-reference

- Refer to Task 148 for editing a Flash button. The same technique applies to Flash text.

Linking to Audio Files

You can link to an audio file, which is the fastest and easiest way to add sound to your Web page.

notes

▪ You have more control over how your sound is played if you actually embed it into your file. Refer to Task 151.

▪ Although it isn't necessary to put the file size in your document, it is still a good idea so the user knows about how long it may take to load. If the user is on a slow connection, the user has the option not to click it (Step 3).

▪ If you'd rather not have the size of the sound file in your document, you could put it in the alt tag of an image if you are using an image (Step 3).

▪ When you select a sound file, you may get a message asking if you want to open the file or save it to disk, along with a warning of a potentially hazardous file (Step 3).

1. Enter the text or image you want to use to link to a sound.

2. Select the text or image, and in the Property inspector, enter a path name or click the Browse button to the right of the Link field, shown in Figure 150-1, to navigate to a sound file within your root folder. Or use my favorite way of linking, which is to use the Point to File icon and drag it to the sound filename in the Files panel.

Figure 150-1: The Property inspector showing the Link field

3. In your document, next to the linking text or image, add the file size of the sound, as shown in Figure 150-2.

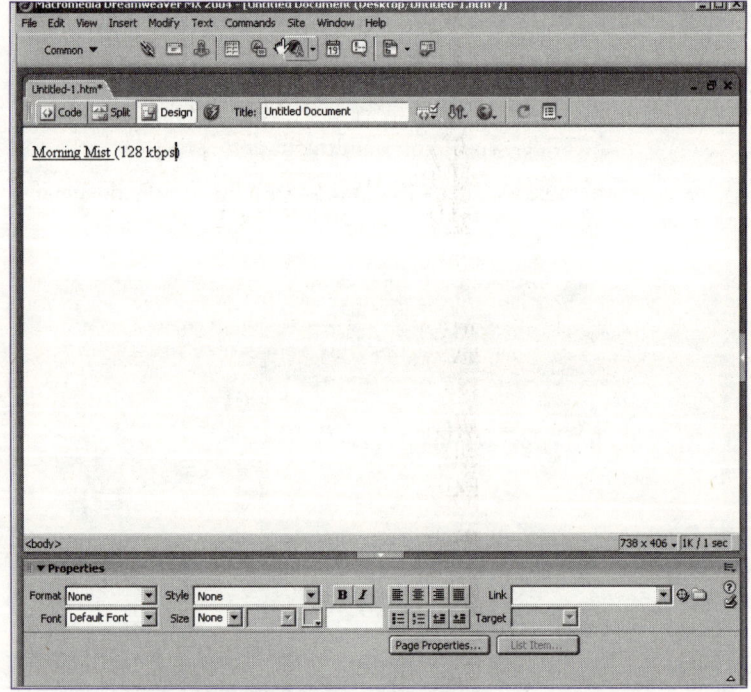

Figure 150-2: The file size added as a courtesy to the user

4. Save the page and preview (F12).

5. Click the audio file link.

6. The program designated to play the file type you've linked to opens in a separate window.

7. Figure 150-3 shows Internet Explorer 6 when the link to the MP3 file was clicked. The browser's default player opens; in this case, it is Winamp.

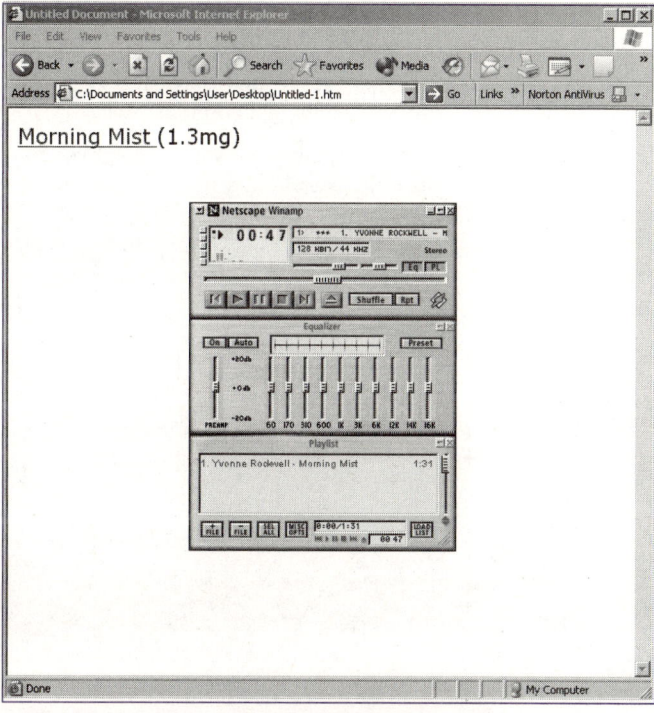

Figure 150-3: The default player for Internet Explorer 6

8. If Real Audio is your default player, it will open.

cross-reference

- For more on linking methods, refer to Tasks 40 and 41 (Step 2).

Embedding Audio Files

Embedding sound using a plug-in (or helper application) will display the controls for playing and stopping a movie if you so choose. Beware that a specific plug-in may not be installed on a user's machine and plug-ins may function differently in different browsers, so test carefully. Refer to Task 126 to learn how to check a user's system for a specific plug-in.

notes

▪ Go to `www.macromedia.com/devnet/activecontent` for the Macromedia utility for media objects to work properly in the new Internet Explorer browser.

▪ If the sound file is not in your root folder, you are prompted to save a copy in your root. Select OK when prompted (Step 3).

▪ If you are using the browser's default player, a size of 144x60 is what you need (Step 5).

1. Open your document you want to embed sound into and click to place your cursor.

2. Choose Insert ⇨ Media ⇨ Plugin, or from the Insert bar, Common category, Media icon, select the menu and click Plugin.

3. In the Select dialog box, navigate to the desired sound file in your root folder, and select it. Notice the placeholder image added to your document (see Figure 151-1).

Figure 151-1: The placeholder added to your document

4. Switch to Code view and notice the `<embed>` tag added, as shown in Figure 151-2. This tag references the audio file and the application to play it.

caution

▪ You may want to convert your sound files into SWF files, since the Flash player is widely supported (Step 3).

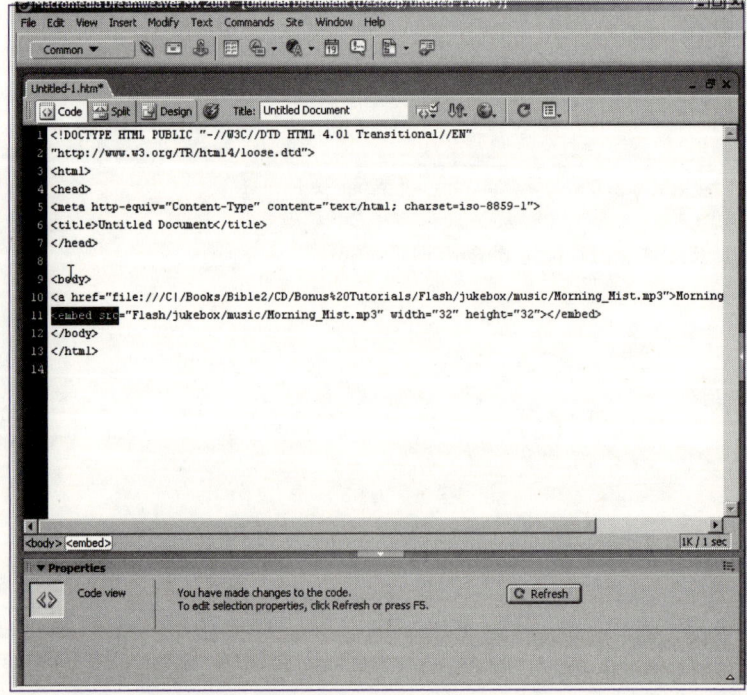

Figure 151-2: The code added with the plug-in

5. To size the plug-in, select the placeholder and drag the resize handles (see Figure 151-3).

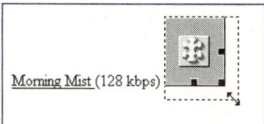

Figure 151-3: The plug-in placeholder being resized

6. Or you can enter specific width (W) and height (H) dimensions in the Property inspector.

7. Use the Align field menu to align text with your media player.

8. Test in your target browsers. Figure 151-4 shows the Real Player in Internet Explorer based on the size I made the plug-in placeholder.

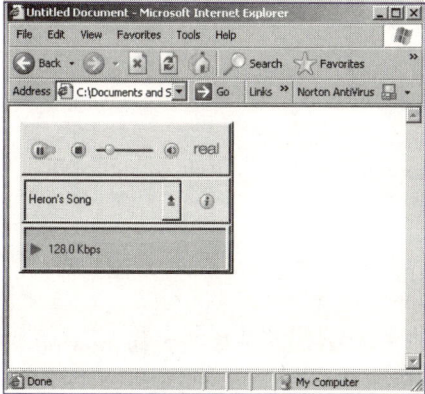

Figure 151-4: The player as seen in Internet Explorer 6 using the RealOne Player

cross-reference

■ See Task 144 for making the media object accessible (Step 2).

Task 152

Playing Background Music Automatically

Adding background music to your page can either enhance the user experience or hinder it. Use sound wisely and use sound suitable to your audience. This task shows you how to add sound without displaying a player.

1. Click at the top of your page to place the cursor.

2. Choose Insert ⇨ Media ⇨ Plugin, or from the Insert bar, Common category, Media icon, select the menu and click Plugin, as shown in Figure 152-1.

notes

- Go to www.macromedia.com/devnet/activecontent for the Macromedia utility for media objects to work properly in the new Internet Explorer browser.

- Check the Code view and note that the media uses <embed> tags, which can be read by both Internet Explorer and Netscape (Step 2).

- Although you want the sound to play automatically and not offer controls, you still need a very small image even if it isn't visible, because some browsers require a height and width (Step 4).

- To test an embedded file, use a browser, not the Play button in Dreamweaver (Step 10).

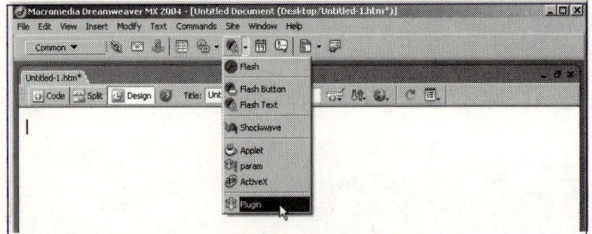

Figure 152-1: Inserting the media plug-in

3. In the Select dialog box, navigate to the desired sound file in your root folder and select it. Notice the placeholder image added to your document.

4. In the Property inspector, type 1 for both the width (W) and height (H).

5. In the Property inspector, click the Parameters button, as shown in Figure 152-2.

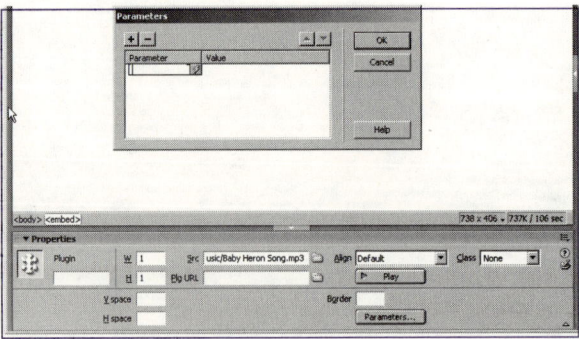

Figure 152-2: The Property inspector showing the Parameters button and the Parameters dialog box

6. In the Parameters dialog box, click the Add (+) button.

7. In the Parameter column, type **hidden**. Tab two times to the Value column and type **true**.

8. Tab two times to get into the Parameter column again (or click the Add sign). Type **autostart**, and then tab two times to the Value column and type **true**, as shown in Figure 152-3.

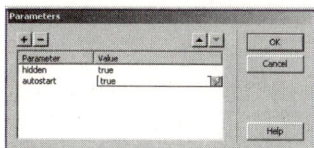

Figure 152-3: The Parameters dialog box being filled in

9. If you want the clip to loop, add a parameter of **loop** and a value of a specific number, or type **true** if you want it to loop indefinitely, as shown in Figure 152-4.

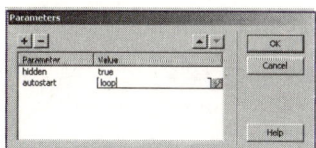

Figure 152-4: The parameters filled in for the sound to loop

10. Click OK to close the Parameter dialog box and test in your browsers.

cross-reference

▪ Refer to Task 150 for linking to audio files (Step 4).

Inserting ActiveX

ctive X is a Windows feature and uses the Windows Media player. You can also use an embed option to make it compatible with Netscape browsers.

1. Click in your document to place the cursor where you want the player to open.

2. Choose Insert ⇨ Media ⇨ Active X, or from the Insert bar, Common category, Media icon, select the menu and click ActiveX.

3. Switch to Code view and notice that there are no `<embed>` tags but `<object>` tags instead, which Netscape browsers will ignore (see Figure 153-1).

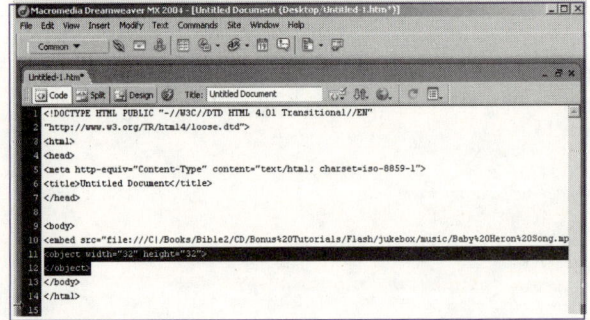

Figure 153-1: The code for ActiveX, which uses `<object>` tags

4. In the Property inspector, in the ClassID text box, type this long line:

CLSID: 22d6f312-bof6-11do-94ab-oo8oc74c7e95

5. Set the width (W) and height (H) in the Property inspector to the size you want, or drag the resize handles to size it visually.

6. Click the Parameters button, and then click the Add (+) button. In the Parameter column, type in **FileName** and tab two times to get into the Value column. Type the path to your music or video file, as shown in Figure 153-2.

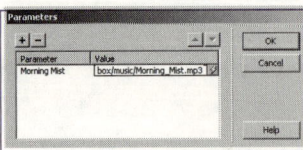

Figure 153-2: The Property inspector and the Parameter dialog box

notes

- Go to `www.macromedia.com/devnet/activecontent` for the Macromedia utility for media objects to work properly in the new Internet Explorer browser.

- You'll only have to type this ID once. It will be available from the drop-down list the next time you need it (Step 3).

- Internet Explorer recognizes the `<object>` tag and Netscape doesn't. But Internet Explorer also recognizes the `<embed>` tag, which Netscape does recognize. If you nest the `<embed>` tag inside the `<object>` tag, each browser will only read one of the tags (Step 8).

7. Set any other parameters and values you'd like. Some of the most used parameters and values are as follows:

   - *AutoStart*. The default value is true, which indicates the file will start playing as soon as it's downloaded. Use false if you want to delay the start.

   - *FileName*. The value is any valid URL to the file you want to load and play in the player.

   - *PlayCount*. The value is any integer, which will set the number of times the file should repeat. The default is 1, and 0 means that it won't loop at all.

   - *SelectionStart*. For the value, enter the number of seconds before the beginning point of the audio clip.

   - *SelectionEnd*. For the value, enter how many seconds before the audio clip will stop playing.

   - *ShowControls*. The default value is true, which will show the display panel.

   - *Volume*. A value of 0 is the loudest; 100 is the softest.

8. Click OK once you've added all your desired parameters to close the Parameter dialog box.

9. For cross-browser compatibility, select the Embed field in the Property inspector. In Code view notice that the `<embed>` tags, using the same parameters you entered for the `<object>` tags of ActiveX, are now entered (see Figure 153-3).

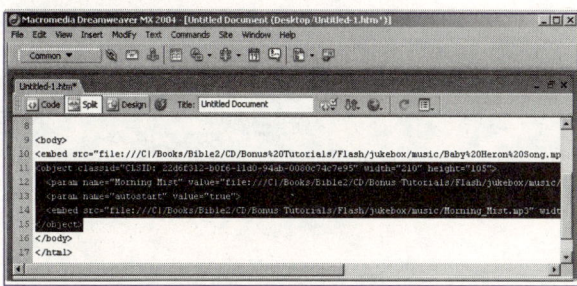

Figure 153-3: The Code view of both the `<object>` and `<embed>` tags

cross-reference

- See Task 144 for making the media object accessible (Step 2).

Inserting Applets

Applets are self-contained programs that can run within a Web page and are platform-independent. Java applets work almost the same as the plug-in and the ActiveX object.

note

- Go to www.macromedia.
  com/devnet/
  activecontent for
  the Macromedia utility
  for media objects to
  work properly in the new
  Internet Explorer browser.

1. Position your cursor in the document and choose Insert ➪ Media ➪ Applet, or from the Insert bar, Common category, Media icon, select the menu and click Applet, as shown in Figure 154-1.

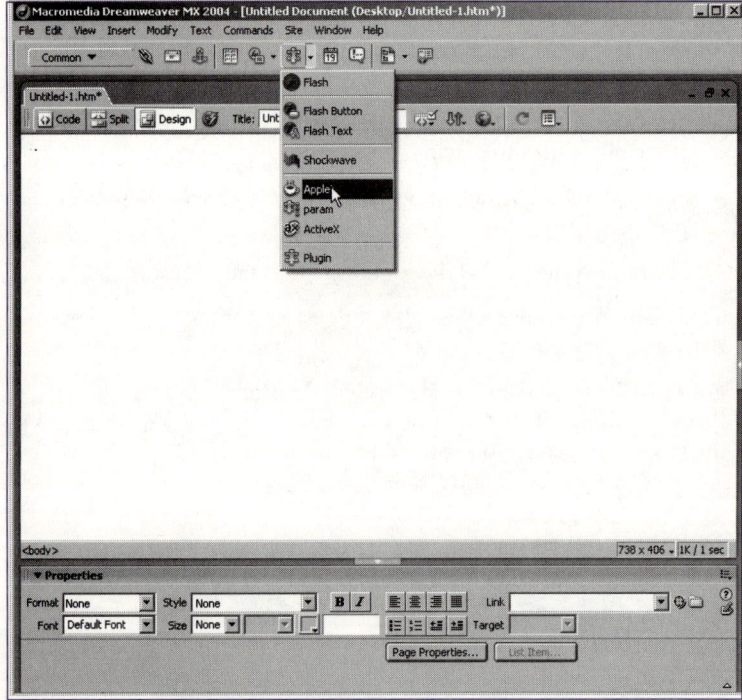

Figure 154-1: The Applet icon in the Insert bar

2. In the Select File dialog box, navigate to the applet and select it. Be sure that the Relative to Document option is selected, as shown in Figure 154-2.

3. A placeholder is added to the document. In the Property inspector, enter the width (W) and height (H) of the Applet object, or use the resize handles to drag the size visually, as shown in Figure 154-3.

4. In the Property inspector, you can add a name for the object, as well as use the alignment options and add horizontal (H Space) and vertical (V Space) space around the object.

5. In the Alt field, enter the path to an image file that will be displayed if the user has disabled Java. If you'd prefer not to replace it with an image, you can enter text into the Alt field.

caution

- An absolute path cannot be used; the path has to be relative to the Web page calling it (Step 2).

- Be aware that many people turn off the ability to see Java in their browsers.

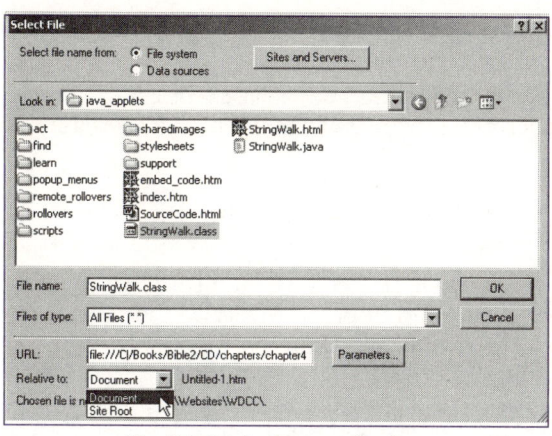

Figure 154-2: The Relative to Document option

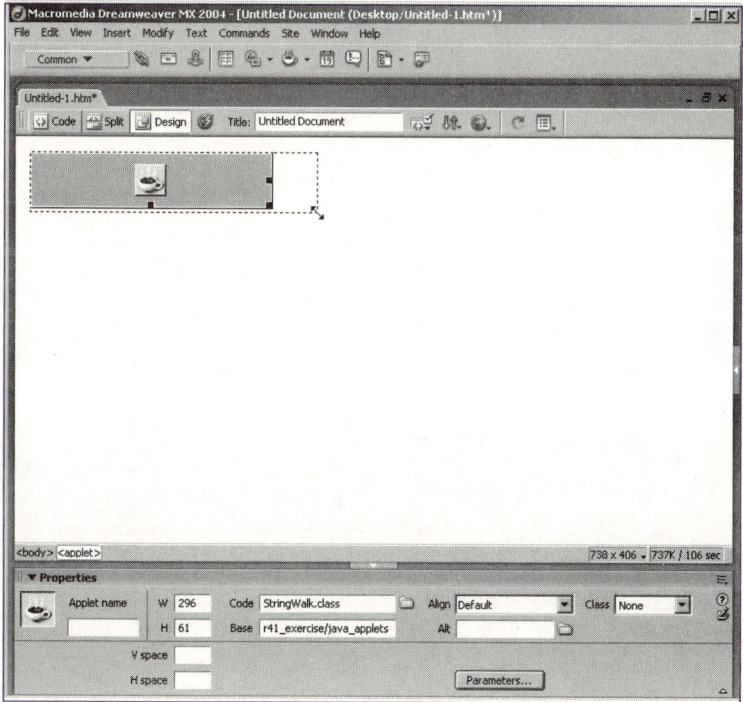

Figure 154-3: The applet added to the page and being resized with the handles

cross-reference

- Task 153 has a list of common parameters to use.

6. Click the Parameters button to add any custom parameters to the applet.

7. Click the Add (+) button and enter a parameter in the Parameter column. Tab twice to activate the Value column, and enter the value.

8. Click the Add (+) button to add additional parameters and values.

Inserting a Shockwave Movie

Insertion of a Shockwave movie is the same as a Flash movie, with the exception of the width (W) and height (H) settings and other specific Shockwave parameters. (Refer to Task 145.)

notes

- Go to `www.macromedia.com/devnet/activecontent` for the Macromedia utility for media objects to work properly in the new Internet Explorer browser.

- You can also adjust the height and width by dragging on the handles of the placeholder.

- The Insert bar will show the last icon used when there is a menu list of objects to choose from.

1. Click in your document to place the cursor in the position you want to insert the Shockwave movie.

2. Choose Insert ⇨ Media ⇨ Shockwave, or from the Insert bar, Common category, click the arrow on the Media icon and select the Shockwave icon, as shown in Figure 155-1.

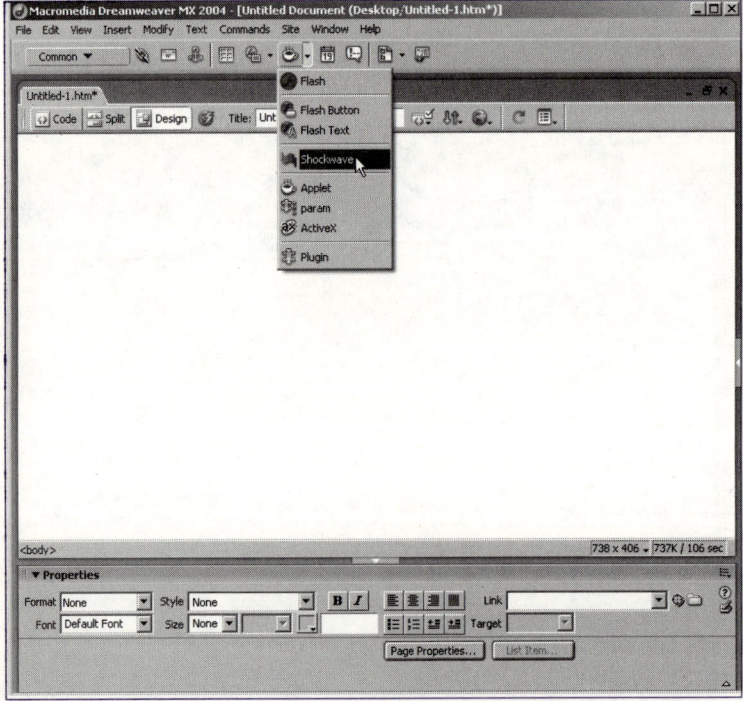

Figure 155-1: The Insert bar showing the Media and Shockwave icons

3. Navigate to a Shockwave file, select it, and click OK.

4. With the placeholder selected, you'll need to type in the width (W) and height (H) of the movie. Click the Parameters button and enter desired parameters. If you don't know the width and height, continue on for an optional way of inserting Shockwave movies.

5. You can take a shortcut by doing some of the work in Director prior to inserting into your HTML page. Once your movie is made, choose File ⇨ Publish Settings.

6. In the dialog box (Format tab), name the HTML file and be sure the Shockwave default template is selected, as shown in Figure 155-2. The HTML file generated will be the same name as your movie.

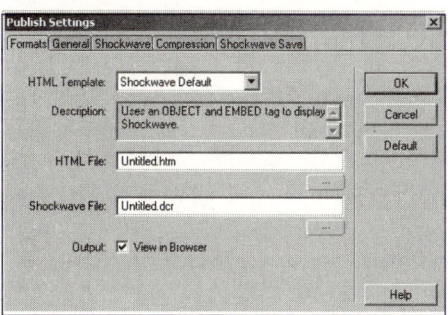

Figure 155-2: The dialog box in Director showing the HTML option

7. You can now open the movie's HTML/HTM file, select the Shockwave object, and copy (Edit ➪ Copy).

8. Open the page in Dreamweaver that you want to insert your movie into and place the cursor.

9. Paste (Edit ➪ Paste) the movie into the document, as shown in Figure 155-3.

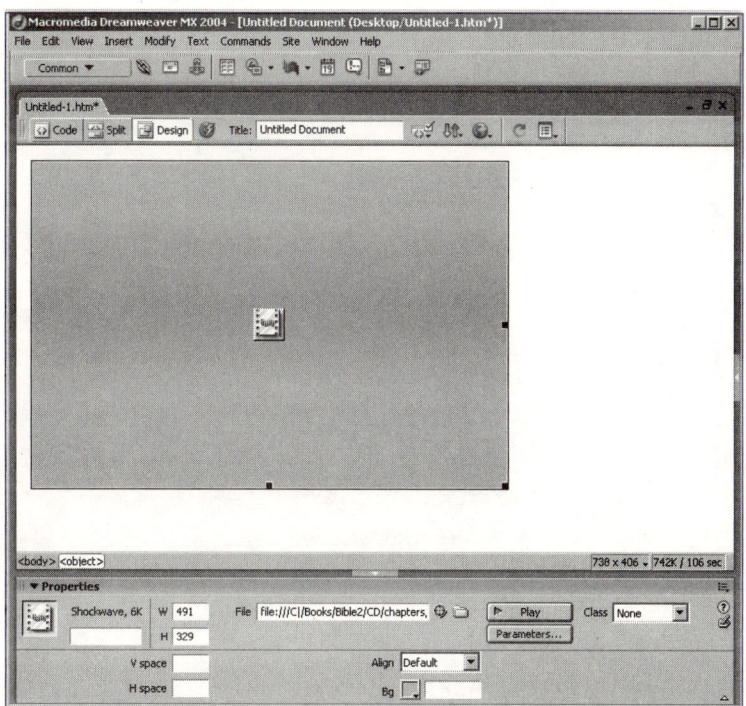

Figure 155-3: The Shockwave movie added to the HTML document

cross-references

- Refer to Task 145 for inserting a Flash movie (Step 1).

- Refer to Task 144 for making the object accessible (Step 4).

Inserting a QuickTime Movie

Both Internet Explorer and Netscape on both Windows and Macintosh platforms can use the QuickTime movies plug-in.

1. Click in your document to place the cursor where you want the player to open.

2. Choose Insert ➪ Media ➪ Plugin, or from the Insert bar, Common category, Media icon, select the menu and click Plugin.

3. In the Select File dialog box, navigate to your movie file and select it.

4. With the plug-in placeholder selected, open the Property inspector and type in the width (W) and height (H) you want. Or drag on the resize handles to resize the display, as shown in Figure 156-1.

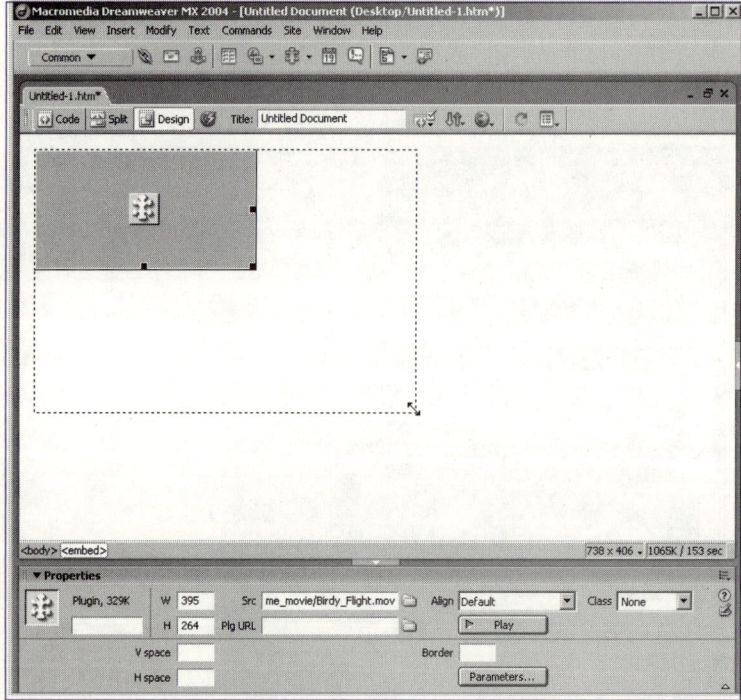

Figure 156-1: The placeholder being resized

5. The Plg URL field in the Property inspector is for the URL that takes users to a location to download the player if they don't have it. Type in **http://www.apple.com/quicktime**, as shown in Figure 156-2.

6. Click the Parameters button and click the Add (+) button to add Parameters and Values (see Figure 156-3). The few parameters available for QuickTime are as follows:

   • *Autoplay.* The value of true plays as soon as it's downloaded; false won't play until the user clicks the play button.

- *Bgcolor.* The value is entered as hexadecimal numbers or valid HTML color names. This determines the color around the player if the player doesn't take up all the space.

- *Controller.* The value is true by default, except for QuickTime VR, Flash, and image files. The controller is displayed when true.

- *Hidden.* Has no value. The QuickTime plug-in does not show a movie, but sound is played.

- *Href.* The value is a URL for a link of where to go when the movie is clicked.

- *Volume.* A value of 0 is the softest; 100 is the loudest.

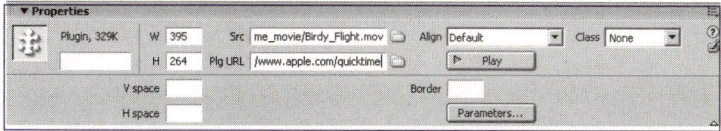

Figure 156-2: The Property inspector showing the Plg URL field

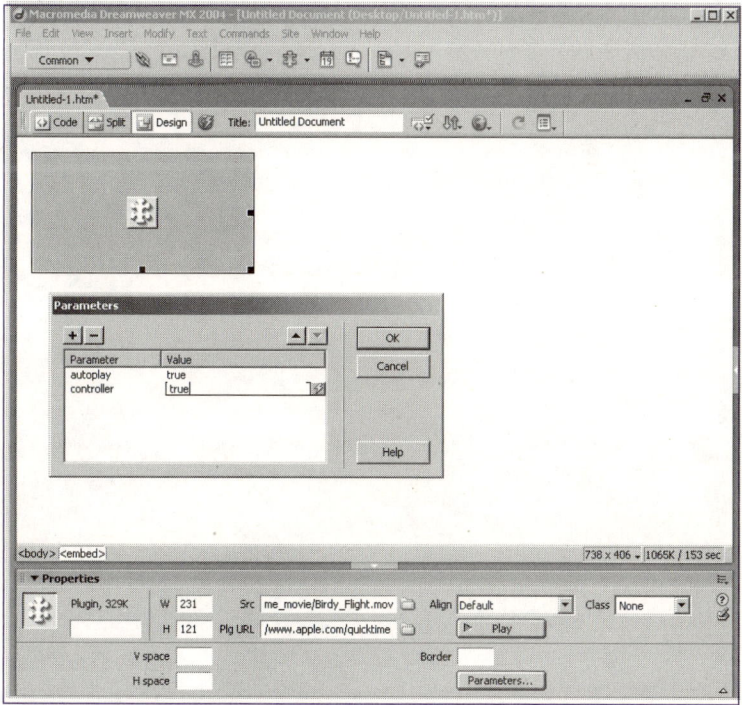

Figure 156-3: The Parameters dialog box filled in

cross-reference
- Refer to Task 144 for making the object accessible.

Part 9: Styling with CSS Styles

Adding a New Style

CSS gives you much more control over the layout and design of your pages than is offered with HTML. Using CSS, you can create highly customizable styles, as well as modify the properties and layout appearance of existing HTML tags. Styles are stored in a style sheet and are either embedded in an HTML document or linked to from an external text file.

1. To add a new style, open a new or existing document to which you wish to add the style.

2. Make the CSS Styles panel visible by selecting Window ➪ CSS Styles (see Figure 157-1).

Figure 157-1: CSS Styles panel

3. Click the New CSS Style button to bring up the New CSS Style dialog box, shown in Figure 157-2.

4. Select the type of style to create by selecting one of the three options in the Type category. Class and Tag are the two most common types of styles. Depending on which type you pick, the first field in the New CSS Style dialog box will be labeled Name, Tag, or Selector.

notes

- You can also bring up the New CSS Style dialog box by selecting Text ➪ CSS Styles ➪ New (Step 2).

- If you chose a linked style, you'll be prompted to provide a name and choose a location for your external style sheet right after you click the OK button (see Task 164 for information on how to create linked style sheets) (Step 6).

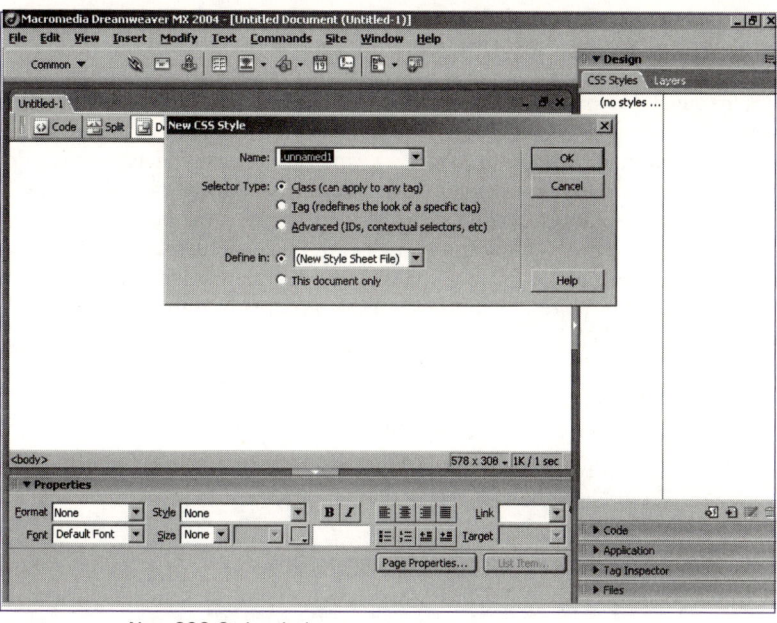

Figure 157-2: New CSS Style window

5. If you select Class, you need to enter a name for the class in the Name field. Class names must always begin with a period. If you select Tag, enter the tag name in the Tag field or select it from the pop-up list that appears next to it, as shown in Figure 157-3.

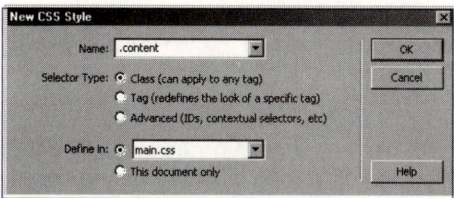

Figure 157-3: Entering a ClassSelect

6. If you select Advanced, enter the selector name in the Selector field or enter it into the pop-up list that appears next to it. Specify whether you want to create a linked style sheet or an embedded style sheet by selecting the New Style Sheet (linked) or This Document Only (embedded) option next to where it says Define In.

7. Click the OK button to create your style and bring up the CSS Style Definition window. After defining your style (see Tasks 158-160 for specific information on defining your styles), click OK or Apply in the CSS Style Definition dialog window to finish creating the style.

cross-reference

▪ Refer to Tasks 164 and 165 for external and embedded style sheets.

Task 158

Defining a Custom Style

Custom styles are the most common type of style used in CSS. They function much the same way that style sheets in word processing and page layout programs function, allowing you to apply formatting to any selection in the document window. Besides applying styles to words and paragraphs, though, CSS allows you to also apply custom styles to forms, tables, images, and many other kinds of page elements, making them an extremely useful addition to any Web designer's arsenal. Using custom styles, you can change many of the presentation properties of your pages, including font colors, sizes, weights, decoration, borders, background colors, and much more.

1. Download the Task 158 folder from www.wiley.com/compbooks/ 10simplestepsorless and open Task 158.htm.

2. Click the New CSS Style button in the CSS Styles panel to bring up the New CSS Style window, as shown in Figure 158-1.

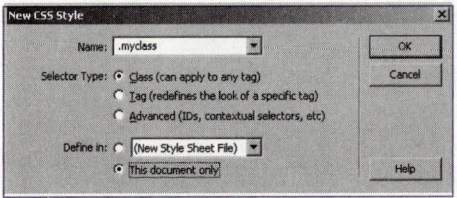

Figure 158-1: New CSS Style window

3. Select Class as the selector type in the New CSS Style window.

4. Type in the name of your class in the Name field. For the purpose of this task, type in the name **.myclass**.

5. Select New Style Sheet File or This Document Only to create either an internal (embedded) or external style sheet. For the purpose of this task, create an internal style sheet by selecting This Document Only.

6. Click the OK button to bring up the CSS Style Definition dialog box for the .myclass style (see Figure 158-2). There are eight different categories of styling attributes, which provide a visual way to edit the many possible attributes of a style, also referred to as rules in CSS. The first category (Type) covers font attributes.

7. In the Font field, select Arial, Helvetica, Sans Serif from the pop-up menu.

8. Select 12 in the Size field, and choose pixels as the unit of measurement from the adjacent pop-up menu.

notes

- Class names in CSS must always begin with a period. If you omit the period, Dreamweaver will add one for you (Step 4).

- When you create a custom class, the styling attributes are only reflected once you apply them to an object or element on a page. See Task 159 to learn how to apply custom styles to elements in a document (Step 10).

- If you have an external style sheet, selecting a property in the CSS Styles panel automatically opens the Rules panel, revealing the properties. You can edit in this panel as well (Step 10).

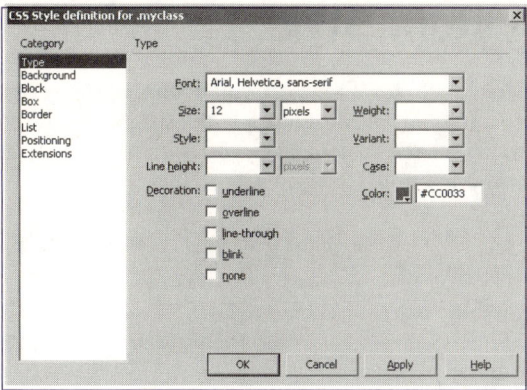

Figure 158-2: CSS Style Definition dialog box

9. Type **#CC0033** in the Color field to assign a red color to the type, and click OK to create the style.

10. Click the plus (+) sign next to `<style>` in the CSS Styles panel to reveal the new style you just defined. Notice that the style properties are also listed in the right column of the CSS Styles panel, as shown in Figure 158-3. When you are finished, save your document by selecting File ⇨ Save.

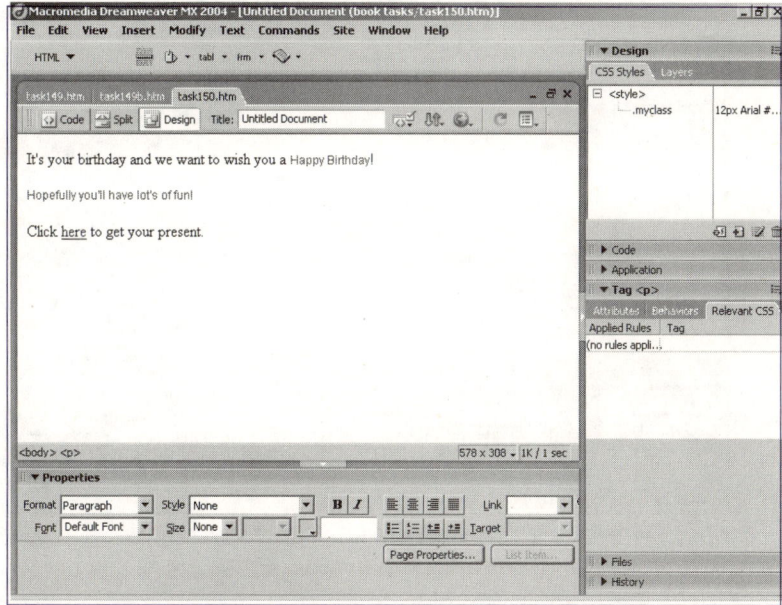

Figure 158-3: Styles that you create are listed in the CSS Styles panel

tip
- You can select many different kinds of measurement units for font sizes in CSS, including pixels, points, picas, millimeters, and more. CSS font sizes are more consistent across computer platforms than HTML-defined sizes (Step 6).

cross-reference
- Refer to Task 164 and 165 for external and embedded style sheets.

Applying a Custom Style

When you define a custom style (see Task 158), you do not alter any of the content on your page until you specifically apply the style to a text selection or other page element. To use the custom style, you need to apply it, a process that is extremely easy and intuitive.

1. Download the Task 159 folder from www.wiley.com/compbooks/ 10simplestepsorless and open Task 159.htm.

2. Display the Styles panel by selecting Window ➪ CSS Styles or by clicking on the Design panel group name and then selecting CSS Styles to make it the active panel.

3. Highlight the words Happy Birthday in the first paragraph. In the next step you apply the .myclass style to this selection of text.

4. Right-click the .myclass style in the CSS Styles panel and select Apply from the pop-up menu, as shown in Figure 159-1. Notice that after you apply the style, the highlighted text takes on the styling attributes of the .myclass style.

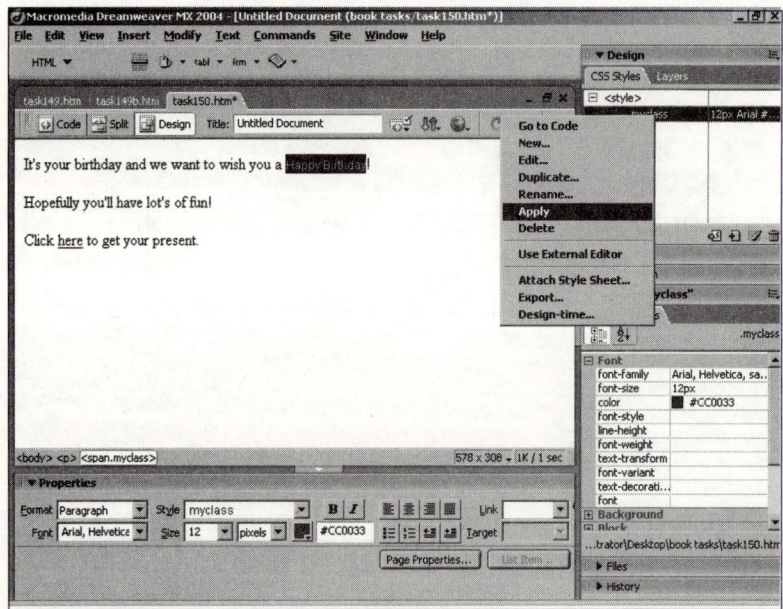

Figure 159-1: Applying a style using the CSS Styles panel

5. Click anywhere in the Happy Birthday text, and look at the Property inspector. You'll notice the style name that is applied, as well as the properties such as font, color, and size.

6. Place your cursor at the beginning of the second paragraph of text in the Task 159.htm page—the one that begins with the word "Hopefully."

7. Click the Style pop-up menu in the Property inspector, and select the .myclass style from the pop-up list. The Property inspector lists all custom styles associated with a document, and this is an alternate way to apply a style to your page. Notice also that the style name previews with its chosen style attributes when it displays in the inspector palette's pop-up menu. In this case, the style is applied to the whole paragraph, because if there is no text highlighted, the entire paragraph inherits the style attributes (see Figure 159-2).

tip

- Yet another way to apply a style to a selection is to right-click it in Design view and select the name of the style from the pop-up list under CSS Styles (Step 6).

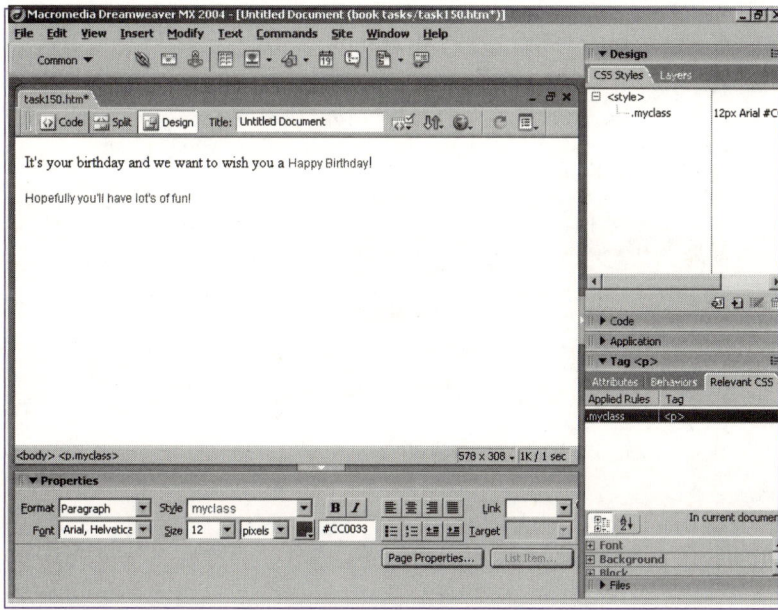

Figure 159-2: Applying a style using the Property inspector

cross-reference

- Refer to Task 158 for defining a custom style.

Redefining an HTML Tag

Besides creating custom class styles with CSS, you can also redefine existing HTML tags. When you redefine a HTML tag, you can control how text and other objects contained inside of specific HTML tags are formatted. When you redefine an HTML tag, you make a global change to your document, because all content contained within the tag you redefine will automatically inherit the style attributes you assign.

notes

- You can apply CSS attributes to any existing HTML tag or any custom tag by entering its name in the Tag field (Step 3).

- When you redefine an HTML tag, the new CSS properties will automatically be applied to every instance of the tag in the document that uses the style sheet (Step 5).

- Not all style properties will preview correctly in Design view. In many cases, you will need to preview your page in a Web browser to see how the style properties display (Step 9).

- Only text in the body will be affected. If you have a table, the text within it won't be changed (Step 9).

1. Download the Task 160 folder from www.wiley.com/compbooks/ 10simplestepsorless, and then open Task 160.htm.

2. Select Windows ⇨ CSS Styles to make the CSS Styles panel visible.

3. Click the New CSS Style button in the CSS Styles panel to bring up the New CSS Style window.

4. Select the Tag option under Selector Type. Use this option whenever you want to redefine an HTML tag.

5. For the purpose of this task, select the body tag from the pop-up menu, as shown in Figure 160-1. Notice that Dreamweaver lists a large number of HTML tags in this menu, all of which can be redefined using CSS.

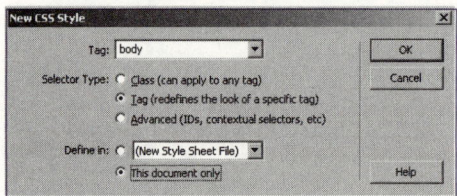

Figure 160-1: The body tag is selected

6. Select New Style Sheet File or This Document Only to create either an internal or external style sheet, and then click the OK button to bring up the CSS Style Definition window, as shown in Figure 160-2.

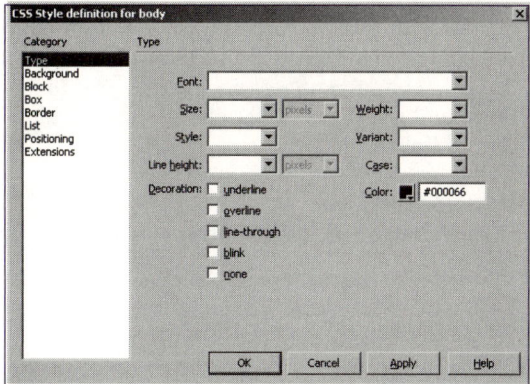

Figure 160-2: CSS Style Definition window

7. Enter the attributes in each category to which you want to apply to the tag. For the purpose of this task, change the color to something else by clicking the Color button and using the color box to select a new color under the Type category. This will make all text on your page display in the color you choose, because any text that appears on your page will be contained within the `<body>` tag.

8. When you are done entering the attributes for the style in the CSS Style Definition window, click OK to apply the style.

9. Since you applied the style to the `<body>` tag, any text in your document's body will now inherit the styling attributes you defined. Notice that the rest of the text that was black before now displays in the color you chose in Step 7. The other text that has the .myclass style applied to it still displays in the color used for that style.

cross-reference

■ Refer to Tasks 164 and 165 for internal and embedded style sheets.

Task # 161

Using Advanced Selectors: Pseudo-Classes

Advanced selectors in Dreamweaver give you access to, among other things, pseudo-classes, which are kind of a combination of a class style and a redefined HTML tag. One of the most common uses of pseudo-classes is to modify the attributes of hypertext links. In this task you'll learn how to use pseudo-classes to change the appearance of your links.

notes

- link.htm is a fake link used just to create a demonstration link on the page (Step 9).

- Be sure and preview your page in a Web browser to accurately view how your custom selector styles display. Not all of these styles display correctly in Dreamweaver.

1. Download the Task 161 folder from www.wiley.com/compbooks/ 10simplestepsorless, and then open Task161.htm.

2. Select Windows ➪ CSS Styles to make the CSS Styles panel visible.

3. Click the New CSS Style button in the CSS Styles panel to bring up the New CSS Style window.

4. Select the Advanced option under Selector Type, as shown in Figure 161-1.

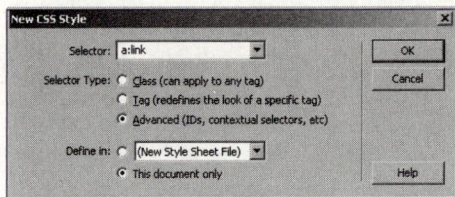

Figure 161-1: New CSS Style window

5. In the Selector pop-up menu, choose the a:link option. For this task, you'll alter the standard link appearance of the anchor tag. Notice that the other options listed in the menu display different states of the link object, including visited, hover, and active.

6. Select New Style Sheet File or This Document Only to create either an internal or external style sheet, and then click the OK button to display the CSS Style Definition window (for the purpose of this task, use an internal style sheet).

7. Change the font weight to Bold by selecting Bold from the pop-up menu in the Type category, as shown in Figure 161-2.

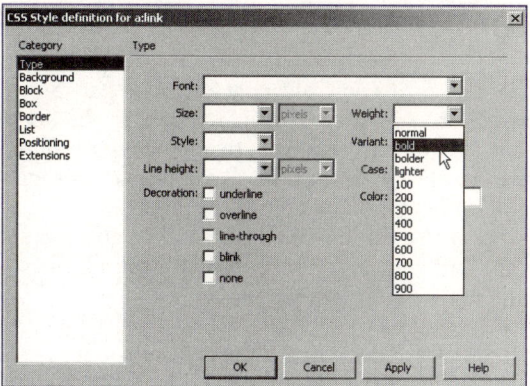

Figure 161-2: Changing the display to bold for the a:link selector

8. Click the OK button to apply your style. Once you apply it to your document, any links on the page appears in bold. Notice that the word "here" in the third paragraph is now bolded.

9. Save the file by selecting File ⇨ Save.

tip

- You can quickly edit your link properties using the Page Properties options available by selecting Modify ⇨ Page Properties. The Page Properties window offers a simplified interface for adjusting your link appearance using pseudo-classes (Step 8).

cross-reference

- Refer to Tasks 164 and 165 for internal and embedded style sheets.

Grouping Selectors

Selectors are either tags or classes that you can apply CSS styling to. Sometimes you'll want to create a style that applies to multiple selectors, whether they are classes, redefined tags, or pseudo-classes. Rather than creating a different style for each selector, you can instead create a style that applies to a group of selectors. Let's say, for example, that you want all your headers, h3 through h6, and two custom classes to appear in a certain font. Instead of creating six styles (four redefined tags styles and two custom styles), you could instead group all the selectors together into a single style. This task shows you how.

1. First, open the page to which you want to add the style. If you are creating a new page, be sure to name the file and save it before proceeding

2. Select Windows ➪ CSS Styles to make the CSS Styles panel visible.

3. Click the New CSS Style button in the CSS Styles panel to bring up the New CSS Style window.

4. Select the Advanced option under Selector Type.

5. Enter as many tags, class names, or pseudo-classes as you want to group together as a style. Be sure to separate each selector with a comma, as shown in Figure 162-1.

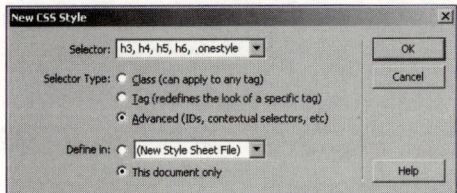

Figure 162-1: Grouping selectors together

6. Select New Style Sheet File or This Document Only to create either an internal or external style sheet, and then click the OK button to bring up the CSS Style Definition window.

7. Use the different categories to set the properties for your style, as shown in Figure 162-2. When you are done, click the OK button to create the style.

note

▪ You can still use the same selectors again in a different style. As long as the styles don't conflict, you can create as many style groupings as needed (Step 8).

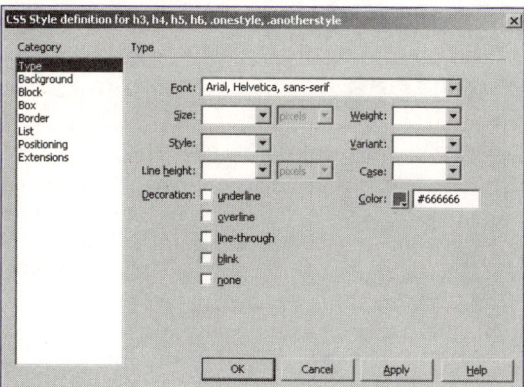

Figure 162-2: Defining the style properties

8. If your style contains custom class selectors, you'll have to apply the classes for them to display; otherwise, any redefined tags (HTML tags) will automatically inherit the style attributes. When you combine styles like this, Dreamweaver groups all the selectors together at the beginning of the style declaration so that it looks like the following code:

```
h1, h2, h3, h4, h5, h6, .onestyle, .anotherstyle {
font-family: Arial, Helvetica, sans-serif;
color: #000080;
}
```

tip

- Grouping selectors can help you simplify your style sheets by cutting down on the number of styles you need to create (Step 5).

cross-reference

- Refer to Tasks 164 and 165 for internal and embedded style sheets.

Styles within Styles: Using Contextual Selectors

note

• You can use any kind of selector when defining contextual selectors—customs classes, redefined HTML tags, or pseudo-classes (Step 5).

Another powerful feature of CSS is that you can specify "conditional" styles that apply only when a certain logic or specific combination of elements has been met. For example, you can specify a style that will apply only to the <i> (italic) tag when it is embedded within a <b> (bold) tag. In other words, if your text is bold and italic, the style would apply, but if it was just italic, the style would not apply. This is called a *contextual selector*, and it is used to define more complex styling scenarios that greatly enhance the level of control you can gain over your presentation.

1. First, open the page to which you want to add the style.

2. Select Windows ➪ CSS Styles to make the CSS Styles panel visible.

3. Click the New CSS Style button in the CSS Styles panel to bring up the New CSS Style window.

4. Select the Advanced option under Selector Type.

5. With contextual selectors, you enter two or more selectors into the Selector field, each separated by a space, as shown in Figure 163-1. A selector that follows another selector is its *descendant*, and the succession of selectors acts like a logic statement. For example, if you entered

   `h1 b`

   all bold tags that occurred inside of an h1 tag would inherit the properties of the style. In this case, b is a descendant of h1. You could also use custom classes and go deeper with a statement like

   `h1 b .myclass`

   In this case, .myclass is now a descendant of b (bold tag), and only text styled with .myclass that is contained within bold tags *and* contained within an h1 tag will inherit the style properties.

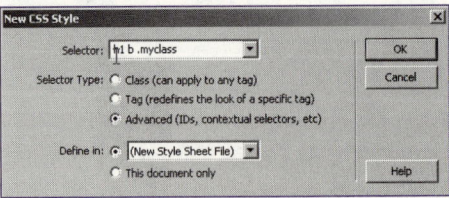

Figure 163-1: Entering selectors

6. Now finish creating the style. Select New Style Sheet File or This Document Only to create either an internal or external style sheet,

and then click the OK button to bring up the CSS Style Definition window.

7. Use the different categories to set the properties for your style, as shown in Figure 163-2. When you are done, click the OK button to create the style.

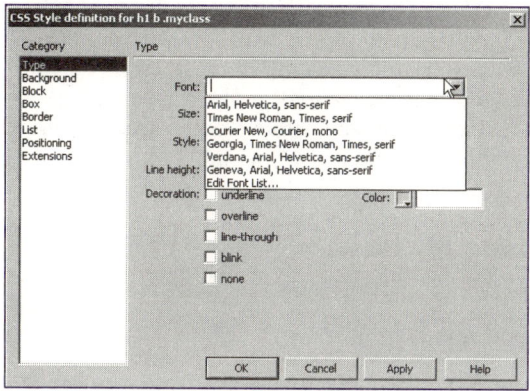

Figure 163-2: Defining the style properties

8. To use any of the styles, apply them in the same manner you would any of the styles as discussed in the previous tasks. When you use contextual styles like this, Dreamweaver groups all the selectors together at the beginning of the style declaration so that it looks like the following code:

```
h1 b .mystyle {
font-family: Arial, Helvetica, sans-serif;
font-size: 12px
color: #660033;
}
```

Task 163

tip

- Using contextual selectors can help you create more precise style sheets because they give you greater control over the options under which style properties are inherited by selectors (Step 8).

cross-references

- Refer to Tasks 164 and 165 for internal and embedded style sheets.

- Refer to Task 159 for applying the style (Step 8).

Task 164

Linking to an External Style Sheet

When you create a style sheet, you have the option of defining the styles inside of the current document or saving them in an external file. When you save your style sheet as an external file, Dreamweaver automatically links it to the page you are currently working on. This link works much the same way that hypertext links work in HTML, because it contains the URL of the style sheet file being linked to. If you've already created an external style sheet, you can link many documents to it. This offers you the ability to control style formatting sitewide by managing a single style sheet file. This makes it easy to make global changes to the styles in your site without having to edit multiple documents—one of the major selling points of CSS.

notes

- External style sheets are saved as separate and distinct text files.

- You can attach multiple external style sheets by repeatedly clicking the Attach Style Sheet button.

- The import option is not used to import a style sheet but rather, most commonly, to link an external style sheet to another external style sheet. Some browsers recognize the import directive from an internal style sheet, but it is best to use the link directive instead, as it offers the best browser compatibility.

1. To create an external style sheet, follow the steps in Tasks 158, 159, or 160 for creating a new style, but select the New Style Sheet File option in the New CSS Style window, as shown in Figure 164-1.

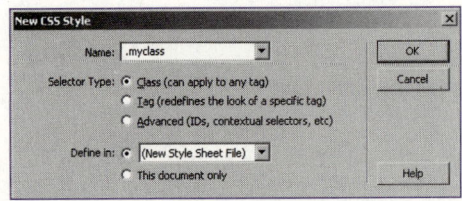

Figure 164-1: Selecting the New Style Sheet File option in the New CSS Style window

2. Click the OK button after you select the New Style Sheet file option to display the Save Style Sheet File As dialog box, shown in Figure 164-2. This allows you to browse for a location on your hard drive to save the external style sheet.

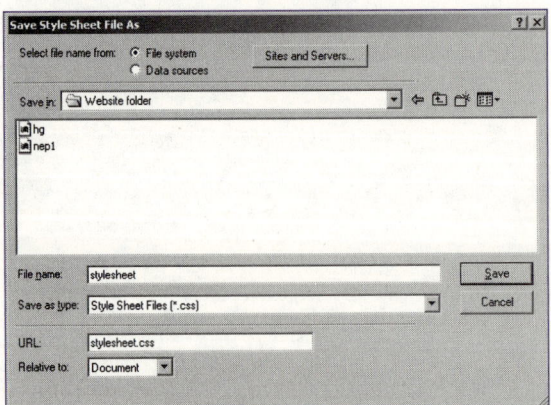

Figure 164-2: Save Style Sheet File As window

3. After you select a location to save the file, name it and append the .css extension. Click the Save button to save it.

4. To link to an existing external style sheet file, open a new or existing document that you want to link to the style sheet.

5. Select Window ⇨ CSS Styles to display the CSS Styles panel.

6. Click the Attach Style Sheet button to bring up the Attach External Style Sheet dialog box, shown in Figure 164-3.

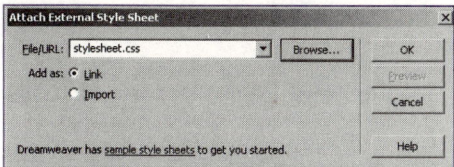

Figure 164-3: Attach External Style Sheet window

7. Enter the filename/URL or click the Browse button to browse for the external file if it exists on your hard drive. Note that you can also link to remote files on the Web by entering the full URL of the style sheet (e.g., **http://www.mysite.com/stylesheets/mystyles.css**).

8. Keep the Link option selected under Add As, since this option is the most widely supported under different browser types.

9. Click the OK button to link the style sheet. Notice that the linked style sheet is displayed in the CSS Styles panel after it has been added.

cross-reference

▪ Refer to Tasks 158, 159, and 160 for information on creating new styles.

Converting an Internal (Embedded) Style into an External Style

Once you've discovered the benefits of external styles over internal ones, chances are you'll most often decide to go with external style sheets. Unless you are only working on a single page that will never share its styles with any other page, it makes much more sense to store your styling information in one single file and link to it from multiple pages. For this reason, if you've already created internal style sheets and wish to convert them to external, the process is very simple.

note

- The import option is not used to import a style sheet but rather, most commonly, to link an external style sheet to another external style sheet. Some browsers recognize the import directive from an internal style sheet, but it is best to use the link directive instead, as it offers the greatest compatibility (Step 7).

1. Open the document containing the internal style that you wish to convert.

2. Select Window ⇨ CSS Styles to display the CSS Styles panel.

3. Highlight the name of the style in the CSS Styles panel that you wish to convert, right-click it, and select Export from the pop-up menu, as shown in Figure 165-1.

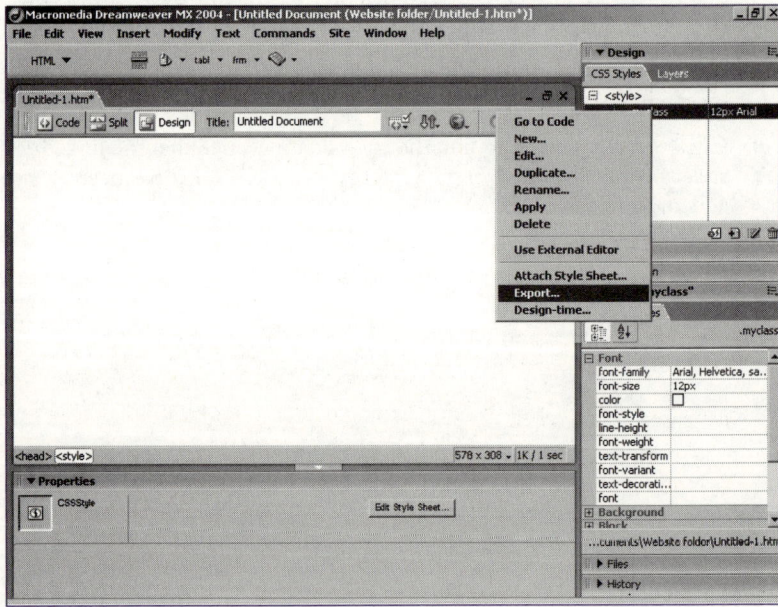

Figure 165-1: Exporting an internal style sheet

4. In the Export Styles as CSS File window, select the location to save the style sheet file (see Figure 165-2). Be sure to select Style Sheet File (*.css) under Save as Type, and click Save to save it to your hard drive.

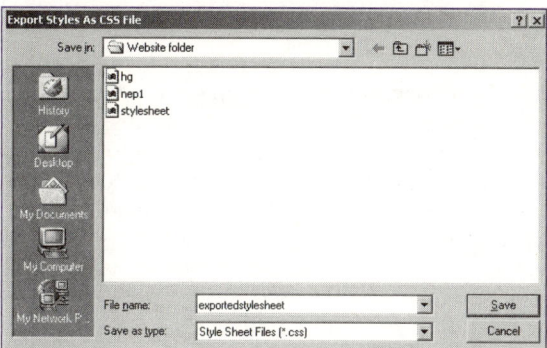

Figure 165-2: Specifying the location of the style sheet

tip

- You can click the Preview button in the Attach External Style Sheet window to see the effect of the new style sheet on the current document before you finish attaching it (Step 6).

5. Now you need to delete the internal style sheet. In the CSS Styles panel, make sure the name of the style you just exported is still highlighted, and click the Trash icon in the panel to delete it.

6. Now it's time to attach the external style sheet you just exported. Click the Attach Style Sheet button to bring up the Attach External Style Sheet dialog box, shown in Figure 165-3. Use the Browse button to locate the file.

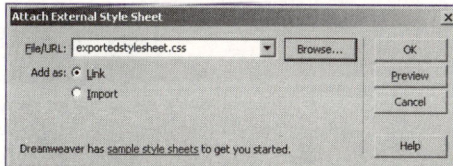

Figure 165-3: Attach External Style Sheet window

7. Keep the Link option selected under Add As, since this option is the most widely supported under different browser types.

8. Click the OK button to finish linking the style sheet. At this point the style will reappear in the CSS Styles panel as an external style sheet.

cross-reference

- Refer to Tasks 158, 159, and 160 for information on creating new styles.

Editing Styles

O nce you create styles, editing them is easily accomplished whether the style sheets are internally or externally located. While you can always edit your style sheets directly in Source view (if you happen to know CSS really well, of course), it's much simpler to use Dreamweaver's excellent visual tools to edit them. Even if the styles were created in another application, they can still be edited using visual tools available in Dreamweaver.

1. Open the page containing the styles you want to edit. You can open the document Task 160.htm if you want to follow along on a page with existing styles.

2. Select Window ⇨ CSS Styles to display the CSS Styles panel, as shown in Figure 166-1.

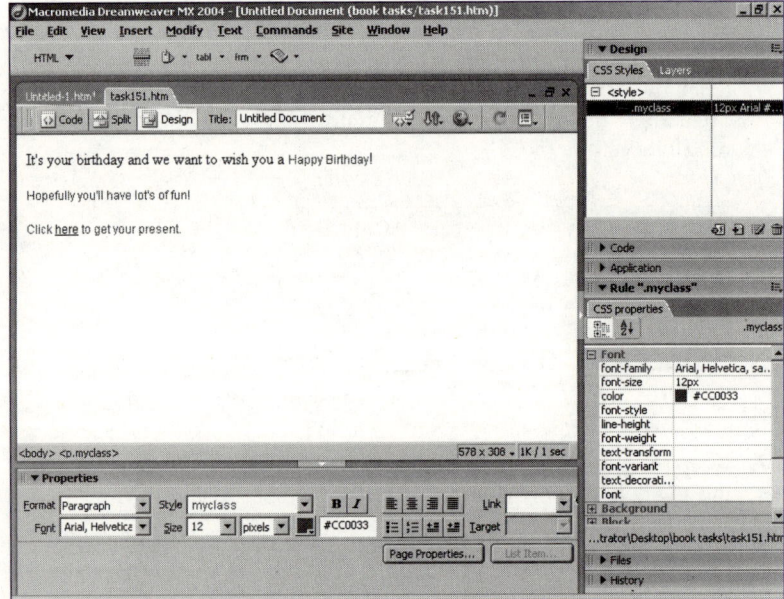

Figure 166-1: The CSS Styles panel displays any current styles in a document

3. Highlight a style you want to edit in the CSS Styles panel, and then click the Edit Style button, also located in the CSS Styles panel. This brings up the familiar CSS Style Definition window.

4. Make the desired changes to your style using the different categories in the CSS Style Definition window. When you are finished, click OK, and the styles are automatically updated in the current document.

5. Another option is to select a style in the CSS Styles panel. If it's in an external style sheet, the Rules panel opens. The Tag inspector

changes to the Rule inspector, as shown in Figure 166-2. The Rule inspector displays all the properties of the highlighted style and allows you to edit any of them by simply typing in a new value in the property sheet.

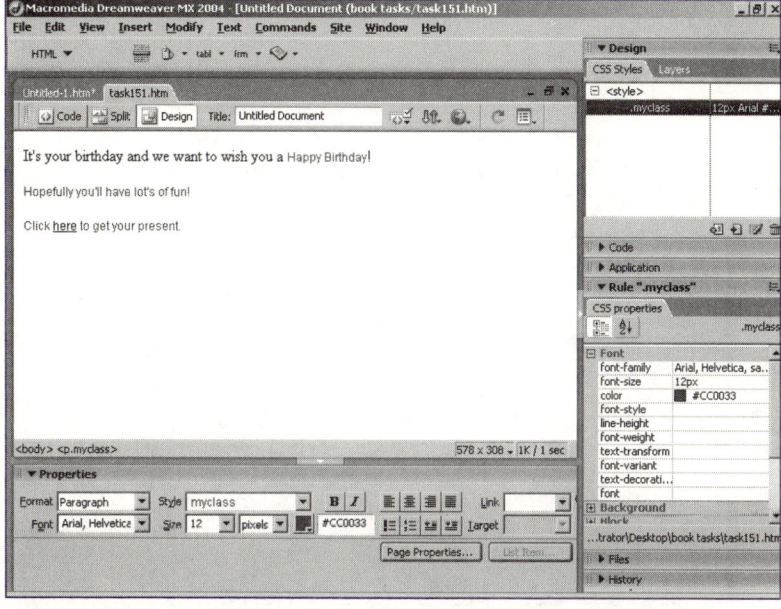

Figure 166-2: The CSS Styles panel displays any current styles in a document

6. For an external style sheet, select the style in the CSS Styles panel, and then open the Tag inspector. You can now use the CSS Relevant panel or the Attributes panel to edit any attribute you desire.

7. When you save and close your page, be sure to save the style sheet if asked to. Sometimes when you are editing, the style sheet may have opened automatically without you realizing it.

tip

▪ Double-click the style property in the left column of the Rule inspector to display the CSS code in either Split view (internal style sheet) or Code view (external style sheet). The cursor automatically positions itself in front of the code for the style being edited, allowing you to directly edit the style's raw code (Step 6).

cross-reference

▪ Refer to Task 164 for more information on external style sheets.

Using a CSS Template

Dreamweaver comes with several professionally designed template pages that use CSS to control layout and formatting for text. You can use any of the templates as a starting point in designing a page that looks great and uses the latest CSS techniques.

notes

- "Halo" is a look-and-feel design similar to Apple's "Aqua" design. It is the new look of the Macromedia site as well (Step 2).

- You can save the templated document anywhere on your hard drive. If you are working on an existing site, be sure to save it within your site's root folder (Step 4).

- External style sheets and their accompanying dependent files are treated just like any other asset in a Web site and should be kept within the root folder of your Web site (Step 5).

1. Select File ⇨ New to bring up the New Document dialog window, shown in Figure 167-1.

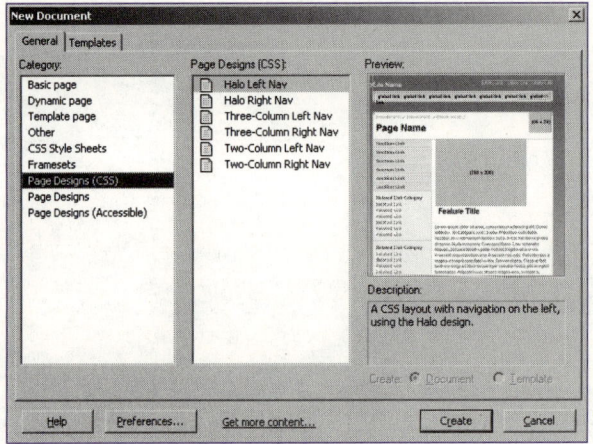

Figure 167-1: New Document window

2. Select Page Designs (CSS) from the General category to display the list of available CSS templates.

3. Scroll through the list of available page designs using the preview window to see what they look like. When you find one you like, highlight it and click the Create button.

4. After you click the Create button, the Save As dialog box appears, prompting you to choose a location to save the document in. Select a location, enter the filename, and click the Save button.

5. After you click the Save button, the Copy Dependant Files dialog box appears, as shown in Figure 167-2, informing you that you need to also copy the style sheet and any other dependent files that accompany the template.

Task **167**

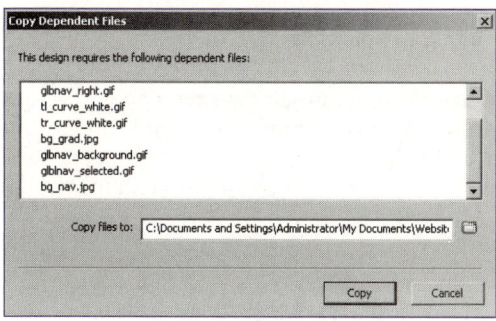

Figure 167-2: Copy Dependant Files window

6. Select a location to copy the files to by clicking the folder icon and browsing your hard drive for an appropriate location. When you are finished selecting the location, click Copy to copy them over to the new location.

7. After the files are copied, the templated page opens in a new document window, as shown in Figure 167-3. You are now ready to begin using the template to design your own page. Simply type over any of the existing text to add your own content to the document, and save it as you would any other document.

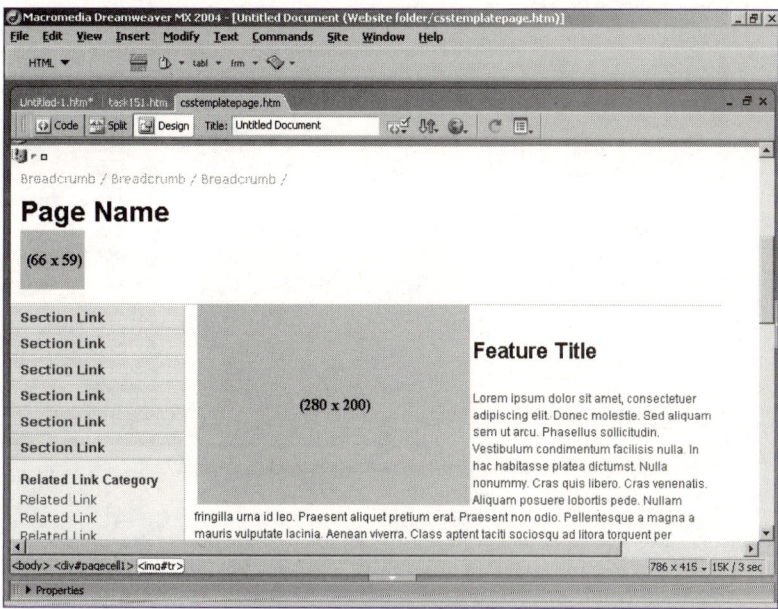

Figure 167-3: CSS template document in Design view

Using the Tag Inspector

The Tag inspector gives you access to all of the properties of your CSS styles by displaying a property sheet where you can both view and edit any of the properties. Using the Tag inspector allows you to quickly edit your style sheets without having to switch out of Design view or navigate through many different dialog windows.

notes

- If you select an item with no relevant CSS styles, the Tag inspector informs you that no rules are applied to the item (Step 4).

- In Category view, the CSS properties are divided into eight different categories. You can expand and collapse the view for each category by clicking on the plus or the minus sign next to the category (Step 7).

1. Open the document 168.htm.

2. Display the Tag inspector by selecting Window ➪ Tag Inspector.

3. Click the Relevant CSS tab in the Tag Inspector panel.

4. Click anywhere in the document (in Design view) to place the cursor inside a word or other element that has a style applied to it. When you do this, the Tag inspector displays all of the rules and CSS properties that are relevant to the item you selected, as shown in Figure 168-1.

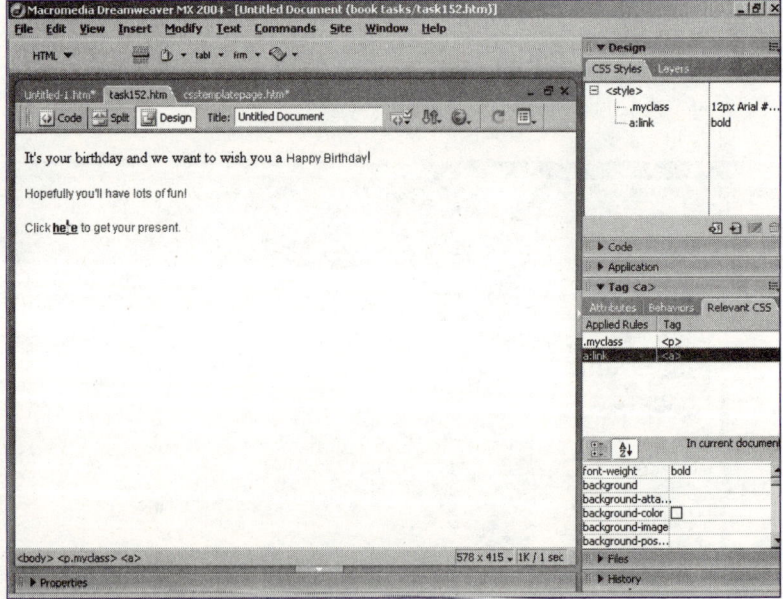

Figure 168-1: The Tag inspector displays relevant styles for the selected item

5. The Tag inspector is divided into two panes, top and bottom, as shown in Figure 168-2. The top pane lists each rule associated with the item you have selected, as well as the tag with which the rule is associated. Because you can have multiple styles associated to a single item, this pane can list several items. The bottom pane lists the actual style properties associated with any rule.

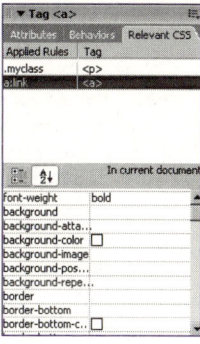

Figure 168-2: Close-up view of the Tag inspector

6. To view or edit properties in a rule, select the rule in the top pane of the Tag inspector and use the property sheet listed in the bottom pane to view or make any necessary changes to the properties, as shown in Figure 168-3.

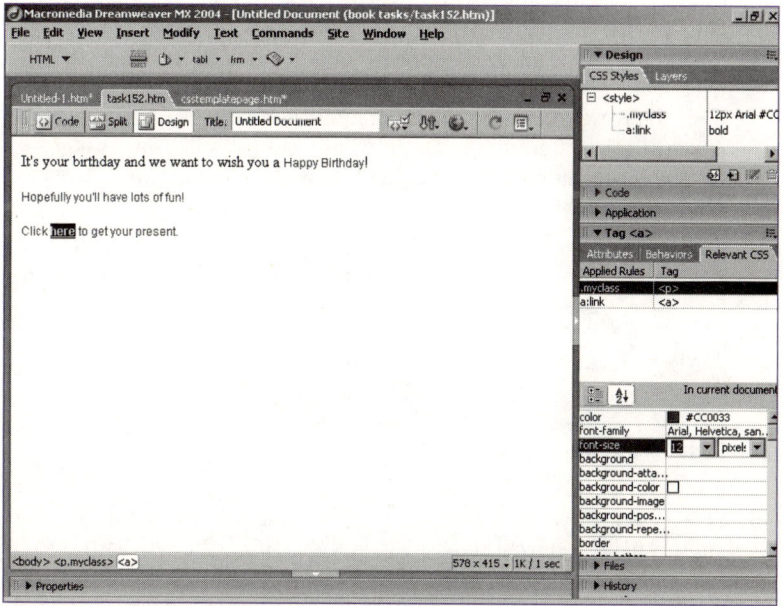

Figure 168-3: Viewing the properties for different rules associated with a selected tag

7. The bottom pane in the Tag inspector has two possible views: Category and List. Category displays the properties sorted by category, and List displays them sorted alphabetically. To switch between the views, click either of the two buttons in the middle of the Tag Inspector panel.

cross-reference

- Refer to Task 166 for information on editing styles.

Formatting Lists Using CSS

One of the more useful features of CSS is the ability to format lists in a much wider variety of ways than you can with HTML. Forget about the boring old bullets and indents you're used to; the list properties in CSS allow you to include many more bullet types, modify their position relative to the text, and even use a custom graphic as a bullet.

1. Open a new or existing document to which you would like to add a formatted list.

2. Make the CSS Styles panel visible by selecting Window ➪ CSS Styles.

3. Click the New CSS Style button in the CSS Styles panel.

4. In the New CSS Style window, select the Tag option under Selector Type. The Tag option is used to redefine existing HTML tags.

5. Now you redefine the HTML tag for list items by attaching custom properties using CSS. To do this, you need to redefine either the `<ul>` or the `<ol>` tag. The `<ul>` tag defines unordered lists and is used when you want to create lists that aren't numbered, such as bulleted lists. The `<ol>` tag defines ordered lists and is used when you want to create lists with sequential numbering. Depending on which type of list you want to create, enter **ul** or **ol** (or select either tag from the pop-up menu) in the Tag list, as shown in Figure 169-1.

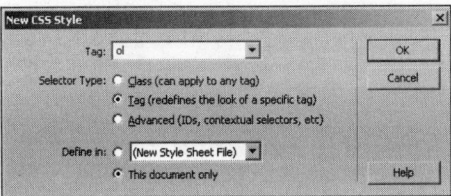

Figure 169-1: Modifying the list tag

6. Select New Style Sheet File or This Document Only to create either an internal or external style sheet, and then click the OK button to bring up the CSS Style Definition window for the tag you selected.

7. In the CSS Style Definition window, click the List category to display the List properties, as shown in Figure 169-2.

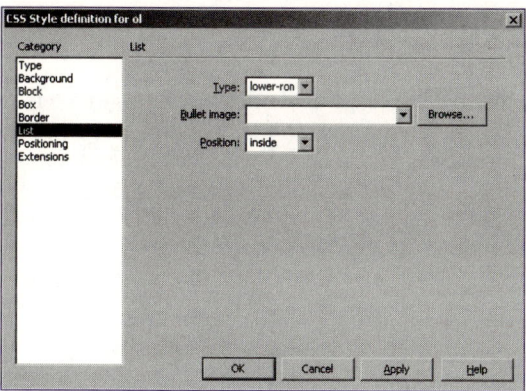

Figure 169-2: CSS properties for lists

tip

- If you use custom graphics for your bullets, be sure to make them small; try to keep them no bigger than one line of type (Step 8).

8. Use the appropriate fields to select the options you want your list to use. The first pop-up list defines how the type will appear or the type of bullet that will be used. The next field is used to browse and specify a custom image you can use as a bullet. Simply use the Browse button to locate any GIF or JPEG image you'd like to use. The final option, Position, defines whether the bullet or number appears inside or outside the list block. After you are done selecting the appropriate options in this window, click the OK button to apply them.

9. In Design view, enter the list items into your document that you want to apply the list to. Use a return after each item in the list.

10. Highlight all the items in the list and select Text ⇨ Lists ⇨ Ordered List or Unordered List (depending on whether you redefined the `<ol>` or `<ul>` tag). After you apply the appropriate list style, your list updates to reflect the properties you created in the new style.

cross-reference

- Refer to Task 32 for using the Property inspector for lists.

Task 170

Adding a Background Style

While HTML allows you to add background colors and images to elements like whole pages, tables, and individual table cells, CSS background properties go much further, allowing you to add background colors and images to words, paragraphs, images, and many other page elements.

1. To add a background style, first open the document to which you want to add the style.

2. Make the CSS Styles panel visible by selecting Window ⇨ CSS Styles, and click the New CSS Style button to open the New CSS Style window.

3. Select either Class or Tag under Selector Type in the New CSS Style window. Use Class if you want to create a custom style that can be applied to any element. Use Tag if you want your background to apply to all instances of a specific HTML tag (see Figure 170-1).

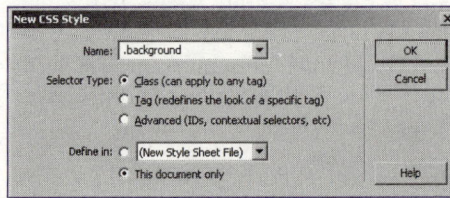

Figure 170-1: Specifying the type of style

4. Select New Style Sheet File or This Document Only, depending on whether you want an internal or external style sheet. Click OK.

5. In the CSS Style Definition window, click the Background category to display the options for background properties, as shown in Figure 170-2.

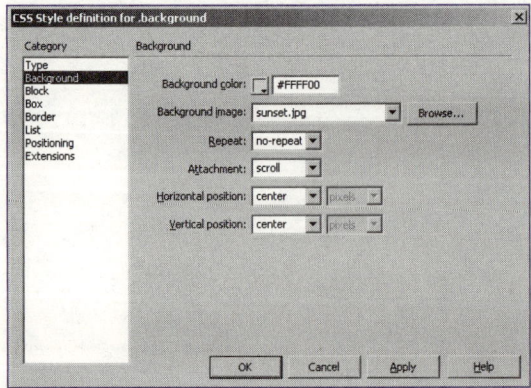

Figure 170-2: Background category in the CSS Style Definition window

6. Select a background color and/or a background image by using, respectively, the color well and the Browse button to locate an image on your drive.

7. The other four pop-up menus refer to different options available when you use a background image. If you are using an image, choose a repeat option by selecting one of the choices from the Repeat pop-up menu. The choices are as follows:

- *Repeat*. Tiles the image horizontal.

- *Repeat x or Repeat y*. Tiles the image horizontally only (x) or vertically only (y).

- *No-Repeat*. No tiling; the image only displays once.

8. Set the attachment pop-up menu to Fixed or Scroll. Fixed causes the background image to stay in place as the page scrolls, whereas Scroll causes it to scroll with the page.

9. Set the horizontal and vertical positions using the corresponding pop-up menus. These refer to the positioning of the background image in relation to the element that the style is applied to. For example, if you apply the style to a paragraph of text, these options define where in the paragraph the background image appears.

10. Click OK to create the style, or modify any of the other categories to continue defining your style. If you created your style as part of a redefined HTML tag, the style appears whenever that tag is used. If you created a custom style, you need to apply the style to an element on your page in order to see it.

Task 170

tip
- Redefining the `<td>` tag is a good way to add a background to every table cell in a table. You could also add the background to every row (`<tr>`) or the entire table itself (`<table>`) using a CSS background style (Step 4).

cross-reference
- Refer to Task 159 for custom classes.

Adding a Border

With HTML, the only elements that can have borders are images, tables, and table cells. With CSS, however, you can add different kinds of borders to a multitude of elements and even control the appearance of each side of the border (top, bottom, left, or right). CSS border properties open up whole new design possibilities that help you move away from tables as a primary design tool.

1. To add a border style, first open the document where you want to add the style.

2. Make the CSS Styles panel visible by selecting Window ⇨ CSS Styles, and click the New CSS Style button to open the New CSS Style window.

3. Select either Class or Tag under Selector Type in the New CSS Style window, as shown in Figure 171-1. Use Class if you want to create a custom style that can be applied to any element. Use Tag if you want your border to apply to all instances of a specific HTML tag.

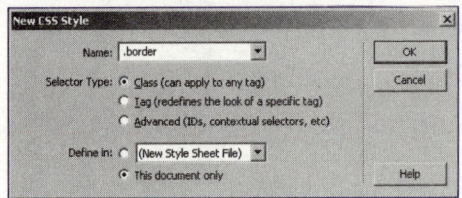

Figure 171-1: Specifying the type of style

4. Select New Style Sheet File or This Document Only, depending on whether you want an internal or external style sheet. Click OK.

5. In the CSS Style Definition window, click the Border category to display the options for border properties, as shown in Figure 171-2.

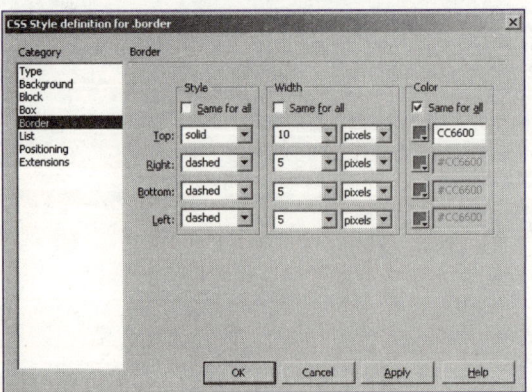

Figure 171-2: Border category in the CSS Style Definition window

notes

- You must select a style from the Style pop-up menu in order to see the border you create. If you leave the Style field set to None, the border will not appear regardless of its width and color settings (Step 6).

- Not all of the options for border styles will preview correctly within Dreamweaver. Make sure you preview your page in your target browser to get an accurate idea of how the style will render in the browser (Step 9).

6. Select the style of border from the Style pop-up menu; there are eight different options. If you keep the Same for All option checked, all four sides of the border will be the same. If you uncheck this option, you can set different borders for each of the four sides. This is also true for the Width and Color settings.

7. Select the border width from the Width pop-up menu. You can choose Thin, Medium, or Thick, or you can specify a custom value measured in a variety of different measurement units.

8. Select the border color from the Color pop-up menu. Click the color well to use the Color Picker to change colors.

9. Click OK to create the style, or modify any of the other categories to continue defining your style. If you created your style as part of a redefined HTML tag, the style appears whenever that tag is used. If you created a custom style, you need to apply the style to an element on your page in order to see it.

cross-references

- Refer to Task 159 for custom classes (Step 3).

- Refer to Task 160 for redefining HTML tags (Step 3).

Task 172

Making Links with No Underlines

One of the most common uses of CSS is to disable the underline option for hypertext links. To do this, you can use the Advanced Selector option to modify the link attribute of the <a> tag, giving you access to the decoration properties for all links displayed on your page. It's a handy technique that is easy to execute and works on all browsers except for Netscape 4 and below.

notes

- You can also remove underlines from links by modifying the Underline Style option in the Page Properties dialog box, accessible by selecting Modify ⇨ Page Properties. This method is less flexible (and has embedded styles) in terms of the kinds of properties you can set, but it does offer quicker access and setup for creating pseudo-classes for your hypertext links.

- The a:link selector style only affects unvisited links. To remove the underlining for visited links as well, you need to also create a style for the a:visited selector (Step 3).

1. Open the document where you want to remove the link underlining.

2. Make the CSS Styles panel visible by selecting Window ⇨ CSS Styles.

3. Click the New CSS Style button to open the New CSS Style window.

4. Select Advanced under Selector Type in the New CSS Style window, and select the a:link option in the Selector pop-up menu, as shown in Figure 172-1. The a:link option is a pseudo-class that affects the link attributes of the <a> tag.

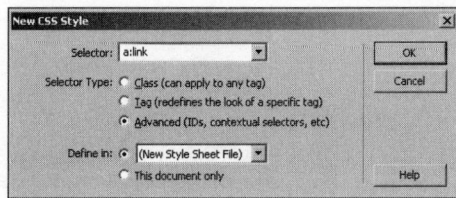

Figure 172-1: Using an advanced selector to modify the link attributes of the <a> tag

5. Select New Style Sheet File or This Document Only, depending on whether you want an internal or external style sheet. Click OK.

6. By default, all links in HTML display with an underline, which in CSS is referred to as a *decoration*. To turn this decoration off, check the None option under Decoration in the Type category of the CSS Style Definition window, as shown in Figure 172-2.

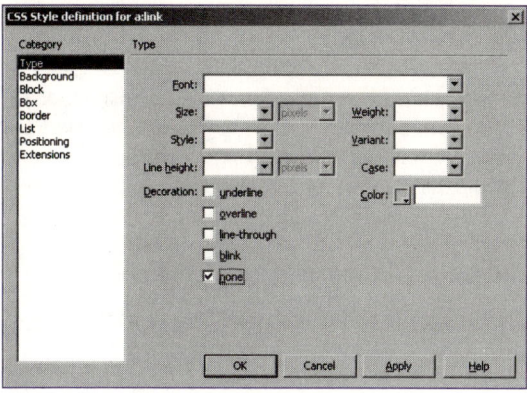

Figure 172-2: Turning off link underlining

7. Click OK to create the style, or modify any of the other categories to continue defining your style. From this point, all links that you create in your document will show up without an underline.

tips

▪ There are several other types of decorative effects that you can apply to your links, such as blink, strikethrough, and so on. With the exception of the underline option, I don't recommend using these other options because they are poorly supported across multiple browsers and because they tend to be pretty unattractive (Step 5).

▪ Create a second style for the a:hover selector, and set the text decoration to Underline. This way your links will display an underline only when a user hovers his or her mouse over the link, creating a professional-looking interactive effect (Step 6).

cross-reference

▪ Refer to Task 161 for pseudo-classes.

Changing Link Colors

While you may not realize it, Dreamweaver now uses CSS instead of HTML to define link colors. To change your link colors, you can use the Page Properties preferences, a convenient shortcut that creates pseudo-classes without using the CSS styling options. This is one very handy shortcut that is new to Dreamweaver MX 2004.

1. Open the document where you want to change the link coloring.

2. Select Modify ⇨ Page Properties to bring up the Page Properties dialog window.

3. Click the Links category to display the Link options, as shown in Figure 173-1.

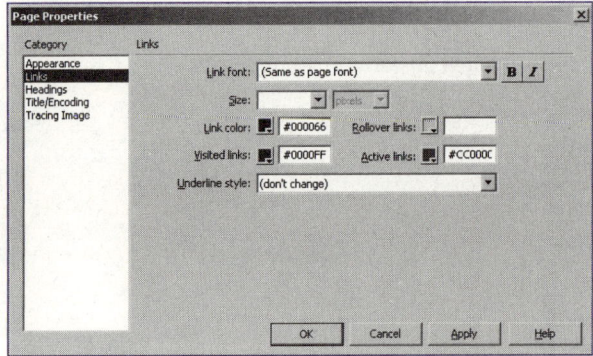

Figure 173-1: Changing link colors is achieved via the Page Properties window

4. Click any of the color wells to bring up the Color Picker, and pick a link color for each link state, as shown in Figure 173-2.

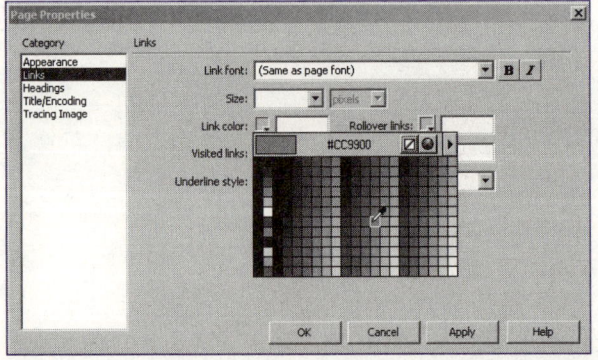

Figure 173-2: Use the Color Picker to alter the colors for each link state

5. Click OK to apply the link coloring. Notice that when you do this, the CSS Styles panel displays the styles for each link as pseudo-classes (see Figure 173-3). A pseudo-class is a different kind of style that is used to alter attributes of tag—in this case the `<a>` tag used to create anchor links. This is indicated by the `a` followed by a colon and then the name of the attribute being modified.

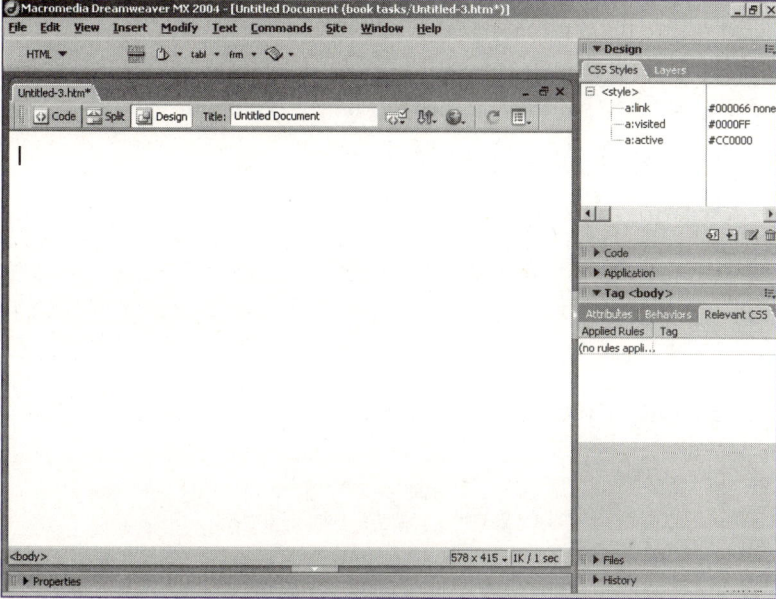

Figure 173-3: Setting link colors with the Page Properties window creates styled pseudo-classes that appear in the CSS Styles panel

cross-reference

• Refer to Task 174 for information about setting link colors using the CSS Styles panel.

Using Different Colors for Different Links

Another useful feature of CSS is that you can apply different colors to different links. Instead of having to use the same color for all your links, you can
customize each link by applying a class with a different custom color. Imagine,
for instance, that you have links that appear in the content area of your site,
which has a white background. You may also have links in a sidebar with a totally
different color background. You'll probably want the link colors different for
each area for easier viewing—depending on your color scheme.

1. Open the document where you want to change the link coloring.

2. Make the CSS Styles panel visible by selecting Window ⇨ CSS
   Styles, and click the New CSS Style button to open the New CSS
   Style window.

3. Select Class under Selector Type in the New CSS Style window, and
   type a name into the Name field, as shown in Figure 174-1.

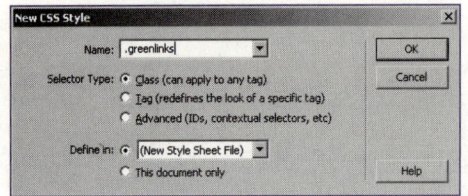

Figure 174-1: Creating a custom class for a link color

4. Select New Style Sheet File or This Document Only, depending on
   whether you want an internal or external style sheet, and then click
   OK to bring up the CSS Style Definition window.

5. In the Type category of the CSS Style Definition window, click the
   Color Well and use the Color Picker to choose a new color for the
   link, as shown in Figure 174-2. Add any other styling attributes you
   want to apply to the link, and click the OK button to create the style.

6. Repeat Steps 2 through 5 to create any additional colored styles to
   use for your links.

7. Create a link on your page to which you want to apply one of the colors by highlighting the text to be linked and typing the link URL
   into the Link field of the Property inspector.

notes

▪ When you use custom
  classes to control the link
  colors, it's best not to apply
  any link colors through the
  page properties, as you
  will end up with conflicting
  style information. Conflicting
  styles in CSS tend to display unpredictably and are
  best avoided (Step 5).

▪ The pop-up Style menu in
  the Property inspector displays the style names in
  the same color they were
  created in, making it easier
  to see what the style will
  look like before you apply it
  to your link (Step 8).

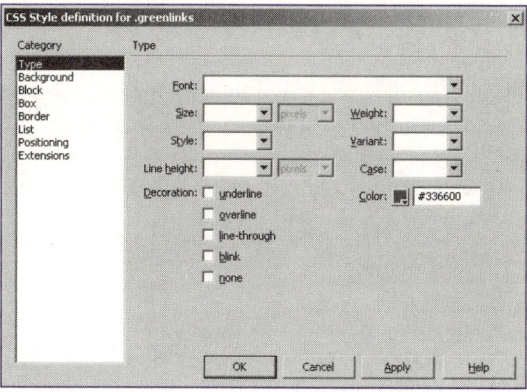

Figure 174-2: Setting the color for the link style

8. Use the pop-up menu in the Style field of the Property inspector to apply the style you created earlier with the custom link color. When you apply the style, the link takes on the color of that style, as shown in Figure 174-3.

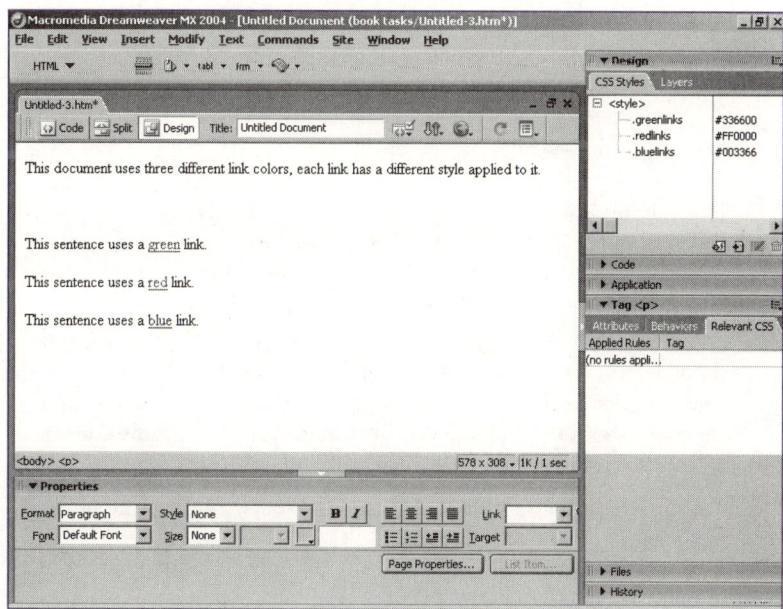

Figure 174-3: Setting up different link colors with different styles

cross-reference

▪ Refer to Task 159 for information about applying styles (Step 8).

Using Design Time Style Sheets

Design Time Style Sheets allow you to show and hide multiple external style sheets without actually attaching them to a document. This enables you to experiment with different style sheets while you are designing in Dreamweaver, without changing the current document in any way. This is really handy for developers that use different style sheets for different computer platforms or browsers. It allows them to see the effects of each style sheet in real time without having to save multiple versions of the page.

note

- Styles that are shown or hidden using Design Time Style Sheets only affect the document as it is viewed in Dreamweaver. Shown or hidden styles will not affect the way the document is viewed in a Web browser (Step 7).

1. To show or hide a style sheet using Design Time Style Sheets, first open the document you wish to design with.

2. Select Text ➪ CSS Styles ➪ Design Time to display the Design Time Style Sheets dialog window, as shown in Figure 175-1.

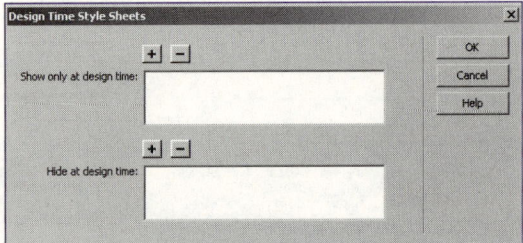

Figure 175-1: Design Time Style sheets window

3. The window consists of two fields: Show Only at Design Time and Hide at Design Time. These fields are used to list the style sheets to either show or hide for the current document. Use the Plus (+) and Minus (–) buttons to add/delete a style sheet to either category.

4. When you click the plus (+) sign for either category, the Select File dialog window appears, as shown in Figure 175-2. This allows you to select a style sheet file anywhere on your hard drive. After locating the style sheet file, click OK to connect it. At this point the styles become either enabled or disabled in the document.

5. You can add as many style sheets as you want by clicking the plus (+) sign repeatedly and adding more styles, as shown in Figure 175-3. Notice that any linked style sheets that have been hidden are listed as "hidden" in the CSS Styles panel.

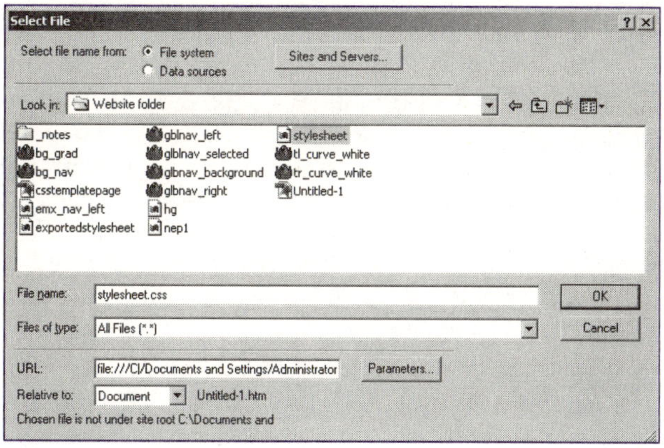

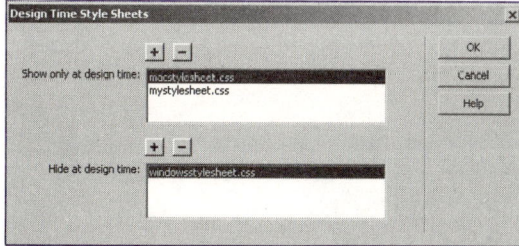

Figure 175-2: Select File window

6. To delete a style in either field in the Design Time Style Sheets window, highlight the style name and click the minus (–) button in either list.

Figure 175-3: Showing/hiding multiple style sheets

7. When you are finished specifying the styles to show or hide, click the OK button to apply the changes. Edits made using Design Time Style Sheet information are kept with the document when you save it.

tip

- Click the Sites and Servers button in the Select File window to quickly access your saved sites and servers (Step 4).

cross-reference

- Refer to Tasks 164 and 165 for internal and embedded style sheets.

Embedding a Layer Using CSS

While you may not realize it, CSS forms the basis of layer positioning in the world of Web design. A CSS layer is sometimes referred to as a `"div"` because the `<div>` tag is used to define layers in CSS. Once you create a layer, you use the positioning properties of CSS to control the size, placement, and other aspects of the layer.

notes

▪ Changes made with the Tag Library Editor are global changes that affect all tags or attributes with the same name (Step 1).

▪ If you insert a `<div>` tag without applying any positioning attributes in the accompanying style, the selection handles will not appear around a layer. The layer will just appear as regular text, though when you mouse over the layer, Dreamweaver displays a red line around it to indicate that it is a layer object (Step 10).

1. To embed a layer and control its properties using CSS, first open the document in which you'd like to embed the layer.

2. Make the CSS Styles panel visible by selecting Window ➪ CSS Styles, and click the New CSS Style button to open the New CSS Style window.

3. Create a new style for the layer by selecting Class under Selector Type in the New CSS Style window, and then enter a name for the style in the Name field.

4. Select New Style Sheet File or This Document Only, depending on whether you want an internal or external style sheet. Click OK to bring up the CSS Style Definition window.

5. Click the Positioning category to display the positioning properties for the style, as shown in Figure 176-1.

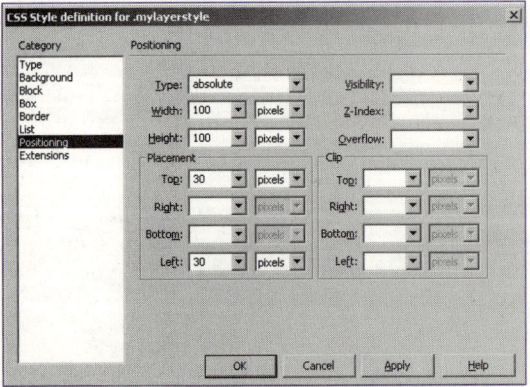

Figure 176-1: Positioning properties control the size and appearance of the layer

6. Set the type of layer positioning by selecting one of the options from the Type pop-up menu. Absolute is used to create a layer that is positioned independently of other layers. Relative allows you to position a layer relative to another layer. Static creates a layer that rests at the location where the `<div>` tag is placed.

7. Enter the width, height, and placement values in the appropriate fields. The Placement options define where on the page your layer appears in relation to the edges of the page (absolute) or the edges of another layer (relative). The other fields are optional and relate to advanced features of layer positioning. Click OK when you are fin-

Task **176**

ished entering the values for the positioning properties to create the layer style.

8. To place the layer on the page, select Insert ⇨ Layout Objects ⇨ Div Tag. This brings up the Insert Div Tag window, as shown in Figure 176-2.

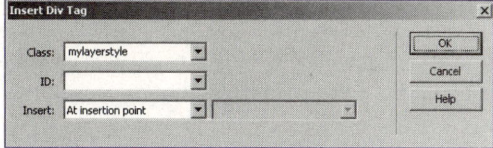

Figure 176-2: Insert Div Tag window

9. In the Class pop-up menu, select the name of the style you created earlier. This applies the positioning properties you defined earlier to the new layer. Click OK to insert the layer on the page.

10. Now you should see the layer defined by a gray border on the page using the values you set in the positioning properties. When you highlight the layer, selection handles and a "handle" in the upper left corner appear. These can be used to reposition the layer on the page (see Figure 176-3). At this point you can also use the Property inspector to change any of the positioning values of the layer, or in the case of moving and resizing the layer, you can simply use the mouse to drag the layer or any of its handles to a new position.

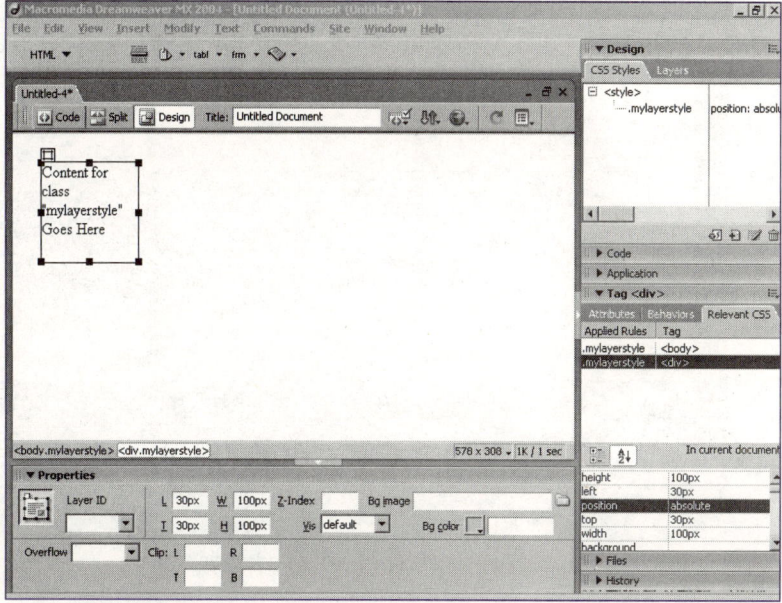

Figure 176-3: Embedded layer displays selection handles

cross-reference

- Refer to Task 159 for information about custom styles and Task 109 for setting layer properties with the Property inspector.

Checking CSS Compatibility with Different Browsers

One of the drawbacks of designing with CSS is that you are working with some of the most cutting-edge technologies in the world of Web design. This is a drawback because the major browser companies still haven't gotten their CSS rendering acts completely together and different browsers offer differing levels of support for various CSS features. The best way to deal with this issue is to check your pages in multiple browsers to ensure that your CSS-designed pages display consistently.

To help the situation, Dreamweaver includes a handy Check Target Browser feature that analyzes all of your CSS code and checks to see if it is compatible with a list of target browsers that can be customized. By default, the list includes most of the major browsers that you are likely to encounter and alerts you to any problems that might occur.

1. To perform a target browser check, open a document that uses CSS and switch to Code view. If Dreamweaver finds any problems with the CSS code, it displays a wavy, red underline beneath the code in question.

2. Position your cursor over any of the red lines to display a ToolTip that gives more details about which browsers do not support the code in question, as shown in Figure 177-1.

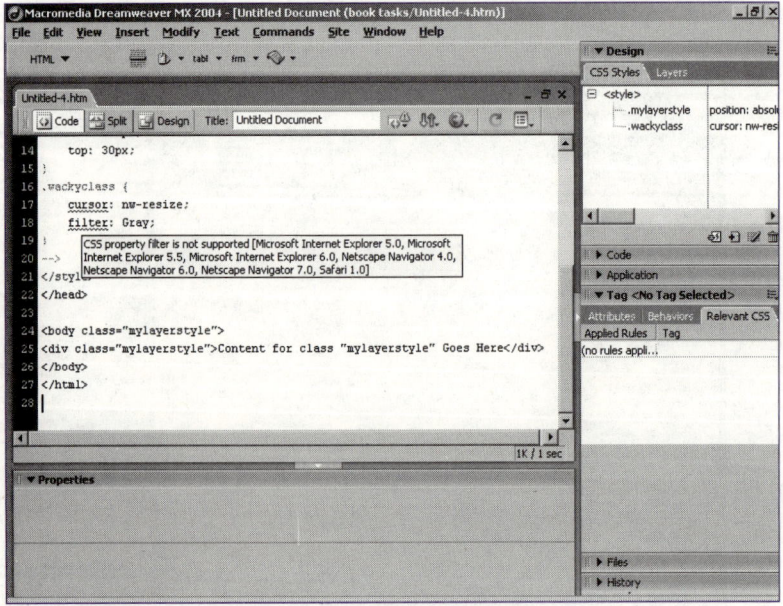

Figure 177-1: Browser check errors displayed in Code view

3. You can also display a list of all of the results of a target browser check by clicking the Check Target Browser button in the document

toolbar and selecting Show All Errors. The results are displayed in a new window, as shown in Figure 177-2.

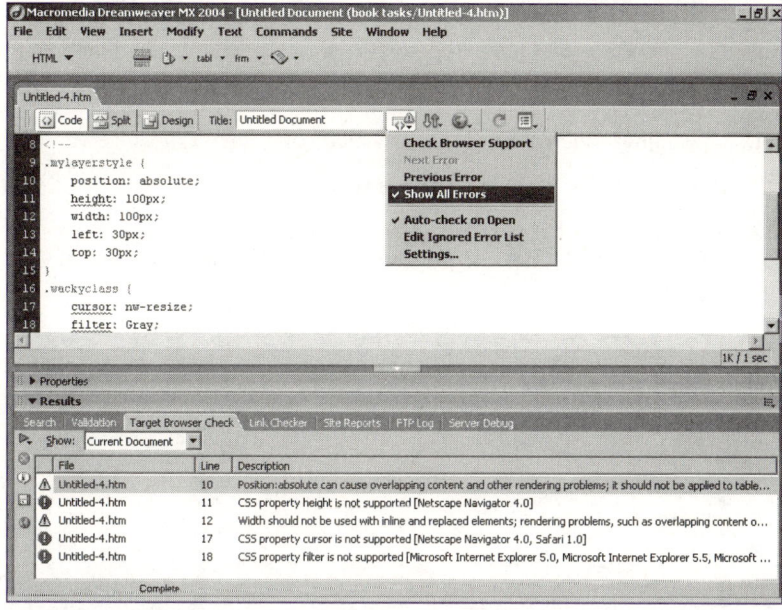

Figure 177-2: Viewing the results of a target browser check

4. Normally, Dreamweaver only performs a check against target browsers when you first open a document. To perform the check manually at any other time on an open document, switch to Code view and select the Check Browser Support option from the pop-up list on the Check Target Browser button. This displays the red, wavy error lines if it finds any problems.

5. To edit the list of target browsers to add or delete new browser versions, select the Settings option in the Check Target Browser button pop-up list. This brings up the Target Browsers dialog window, shown in Figure 177-3. You can edit this list by checking or unchecking browsers and selecting version numbers from the corresponding pop-up menus.

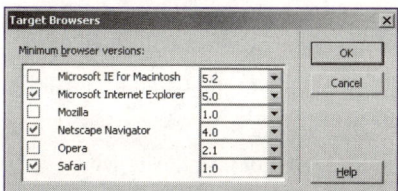

Figure 177-3: Target Browsers settings

cross-reference

- Refer to Task 7 for setting up testing browsers.

Inserting Content Blocks (DIVs)

Inserting DIVs (in the Layout Object group) is different than adding a layer in Dreamweaver. When you add or draw a layer, it is absolutely positioned and inline. The DIV you add here is a content block that you can and will control using CSS styles.

note

- A DIV is a container to hold content. You can control position and styling using a CSS style sheet (Intro).

1. Open a new document or one to which you want to add a `<div>` tag.

2. Place your cursor where you want the `<div>` tag to appear.

3. Select Insert ⇨ Layout Object ⇨ Div Tag, or from the Insert bar's Layout category, click the Div Tag button, as shown in Figure 178-1.

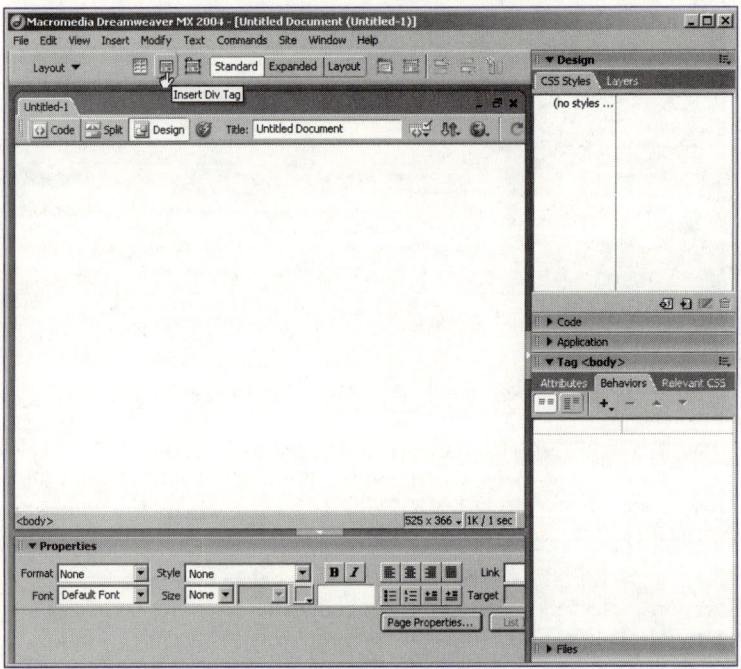

Figure 178-1: A new document is open and the Div Tag object is selected in the Layout category of the Insert bar

4. In the Insert Div Tag dialog box, select a class from the menu if you'd like. Any classes you have defined in your style sheet will show up.

5. Select an ID if you'd like from the ID menu. Only defined IDs, not used ones, will be visible to select.

6. Select an insertion point from the Insert menu to indicate where you'd like to place the `<div>` tag (see Figure 178-2).

7. If you select anything other than At Insertion Point, the field on the right is populated with additional options, as shown in Figure 178-3. Click OK when you are finished.

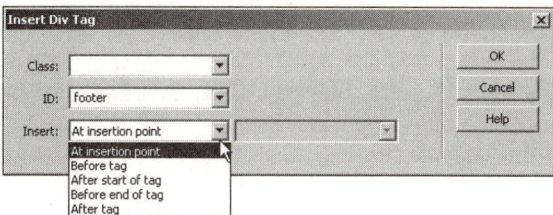

Figure 178-2: The Insert options

8. Pass your cursor over the area where you see the placeholder text. You see a highlight of the box or container as your mouse passes over it, as shown in Figure 178-4.

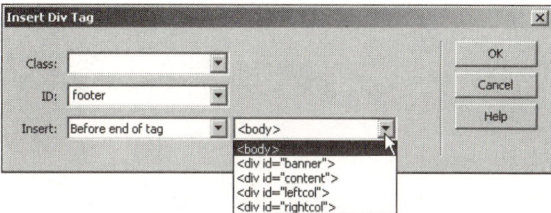

Figure 178-3: Some of the Insert DIV tag Insert options

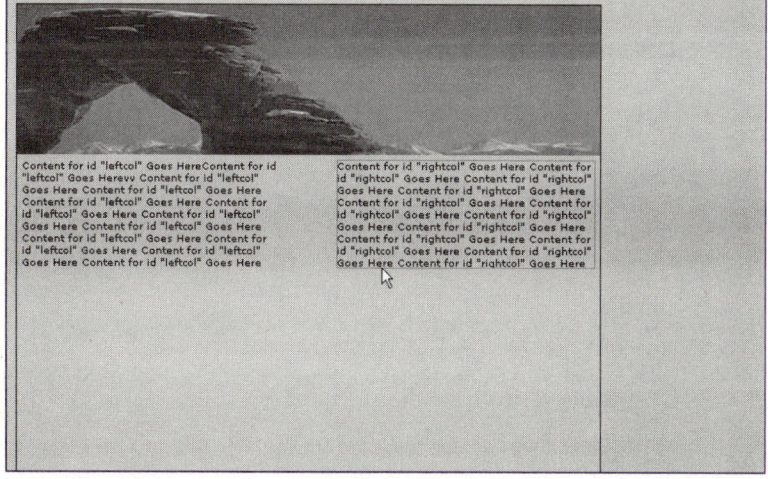

Figure 178-4: The box or container highlighted as your mouse passes over it

tips

▪ Attach a CSS style sheet and use positioning styles to use with your `<div>` tags (Step 1).

▪ You can also use CSS starter pages by choosing Page Designs (CSS) from the Create from Samples section of the Start Page. This opens the New dialog box, where you can select the desired design (Step 2).

cross-reference

▪ Refer to Task 108 for drawing and inserting Dreamweaver layers (Intro).

Creating a Container to Hold a Banner (ID Selector, DIV, Background Image)

notes

- The starter file has page properties added; then the styles were exported to the practice.css style sheet. Refer to Tasks 31 and 165 (Step 1).

- In this example you didn't add a border to the bottom of the DIV because another container for the content is going to be positioned below the banner (Step 5).

When you design without tables, the container of choice is a DIV. You'll need to define class and ID selectors to position and format DIVs. ID selector names begin with a # sign and can only be used once. You can have multiple ID selectors, but they must be unique names. In this task you define an ID selector and create a new DIV.

1. Open the Task 179.htm file from the Part 9 Task 179 folder, which you can get at www.wiley.com/compbooks/10simplestepsorless.

2. In the CSS Styles panel (Window ⇨ CSS Styles), click the New CSS Style button to open the New CSS Style dialog box. Use the following settings (also see Figure 179-1):

   Select Advanced (IDs, contextual selectors, etc.) as the Selector Type.

   Name the style **#banner**.

   Select the external style sheet practice.css for the Define In section.

   Click OK to open the New CSS Style Definition dialog box.

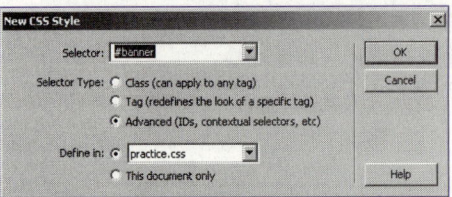

Figure 179-1: The ID style settings

3. Select the Background category and use these settings:

   Click the Browse button next to Background image and select background.jpg from the Task 179 folder.

   Select No-Repeat from the Repeat drop-down menu.

4. Select the Box category and use these settings:

   Enter **600** pixels for the width and **150** pixels for the height.

   Uncheck the Same for All check box. In the Margin area, type **10** for everything except Bottom.

5. Select the Border category and use these settings:

   Uncheck all of the Same for All check boxes.

   Select Solid from the Top, Right, and Left Style drop-down menus.

Enter 1 pixel for the Top, Right, and Left Widths.

Enter #000066 for the Top, Right, and Left Color.

6. Click OK to save the style.

7. Select Insert ⇨ Layout Objects ⇨ Div Tag to open the Insert Div Tag dialog box.

8. Select banner in the ID drop-down menu, as shown in Figure 179-2.

Figure 179-2: Selecting the banner ID

9. Select At Insertion Point in the Insert drop-down menu, and click OK.

10. Select and delete the text that Dreamweaver automatically inserts in the DIV. Figure 179-3 shows the banner DIV added to the page.

Figure 179-3: The banner DIV added to the page

tip

▪ ID names must begin with # (Step 2).

cross-references

▪ Refer to Task 178 for using the Insert DIV function (Intro).

▪ Refer to Task 180 for adding columns to this exercise's DIV container (Step 10).

Creating a Container to Hold Columns

This task builds on Task 179, where you added a banner image to a Web page. In this task you add a container that will hold columns that you create in Task 181. The DIV container will have a background and a border to match the banner.

1. Open the Task 180.htm file from the Part 9 Task 180 folder, which you can get at www.wiley.com/compbooks/10simplestepsorless.

2. Open the CSS Styles panel (in the Design panel group) and click the New CSS Style button.

3. In the New CSS Style dialog box, use these settings (also see Figure 180-1):

    Select Advanced (IDs, contextual selectors, etc.) as the Selector Type.

    Name the style **#content**.

    Select the external style sheet practice.css for the Define In section.

    Click OK.

note

- No border was added to the top of this container because it is going below the banner and we want a seamless look (Step 4).

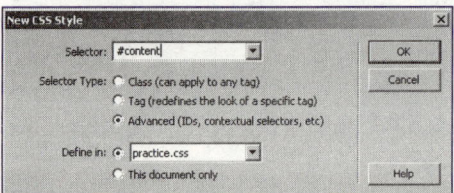

Figure 180-1: The settings for the content ID selector

4. In the New CSS Style Definition dialog box, set the following in each listed category:

    Box category:

    Width. 600 pixels

    Height. 400 pixels

    Uncheck the Same for All check box in the Margin section. Set the Right Margin to 10 pixels and the Left Margin to 10 pixels.

    Border category:

    Uncheck the Same for All check box in all of the sections.

    Set the Right, Left, and Bottom Style to Solid.

    Set the Right, Left, and Bottom Width to 1 pixel.

    Set the Right, Left, and Bottom Color to **#000066**.

5. Click OK to save the style definition.

6. In Code view, position the insertion point after `<div id="ban-ner"></div>`, as shown in Figure 180-2.

```
1  <!DOCTYPE HTML PUBLIC "-//W3C//DTD HTML 4.01 Transitional//EN"
2  "http://www.w3.org/TR/html4/loose.dtd">
3  <html>
4  <head>
5  <title>Untitled Document</title>
6  <meta http-equiv="Content-Type" content="text/html; charset=iso-8859
7
8  <link href="practice.css" rel="stylesheet" type="text/css">
9  </head>
10
11 <body>
12 <div id="banner"></div>
13 </body>
14 </html>
15
```

Figure 180-2: Positioning the cursor for the next `<div>` tag

7. Select Insert ⇨ Layout Objects ⇨ Div Tag.

8. Select content from the ID drop-down menu.

9. Select At Insertion Point in the Insert drop-down menu, and click OK.

10. Select and delete the text that Dreamweaver automatically inserts in the DIV. Figure 180-3 shows the content DIV added. Notice how the border lines up nicely with the banner DIV.

Figure 180-3: The content DIV added

tip

▪ ID selector names must start with # (Step 3).

cross-references

▪ Refer to Task 179 for adding the banner DIV (Intro).

▪ Refer to Task 181 for adding two columns into the DIV you added in this task (Step 10).

Adding Two Columns to a DIV Container

In this task you add columns to the container you built in Task 180. The columns will use the `float` property, which enables containers like DIVs to float beside other elements, like images can.

1. Open the Task 181.htm file from the Part 9 Task 181 folder, which you can get at www.wiley.com/compbooks/10simplestepsorless.

2. Click the **New CSS Style** button, and use these settings in the New CSS Style dialog box:

   Select Advanced (IDs, contextual selectors, etc.) as the Selector Type.

   Name the style **#leftcol**.

   Select the external style sheet practice.css for the Define In section.

   Click OK.

3. In the New CSS Style Definition dialog box, enter the following settings for the Box category, as shown in Figure 181-1:

   Width. 45 and select % from the drop-down menu

   Float. Left

   Uncheck the Same for All check box in the Margin section.

   Set the Top, Left, and Bottom margins to **5** pixels.

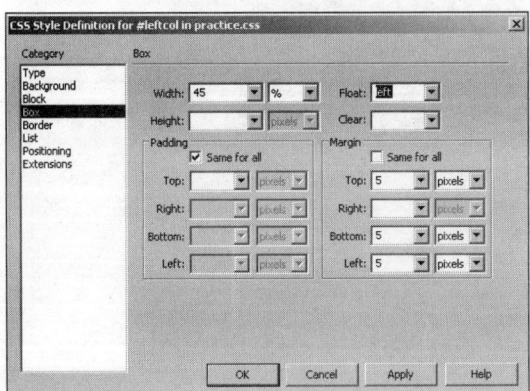

Figure 181-1: The Box category filled in for the floating container

4. Click OK to save the style definition.

5. In Code view, position the insertion point `<div id="content"></div>`, as shown in Figure 181-2.

6. Select Insert ⇨ Layout Objects ⇨ Div Tag, and select leftcol from the ID drop-down menu. Select At Insertion Point and click OK. Figure 181-3 shows how the column looks in Design view.

```
1  <!DOCTYPE HTML PUBLIC "-//W3C//DTD HTML 4.01 Transitional//EN"
2  "http://www.w3.org/TR/html4/loose.dtd">
3  <html>
4  <head>
5  <title>Untitled Document</title>
6  <meta http-equiv="Content-Type" content="text/html; charset=iso-8859
7
8  <link href="practice.css" rel="stylesheet" type="text/css">
9  </head>
10
11 <body>
12 <div id="banner"></div>
13 <div id="content">|</div>
14 </body>
15 </html>
16
```

Figure 181-2: The insertion point within the content DIV

tip
- ID selector names always begin with a # sign. Also, each ID must be unique and can be used only once (Step 2).

7. Repeat Steps 2 to 6, except name the ID selector **#rightcol** and in the Box category, set the float to Right. Also set the right margin to **5** pixels and the left margin to **0**.

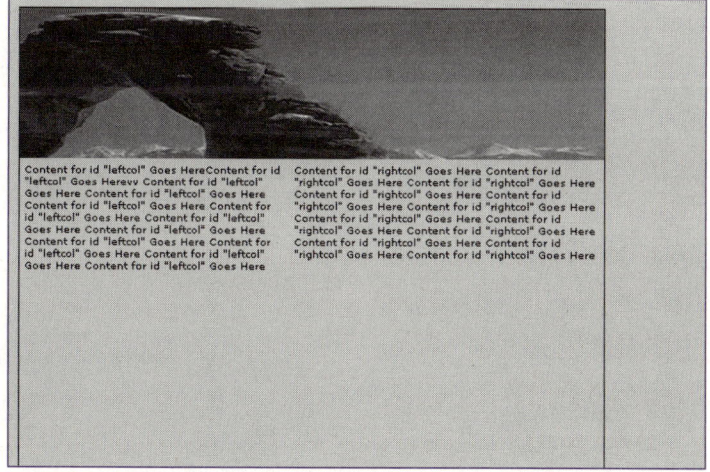

Content for id "leftcol" Goes HereContent for id "leftcol" Herevv Content for id "leftcol" Goes Here Content for id "leftcol" Goes Here Content for id "leftcol" Goes Here Content for id "leftcol" Goes Here Content for id "leftcol" Goes Here Content for id "leftcol" Goes Here Content for id "leftcol" Goes Here Content for id "leftcol" Goes Here Content for id "leftcol" Goes Here Content for id "leftcol" Goes Here Content for id "leftcol" Goes Here

Content for id "rightcol" Goes Here Content for id "rightcol" Goes Here Content for id "rightcol" Goes Here Content for id "rightcol" Goes Here Content for id "rightcol" Goes Here Content for id "rightcol" Goes Here Content for id "rightcol" Goes Here Content for id "rightcol" Goes Here Content for id "rightcol" Goes Here Content for id "rightcol" Goes Here

Figure 181-3: The left column added with text

8. In Code view, position the insertion point after the `lefcol </div>` tag and before the `</div>` tag of the content block.

9. Select Insert ⇨ Layout Objects ⇨ Div Tag to open the Insert Div Tag dialog box. Select rightcol from the ID drop-down menu and select At Insertion Point.

10. Click OK.

cross-references
- Refer to Task 180 for adding the container that holds the two columns (Intro).
- Refer to Task 179 for adding the DIV that holds the banner (Intro).

Part 10: Automating with Library Items and Templates

Saving as a Library Item

A Library item in Dreamweaver provides a means of reusing "standard" content on multiple pages. Changes to a Library item are automatically propagated to all pages containing that Library item. The appeal of this kind of automation is considerable.

Before you actually commit to Library items, however, you need to understand the disadvantage of using them as well. Library items are *design time* tools only. This means that they only affect files in your local site on your computer. For those changes to be reflected on the Web, the changed files must be uploaded to the hosted site. On a site with many files, each containing a Library item, each file must be uploaded after each change to that Library item. Library items themselves (i.e., the *.lbi files) have no function on the server and should only be uploaded if you want to share them with someone.

This task teaches you how to create a Library item so that you can insert it on other pages as needed (note that this is just one of many ways to create a Library item).

1. Create a new page in Dreamweaver by choosing File ⇨ New (Ctrl/Command+N).

2. The General tab should be selected in the New Document dialog box. Select Basic Page under Categories (the left pane), and select HTML under Basic Page (the right pane), as shown in Figure 182-1. Click the Create button.

note

- There are at least five distinct ways to create Library items in Dreamweaver: (1) use the File ⇨ New procedure (shown here), (2) use the File ⇨ Save As option and select Library Files (*.lbi) from the list, (3) select content already existing on a page and use Modify ⇨ Library ⇨ Add Object to Library, (4) use the Group menu on the Library section of the Asset panel to select New Library Item, or (5) select the object in Dreamweaver's Design view, and drag and drop it into the Library (file) section of the Asset panel (Intro).

caution

- A Library item should be a code fragment *only*. It should not contain (a) `<html>`, `<head>`, or `<body>` tags; (b) any content that would otherwise be in the head of the document; or (c) JavaScript or style sheet information (unless you *really* know what you are doing!). If you are having trouble with a Library item, this is the first place to look.

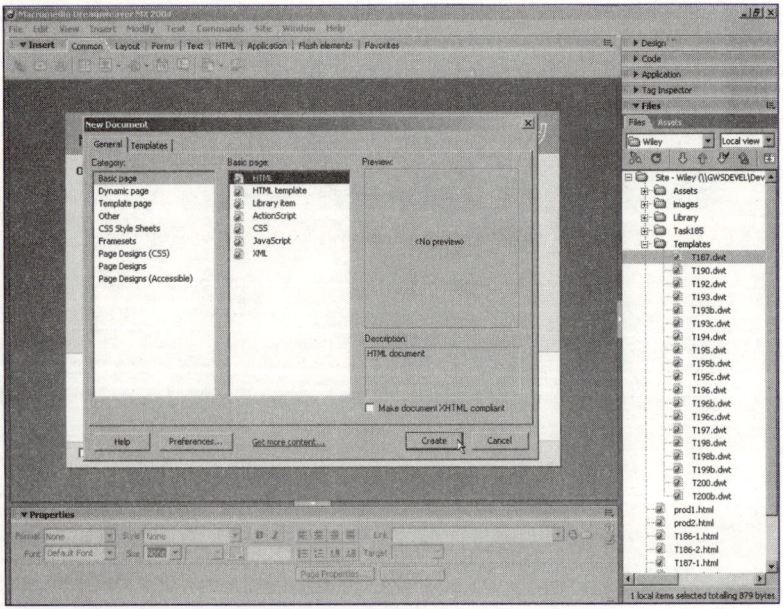

Figure 182-1: New Document dialog box for creating a new page

Task 182

3. With your insertion point in the Design View pane, enter the following text:

Copyright (C) 2003 – My Big Company, Inc.

4. Because you want this copyright notice to also link to My Big Company's Web site, select the company name and click in the Link field of the Property inspector so that you can add a hyperlink.

5. With the company name selected and the cursor positioned in the Link field of the Property inspector, enter the absolute link **http://www.mybigcompany.com** and press Enter/Return on the keyboard.

6. You now have a page containing a copyright statement and a link. In Design view, select that entire line of text that you entered (beginning with "Copyright" and ending with "Inc."), and select Modify ⇨ Library ⇨ Add Object to Library. Note that this creates a file in your Assets panel called "Untitled"; rename this file **T182-1** (see Figure 182-2).

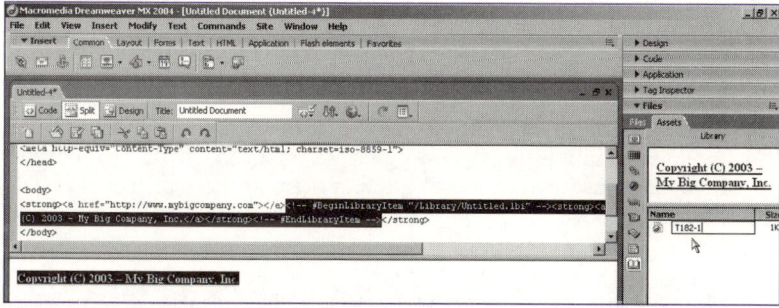

Figure 182-2: Adding your selection to the site's Library

7. Verify the correct location of the file you just saved by examining the Files panel in Dreamweaver. Check that the file is indeed named correctly (T182-1.lbi) and that it is placed in the Library folder at the root level of the site (see Figure 182-3).

You have created a Library item from a page element and saved it in the site's Library for future use.

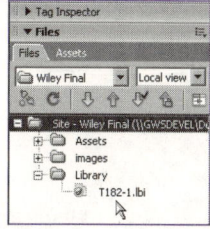

Figure 182-3: Verify the placement of the Library item in the site

tips

▪ If you have just opened Dreamweaver, it is possible that you will be looking at the Start Page. To arrive at the point where this step ends, just click the More option, below the Create New heading (Step 1).

▪ Even though you have used File ⇨ Save (Ctrl/Command+S), the panel that opens is called Save As and the suggested name is Untitled-1.lbi. This reflects the fact that Dreamweaver already knows that the file is a Library item and has added the required file extension of .lbi (Step 6).

▪ Depending on your preferences, you may need to refresh the site's File list to see newly created Library items properly (Step 7).

cross-reference

▪ Details of working with Library items are covered in the next four tasks, as well as in Task 189.

Using Simple Library Items

This task teaches you how to use simple Library items—that is, Library items that do not contain behaviors, JavaScript, or CSS. You need to use the Library item that you created in the previous task (Task 182), or you can download the T182-1.lbi file (make sure you place it within the Library folder in your site when you download it) from the partX task182 folder at www.wiley.com/compbooks/10simplesteps.

notes

- Be aware that Dreamweaver's link management will adjust any links within your site that appear in your Library items. This means that if you have a link to an image or another page in your Library item, that link will be correctly made even though the target pages are at different folder levels (Step 5).

- Library items on your page are dealt with as if they were a single entity. If you want to edit a Library item, you can do that by using the Open button on the Property Inspector in addition to actually opening the file itself. See Tasks 185 and 186 for more details on editing Library items (Step 6).

1. Create a new basic HTML page in Dreamweaver by choosing File ➪ New (Ctrl/Command+N).

2. Enter some content on this page. It is often convenient to copy generic content from a site like www.lipsum.com for the purpose of filling a page (you can also copy this "Greek" text from the file called loremipsum.txt from the partX Task183 folder at www.wiley.com/compbooks/10simplesteps.

3. Make sure you have Dreamweaver's Design view enabled and the insertion blinker showing in Design view. Click below the content you have just added, and insert a paragraph space by pressing the Enter/Return key.

4. Insert the Library item called T182-1 at this point by opening the Asset panel (if it is not already open), selecting the T182-1 Library item, and clicking the Insert button at the bottom of the panel (see Figure 183-1).

caution

- If you have not yet saved the page within the site, you will not see the Library item filenames appear in the Assets panel. This is because Dreamweaver does not yet know to which site this file belongs (Step 4).

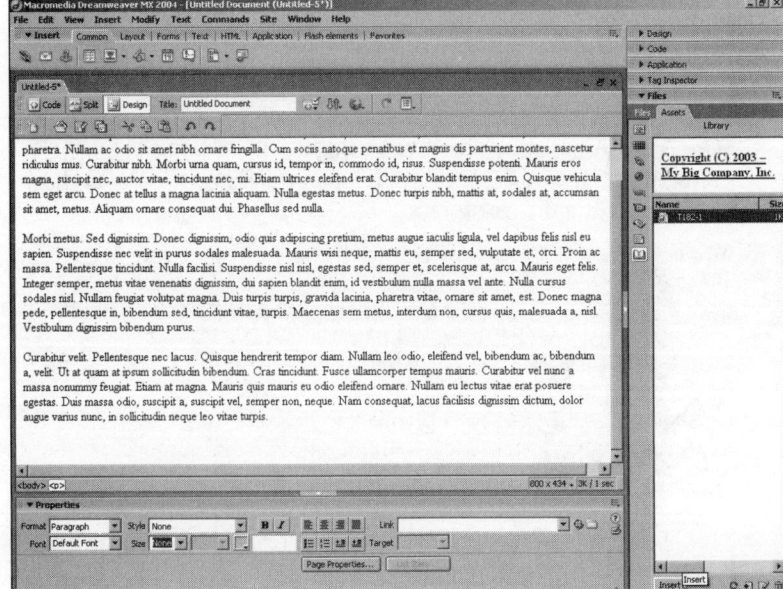

Figure 183-1: The Library section of the Assets panel showing the Library filenames and contents

Task **183**

5. Your basic page should now contain a single Library item, as shown in Figure 183-2. When you view this page in Dreamweaver's Design view, you should see the words "Copyright (C) 2003 – My Big Company, Inc." highlighted in a straw color, indicating that it is a Library item. Selecting the words (you cannot click within them, since the entire selection is controlled by the Library) exposes a specific Library item Property inspector. This inspector allows you to open the Library item, to detach this instance from the Library, or to re-create the Library item from this instance (you would use this if you had lost your original Library item, for example).

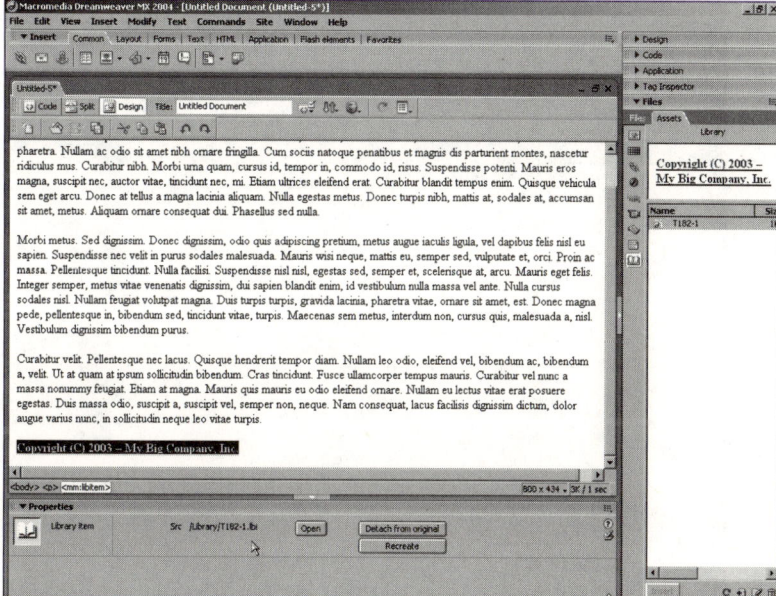

Figure 183-2: A page containing a Library item and its Property inspector

6. Enable Split view (by clicking on the Split View icon on Dreamweaver's toolbar), and note that the code for the Library item is also highlighted with a straw color in the Code view. In addition, note that some HTML comments have been added to the page identifying which Library item is the parent for this code. This use of comments in the code is the umbilical cord that links this particular instance of that Library item to its parent file in the Library, and it's what allows Dreamweaver to propagate changes from the parent file in the Library into each page containing that Library item.

cross-reference

- Refer to Task 182 for a simple way to make Library items.

Using Complex Library Items

A complex Library item is one that contains behaviors, JavaScript, or CSS. This task teaches you how to use a Library item containing a behavior.

1. Create another new page as before. Enter the word **LINK** on the page, select the word LINK, and make it a null link by entering **javascript:;** in the Link field of the Property inspector and then pressing Enter/Return (see Figure 184-1). You can now apply behaviors to this null link (you cannot do so with plain text).

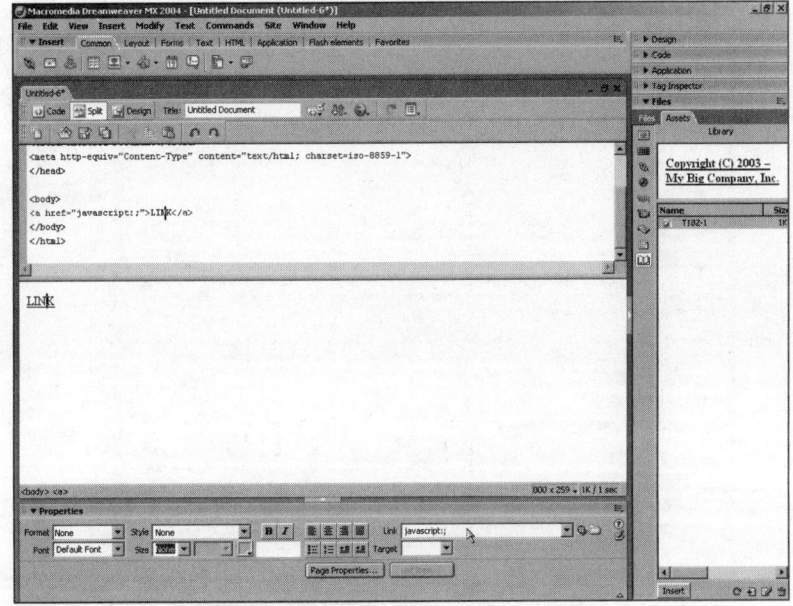

Figure 184-1: Creating a null link on the page

2. With this null link selected, apply Dreamweaver's Popup Message behavior, and enter **Thank You for Clicking!** in the Message field before clicking on the behavior's OK button. Note that this has now added some JavaScript to the head of your page, which you can see in Code view and in Figure 184-2.

3. With the word LINK selected, save as a Library item just as you did in Step 6 of Task 182 (use **T184-1.lbi** for the name).

    This second file is a more complex Library item simply because it contains a link to which a behavior has been applied.

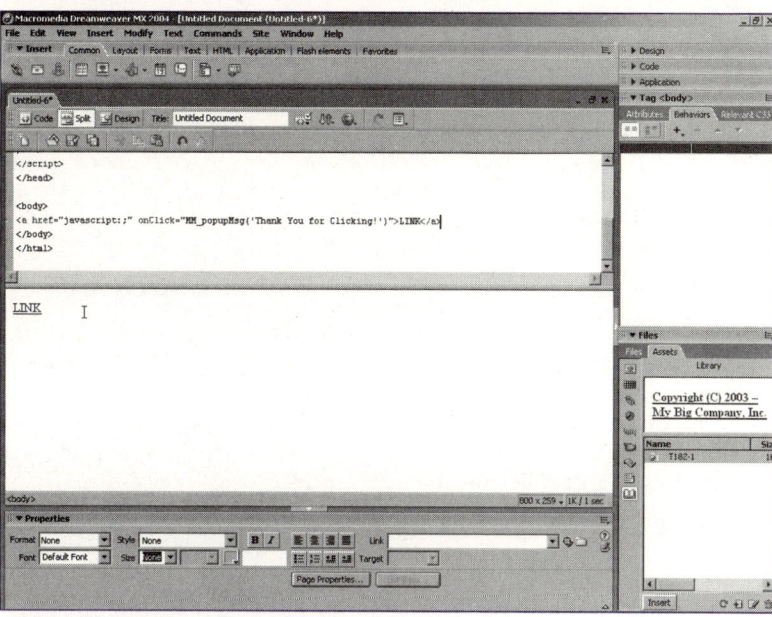

Figure 184-2: After applying a behavior to the link

4. Select the Library item on this page that you have just created and click the Open button on the Property inspector. Look at the code on this Library item's page. Are you surprised to discover that there is no JavaScript there? I was the first time I did this. What this means is that Dreamweaver MX 2004 is smart enough to *not* copy the JavaScript from the parent page into the Library item. But is the reverse also true? Is it smart enough to make sure that the receiving page gets that JavaScript? Let's try it.

5. Create a new page in Dreamweaver MX 2004 and click in the Design view. Make sure that you have selected the Split View icon on the toolbar.

6. Find the Library item named T184-1.lbi in your Asset panel, select it, and insert it on the page by clicking the Insert button.

7. Once again, look at the code on the page, and note that DMX 2004 has indeed inserted the required support JavaScript on the page.

8. Preview this page containing the Library item by pressing F12, and note that when you click LINK, the alert message appears as expected. This means that the behavior you applied in Step 2 is working properly when that Library item is used on a page.

9. You can expect Library items to behave like this in the future—making a Library item from a page element to which a behavior has been applied will *not* also copy the associated support JavaScript functions into the Library item file. Instead, it will cause the required JavaScript to be copied to the target pages containing the Library items, if that JavaScript is not already there.

cross-reference

- Refer to Tasks 185 and 186 for ways to edit Library items, and to Task 182 for a simple way to make a Library item.

Task 185

Making Simple Edits to Library Items

For this task and the following one (Task 186), a simple edit is considered one that changes only the appearance or the structure of the item, and a complex edit is one that changes the function of the item.

1. Begin this task by creating a new page in Dreamweaver, as described previously.

2. Insert filler content on this page by copying and pasting from the loremipsum.txt file.

3. Insert a Library item on this page by first clicking in Design view to set your insertion point and then selecting T182-1 in the Library view of the Asset panel and pressing Insert. Your page now contains the hyperlinked words "Copyright (C) 2003 – My Big Company, Inc." as a Library item.

4. Save this page as **T185-2.html** and close it.

5. Edit that Library item by finding and double-clicking its name in your Asset panel's Library display (see Figure 185-1).

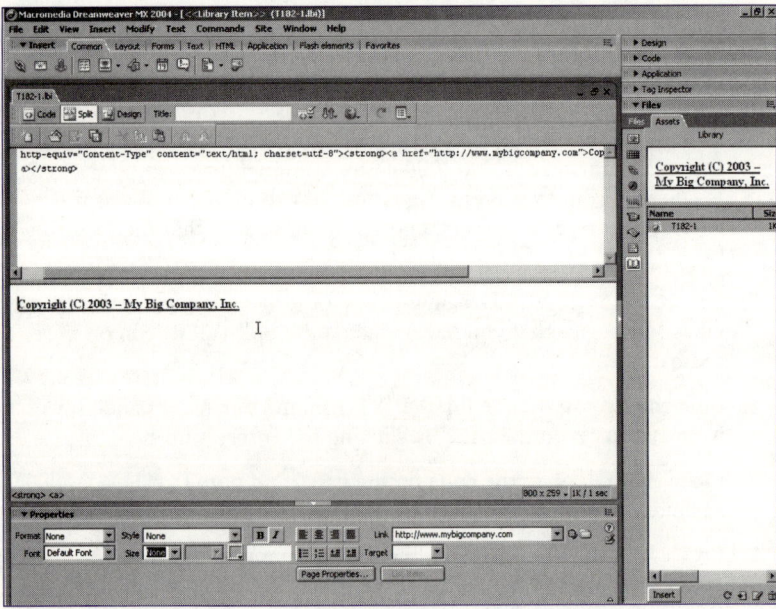

Figure 185-1: Preparing to edit a Library item

6. Select the entire phrase "Copyright (C) 2003 – My Big Company, Inc." and center-align it by clicking on the Center Align icon in the Property inspector. In the Code view pane, note that the selection is now wrapped in a `<div>` tag, with alignment set to Center (see Figure 185-2). This is the best way to center-align text on your page.

note

- Filler text is called Greek text even though it looks more like Latin! It is a holdover from the days of print/typography and is actually based on the obscure writings of Cicero, except altered to reflect English letter frequencies (Step 2).

caution

- When you are making and then saving changes to Library items, all pages containing instances of that Library item will also be changed. If these pages are already open in Dreamweaver when you make your changes to the Library item, you must remember to save the pages as well, since they will have also been modified. If the pages containing the Library item are closed when you save changes to the Library item, the changes you make will be propagated directly to the saved files, and you will not have to remember to save them. This is good and bad, since it is not possible to reverse such saved file changes. Be careful! (Step 7)

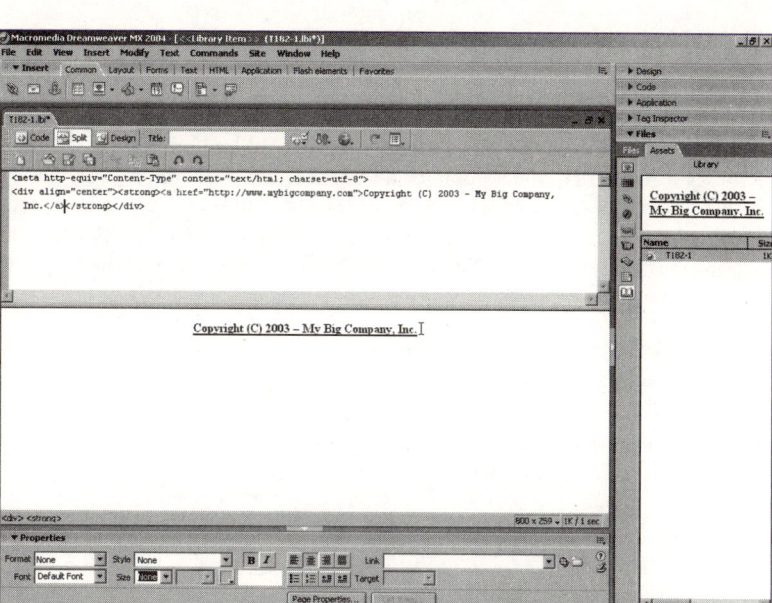

Figure 185-2: Center-aligning the Library item's contents

7. Save the Library item page.

When you save the Library item you just changed, each page in the site containing that Library item is correspondingly changed—that is, the change you just made is propagated to all instances of the Library item (see Dreamweaver's alert in Figure 185-3 asking if this should be done). This is one of the real conveniences of using Library items. Later you will see that templates work this way too. You can check to see that this happened by opening the file you saved earlier (T185-2.html) and verifying that the Library item's contents are now center-aligned.

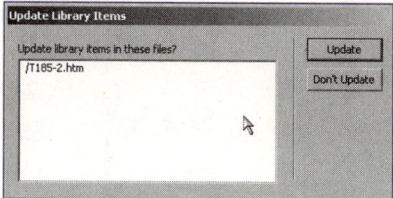

Figure 185-3: Update Library Items alert panel

cross-reference

▪ Refer to Task 182 for making Library items and Task 186 for complex editing (Intro).

Task 186

Making Complex Edits to Library Items

Beware! This task is definitely in the danger zone. Making complex edits to Library items is . . . well . . . complex. The problem arises from the fact that a Library item is merely a snippet of code—it is not a full Web page. This means that it does (should) not contain some of the structural tags that a complete Web page does—for instance, `<html>`, `<head>`, or `<body>`. The result of this is that you will always have problems trying to apply styles and behaviors when editing an *existing* Library item.

If you do need to do this (and it may be something that all of us need to do at one time or another), the best procedure is as described in the following, which requires Task186-1.html, the image files (image1_up.gif and image1_over.gif), and the corresponding Library item (T186-1.lbi) from the partX task186 folder at `www.wiley.com/compbooks/10simplesteps`.

1. Open the task186-1.html file and note that this file contains a single image as a Library item—nothing more. In this task, you add a rollover behavior to this image.

2. Select the image in Task186-1.html, and click the Detach from Original button on the Property inspector (see Figure 186-1). Read, but ignore, the subsequent alert regarding the consequences of detaching this image from its parent Library item (see Figure 186-2). This image is now treated as a simple page element to which behaviors can be applied.

notes

- It is unfortunate that Dreamweaver doesn't offer any way to edit behaviors already applied to Library items. Perhaps future versions will be more tolerant (Intro).

- Behaviors cannot be applied direct to Library items, so it is necessary to detach the Library item before proceeding with this task (Step 2).

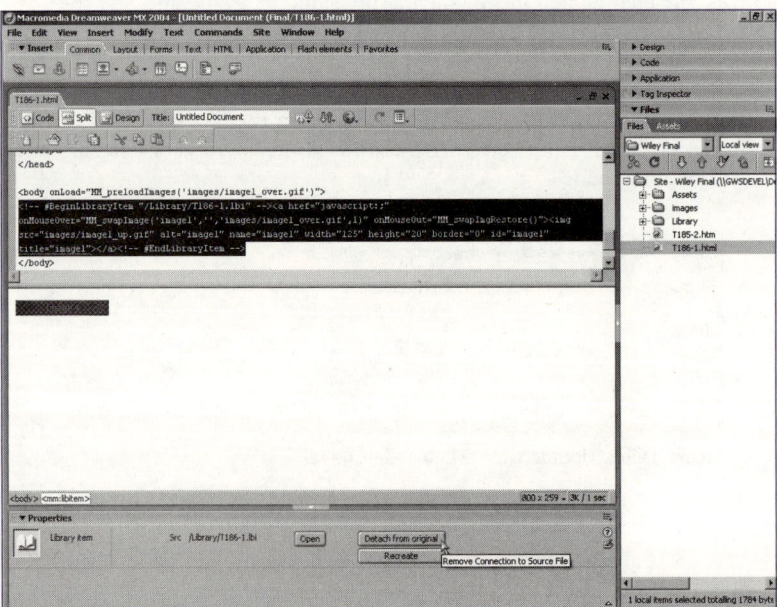

Figure 186-1: Detaching a Library item

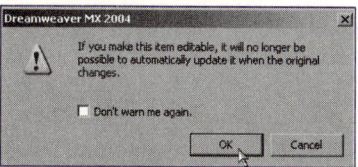

Figure 186-2: Dreamweaver's Alert after detaching a Library item

3. Select the image again, and apply a Swap Image behavior. Elect to swap this image with the one that you copied from the Wiley site called image1_over.gif. You may ignore the setting of the automatic restore and the preload image options for this task (see Figure 186-3).

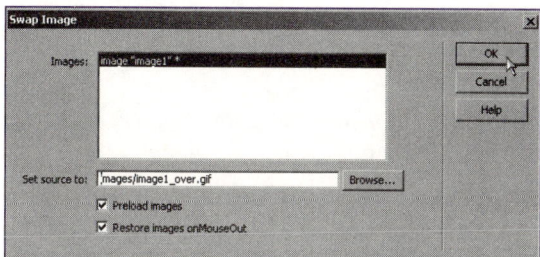

Figure 186-3: Completing the Swap Image behavior

4. Select the image again and create a new Library item from it, using Modify ⇨ Library ⇨ Add Object to Library. Name this Library item T186-2. Examine Code view for this page and note that Dreamweaver MX 2004 has now added quite a bit more code, both to the Library item and to the head region of the page.

5. Close page T186-1.html without saving it. Now reopen this page, select the Library item, and press the Delete key to delete it from the page. Find T186-2 in the Asset panel's Library, select it, and press the Insert button to insert the new Library item on the page. Note that when you do this, the required JavaScript is automatically inserted in the head region of the page. Save the page now as **T186-2.html**. Preview the page and note that the rollover works as expected.

cross-reference

• Refer to Task 120 for complete instructions for adding a Swap Image behavior (Step 3).

Creating a Dreamweaver Template

A template is a "cookie cutter" for your site. It allows you to create many identical pages, each of which can be independently edited. The inside area of a cookie cutter allows each cookie to be made with unique decorations, just as special areas in a template allow each page to have unique content. Unlike a cookie cutter, however, a Dreamweaver template remembers each page made from it (child page) and can continue to "nurture" its child pages as your site develops and changes.

This task teaches you how to build a simple template page. You may also want to download logo.gif from the partX task187 folder at www.wiley.com/compbooks/10simplesteps and place it in the images folder of your site.

1. Create a new page in Dreamweaver by choosing File ⇨ New (Ctrl/Command+N)

2. Choose File ⇨ New ⇨ Basic Page under Category, and HTML Template under Basic Page Click the Create button.

3. In Design view choose Insert ⇨ Table (Ctrl/Command+Alt/Option+T) to add a table to the document. For this exercise, enter the values shown in Figure 187-1 (make sure that the None option under Header is selected) and click OK.

notes

- When you open a template page, open Code view and you'll see this code:
  ```
  <!-- TemplateBegin
  Editable name="
  doctitle" --><title>
  Untitled Document
  </title><!--
  TemplateEndEditable
  ```
  This is how Dreamweaver "declares" that the `<title>` tag is within an editable region (named `doctitle`). Being in an editable region means that you can change the title on each child page produced from this template (Intro).

- You could also add an editable region by selecting your content right-/Control+clicking, then in the context menu that appears, selecting Templates ⇨ New Editable Region (Step 7).

- Since Dreamweaver already knows that this is a template page, it obligingly opens the Templates folder and fills in the dwt suffix for you automatically when you save it (Step 9).

caution

- Only changes to noneditable regions of your template file will propagate their child pages. Do not expect to make a change to an editable region in a template page and have that change appear in any existing child pages (Step 9).

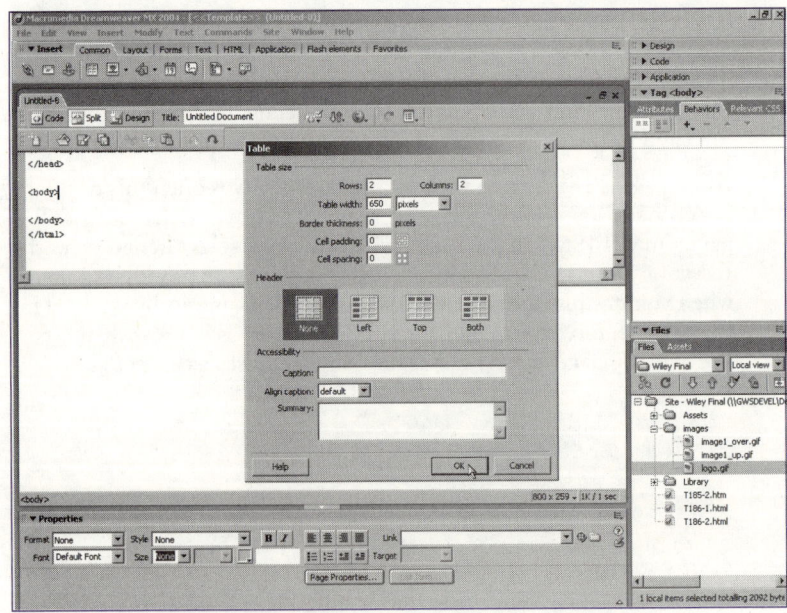

Figure 187-1: The Insert Table panel for inserting the table on the page

Task **187**

4. Click in the upper left cell of this table and insert logo.gif (the file you downloaded from the Wiley site—click through the alert about file paths); assume that this is your company's logo image. Click in the upper right cell of this table and enter **A Really Good Company**; assume that this is the company masthead. You will want both of these cells to appear on every page in the site, since they contain information that is common to the message of the site.

5. Click in the lower left cell of this table and enter the following items, pressing Enter/Return after each one:

> **HOME**
>
> **Services**
>
> **Contact**

These will serve as the start for a site's navigation scheme. It's mighty ugly, but it gets the point across.

6. Click in the lower right cell. This is where you will put content that is unique to each page. You'll want to be able to change the content on each page, so you need to make an editable region here.

7. Choose Insert ⇨ Template Objects ⇨ Editable Region (Ctrl/Command+Alt/Option+V). Name the new editable region **mainContent** and press OK (see Figure 187-2).

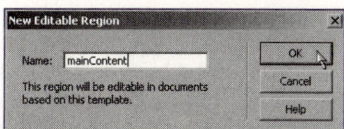

Figure 187-2: The New Editable Region dialog panel

8. You have completed a template page. Save it by Choosing File ⇨ Save, and use the name **T187**. Close this file to end the task.

To appreciate the functionality of templates, you must do more than create them. You must use them as the template on which you create (or "spawn") child pages, as you'll see in the next task.

cross-references

- See the Caution in Task 184 regarding making links using the Browse icon in the Property inspector.

- See the Caution in Task 189 regarding placing any other files in either templates or Library folders.

Using a Template to Create Child Pages

The real power of templates in Dreamweaver MX is realized with the ease of maintenance of the child pages that are dependent on these templates. To demonstrate this, you'll use the template you created in the previous task—or you can download T187.dwt from the partX task188 folder at www.wiley.com/compbooks/10simplesteps (make sure you place the file in the Templates folder of your site). The remainder of this task makes use of this template file.

1. Start the process of creating (or "spawning") a child page by selecting File ⇨ New from the Dreamweaver MX menu.

2. In the New File panel, select the Templates tab, and then find and select the site name within which you have saved this task's template file. When you do this, you should see a list of all the template files that are available to you in this site, and you can preview any selected template files to the right. Select T187 in the list of templates available, and make sure that you have checked the Update Page When Template Changes check box. Then click the Create button to spawn a child page (see Figure 188-1).

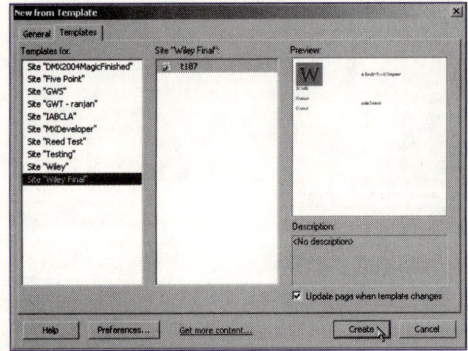

Figure 188-1: Creating a new child page from a template

3. You should now be looking at a page that is an exact replica of the template page. All of the layout elements are in place as on the parent template. The only difference is that you can only edit content that is within your editable region (mainContent). If you try to click anywhere else on the page, you will only see the slashed circle as a pointer, meaning that you cannot do this (see Figure 188-2). Use the loremipsum.txt file from Task 183 (or download it from the Wiley site referenced at the beginning of the task) to paste some filler text content (try adding three or four sentences of content) into this editable region (to replace the mainContent text already there). Save this file as **T188-1.html**, and then close it.

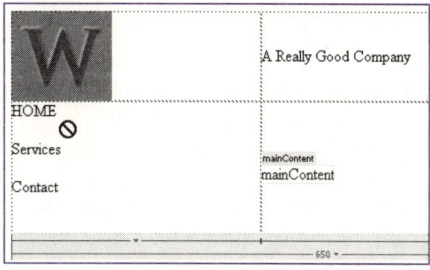

Task 188

Figure 188-2: Attempting to edit a noneditable region

4. At this point, you should have no files open. Now open T187.dwt for an edit. Change "A Really Good Company" to "A Really, Really Good Company," and save the file. When you save, you are prompted as to whether you want to update this template's child pages, and you should accept that offer. You are then shown the progress and results of that update process (in this case, you should see one file has been updated, as shown in Figure 188-3).

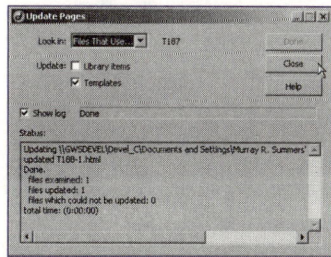

Figure 188-3: Update Pages dialog box

5. To check on this update, open T188-1.html and note that the masthead content on the page has been changed to reflect the edits made to the parent template page. Also note that the contents of the editable region have been left untouched. This is the power of templates.

Be aware that templates (and Library items) are *design time tools*. Any files changed by updates to templates or Library items must still be uploaded to the server in order for their changes to be reflected on your Web site.

Applying a Template to an Existing Page

In the previous task, you spawned a child page from a template using the File ⇨ New approach. This is the best (and most trouble-free) method for creating child pages; however, there are other ways to accomplish this goal. You can also apply a template to an existing page. This latter method is best used on new pages (i.e., ones that do not contain any unique content yet), although it can be used on any existing page.

This task teaches you how to create child pages from a template by applying the template to a page. It also demonstrates one of the problems with this method.

For this task, you need to have access to the both the template page created in Task 187 (T187.dwt), and the file named T189-1.html, which you can download from the partX task189 folder at `www.wiley.com/compbooks/10simplesteps` (make sure you place the T187.dwt file in the Templates folder of your site).

1. To begin, create a new page using File ⇨ New and select a Basic HTML page.

2. Select Modify ⇨ Templates ⇨ Apply Template to Page. Make sure that you are in the correct site, and select the template file named T187 in the Template list that appears for the site you have selected. Also make sure that the Update Page When Template Changes check box at the bottom of the selection panel is checked (see Figure 189-1). Click Select, and note that you now have a new instance of the exact layout specified in T187.dwt. In all ways, this child page will behave identically to the one created in Task 188. You may close this page without saving it.

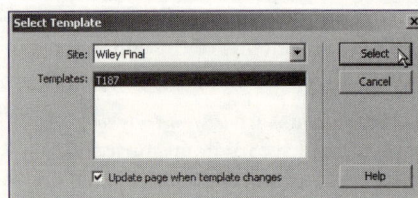

Figure 189-1: Select Template dialog box when applying a template to a new page

The process you used here is to create a new page and immediately apply the template to it. But what if you have an existing page that already contains some layout elements?

3. Open the file named T189-1.html, and note that it is a copy of the template's layout, but it is not a child of that (or any) template (note the absence of template markup on the page and the missing template marker in the upper right-hand corner of the page). With this page open, again apply the template using Modify ⇨ Templates ⇨ Apply Template to Page and proceed as before.

note

- Whenever you or Dreamweaver make changes to a page, an asterisk is appended to the filename in several places on the Dreamweaver screen. This alerts you that the file has been changed and needs to be saved. If you try to close the file without saving it, you will be prompted to do so (Step 4).

cautions

- If you were to forget to select that Update Page When Template Changes check box, you would lose one of the main benefits of using templates—although that may be what you want. At any rate, make sure that you verify this check box each time you create a child page (Step 2).

- Be aware that the Library items and the Templates folders are sacred territory. There should be no files in either of these folders other than Library items and templates, respectively. Saving HTML or CSS or image files, for example, in either folder will confuse Dreamweaver's link management routines and may cause some big problems for you (Step 4).

4. This time, since your page already contains layout elements, a new dialog box appears, asking you where to put the material that it finds on this page. When you follow this dialog box's instructions by selecting Document Body and you examine the options listed under Move Content to New Region, you see that you can only select a single region to receive the page's content (see Figure 189-2). In the case of this page, no matter what you select, you will not get very acceptable results.

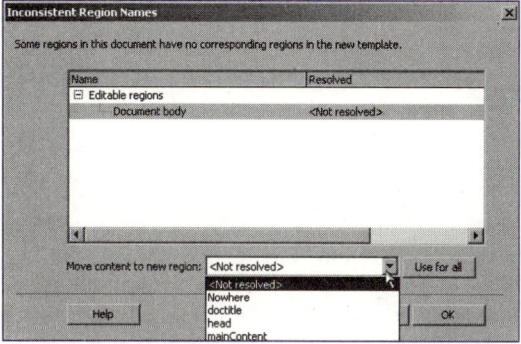

Figure 189-2: Selecting the destination region for a page's existing content

Obviously, you must place this page's contents in the mainContent editable region (none of the other options make any sense), so make that selection and click OK. You can see one of the reasons why this may not be a good approach. The entirety of this page's layout has been placed into the template's region named mainContent (see Figure 189-3).

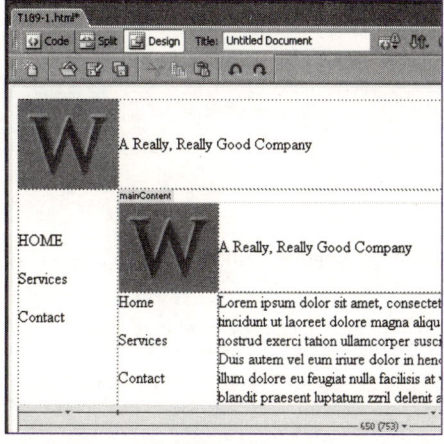

Figure 189-3: Ouch! The consequences of applying a template to a page with existing content

cross-reference

▪ While this task is interesting, see Task 188 for a much safer way to create child pages (Intro).

It can get worse. Imagine if your template file contained several editable regions. Well, let's not dwell on such unpleasant thoughts . . .

Converting a Static Page to a Template Instance

It is not uncommon to discover that you need to bring your site under template control only after you have already created some pages in the site. Given the lessons learned in the previous task regarding applying templates to existing pages, what is the best way to go about this conversion? Unfortunately, the best method is also the most tedious. There is no substitute for doing this conversion a page at a time.

This task teaches you that method. It requires that you have the files from the partX task191 folder, available at `www.wiley.com/compbooks/10simplesteps` (make sure you place the file—T190.dwt—in the Templates folder of your site). You can place the remaining file at the root level of the site (T190-1.html).

1. To begin, open and examine the template file—T190.dwt. Note that this file has two editable regions: mainContent and wordsWisdom (see Figure 190-1). Since this template contains two editable regions, you can already anticipate that using the method of applying the template to any existing child pages will not work well.

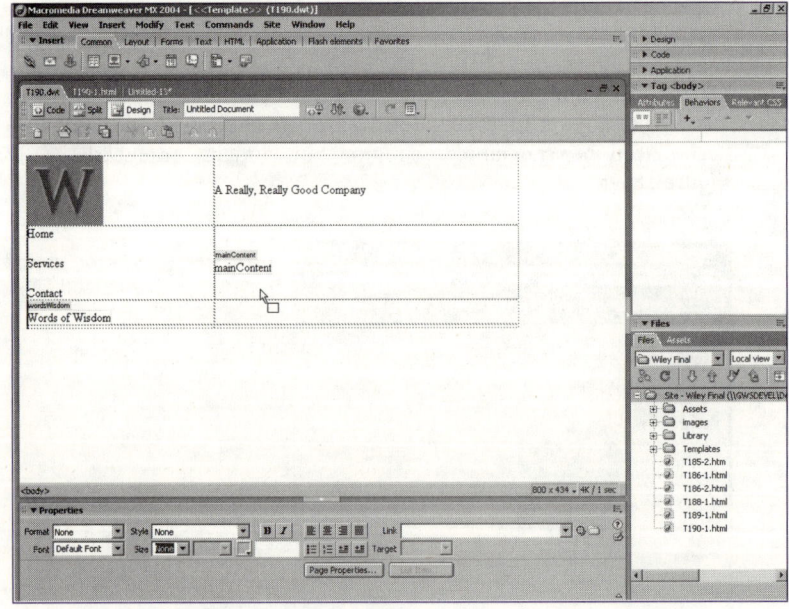

Figure 190-1: The template's editable regions

2. Next, open the HTML file and examine it (T190-1.html). Note that it contains unique content where both of the template's editable regions would be. To complete this task, you now bring T190-1.html under template control.

3. Create a new child page from the T190 template using the File ⇨ New menu option.

4. With T190-1.html open, copy the phrase "This is the content on page T190-1.html" and paste it in place of the words "mainContent" in the mainContent editable region on the new child page. Also, copy the words "A stitch in time saves nine." and paste them in place of the "Words of Wisdom" content that is in the similarly named editable region. With this operation completed, you can close T190-1.html.

5. Now save the new child page as **T190-1.html** (in other words, you overwrite the existing file). You save the new child page with the same name as the existing page to preserve any links that may already exist elsewhere in this site (T190-1.html). See Figure 190-2.

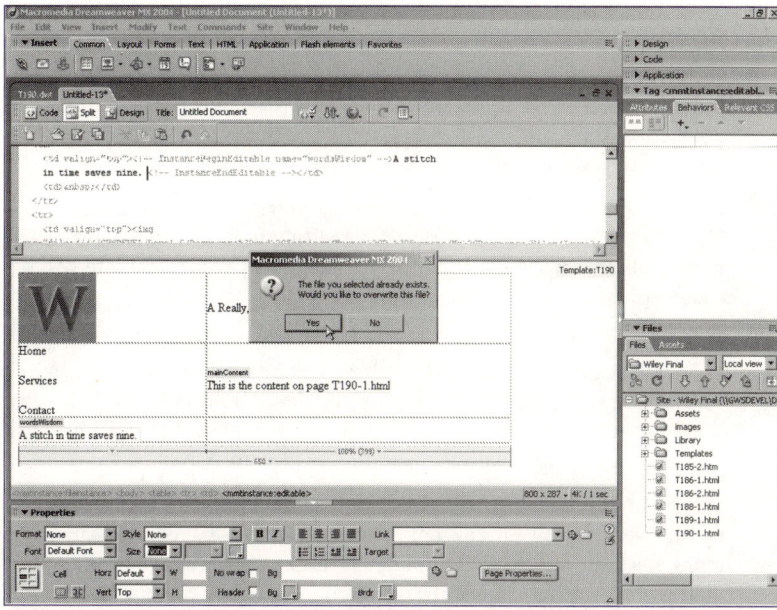

Figure 190-2: The alert that appears when saving the child page

You have changed a static page into a template-managed page by performing this copy-and-paste operation. While tedious (if there are many pages), it is guaranteed to allow you to place content as desired in the new child pages, particularly if the template and the layout is complex.

cross-references
- Refer to Task 61 for inserting tables (Intro).
- Refer to Task 187 for adding editable regions (Step 2).

Task **190**

Detaching a Template by File or Sitewide

Now that you know how to bring files under the control of a template, it's time to look at the other side of the coin. There may come a time when you need to detach a page (or an entire site) from its controlling template (see the discussion at the end of this task for possible scenarios). This task teaches how to perform this action.

Let's do this with the new template child page you created in the previous step. If you didn't do Task 190, you can get the necessary file (T190-1.html) from the partX task191 folder at www.wiley.com/compbooks/10simplesteps.

1. Open this page (T190-1.html). Start the detachment process by choosing Modify ➪ Templates ➪ Detach from Template.

2. As quickly as that, the template-specific markup is removed from the page. You can confirm this by noting that the template marker is gone from the upper right-hand corner of the document and by examining the code of the page.

3. If you now save this page in your site, you will have completely removed any association of that page with a template. Changes made to noneditable regions of that page's previous parent template will no longer propagate to this page.

   You might want to do this detachment to make changes on the page in some area that is blocked by it being a child to the template. While this is one way to deal with such needs, there are other—and likely much better—ways to do so (these other methods involve using some of the advanced templating capability of Dreamweaver MX).

4. If instead of detaching a single page, you decide you want to "detach" the entire site, you can do that as well. With any page in the site open, choose Modify ➪ Templates ➪ Export without Markup. The dialog panel in Figure 191-1 appears. Complete the export process by browsing to a new location on your hard drive that is to receive the "detached' site," and click OK.

5. Opening a file in the new export location reveals the complete absence of any template markup (see Figure 191-2).

   Why would you want to export the entire site without template markup? One reason might be to slim down the pages; Dreamweaver's template features are driven by proprietary code placed on the page within HTML comment tags. While this markup can get somewhat voluminous on template pages, most child pages will not be overly burdened by it.

   Another reason might be to remove some of the logic of the operation of templates from the public site. If your template methodology involves some of the more advanced capabilities of Dreamweaver, by

notes

- Because this file is still open, you can undo the removal of markup that you just triggered by clicking on the Undo arrow in the Dreamweaver Standard toolbar (you did add that to the View options, didn't you?), or by using Edit ➪ Undo Edit Source (Ctrl/Command+Z) (Step 2).

- The two check boxes on the Export Site without Template Markup dialog panel are advanced options—the first applies if you want to additionally save the exported files as XML data files; the second applies if you had previously exported the site to this same location and only want to export those files that had changed since the last export (Step 4).

caution

- Do not perform this lightly! It is generally a one-way street, since the way back can be difficult and tedious, particularly if your template file contains more than one editable region. In fact, if you have used any of the advanced template features discussed in later tasks and you remove template markup from your pages or you inadvertently delete your template, you may not be able to recover it (Step 1).

Task **191**

removing the markup from the site, you will have removed the key to the way in which these capabilities were used. Make sure you have a good backup of the site when you do this.

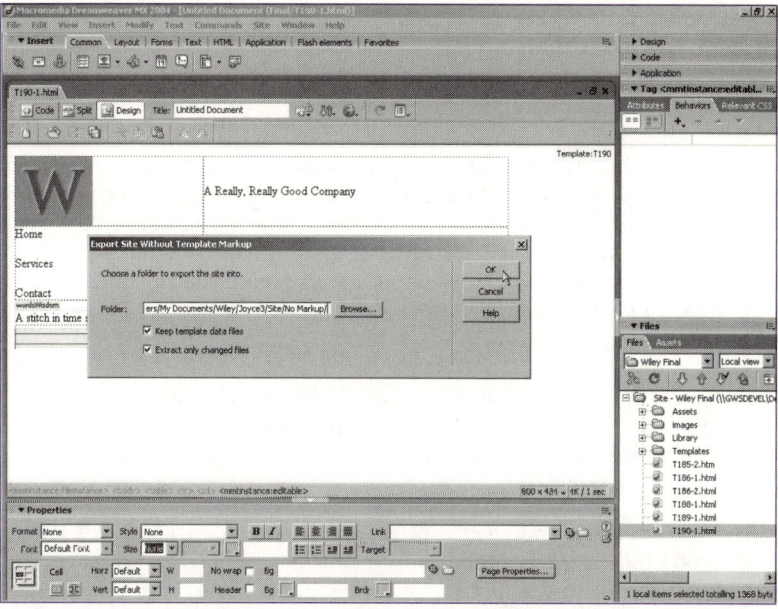

Figure 191-1: The Export Site without Template Markup dialog panel

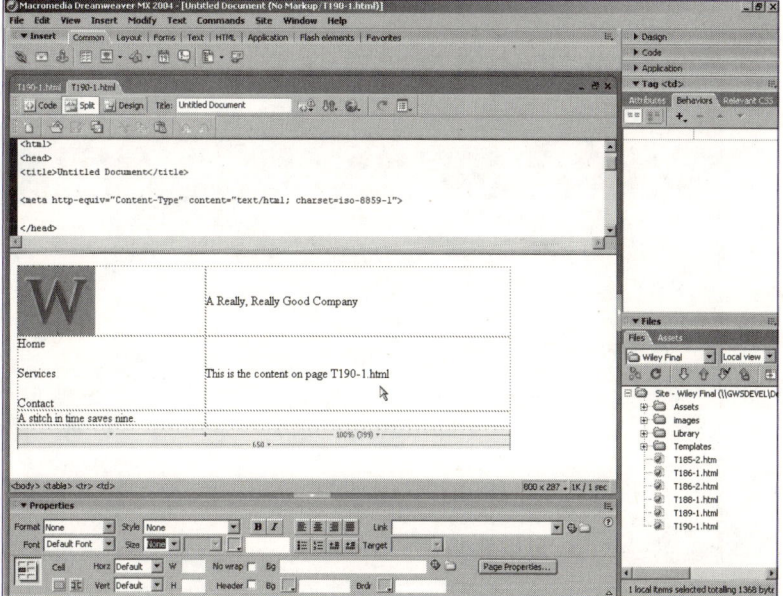

Figure 191-2: The exported site—no template markup here!

tip

- Although you have exported the site with no template markup, to use this new site in Dreamweaver, you must now create a new site definition that points into the folder housing the exported files. This operation does not automatically create that new site for you (Step 5).

cross-reference

- To read more about the advanced template features, visit Tasks 193 through 200. Each of these would be difficult to recover from a page whose template markup had been removed (Step 3).

Working with Library Items in Templates

You now return to Library items for a single task focused on the integration of Library items with templates.

A Library item into a template is a convenient way to have a section-specific subnavigation menu in a single template file's editable region. By containing the subnavigation menus in Library items, you gain the maintenance advantage of sitewide propagation of changes. On the other hand, having them in an editable region allows a different Library item to be used on various pages. This task requires files from the Wiley site, so download all files from the partX task192 folder at `www.wiley.com/compbooks/10simplesteps`. Place T192.dwt into the Templates folder, and both T192-prod1.lbi and T192-prod2.lbi into the Library folder of your site.

1. Open the Template file (T192.dwt) and note that the file contains a navigation element across the top and a single editable region, called SectionNav, below, which will be used to house the section-specific navigation for the site.

2. Now open and examine the other two files you downloaded, T192-prod1.lbi and T192-prod2.lbi. The former contains only a set of links specific to Product 1, while the latter contains only a set of links specific to Product 2 (see Figure 192-1). These are product-specific Library items to be used on child pages, which will be accessed when the global Product link is clicked. Close these pages.

notes

- Copying files into and out of either the Templates or the Library folder can confuse Dreamweaver as it tries to track parent and child relationships among your files. Refresh the site cache periodically (Site ⇨ Advanced ⇨ Recreate Site Cache)! (Intro)

- Don't be concerned if you find that some of these demonstration pages don't link to other files. In some cases, those other files simply do not exist, and the links have been made purely for tutorial purposes (Step 2).

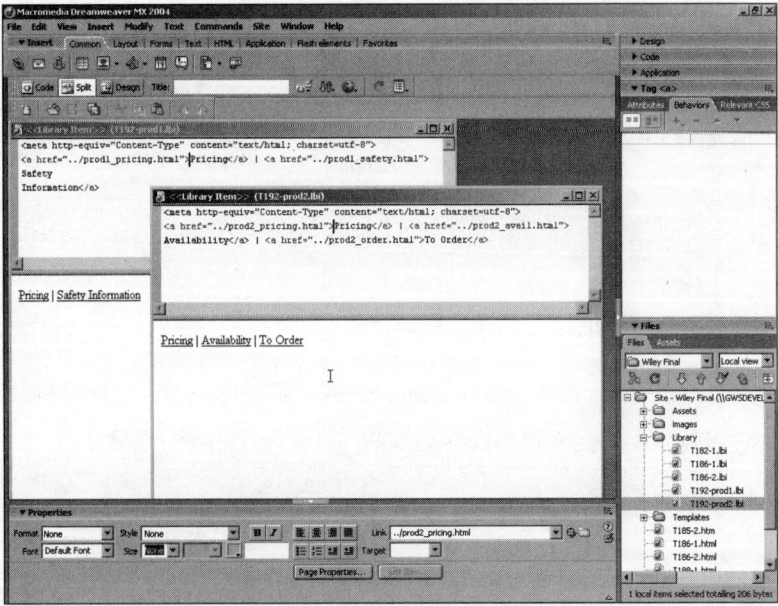

Figure 192-1: The two product-specific navigation element Library items

3. Use File ➪ New ➪ Templates ➪ Site Name ➪ T192 twice to spawn two new child pages from this template (make sure that you select the Update Page When Template Changes check box so that your changes to the template file are propagated to each child page).

4. With one of your new child pages showing in Dreamweaver MX's Design view, note that you are not able to change anything in the global navigation content (the links for About Us, Product 1, etc.). Click in this editable region, remove the text showing the region's name, select the Asset panel, and then click the Library icon (this may already be selected for you). Select T192-prod1 in the Library, and use the Insert button to insert Product 1's specific navigation. Save this page as **T192-prod1.html** (see Figure 192-2).

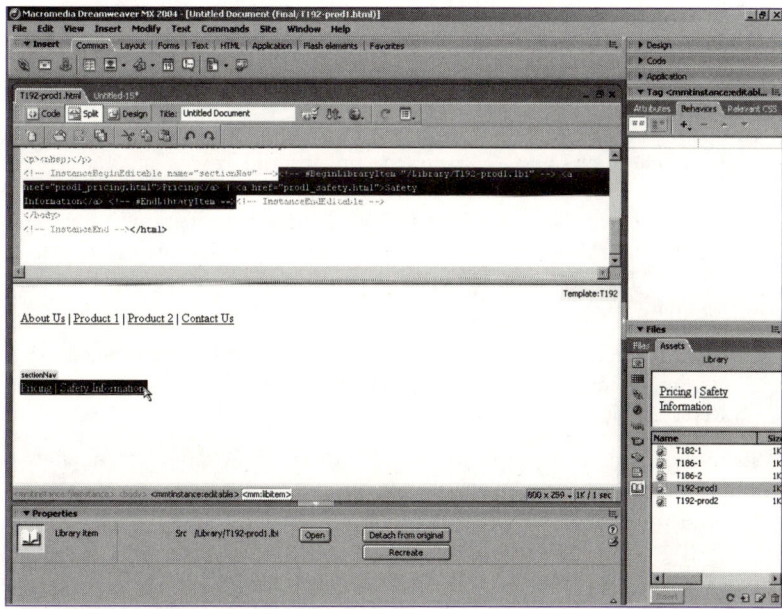

Figure 192-2: After saving T192-prod1.html

5. Select the other child page you spawned, delete the editable region's text, and insert the T192-prod2 Library item in its place. Save this page as **T192-prod2.html**.

6. To test this, open T192.dwt (if it is not already open) and change the words "Contact Us" to **Contact Information**, in the primary navigation element. Save T192.dwt, and allow the child pages to be updated.

7. Now switch to T192-prod1.html. Select the Library item and press Open on the Property inspector, so that the item can be edited. Now add | **Availability** to the end of the links in this Library item, and save and close the page. Note that the change you just made is now also shown on T192-prod1.html, but not on T192-prod2.html.

cross-reference

- You can read more about Library item creation and editing in Tasks 182 to 186 (Step 7).

Using Optional Regions

An optional region is an excellent way to include content on a template page that may or may not be displayed on any given child page. A good example of this kind of content would be a "breadcrumb" location element—the Web equivalent of the "you are here" note on a map. The advantage of an optional region is that it is treated as part of the template's noneditable content so that any links or file references within it would be automatically propagated to child pages by Dreamweaver's template engine if they should be changed in the template file. Yet you still have control over the display of these regions on each individual child page.

To illustrate this, you will use a special image on a page, announcing that something is "Coming Soon." Since this image might change periodically, it would be convenient to have the filename change propagated to all other child pages in the site. To complete this task, you need files from the Wiley site, so download all files from the partX task193 folder at www.wiley.com/compbooks/ 10simplesteps. Place T193.dwt into the Templates folder of your site, and copy the image file (coming.gif) into the Images folder.

1. Open the template page called T193.dwt for examination. Note that there is an image in the lower right of the page announcing "Coming Soon!" You will make this image part of an optional region on the template page.

2. With this template page open in Design view, select the replace-ableimage image and use Insert ⇨ Template Objects ⇨ Optional Region to initiate this process.

3. In the dialog box that follows, and with the Basic tab selected, enter **comingSoon** as the name of the optional region, and uncheck the Show by Default check box (see Figure 193-1). Click OK to complete the process. Now save the template file with this modification (using File ⇨ Save As and T193b.dwt as a filename) and close the file.

You have created an optional region that will *not* be shown by default on any child page. However, you *will* be able to exercise your "Option" to change its visibility on selected pages as needed. The details of the process by which this occurs is addressed in later tasks.

notes

- Region names are used only by the Dreamweaver template engine. As a result, it is not a problem if these names sometimes conflict with other page content or even with other "reserved" names (Intro).

- When you make a link to a file, Dreamweaver always makes that an absolute link to the physical location of the file on your hard drive. Once you save your page, Dreamweaver then adjusts those links to either document- or root-relative links (depending on how you have set the link method). Therefore, if a file has not yet been saved, you should not be concerned about seeing absolute links that reference files on your drive—for instance, file://...—in the code (Intro).

- It is possible to select an entire table by slowly mousing over the table's structure in Design view. As you pass close to one of the outer borders of the table, you will see a checkerboard pointer on your mouse arrow; this means that if you click at that point, you will select the table itself (Step 4).

- When you open this child page, you will *not* see the image that you inserted on the template. If you examine the code for this page, you see that the image is not even mentioned in the code! This is because you *elected not to show the region by default* when you created the optional region in the parent template (Step 5).

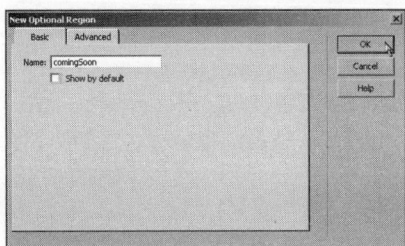

Figure 193-1: Defining a new optional region

4. Spawn a child page from this template (T193b, as you have done before) using File ⇨ New ⇨ Templates ⇨ Site ⇨ T193b, and note immediately that the replaceableimage image is not shown at all. In fact, if you examine the code on the page using Code view, you see that the code for this image and its containing table is not on the page! Save this page in your site as **T193-1.html**. In the next step you toggle the visibility of this image.

5. With T193-1.html still open, select Modify ⇨ Template Properties, select comingSoon (it will likely already be selected), and select the Show comingSoon check box (see Figure 193-2). Before closing this panel, note that successive clicks in this check box toggle the boolean shown under the word Value in the text area above the check box. Leave this check box enabled and click the OK button. The page now displays the replaceableimage image.

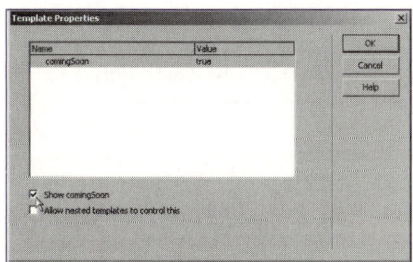

Figure 193-2: Using Modify ⇨ Template Properties to toggle the visibility of an optional region

Because this image is in an optional region, its display on any page can be toggled on or off. Because the optional region is within the noneditable part of the template page, inserting a new image in place of the one there currently causes that new image link to be propagated to all pages on which this optional region is shown. This is a very graphic illustration of the power of optional regions.

cross-references

- Remember that you need to define a site when using sample folders. Refer to Tasks 10 and 11 to define a site (Step 1).

- Refer to Task 188 for creating new child pages (pages based on your template) (Step 4).

Task 194

Using Editable Optional Regions

This region is precisely what the name implies:It is an optional region that has editable content. In Task 193, you inserted an announcement image using an optional region, and you build on that in this task.

An image on your page needs a caption to be fully understood. You also might want this caption to be worded differently on different pages in the site. By placing a caption area into an editable portion of the optional region, you can achieve this flexibility. This task teaches one way to do that and requires that you have the template and image files used in Task 193, which you can download from the partX task194 folder at www.wiley.com/compbooks/10simplesteps. Place T193b.dwt into the Templates folder of your site and the image file (coming.gif) into the images folder.

1. Open the template file (T193b.dwt) for inspection. Note (by using Code view) that the replaceableimage image is contained in a single-cell table. You will add another cell to this table below the image to show a caption, and you will make this caption part of a new editable optional region.

2. Select the replaceableimage image, and press the keyboard's right arrow once to move the insertion point to the right of the image. Now use Insert ⇨ Table Objects ⇨ Insert Row Below to insert a new row beneath the image (see Figure 194-1). You will use this row to hold your caption.

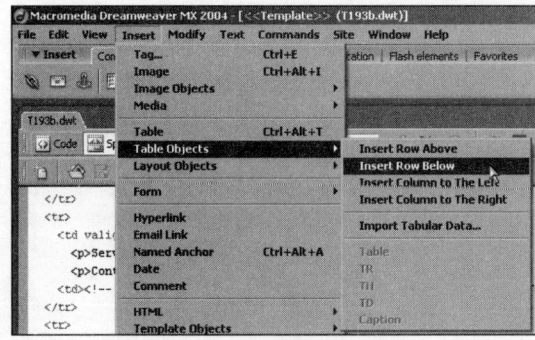

Figure 194-1: Inserting a new table row

3. Since you want this caption to be part of an editable optional region, you first add that new region. With the insertion point in the new row added in Step 2, use Insert ⇨ Template Objects ⇨ Editable Optional Region. In the ensuing dialog box, name this region **comingCaption** and also deselect the check box for Show by Default.

notes

- When inserting editable optional regions, you do not get to name the editable region inserted within the optional region (Step 3).

- By using this procedure, you have created an optional region that will only be shown when the value of the parameter called comingCaption is true. This is how template expressions and parameters work, and you will see more about this in subsequent tasks (Step 5).

- You will see that some of your child pages are updated to contain this new editable optional region, while some may not be updated (depending on which child pages you have spawned). The ones that will be updated are those for which you have used the Modify ⇨ Template Properties method to set the value of the comingCaption parameter to true (Step 5).

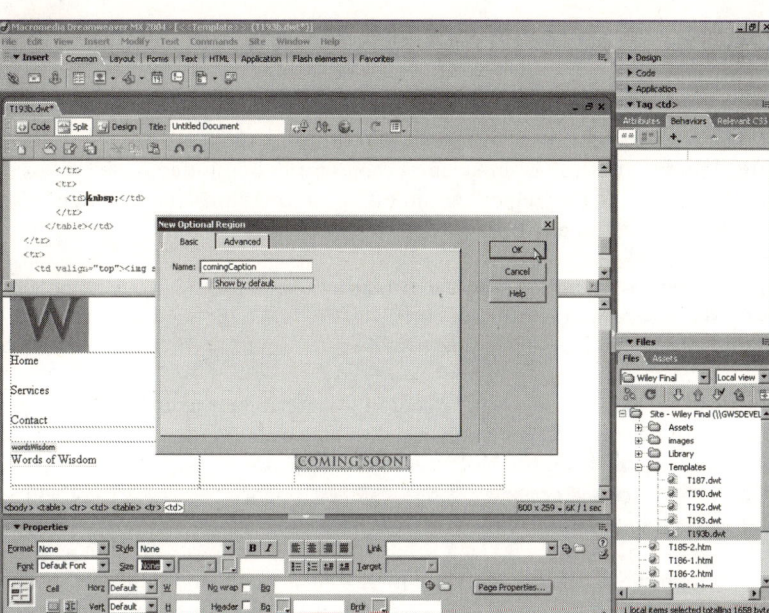

Figure 194-2: Creating the editable optional region

4. Click within the editable region that was inserted by this action and enter **Caption Here**. This will serve as a reminder to enter a caption when you elect to have this region shown. Save this page as **T194.dwt** and close the file.

5. Spawn a new child page from T194 and note again that in the default state, neither of the optional regions are displayed. By using Modify ⇨ Template Properties, you can elect to display one or both of your optional regions. In the event that you elect to display comingCaption, only then will you have access to the editable region that is part of this optional region.

   This process allows you to show the image either with or without the caption, as well as allowing you to customize that caption on each individual page.

cross-reference

• Remember that you need to define a site when using sample folders. Refer to Tasks 10 and 11 to define a site (Step 1).

Using Repeating Regions

A repeating region might be used to create an area of the page that could be repeated one, two, or more times, depending on the content to be displayed. In its strict sense, a repeat region's entries are not editable (unless you then insert an editable region within one), and therefore they would carry the advantages of automatic propagation to child pages.

As an example, you might want to display a rating of some products or services, using star images to denote that entry's score. In a template page, it would be convenient to do this with a repeat region.

For this task, you use a repeating region to determine the number of stars to display after a product name. You need to use the T195.dwt template file and the star.gif image file from the Wiley site. You can find them in the partX task195 folder at www.wiley.com/compbooks/10simplesteps. Place T195.dwt in the Templates folder and star.gif in the Images folder of your site.

1. Open the T195.dwt template file for inspection, and note that a new row has been added to the bottom of the table. This row contains two product names: Product 1 and Product 2. You will use a repeating region to repeat a star image to the right of each product name.

2. In Design view, click to the right of Product 1, and use Insert ⇨ Template Objects ⇨ Repeating Region to insert the first repeating region here. Name this region **stars1** (see Figure 195-1).

note

- As configured in this task, the repeating region will be shown on every page in the site. It would make a lot of sense to wrap an optional region around it so that it is only shown on those pages that also show the announcement image and caption. Can you figure out how to do that? (Step 9)

caution

- When you are using straight repeating regions, once added, a repeating entry cannot be deleted. Be very careful when using this capability! (Intro)

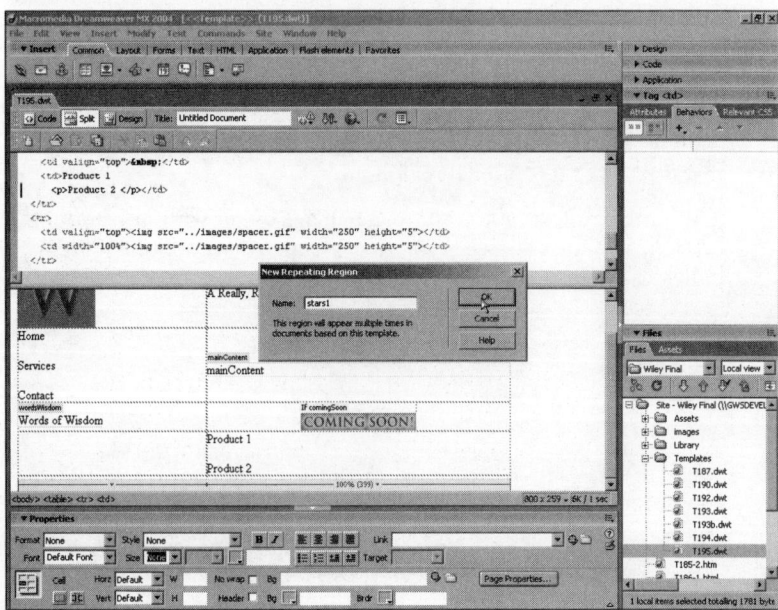

Figure 195-1: Creating the stars1 repeating region

3. Click to the right of Product 2 and repeat Step 2 to add a repeating region to the right of this product's name. Name this region **stars2**.

4. In stars1, select the word stars1 and delete it. In its place, insert the star.gif image, so that you see a single star image to the right of Product 1.

5. Repeat this process for stars2.

6. You now have two product names, each followed by a repeating region, each of which contains a single star image.

7. Save the template file as **T195.dwt.**

8. Spawn a child page from this template using File ⇨ New ⇨ Templates ⇨ Site Name ⇨ T195 ⇨ Create.

   Note that you now see a mini user interface positioned to the right of each repeat region's name tab. This interface allows you to add new instances of the element contained within the repeat region to the page.

9. For stars1, click the plus (+) sign in the mini user interface. This adds a second star to the rating of Product 1. You can click additional times to add more stars if you like (see Figure 195-2).

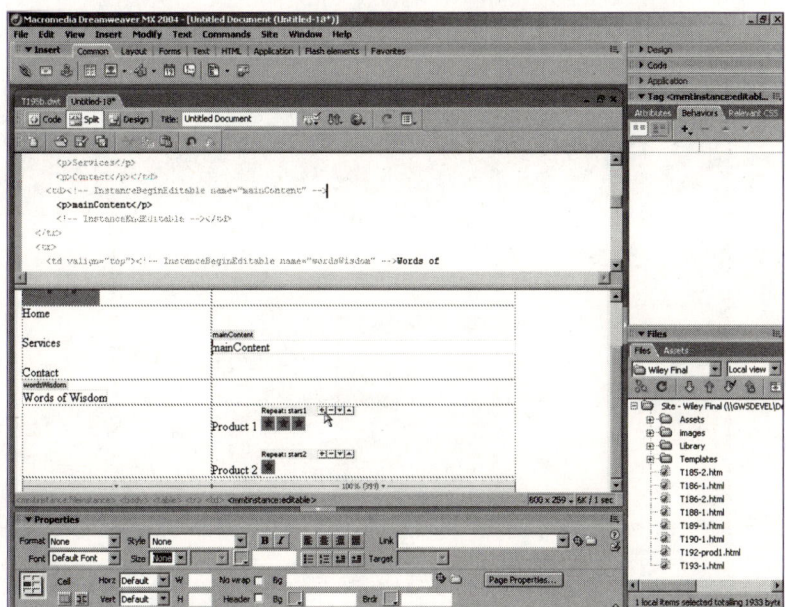

Figure 195-2: Rating the products with repeating regions and the mini-user interface

10. Repeat this process for stars2. You have now used a repeating region to add a variable number of instances of the star image.

cross-references

- Remember that you need to define a site when using sample folders. Refer to Tasks 10 and 11 to define a site (Step 1).

- Refer to Task 61 for inserting tables (Step 2).

Using Repeating Tables

A repeating table is really nothing different than the repeating region that was just built in Task 195 except that the whole process is more integrated, and a bit more flexible. This task teaches you how it works. To complete this task, you need to use two files that you can get from the partX task196 folder at www. wiley.com/compbooks/10simplesteps. Place T196.dwt in the Templates folder and star.gif in the Images folder of your site.

1. Begin by opening T196.dwt. Note that the repeating regions from the previous task have been removed from this template, and the row in which they were placed is not empty. This is where you will place your repeating table.

2. Click in the row below the replaceableimage image, and select Insert ⇨ Template Objects ⇨ Repeating Table to open the Repeating Table dialog panel. Examine this dialog panel carefully, and note that in addition to the standard table parameters, you can also specify which rows will constitute the repeating element of the table. For this task, select a table that is 300 pixels wide and has one row and two columns. Enter o in the Cell Spacing, Cell Padding, and Border fields. Finally, enter 1 in the Starting Row and Ending Row fields, and name the region **productRanking** (see Figure 196-1). Click OK to insert the region.

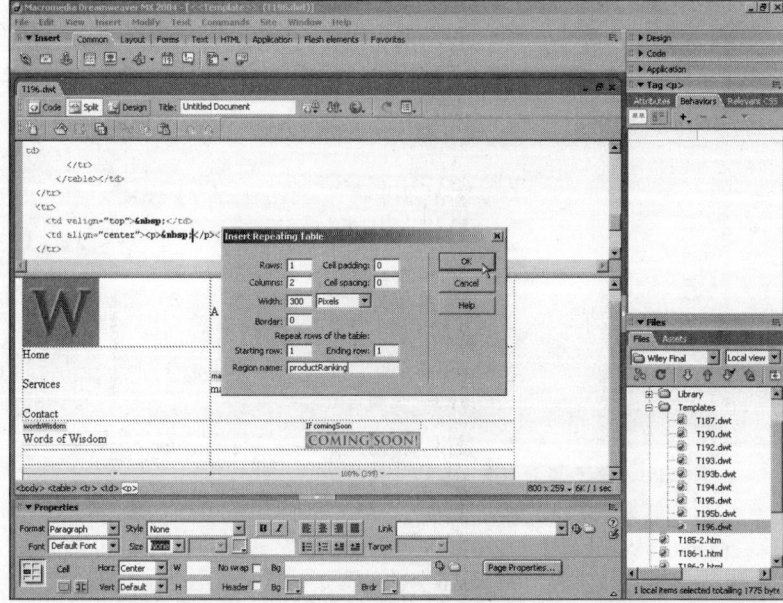

Figure 196-1: The details of the repeating table insertion

3. Click within the new editable region in the left-hand cell of the repeating table, and enter **Product** (this will remind you to enter a product name when you spawn a child page). Click within the right-hand cell and insert the star.gif image. Since this image is now within an editable region, you have to manually insert the proper number for your rankings rather than use a mini user interface to do this for you.

4. Save this page as **T196.dwt** and spawn a child page from it using File ⇨ New ⇨ Templates ⇨ Site Name ⇨ T196 ⇨ Create. Again, you see a mini user interface with which you can specify the number of times to repeat the rows.

5. In this child page, you can enter a product name in the left-hand cell and insert additional stars in the right-hand cell as needed. In addition, it is a simple matter to add new products to the list. For this task, enter a rating for Product 1 and Product 2. You can decide how many stars to award each product. (See Figure 196-2.)

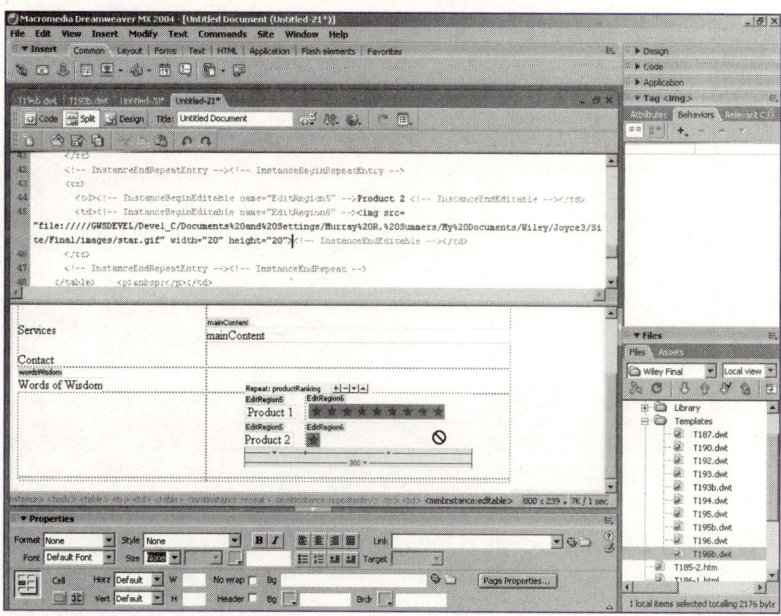

Figure 196-2: A really good rating

tips

- When Dreamweaver inserts a repeating table, it also puts an editable region into each cell of the repeating region. If the table that you insert has more than one column, each cell of each row (within the repeat region) would automatically receive the editable region.

- If you want to remove a repeated instance of a row, you must first select some content within that row's editable region before the "–" on the mini user interface will actually delete anything without an error alert.

cross-reference

For more information about working with tables in Dreamweaver, see Part 3.

Using Parameters

Much of the cool stuff that Dreamweaver MX is able to do with templates is mediated behind the scenes by the use of template parameters. You have used them yourself in this section, although you may not know it. Let's look at some of those you may have already used.

1. In Code view, examine the head region of your optional region template page from Task 193 (T193b.dwt) or use the one from the partX task193 folder at www.wiley.com/compbooks/10simplesteps. Figure 197-1 shows a template parameter declaration.

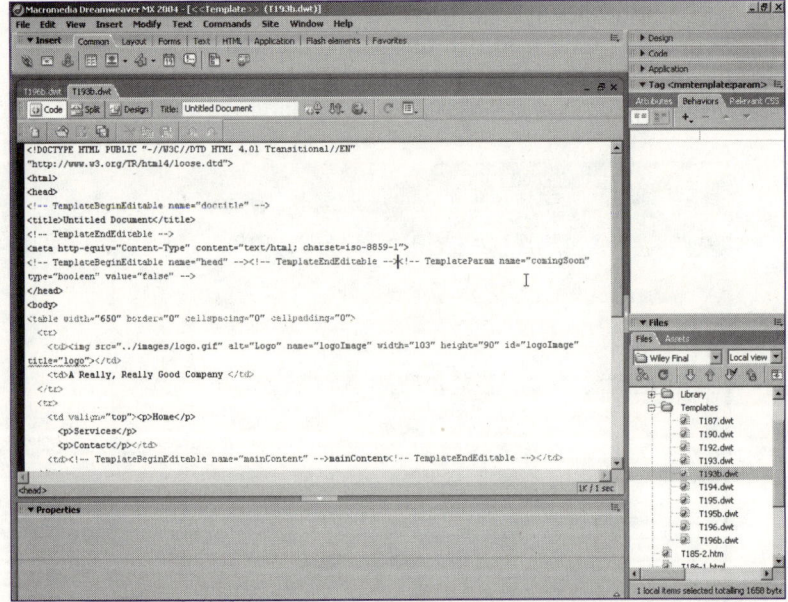

Figure 197-1: A view of the head region showing a template parameter declaration

This is what a template parameter looks like. For this optional region, Dreamweaver selected a boolean type, and since you selected the check box that prevented this region to be shown by default when you originally built this page, its value is false.

2. If you want to use parameters yourself without having Dreamweaver doing it for you, create a new template page in DMX04 using File ⇨ New ⇨ General ⇨ Template Page ⇨ HTML Template.

3. Open Code view and type the following line of code just *above* the `</head>` tag.

```
<!-- TemplateParam name="showMe" type="boolean"
value="false" -->
```

This puts a boolean parameter on the page that contains a default value of false. This value can be used to put specific content on each child page.

4. Switch back to Design view. Click the Insert Table icon in the Common category of the Insert bar to add a table. Give it two columns and two rows, and make it 300 pixels wide.

5. To avoid Dreamweaver's nagging about not having an editable region on a template page, insert an editable region (Insert ➪ Template Objects ➪ Editable Region) in the upper left-hand corner cell. It doesn't matter what you call it.

6. Click in the upper right-hand cell and enter **showMe is true**. Select that entire phrase and insert an optional region using Insert ➪ Template Objects ➪ Optional Region. Instead of giving this optional region a name using the Basic tab, click the Advanced tab, select the Use Parameter radio button, and in the drop-down list, find and select showMe, as shown in Figure 197-2. (If you do not find this parameter's name listed, check the syntax of your manually entered code in Step 3).

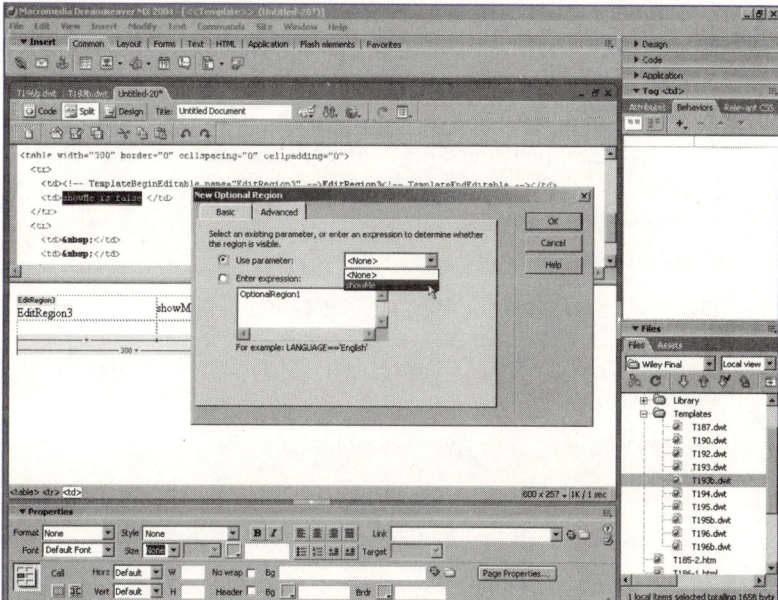

Figure 197-2: Using the Advanced tab to select a parameter's controlling value

7. Click OK to accept this optional region, and save the template page as **T197.dwt**.

8. Spawn a child page from this template, and note that there is no text in the table. This is because the optional region is using the value of the parameter called showMe to determine the visibility of the text you entered in Step 6, and so far, that value is false. Change that value using Modify ➪ Template Properties, selecting showMe, and setting it to display—that it, to true. Notice that at soon as you press OK, the text is displayed.

Dreamweaver MX has tested the value of the parameter that you entered manually, and has made a decision about whether to display the optional region. This demonstration has only scratched the surface of the things that can be done with parameters.

tips

- Dreamweaver MX and Dreamweaver MX 2004 have no user interface for inserting template parameters in your code. There are only two ways to do this: (1) by using the manual method described here or (2) by clicking on your page, inserting an optional region, and then deleting the optional region you just inserted. This latter method deletes the optional region's code from the <body> section, but it will leave the parameter defined in the <head> section. You can then edit this parameter to be any type with any default value (Step 1).

- A template parameter by itself has no function on the page. Template parameters act just like program variables. You can create them, but nothing will happen until you apply some logic to them and make decisions based on their values (Step 6).

cross-references

- Refer to Task 61 for inserting tables.

- Refer to Task 188 for making child pages (Step 8).

Using Expressions

To extract the full power of Dreamweaver's template features, you need to understand how to use both template parameters and template expressions together. You can think of this pair of concepts as the variables and the logic for your pages, respectively. There is *no* user interface for entering template expressions into your pages. As explored in Task 197, there is a "backdoor" way of entering an expression by inserting an optional region in your page (the expression is the part you enter in the Advanced tab of the dialog panel). A template expression can take two forms. You have already used one of them (look back at Task 197): an "implied" expression (the test to see if showMe is true or false). In this task, you use an explicit expression. To complete this task, you need T198.dwt from the partX task198 folder at www.wiley.com/compbooks/ 10simplesteps. Save this file in the Templates folder in your site. This file already has a template parameter added to the head of the document, specifying a name of pagenumber and a default value of 1.

1. Open T198.dwt and click in the upper right-hand cell of the table so that the cursor is positioned immediately before the "P" of PAGE. Now go into Code view.

2. With the cursor positioned before the "P" and with the Code view pane having focus (i.e., you clicked there), enter the first part of a template expression:

   ```
   @@(pagenumber=="1"
   ```

   This is the first part of an IF/THEN/ELSE expression, and it is testing the value of the pagenumber parameter. If the expression finds that the value is 1, then the next part of the test will evaluate (the THEN clause).

3. Continue building the expression so that it reads

   ```
   @@(pagenumber=="1"?'first '
   ```

   which will output the word "first" to the page when the test succeeds.

4. Next, continue building the expression as follows:

   ```
   @@(pagenumber=="1"?'first ':'')@@
   ```

   which says to write a null string if the test fails (i.e., the ELSE part). Your code should now look like Figure 198-1. Save this page (remember, it's a template page), and then spawn a child page from it. Do you see the word "first"? You should.

notes

- Expression syntax is as follows: @@(xxxxx)@@. The opening @@(and closing)@@ will always be the same. What is placed between these two constant character strings is what defines the logic and the function of the expression. Template expressions use a JavaScript-like language. You can find much more about this using Dreamweaver's F1 Help files (Step 2).

- When a template expression is placed on a template page, it is shown in Design view with a special icon: @@ . By selecting this icon on the Design view page, you select the entire template expression (Step 3).

caution

- Template expressions are very strict in their syntax requirements. If you are having trouble following the instructions in this task because of error messages from Dreamweaver, the first thing to check is the syntax of the expressions you have manually entered (Step 5).

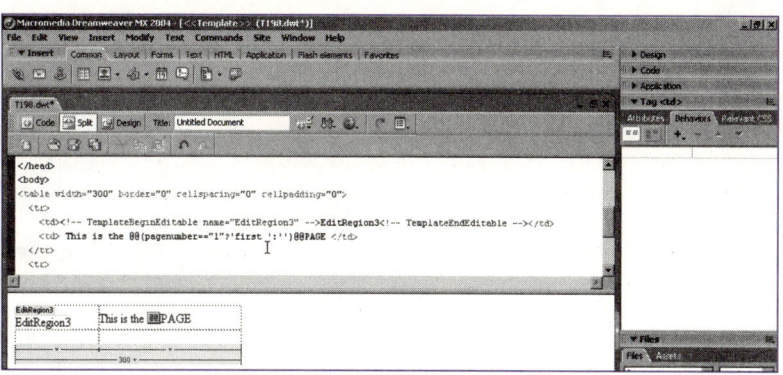

Figure 198-1: The first template expression, completed

5. Continue in this same page with two additional expressions, identical in form and function to the first, but added to the ELSE portion of the current expression. Change this:

```
@@(pagenumber=="1"?'first ':'')@@
```

to this:

```
@@(pagenumber=="1"?'first ':pagenumber=="2"?'second '
:pagenumber=="3"?'third ':'')@@
```

You have concatenated the three tests into a single statement that can be represented as IF/THEN/ELSEIF/THEN/ELSEIF/THEN/ENDIF. Save this page and return to your child page.

6. In the child page, use Modify ➪ Template Properties to set the value of pagenumber first to "2" and then to "3". Press OK after each and watch as the child page automatically adjusts to show the proper page number (see Figure 198-2).

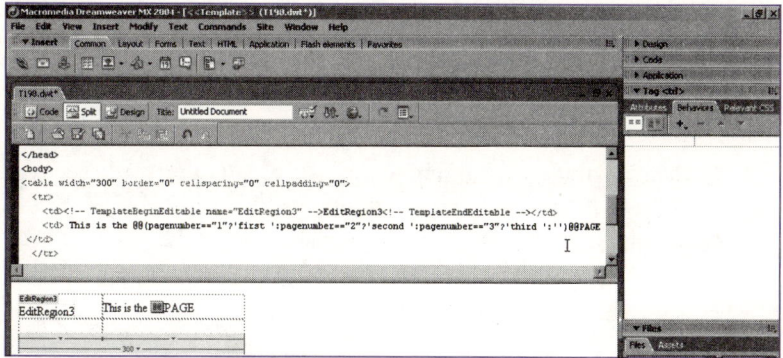

Figure 198-2: The final template expression

cross-reference

▪ You can read more about template parameters in Task 197 (Step 6).

Using MultipleIf Conditional Regions

If you've been doing these tasks in order, you should now have optional regions, parameters, and expressions under your belt. If so, you are ready for nearly anything Dreamweaver templates can throw at you. The previous task took you pretty deeply into the heart of the template features of Dreamweaver by examining how to achieve a series of complex IF/THEN tests—and the use of that capability will allow similarly complex logic on a page. Another logical tool that is quite useful is a structure similar to the case statements, where a series of conditions are listed and then tested from the top down. The first to succeed is the one that gets executed. MultipleIf conditional regions offer such a logical structure.

We are really on our own here—there is no user interface and no way to insert this code other than to do it manually. From the partX task198 folder at `www.wiley.com/compbooks/10simplesteps`, save the T198.dwt file in the Templates folder in your site.

1. Open T198.dwt in preparation for the next steps. Note that this page has a parameter in the head with a name of `pagenumber`, a type of `number`, and a value of `1`.

2. With the cursor positioned before the "P" of PAGE, and with the Code view pane having focus (i.e., you clicked there), insert (in Code view) a three-case, MultipleIf condition skeleton by entering the following code (all on one line):

```
<!-- TemplateBeginMultipleIf -->
<!-- TemplateBeginIfClause cond="" -->@@("")@@
<!-- TemplateEndIfClause -->
<!-- TemplateBeginIfClause cond="" -->@@("")@@
<!-- TemplateEndIfClause -->
<!-- TemplateBeginIfClause cond="" -->@@("")@@
<!-- TemplateEndIfClause --><!-- TemplateEndMultipleIf -->
```

3. Click between the first pair of double quotes (just after `cond=`) in the code you just inserted, and enter the following condition:

```
pagenumber=='1'
```

Then enter **first** , making sure to put a space after the word. Repeat this process for the next two conditions, using

```
pagenumber=='2'
```

and

```
pagenumber=='3'
```

for the next two conditions, use and **second** and **third** for the next two results. Your final code should look like Figure 199-1.

notes

- A snippet is available at `www.dreamweavermx-templates.com` that you can use instead of typing all the skeleton MultipleIf code manually (Step 2).

- A trailing space has been left after each of the output strings in the MultipleIf expression for proper screen display—in other words, `"first^"`, `"second^"`, and so on (spaces are shown here with the carat character—^) (Step 3).

- The scope of capabilities of template expression scripting is quite large. You can read more about this using Dreamweaver's F1 Help and reading the sections on template parameters and expressions (Step 4).

caution

- Refer to the Caution in the previous task about template expression syntax (Step 3).

Task **199**

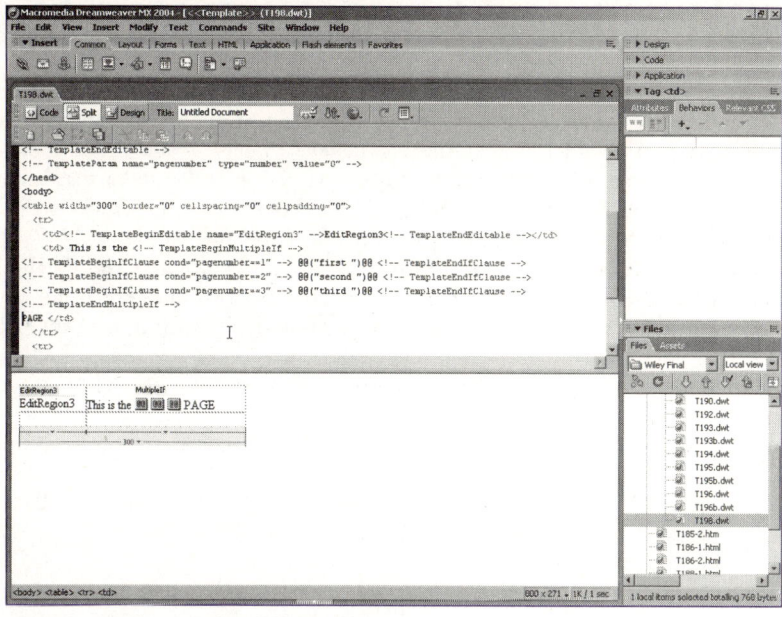

Figure 199-1: The completed MultipleIf region

4. Save this page as T199.dwt, and spawn a new child page from it. Test the functionality of your code by using Modify ➪ Template Properties to change the value of `pagename` successively from **1** to **2** to **3**, and watch the page's contents adjust accordingly.

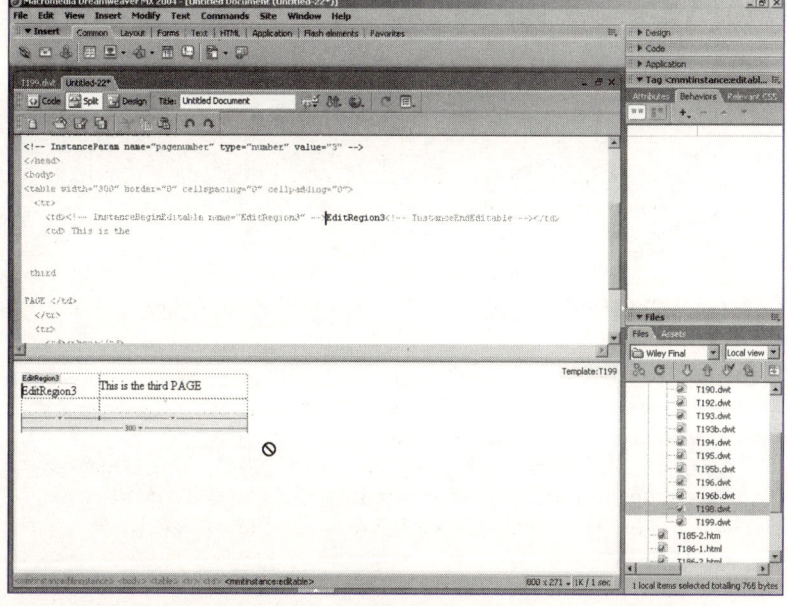

Figure 199-2: Taa-daa! A successful MultipleIf output with a parameter value of 3.

cross-reference

▪ Refer to Task 206 for using snippets (Step 2).

Making the Body onLoad Event Editable

There are many things you might want to do to template child pages to accommodate the needs of a site, but one of the most problematic is trying to apply a behavior to a child page when that the behavior needs to add an event handler to the `<body>` tag. In a template child page, it is not possible to have an editable region around the `<body>` tag, so it would seem that you cannot make such edits. But this is not the case with Dreamweaver MX/MX 2004 for the `<body>` tag— or for any other tag on the page for that matter. While this task specifically addresses the `<body>` tag, the same methods may be applied to any other tag on your page. For this task, download T200.dwt and T200-1.html from the partX task200 folder at www.wiley.com/compbooks/10simplesteps. Save T200.dwt in the Templates folder, and the HTML page in the root of your site.

In this task, you add a pop-up message to the `<body>` tag of a template child page.

1. Open T200.dwt and select the `<body>` tag on the Tag Selector at the bottom of the Document window.

2. Use Modify ⇨ Templates ⇨ Make Attribute Editable to open the Editable Tag Attributes dialog panel.

3. Since this `<body>` tag has *no* existing attributes on this page, you have to manually add one. Click the Add button on the dialog panel to do this. In the dialog box that opens, enter **onLoad** and press OK (see Figure 200-1). Make sure that ONLOAD is shown in the Editable Tag Attributes dialog panel and that the Make Attribute Editable check box is enabled.

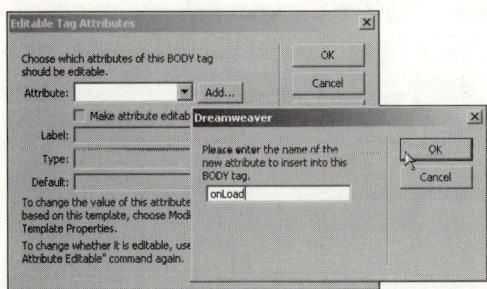

Figure 200-1: Adding onLoad to the Editable Attribute dialog box

4. The value that you enter for Label will actually be used to name a parameter that this process will add to the template page. Enter **loadParam** here. Leave the Type as Text, and leave the Default value at null (or blank), as shown in Figure 200-2. Press OK. Save this template as **T200.dwt** and examine the code on the page.

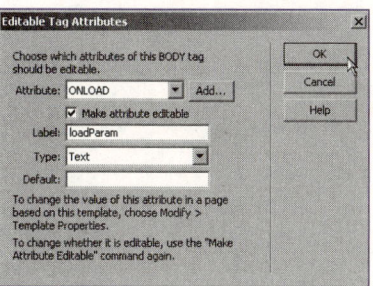

Figure 200-2: Completing the Editable Attribute dialog box for the `<body>` tag

This editable attribute process does two things. The first is to insert a parameter in the head of the document:

```
<!-- TemplateParam name="loadParam" type="text" value="" -->
```

The second is to add an expression to the `<body>` tag (look at the code):

```
<body onLoad="@@(loadParam)@@">
```

This causes each child page to evaluate `loadParam`'s value and place it in the onLoad event in the `<body>` tag. In most cases, this value is null, and so nothing happens. On some pages, however, by assigning a non-null value to `loadParam`, you can give that onLoad event handler something to do!

5. Spawn a child page from this template and save it as **T200-2.html**. Keep this page open so that you can manipulate the value of its parameter.

6. Open T200-1.html. This page has already had the Popup Message behavior applied to it. Look at the `<body>` tag and copy the contents of the onLoad event call by selecting `MM_popupMsg('Hello World!')`.

7. Return to T200-2.html and use Modify ➪ Template Properties to allow you access to the `loadParam` parameter's value. Click in the Value entry field, and paste in the contents of the clipboard. When you click OK, the page should now contain this `<body>` tag:

```
<body onLoad="MM_popupMsg('Hello World!')">
```

When you preview this page, you see the alert, as shown in Figure 200-3. If you do not, check the contents of the event call that you pasted into the Template Properties dialog box.

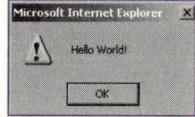

Figure 200-3: Hello World!

cross-reference

- To read more about linking to external files, go to Task 41.

Part 11: Working with Code

Finding and Replacing Code and Text

Rather than having to manually search for a word or specific section of code, with the Find and Replace feature, you can instantly find all instances of a given string in either the current document or any number of unopened documents. You can also replace what you find with a new string if necessary. When you are working with multiple pages or large Web sites, Find and Replace is one of the most powerful and time-saving features, since it enables you to make many, many repetitive changes with just the click of a button.

1. Select Edit ➪ Find and Replace to open the Find and Replace dialog box, as shown in Figure 201-1.

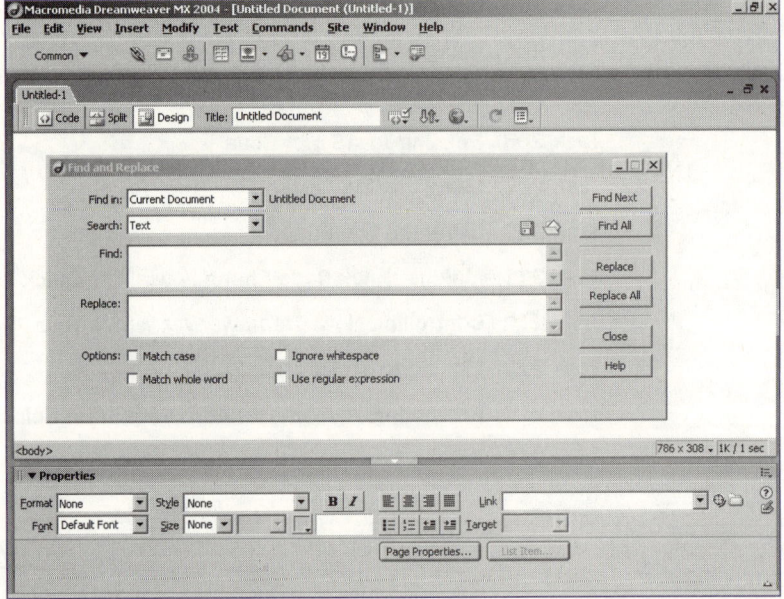

Figure 201-1: Find and Replace dialog box

2. Define where you would like to search for the text by selecting one of the options in the pop-up list of the Find In field.

3. Select either the Source Code option or the Text option from the Search pop-up list.

4. Enter the text to search for in the Find field.

5. To continue with a find operation only, press the Find Next or Find All buttons. When you press the Find Next button, Dreamweaver jumps to the next instance of the search string and opens any unopened document, if necessary. If you press the Find All button, the task is completed without opening any unopened documents, but the results are displayed in the Results panel, as shown in Figure 201-2.

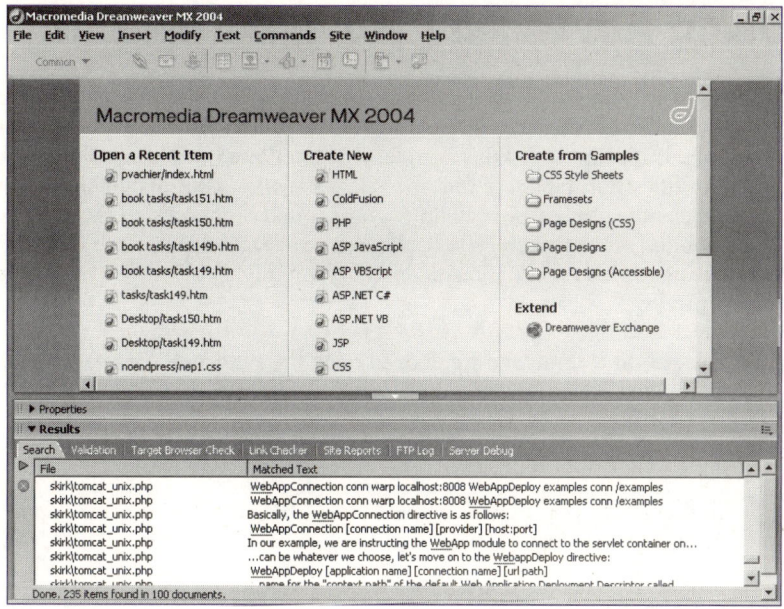

Figure 201-2: Results panel showing results of a Find All command for the word "web"

tip
- You can save search-and-replace queries you use by clicking the Save Query button in the Find and Replace dialog box. To use a saved query in the future, click the Load Query button. Queries are saved as standalone Dreamweaver files that can be stored anywhere on your hard drive (Step 4).

6. To open a file listed in the Results panel after a Find All command, double-click the entry in the Results panel.

7. To replace the text you find with new text (optional), enter your new text in the Replace field after filling in the search text in the Find field.

8. Press either the Replace or Replace All buttons. If you press the Replace button, the first instance of the search string is replaced with the new text. If you press the Replace All button, Dreamweaver works in the background on unopened documents and displays the results of the Find and Replace in the Results panel.

cross-reference
- Refer to Task 202 for more advanced searches.

Using Advanced Find and Replace

The Find and Replace command also offers advanced text and tag search capability, making it easy to confine a search to specific HTML tags or text inside or outside of specific tags. For example, you could use the advanced text search feature to find all instances of the word "Car" in all of your document's `<title>` tags, and change only those matching words found in the title to the word "Automobile." Alternatively, you could use the advanced tag search feature to find all instances of a specific tag and replace/modify those tags in a variety of different ways.

1. Select Edit ➪ Find and Replace to open the Find and Replace dialog box.

2. Define where you would like to search for the text by selecting the appropriate option in the pop-up list of the Find In field.

3. In the Search pop-up menu, select Text (Advanced) or Specific Tag to display the advanced search options for each type of search.

4. For advanced text searches, select the option Inside Tag or Not Inside Tag to define where you want to search for the text string, and then select the desired tag from the corresponding pop-up menu, as shown in Figure 202-1. Make sure to also enter the text to search for in the Find field.

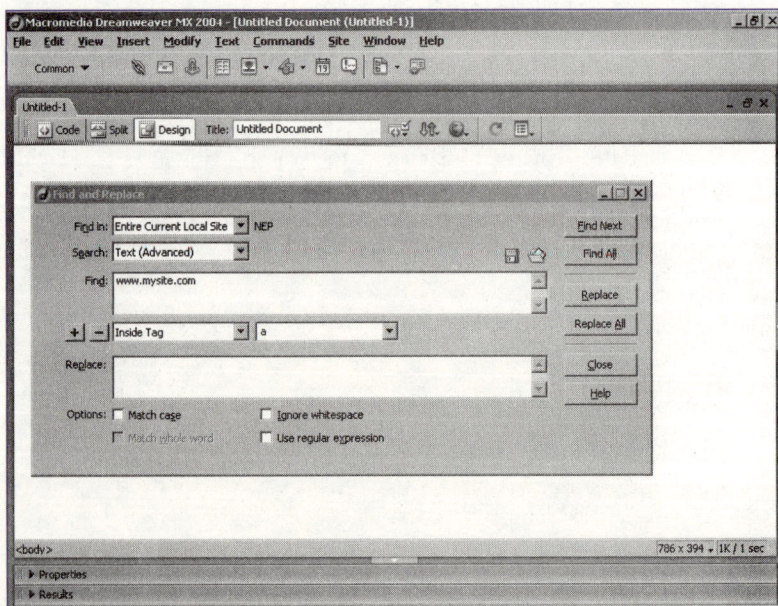

Figure 202-1: The advanced text search options

5. To search for a specific tag, select the Specific Tag option in the Search field instead, and then select the desired tag from the corresponding pop-up menu, as shown in Figure 202-2.

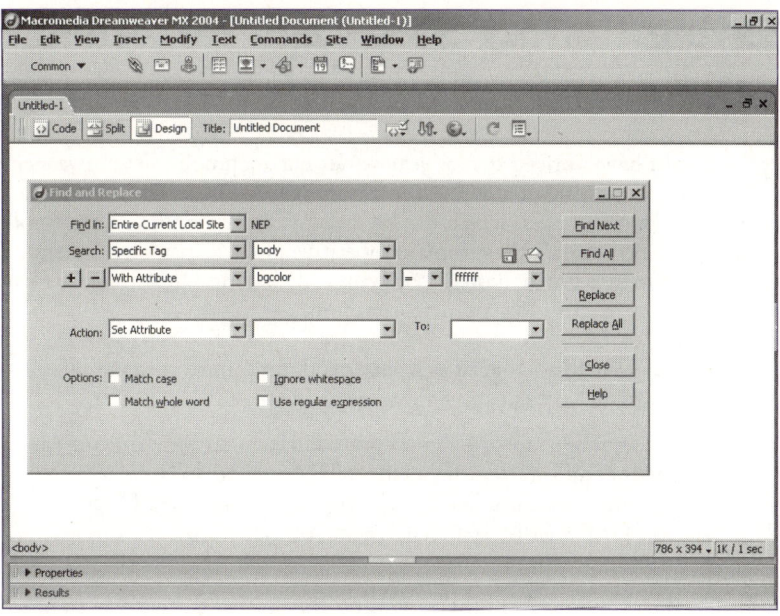

Figure 202-2: The specific tag search options

6. To add additional criteria to either search, click the Plus (+) button and choose additional options as needed from the available menus. For example, you can search for specific attributes of an HTML tag or for tags within tags by choosing new options from the corresponding pull-down menus. To delete extra search criteria, click the Minus (–) button.

7. When using the specific tag search option, you define the parameters to look for and then set an action to perform from the Action pop-up menu while specifying replacement text, as shown in Figure 202-3.

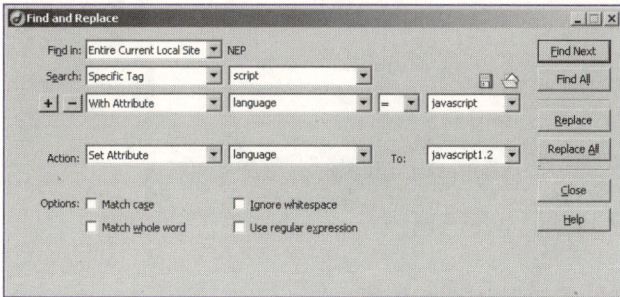

Figure 202-3: Defining options for a specific tag find and replace

8. Use the Find Next/Find All or Replace/Replace All buttons to complete the operation.

Task 202

tips

- Advanced text searches are best used for finding/replacing text that occurs only inside or outside of a specific HTML tag. To find text inside an entire HTML document including all its tags, choose the `<body>` tag in the tag list (Step 4).

- You can create complex and powerful search queries by adding more criteria to your search. Remember, you can save your queries by clicking the Save Query button so that they can be quickly accessed again at a later date (Step 6).

- Remember that in most cases opening and closing HTML tags contain lots of content that you may not want to delete or change. The Strip Tag action is a good one to use if you just want to delete the opening and closing HTML tags, but not the content inside of them (Step 6).

cross-reference

- Refer to Task 201 for instructions on using basic find and replace.

Saving History Steps and Recording a Command

notes

■ Commands that you create are saved as text files in the Dreamweaver/ Configuration/Commands folder or in a specific user's Commands folder on multi-user operating systems (Step 5).

■ Some mouse actions, such as clicking to select items in a page or dragging items around on the page, cannot be recorded (Step 6).

You might have noticed that as you work on a document, Dreamweaver keeps track of everything you do in the History panel. Each document you work on has its own history list, which can be saved as a new command and applied to other documents to quickly automate repetitive tasks, much like a macro command. You can also create custom commands by having Dreamweaver record your actions in real time as you perform them.

1. To save your history steps as a command, first make sure the History panel is visible by selecting Window ⇨ History.

2. If you're going to record a new command, you might want to clear your history and start with an empty History panel. To clear your history, you can right-click the History panel and select Clear History. If the history is already clear, you can continue without performing this step.

3. Go ahead and perform the actions on the document that you want to save as a new command. As you perform each action, Dreamweaver inserts a new entry in the History panel, as shown in Figure 203-1.

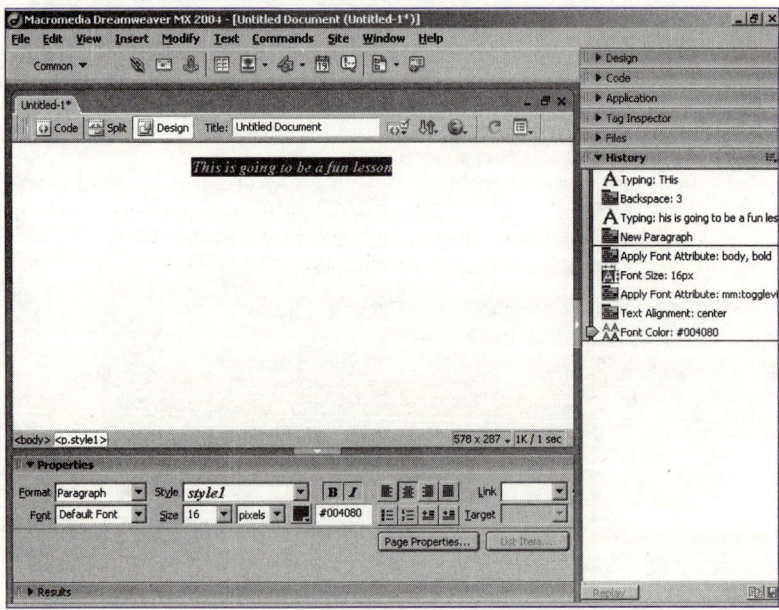

Figure 203-1: The History panel

4. Once you've completed all the steps you want to save, highlight them in the History panel and click the disk icon in the lower right corner of the panel to save them as a command. Only steps that do not have a red X through them or do not have a separator line between them can be saved as a single command.

5. After you click the Save Command icon, the Save as Command dialog box appears, as shown in Figure 203-2, allowing you to choose a name for the command. Pick a name and click OK. Once the command has been saved, it will then appear in the Commands menu. You can delete or rename commands that appear in this menu by selecting Commands ⇨ Edit Commands List.

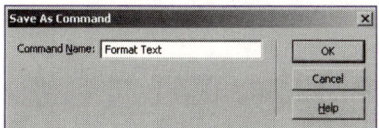

Figure 203-2: Save as Command dialog box

6. To have Dreamweaver automatically record a series of steps for you and save it as a temporary command, select Commands ⇨ Start Recording and begin performing the actions you want to record. After you select this command, the cursor displays a cassette tape icon letting you know that you are in Record mode.

7. When you are done, select Commands ⇨ Stop Recording.

8. To run the command, select Commands ⇨ Play Recorded Command.

9. After you run the command, a Run Command entry appears in the History panel. To save this as a permanent command that you can name and reuse for future use, highlight it and click the disk icon in the History panel as described in Steps 4 and 5.

Task 203

tip
- Select Get More Commands in the Commands Menu to visit the Dreamweaver Exchange site, where you can download more commands for use with Dreamweaver (Step 3).

cross-reference
- Refer to Task 201 for instructions on using basic find and replace.

Commenting Your Code

Code comments are useful for making notes about your code, since they are only visible in Source mode and not to regular visitors viewing your Web page in a browser. They can help you keep track of your code and provide information both to yourself and to others working on your pages in a multiuser environment.

1. Open the page to which you want to add a comment.

2. Normally, comments are entered manually when you are writing code. The standard way to include a comment is to enter the text and enclose it between an opening and closing comment tag:

   ```
   <!-- This is a comment that will appear invisible in the
   browser because it is contained within comment tags -->
   ```

   Dreamweaver, however, allows you to enter comments either in Design view or Source view.

3. To insert a comment in Design view, select Insert ⇨ Comment or click the Comment icon in the Common Items Insert menu. This brings up the Comment dialog box, shown in Figure 204-1.

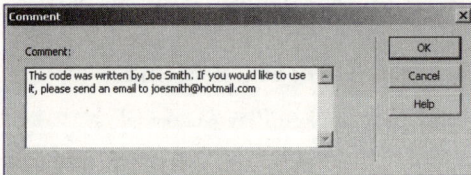

Figure 204-1: Comment dialog box

4. Enter the comment you want to include in the Comment dialog box and click OK. When you do this, Dreamweaver warns you that you won't be able to see the comment in Design view unless you turn on Invisible Elements and set the correct preference.

5. To make comments visible in Design view, select Preferences ⇨ Invisible Elements and make sure that Show Comments is checked (it's off by default). Then make sure that the Invisible Elements option is checked in the View ⇨ Visual Aids menu (it's on by default). Comments appear as a yellow marker in Design view and can also be edited using the Properties panel, as shown in Figure 204-2.

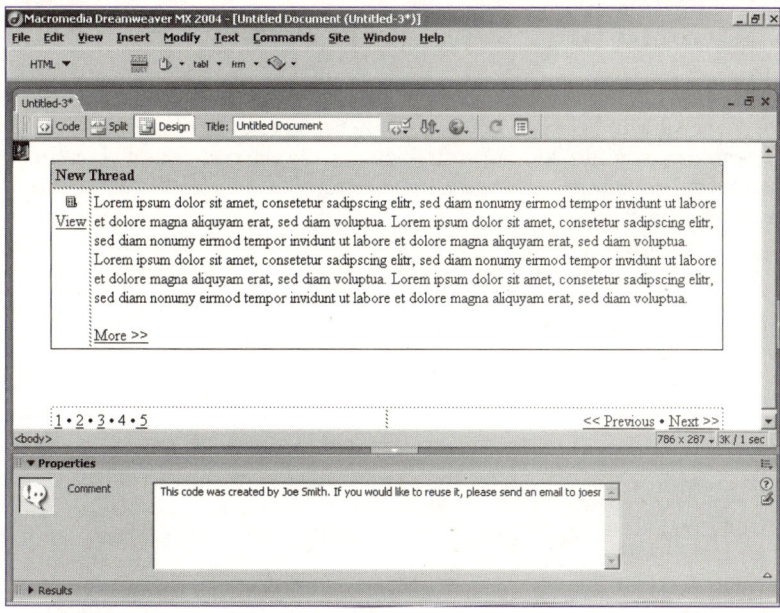

Figure 204-2: Viewing comments in Design view

6. To insert a comment in Code view, place the cursor anywhere in the code where you want to insert the comment.

7. Select Insert ➪ Comment or click the Comment icon in the Common Items Insert menu. When you do this, Dreamweaver inserts opening and closing comment tags and leaves the cursor blinking inside the tags, ready for you to type your comment.

8. Type in your comment to finish inserting it.

cross-reference

▪ Refer to Task 205 for customizing the Code view.

Customizing the Code View

You may have noticed that Dreamweaver automatically colors the code in Code view to help you differentiate between tags, attributes, content, and so forth. If you want, you can customize the way the coloring of your code is displayed through the code preferences settings, as well as the font that is used to display the code.

1. To change the code coloring, select Edit ⇨ Preferences (Dreamweaver ⇨ Preferences on the Mac) to display the Preferences dialog box.

2. Click the Code Coloring category to display the code coloring preferences, as shown in Figure 205-1.

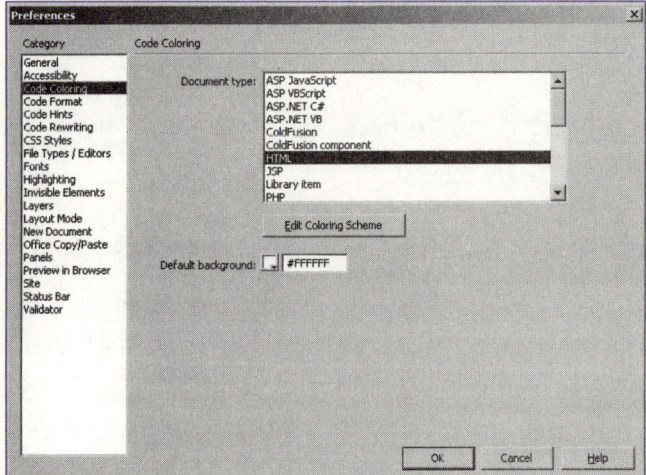

Figure 205-1: Code Coloring preferences

3. Click the type of code that you would like to change. The default is HTML, but you can select many other kinds of code to alter. For now, keep the HTML document type selected.

4. Click the Edit Coloring Scheme button to alter the current color scheme for HTML. This displays the Edit Coloring Scheme dialog box, as shown in Figure 205-2. Notice that each type of HTML tag and attribute can have a color and style properties assigned to it.

5. Browse through the different styles and notice how each one uses a different color to set it off from the rest. The Preview area shows how the code looks in Code view with the current settings. To change a style property, simply change either the text color, background color, or style attributes. Notice that the Preview area offers a live update of how the changes affect your Code view.

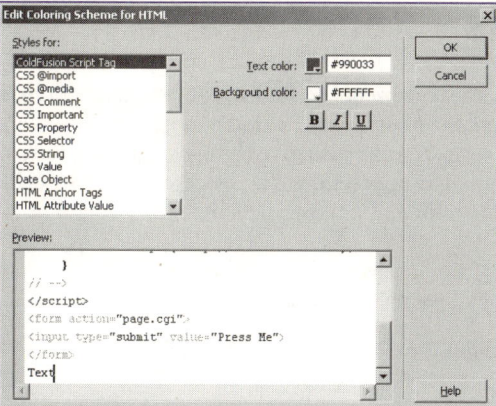

Figure 205-2: Edit Coloring Scheme dialog box

6. When you are satisfied with your changes, click OK to accept them or Cancel to dismiss the window.

7. To change the font display option for your code, click the Fonts category in the Preferences window to display the Fonts preferences shown in Figure 205-3.

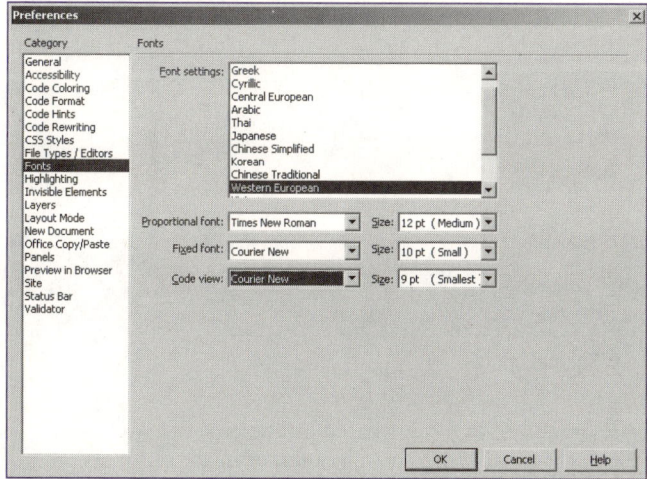

Figure 205-3: Fonts preferences

8. While you can control many of the different font settings used throughout the application from this window, the selection you make in the Code View field only affects how code appears in Code view. Select an appropriate font and size from the pop-up menus to customize the display to your preferred font.

9. When you are finished setting the font preferences, click OK to accept your changes or cancel to dismiss the window.

tip

- I recommend using mono-spaced fonts such as Courier or Monaco for Code view, since they make it easier to count characters when you need to debug your code (Step 8).

cross-reference

- Refer to Task 201 for finding and replacing specific text.

Using Snippets

Code snippets enable you to store bits of code that you can quickly reuse when needed. Snippets can consist of any kind of code, including HTML, JavaScript, ASP, PHP, and more. You can also save things like tables, forms, special characters, and just about anything else that can be represented by code. Dreamweaver comes with lots of predefined snippets that are ready to use right out of the box.

note

- Many snippets contain Greek placeholder text. You can replace the Greek text and maintain the formatting by typing over it (Step 7).

1. Open the page where you want to add a snippet.

2. Select Window ⇨ Snippets to display the Snippets panel, as shown in Figure 206-1.

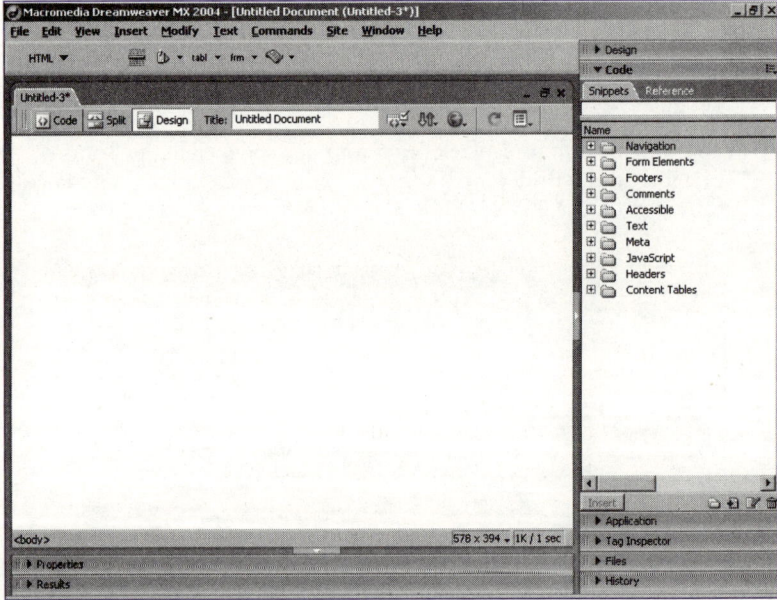

Figure 206-1: Snippets panel

3. Snippets are organized in folders based on the type of code they contain. Click the plus (+) sign next to a folder in the Snippets panel to expand the view and see the contents of any folder. Since Dreamweaver ships with a lot of predefined snippets, you'll see lots of them in the Snippets panel.

4. For this task, expand the Content Tables folder to view its contents. Notice that snippet folders can contain snippet files that look like little page icons with an "s" on them, as well as other folders. The folders are used strictly to organize the snippets by type.

5. Expand the Icon folder located inside the Content Tables folder by clicking the plus (+) sign, as shown in Figure 206-2.

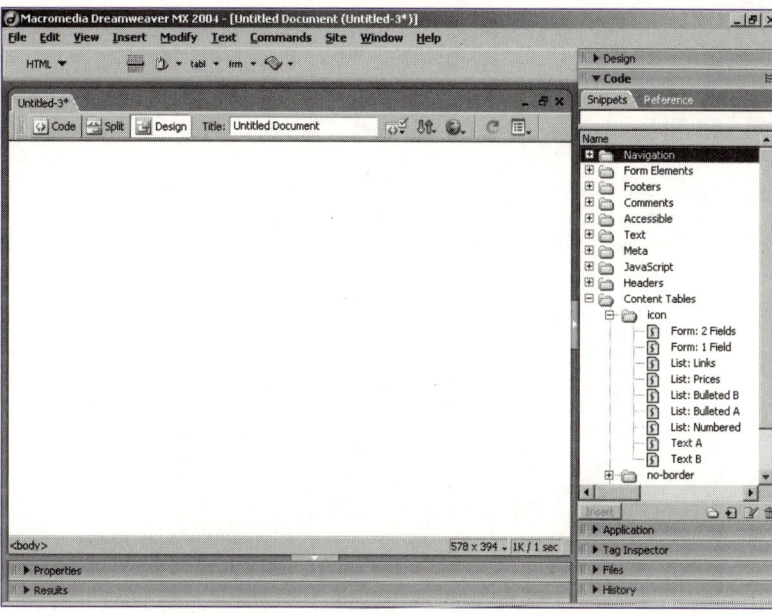

Figure 206-2: Expanding the snippet folders to view their contents

6. The Icon folder contains numerous formatted tables saved as snippets. When you click a snippet, a preview appears in the top pane of the Snippets panel.

7. To use a snippet, click its name in the Snippet panel and then click the Insert button at the bottom left of the panel. Try inserting the first snippet labeled Form: 2 Fields. When you do this, Dreamweaver inserts the table into the Design view, as shown in Figure 206-3.

8. Experiment with some of the other snippets to see what kinds of goodies are included in the Snippets panel. You'll find that there are lots of time-saving snippets that offer plenty of shortcuts for working in Dreamweaver.

Figure 206-3: Table inserted into Design view

tip

- Other ways to insert a snippet include dragging it from the Snippets panel into a document, double-clicking it, or right-clicking and selecting Insert (Step 5).

cross-reference

- Refer to Task 207 to see how to save custom snippets.

Saving Snippets

Any code you want to reuse again can easily be saved as a snippet and made available in the Snippets panel, where it can be accessed with a single click.

1. In the Snippets panel, highlight the folder where you want the new snippet to go. If you want to create a new folder, click the New Folder button in the Snippets panel first.

2. Click the New Snippet icon in the Snippets panel to open the Snippet dialog box, shown in Figure 207-1.

note

- Many snippets contain Greek text to serve as placeholder copy that can be replaced by just typing over it.

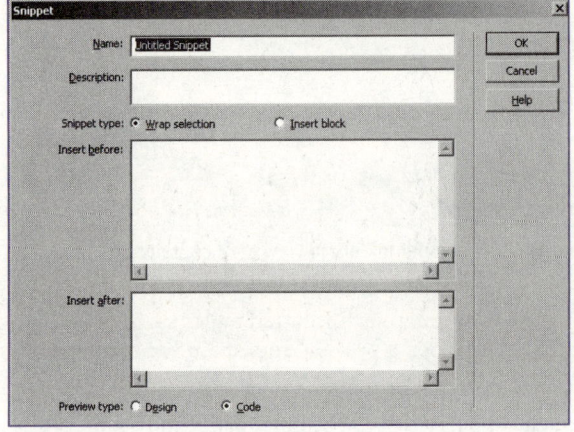

Figure 207-1: Snippet dialog box

3. Enter a name and description (optional) for the snippet.

4. Select the snippet type. Wrap Selection is used for items like opening and closing tags that can be automatically wrapped around blocks of text. Insert Block is used when you just want to insert a single block of text or code.

5. If you choose Wrap Selection, type or paste your code into both the Insert Before and Insert After fields. For example, if you want your snippet to serve as a wrapper for generic scripts, you would insert `<script` in the Insert Before field and `</script>` in the Insert After field.

6. If you choose Insert Block, type or paste your code into the Insert Code field, as shown in Figure 207-2. Remember that you can only insert code into this field, so if you want to copy a table or other complex element, you must select it in Source view and then copy all of its code before pasting it here.

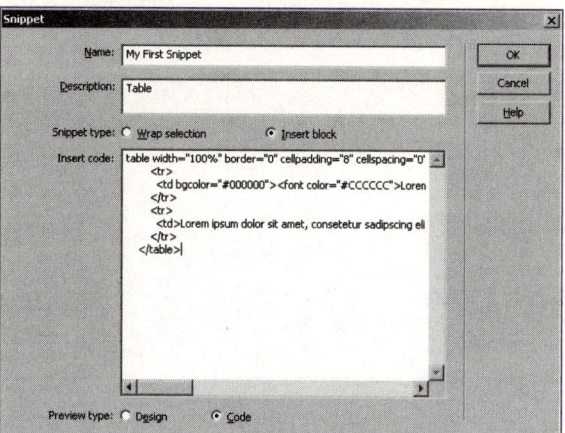

Figure 207-2: Inserting a block of code as a snippet

tip
- You can also drag a snippet from the Snippet panel
  into a Dreamweaver document or double-click to
  insert it (Step 5).

7. Select the Design or Code option under Preview type. This option affects how the snippet displays in the Snippet panel preview pane. Selecting Design previews the snippet as it would appear in Design view, while selecting Code previews the snippet as it would appear in Code view.

8. Click OK to finish creating the snippet. The new snippet appears in the folder you selected when you first clicked the New Snippet icon (see Figure 207-3). You can also drag and drop the snippet to a differ-ent folder if needed.

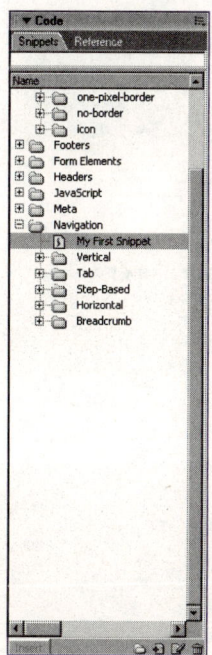

Figure 207-3: The new snippet added to the Snippets panel

cross-reference
- Refer to Task 206 for using
  snippets.

Task 208

Reusing JavaScript Code

You can use snippets to save and quickly apply commonly used JavaScript code. In this task you save an existing script as a snippet and then reuse it in a new document.

1. Download the task208 folder from `www.wiley.com/compbooks/10simplestepsorless` and open the task208 .htm file.

2. Switch to Code view and highlight the JavaScript code, as shown in Figure 208-1.

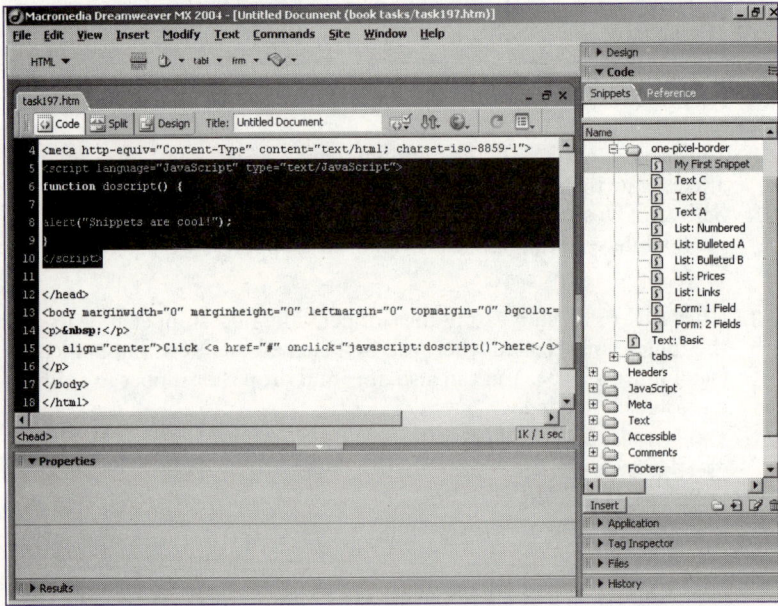

Figure 208-1: Highlighting the code to use as a snippet

3. With the code highlighted, right-click it and select Create New Snippet from the pop-up menu. This brings up the Snippet dialog window shown in Figure 208-2.

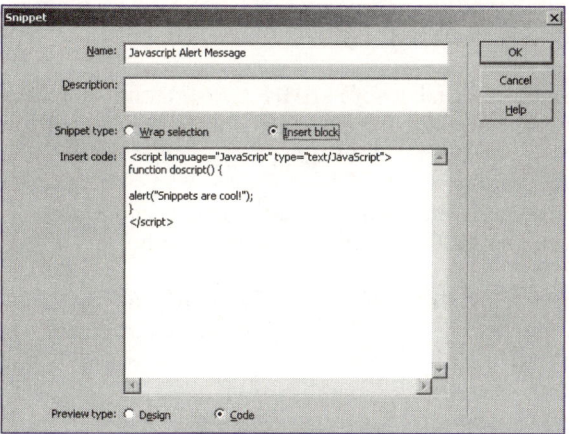

Figure 208-2: Snippet dialog window

4. Make sure the Insert Block radio button is checked.

5. Enter **Task 208 Script** for the name and click OK.

6. Display the Snippets panel by selecting Window ⇨ Snippets.

7. You'll notice the snippet was created in whatever folder you were last working within in the Snippets panel. Drag and drop the Task 208 Script snippet into the JavaScript folder in the Snippets panel. Your snippet is now saved, organized in the JavaScript folder, and ready to use again.

8. To reuse the snippet, open a new document and switch to Code view.

9. Place your cursor between the document's `<head>` tag and `<body>` tag (or anywhere else you want to place the script).

10. Make sure the Task 208 Script snippet is highlighted in the Snippets panel, and then click the Insert button to insert the script.

tips

- You can reorganize the folders in the Snippets panel in any way to help you keep track of your custom code snippets (Step 7).

- You can also drag a snippet from the Snippet panel into a Dreamweaver document or double-click to insert it (Step 10).

cross-reference

- Refer to Tasks 206 and 207 for using and saving snippets.

Task 209

Using the Tag Library

The Tag Library is a master database of HTML tags containing information that controls how Dreamweaver globally handles tag formatting. By editing the information contained in the Tag Library, you can completely customize how tags are formatted. Once tags have been defined and their formatting specified in the Tag Library, the formatting information is automatically applied by Dreamweaver as it generates code whenever you edit a document.

notes

- Changes made with the Tag Library Editor are global changes that affect all tags or attributes with the same name (Step 1).

- Most people won't need to make any changes to the tag formatting handled by Dreamweaver. However, if you create new tags or need to change the formatting of specific existing tags, the Tag Library Editor is the way to go (Step 2).

1. To edit or add tags to the Tag Library, you need to use the Tag Library Editor. To open the Tag Library Editor, shown in Figure 209-1, select Edit ➪ Tag Libraries.

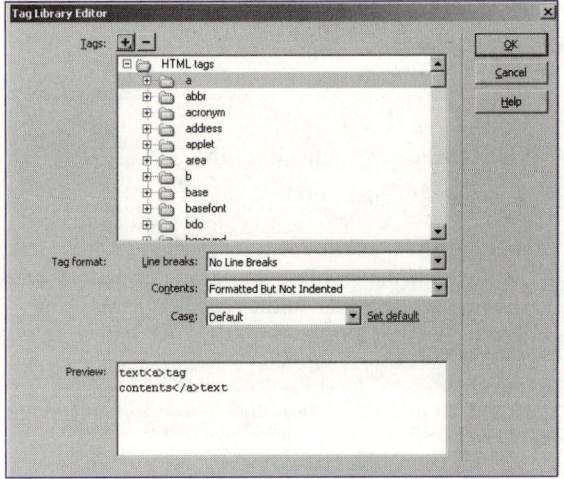

Figure 209-1: The Tag Library Editor

2. To modify existing tags, first select a category of tags to edit in the Tags field, such as HTML tags. Notice that many different custom tags are included already in this list and they are organized into several different folder categories.

3. Try viewing the list of HTML tags, the first folder listing in the Tags field, by clicking the plus (+) sign to expand the HTML Tags folder.

4. Select any of the tags displayed in the list of HTML tags. When you select a tag, the tag formatting options are displayed in pop-up menus in the Tag Library Editor, as shown in Figure 209-2. For any tag listed, you can edit line breaks, whether or not the tag is formatted and/or indented (Contents), or its letter case. Notice that the Preview field allows you to preview how a tag is formatted given the options that you have set for it.

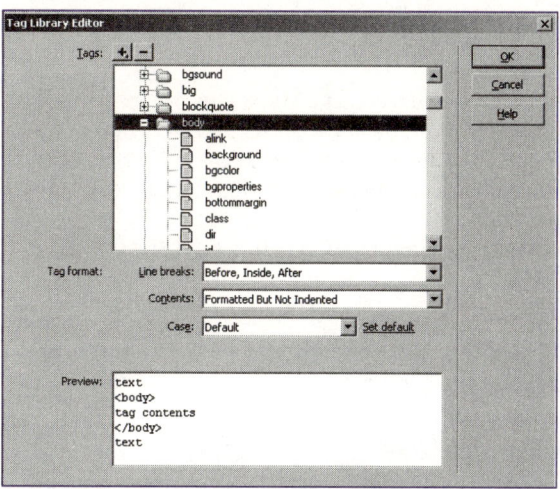

Figure 209-2: Tag formatting options displayed in the Tag Library Editor

5. You can also edit a tag's attributes by clicking the plus (+) sign next to a tag's folder to expand the view to include its attributes. Selecting a tag attribute in the Tag Library Editor also allows you to change its case or attribute type using the pop-up menus that appear whenever an attribute is selected, as shown in Figure 209-3.

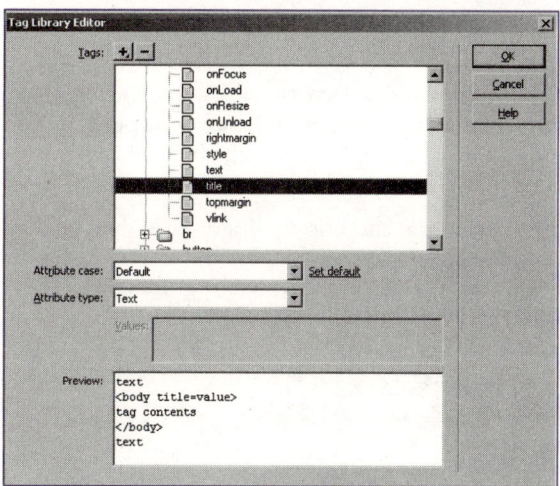

Figure 209-3: Editing a tag's attributes

cross-reference

▪ Refer to Task 210 for using the Tag Editor.

Using the Tag Editor

The Tag Editor offers a quick way to access the various properties and attributes of a tag and change them on the fly whether you are working in Code view or Design view. Changes made with the Tag Editor only affect specific tags that you select in a specific document, rather than affecting all your tags globally.

notes

- If the Edit Tag option is not available in the pop-up menu when you right-click a tag, the tag is not recognized and it cannot be edited using the Tag Editor (Step 1).

- You can also right-click element objects in Design view to edit them with the Tag Editor (Step 2).

1. Open a new or existing document and switch to Code view by clicking the Code View button.

2. For the purpose of this task, right-click the <body> tag in Code view and select Edit Tag <body> from the pop-up menu. This opens up the Tag Editor, as shown in Figure 210-1.

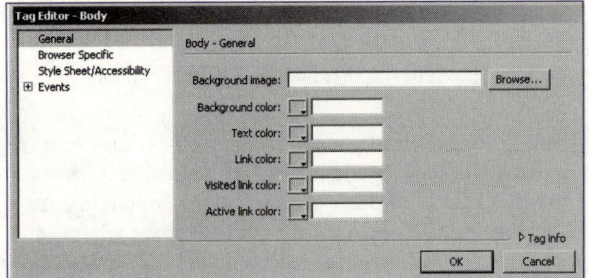

Figure 210-1: The Tag Editor

3. The Tag Editor allows you to change the properties and attributes of many common tags. Its contents will vary depending on the tag that you select to edit. Notice that in this case, the Tag Editor gives you a quick visual way to edit all of the options and attributes associated with the <body> tag.

4. Click Cancel in the Tag Editor, and this time right-click the <html> tag and select Edit Tag <html> from the pop-up menu. Notice how the Tag Editor's fields and options change, as shown in Figure 210-2, to reflect the specific options associated with the <html> tag.

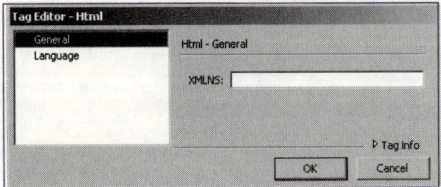

Figure 210-2: The Tag Editor with different fields and options

5. Click the triangle next to Tag Info label to open up the tag information pane. This pane, shown in Figure 210-3, displays information about the tag you are editing from the O'Reilly HTML Reference

Library that ships with Dreamweaver. The O'Reilly HTML Reference provides an excellent database of information about most HTML tags in a convenient and easily accessible format.

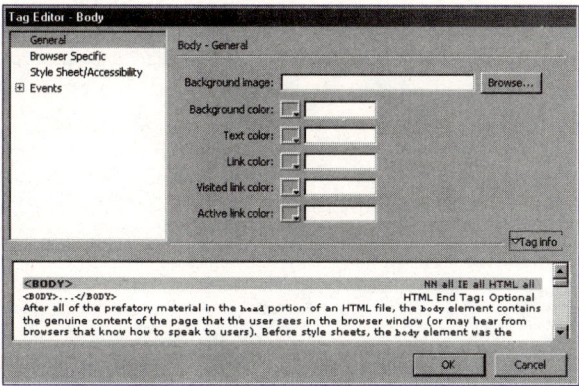

Figure 210-3: The Tag Editor showing information for the `<body>` tag

6. To make changes to a tag with the Tag Editor, edit the options listed in the dialog window and click OK to apply them.

tip

• You can also display the O'Reilly HTML Reference information for any tag by selecting Window ➪ Reference (Step 5).

cross-reference

• Refer to Task 209 for using the Tag Library and to Task 211 for making quick changes using the Tag Editor.

Task 211

Making Quick Code Changes with the Quick Tag Editor

U sing the Quick Tag Editor allows you to access your code from the Property Inspector without having to switch to Code view. It provides a quick and convenient method to make minor changes to your code that aren't normally available in the Property Inspector.

note

• The `title` attribute displays its value as a ToolTip when viewed in most modern browsers (Step 2).

1. Download the task211 folder from `www.wiley.com/compbooks/ 10simplestepsorless` and open the file task211.htm as shown in Figure 211-1.

Figure 211-1: You'll edit the code for the image tag in this document using the Quick Tag Editor

2. Click the image on the page to select it. Using the Quick Tag Editor, you'll now add a `title` attribute to the image tag.

3. Select Window ⇨ Properties to display the Properties Inspector if it is not already visible.

4. In the Properties Inspector, click the Quick Tag Editor icon, as shown in Figure 211-2, to display the code for the image tag.

Figure 211-2: Using the Quick Tag Editor

5. Move your cursor just before the closing bracket (>) and add the following code using the Quick Tag Editor. The resulting code is shown in Figure 211-3.

```
title="Lightning Storm"
```

6. Hit Return/Enter to accept the code changes.

Figure 211-3: After adding the `title` attribute

Controlling How Dreamweaver Writes Your Code

notes

- Dreamweaver will not apply code formatting preferences to code written in Code view while you are working in Code view, but it will reformat your code based on your preferences when you switch back to Design view and begin editing your code (Step 1).

- You can force Dreamweaver to apply the new source formatting preferences to an open document by selecting Commands ⇨ Apply Source Formatting (Step 5).

When you are creating a page in Design view, Dreamweaver formats code based on a set of preferences that you can alter through the Preferences window. By altering the Code Formatting preferences, you can control many of the aspects of code formatting, including indents, tag size, code wrapping, line breaks, letter case, and so on. This allows you quick, global control over the appearance of all the code that Dreamweaver outputs.

1. Select Edit ⇨ Preferences (Dreamweaver ⇨ Preferences on the Mac) to display the Preferences dialog box.

2. Click the Code Format category to display the dialog box shown in Figure 212-1.

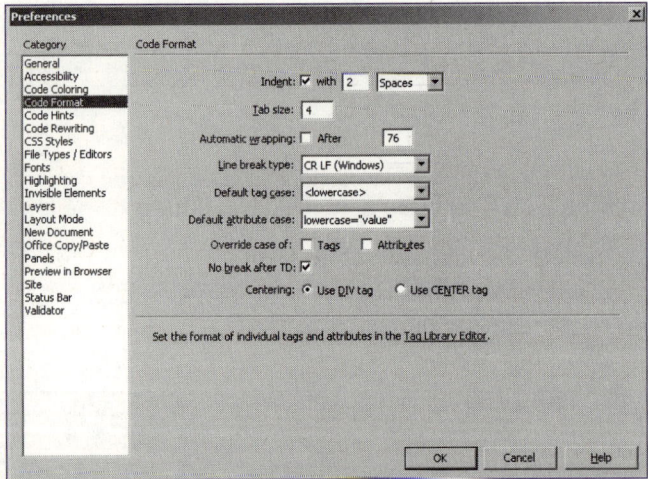

Figure 212-1: Code Format preferences

3. Change the formatting options displayed in the dialog box as necessary. For example, you can change the indent size from its default of two spaces to a larger amount if you wish to increase the indents for your code, as shown in Figures 212-2 and 212-3.

4. Click OK to apply your changes.

5. If you have an open document you want to apply the formatting changes to, make sure you are in Design or Split view and edit your document to force Dreamweaver to update the code. If you are applying formatting options to an existing document, the formatting changes will not be reflected until you make changes to the document in Design view.

Task 212

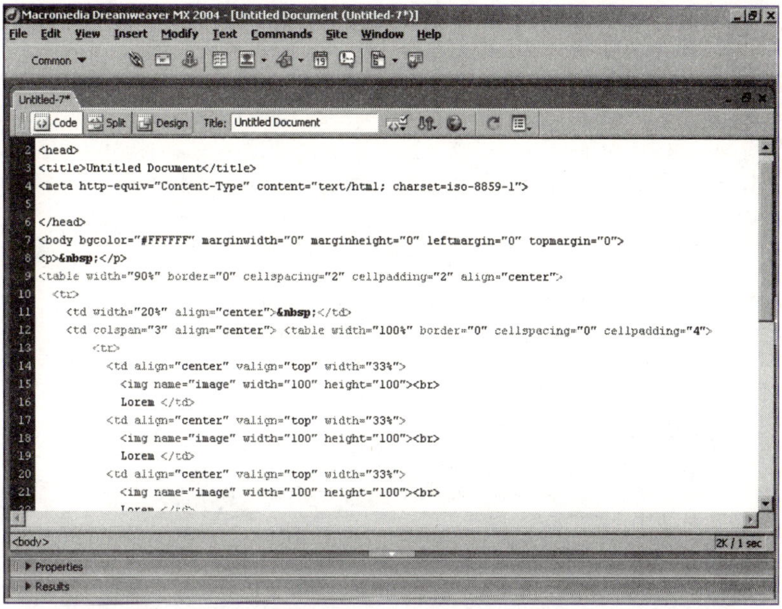

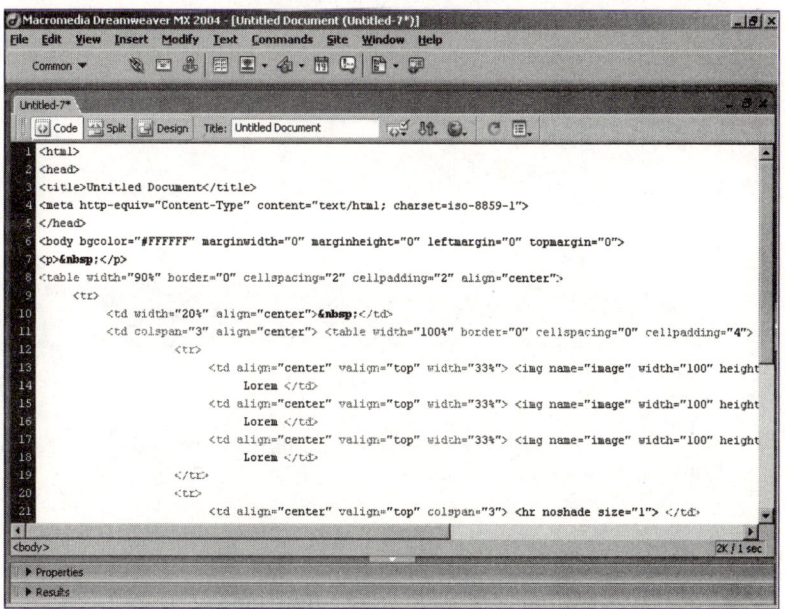

Figure 212-2: Code with a standard two-space indent

Figure 212-3: Code with indent space increased to five spaces

cross-reference

- Refer to Task 214 for information on how to protect your code (Step 1).

Linking to an External Script

Besides including scripts directly in your code, you can also link to external scripts written in languages such as JavaScript, VBScript, PHP, and more.

1. Open the document where you wish to add the script.

2. Switch to Code view and place you cursor at the point where you would like to add a linked script.

3. Select the HTML option from the pop-up list in the Insert window (Window ➪ Insert) to display the insert buttons for HTML items, as shown in Figure 213-1.

note

- Linked scripts allow you to store your scripts outside of the current HTML document, which is useful if you want to link several documents to a single script so that modifications to the script are more easily managed (Step 2).

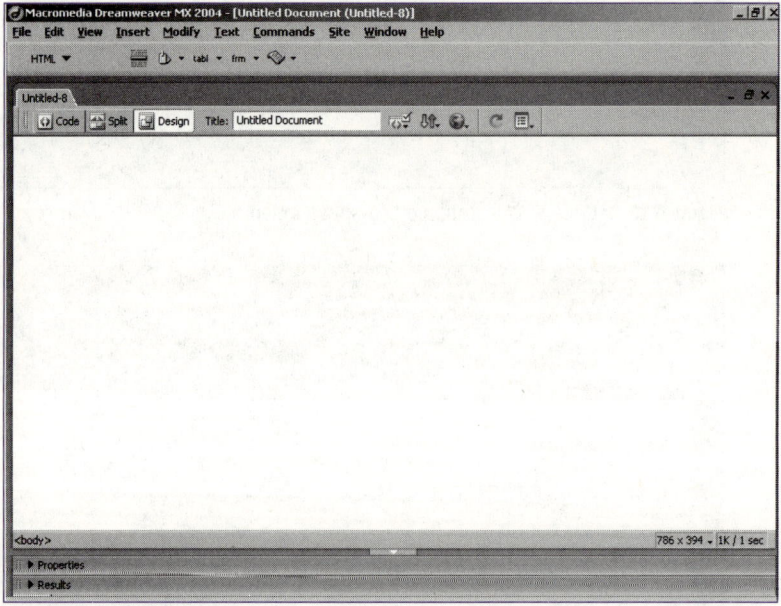

Figure 213-1: Insert palette

4. Click the Script icon and select Script from the pop-up menu to bring up the Insert Script dialog box, as shown in Figure 213-2.

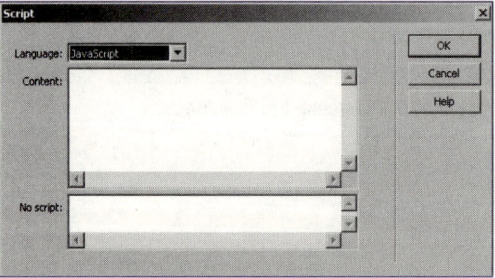

Figure 213-2: Insert Script dialog box

5. Select either JavaScript or VBScript in the Language pop-up menu and then OK to insert the script.

6. Right-click the `<script>` tag in Code view and select Edit Tag `<script>` to bring up the Tag Editor, as shown in Figure 213-3.

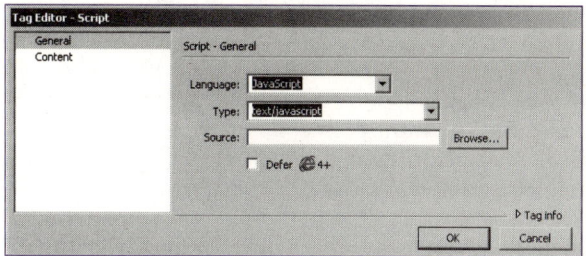

Figure 213-3: Tag Editor

7. Click the Browse button next to the Source field to locate the external script you want to link to. Note that you can also change the script type in this dialog box to other kinds of scripts, including JScript, LiveScript, and PHP.

Task **213**

tip

- If you have set your preferences to display scripts as invisible elements in Design view, you can highlight the script and set its source using the Property Inspector (Step 6).

cross-reference

- Refer to Task 208 for working with JavaScript code.

Preventing Your Handwritten Code from Being Modified

Dreamweaver's Roundtrip HTML feature does a very good job of keeping your handwritten code safe from being rewritten. However, sometimes Dreamweaver will attempt to fix code that appears improperly structured based on its understanding of HTML syntax and rules. This can be a good thing in general, but there are times when you don't want this to occur, especially when working with proprietary tags and third-party scripting languages. You can still have Dreamweaver fix improperly structured code while telling it to leave file types with certain extensions completely alone.

note

▪ This warning only appears after Dreamweaver has fixed or removed any tags, so the only way to undo the changes if you don't want them is to immediately close the document without saving the changes, disable the Code Rewriting preferences, and then reopen the document (Step 6).

1. You can control how and when code is rewritten by modifying the Code Rewriting preferences. To access these preferences, select Edit ⇨ Preferences to display the Preferences dialog box.

2. Click the Code Rewriting category to display the dialog box shown in Figure 214-1.

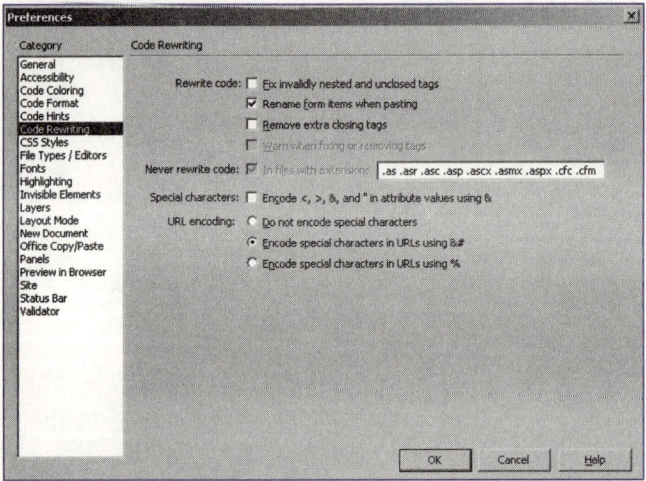

Figure 214-1: Code Rewriting preferences

3. Normally, the Rewrite Code options are turned off by default. To never make any changes to your code, leave the options set to their default.

4. To fix invalidly nested and unclosed tags or to remove extra closing tags, check the appropriate options. Once you check either of these options, the Never Rewrite Code option will no longer be grayed out (see Figure 214-2).

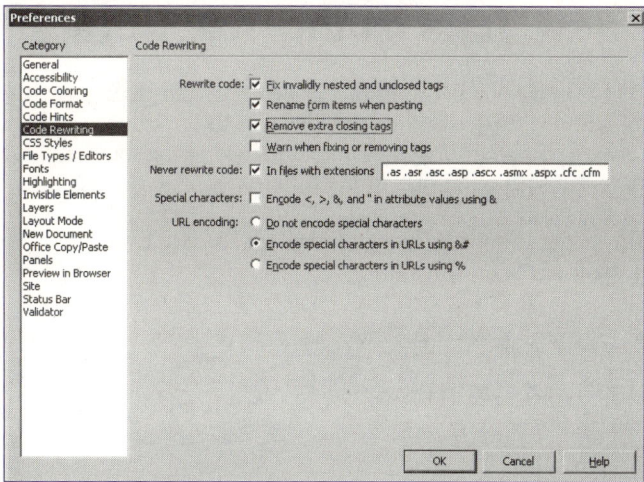

Figure 214-2: Enabling Code Rewriting

5. The Never Rewrite Code option allows you to specify files to leave alone under all circumstances. Enter the extension of the files that you want Dreamweaver to leave alone in the field next to the check box. Notice that you can include many different extension types as long as they begin with a period and each is separated by a space.

6. Check the Warn When Fixing and Removing Tags option, as shown in Figure 214-3.

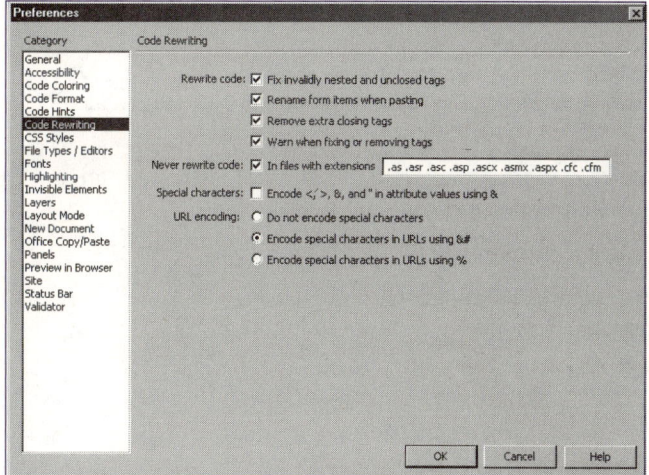

Figure 214-3: The Warn When Fixing and Removing Tags option selected

7. Click OK to apply the changes.

tip

- If you leave the Code Rewriting preferences turned off, Dreamweaver highlights any improperly structured code in yellow in Design view. Double-clicking the highlighted code displays a brief explanation of what problems were found (Step 3).

cross-reference

- Refer to Task 212 for controlling how Dreamweaver writes your code.

Adding New Tags to the Tag Library

While the Tag Library offers a comprehensive list of tags that you can set the formatting options for, it's easy to add new tags to the Library at any time. This will help ensure that additional tags not contained in the standard list are formatted consistently with other tags in the Library.

notes

▪ Changes made with the Tag Library Editor are global changes that affect all tags or attributes with the same name (Step 1).

▪ Most people won't need to make any changes to the tag formatting handled by Dreamweaver. However, if you create new custom tags and/or need to change the formatting of specific existing tags, the Tag Library Editor is the way to go (Step 2).

1. Select Edit ⇨ Tag Library to bring up the Tag Library Editor, as shown in Figure 215-1.

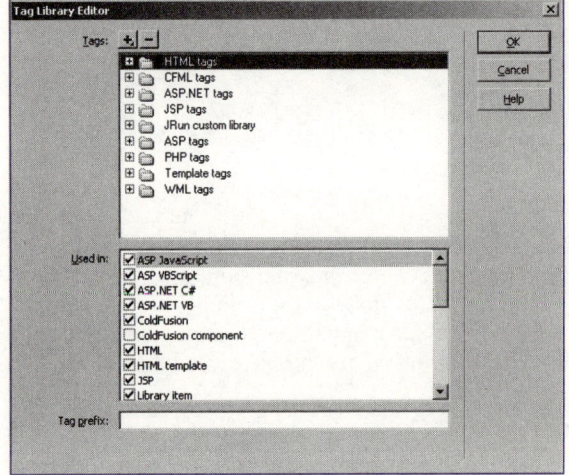

Figure 215-1: Tag Library Editor

2. Click the large plus (+) sign next to the Tags label and select New Tags, as shown in Figure 215-2, to bring up the New Tags dialog box.

3. In the New Tags dialog box, select the Tag Library that you want to add the new tag to from the pop-up list. The HTML tags option listed by default is the most common Library to use.

4. Enter a name for your tag in the Tag Names field.

5. If your tag requires a closing tag (most tags do), check the Have Matching End Tags option, as shown in Figure 215-3.

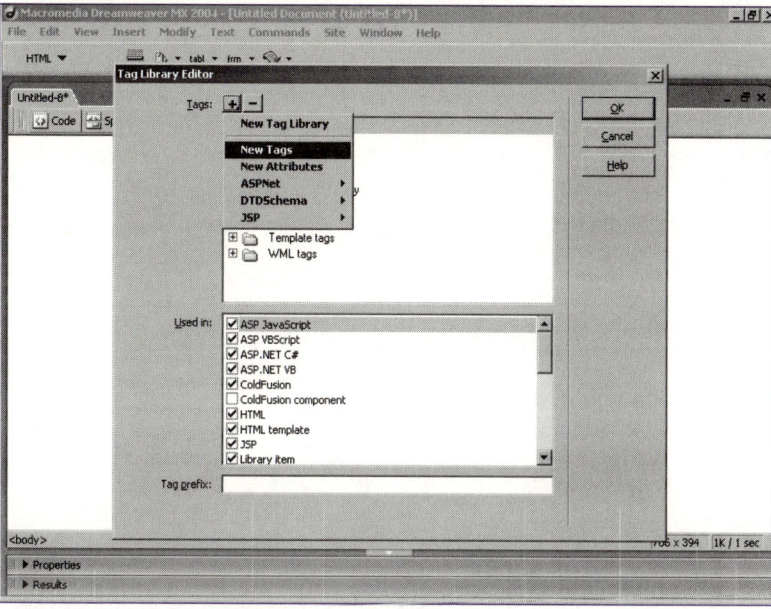

Figure 215-2: Selecting the New Tags option

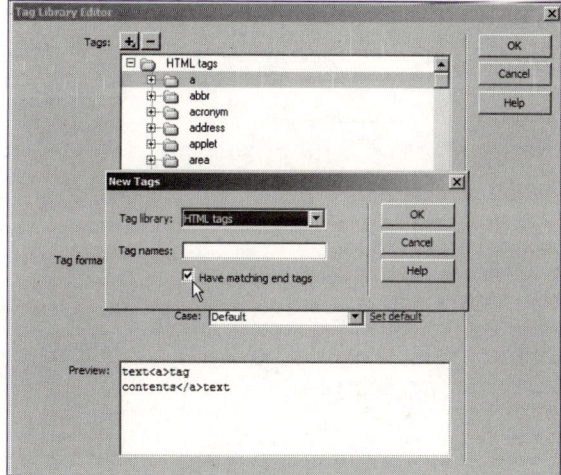

Figure 215-3: The closing tag option selected

cross-reference
- Refer to Task 210 for using the Tag Editor.

6. Click the OK button to add the new tag. The tag is then listed alphabetically in the list of tags in the Tag Library Editor.

7. Click the new tag's name and enter its formatting options in the Tag Library Editor.

Part 12: Setting Up Web Applications

Installing IIS and PWS

Although this task isn't technically part of Dreamweaver, it is something you need to do to test a dynamic site locally. If you are going to use ColdFusion, you won't need this procedure, but you will need it to test ASP (Active Server Pages) locally. In this part of the book and the following part (Part 13), you see how to build dynamic pages for ASP and ColdFusion only. Dreamweaver does support many other server technologies, and many will be very similar to the ColdFusion examples used.

IIS (Internet Information Server) is the preferred application to install, but if you are using Windows 98, you need to install PWS (Personal Web Server).

1. Check your computer to see if you can find an Inetpub folder. If not, you need to install PWS or IIS, or opt to use a hosting service.

2. Double-click the PWS installation file on the Windows 98 CD. Or double-click the file downloaded from the Microsoft Web site. The installation wizard opens, as shown in Figure 216-1.

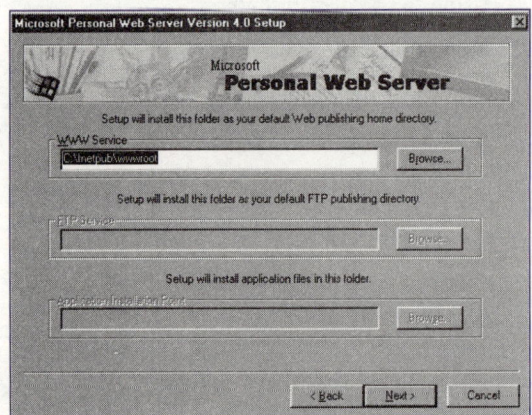

Figure 216-1: The Personal Web Server Installation Wizard

3. Follow the installation wizard directions.

4. When asked for the default Web publishing home directory, accept the default C:\Inetpub\wwwroot and click Finish.

5. In Windows 2000 and Windows XP, choose Start ⇨ Settings ⇨ Control Panel ⇨ Add/Remove Programs, as shown in Figure 216-2.

notes

- Sun's Java System ASP (formerly Sun ONE ASP) and Chili!Soft ASP may be used on Windows, Linux, and Solaris platforms. Macintosh users need to use a Web-hosting service with ASP 2.0 support or install IIS or PWS on a remote (Windows) computer (Step 1).

- Be sure your Web server allows you access to a database. And check that your database type is supported.

- If you'd rather use a hosting service and not test locally, you don't need either of these applications installed.

caution

- If you are going to install ColdFusion but also want or need to have IIS or PWS, install them first, and then ColdFusion.

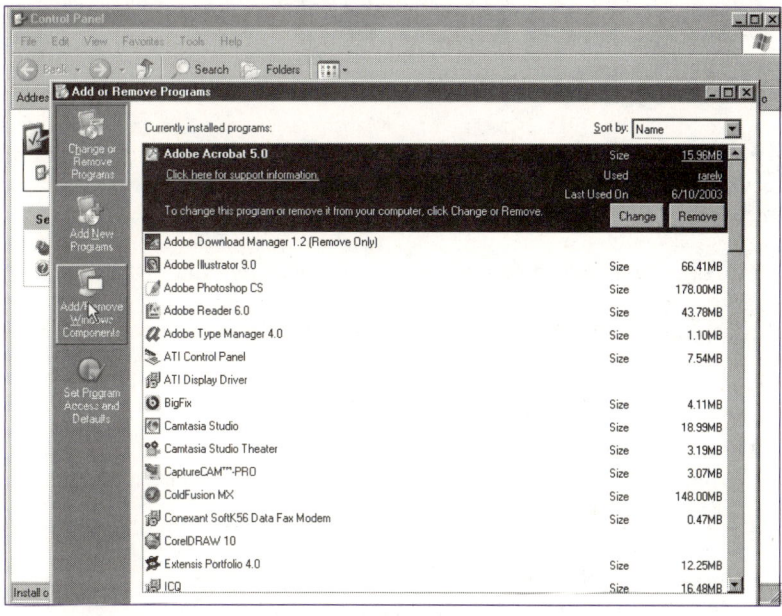

Figure 216-2: The Add/Remove Windows Components option

6. Choose Add/Remove Windows Components.

7. Select the IIS box (see Figure 216-3).

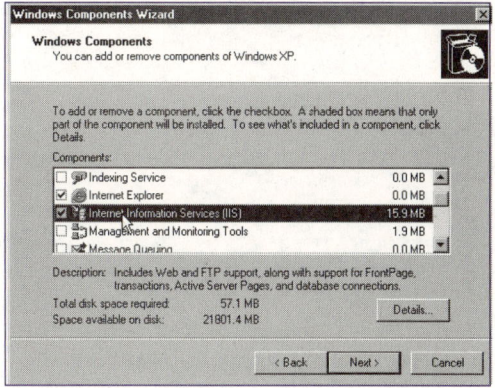

Figure 216-3: The Windows Components Wizard

cross-reference

- Refer to Task 219 for installing ColdFusion MX (Intro).

8. Click Next.

9. Follow the installation steps.

Setting Up a Local Web and Testing Server

PC users can test locally using IIS, PWS, and ColdFusion Developer Edition. Only ASP and ColdFusion server technologies are going to be discussed in this book.

1. Copy the task217 folder to your hard drive. You can get the files from www.wiley.com/compbooks/10simplestepsorless. This folder contains a starting root folder (admin) for a dynamic site.

2. PC users who are testing locally need to copy and paste the admin (task 217) folder in the C:\Inetpub\wwwroot folder.

3. Open Dreamweaver MX 2004 and click Site ⇨ Manage Sites. Then click the New button, select Site, and select the Advanced tab, if it isn't already (see Figure 217-1).

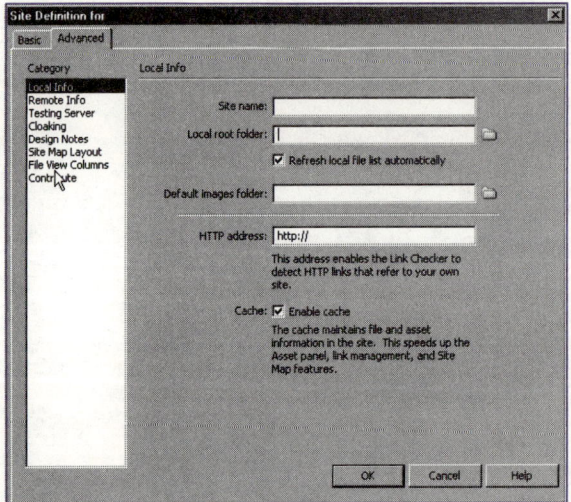

Figure 217-1: The Advanced tab on the Site Definition dialog box

4. Fill in the site name. Click the yellow folder for the Local Root Folder, and navigate to the location where you saved your site's files. Open admin, and then click Select. The filled-in dialog box looks like Figure 217-2.

5. Select the Testing Server category. Choose a server model from the drop-down menu.

6. To the right of the Access field, click the arrow to open the menu of Access options and select Local/Network. The Testing Server folder should be populated already with the same folder you added in the Remote category (see Figure 217-3). The URL prefix should be http://localhost/foldername.

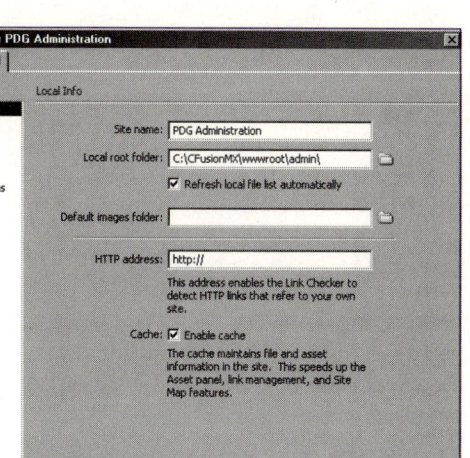

Figure 217-2: The local site information filled in

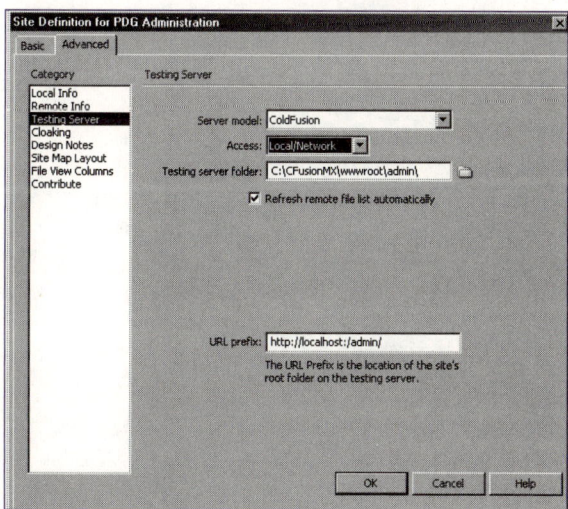

Figure 217-3: The Testing category filled in

7. Click the Basic tab and click Next until you see the Test URL button. If you are using ColdFusionMX standalone, the URL won't work. You'll need to add **8500** to the URL. It should be `http://localhost:8500/admin/`.

8. Click the Advanced tab and click OK to close the Site Definition dialog box. Click Done in the Edit Sites dialog box. The site's cache is created and the dialog box closes.

cross-reference

▪ Refer to Task 11 for defining a site (Step 1).

Task 218

Defining a Remote Web and Testing Server

Macintosh users need to use a remote server option rather than a local one. The exception is if Macintosh users install ColdFusionMX for Macs. Windows users who would rather test on a remote server should also set up for using a remote testing server.

1. Open any local site you may have defined. If you want to use a sample, get the task217 folder from www.wiley.com/compbooks/ 10simplestepsorless and copy the admin folder onto your hard drive. Complete Steps 2 to 4 of this task and proceed.

2. Choose Site ➪ Manage Sites, click a site name, and select Edit or click the New button and select Site. Select the Advanced tab if it isn't already. If this is a new site, be sure to fill in the local information. Figure 218-1 shows the Manage Sites dialog box with the local information filled in.

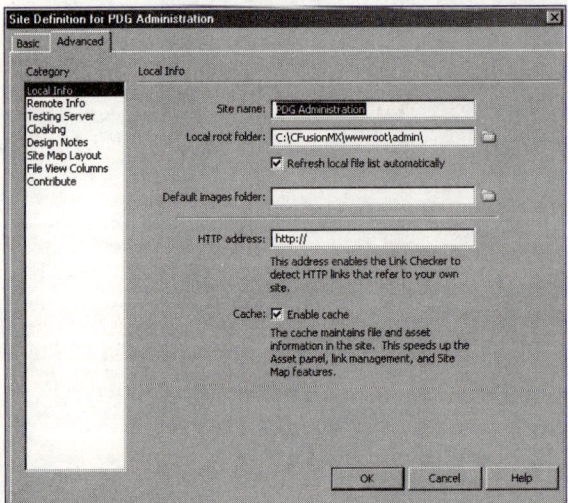

Figure 218-1: The Manage Sites dialog box

3. Select the Remote Info category. From the Access drop-down menu, select FTP.

4. Type in the name of your domain or whatever your hosting server requires to access it, as shown in Figure 218-2. Sometimes it may be the domain name or an IP address. If you aren't sure, ask your hosting server.

5. Enter your username and password and check Passive FTP.

6. If you are online, you can click the Test button to be sure you entered everything properly and that the connection can be made.

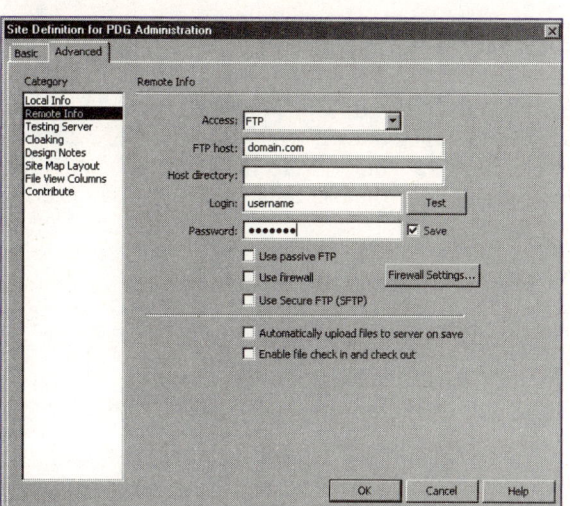

Figure 218-2: FTP selected and host information added

7. Select the Testing Server category.

8. Select the Server Model you want, and then select FTP from the Access drop-down menu.

9. The fields are filled in automatically from the Remote Server category, as shown in Figure 218-3.

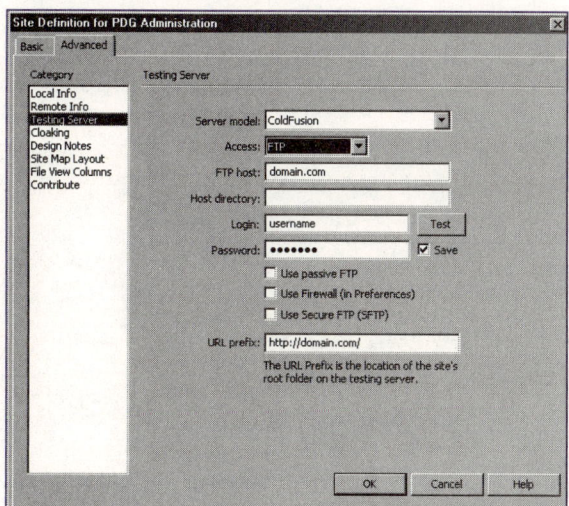

Figure 218-3: The Testing Server category filled in

cross-references
- Refer to Task 82 for putting files.
- Refer to Task 217 for setting up the local information (Step 1).

10. Click the Test button if you are online. Be sure to check the URL prefix and make sure that's correct. You can click OK to close the dialog box and then click Done to exit the Site Manager.

Installing ColdFusion MX

After you install either PWS or IIS, you are ready to install ColdFusion MX. You can install ColdFusion on Windows, Unix, and Mac OSX. This tutorial covers Windows only. The Mac installation needs JEE Run. Although it can be done and the instructions are on Macromedia's site, it isn't an easy job and goes beyond the scope of this book.

notes

- ColdFusion will operate as the Enterprise version for 30 days. If you don't enter a serial number, it will then revert to the Developer Edition (Step 4).

- The Developer Edition means you can use it to test and develop on your machine, but it can't be used to serve files from your computer (Step 4).

1. Download ColdFusion Server from www.macromedia.com.

2. Once downloaded, locate the ColdFusion MX installer.exe file and double-click it. Click Next in the Welcome window.

3. Click I Accept the Terms in the License Agreement after you've read it; then click the Next button.

4. Fill in the customer information. If you've purchased the full version of ColdFusion, enter the serial number. If not, leave it blank, and it will operate as the free Developer Edition. Then click Next (see Figure 219-1).

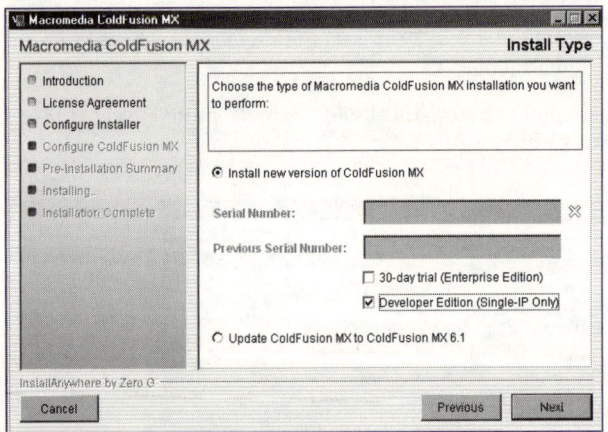

Figure 219-1: The customer information

5. In the Server Configuration dialog box, leave Server Configuration checked unless you are using J2EE. Click Next.

6. In the Web Server Selection dialog box, leave the Built-in Web Server option checked and click Next.

7. Enter a password for the ColdFusion MX administrator, and enter it again in the Confirm field (see Figure 219-2). Click Next. In the Installation confirmation dialog box, click the Install button.

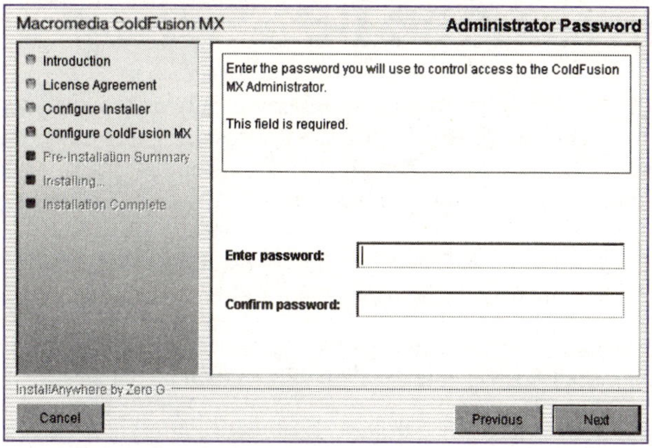

Task **219**

Figure 219-2: The password fields

8. The Install Wizard Completed dialog box opens; click Finish. Click the red x in the upper right corner to close the install interface.

9. If the Administrator window opens, type in the password you entered in Step 7. The window that opens next contains links to a lot of documentation and a sample.

cross-references

- Refer to Task 227 for setting up a ColdFusion DSN (data source name).

- Refer to Task 216 for installing IIS or PWS (Step 1).

Setting Up an ODBC Driver

You only need to do this task if you plan on testing locally or remotely using a DSN connection (refer to Task 221 or 222). Access databases require an ODBC (Open Database Connectivity) driver. If you need another kind of driver for your particular database, substitute it in this task.

notes

- If you are using ColdFusion, put the site files in the ColdFusionMX/www.root folder (Step 5).

- The ODBC Data Source Administrator dialog box now shows the database you added (Step 6).

1. Open Dreamweaver to the defined site you are using with a database. To set up an ODBC driver, choose one of the following options:

   - *Windows 98.* Click Start ⇨ Settings ⇨ Control Panel. Then double-click the ODBC Data Source (32 bit) name to open it.

   - *Windows NT.* Click Start ⇨ Settings ⇨ Control Panel. Double-click the ODBC icon to open it.

   - *Windows 2000.* Click Start ⇨ Settings ⇨ Control Panel. Double-click Administrative Tools, and then double-click the Data Sources (ODBC) to open the ODBC Data Source Administrator.

   - *Windows XP.* Click Start ⇨ Control Panel. Double-click Administrative Tools, and then double-click the Data Sources (ODBC) to open the ODBC Data Source Administrator, as shown in Figure 220-1.

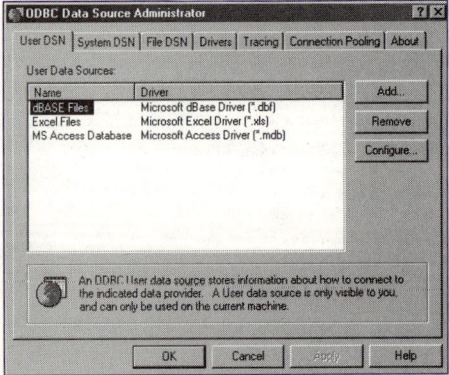

Figure 220-1: The ODBC Data Source Administrator as seen in Windows XP

2. Select the System DSN tab and click the Add button. If you are using Microsoft Access, select Microsoft Access Driver (*.mdb), as shown in Figure 220-2, and click Finish.

3. Type the name of your database in the Data Source Name field.

4. Type a description of your database in the Description field (see Figure 220-3).

5. In the Database area, click the Select button and navigate to the C:\InetPub\wwwroot\(your folder) and select the database file. Click OK.

Task **220**

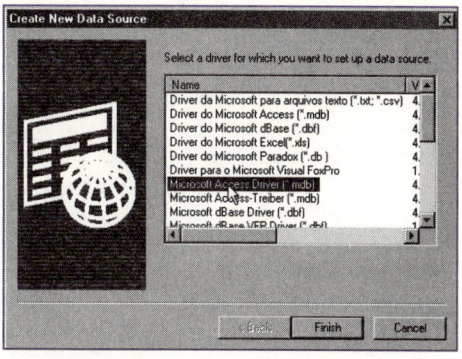

Figure 220-2: Creating a new data source

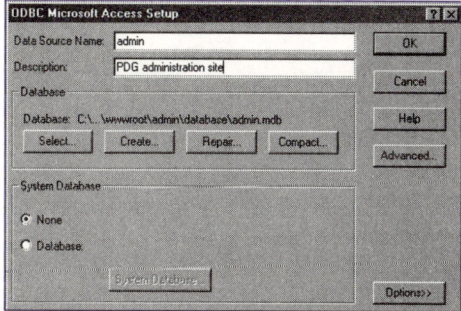

Figure 220-3: The ODBC Microsoft Access Setup dialog box

6. Back in the ODBC Microsoft Access Setup dialog box, click the Options button. Type **4000** in the Page Timeout field and click OK (see Figure 220-4).

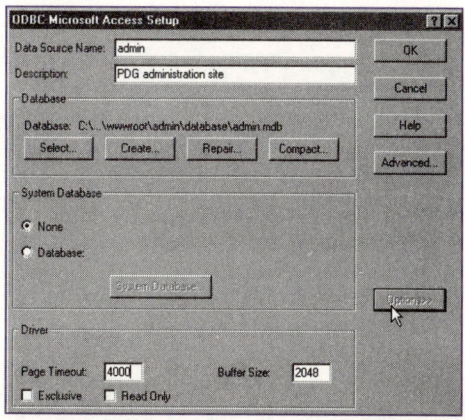

Figure 220-4: The Options area of the ODBC Microsoft Access Setup dialog box

7. Select the name you entered for your database and click OK to complete the setup.

cross-reference

- You can use either a DSN connection (Task 221) or a connection string (Task 223) after you've set up your appropriate drivers to test locally.

Setting Up a Local DSN Connection

A data source name (DSN) needs to be created in order to connect to a database. Then you'll need to get Dreamweaver to connect to the DSN. This task is for Windows users who want to test locally using IIS or PWS. A DSN is a one-word identifier that points to a database. If you are using ColdFusion, refer to Task 227.

If you are using ColdFusion, refer to Task 227.

1. Open your defined site in the Files panel.

2. Double-click one of your ASP files or another appropriate file to open it.

3. Expand the Application panel group by selecting it, and select the Databases tab to make it the active panel (see Figure 221-1).

notes

- You may want to use conn(name). The conn in the front of the name helps identify that this is a connection name when and if you need to edit the code.

- In the Databases panel, you can click the plus (+) sign next to the connection name to see what is available for you to access from the database (Step 10).

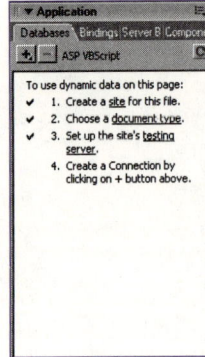

Figure 221-1: The Application panel group with the Databases panel active

4. Click the Add (+) button.

5. Click Data Source Name (DSN), as shown in Figure 221-2.

caution

- If you are developing for ColdFusion, you must perform Task 226 first.

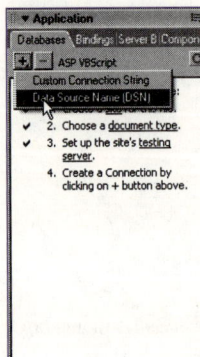

Figure 221-2: The Data Source Name menu option

6. Type a name in the Connection Name field.

7. Click the down arrow for Data Source Name (DSN), and select the name you entered for your database, as shown in Figure 221-3.

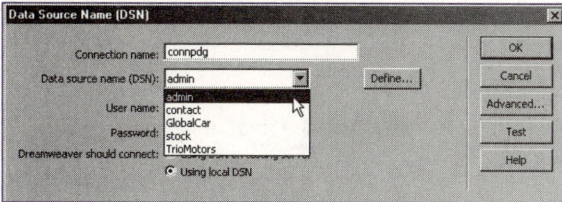

Figure 221-3: Naming the connection

8. Click the Using Local DSN radio button to select it.

9. Click the Test button. You should get a successful connection, as shown in Figure 221-4. Click OK for the connection.

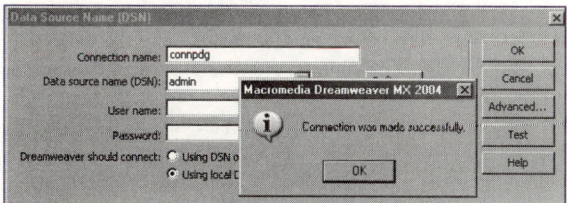

Figure 221-4: The connection is made successfully

10. Click OK to close the dialog box.

cross-reference

• Refer to Task 222 for setting up a DSN if you are using a remote server.

Setting Up a Remote DSN Connection

This task is for Macintosh users and PC users who are testing on a remote server, and it presumes you own a domain and it is hosted with a server provider. This is one of the more difficult tasks, since there are so may variables depending on your own host. Your host does need to set up the DSN name for you.

notes

- Once you select FTP, the dialog box is populated with fields for you to fill in that are appropriate to the access type (Step 3).

- Check In/Out is used when working in a team environment. If this option is selected, it will lock files in use (Step 6).

- This is the server technology that is being used to communicate with the database (Step 7).

1. Open your defined site in the Files panel. Click the site definition down arrow and select Manage Sites. Select your site, and click the Edit button.

2. Select the Advanced tab if it isn't active already, and select the Remote info category.

3. Click the arrow for Access and select FTP. Enter your FTP host connection information in the FTP Host field.

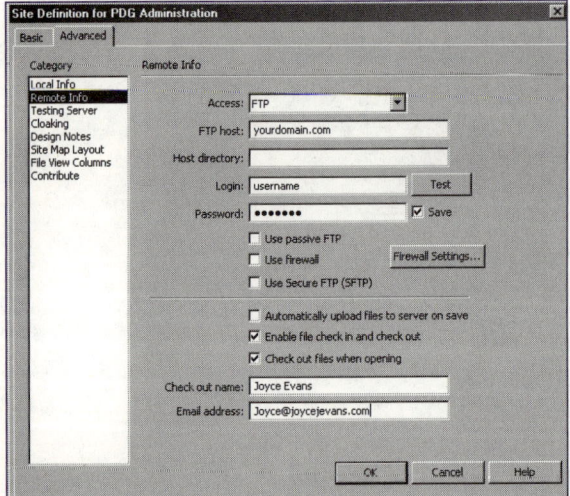

Figure 222-1: The Remote info category

caution

- If you are developing for ColdFusion, you must perform Task 226 first.

4. Type the directory of your database files. If you are unsure, check with your host.

5. Enter your login and password information.

6. If you work with others who may be accessing the same files, select the Check In/Out option. When you are done, click the Test button. A success message should appear, as shown in Figure 222-2.

Macromedia Dreamweaver MX 2004 ✕

ⓘ Macromedia Dreamweaver MX 2004 connected to your Web server successfully.

OK

Figure 222-2: The results of the Test button if it is set up properly

7. Select the Testing Server category. Click the down arrow for the Server Model field and click ASP VBScript. The FTP Host information is automatically added if you've already filled it in with the data you entered in the Remote Info category.

8. Click OK and then Done.

9. Open your site's index page (or appropriate file), and open the Applications panel. Select the Databases panel and set up a connection to your site as in Task 221 (see Figure 222-3).

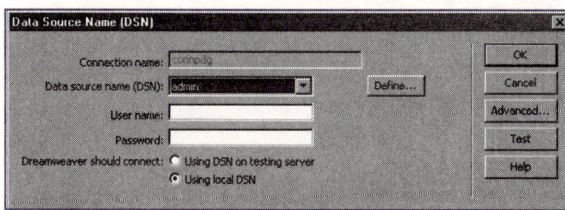

Data Source Name (DSN) ✕

Connection name: connpdq
Data source name (DSN): admin   Define...
User name:
Password:
Dreamweaver should connect: ○ Using DSN on testing server
                             ● Using local DSN

OK
Cancel
Advanced...
Test
Help

Figure 222-3: The Connections dialog box

cross-reference

▪ Refer to Task 217 if you want to test locally (Step 3).

Task 223

Setting Up a DSN-less Connection

Both PC and Mac users can use the DSN-less connection method of setting up a DSN name. You will need to get your server to set the proper permissions for your database folder. You'll also need to know what the full path to your database is (ask your host). Or you can use the MapPath method in Task 224 to determine the path.

notes

- You don't need to define a DSN name.

- Type the path in one line; don't use breaks or paragraph spaces (Step 6).

- You need to be connected to the remote server for the Test button to work. You should get a success message. If not, you need to check your string. Check with your provider that the string is correct and that they are using the latest Microsoft drivers (Step 8).

1. Open a page from your defined site.

2. Click the expander arrow to open the Application panel group. Click the Databases tab to make it the active panel.

3. Click the Add (+) button.

4. Click Custom Connection String, as shown in Figure 223-1.

Figure 223-1: The Custom Connection String dialog box

5. Name your connection (see Figure 223-2).

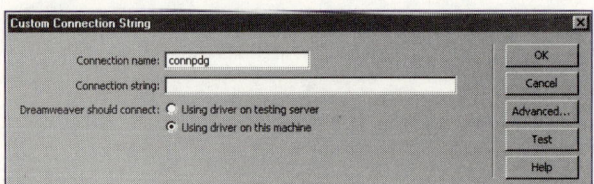

Figure 223-2: Naming the connection

6. In the Connection String field, type in the full path to your database (see Figure 223-3). It'll look similar to this:

```
"DBQ=d:\mydomain.com\wwwroot\Database\assets.mdb;
DRIVE={Microsoft Access Driver (*.mdb)}"
```

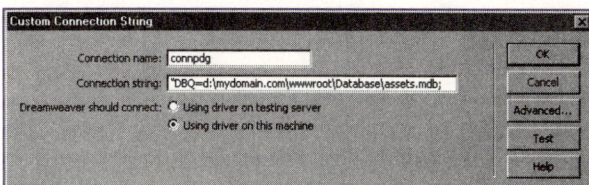

Figure 223-3: The string entered

7. PC users, select the Using Driver on Testing Server option.

8. Click the Test button.

9. Click OK. Figure 223-4 shows the connection added in the Databases panel.

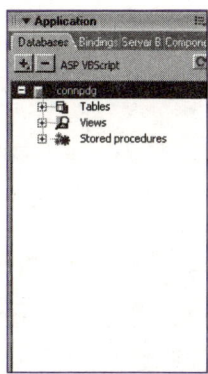

Figure 223-4: The connection added

cross-reference

▪ Refer to Task 225 for uploading your files to a server.

Using the MapPath Method

If for some reason you can't get your hosting service to provide you with the full path—or more likely they are too slow about it—you can use the MapPath method. This determines the full path of your database. Use only one of the methods described in Tasks 221 to 224. You will need to have a database folder with your database in it.

1. Upload your files to the remote server, and make a note of the virtual path. Virtual paths usually use your domain name, such as:

   www.mydomain.com/database/contact.mdb

2. Open a site page from the local site root folder using the Files panel, as shown in Figure 224-1.

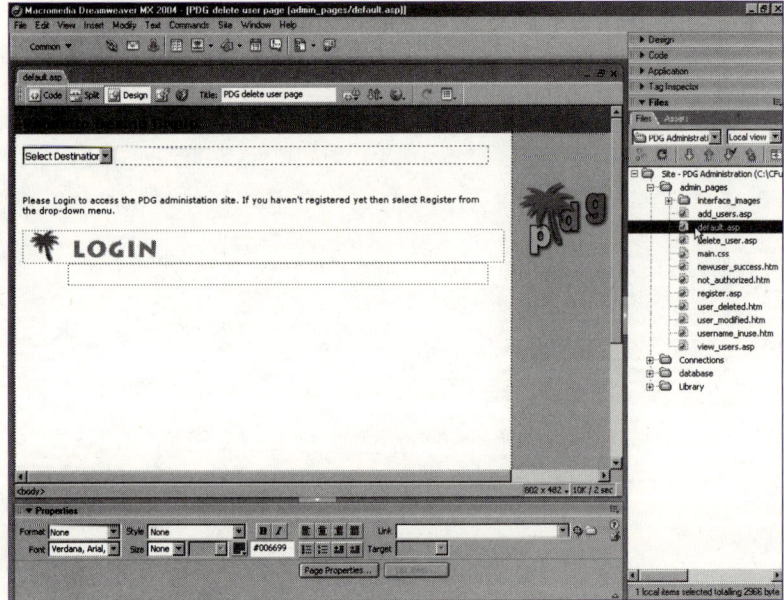

Figure 224-1: A page opened in a defined site using the Files panel

3. Click the Databases panel in the Application panel group, as shown in Figure 224-2.

Figure 224-2: The Databases panel

4. Click the Add (+) button.

5. Click Custom Connection String.

6. Name the connection.

7. In the Connection String field, add the following, substituting your folder names (also see Figure 224-3):

```
"DRIVER={Microsoft Access Driver (*.mdb)};DBQ=" &
Server.MapPath("yourfolder\ database\(databasename).mdb")
```

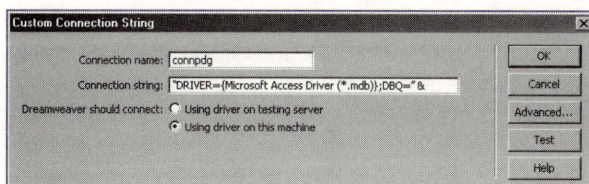

Figure 224-3: The Connection dialog box

8. PC users select the Using Driver on Testing Server option.

9. Click the Test button.

10. If the connection is successful, close the dialog box by pressing OK (see Figure 224-4).

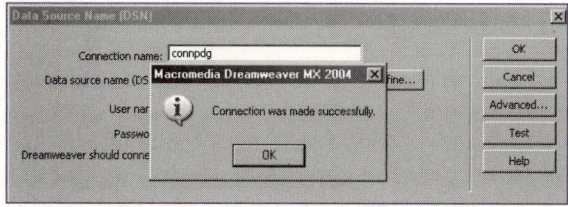

Figure 224-4: A successful connection

cross-reference

- Refer to Task 221 for setting up a local DSN (and not use MapPath) (Step 1).

Transferring Files to a Server

Your files (including the database) need to be transferred to either the local testing server or the remote testing server. To transfer your files to a remote server, you need to be online.

1. Press F8 to open the Files panel (see Figure 225-1).

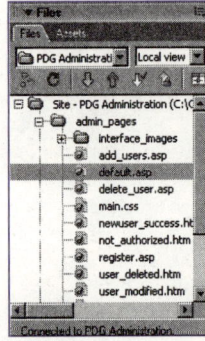

Figure 225-1: The Files panel

2. Click the Expand/Collapse icon to expand it to view both the local and remote root folders, as shown in Figure 225-2.

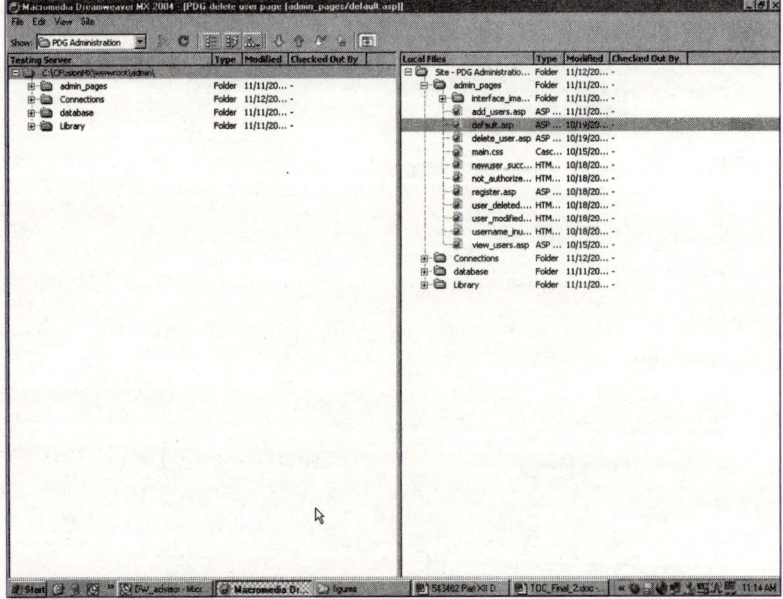

Figure 225-2: The Files panel expanded

3. Click either the Connect or the Refresh icon to connect.

notes

- If you are using a remote site, you see a note about clicking the icon in the toolbar to connect to the server. If you are developing locally, the text will say to click the Refresh icon (Step 3).

- The other arrow next to Put is Get. Get moves selected files or folders from the remote root folder to the local root folder (Step 5).

- If you select a file to put that is within another directory, Dreamweaver uploads to the proper directory—or it will add one if necessary. This is one of the greatest advantages of Dreamweaver's site management capabilities (Step 5).

caution

- If the Files panel is already open, pressing F8 toggles it closed (Step 1).

4. On the right side are you local files. Select the root folder if you want to upload (put) the entire site. Figure 225-3 shows the root folder in the Local view selected.

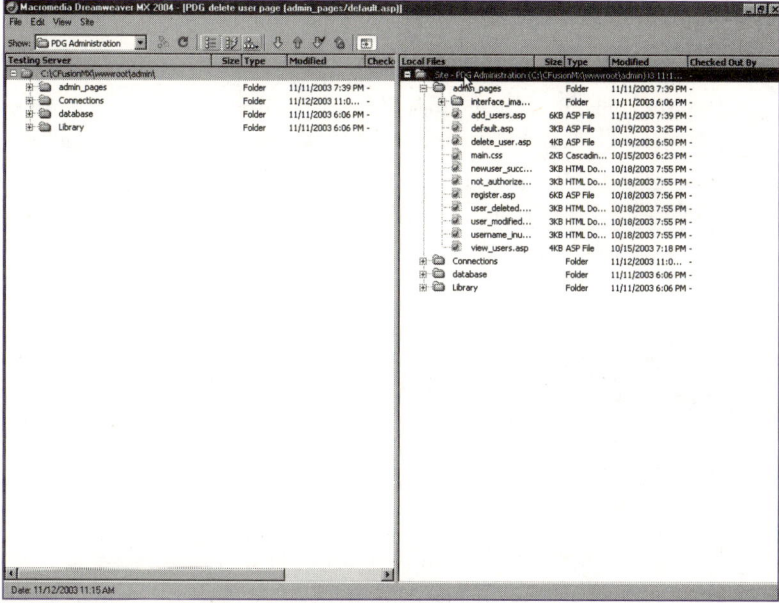

Figure 225-3: The root folder selected for upload

5. Click the Put icon (the blue up arrow in Figure 225-4) to place all your files onto the remote Web server.

6. Click OK for the message asking if you are sure you want to put the entire site.

7. Click the Expand/Collapse button to return the Files panel to its collapsed state.

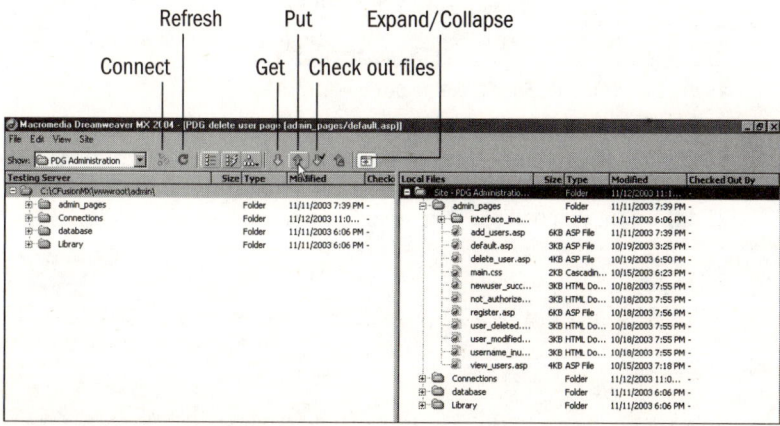

Figure 225-4: The Files panel

cross-reference

▪ Refer to Task 22 for checking files in and out (Step 6).

RDS Login for ColdFusion

Remote Development Services (RDS) must be configured before you set up a DSN for connecting to your database. The RDS login is enabled in ColdFusion MX 2003 Server by default. When you installed it, you had to enter a password.

notes

- You don't need to define a DSN name (see Task 221 or 222). Add a ColdFusion data source if you use this method.

- If you don't have a page open when you access the Databases panel, the links are grayed out (Step 2).

- Once you log in, the Databases panel shows the predefined data sources (Step 5).

1. Double-click one of your site's files in the Files panel to open it. Your site files will be ColdFusion pages with a .cfm extension, not .asp.

2. Press Ctrl+Shift+F10 to bring up the Databases panel in the Application panel group.

3. Click the RDS login link, which is number 4, as shown in Figure 226-1.

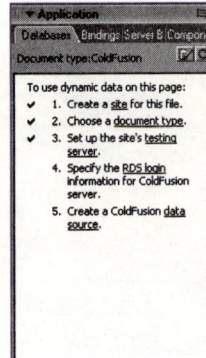

Figure 226-1: The Databases panel showing the RDS login link

4. Type your RDS login, as shown in Figure 226-2.

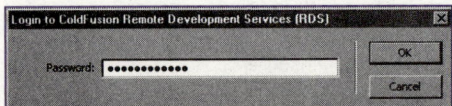

Figure 226-2: The RDS login dialog box

5. Click OK. Figure 226-3 shows any databases defined in ColdFusion. If you have installed the sample databases that shipped with ColdFusion, you will see them listed.

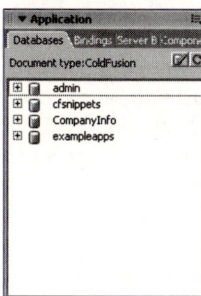

Figure 226-3: The Databases panel showing the predefined data sources

cross-references

- Refer to Task 217 or 218 for setting up a testing server. This has to be done prior to the RDS login (Step 2).

- Refer to Task 227; you'll need to set up the ColdFusion data sources.

Adding a ColdFusion Data Source

In this task, you create a DSN (data source name) to add a data source for your ColdFusion site in Dreamweaver. Be sure you have installed ColdFusion first (see Task 219). If you are using ColdFusion and testing remotely, this is not the correct task for you.

notes

- The Bindings panel is part of the Applications panel group (Step 1).

- The new data source is available in your Data Sources table. The small icons to the left of each data source allow you to edit, verify, and delete the data source (Step 7).

1. Open one of your site's pages from the Files panel. Press Ctrl/Command+F10 to open the Bindings panel.

2. Click the data source link (number 5 on the list). If the link isn't present, click the Modify Data Sources icon, as shown in Figure 227-1.

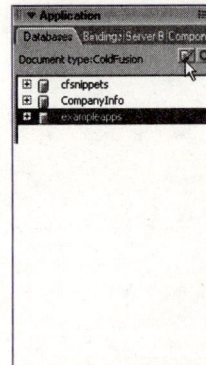

Figure 227-1: The Modify Data Sources icon

3. Enter the login password you set up when you installed ColdFusion MX Server. This opens the ColdFusionMX Administrator, as shown in Figure 227-2.

4. In the Data Sources dialog box, type your database name into the Data Source Name field and choose Microsoft Access as the driver type, as shown in Figure 227-3.

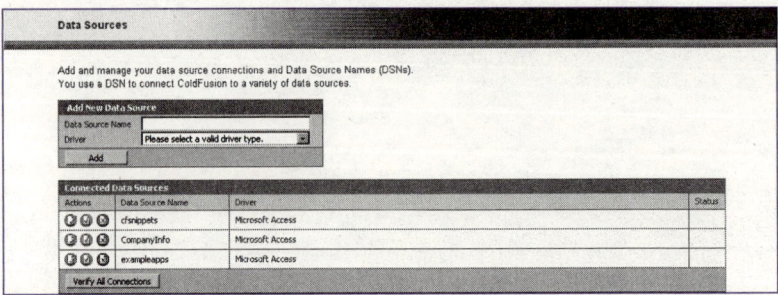

Figure 227-2: The ColdFusionMX Administrator

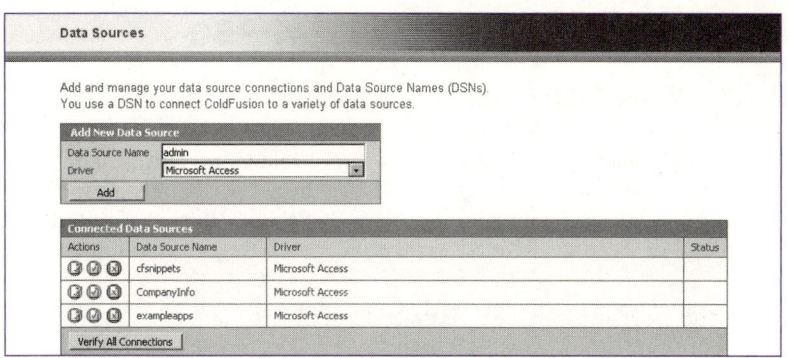

Figure 227-3: Selecting the data source name and the driver type

5. Click the Add button on the Microsoft Access screen.

6. Click the Browse button for the database file, navigate to your C:\CFusionMX\wwwroot\(yourfolder)\database folder, and select the yourdatabase.mdb database file (see Figure 227-4).

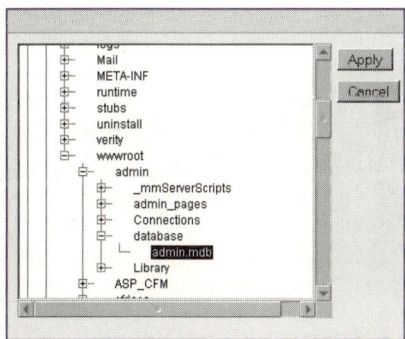

Figure 227-4: Select your database file

7. Click the Apply button.

8. Click the Submit button to build the new DSN.

9. Log out and close the CFMX Administrator.

cross-reference

- Refer to Task 218 if you are testing remotely.

Applying Directory Database Permissions

When you have your database in your root folder and testing and/or remote server locations, you'll need to be sure the proper permissions are set so that users can interact with your database. By default, IIS allows visitors to read your files. You need to add read/write privileges to the database folder.

notes

• If you get errors such as "your recordset must use updateable query" or "the system could not lock your file" or the "database is read-only," your permissions are not set properly.

• This task is for NTFS volumes only. If you have FAT32, you won't need to do this. But you may need to check the permissions on a remote server.

1. Use Windows Explorer or My Computer to browse to your site's root folder.

2. Right-/Control+click the database folder and select Properties. Depending on your operating system, the dialog box may vary.

3. In the Properties dialog box, select the Sharing tab. Select Share This Folder, type in the database name, and select the user limit of Maximum Allowed, as shown in Figure 228-1.

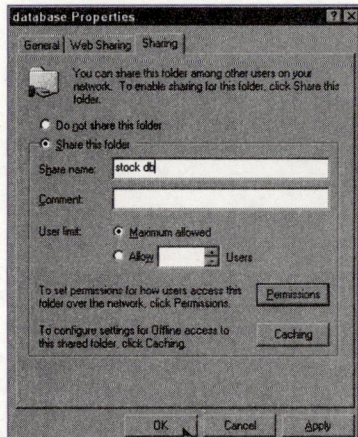

Figure 228-1: The Sharing tab dialog info filled in

4. Click the Permissions button. In the Permissions dialog box, click Add to open the Select Users, Computers, or Groups dialog box. Select the IUSR account from the list in the upper window. This activates the Add button. Click the Add button to move the account into the lower window, as shown in Figure 228-2. Then click OK to return to the Permissions dialog box.

5. The Permissions for your database name (I used stock db) dialog box now has Internet Guest Account added and active. Select Full Control under the Allow heading, as shown in Figure 228-3, and click OK.

6. For Windows XP users, simply open Windows Explorer, click the Tools menu, select Folder Options. Click the View tab, and in the Advanced Settings panel, uncheck the Use Simple File Sharing box to deselect it, as shown in Figure 228-4. Click OK.

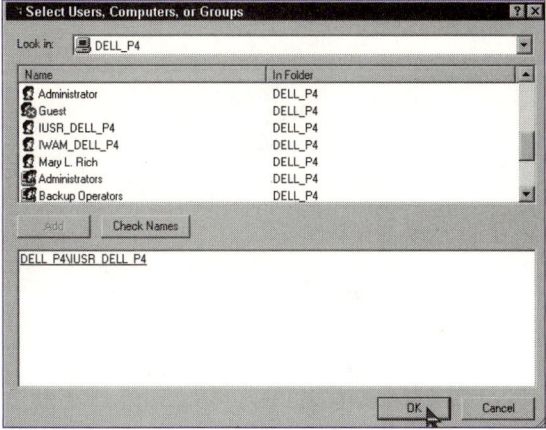

Figure 228-2: An IUSR account being added

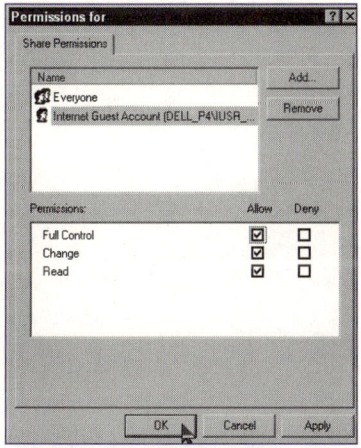

Figure 228-3: The permissions are set for full control.

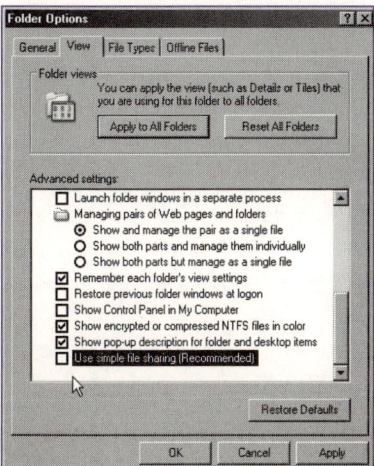

Figure 228-4: Permissions being set for Windows XP

cross-reference

- Refer to Part 13 for adding information to and retrieving information from the database (Step 6).

Part 13: Making Your Site Dynamic

Task **229**

Adding a Recordset

note

▪ Notice that the columns correspond to the headings you see in the sample document. The text and image will be supplied dynamically from a database (Step 8).

A *recordset* is a query that extracts information from a table. Before adding a recordset, you need to perform Task 222. You can use the sample Shopping Cart site (detail folder) if you'd like. You also need to set the DSN. You'll find the necessary file in the task229 folder at `www.wiley.com/compbooks/ 10simplestepsorless`.

1. If you are using the sample files, define the site and then open the product_details.asp page. Or open any page where you want to add a recordset. You have your testing server set up as well.

2. Open the Applications panel group and select the Bindings panel (Window ➪ Bindings).

3. Click the Add (+) button and select Recordset (Query), as shown in Figure 229-1.

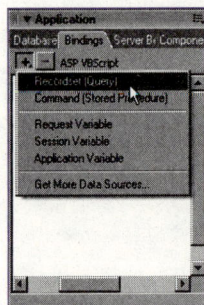

Figure 229-1: Selecting the Recordset (Query) option

4. Name the recordset. For this example I used rsDetails.

5. Select the Connection. For this sample select stock. If you don't see tables for Jewelry and Ornaments, click the Define button and be sure the correct DSN name is selected. Select the Ornaments table.

6. If you want all the columns, leave the All option selected. For this sample Task, select Selected and select everything except OrnamentID, Instructions, and OrnamentPrice.

7. Figure 229-2 shows the completed Recordset dialog box. Click OK to close it.

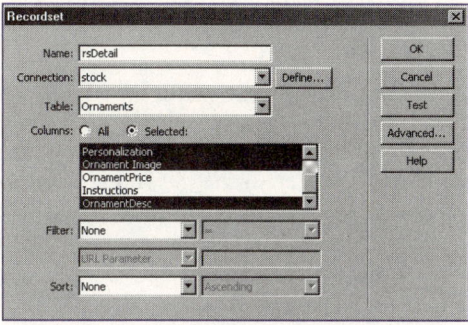

Figure 229-2: The completed Recordset dialog box

8. In the Bindings panel, click the plus (+) sign next to the recordset. You'll see the columns of the table you selected, as shown in Figure 229-3.

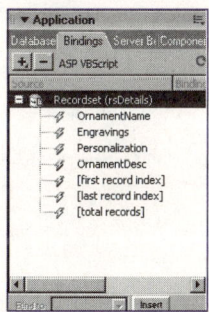

Figure 229-3: The recordset is added to the page

9. Save your document.

cross-references

▪ Refer to Task 217 or Task 218 for setting up your remote and testing servers (Step 1).

▪ Refer to Tasks 230 and 231 for adding the dynamic text and images to the details page (Step 9).

Adding Dynamic Text

In Dreamweaver, you can place dynamic data in most places on a Web page or in its source code. Dynamic data can be placed in a specific point on a page, or it can replace a string of text or be put in the properties of form objects, images, or other objects to make them dynamic. If you are using the sample files from www.wiley.com/compbooks/10simplestepsorless in the task229 details folder, you can add the dynamic text to the product_details page. If you are using the sample files, you'll need to perform Task 229 first.

1. If you are using the sample files, define the site and then open the product_details.asp page in the detail\html subfolder. Or open any page you want to add dynamic text to. This task assumes you've defined a site, set up the DSN name (Database tab), set up the testing server, and added a recordset.

2. Open the Applications panel group and select the Bindings panel (Window ⇨ Bindings).

3. Make sure the Bindings panel lists the content source you want to use. Click the plus (+) sign to check the columns defined. Figure 230-1 shows the Bindings panel for the product_details.asp page.

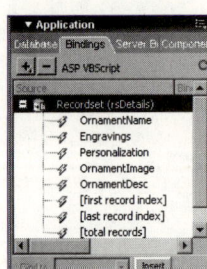

Figure 230-1: The Bindings panel for the products_details.asp page.

4. In Design view, select text on the page, or click where you want to add dynamic text. For the sample page, click below the Ornament Name heading.

5. In the Bindings panel, select a content source from the list. If you select a recordset, specify the column you want in the recordset. For the products_detail page, select OrnamentName.

6. Click Insert, or drag the content source onto the page. Figure 230-2 shows the OrnamentName selected, as well as the Insert button and the code, highlighted in blue, added to the document.

note

- To get your cursor below the Ornament Name heading, place it behind the heading and press Enter/Return (Step 5).

caution

- If you have problems previewing, be sure you have the correct permissions set to the database folder. You need read for the folder and write for the database file. Another thing to check is the DSN setup; change the timeout to 5,000 (Step 8).

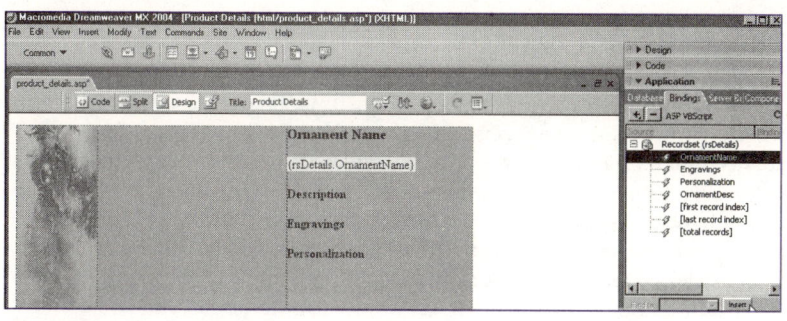

Figure 230-2: The code added to the document that tells the database what information to insert

7. If you are using the sample file, repeat for the other headers, selecting the appropriate column name.

- *Description*. OrnamentDesc

- *Engravings*. Engravings

- *Personalization*. Personalization

8. Test in a browser and you'll see the text added to the fields, as shown in Figure 230-3.

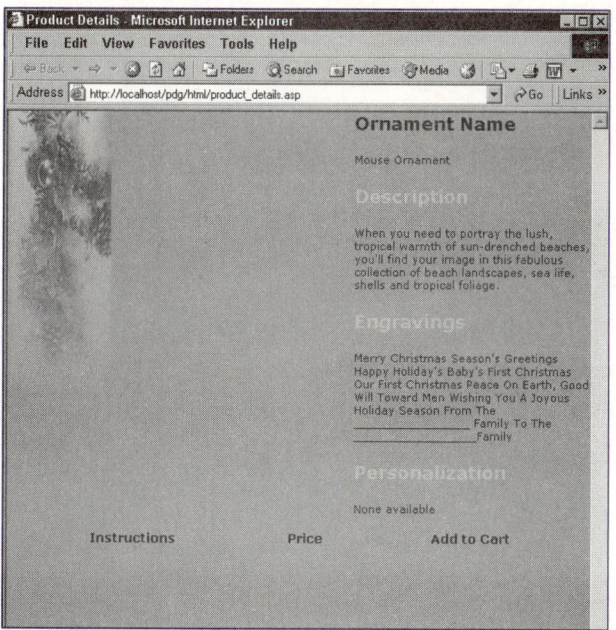

Figure 230-3: Text added dynamically to the page

cross-references

- Refer to Task 222 for setting up the DSN name and timeout (Step 5).

- Refer to Task 231 for adding dynamic images and data (Step 5).

Adding Dynamic Images

Y ou can make images on your page dynamic. If you are using the sample files from www.wiley.com/compbooks/10simplestepsorless in the task229 details folder, you can add the dynamic image to the product_details page.

1. If you are using the sample files, define the site and then open the product_details.asp page. Or open any page where you want to add dynamic text. This task assumes you've defined a site, set up the DSN name (Database tab), set up the testing server, and added a recordset.

2. With the page open in Design view (View ➪ Design), place the insertion point where you want the image to appear on the page. For the sample products_details page, place the cursor in the center column.

3. Select Insert ➪ Image. The Select Image Source dialog box appears, as shown in Figure 231-1. Navigate to the folder that contains your images. Copy the URL path.

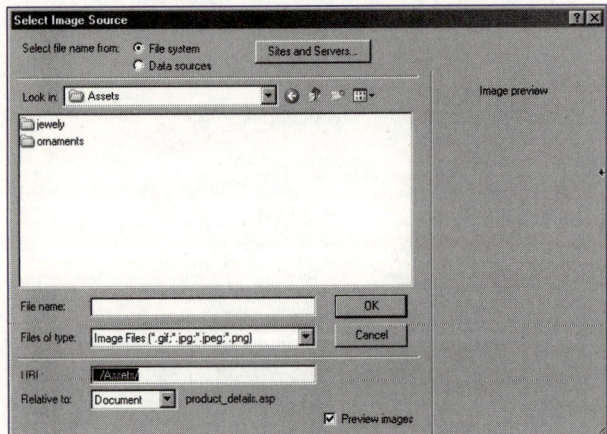

Figure 231-1: The Select Image Source dialog box

4. Click the Data Sources option (Windows) or the Data Source button (Macintosh) at the top of the dialog box. A list of content sources appears, as shown in Figure 231-2.

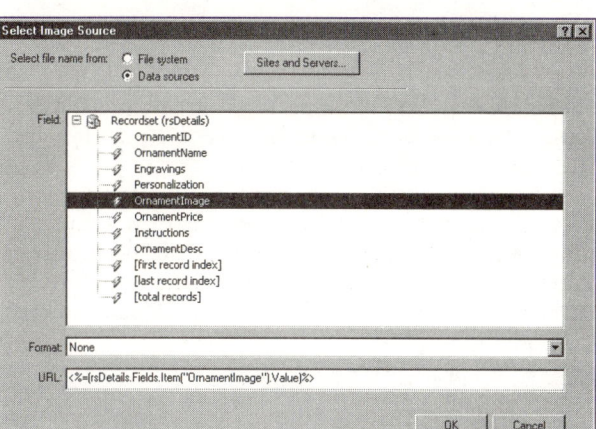

Figure 231-2: The data sources selected and the OrnamentImage selected

5. Select a content source from the list. For this example, select OrnamentImage, as shown in Figure 231-2.

6. Place your cursor in front of the URL field and type in the path to your images. For this sample, my path is ../Assets/ornaments/.

7. Click OK.

8. Test in a browser. It will look like Figure 231-3.

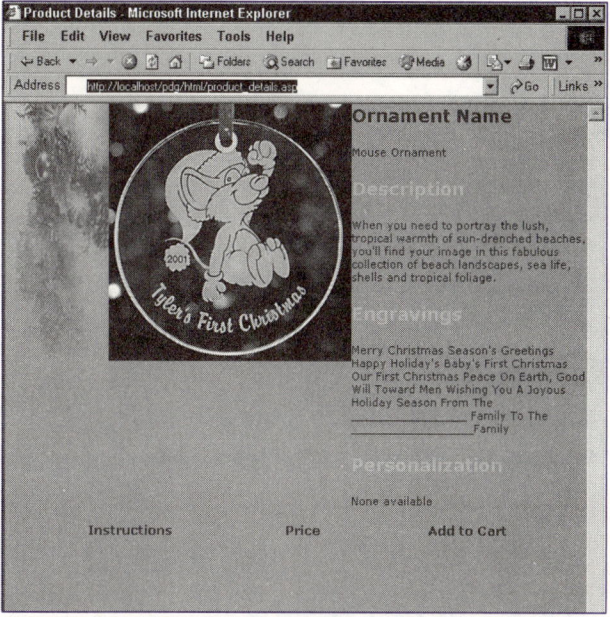

Figure 231-3: The image is added to the page dynamically

cross-references

- Refer to Task 229 for adding a recordset.

- If you want to make existing images dynamic, refer to Task 232.

Making HTML Attributes Dynamic

Dynamic data may include sources such as images, form objects, Flash, Active X, and other objects supported by Macromedia Dreamweaver.

1. To make attributes dynamic with the Property inspector, select an HTML object in Design view and open the Property inspector (Window ⇨ Properties). You can use the products_details1.asp page (Task 229 folder at the companion Web site) to practice on if you'd like. It has a placeholder image inserted, as shown in Figure 232-1.

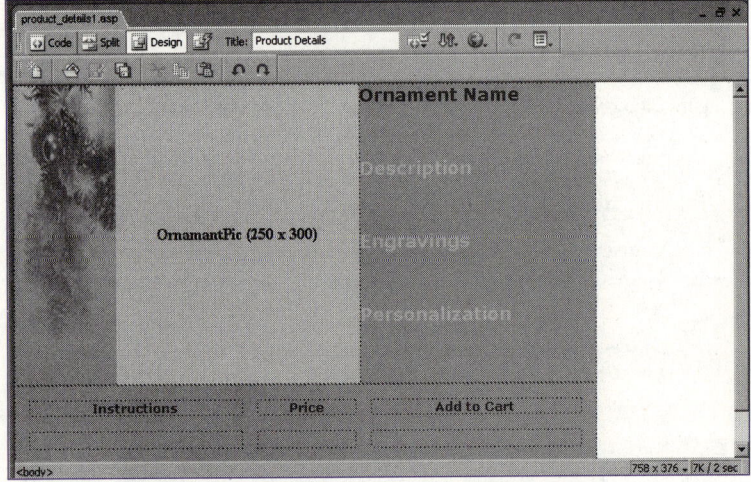

Figure 232-1: A sample file with a placeholder image inserted

2. To bind a dynamic content source to the HTML attribute, click the folder icon to open a file selection dialog box; then click the Data Sources option to display a list of data sources, as shown in Figure 232-2. Refer to Task 231.

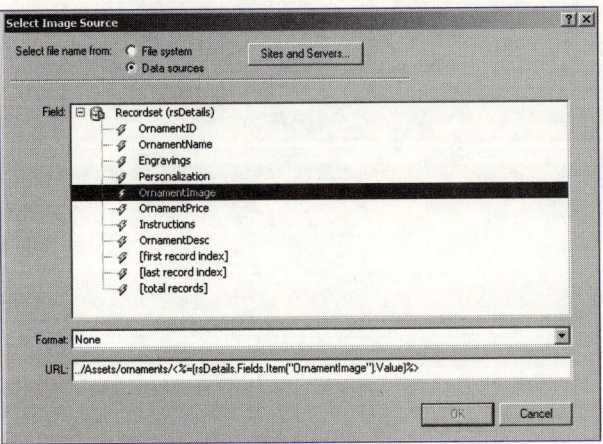

Figure 232-2: Binding the attribute

3. To make the attribute's value dynamic using the Tag inspector, open the Tag inspector and select Attributes to activate its panel. Select the Show List view icon, and then select the desired attribute. Click the lightning bolt icon or folder at the end of the attributes row. Figure 232-3. shows a lightning bolt selected and the list of data sources that opens.

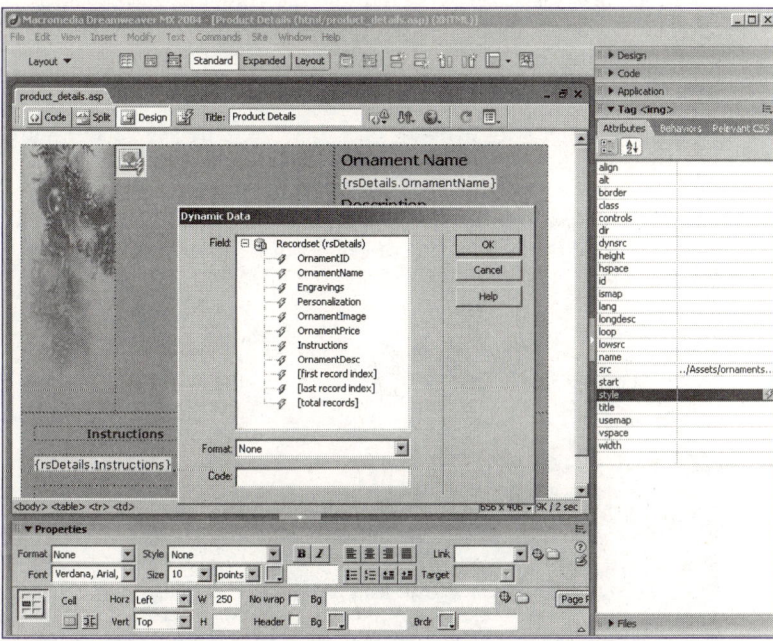

Figure 232-3: A list of the data sources available for the selected object

4. Select a source of content (column from your table) from the list of content sources. The content source should hold data that's appropriate for the HTML attribute you want to bind. If no content sources appear in the list, or if the available content sources don't meet your needs, define a new content source. Click OK.

cross-reference

- Refer to Task 222 for setting up the DSN name, which is where you select the database.

Formatting Dynamic Data

You can format how your dynamic data displays just like any other page elements. You format the table as well as the text that is returned for dynamic text.

1. If you've done Tasks 229 and 230 using the sample files, you can open the products_details.asp page, which is part of the Shopping Cart site (partXIII task229 details folder at www.wiley.com/compbooks/10simplestepsorless).

2. Or open any page with dynamic data that you want to format. Figure 233-1 shows the products_details.asp page as viewed in Live Data view in Dreamweaver. The highlighted text is what is being pulled from the database. Notice how the highlighted text is right next to the image, and the text in the bottom portion (order section) is too close together as well.

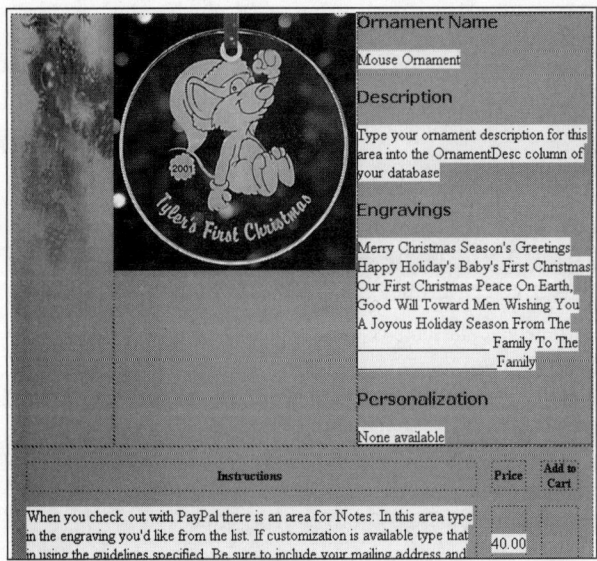

Figure 233-1: The dynamic data against the image

3. Click the text and look at the Tag Selector. You'll notice the text has `<p>` paragraph tags and it's in a column/cell that has a `<td>` tag. To add a CSS style, you need to define the paragraph and the cell tags. Of course, this style will affect all paragraphs and cells in the document unless you apply a separate style to other areas—which you'll do.

4. Add a new style and group `<p>` and `<td>` tags. I'm making my font 10-point Verdana and in the Box category, setting all the margins to 8. This moves the text away from the image but not the titles.

notes

- A workaround for too much text is to add an additonal column to the database and add the server logic to pull it from the database right after the current content (Step 6).

- If your spacer is next to the Add to Cart text, forcing it to the left, place it before the text (Step 8).

caution

- When you edit a style, the style sheet opens without your knowing it. Be sure to save the file before you close it or your changes won't take effect. (Save All will do the job.) [Step 3]

5. Repeat Step 4 for the heading tags (the example has h3 and h4 tags).

6. The Engravings section needs line breaks in the entry. This needs to be fixed in the database. I added `<br>` tags after each entry. But Access has a 255-character limit, so I moved part of the text to the Personalization section, as shown in Figure 233-2.

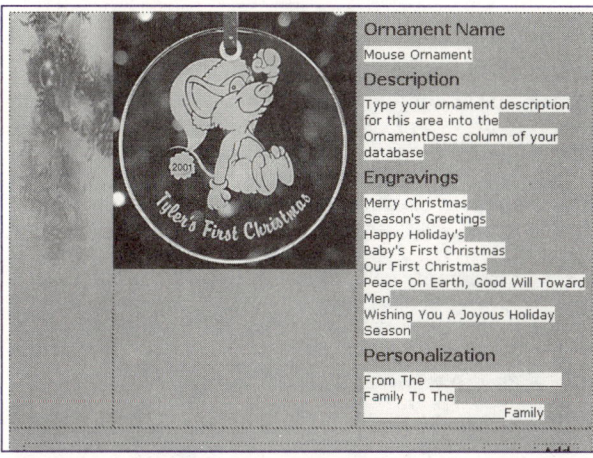

Figure 233-2: The text in the ornament column newly formatted

7. Click anywhere in the row with the instructions and price in it, and select the `<tr>` tag in the Tag Selector to select the entire row. In the Property inspector, set the Vert alignment to Bottom. This forces the price to go to the bottom of the cell.

8. Insert your cursor in the Price cell (where the text is) and insert a spacer.gif, making it 50 pixels wide. Insert your cursor in the Add to Cart column and set the width (W) to 100 pixels.

9. Insert your cursor where the price number is and set the Horz cell alignment to Center.

10. View your page and see how much better it looks.

cross-reference

- Refer to Task 162 for grouping tag selectors and making a new style (Step 4).

Viewing a Record from a Database

I'll use the PDG administration site to demonstrate this technique. You'll need to define the site, set the DSN, and add a recordset; then you'll be ready to go. You can get the file at www.wiley.com/compbooks/10simplestepsorless in the task229 folder.

note

▪ For the recordset for this page, all you need to select is the last name, first name, and e-mail address (Step 2).

1. If you are using the sample files, copy the admin folder into the Inetpub/wwwroot folder, define the site, and then open the view_users.asp page in the admin/html/admin_pages folder. Or open any page you want to use. You have to have your testing server set up as well. The DSN name should be set and a recordset added.

2. Open the Applications panel group and select the Bindings panel (Window ➪ Bindings). Expand the recordset to view all the columns.

3. Place your cursor in the empty cell below the Last Name column, as shown in Figure 234-1.

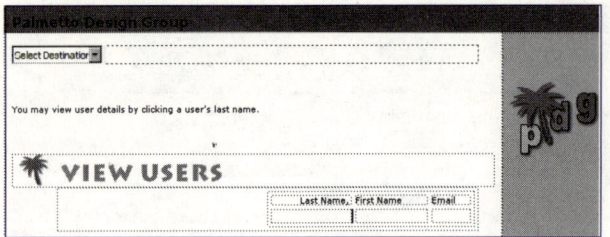

Figure 234-1: The cursor set where you want to add the dynamic code to pull the Last Name from the database

4. In the Bindings panel, select the LastName column and click the Insert button. Figure 234-2 shows what it looks like in your document. If you preview in your browser, you see one last name from the database displayed.

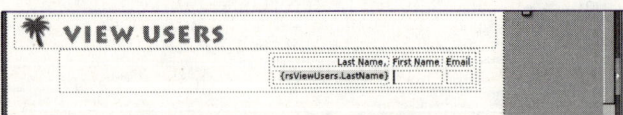

Figure 234-2: The dynamic code added to your document between {}

5. Click in the second cell under the first name column, select FirstName from the Bindings panel, and click the Insert button.

6. Click to place your cursor in the cell below the Email column. Type **Send Email** and highlight it to select it. In the Property inspector, type **mailto:** into the Link field, as shown in Figure 234-3.

7. Save the page.

Task **234**

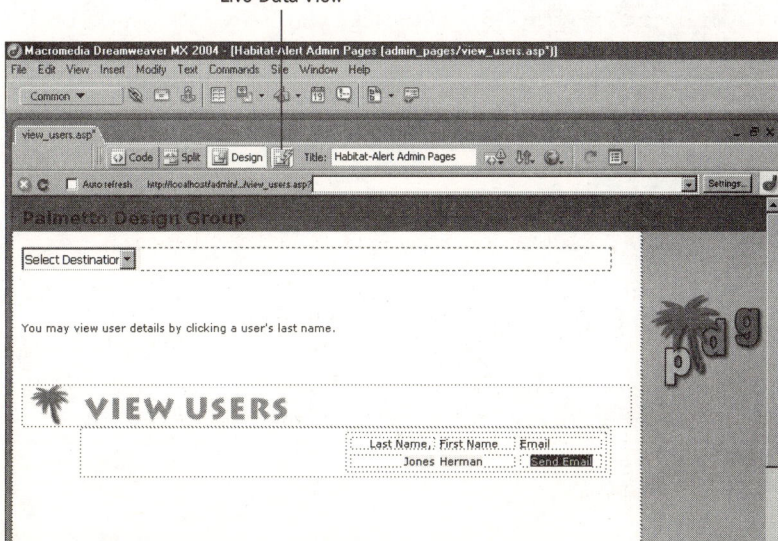

Figure 234-3: The e-mail text added and a link placed in the Property inspector

8. Click the Live Data View icon (it may take a while) to view one entry
   from your database. To view more than one record, you need to add a
   Repeat Region behavior. Figure 234-4 shows Live Data view.

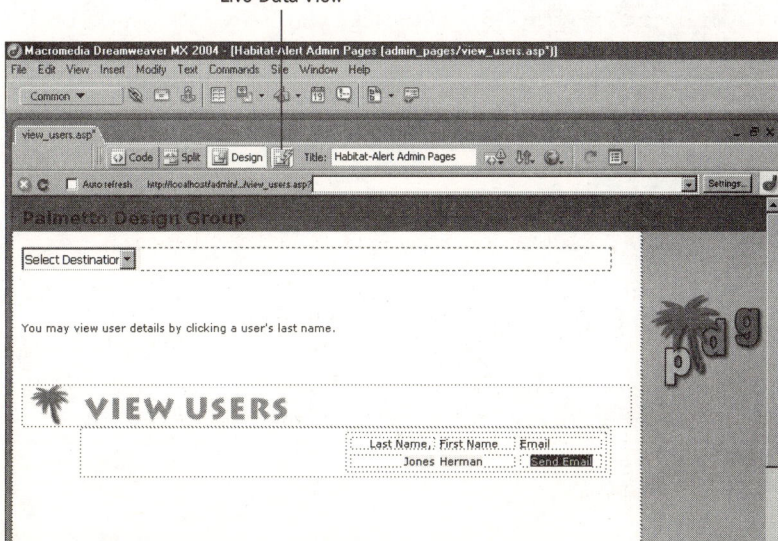

Live Data View

Figure 234-4: A page as seen in Live Data view

cross-references

- Refer to Task 222 to set up
  the DSN name and Task
  229 for adding a recordset
  (Step 1).

- Refer to Task 235 for making the e-mail link dynamic
  (Step 6).

- Refer to Task 236 for
  adding repeat regions to
  display more than one
  entry from the database
  (step 6).

Making an E-mail Link Dynamic

I'll use the PDG administration site to demonstrate this technique. You can get the file at www.wiley.com/compbooks/10simplestepsorless in the partXIII admin folder. In this task you see how to make an e-mail text that is pulled from the database and how to generate a link as well.

note

- The Attributes tab of the Tag inspector shows attributes in various categories of your document. For the href link, we used the General category (Step 3).

1. If you are using the sample files, copy the admin folder into the Inetpub/wwwroot folder, define the site, and then open the view_users.asp page. Or open any page you want to use (or use the view_users.asp page). You have your testing server set up as well. If you use the sample file, do Task 234 first.

2. Open the Applications panel group, select the Bindings panel (Window ➪ Bindings), and expand the recordset to view all the columns (for this page, the only columns you need are LastName, FirstName, and EmailAddress).

3. Click your cursor in the Send Email text and select the <a> tag from the Tag Selector, as shown in Figure 235-1.

```
<body> <table> <tr> <td.background> <div> <div> <table> <tr> <td> <table> <tr> <td> <a>
```

Figure 235-1: The <a> tag selected in the Tag Selector

4. Open the Tag Inspector panel, click the Attributes tab, and click the Show Category View icon. Select the href entry. Notice the mailto: you typed into the Property inspector shows here (see Figure 235-2). If you select the e-mail area, you see that it becomes an active field where you could also type in the mailto if you hadn't done so already.

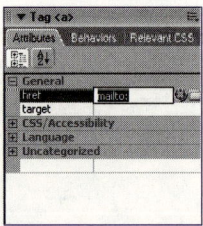

Figure 235-2: The Tag Inspector with href selected and the mailto: added

5. Click in the box to the right of Target. You'll see a lightning bolt, as shown in Figure 235-3. Click it.

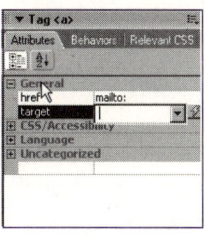

Figure 235-3: The lightning bolt icon appear when you select Target or the field to the right of it

6. The Dynamic Data dialog box opens. Select Email as shown in Figure 235-4. Click OK to close the dialog box.

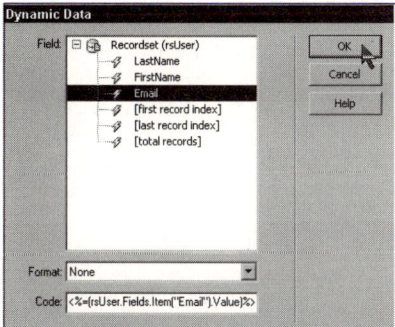

Figure 235-4: The Dynamic Data dialog box with Email selected

7. Save your page and preview in a browser. If you click Send Email, it will open the e-mail client with the user's e-mail entered.

cross-references

- Refer to Task 209 for using the Tag Selector (Step 3).

- Refer to Task 236 for adding more than one record to the View Users page (Step 3).

Task 236

Adding Repeat Regions

The most common use of a repeat region is when you wish to display multiple records on the page. Most uses of repeat regions are displayed through a table containing dynamic data. To follow along with a sample page, you can do Tasks 234 and 235 or open view_users3.asp from the task229 admin folder found at www.wiley.com/compbooks/10simplestepsorless in the task229 folder. You need to define the site, set up the DSN name, and add a recordset. If you are going to use the sample file, perform Tasks 234 and 235 first.

1. Open view_users.asp or view_users3.asp from the sample site or any page you want to add a repeating region to in order to show multiple entries from a database.

2. Click in any of the table cells that contain the dynamic data.

3. Select the table's `<tr>` tag in the Tag Selector.

4. Open the Applications panel and select the Server Behaviors tab to activate that panel.

5. Click the Add (+) button and select Repeat Region, as shown in Figure 236-1.

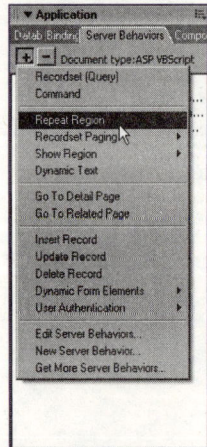

Figure 236-1: Selecting the Repeat Region behavior from the Server Behaviors panel

6. In the Repeat Region dialog box, select the recordset and choose the All Records option, since we don't have many in the sample database. You may choose to show however many entries you'd like displayed on a page. Click OK to close the dialog box.

7. Save and test. You see all the entries that are in the database, as shown in Figure 236-2. You'll notice the e-mail links are all set as well because this sample file has the dynamic e-mail added.

notes

▪ You'll notice a little gray tab added to your table that says Repeat (Step 9).

▪ The Dynamic Table dialog box retains the values you enter for table borders, cell padding, and cell spacing. If you are working on a project that needs several dynamic tables requiring the same look, you may want to enter the table layout values, as this will further simplify page development. Note that after inserting the table, you can adjust these values using the table Property inspector (Step 9).

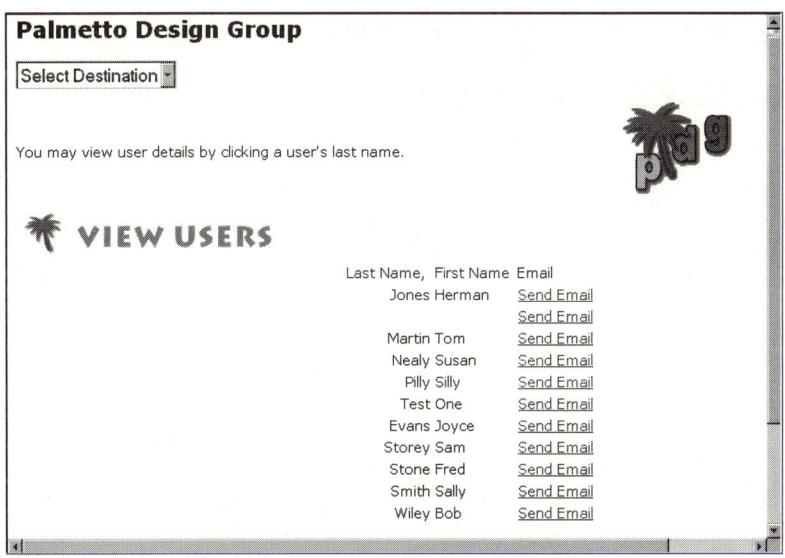

Figure 236-2: All the records are displayed from the database

8. You can also automatically add tables if you don't have a starter table like the sample page. Open a new ASP page (File ⇨ New ⇨ Dynamic Page ⇨ ASPVBscript). Save the page and add a recordset. For this example, I'm using the same three fields of last name, first name, and e-mail address.

9. From the Application category of the Insert bar, select the Dynamic Data arrow and select Dynamic Table. In the Dynamic Table dialog box, select the recordset you want to use from the Recordset pop-up menu. Select the number of records to display per page. Input values for the table border and so on if desired, as shown in Figure 236-3. Click OK.

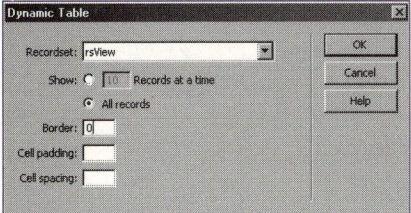

Figure 236-3: The Dynamic Table dialog box

10. A table and placeholders for the dynamic content defined in its associated recordset are inserted into the page. The bottom portion shows how it looks viewed in a browser. The table needs some formatting, but it's a quick way to get a repeating table into your document.

cross-reference

▪ Refer to Task 237 for deleting a record. You'll notice that there is a bad record in the database—it's blank with just an e-mail address link (Step 10).

Inserting Records into a Database (Add Instant Form)

Y ou can create a basic insert page in a single operation using the Record Insertion Form application object. The application object adds both an HTML form and an Insert Record server behavior to the page.

notes

- If you are using a different server technology, select it from the Dynamic Page column instead of ASP (Step 1).

- You can use the sample site's (www.wiley. com/compbooks/ 10simplestepsorless) register.asp page and just delete the form that is in it. Add this object instead (Step 6).

1. Open any page you want to use to add information to a database. Or choose File ➪ New, select Dynamic Page and then ASP VBScript, and click Create, as shown in Figure 237-1.

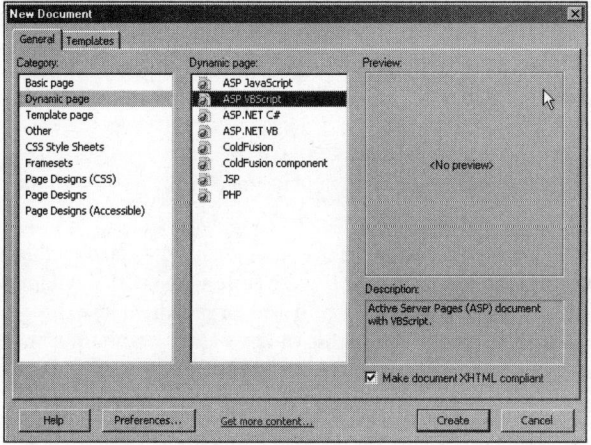

Figure 237-1: Adding a new ASP page

2. Before you can add the Insert Record Behavior, you need to add a DSN name and a recordset to the page.

3. Select the Insert Record Behavior by going to Insert ➪ Application Objects ➪ Insert Record ➪ Record Insertion Form Wizard. The Record Insertion Form window, shown in Figure 237-2, opens.

4. Fill in the following options (also see Figure 237-3):

   - *Connection.* Choose the database from the list. If you did Task 222, it will be listed.

   - Select the appropriate table you want to insert into.

   - Click the Browse button and navigate to the page you want the user brought to after inserting a record into the database.

   - In the Form Fields box, select any entry that you do not want in the form and click the Minus (–) button.

   - Change the label and type of entry if you desire.

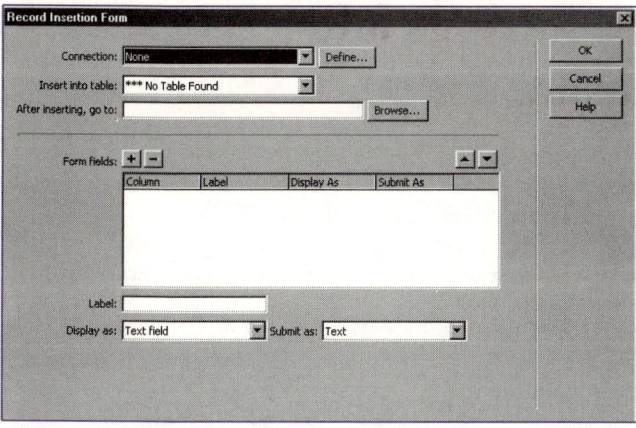

Figure 237-2: Record Insertion Form window

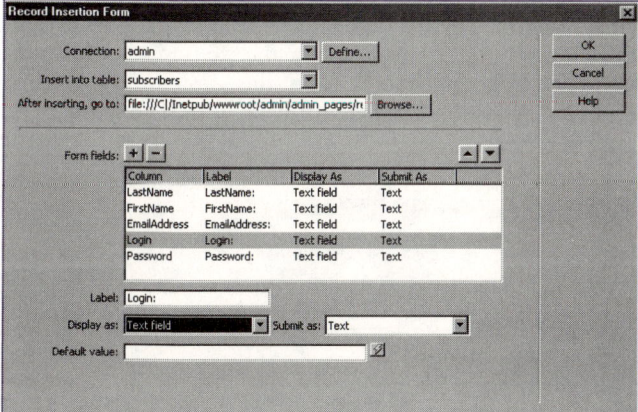

Figure 237-3: Record Insertion Form Wizard

5. Click OK.

6. Title your page and add any design elements you'd like. Dreamweaver adds both an HTML form and an Insert Record server behavior to your page. The form objects are laid out in a basic table, as shown in Figure 237-4.

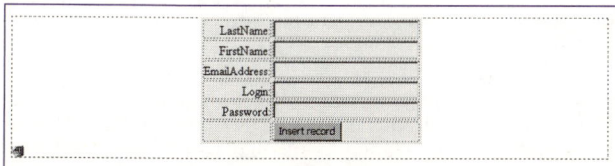

Figure 237-4: Insert Record finished product

cross-references

▪ Refer to Task 222 for defin-ing the DNS and Task 229 for adding a recordset (Step 2).

▪ Refer to Task 238 for using an existing form and adding a server behavior.

▪ Refer to Task 239 for checking for duplicate usernames.

Inserting Records into a Database (Use Existing Form)

notes

- In the sample file, each form field is named. It's not required that the form fields match the names of the database columns; it just makes it easier for selection (Step 2).

- You need to think through what needs to happen with each page. Since the users are adding information into the database, you want them to know they were successful, so you prepare the success and failure pages ahead of time that you need to link to (Step 3).

You have a site structure set up, you've added a form to your page, and you want to use it to gather information from the user. This task shows you how to insert the user information into the database using the form you've already built and designed. You can use the sample site from `www.wiley.com/compbooks/10simplestepsorless` in the task229 details folder if you'd like. Remember to define the site.

1. Open add_users.asp from the admin pages folder in the Files panel. You need to download the admin folder from `www.wiley.com/compbooks/10simplestepsorless` in the task229 folder and define the site if you haven't already. For everything to test at the end of this task, you need to perform Tasks 234, 235, and 236 first.

2. Before you can add the Insert Record behavior, you need to add a recordset to the add_users.asp page. Name the recordset **rsAddUsers** and choose the connection you defined for the admin database. Click Select, and select last name, first name, e-mail, login, and password, as shown in Figure 238-1.

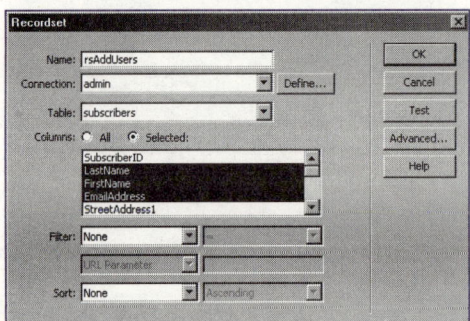

Figure 238-1: A recordset added to the add_users.asp page

3. Open the Server Behaviors panel and click the Add (+) button. Select Insert Record. In the Insert Record dialog box, choose the connection you defined for the admin database and the subscribers table.

4. Click the Browse button for the Go To field and navigate to the page you want users taken to when they add a user successfully. For this example, navigate to the newuser_success.htm page and select it.

5. The Get Values From field should say FormNewUser, which is the name of the sample form. (Of course, if you are using your own file, this will be different.)

6. Check through the list of form elements and look for any that say `<ignore>`. If you see one, select it and then select the corresponding column name from the Form Elements list, as shown in Figure 238-2.

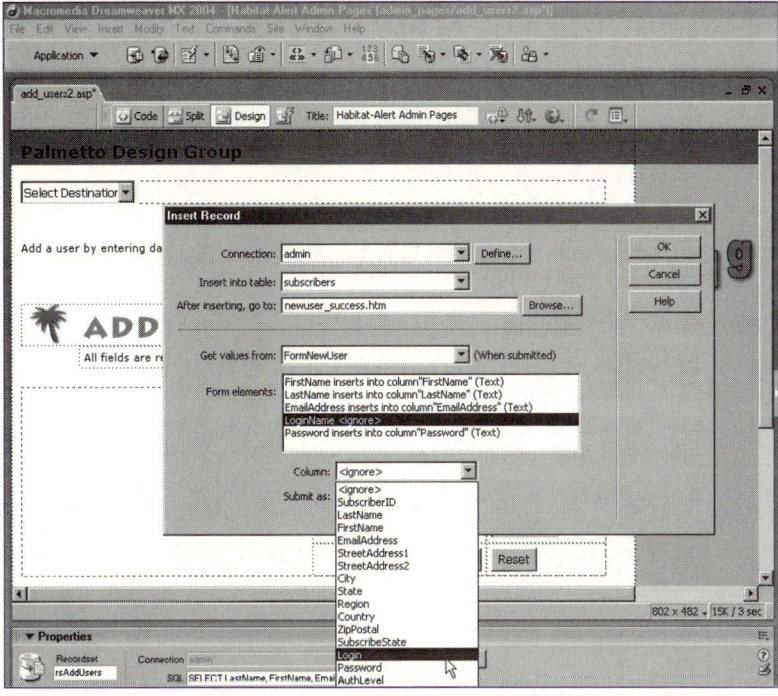

Figure 238-2: The Insert Record dialog box filled in

7. Save the page and test in a browser. To test it, fill in the form with your name and so on and click the Add New User button. You should see the New User Added Successfully page, as shown in Figure 238-3.

Figure 238-3: The Add User success page

cross-reference

- Refer to Task 240 for removing entries from the database (Step 8).

8. From the drop-down menu, select View Users to see your name added.

Authenticating Username

Your Web site should contain a page that users can use to register the first time they come to your Web site. A registration page (or an Add User page) contains four basic parts:

note

- You can select whichever field you want to authenticate. If you have more than one, repeat the behavior (Step 4).

- A table in your database to store user records

- An HTML form that lets users input registration information, such as username and password

- An Insert Record behavior

- A Check New Username server behavior

1. Open a new page or open the add_users.asp page. Perform Task 238 if using the add_users.asp page.

2. Select the Server Behaviors panel by going to Window ⇨ Server Behaviors

3. Click the Plus (+) button and select User Authentication ⇨ Check New Username from the pop-up menu that appears, as shown in Figure 239-1.

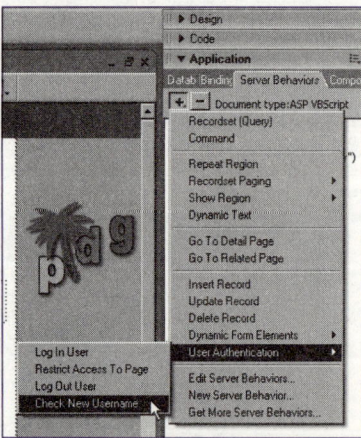

Figure 239-1: Selecting the Check New Username behavior

4. In the Username Field pop-up menu, select the form text field your visitors use to enter a username. The login name is the one you don't want repeated, so select LoginName from the drop-down menu, as shown in Figure 239-2.

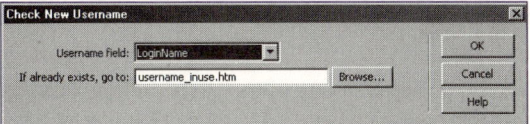

Figure 239-2: LoginName selected from the drop-down menu

5. In the If Already Exists, Go To text box, specify a page to open if a matching username is found in the database table. The opened page should alert the user that the username is already taken and let the user try again.

6. Click OK. Test in the browser by entering your name and password. Repeat using the same username. You should get the page in Figure 239-3 if using the sample file.

Figure 239-3: A page showing that the username is already taken

cross-references

- Refer to Task 238, where the user is taken to a success page when registering or adding a new user.

- Refer to Task 241 for updating or modifying pages.

Deleting Records

Your application can contain a page that lets users delete existing records in a database table. A delete page is usually a detail page working in tandem with a results page. The results page lets the user select a record to delete and then passes the choice to the delete page.

note

- The delete page can contain only one record-editing server behavior at a time. For example, you cannot add an Insert Record or an Update Record server behavior to the delete page.

1. If you want to use the PDG administration site, open delete_user.asp from the admin_pages folder in the Files panel.

2. In the Bindings panel, add a new recordset. Name the recordset **rsDeleteUser**, and choose the admin connection. Be sure that the subscribers table is displayed in the Table menu. Select the All Columns option. Sort the results by LastName. Click OK to close the dialog box. Figure 240-1 shows the delete_user.asp page with a form already added to it.

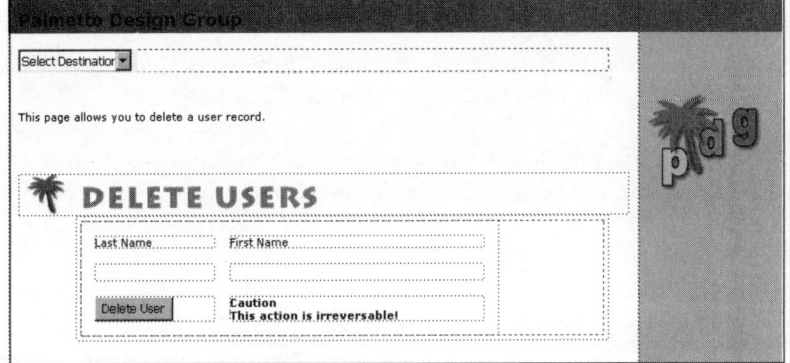

Figure 240-1: The Delete Users page

3. Place your cursor in the first cell of the second row (below Last Name cell). In the Bindings panel, open the recordset, select LastName, and click the Insert button.

4. Tab to the second cell and select FirstName from the Bindings panel. Click the Insert button. Figure 240-2 shows the server logic added to the form for the username.

5. Click in the page and open the Server Behaviors panel. Click the Add (+) button and select Delete Record.

6. In the Delete Record dialog box, select the admin connection. In the Delete from Table field, select Subscribers. Select the rsDeleteUser (or whatever your recordset is named) from the Select Record From field. Set the Unique Key Column to SubscriberID, and check Numeric.

Task 240

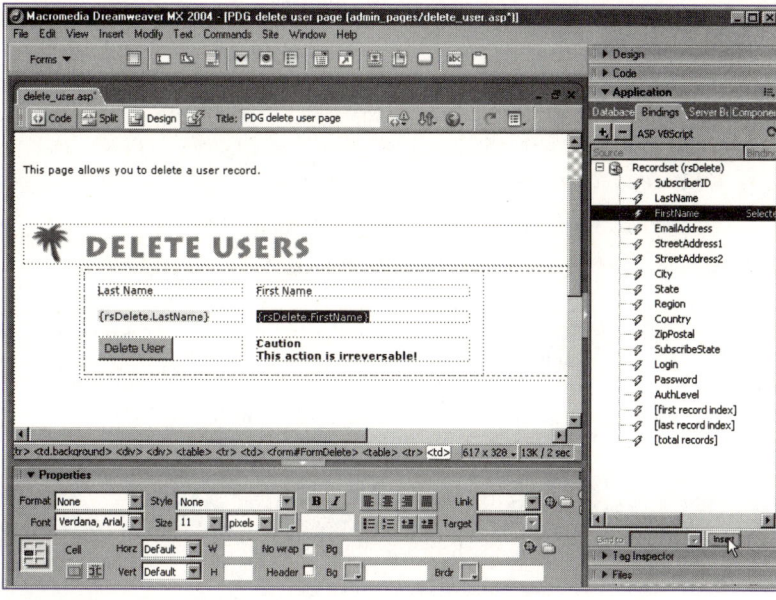

Figure 240-2: The server logic added to the Delete User form

7. In the Delete By Submitting field, select your form's name from the pop-up list. Set the After Deleting, Go To field to **user_deleted.htm**, and click OK to close the dialog box. Figure 240-3 shows the Delete Record dialog box filled in.

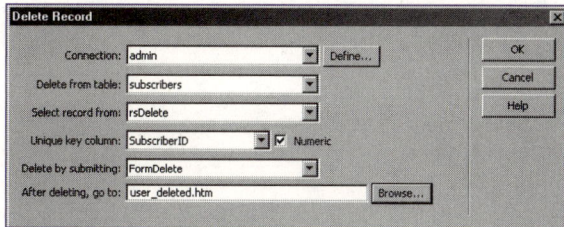

Figure 240-3: The Delete Record dialog box filled in

8. Save and test the file. You are presented with one username. If you click the Delete User button, the record is deleted and you are sent to the user-deleted page.

cross-references

▪ Refer to Task 229 for adding a recordset (Step 2).

▪ Refer to Task 243 for adding a recordset navigation bar that you can use to navigate through the records (Step 8).

Updating Records

An update page has three parts:

- A filtered recordset to retrieve the record from a database table
- An HTML form to let users modify the record's data
- An Update Record server behavior to update the database table

You can add the final two building blocks of an update page in a single operation using the Record Update Form application object. The application object adds both an HTML form and an Update Record server behavior to the page. If you want to use the sample administration site, open that defined site now.

1. Open a new page (ASP for the sample administration site) in Design view, and save as **modify.asp** into the admin pages folder.

2. Add a recordset to it, as shown in Figure 241-1.

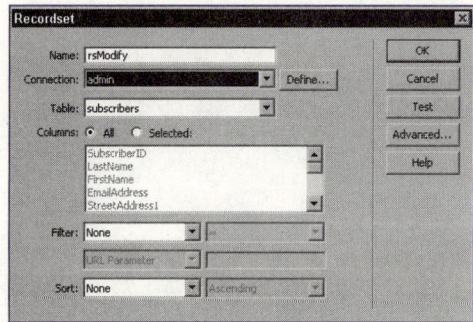

Figure 241-1: A recordset being added for the new ASP page opened in the PDG administration site

3. Select the Update Record Behavior by going to Insert ⇨ Application Objects ⇨ Update Record ⇨ Record Update Form Wizard, as shown in Figure 241-2.

4. Fill in the Record Update Form dialog box. Select your connection, the table, the recordset name, your unique key, and then the page that the users are taken to after they update or modify a record, as shown in Figure 241-3.

5. In the Form Fields column, select and delete any entries you don't want to be modified. In this example, I selected subscriberID and deleted it, as shown in Figure 241-3.

6. Click OK to close the dialog box and add the HTML form to your page.

7. Open the Server Behaviors panel and you'll see that the Update Record behavior has been added.

note

- As you can see, there is only one user record shown. There are a couple of different ways to access a specific user. Refer to the Cross-Reference notes to go to different tasks to accomplish the method you prefer (Step 7).

Task 241

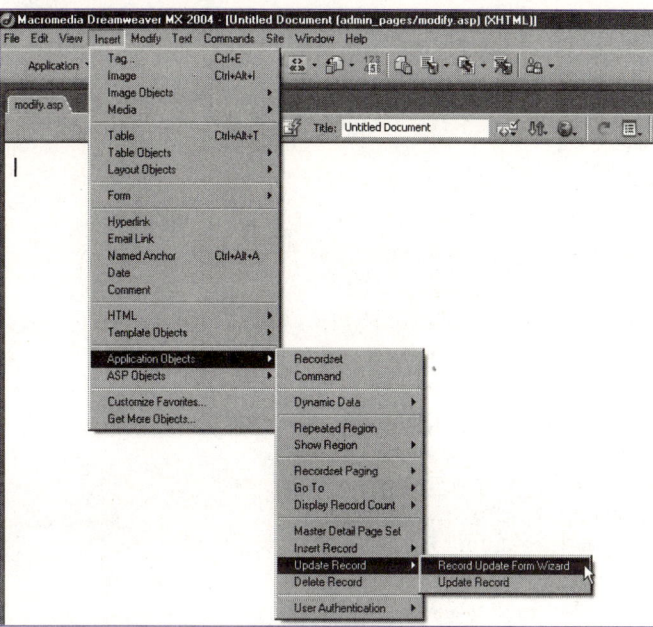

Figure 241-2: Selecting the Record Update Form Wizard

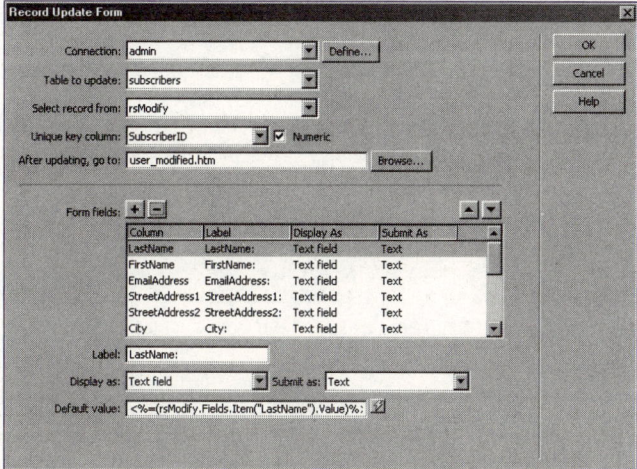

Figure 241-3: Record Update Form Wizard

8. The next step would be to add some design elements to this page—perhaps attach a template.

9. Now test the page in a browser. If you used the PDG administration site and saved the modify.asp page into the admin pages folder, after you make a change and click the Update Record button, you are brought to the Modify Users success page.

10. The PDG administration site uses a Library item for the menu. Since a new page has been added, it would need to be added to the menu so that users of the administration site could access it.

tip

- An easy way to add a new page to an established site is to open an existing page and save it with a new name. If it contains server logic you don't want for the new page, select the behavior in the Server Behaviors panel and click the Minus (–) icon to remove it. Remove or update any recordsets (Step 7).

cross-references

- Refer to Tasks 242 and 243 for adding a navigation bar to navigate through the users on the Modify Users page (Step 8).

- Refer to Task 245 for making usernames link to the Modify page.

Building a Recordset Navigation Bar

This navigation bar can be added to any page, but in this task, you use the sample PDG administration site to add navigation to the Modify User page built in Task 241.

1. Open the modify.asp page you built in Task 241 or open any page where you'd like to add a navigation bar. Place your cursor below the Update Record table.

2. Choose Insert ➪ Application Objects ➪ Recordset Paging ➪ Recordset Navigation Bar, as shown in Figure 242-1.

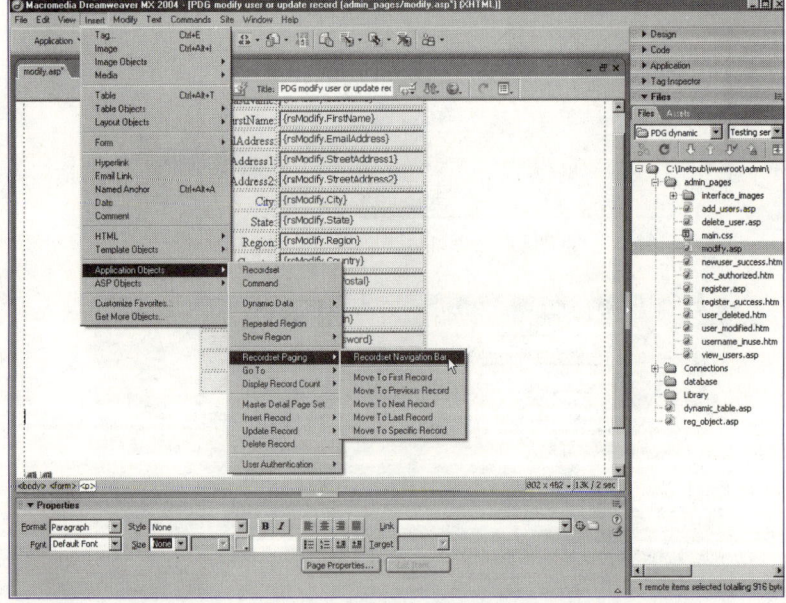

Figure 242-1: Selecting the recordset navigation bar from the Insert menu

3. In the Recordset Navigation Bar dialog box that opens, choose the Text option, as shown in Figure 242-2. Notice that you select the recordset you want to navigate through.

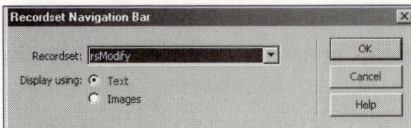

Figure 242-2: The Recordset Navigation Bar dialog box filled in

4. Click OK to insert the text-based navigation bar. Figure 242-3 shows how it looks in your document.

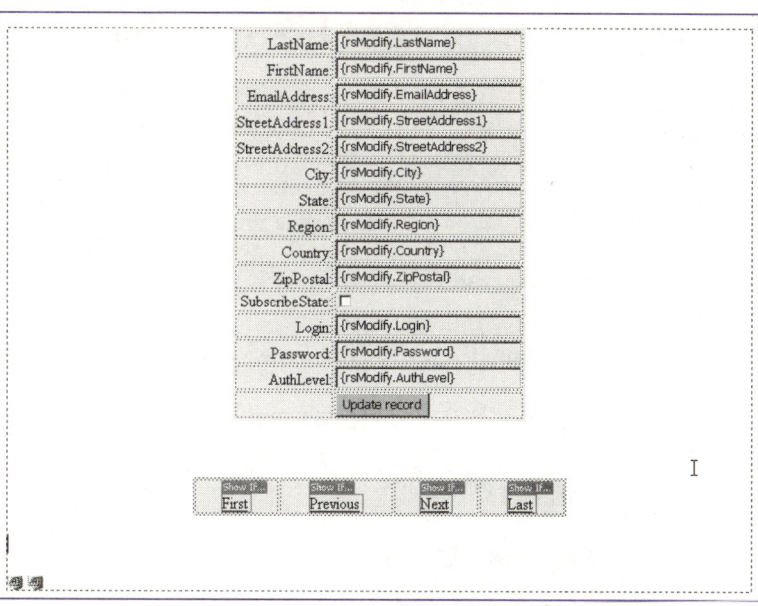

Figure 242-3: The recordset navigation bar inserted into your document

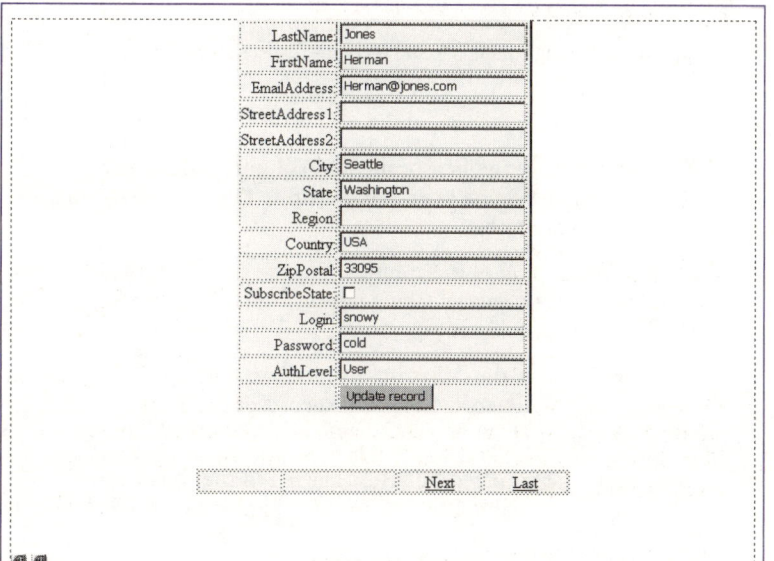

Figure 242-4: The menu as viewed in Live Data view

5. Click the Live Data view, and as you can see in Figure 242-4, only the Next and Last menu options are available.

6. Preview in a browser and click Next. Now the other menu options are available. You also see the next entry in the database.

cross-reference

▪ Refer to Task 243 for adding a status record to the recordset navigation bar (Step 3).

Setting the Recordset Navigation Status

I n this task you add a record that shows which record you are viewing. This task uses the recordset navigation bar from Task 242. To maintain the design element of the recordset navigation bar, you put the status in the same table.

1. Open the modify.asp page completed in Task 242 or any page with a recordset navigation bar.

2. Insert your cursor into the last cell of the Recordset Navigation Bar table.

3. Right-/Control+click and select Table ➪ Insert Rows or Columns. Select Columns, enter the value of **2**, and choose After Current Column, as shown in Figure 243-1.

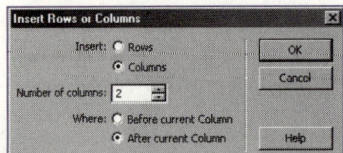

Figure 243-1: Adding columns to the recordset navigation bar

4. Click OK to add the new columns.

5. With your cursor in the first of the new columns, add either a backslash (\) or a pipe (|) line to visually separate the status text from the rest of the navigation bar.

6. With your cursor still in the column with the slash or pipe, choose Insert ➪ HTML ➪ Special Characters ➪ Non-Breaking Space to add a space in this column.

7. Place your cursor in the last column and choose Insert ➪ Application Objects ➪ Display Record Count ➪ Recordset Navigation Status, as shown in Figure 243-2.

8. Check to see that your record set is selected in the Recordset Navigation Status dialog box, as shown in Figure 243-3. Click OK to close.

9. Save your page and preview. Click the next text and notice the status changes, as shown in Figure 243-4.

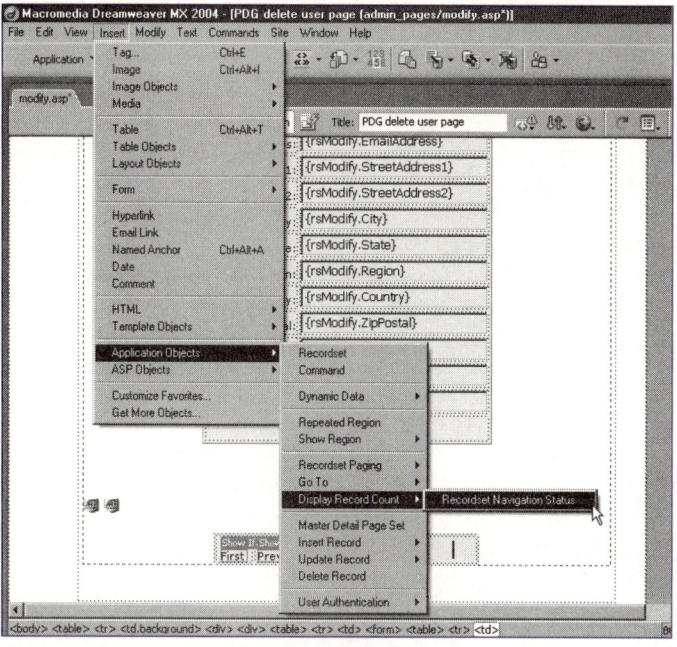

Figure 243-2: Adding the Recordset Navigation Status behavior

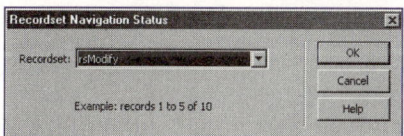

Figure 243-3: The Recordset Navigation Status dialog box

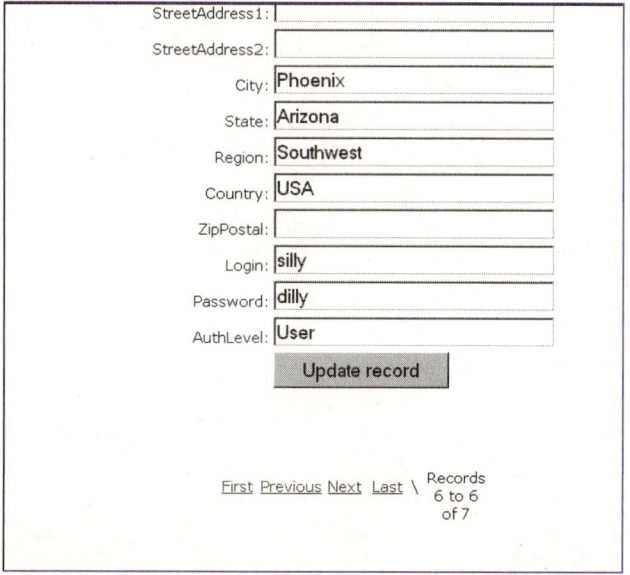

Figure 243-4: The recordset navigation bar and status as seen in a browser

cross-reference

- This navigation bar could use some formatting, especially to make the text look better. Refer to Task 233 for formatting (Step 8).

Building Login Pages

S ince this is an administration site, the default page should open to a login window. If a user hasn't yet registered, he or she can use the menu to go to the Register page. For most sites you'll probably have your login page on the home page with other content.

1. Open any page where you'd like to add a login. You can use the PDG administration site (part13/admin folder) if you'd like. Open the default.asp page from the admin_pages folder in the Files panel.

2. Place your cursor where your want to add a form. In the default page, insert your cursor in the table below the title and choose Insert ⇨ Form ⇨ Form.

3. In the Property inspector, name the form **FormLogin**, as shown in Figure 244-1.

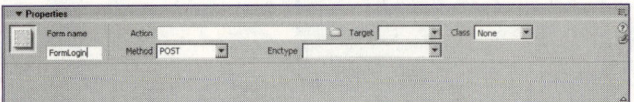

Figure 244-1: The form field added and named in the Property inspector

4. Type the words **User Name** and press Enter/Return. Choose Insert ⇨ Form ⇨ TextField, and name the TextField **LoginName** in the Property inspector, as shown in Figure 244-2.

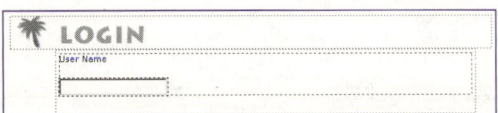

Figure 244-2: The TextField for the username is added and named

5. Place your cursor to the right of the TextField, press Enter/Return, and type **Password**. Press Enter/Return again.

6. Choose Insert ⇨ Form ⇨ TextField. Name this one **Password** (see Figure 244-3). Press Enter/Return after the TextField.

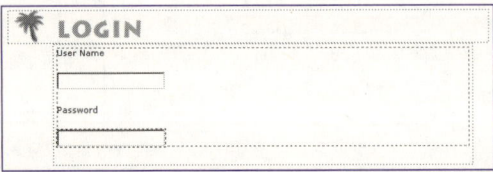

Figure 244-3: Both the username and password fields added

7. Choose Insert ⇨ Form ⇨ Button. Select the button, and in the Property inspector, change the label to **Log In**, as shown in Figure 244-4.

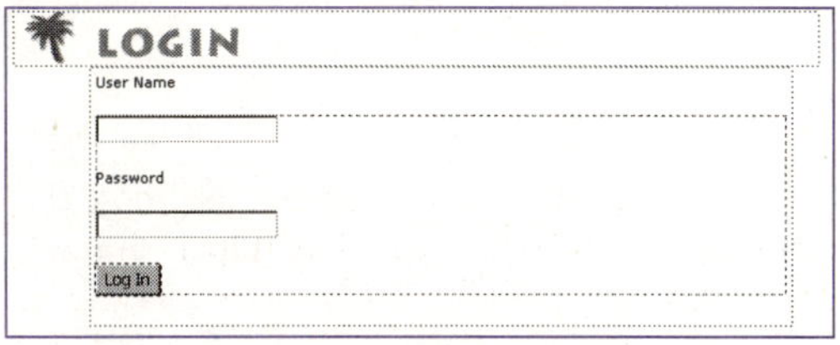

Figure 244-4: The Log In button added

8. Open the Bindings panel, click the Add (+) button, and add a record-set. Select only the Login and Password columns. Save the page. This form isn't ready yet; you'll need to do Task 245 to tell the form what action to take and the method to use.

cross-references

- Refer to Tasks 97 and 98 for inserting forms and form elements (Step 2).

- Refer to Task 245 to validate the information the user enters into the login form (Step 10).

Validating the Login Entries

This task assumes you've built a login page. You can use the one built in Task 244 if you'd like. A server behavior is added to a login page to check if the username and password match what is in the database.

notes

■ The success and failure pages are not included in the PDG administration site sample (Step 7).

■ If the users try to enter a page, you may have the page restricted and tell them they need to log in. Once they log in, the Go to Previous URL options return them to the page they tried to access (Step 8).

1. Open the default.asp page in the sample site or any page with a login form. Open the Server Behaviors panel, click the Add (+) button, and select User Authentication ⇨ Log In User. The Log In User dialog box opens, as shown in Figure 245-1.

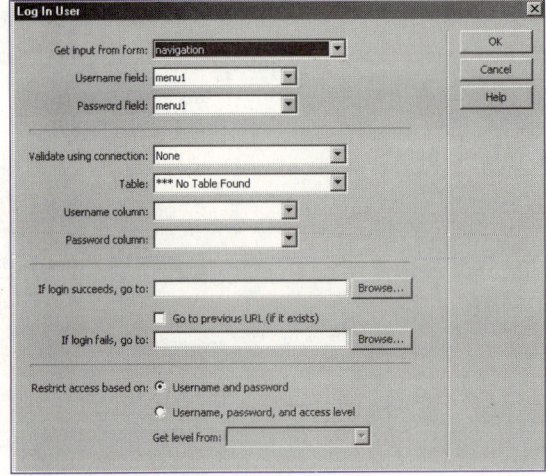

Figure 245-1: The Log In User dialog box

2. In the Get Input from Form field, select your form's name. The sample default pages form name isFormLogin.

3. The form field's names for the username and password will most likely fill in automatically. If they don't, select them from the drop-down list.

4. In the Validate Using Connection field, select the name of your connection (admin for the PDG administration site).

5. Select the table name subscribers from the drop-down menu.

6. Select the name of the username column from the drop-down menu. In the PDG administration site, this column is named login, as shown in Figure 245-2.

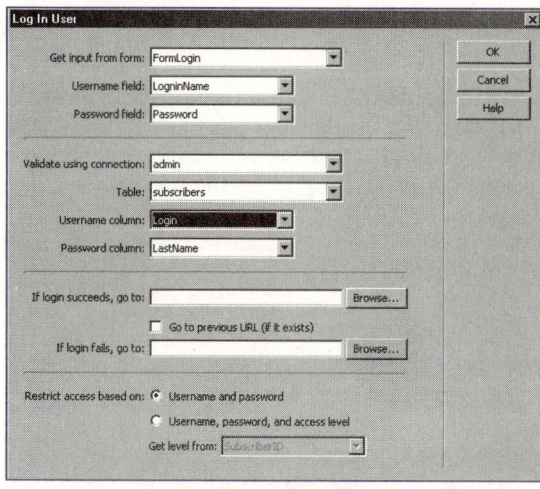

Figure 245-2: The Log in User form filled out to the Password Column field

7. Click the Browse button for the If Login Suceeds, Go To field and navigate to a file you've already made that you want the user directed to if the login succeeds.

8. If you want users to be able to go back to a page that they may have entered prior to the login page, check the Go to Previous URL (If It Exists) option.

9. Click the Browse button next to the If Login Fails, Go To field, and browse to a page that gives the user another chance to log in.

10. Select the Restrict Access Based on Username and Password. Figure 245-3 shows the completed dialog box. Click OK.

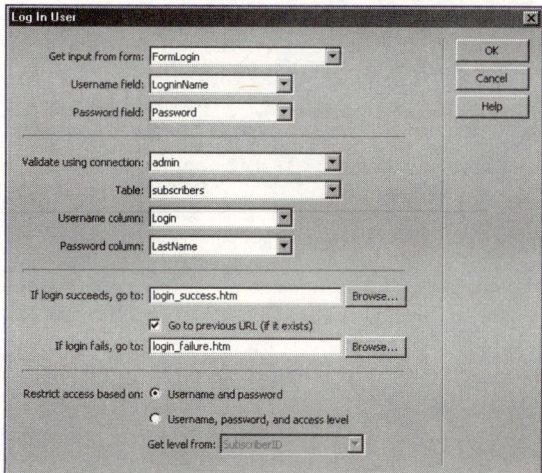

Figure 245-3: The Log In User dialog box filled in

cross-reference

- Refer to Task 246 for another method of restricting access to a specific page based on user access rights (Step 10).

Restricting Access to a Specific Page

You can restrict access to specific pages in your site by using the Restrict Access to Page server behavior. This behavior needs to be added to each page you want to protect. This task sets the Restrict Access behavior to check the user's authorization based on not only the login name and password but an authorization level as well.

1. Open a page you want to restrict.

2. Open the Server Behaviors panel and click the Add (+) button.

3. Select User Authentication ➪ Restrict Access to Page. The Restrict Access to Page dialog box opens, as shown in Figure 246-1.

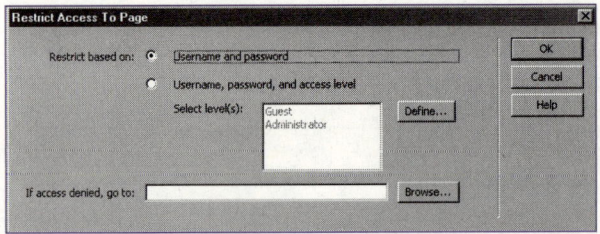

Figure 246-1: The Restrict Access to Page dialog box

4. Select whether you want to restrict only using a username and password or by an access level as well.

5. If you choose to restrict access by authorization level, you need to select the level of access from the list, as shown in Figure 246-2.

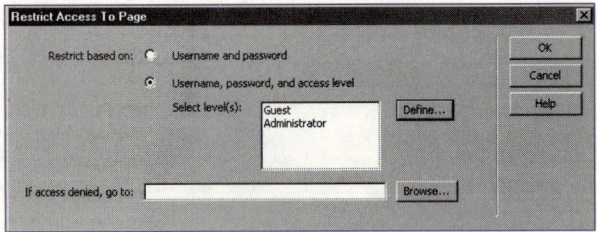

Figure 246-2: The Select Level(s) field with options visible

6. If you don't see any access level options, click the Define button. Click the Add (+) button and add the levels needed, as shown in Figure 246-3. These levels need to be the same as levels you've entered into the database. Click OK.

Figure 246-3: The Define Access Levels dialog box

7. Browse to the page that users are brought to if their login fails, as shown in Figure 246-4. Click OK to close the dialog box.

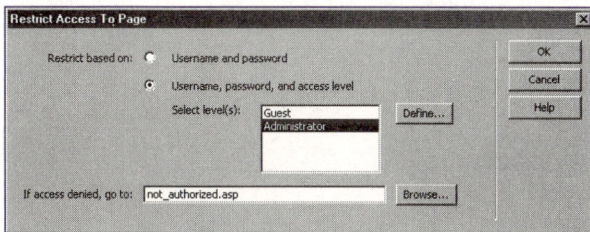

Figure 246-4: TheRestrict Acces To page dialog box filled in

Logging Out Users

When a user logs in successfully, a session variable is created that consists of the username. When the user leaves your site, you can use the Log Out User server behavior to clear the session variable and redirect the user to another page (usually a "goodbye" or "thank-you" page). You can invoke the Log Out User server behavior when the user clicks a link or when a specific page loads.

notes

- You don't need to place your cursor if you are adding this behavior to a page that will automatically log users out. You'll see this option in Step 4 (Step 1).

- You can also make your logout page a separate pop-up window if you'd like.

1. Open a page that you want to use as a logout page. Place your cursor in the document where you'd like logout text to go (if you want text added).

2. Open the Server Behaviors panel and click the Add (+) button.

3. Select User Authentication ➪ Log Out User. The Log Out User dialog box opens, as shown in Figure 247-1.

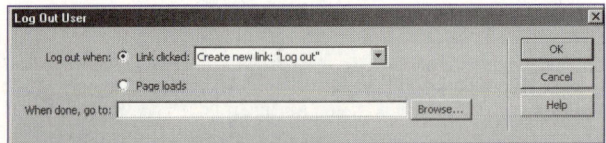

Figure 247-1: The Log Out User dialog box

4. You need to choose a log out method. You can select either to log out when the text is clicked or when the page loads.

5. Enter a page URL that the login will take the users to. It's typically a thank-you page. Click OK. Figure 247-2 shows the dialog box filled in.

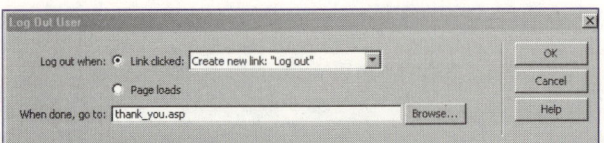

Figure 247-2: The Log Out User dialog box filled in

6. In your document, if you select the Link Clicked option, you see the text added automatically, as shown in Figure 247-3.

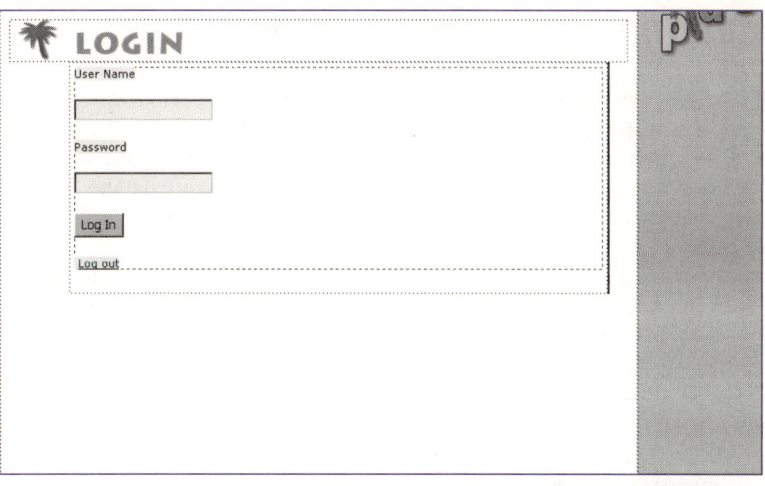

Figure 247-3: The logout text added into the document by the server behavior

7. If you've linked to a logout page, the user will be brought to it, as shown in Figure 247-4.

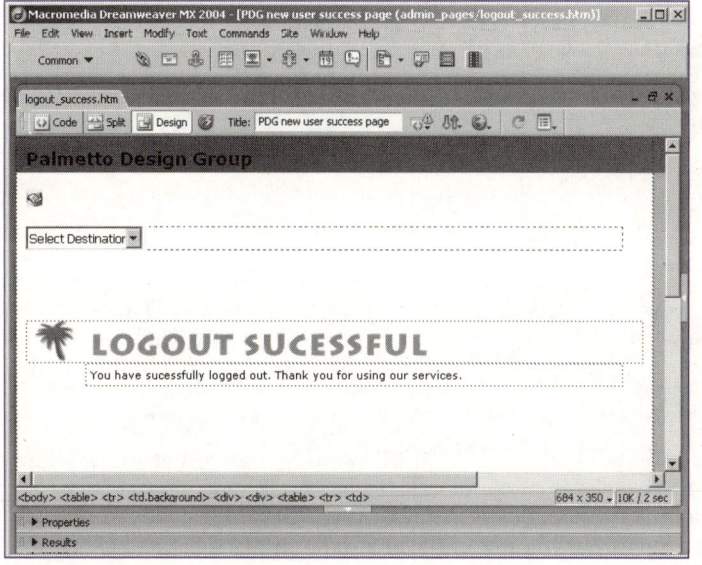

Figure 247-4: A logout page

cross-reference

■ Refer to Task 244 for building a login page (Step 4).

Building Dynamic Menus

This task shows you how to make a drop-down list menu dynamic. You can automatically populate a menu or list from a database. This is a great way to add products to a list dynamically, and it sure beats having to manually update your links every time a new product is added. In the detail/database folder is a small database named stock with a Jewelry table. Define the site and set a DSN name if you haven't done so yet.

1. You need to have a menu in an ASP (or other server technology page) built before you begin. You also have to add a recordset. If you use the stock sampledatabase, select the stock connection and then the jewelry table. Now select just the AssetFileName and click OK, as shown in Figure 248-1.

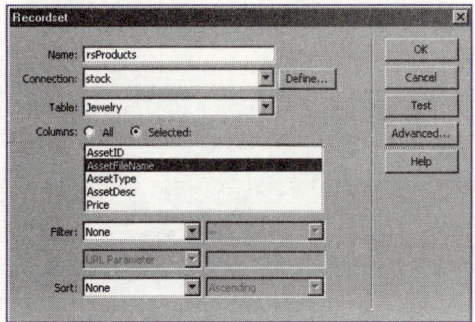

Figure 248-1: The recordset for the dynamic menu

2. Insert a form (name it **FormMenu**) and insert a List/Menu field (name it **ProductMenu**). Don't add any list values.

3. In Property inspector, click the Dynamic button. The Dynamic List/Menu dialog box opens, as shown in Figure 248-2.

4. You should see your form in the Form field. If you have more than one form on the page, be sure the correct one is selected.

5. In the Static Options field, click the plus (+) sign to add an entry line. Then insert your cursor in the area below the Label text and type **Select A Product**. The label is what is seen in the menu. You can click the Add (+) button to add any static entries that aren't going to change. Enter the links into the Value column.

Task **248**

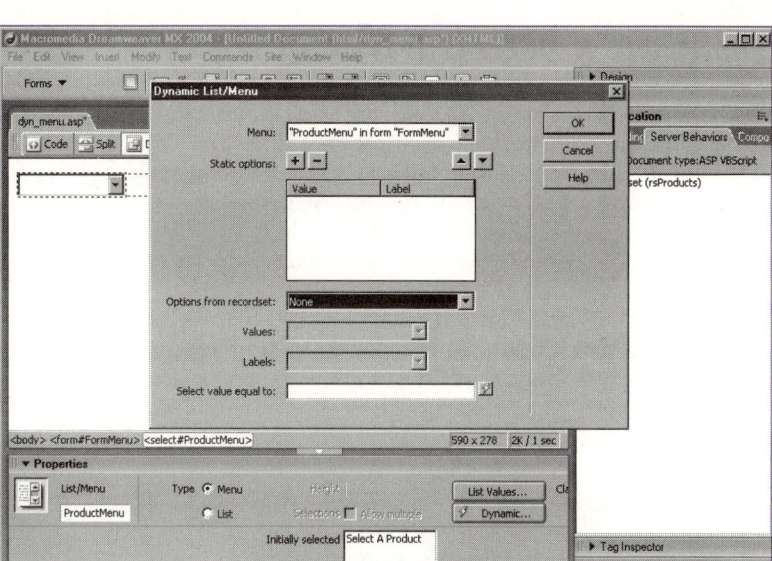

Figure 248-2: Click the Dynamic button to open the Dynamic List/Menu dialog box

6. In the Options from Recordset field, select the recordset you defined.

7. Select the recordset column that contains the label and the values. In this example they are both the same, because the sample database doesn't contain links for a menu. But if you designed your database for a dynamic menu, one of the columns would contain links.

8. If you want a particular menu item to be selected when the page opens in a browser or when a record is displayed in the form, enter a value equal to the menu item's value in the Select Value Equal To box.

9. Click OK. Figure 248-3 shows the Dynamic List/Menu dialog box filled in.

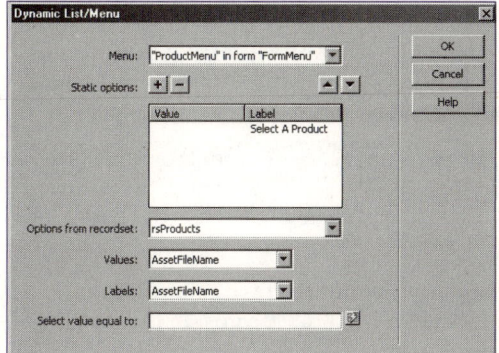

Figure 248-3: The Dynamic List/Menu dialog box filled in

10. Save the page and test in a browser.

cross-references

- Refer to Task 229 for adding recordsets (Step 2).

- Refer to Task 102 for making a drop-down list menu (Step 2).

Building a Master-Detail Page

Dreamweaver has some application objects that can really speed up your Web development time. In this task you see how to use the Master-Detail Page Set application object. You can build a complete set of dynamic pages by filling in one or two dialog boxes. The method you use is identical for ColdFusion, ASP, JSP, and PHP pages. You can use the sample admin site folder if you'd like from www.wiley.com/compbooks/10simplestepsorless in the Part XIII folder.

notes

- You can format the page anyway you'd like—even attach a style sheet.

- Delete any column entries you want before you build the master and detail pages. In the sample file you'd probably want to delete everything except the first and last name in the master page.

1. Open a new dynamic page (File ⇨ New ⇨ Dynamic, select a file type, and click Create). For the sample admin folder, make a new ASP page and save it as master_detail.asp.

2. Open the Bindings panel (Ctrl/Command+F10), click the Plus (+) button, and select Recordset (Query).

3. Fill in the information for the recordset, as shown in Figure 249-1.

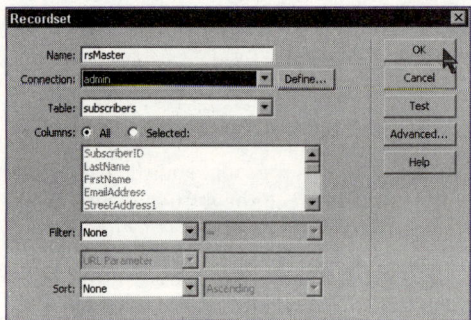

Figure 249-1: Add a recordset to the master_detail page

4. Choose Insert ⇨ Application Objects ⇨ Master Detail Page Set. The Insert Master-Detail Page Set dialog box opens, as shown in Figure 249-2.

5. In the Master Page Fields area, select the recordset columns to display on the master page. By default, all the columns in the recordset are selected. Delete the record ID (subscriberID for the sample files) by selecting the name and clicking on the Minus (–) button. You may want to display only the first and last names on the master page.

6. In the Link to Detail From pop-up menu, select the column in the recordset that will link to the detail page. For instance, the last name of each person will link to the detail page if you select the Last Name column.

7. In the Pass Unique Key pop-up menu, select the column in the recordset containing values identifying the records. In the sample, it is subscriberID.

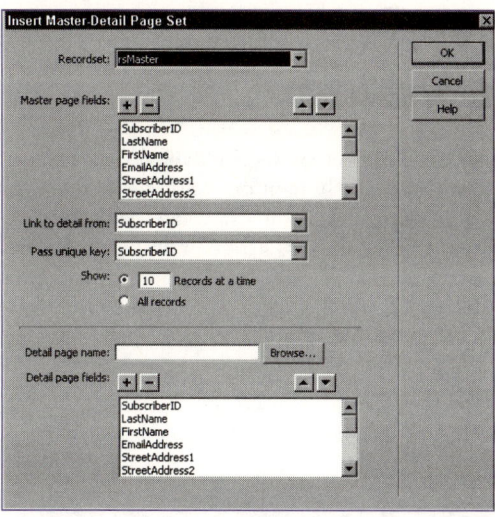

Figure 249-2: The Insert Master-Detail Page Set dialog box

8. Specify the number of records to display on the master page. In the Detail Page Name text field, you can enter a page you've already created or type a new name, and the application will create the new page.

9. In the Detail Page Fields area, select the columns to be displayed on the detail page. Again, if you have a recordID, delete it. When you are done filling in the dialog box, click OK. A detail page opens, as shown in Figure 249-3.

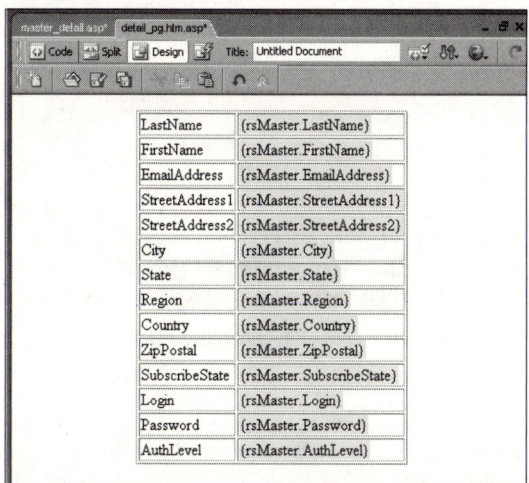

Figure 249-3: The detail page that is generated automatically

10. Select the master_detail page, and you see the dynamic content and server behaviors that have been added to the page automatically.

Viewing One Record (Passing Single Values)

In earlier tasks in this part, you built pages that display dynamic data, repeat the data from its content source, and show or hide information depending on what is the database. The next step is to pass values from one page to another. For example, say you have a repeated list that shows a group of employees. Suppose you want to be able to view a particular employee's record by itself and get more detailed information. To do this, you have to set up a a link that passes the value of that record from your master page to your employee detail page.

1. Open the file view_users4.asp.

2. Click the dynamic text called {rsUsers.LastName}. See Figure 250-1.

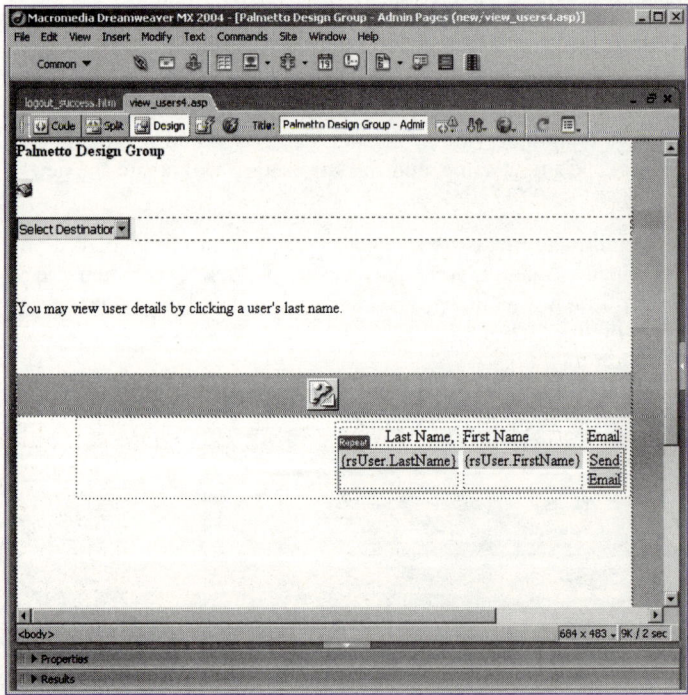

Figure 250-1: The view_users.asp page with the dynamic text selected

3. Select Window ⇨ Server Behaviors.

4. Click the Plus (+) button. The Server Behaviors window appears.

5. Select Go to Detail Page from the menu.

6. The Go to Detail Page pop-up menu appears, as shown in Figure 250-2.

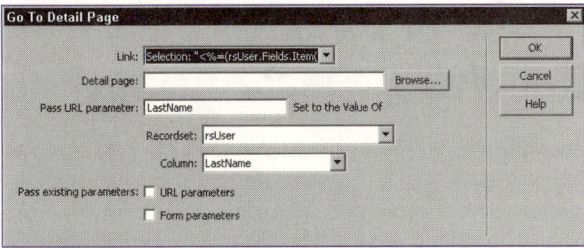

Figure 250-2: The Go to Detail Page dialog window

7. Click Browse and select the page called view_users_detail.asp.

8. Click in the Column field and select SubscriberID. The filled-out dialog box is shown in Figure 250-3.

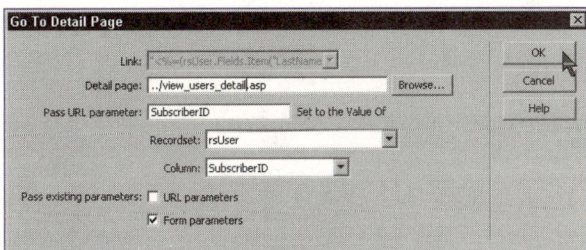

Figure 250-3: The Go to Detail Page dialog box filled in

9. Click OK, save your page and preview in a browser. The final page is shown in Figure 250-4.

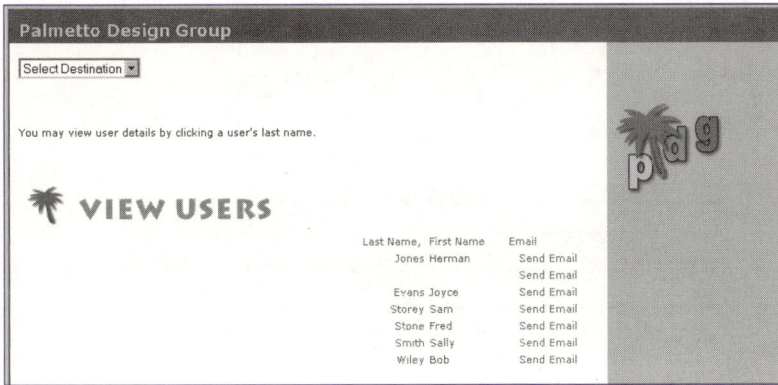

Figure 250-4: The selection page as viewed in the browser

Task **251**

Building a Page to Receive Data from Another (Receiving Single Values)

notes

- The sample file you can use is in the Part 13/ admin folder.

- The rs in front of the recordset name is not required. It is simply a naming convention to distinguish that it is a recordset.

Since you have now built a page that will send a single value, you must now build the page that will receive that value and display the relevant data. You need to build a query that displays more detailed information than what is being show in view_users.asp. In all of your other pages, you displayed whatever is the database. Now you must change your recordset to filter the database to show a specific set of data.

1. Open the file called view_users_detail.asp.

2. Select Windows ⇨ Server Bindings.

3. Double-click the recordset called rsUsers.

4. Go down to where it says Filter and change the second box to URL Parameter and SubscriberID (see Figure 251-1).

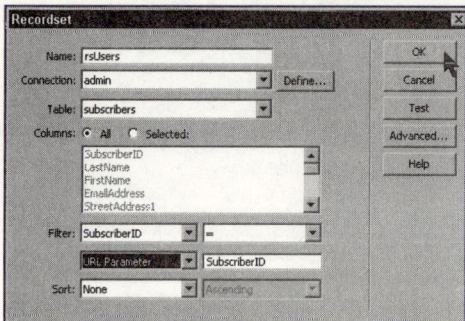

Figure 251-1: The URL and SubscriberID changed

5. Test the connection. It asks you for a number. Type in **12** and click OK (see Figure 251-2).

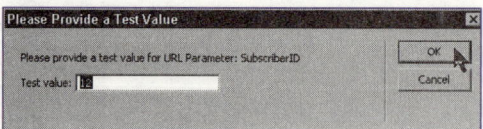

Figure 251-2: Enter a **12** into the Please Provide a Test Value box

6. The Test SQL Statement box shows the database record with SubscriberID number 12 if the test was successful (see Figure 251-3). Click OK to close the text window, and click OK again to close the Recordset window.

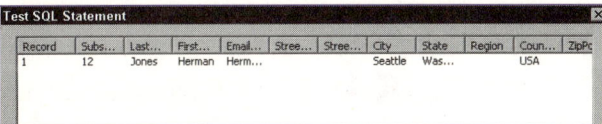

Figure 251-3: The successful test

7. You can insert all of the fields from the Subscriber database onto the page (see Figure 251-4).

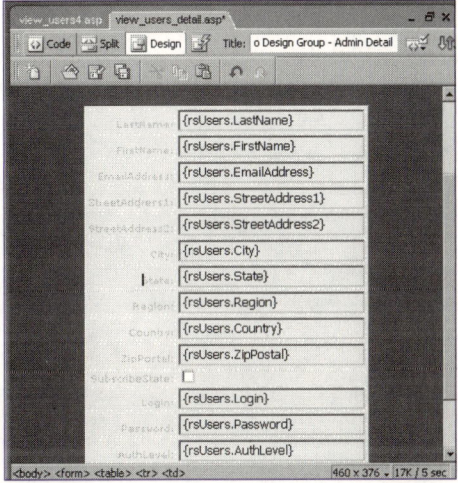

Figure 251-4: The page with all of the fields added

8. Save the file and test it your browser. Starting with the view_users3. asp page you made in Task 250, click one of the subscriber's last names. The view_users_detail page should open with the detailed data about the subscriber.

cross-reference

- Refer to Task 229 for setting up a recordset.

Task 252

Creating Search Pages

A search page on the Web typically contains form fields in which the user enters search parameters. At a minimum, your search page must have an HTML form with a Submit button. Next, you tell the form where to send the search parameters when the user clicks the Submit button.

1. Open a file you want to include a search form on, or create a new page. You can use the search.asp file in the Part XIII folder at `www.wiley.com/compbooks/10simplestepsorless` if you'd like.

2. Select Insert ⇨ Form ⇨ Form. An empty form is created on the page.

3. Select Insert ⇨ Form ⇨ Text Field.

4. Click the text field that you have inserted, go down to the Property inspectory, and call it **LastName**. See Figure 252-1.

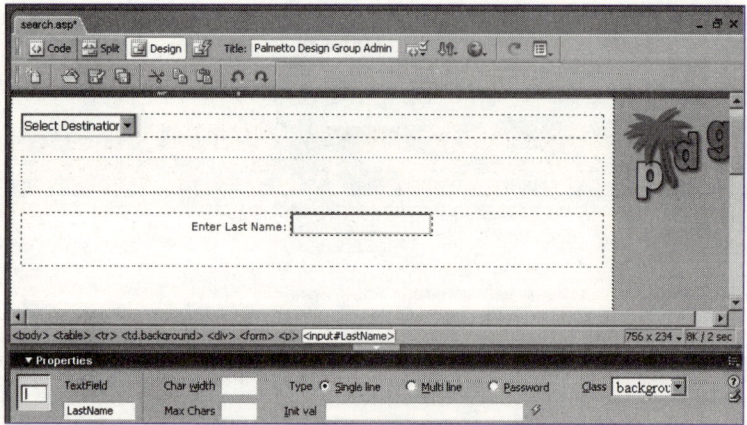

Figure 252-1: The LastName text field and the Property inspector where the field is named

5. Add a Submit button to the form (Insert ⇨ Form ⇨ Button).

6. Select the form by selecting the `<form>` tag in the Tag Selector in the Status toolbar at the bottom of the Document window, as shown in Figure 252-2.

notes

- If you want, change the label of the Submit button by selecting the button, opening the Property inspector (Window ⇨ Properties), and entering a new value in the Label text box (Step 5).

- GET sends the form data by appending it to the URL as a query string. Because URLs are limited to 8,192 characters, don't use the GET method with long forms. POST sends the form data in the body of a message. Default uses the browser's default method (usually GET) (Step 7).

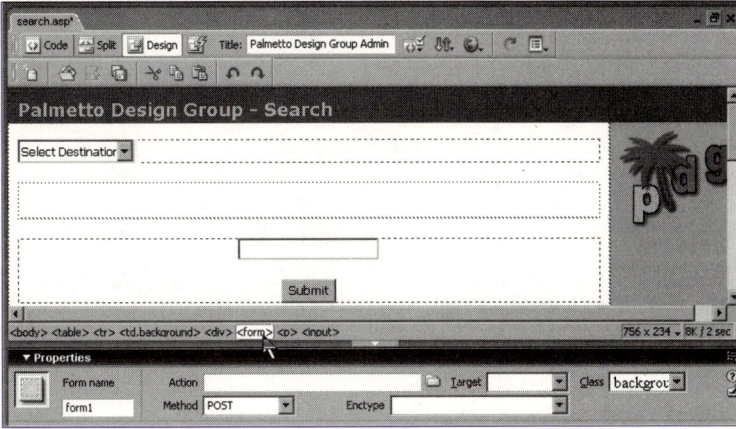

Figure 252-2: Selecting the `<form>` tag using the Tag Selector

7. In the Action text box in the form's Property inspector, enter the file-name of the results page that will conduct the database search (see Figure 252-3).

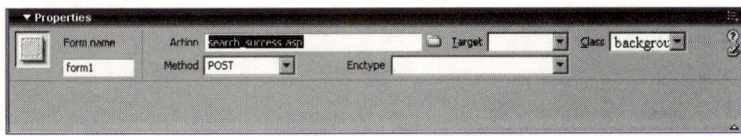

Figure 252-3: The Form Property inspector with the action

cross-reference

- Refer to Task 251 for build-ing a page to receive the data from the search.

Building a Results Page

In this task you create a page that shows the result of your search.

1. Open the page you want your search results to appear on in the Document window. If you don't have a results page yet, create a blank dynamic page (File ➪ New ➪ ASP VBScript).

2. Create a new recordset by opening the Bindings panel (Window ➪ Bindings), clicking the Plus (+) button, and selecting Recordset from the pop-up menu. The connection should be to a database containing data you want the user to search.

3. In the Table pop-up menu, select the table to be searched in the database. Select the desired columns by Ctrl/Command+clicking them in the list. You should include only the columns containing information you want to display on the results page. Leave the Recordset dialog box, shown in Figure 253-1, open for now. You'll use it next to retrieve the parameters sent by the search page and create a recordset filter to exclude records that don't meet the parameters.

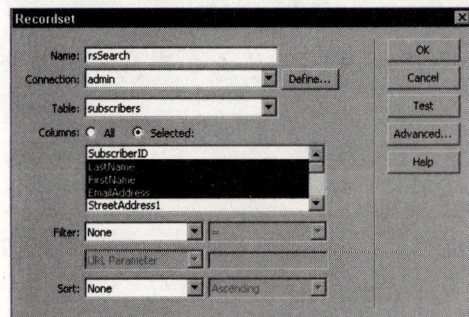

Figure 253-1: The Recordset dialog box with the subscribers table selected

4. To create the recordset filter, in the first pop-up menu in the Filter area, select a column in the database table in which to search for a match. For example, if the value sent by the search page is a city name, select the column in your table that contains city names.

5. From the pop-up menu beside the first menu, select the equal sign (it should be the default).

6. From the third pop-up menu, select Form Variable if the form on your search page uses the POST method, or select URL Parameter if it uses the GET method. The search page uses either a form variable or a URL parameter to pass information to the results page.

7. In the fourth text box, enter the name of the form object that accepts the search parameter on the search page.

notes

▪ In a single-parameter search, you can search for records in only a single table. To search more than one table at a time, you must use the advanced Recordset dialog box and define a SQL query (Step 3).

▪ The name of the object doubles as the name of the form variable or URL parameter. You can get the name by switching to the search page, clicking the form object on the form to select it, and checking the object's name in the Property inspector (Step 4).

8. If you want, click Test, enter a test value, and click OK to connect to the database and create an instance of the recordset. Click OK to close the test recordset. The filled-in dialog box is shown Figure 253-2.

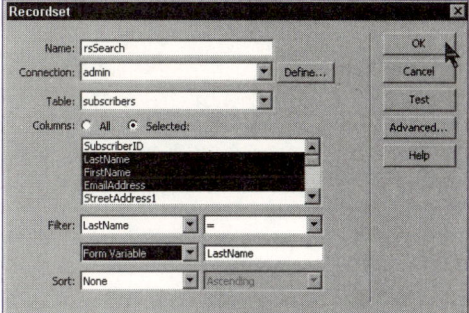

Figure 253-2: The filled-in Recordset dialog box

9. Dreamweaver inserts a server-side script on your page that, when run on the server, checks each record in the database table. If the specified field in a record meets the filtering condition, the record is included in a recordset. In effect, the script builds a recordset containing only the search results.

10. Save the page and test it in your browser. Open search.asp (from Task 252) and enter a last name. Click the Submit button. If the last name exists in the database, the search_success.asp page displays the fields you specified, as shown in Figure 253-3.

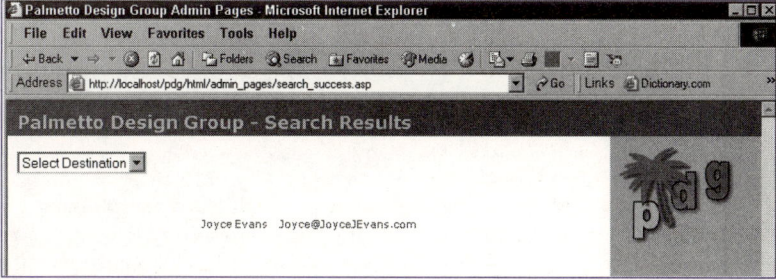

Figure 253-3: A successful search

cross-reference

• Refer to Task 252 for building the search form.

Index